CONSTITUTIONAL LAW FOR CRIMINAL JUSTICE

George T. Felkenes

Director, School of Criminal Justice
Michigan State University

Prentice-Hall, Inc., Englewood Cliffs, New Jersey 07632

Felkenes, George T
    Constitutional Law for Criminal Justice
    "Appendix A: The Constitution of the United States
of America": p.
    1.   United States—Constitutional law—Cases.
I. United States. Constitution. 1977. II. Title.
KF4549.F4   342'.73'.02   77-11156
ISBN 0-13-167833-7

Prentice-Hall Series in Criminal Justice
James D. Stinchcomb, *Editor*

Printed in the United States of America

10   9   8   7   6   5   4   3   2   1

Prentice-Hall International, Inc., *London*
Prentice-Hall of Australia Pty. Limited, *Sydney*
Prentice-Hall of Canada, Ltd., *Toronto*
Prentice-Hall of India Private Limited, *New Delhi*
Prentice-Hall of Japan, Inc., *Tokyo*
Prentice-Hall of Southeast Asia Pte. Ltd., *Singapore*
Whitehall Books Limited, *Wellington, New Zealand*

ACKNOWLEDGMENTS

An author needs assistance when preparing a book. It is seldom the efforts of a single person. I am no exception. Consequently I want to thank the following persons for their assistance and encouragement: Mrs. Patricia Riley for her typing and editorial help; Mr. Scott Langer for assistance in legal research; and Dr. C. Allen Graves for his criticism of the manuscript. Also worthy of special note are the large number of unknown manuscript reviewers who offered many valuable suggestions. One last person helped me immensely with her criticisms, often biting, but nevertheless accurate—my wife Sandra. This book is partly her effort.

CONTENTS

Chapter 12

EIGHTH AMENDMENT   340

Bail   Cruel and Unusual Punishment

PREFACE

There is a need in the criminal justice and social and behavioral science fields for a comprehensive text on the Constitution. There is a need for a Constitutional law text that develops the Constitutional aspects of criminal law and procedure as well as the more traditional Constitutional problems, i.e., commerce clause, speech, and religion. There is a need for a text with a logical, historically accurate, and understandable sequence of Constitutional development. There is a need for a text including only those cases that properly illustrate the points of law being covered without an excessive number of cases which merely add unnecessary surplusage. I have attempted to provide this kind of book on the Constitution.

This book presents introductory material for each chapter which give both a historical perspective and an overview of what will be covered. Because of the changing philosophies of the United States Supreme Court as society itself has changed, both of these features are essential to the student's understanding of the subject. I have also drastically edited the long Supreme Court opinions so that the student will not have to labor over ponderous opinions to extract the Constitutional principles involved. This Constitutional law text has included sections on corrections and juvenile issues that have been addressed by the Supreme Court as a feature of great importance to the criminal justice student.

The Constitution is a living document that should interest and stimulate the student of today. It touches in some way many of our daily activities from the purchase of a carton of milk at the local grocery to making an arrest at a shopping center of a person passing out political leaflets.

During the past two decades, the "liberal" or "conservative" interpretation of the Constitution has resulted in a national debate over the powers of the United States Supreme Court. I have attempted to include cases of historical significance to example how the attitude of the court changes in its Constitutional philosophy. The student should read carefully chapters 9 and 10 to taste the full flavor of changes that Constitutional decisions can make in our society.

I wish each student who uses this text good luck. Now let's begin.

George T. Felkenes

Michigan State University

CONSTITUTIONAL
LAW FOR
CRIMINAL JUSTICE

1

THE CONSTITUTION: AN OVERVIEW

Historical Context

The origin of the Constitution is found in the heritage of England and America. Underlying the Constitution, especially in terms of specific protections, are the effects of the Magna Charta of 1215. English common law is also seen in the context of the limited authority given elected officials in governing the people. The Americans knew all too well the dangers and abuses of governmental authority and realized that in order to protect basic freedoms it was necessary to have written documents stating explicitly the powers of the government as well as the rights of the people. Because of their experience with English institutions the colonies were constantly attempting to adapt their knowledge and experience to the new, sometimes dangerous, and unknown conditions in the new world.

English society was highly structured; therefore, laws were often developed with regard to these rigidly structured class conditions. The colonies, however, were relatively free from a class system. Consequently, it became clear that the colonists were opposed to the idea that English laws should be used in governing their colonies. They did not see themselves as subordinate to King George III's England. Instead, they felt entitled to self-government on the basis of an equal partnership within the Dominion. They could not view themselves as being subject to taxation by Parliament with no voice in the Parliament. The laws of England simply could not apply to the New World.

One of the major irritations was the constant administrative interference by English officials. The colonists' protests, demonstrations, and petitions against

English autocracy were at best given a hearing; at worst, they were ignored. The colonies, seeking to exert what pressures they could, refused to import or use English goods, in an attempt to influence and inform Parliament of their plight and dissatisfaction with English rule. Nothing worked. The ultimate step was taken—resort to arms in 1775.

The Revolutionary War began at Lexington and Concord. A few weeks after the first shots were fired, the Second Continental Congress convened in Philadelphia to consider prosecution of the war against England. This body hardly represented the people of the Colonies. Instead, it was made up of American radicals and revolutionists who were present at the request of various revolutionary and patriotic groups. Their main task was to determine how best to provide for the common defense; therefore, an army and navy were established. Money was borrowed in the name of the newly established government. Assistance from other European countries was solicited in the struggle against the English Crown. Of major constitutional significance, the second Constitutional Congress drew up the Articles of Confederation in addition to adopting a Declaration of Independence.

During these turbulent times the country was in an upheaval. Most Americans hoped that England and America could eventually resolve their differences and come together. King George, however, squashed any reconciliation by claiming that the colonies were in a state of rebellion after the Second Continental Congress on June 6, 1775. At this time he also issued a document outlining the grievances of the colonies, but denying any intention they might have to become separate from England. In the colonies the more moderate leaders now became convinced that the only solution was separation and independence.

As a result of growing dissatisfaction, Congress appointed a committee on June 10, 1776 to draw up a declaration of independence. On July 4, 1776 the Declaration of Independence was signed by John Hancock, President of the Congress. The Declaration became a rallying point for the revolution because it rationally justified resorting to war as a means of achieving independence. Another stimulus that inspired patriotic fervor was the implication that the conflict was being fought to set up a government that would be run according to the will of the people.

Problem of Unity

Like the Second Continental Congress, revolutionaries and patriotic groups authored most of the state constitutions. These written constitutions, while different in wording, all possessed some common features: demise of a strong executive, legislative supremacy, limited governmental power, and the voice of the people as the primary source of governmental power.

The Congressional resolution that authorized the drafting of the Declaration of Independence also proposed development of a plan for a confederation of the several states. The Congress, after much haggling over the selfish interests of individual states, finally adopted the Articles of Confederation on March 1, 1781. The Articles created the framework for a cooperative form of government. In reality, this government was nothing more than a form of confederacy which pledged cooperation among the states which signed the Articles. Each state retained its independence. There were no provisions for an executive or permanent judiciary. The Articles provided little opportunity for change because unanimous approval was required to amend. The Congress was the primary governmental organ. It was comprised of from two to seven persons from each state who were elected annually. The state paid the delegates and the delegates could be recalled by the State. Each state was permitted one vote, and the affirmative vote of nine states was needed to approve important matters.

The Articles contained several provisions that were aimed at unity among the states. Examples of these were a full faith and credit clause and a privilege and immunities provision. The major defects in the Articles, however, would prove fatal. There was no provision for a strong executive. Congress was given no power to control interstate and foreign commerce or to raise funds by taxation. The method authorized for the central government to raise revenue was as unique as it was ineffective. Congress could only issue requisitions to states which would in turn levy taxes and remit the necessary funds. Hence, it was impossible to operate a treasury. More than any other factor, the inability to raise revenue doomed the Articles as a viable instrument of government for the colonies. Because of the failure to raise adequate funds for domestic purposes foreign countries hesitated to enter into commercial treaties because they felt that the colonies could not fulfill their financial obligations.

Amendments to the Articles were proposed to remedy the revenue raising problem, but this process was also doomed to failure because of the Article requiring ratification of amendments by all states. State interests prevailed and various political groups came to recognize that the Union would disintegrate because of the defects in the Articles.

On May 14, 1781 a convention was called in Philadelphia for the purpose of remedying the deficiencies of the Articles. After delays in selecting state delegates, the convention convened with 55 delegates on May 25, 1787. Among the delegates were some of the ablest men in America: John Rutledge, the Pinckneys of South Carolina, Benjamin Franklin, George Washington, James Madison, and Gouverneur Morris. Washington was elected presiding officer.

Development of the Constitution

Before beginning their deliberations the delegates set some ground rules. Each state delegation was to have one vote. They agreed to keep their deliberations secret because they wanted to have a free exchange of debate without the fear of being criticized publicly for their individual ideals. The end result was to be as complete a document as possible for the new government. About the only account of the convention proceedings are the notes of James Madison who was the only person who prepared an accurate record.

The first major issue to arise was the organization structure of the new government. Virginia immediately proposed a plan in which the legislative branch would be supreme, a system of national courts, and a national executive. The legislature was to be comprised of two houses, each chosen based on population and the amount of their contributions to the central government. One house was to be elected by popular vote. The second was to be chosen by the first house from persons elected by the state legislatures. This plan, the Virginia Plan, met with strong objection from the smaller states. An alternate plan was proposed and called the New Jersey Plan.

The New Jersey Plan proposed that the Convention concern itself with proposing amendments to the Articles. It suggested that various difficulties with the Articles be eliminated. Congress should be given the power to collect taxes on foreign imported goods, to impose a stamp tax on documents, and to control collection of both. Congress should also be permitted to collect revenues requisitioned from states but as yet unpaid. Treaties made by Congress should be the supreme law of the land. A plural executive, chosen by Congress, was suggested to carry out executive functions. The executive was given the authority to appoint a supreme court. This court was to have jurisdiction over trade regulation acts, collection of revenue, and controversies over the construction of treaties.

With the proposal of these two plans, the lines were drawn between the large and the small states. The Convention was deadlocked over the issue of representation: The small states feared being swallowed up by the large states and the large states refused to yield on the issue of proportional representation. A third plan, the Connecticut Plan, was introduced as a compromise. It proposed that one house be comprised of states having equal votes and that the other house be chosen according to population and have authority to originate revenue bills. The Great Compromise averted dissolution of the convention.

The concept of limited power was written into the new Constitution by listing the specific powers of the new Congress. The grants of power were taken from various state constitutions as well as the Articles of Confederation. Among the most salient specific powers granted were a very broad taxing power and a necessary and proper clause that permitted Congress to choose the means of carrying out the specific powers given to it.

The various Articles proposed by the Convention outlined the governmental organization of the new nation.

Article I

Article I, the legislative article, comprises about one-half of the 1787 Constitution. This Article in effect limits everything else in the complete document. The powers of the general government were determined by the Philadelphia delegates. The supremacy of the legislature was assured by specifying Congress as the law-making body. Woven into the Constitution is the thread of primacy of the state legislatures in the governmental concept. Examples of this concept are found in several Articles. Article I, Section 8 stipulates that state legislatures shall look to the government for military and other necessary purposes. Article II, Section 1 allows state legislatures to direct the mode of appointment of presidential electors. The state legislatures may apply for federal help for protection against domestic violence as provided in Article IV, Section 4.

It is clearly implied by the opening words of the Constitution that the legislature is the primary arm of government, "We the People of the United States." The Congress is the closest to the people. It writes the laws which others apply. A quick reading of Article I reveals that rules and regulations for the country as a whole are promulgated. In its broadest scope, Article I permits dealing with foreign governments in either peaceful matters or in making war. It deals with the problems of diplomacy, tariffs on imports, maritime offenses on the high seas, and commercial intercourse with foreign nations.

Domestically, Article I provides powers for dealing with commerce between states, claims by a citizen of one state against a citizen of another, post offices, bankruptcy, weights and measures, money, and patents. In order to have a cohesive nation, the Article is primarily concerned with matters on a country-wide basis, particularly in the area of commerce to permit easier intercourse between states and sections of the country.

Limitations on governmental powers are also contained in Article I. No government, state or federal, can grant titles of nobility, impose duties on exports, pass bills of attainder, or enact *ex post facto* laws. States are prohibited from exercising treaty powers and interfering with the country's money supplies. Congress is also warned not to discriminate for or against one state over another.

Article II

Article II, defining executive power, is the second longest in the Constitution. It describes in detail how the country's chief executive is selected. This process was obviously of great importance to the founders' attempts to keep the states involved in choosing the chief executive through their designation of the body which ultimately does the selection. The president is vested with "the executive power." He executes the laws enacted by Congress. Because quick governmental reaction is of major importance in dealing with foreign nations, the President is designated as the Commander-in-Chief of the armed forces, thereby insuring rapid response to emergencies which may arise in the field of foreign relations. The legislature once again may check this duty by utilizing its "power of the purse" to regulate the size of the armed forces and also provide the rules and regulations for both land and naval forces. Congress is given the sole power to declare war. Additionally, presidential appointments of diplomats to represent the United States in foreign nations are subject to Senate approval.

A president is subject to removal by impeachment and conviction by Congress. This provision of Article II gives the country the opportunity to correct mistakes since there are very few qualifications required to be elected president.

Article III

The judiciary is covered by Article III. The Supreme Court is established but placed under certain Congressional controls. The general jurisdiction of the federal courts is fixed. As mentioned, the courts are subject to a large amount of Congressional control. It determines the size of all courts, as well as the Supreme Court's jurisdiction. The growth, retrenchment, or demise of inferior federal courts is a subject of Congressional control. To prevent Congressional control from becoming overbearing, Article III provides for a lifetime tenure in judicial office and no reduction in pay.

While Article III is silent about the power of federal courts to review the constitutionality of Congressional acts, Article VI seems to indicate that federal courts have the power to review state laws and constitutions.

Also provided in Article III is an elaboration of the law on treason. Strict rules provide for free ideas and expression of the governed to protect against their being capriciously charged with treason or crimes derivative therefrom, i.e., sedition.

Article IV

General relationships between states are covered by Article IV. "Full Faith and Credit shall be given in each State to the public Acts . . . of every other State." Discrimination against the citizens of one state by another is prohibited. Fugitives from one state may be extradited to the state from which they fled. This Article also provides Congressional power to form and admit new states to the nation.

According to Article IV, the people are guaranteed a republican form of government in all states. This means that the same kind of people who control the general government also control the state governments. Within this broad, general guideline the state is left free to provide its people with solutions to problems of local interest, i.e., divorce laws and criminal sanctions.

Article V

Ratification of amendments is covered by Article V. One is struck by the central role that the states play in the amending process. If two-thirds of the states apply for a convention to propose amendments to the Constitution, Congress must comply. The states have the final word, either through their state legislatures or through conventions called by the state legislatures for ratification of constitutional amendments.

Article VI

The supremacy of the Constitution and the laws and treaties of the United States is confirmed in Article VI. The various local, state, and federal governmental officers are obligated to support the Constitution, but this Article forbids religious tests to be required as a qualification to hold any office or position of trust under the United States.

Article VII

Article VII simply provides:

The Ratification of the Conventions of nine States, shall be sufficient for the establishment of this Constitution between the States so ratifying the Same.

It should be noted that conventions of the people of the states, not the state legislatures were to ratify the Constitution. It is interesting to note that Article VII permitted the Constitution to be ratified by less than three-quarters of the states required for final ratification of amendments. However, ratification of the Constitution only affected those states ratifying it, whereas all states which join the nation are bound by amendments.

Bill of Rights

The original Constitution was criticized because of the absence of a declaration of individual rights. The delegates to the various state ratifying conventions were assured that as soon as there was a new Congress under the Constitution, one of the first orders of business would be consideration of amendments to the Constitution which would guarantee individual rights.

The First United States Congress adopted ten amendments which were subsequently ratified by the states. The Bill of Rights, as these amendments came to be known, have had a tremendous impact on the nation. The amendments' provisions included: the prohibition of laws respecting the establishment of religion and its free exercise; the abridgment of freedom of speech or the press and the right to peacefully assemble and petition the government; the prohibition of unreasonable searches and the requiring that warrants be issued only upon a showing of probable cause supported by oath or affirmation; the prohibition of a person's being placed twice in jeopardy, being compelled to be a witness against himself in a criminal case, or being deprived of life, limb, or property without due process of law; the right to a speedy and public trial by an impartial jury; the right to confront one's accusers; the right to have compulsory process for obtaining witness in his favor, the right to have assistance of counsel; and the guarantee against the imposition of excessive bail, fines, or cruel and unusual punishments.

In early interpretations of the Constitution by the United States Supreme Court, the Bill of Rights was held to apply only to the national government. This interpretation has stood the weather of time and is still the position today, although in recent years numerous provisions in the first ten amendments have been made applicable in the states through the due process clause of the Fourteenth Amendment.

Basically, the Bill of Rights guarantees both substantive (speech, press, assembly, and petition) and procedural (due process of law, jury trial, counsel, searches and seizures, self-incrimination, double jeopardy, cruel and unusual punishments) rights. The substantive freedom and procedural safeguards were deemed by the framers of the Constitution to be crucial in a democratic form of government because they embody the basic idea of constitutionalism itself: a limitation of governmental power and a protection of individual liberty.

The Constitution has endured longer than any other written constitution in the world. It has set up the basic structure, powers, and limitations of a national government. Broad, general language is used in order to achieve interpretations of the document's provisions in relation to changing circumstances, thus giving the document the ability to last. The constitutional writers had two choices: (1) creation of a document guaranteeing the *status quo* by attempting to set forth every conceivable situation requiring a governmental solution or (2) development of a document that could survive by providing broad guidelines and addressing only those basic matters of governmental concern. The latter option was chosen.

The Concept of Federalism

Federalism involves the division of governmental authority between governments. In the United States Constitution the division is between the national and state governments. Each one has its own sphere of power and authority. The individual, however, is subject to the authority of both. Of importance in the federal system of government is that powers are delegated—some exclusively to the national government, such as the war power—and some are held concurrently by the national government and the states, such as the power to tax. The Constitution presents a "necessary and proper" grant of power to the national government, under which power flows by implication from those enumerated powers explicitly stated.

The powers given to the states are not enumerated. States, however, are inherently prohibited from certain powers by the Constitution. Since the powers granted the state governments are not included, the Constitution, in actuality, is only half complete. The Tenth Amendment, however, does state that all powers "not prohibited by it to the states, are reserved to the states respectively, or to the people.'' Thus, the states retain a substantial amount of power through the Tenth Amendment and their concurrent powers. States, however, are prohibited from becoming involved in the conduct of foreign relations because under the Constitution, entering into treaties with foreign countries falls within the power of the national government. This limitation places a restriction on the power of the industrial state.

In conclusion, the concept of federalism is an allocation of powers between the national and state governments. The powers of both are limited by dividing various governmental powers between the two.

Separation of Powers

Both federalism and separation of powers are structural principles that have a dual purpose. They provide a constitutional guarantee of protection of individual liberty while also allowing each level of government to achieve its goals. The doctrine of separation of powers provides a functional distribution of power among the branches of government—legislative, executive, and judicial. Each department is given its own powers, is independent, and is the equal to the others. A unique system in the Constitution, however, provides for ''checks and balances'' of each branch by the other two branches. For example, the Supreme Court may check the Congress or the executive by ruling on the constitutionality of their actions, while the Congress and the executive may review the activities of the Supreme Court through Congress' power to appropriate funds. This system of checks and balances is intricate and should be reviewed by the student of constitutional law.

The framers of the constitution feared governmental power. The purpose of the separation of powers concept is to prevent concentration of governmental authority in the hands of a single governmental person or body. By this device, they assured that there would always be a limitation upon the exercise of power because one power can ''check'' the other.

Supreme Court Decisions and Constitutional Development

The United States Supreme Court has the final authority to interpret the Constitution. The Court places its approval on basic laws by determining their constitutionality. Supreme Court decisions therefore establish policy. The Court's decisions encompass a wide range of alternatives found in case precedents. These are molded by each justice to fit his own view and when a majority of the justices agree, this view becomes the new policy. In short, the Supreme Court has great decision-making power and as an active participant in government it wields that power.

Many people scoff at the idea that the Supreme Court is a political agency of government. It is, however, a strong political force that can and has shaped national, state, and local governmental exercises of power. The economic, social, religious, and political philosophies show through the written opinions. The philosophies can readily be seen in the following case opinions. The power of the Court has often been criticized as undemocratic because it sometimes overrules the pronouncements of a president or Congress. In reality, the Supreme Court should be the weakest of the three coordinate branches of government, but it continues to be held in high esteem by the people because, taken as a whole, the pronouncements of the Court continually interpret the Constitution according to the needs of the people and the nation. These interpretations generally conform to the common will of the people.

Supreme Court decisions on cases and controversies are the basis for the constitutional development noted in this brief section. One should not, however, make the assumption that only the Supreme Court is involved in constitutional development. Congress contributes by establishing many of the features and organs of government, a good example being the 1964 Civil Rights Act which, while ultimately interpreted by the Court, supplied a completely new aspect of constitutional development. The president shapes the Constitution by the position he takes during national emergencies.

In the remainder of this book the reader will be studying materials from decisions by the Supreme Court. The cases have been chosen to demonstrate the dynamic process of constitutional development by means of Supreme Court decisions. The idea that the law is alive becomes immediately apparent as we discuss the major political, economic, social, racial, criminal, war, and civil liberty issues of the day.

QUESTIONS

1. What was the major concern of the framers of the Constitution? How did they specifically deal with this issue?

2. Article III of the Constitution sets the general jurisdiction of the federal courts. What is this jurisdiction?

3. Discuss the concept of federalism as it applies to the Constitution.

4. Describe the system of "checks and balances." Give some specific examples.

2

CONSTITUTIONAL CHALLENGE: THE JUDICIAL REVIEW CONTROVERSY

The United States Supreme Court has been a center for many of the political storms that have raged throughout our history as a nation. The involvement of the Supreme Court in political matters stemmed from its very beginnings. The Constitution of the United States established a high court which was unique to any previous judicial body in the following characteristics:

1. The Court was not only empowered with the final authority in interpreting federal laws but was also given the authority for determining the constitutionality of state laws.

2. The Court was placed in the difficult position of acting as a referee of serious questions regarding the allocation of federal power between the federal executive branch and Congress and between the state and the federal governments.

3. Because of its pivotal position in our government, the Supreme Court may at any time be presented a problem requiring a solution involving fundamental political issues. Frequently these issues take the form of interpreting the provisions of the United States Constitution. When the Court performs the task of applying statutes and ascertaining whether or not they violate the Constitution, the Court is practicing judicial review.

There is no clear provision in the Constitution that specifies that any court can declare to be unconstitutional a federal law enacted in a due manner. The principle that the courts do have this power was established in 1803 in *Marbury* v *Madison*, 5 U.S. 137 (1803). It must be remembered that *Marbury* dealt with federal law. When state laws are involved it seems that under the supremacy clause in Article VI of the Constitution, the Court has the power to declare state laws unconstitutional. However, as some of the cases in this chapter indicate, questions concerning the legitimacy of the power of the United States Supreme Court to declare state and federal laws unconstitutional still arise.

The political issues surrounding judicial review initially concerned the existence of such a power in the Supreme Court; now these issues are primarily directed toward the nature and scope of the Court's function in construing the Constitution. One of the main controversies surrounds the ambiguous clauses in the Constitution, for example, the due process and equal protection clauses of the Fourteenth Amendment. There is no concensus on how these clauses should be interpreted by the Court. In short, the concept of judicial review focuses on the extent to which the Supreme Court should bow to the judgments of the legislatures on ambiguous, doubtful, and complex issues when the constitutionality of a state or federal law is in question.

Is Judicial Review Legitimate?

Most scholars have concluded that Article III of the Constitution (judicial power grant) was meant to provide the Supreme Court with the power to declare both federal and state laws unconstitutional. Still, there are a number of scholars and politicians who have charged that the Supreme Court on specific occasions usurped the power of judicial review.

Outside of *Marbury* v *Madison,* interpretations of Article III have recognized the idea of judicial review as part of the judicial power to decide "cases . . . arising under this Constitution." In issues concerning the constitutionality of state laws, the supremacy clause clearly recognizes the power of the judiciary to declare these laws to be invalid. Consequently, state court judges are bound by the United States Constitution when there is a conflict between a state law and the Constitution. Furthermore, Article III recognizes that the Supreme Court has appellate jurisdiction over state court decisions with regard to cases arising under federal laws or under the United States Constitution. Additionally, ever since the initial Judiciary Act of 1789 Congress has continually given the Supreme Court the power to review state court decisions which interpret the Constitution. As a practical matter, this procedure is essential in avoiding conflicting opinions among states concerning the same clauses in the Constitution. Therefore, the United States Supreme Court has the final review power over the constitutionality of state laws.

Although there has been some doubt whether the Supreme Court possessed the power of judicial review, statements contained in the records of the Constitutional Convention, and the Federalist Papers reveal that the drafters of the Constitution generally understood that the judiciary would act as a barrier protecting against federal laws that transgressed the federal powers in the Constitution. The records reflect an assumption that there would be a judicial review of the constitutionality of federal law by the Supreme Court.

How Judicial Review Works

Today, there are few assaults on the legitimacy of judicial review *per se,* but the manner in which powers are exercised is the subject of frequent questions. This is understandable because of many strong and divergent views on the broad and ambiguous provisions of many parts of the Constitution. Within the Constitution itself is found the only limitation on the power of judicial review. This mandate is that the Supreme Court construe the Constitution only within the framework of a "case or controversy." This requirement found in Article III is very technical and has led to the position that the Court will not give advisory opinions on Constitutional issues. The technical approach has some very important consequences insofar as it prevents the Court from deciding issues which may be of substantial Constitutional importance. For example, in 1923 the Court held that an individual federal taxpayer could not complain about what were thought to be unconstitutional expenditures because the impact of the amount paid by the taxpayer was infinitesimal compared to the total expenditure. *Frothingham* v *Mellon,* 262 U.S. 447 (1923).

A few states permit the state supreme court to give advisory opinions on proposed state laws or their constitutionality under the state constitution. The rationale for this procedure is that it would be wasteful to enact a law that would subsequently be declared invalid. However, this rationale has not been accepted so as to permit the United States Supreme Court to give advisory opinions to other branches of the federal government. One reason is that the Court is an institution designed to test and judge governmental actions already taken, not to act as an implementer or designer of governmental activity. Therefore, before judicial review may take place, there must be a case or controversy.

Judicial Restraint

The concept of judicial restraint has a strong input into judicial review. By this is meant that the Court sets its values against the judgment of those in the legislature when it decides a question involving competing interests and values. One must remember that the Supreme Court is made up of nine members who are appointed for life. Because the Court's members are likely to be strong-willed and independent individuals, there is always the possibility of conflict between the Court and the lawmakers on important questions of policy. Judicial restraint is involved when a legislative judgment is made on issues involving Constitutional matters, for example, those involving individual liberties. Traditionally, the Court has upheld the legislative scheme as long as it is neither arbitrary nor totally unreasonable.

Frequently the argument for judicial restraint involves application of the Bill of Rights and the adjustment of conflicting social values. Judicial restraint postulates that since this is a democratic society, the will of the periodically elected legislature as the representatives of the people ought to prevail and not that of the Court which is chosen for life and is not in tune with societal concerns. The opponents of this position express the feeling that those who argue for the widest use of judicial restraint reject the concept of judicial review. They ask why there should be a written constitution with broad personal liberty guarantees if, for example, these guarantees are subject to the fluctuations of a momentary majority in the legislature.

In summary, the arguments for and against judicial restraint closely parallel those for and against judicial review. The question then becomes whether the elected official or the appointed Court should be the final guarantors of the Constitution. It is safe to say that so long as judicial review is a viable concept, the appropriate scope of judicial power will continue to be a troublesome issue.

Exercising Judicial Review

A perplexing question in the field of constitutional law is *how* a court should exercise its power of judicial review once it has been accepted as a function of the judiciary. Although this point has been the subject of controversy, in the final analysis it may depend on how much judicial review is accepted as a concept.

Just how the courts apply judicial review has been expressed in several different ways. One of these is to interpret the Constitution on an historical basis, but this is at best an uncertain guide. For example, history may indicate that the drafters of the Constitution believed that protection against unreasonable searches and seizures was of greatest importance. But they gave no indication when searches may be conducted in cases in which the national security is involved or in which sophisticated electronic devices are used to overhear conversations several hundred yards distant.

Another way of carrying into effect judicial review was expressed by the United States Supreme Court in 1936 in the following words: "When an act of Congress is appropriately challenged in the courts as not conforming to the constitutional mandate the judicial branch of the Government has only one duty—to lay the article of the Constitution which is invoked beside the statute which is challenged to decide whether the latter squares with the former. . . . This court neither approves nor condemns any legislative policy. Its delicate and difficult office is to ascertain whether the legislation is in accordance with, or in contravention of, the provisions of the Constitution, and having done that, its duty ends." *United States* v *Butler,* 297 U.S. 1 (1936).

How this simple statement can be practically applied in the reality of a case or controversy is a very difficult problem. Cases do not often arise in which there is a clear constitutional mandate for the Court to interpret. For example, each state is entitled to two senators, no matter what its size or importance. It is very unlikely that a need for a constitutional interpretation on this point be made. But the Constitution is full of broad language that is susceptible to conflicting interpretations. For example, the Bill of Rights does not discuss the meaning of due process, free exercise of religion, cruel and unusual punishments, and equal protection. Obviously, these concepts do not have a simple, single, clear meaning. Therefore, in reviewing laws the Court just does not lay the law and Constitution side by side and square the two. The problem is much more complex than *Butler* would seem to indicate.

The remainder of this chapter discusses cases that have shaped the nature and scope of judicial review as a working mechanism employed by the United States Supreme Court. The selected cases show the Supreme Court in action in wrestling with serious constitutional problems. One of the salient political issues surrounding the Supreme Court, involvement in political issues, is presented to express the problem involving judicial review of laws that have a direct relationship to the political organization of the various forms of government. Judicial review of statutes in this one area has been a bold step that has had far reaching consequences in our constitutional form of government.

DEVELOPMENT OF CONCEPT AND DEFINITION

Marbury v *Madison*
5 U.S. (1 Cranch 137) 2 L.Ed. 60 (1803)

Judicial review was being sharply challenged at the beginning of the history of the United States. In 1803 Chief Justice Marshall met the challenge head on. During the Federalist administration strong Republican opposition to the federal judiciary developed. In the closing days of the Federalist administration the famous Law of the Midnight Judges was enacted to create new federal judicial positions. The law received this name because Secretary of State, John Marshall, who already had been confirmed as the new Chief Justice of the United States Supreme Court, signed the commissions for the new judges late in the evening before Jefferson's inauguration. The Jeffersonians were outraged by the appointments of 42 justices of the peace for the District of Columbia. These commissions had been signed and sealed but not delivered. President Jefferson directed his Secretary of State, James Madison, not to deliver 17 of the commissions among whose was William Marbury. Marbury subsequently brought an action to compel Secretary Madison to deliver his commission as a justice of the peace.

The Law of the Midnight Judges was repealed by the Jeffersonians in 1802. The question of the power of judicial review became a matter of serious debate between the Jeffersonians and the Federalists. The Federalists argued that the repeal of the act was unconstitutional because it violated Article III, Section 1 of the Constitution, that federal judges shall hold their offices for life during good behavior. The Federalists doubted that federal courts had the power to judge the constitutionality of acts of Congress. Republicans believed that the Marshall Court would declare the Repeal Act unconstitutional, thereby creating a direct confrontation between the Court and Republican Congress and President Jefferson.

Chief Justice Marshall announced the opinion of the Court:

At the last term on the affidavits then read and filed with the clerk, a rule was granted in this case, requiring the secretary of state to show cause why a mandamus should not issue, directing him to deliver to William Marbury his commission as a justice of the peace for the county of Washington, in the District of Columbia.

No cause has been shown, and the present motion is for a mandamus. The peculiar delicacy of this case, the novelty of some of its circumstances, and the real difficulty attending the points which occur in it, require a complete exposition of the principles on which the opinion to be given by the court is founded.

These principles have been, on the side of the applicant, very ably argued at the bar. In rendering the opinion of the court, there will be some departure in form, though not in substance, from the points stated in that argument.

In the order in which the court has viewed this subject, the following questions have been considered and decided.

1st. Has the applicant a right to the commission he demands?

2d. If he has a right, and that right has been violated, do the laws of his country afford him a remedy?

3d. If they do afford him a remedy, is it a mandamus issuing from this court?

The first object of inquiry is,

1st. Has the applicant a right to the commission he demands?

. . .

It is, therefore, decidedly the opinion of the court, that when a commission has been signed by the President, the appointment is made; and that the commission is complete when the seal of the United States has been affixed to it by the Secretary of State.

. . .

Mr. Marbury, then, since his commission was signed by the President, and sealed by the Secretary of State, was appointed; and as the law creating the office, gave the officer a right to hold for five years, independent of the executive, the appointment was not revocable, but vested in the officer legal rights, which are protected by the laws of his country.

To withhold his commission, therefore, is an act deemed by the court not warranted by law, but violative of a vested legal right.

This brings us to the second inquiry; which is,

2d. If he has a right, and that right has been violated, do the laws of this country afford him a remedy?

The very essence of civil liberty certainly consists in the right of every individual to claim the protection of the laws, whenever he receives an injury. One of the first duties of government is to afford that protection.

. . .

The government of the United States has been emphatically termed a government of laws, and not of men. It will certainly cease to deserve this high appellation, if the laws furnish no remedy for the violation of a vested legal right.

If this obloquy is to be cast on the jurisprudence of our country, it must arise from the peculiar character of the case.

It behooves us, then, to inquire whether there be in its composition any ingredient which shall exempt it from legal investigations, or exclude the injured party from legal redress.

. . .

Is it in the nature of the transaction? Is the act of delivering or withholding a commission to be considered as a mere political act, belonging to the executive department alone, for the performance of which entire confidence is placed by our Constitution in the supreme executive; and for any misconduct respecting which the injured individual has no remedy?

That there may be such cases is not to be questioned; but that every act of duty, to be performed in any of the great departments of government, constitutes such a case, is not to be admitted.

. . .

It follows, then, that the question, whether the legality of an act of the head of a department be examinable in a court of justice or not, must always depend on the nature of that act.

. . .

By the Constitution of the United States, the President is invested with certain important political powers, in the exercise of which he is to use his own discretion, and is accountable only to his country in his political character and to his own conscience. To aid him in the performance of these duties, he is authorized to appoint certain officers, who act by his authority, and in conformity with his orders.

. . .

But when the legislature proceeds to impose on that officer other duties; when he is directed peremptorily to perform certain acts; when the rights of individuals are dependent on the performance of those acts; he is so far the officer of the law; is amenable to the laws for his conduct; and cannot at his discretion sport away the vested rights of others.

The conclusion from this reasoning is, that where the heads of departments are the political and confidential agents of the executive, merely to execute the will of the President, or rather to act in cases in which the executive possesses a constitutional or legal discretion, nothing can be more perfectly clear than that their acts are only politically examinable. But where a specific duty is assigned by law, and individual rights depend upon the performance of that duty, it seems equally clear that the individual who considers himself injured, has a right to resort to the laws of his country for a remedy.

· · ·

It is, then, the opinion of the Court,

1st. That by signing the commission of Mr. Marbury, the President of the United States appointed him a justice of peace for the county of Washington, in the District of Columbia; and that the seal of the United States, affixed thereto by the Secretary of State, is conclusive testimony of the verity of the signature, and of the completion of the appointment, and that the appointment conferred on him a legal right to the office for the space of five years.

2d. That, having this legal title to the office, he has a consequent right to the commission; a refusal to deliver which is a plain violation of that right, for which the laws of his country afford him a remedy.

It remains to be inquired whether,

3d. He is entitled to the remedy for which he applies. This depends on,

1st. The nature of the writ applied for; and,

2d. The power of this court.

1st. The nature of the writ.

· · ·

This writ, if awarded, would be directed to an officer of government, and its mandate to him would be, to use the words of Blackstone, "to do a particular thing therein specified, which appertains to his office and duty, and which the court has previously determined, or at least supposes, to be consonant to right and justice." Or, in the words of Lord Mansfield, the applicant, in this case, has a right to execute an office of public conern, and is kept out of possession of that right.

These circumstances certainly concur in this case.

· · ·

This, then, is a plain case for a mandamus, either to deliver the commission, or a copy of it from the record; and it only remains to be inquired,

Whether it can issue from this court.

The act to establish the judicial courts of the United States authorizes the Supreme Court "to issue writs of mandamus in cases warranted by the principles and usages of law, to any courts appointed, or persons holding office, under the authority of the United States."

The Secretary of State, being a person holding an office under the authority of the United States, is precisely within the letter of the description, and if this court is not authorized to issue a writ of mandamus to such an officer, it must be because the law is unconstitutional, and therefore absolutely incapable of conferring the authority, and assigning the duties which its words purport to confer and assign.

The Constitution vests the whole judicial power of the United States in one Supreme Court, and such inferior courts as Congress shall, from time to time, ordain and establish. This power is expressly extended to all cases arising under the laws of the United States; and, consequently, in some form, may be exercised over the present case; because the right claimed is given by a law of the United States.

In the distribution of this power it is declared that "the Supreme Court shall have original jurisdiction in all cases affecting ambassadors, other public ministers and consuls, and those in which a state shall be a party. In all other cases, the Supreme Court shall have appellate jurisdiction."

It has been insisted, at the bar, that the original grant of jurisdiction, to the Supreme and inferior courts, is general, and the clause assigning original jurisdiction to the Supreme Court contains no negative or restrictive words, the power remains to the legislature, to assign original jurisdiction to that court in other cases than those specified in the article which has been recited; provided those cases belong to the judicial power of the United States.

If it has been intended to leave it in the discretion of the legislature to apportion the judicial power between the supreme and inferior courts according to the will of that body, it would certainly have been useless to have proceded further than to have defined the judicial power, and the tribunals in which it should be vested. The subsequent part of the section is mere surplusage, is entirely without meaning, if such is to be the construction. If congress remains at liberty to give this court appellate jurisdiction, where the Constitution has declared their jurisdiction shall be original; and original jurisdiction where the Constitution has declared it shall be appellate; the distribution of jurisdiction, made in the Constitution, is form without substance.

Affirmative words are often, in their operation, negative of other objects than those affirmed; and in this case, a negative or exclusive sense must be given to them, or they have no operation at all.

It cannot be presumed that any clause in the Constitution is intended to be without effect; and, therefore, such a construction is inadmissible unless the words require it.

If the solicitude of the convention, respecting our peace with foreign powers, induced a provision that the Supreme Court should take original jurisdiction in cases which might be supposed to affect them, yet the clause would have proceeded no further than to provide for such cases, if no further restriction on the powers of Congress had been intended. That they should have appellate jurisdiction in all other cases, with such exceptions as Congress might make, is no restriction; unless the words be deemed exclusive of original jurisdiction.

When an instrument organizing fundamentally a judicial system divides it into one supreme, and so many inferior courts as the legislature may ordain and establish; then enumerates its powers, and proceeds so far to distribute them, as to define the jurisdiction of the Supreme Court by declaring the cases in which it shall take original jurisdiction, and that in others it shall take appellate jurisdiction; the plain import of the words seems to be, that in one class of cases its jurisdiction is original, and not appellate; in the other it is appellate, and not original. If any other construction would render the clause inoperative, that is an additional reason for rejecting such other construction, and for adhering to their obvious meaning.

To enable this court, then, to issue a mandamus, it must be shown to be an exercise of appellate jurisdiction, or to be necessary to enable them to exercise appellate jurisdiction.

It has been stated at the bar that the appellate jurisdiction may be exercised in a variety of forms, and that if it be the will of the legislature that a mandamus should be used for that purpose, that will must be obeyed. This is true, yet the jurisdiction must be appellate, not original.

It is the essential criterion of appellate jurisdiction, that it revises and corrects the proceedings in a cause already instituted, and does not create that cause. Although, therefore, a mandamus may be directed to courts, yet to issue such a writ to an officer for the delivery of a paper, is in effect the same as to sustain an original action for that paper, and, therefore, seems not to belong to appellate but to original jurisdiction. Neither is it necessary in such a case as this, to enable the court to exercise its appellate jurisdiction.

The authority, therefore, given to the Supreme Court, by the act establishing the judicial courts of the United States, to issue writs of mandamus to public officers, appears not to be warranted by the Constitution; and it becomes necessary to inquire whether a jurisdiction so conferred can be exercised.

The question, whether an act, repugnant to the Constitution, can become the law of the land, is a question deeply interesting to the United States; but, happily, not of an intricacy proportioned to its interest. It seems only necessary to recognize certain principles, supposed to have been long and well established, to decide it.

That the people have an original right to establish, for their future government, such principles, as, in their opinion, shall most conduce to their own happiness is the basis on which the whole American fabric has been erected. The exercise of this original right is a very great exertion; nor can it, nor ought it, to be frequently repeated. The principles, therefore, so established, are deemed fundamental. And as the authority from which they proceed is supreme, and can seldom act, they are designed to be permanent.

This original and supreme will organizes the government, and assigns to different departments their respective powers. It may either stop here, or establish certain limits not to be transcended by those departments.

The government of the United States is of the latter description. The powers of the legislature are defined and limited; and that those limits may not be mistaken, or forgotten, the Constitution is written. To what purpose are powers limited, and to what purpose is that limitation committed to writing, if these limits may, at any time, be passed by those intended to be restrained? The distinction between a government with limited and unlimited powers is abolished, if those limits do not confine the persons on whom they are imposed, and if acts prohibited and acts allowed, are of equal obligation. It is a proposition too plain to be contested, that the Constitution controls any legislative act repugnant to it; or, that the legislature may alter the Constitution by an ordinary act.

Between these alternatives there is no middle ground. The Constitution is either a superior paramount law, unchangeable by ordinary means, or it is on a level with ordinary legislative acts, and, like other acts, is alterable when the legislature shall please to alter it.

If the former part of the alternative be true, then a legislative act contrary to the Constitution is not law: if the latter part be true, then written constitutions are absurd attempts, on the part of the people, to limit a power in its own nature illimitable.

Certainly all those who have framed written constitutions contemplate them as forming the fundamental and paramount law of the nation, and, consequently, the theory of every such government must be, that an act of the legislature, repugnant to the constitution, is void.

This theory is essentially attached to a written constitution, and, is consequently, to be considered, by this court, as one of the fundamental principles of our society. It is not therefore to be lost sight of in the further consideration of this subject.

If an act of the legislature, repugnant to the constitution, is void, does it, notwithstanding its validity, bind the courts, and oblige them to give it effect? Or, in other words, though it be not law, does it constitute a rule as operative as if it was a law? This would be to overthrow in fact what was established in theory; and would seem, at first view, an absurdity too gross to be insisted on. It shall, however, receive a more attentive consideration.

It is emphatically the province and duty of the judicial department to say what the law is. Those who apply the rule to particular cases, must of necessity expound and interpret that rule. If two laws conflict with each other, the courts must decide on the operation of each.

So if a law be in opposition to the Constitution; if both the law and the Constitution apply to a particular case, so that the court must either decide that case conformably to the law, disregarding the Constitution; or conformably to the Constitution, disregarding the law; the court must determine which of these conflicting rules governs the case. This is of the very essence of judicial duty.

If, then, the courts are to regard the Constitution, and the Constitution is superior to any ordinary act of the legislature, the Constitution, and not such ordinary act, must govern the case to which they both apply.

Those, then, who controvert the principle that the Constitution is to be considered, in court, as a paramount law, are reduced to the necessity of maintaining that courts must close their eyes on the Constitution, and see only the law.

This doctrine would subvert the very foundation of all written constitutions. It would declare that an act which, according to the principles and theory of our government, is entirely void, is yet, in practice, completely obligatory. It would declare that if the legislature shall do what is expressly forbidden, such act, notwithstanding the express prohibition, is in reality effectual. It would be given to the legislature a practical and real omnipotence, with the same breath which professes to restrict their powers within narrow limits. It is prescribing limits, and declaring that those limits may be passed at pleasure.

That it thus reduces to nothing what we have deemed the greatest improvement on political institutions, a written constitution, would of itself be sufficient, in America, where written constitutions have been viewed with so much reverence, for rejecting the construction. But the peculiar expressions of the Constitution of the United States furnish additional arguments in favour of its rejection.

The judicial power of the United States is extended to all cases arising under the Constitution.

Could it be the intention of those who gave this power, to say that in using it the Constitution should not be looked into? That a case arising under the Constitution should be decided without examining the instrument under which it arises?

This is too extravagant to be maintained.

In some cases, then, the Constitution must be looked into by the judges. And if they can open it at all, what part of it are they forbidden to read or to obey?

There are many other parts of the Constitution which serve to illustrate this subject.

It is declared that "no tax or duty shall be laid on articles exported from any state." Suppose a duty on the export of cotton, of tobacco, or of flour; and a suit instituted to recover it. Ought judgment to be rendered in such a case? Ought the judges to close their eyes on the Constitution, and only see the law?

The Constitution declares "that no bill of attainder or *ex post facto* law shall be passed."

If, however, such a bill should be passed, and a person should be prosecuted under it; must the court condemn to death those victims whom the Constitution endeavors to preserve?

"No person," says the Constitution, "shall be convicted of treason unless on the testimony of two witnesses to the same overt act, or on confession in open court."

Here the language of the Constitution is addressed especially to the courts. It prescribes, directly for them, a rule of evidence not to be departed from. If the legislature should change that rule, and declare one witness, or a confession out of court, sufficient for conviction, must the constitutional principle yield to the legislative act?

From these, and many other selections which might be made, it is apparent, that the framers of the Constitution contemplated that instrument as a rule for the government of courts, as well as of the legislature.

Why otherwise does it direct the judges to take an oath to support it? This oath certainly applies in an especial manner, to their conduct in their official character. How immoral to impose it on them, if they were to be used as the instruments, and the knowing instruments, for violating what they swear to support!

The oath of office, too, imposed by the legislature, is completely demonstrative of the legislative opinion on this subject. It is in these words: "I do solemly swear that I will administer justice without respect to persons, and do equal right to the poor and to the rich; and that I will faithfully and impartially discharge all the duties incumbent on me as ———, according to the best of my abilities and understanding agreeably to the Constitution and laws of the United States."

Why does a judge swear to discharge his duties agreeably to the Constitution of the United States, if that Constitution forms no rule for this government? If it is closed upon him, and cannot be inspected by him?

If such be the real state of things, this is worse than solemn mockery. To prescribe, or to take this oath, becomes equally a crime.

It is also not entirely unworthy of observation, that in declaring what shall be the supreme law of the land, the Constitution itself is first mentioned; and not the laws of the United States generally, but those only which shall be made in pursuance of the Constitution, have that rank.

Thus, the particular phraseology of the Constitution of the United States confirms and strengthens the principle, supposed to be essential to all written constitutions, that a law repugnant to the Constitution is void; and that courts, as well as other departments, are bound by that instrument. (Requested rule discharged.)

CONSTITUTIONAL CONTROVERSIES INVOLVING JUDICIAL REVIEW AFTER *MARBURY* v *MADISON*

Criticism of Judicial Review

Cooper v *Aaron*

385 U.S. 1, 78 S.Ct. 1401, 3 L.Ed. 2d5 (1958)

Infra Chapter 7, p. 188

Jurisdiction of Federal Courts

Martin v *Hunter's Lessee*

14 U.S. (1 Wheat 304) 4 L.Ed. 97 (1816)

The United States Supreme Court directed the Virginia Court of Appeals to revise one of its decisions because of an error in the case. The case itself was reversed by the Supreme Court and remanded. The opinion ended with the statement, "You therefore are hereby commanded that such proceedings be had in said cause, as according to right and justice, and the laws of the United States, and agreeable to said judgment and instructions of said Supreme Court ought to be had, the said writ of error notwithstanding." *Martin* v *Hunter's Lessee* came on a writ of error to the United States Supreme Court from the Virginia Court of Appeals, which refused to obey the above mandate of the Supreme Court. The Court held that federal appellate power extends to cases pending in state courts.

The Virginia Court of Appeals had delivered an opinion stating:

> The court is unanimously of an opinion that the appellate power of the Supreme Court of the United States does not extend to this court, under a sound construction of the construction of the Constitution of the United States; that so much of the 25th section of the act of Congress to establish the judicial courts of the United States, as extends the appellate jurisdiction of the Supreme Court to this court, is not in pursuance of the Constitution of the United States; that the writ of error, in this cause, was improvidently allowed under the authority of that act; that the proceedings thereon in the Supreme Court were, *coram non judice,* in relation to this court, and that obedience to its mandate be declined by the court.

Addressing this issue of jurisdiction, Justice Story cites Article III of the Constitution which creates and defines the judicial power of the United States:

> It is the voice of the whole American people solemnly declared, in establishing one great department of that government which was, in many respects, national, and in all, supreme. It is a part of the very same instrument which was to act not merely upon individuals, but upon states; and to deprive them altogether of the exercise of some powers of sovereignty, and to restrain and regulate them in the exercise of others.
>
> Let this article be carefully weighed and considered. The language of the article throughout is manifestly designed to be mandatory upon the legislature. Its obligatory force is so imperative that Congress could not, without a violation of its duty, have refused to carry it into operation. The judicial power of the United States shall be vested (not may be vested) in one supreme court, and in such inferior courts as Congress may, from time to time, ordain and establish. Could Congress have lawfully refused to create a supreme court, or to vest it in the constitutional jurisdiction?

It was the opinion of the Court that if it was the duty of Congress to vest the judicial power of the United States, it is its duty to vest the whole judicial power. This judicial power must be vested in the Supreme Court and in inferior courts. If this were not the case, then the injunction of the Constitution that the judicial power "shall be vested" would be disobeyed. It is therefore seen to be imperative that the whole judicial power of the United States:

be, at all times, vested either in an original or appellate form, in some courts created under its authority. . . . The appellate power is not limited by the terms of the third article to any particular courts. The words are, ''the judicial power (which includes appellate power) shall extend to all cases,'' etc., and ''in all other cases before mentioned the Supreme Court shall have appellate jurisdiction.'' It is the case, then, and not the court, that gives the jurisdiction. If the judicial power extends to the case, it will be in vain to search in the letter of the Constitution for any qualification as to the tribunal where it depends. It is incumbent, then, upon those who assert such a qualification to show its existence by necessary implication, if the text be clear and distinct, no restriction upon its plain and obvious import ought to be admitted, unless the inference be irresistible.

The opinion of the Court went on to assert that

Under the present Constitution, the prize jurisdiction is confined to the courts of the United States; and a power to revise the decisions of state courts, if they should assert jurisdiction over prize causes, cannot be less important, or less useful than it was under the confederation.

In this connection we are led again to the construction of the words of the Constitution, ''the judicial power shall extend,'' etc. If, as has been contended at the bar, the term ''extend'' have a relative signification, and mean to widen an existing power, it will then follow that, as the confederation gave an appellate power over state tribunals, the Constitution enlarged or widened that appellate power to all the other cases in which jurisdication is given to the courts of the United States. It is not presumed that the learned counsel would choose to adopt such a conclusion.

. . .

This is not all. A motive of another kind, perfectly compatible with the most sincere respect for state tribunals, might induce the grant of appellate power over their decisions. That motive is the importance, and even necessity of uniformity of decisions throughout the whole United States, upon all subjects within the purview of the Constitution. Judges of equal learning and integrity, in different states, might differently interpret a statute, or a treaty of the United States, or even the Constitution itself.

If there were no revising authority to control these jarring and discordant judgments, and harmonize them into uniformity, the laws, the treaties, and the Constitution of the United States would be different in different states, and might, perhaps, never have precisely the same construction, obligation, or efficacy, in any two states. The public mischiefs that would attend such a state of things would be truly deplorable; and it cannot be believed that they could have escaped the enlightened convention which formed the Constitution. What, indeed, might then have been only prophecy, has now become fact; and the appellate jurisdiction must continue to be the only adequate remedy for such evils.

Thus the jurisdiction of the federal courts, as stated by the Constitution, was defined by the Supreme Court in this case.

Advisory Opinions

Muskrat v United States
219 U.S. 346, 31 S.Ct. 250, 55 L.Ed. 246 (1911)

In 1902 Congress enacted legislation allotting lands to certain Cherokee Indians. The number of Indians who were entitled to share in this distribution of land was increased by later legislation. This legislation also imposed a restriction prohibiting the Indian landowners from encumbering, disposing of, or selling the land for a period of 25 years. In 1907 Congress enacted a statute explicitly authorizing Muskrat and three others to bring class action suits against the United States in the courts of claims and in the United States Supreme Court. This action was an attempt by Congress "to determine the validity of any acts of Congress passed since the said Act (1902)." In order to ensure speedy disposition of the suits, these claimants were to be given preference in the courts and their legal fees were to be provided by the United States Treasury from "tribal funds."

The first question addressed by Justice Day, who wrote the opinion for the court, was one of jurisdiction. The answer to this question hinges upon whether the jurisdiction conferred is within the power of Congress, having in view the limitations of judicial power, as established by the Constitution.

In the early days of the government, the right of Congress to give original jurisdiction to the Supreme Court, in cases not enumerated in the Constitution, was maintained by many jurists, and seems to have been entertained by the learned judges who decided Todd's Case. But discussion and more mature examination has settled the question otherwise; and it has long been the established doctrine, and we believe now assented to by all who have examined the subject, that the original jurisdiction of this court is confined to the cases specified in the Constitution, and that Congress cannot enlarge it. In all other cases its power must be appellate.

Upon settlement of the question of jurisdiction, the Court responded to the major issue of this case (i.e., could the Supreme Court respond to a constitutional question raised by Congress in a purely advisory capacity?). The opinion of the Court was that these citizens, were

authorized and empowered to institute suits in the courts of claims to determine the validity of acts of Congress passed since the act of July 1, 1902, in so far as the same attempt to increase or extend the restrictions upon alienation, encumbrance, or the right to lease the allotments of lands of Cherokee citizens, or to increase the number of persons entitled to share in the final distribution of lands and funds of the Cherokees beyond those enrolled for allotment as of September 1, 1902, and provided for in the said act of July 1, 1902.

However, and herein lies the crux of this decision:

the object and purpose of the suit is wholly comprised in the determination of the constitutional validity of certain acts of Congress; and furthermore, in the last paragraph of the section, should a judgment be rendered in the courts of claims or this court, denying the constitutional validity of such acts, then the amount of compensation to be paid to attorneys employed for the purpose of testing the constitutionality of the law is to be paid out of funds in the Treasury of the United States belonging to the beneficiaries, the act having previously provided that the United States should be made a party, and the Attorney General be charged with the defense of the suits.

The object in this case was not to assert a property right as against the government, or to demand compensation for alleged wrongs because of action upon its part. Instead, it was an attempt to settle the doubtful character of the legislation in question. To this issue the Court addressed itself and stated:

In a legal sense the judgment could not be executed, and amounts in fact to no more than an expression of opinion upon the validity of the acts in question. Confining the jurisdiction of this court within the limitations conferred by the Constitution, which the court has hitherto been careful to observe, and whose boundaries it has refused to transcend, we think the Congress, in the act of March 1, 1907, exceeded the limitations of legislative authority, so far as it required of this court action not judicial in its nature within the meaning of the Constitution.

Supreme Court policy on advisory opinions was now defined.

Ripeness of the Controversy

Massachusetts v *Mellon*
Frothingham v *Mellon*
262 U.S. 447, 43 S.Ct. 597, 67 L.Ed. 1078 (1923)

This decision was based on two challenges to the Maternity Act of 1921. Both suits sought to enjoin Secretary of the Treasury Mellon from allocating funds, as provided in the Act, to those states which undertook programs to reduce maternal and infant deaths. These cases were argued, considered, and disposed of together. *Massachusetts* v *Mellon* was an original suit in the Supreme Court. *Frothingham* v *Mellon* was first heard in the Supreme Court of the District of Columbia. *Frothingham* v *Mellon* was brought to the Supreme Court on appeal.

Both cases challenge the constitutionality of the Act of November 23, 1921, 42 Stat. 224, c. 135, commonly called the Maternity Act. Briefly, it provides for an initial appropriation and thereafter annual appropriations for a period of five years, to be apportioned among such of the several states as shall accept and comply with its provisions, for the purpose of co-operating with them to reduce maternal and infant mortality and protect the health of mothers and infants. It creates a bureau to administer the act in co-operation with state agencies, which are required to make such reports concerning their operations and expenditures as may be prescribed by the federal bureau. Whenever that bureau shall determine that funds have not been properly expended in respect of any state, payments may be withheld.

In the words of Justice Sutherland who delivered the opinion of the Court:

In the Massachusetts Case it is alleged that the plaintiff's rights and powers as a sovereign state and the rights of its citizens have been invaded and usurped by these expenditures and acts, and that, although the state has not accepted the act, its constitutional rights are infringed by the passage thereof and the imposition upon the state of an illegal and unconstitutional option either to yield to the federal government a part of its reserved rights or lose the share which it would otherwise be entitled to receive of the moneys appropriated. In the Frothingham Case plaintiff alleges that the effect of the statute will be to take her property under the guise of taxation, without due process of law.

We have reached the conclusion that the cases must be disposed of for want of jurisdiction, without considering the merits of the constitutional questions.

The complaint of the states was that Congress had usurped the reserved powers of the states by enacting a statute. However, the Court points out that nothing had been done and nothing was to be done without the states consent. Therefore:

it is plain that that question, as it is thus presented, is political, and not judicial in character, and therefore is not a matter which admits of the exercise of the judicial power.

The complaint in the Frothingham case is essentially the same, but this plaintiff also alleged that as a taxpayer of the United States the appropriations complained of would increase the burden of future taxation and therefore take her property without due process of law.

In answer to this complaint the Court said:

The administration of any statute, likely to produce additional taxation to be imposed upon a vast number of taxpayers, the extent of whose several liability is indefinite and constantly changing, is essentially a matter of public and not of individual concern. If one taxpayer may champion and litigate such a cause, then every other taxpayer may do the same, not only in respect of the statute here under review, but also in respect of every other appropriation act and statute whose administration requires the outlay of public money, and whose validity may be questioned. The bare suggestion of such a result, with its attendant inconveniences, goes far to sustain the conclusion which we have reached, that a suit of this character cannot be maintained.

Summarizing the opinion of the court, Justice Sutherland states:

If a case for preventive relief be presented, the court enjoins, in effect, not the execution of the statute, but the acts of the official, the statute notwithstanding. Here the parties plaintiff have no such case. Looking through forms of words to the substance of their complaint, it is merely that officials of the executive department of the government are executing and will execute an act of Congress asserted to be unconstitutional; and this we are asked to prevent. To do so would be, not to decide a judicial controversy, but to assume a position of authority over the governmental acts of another and coequal department, an authority which plainly we do not possess.

In *Doremus* v *Board of Education,* 342 U.S. 429, 72 S.Ct. 394, 96 L.Ed. 475 (1952), the United States Supreme Court refused to consider the constitutionality of prayer in public schools because the case brought to the court lacked the necessary standing to raise a federal question. A group of citizens, one of whom had a child graduated from the public school system in question, filed a suit in state court against the use of prayer in public school. As a basis for standing, the group asserted its status as taxpayers and therefore supporters of the public school system. Since the one petitioner who had a direct interest in the practice had lost his status as a parent with a child in the school system because the child had graduated, the Court could not find an ongoing federal question through the case. Further, the taxpayer status could not provide the direct interest in the suit, since there was no evidence that the school prayers increased the cost of education and no specific monies were set aside to support the practice of prayer in the schools. Therefore, no specific injury to the petitioners could be found by the Supreme Court and the case was dismissed.

Under the Tennessee declaratory judgments act, the railroad in *Nashville, Chattanooga, and St. Louis Railways* v *Wallace,* 288 U.S. 249, 53 S.Ct. 345, 77 L.Ed. 730 (1933), sought a declaratory judgment that a state excise tax levied on gasoline stored in Tennessee violated the Commerce Clause and the Fourteenth Amendment. The Tennessee Supreme Court upheld the tax and the railroad appealed claiming that the declaratory judgment procedure did not raise a case or controversy within the judicial power conferred by Article III. In holding the state procedure valid, the United States Supreme Court stated that a declaratory judgment may constitute a case or controversy within the appellate system "so long as the case retains the essentials of an adversary proceeding, involving a real not hypothetical, controversy, which is finally determined by the judgment below."

In a case which considered the constitutionality of a New York law, the definition of "standing" or "ripeness" seems to have been implicitly expanded. The petitioner in *Adler* v *Board of Education,* 342 U.S. 485, 72 S.Ct. 380, 96, L.Ed. 517 (1952), was a group comprised of parents and teachers who had an interest in the New York public school system. They challenged the constitutionality of a law that allowed the school authorities to dismiss or to refuse to hire any teacher who "advocates, advises or teaches" the overthrow of the government by force or violence or, knowing the purpose of an organization to be the overthrow of the government by such means, joins the organization. The petitioners made no claim that the law personally inhibited their activities or beliefs, rather, that the law was an undue restriction on teachers in general. Even so, the case was decided on its merits alone; the law was found to be constitutional. The only consideration of standing was voiced in a dissent to the majority opinion.

Poe v *Ullman*
367 U.S. 497, 81 S.Ct. 1752, 6 L.Ed. 2d 989 (1961)

Connecticut statutes prohibited the use of certain contraceptive devices and the giving of medical advice on the use of such devices. Mr. and Mrs. Poe consulted a doctor after Mrs. Poe had three consecutive pregnancies terminating in infants born with congenital defects of which they shortly died. For their emotional and physical well-being the doctor indicated that preventive conception was recommended. The Poes were unable to secure medical advice on preventing contraception because Connecticut would consider use of such advice an offense. The Poes asked for a declaratory judgment that the Connecticut statute was unconstitutional because it deprived them of life and liberty without due process of law. The state courts upheld demurrers by the state. On appeal the United States Supreme Court held that the record disclosed no justiciable constitutional question.

Justice Frankfurter announced the opinion of the court in which the Chief Justice and Justices Clark and Whittaker joined:

Appellants' complaints in these declaratory judgment proceedings do not clearly, and certainly do not in terms, allege that appellee Ullman threatens to prosecute them for use of, or for giving advice concerning, contraceptive devices. The allegations are merely that, in the course of his public duty, he intends to prosecute any offenses against Connecticut law, and that he claims that use of and advice concerning contraceptives would constitute offenses. The lack of immediacy of the threat described by these allegations might alone raise serious questions of non-justiciability of appellants' claims. . . . But even were we to read the allegations to convey a clear threat of imminent prosecutions, we are not bound to accept as true all that is alleged on the fact of the complaint and admitted, technically, by demurrer, any more than the Court is bound by stipulation of the parties. . . . Formal agreement between parties that collides with plausibility is too fragile a foundation for indulging in constitutional adjudication.

The Connecticut law prohibiting the use of contraceptives has been on the State's books since 1879. . . . During the more than three-quarters of a century since its enactment, a prosecution for its violation seems never to have been initiated, save in *State* v *Nelson,* 126 Conn. 412, 11 A.2d 856. The circumstances of that case, decided in 1940, only prove the abstract character of what is before us. There, a test case was brought to determine the constitutionality of the Act as applied against two doctors and a nurse who had allegedly disseminated contraceptive information. After the Supreme Court of Errors sustained the legislation on appeal from a demurrer to the information, the State moved to dismiss the information. Neither counsel nor our own researches have discovered any other attempt to enforce the prohibition of distribution or use of contraceptive devices by criminal process. The unreality of these lawsuits is illumined by another circumstance. We were advised by counsel for appellants that contraceptives are commonly and notoriously sold in Connecticut drugstores. Yet no prosecutions are recorded; and certainly such ubiquitous, open, public sales would more quickly invite the attention of enforcement officials than the conduct in which the present appellants wish to engage—the giving of private medical advice by a doctor to his individual patients, and their private use of the devices prescribed. The undeviating policy of nullification by Connecticut of its anti-contraceptive laws throughout all the long years that they have been on the statute books bespeaks more than prosecutorial paralysis. What was said in another context is relevant here. "Deeply embedded traditional ways of carrying out state policy . . ."—or not carrying it out—"are often tougher and truer law than the dead words of the written text."

· · ·

The restriction of our jurisdiction to cases and controversies within the meaning of Article III of the Constitution, . . . is not the sole limitation on the exercise of our appellate powers, especially in cases raising constitutional questions. The policy reflected in numerous cases and over a long period was thus summarized in the oft-quoted statement of Mr. Justice Brandeis: "The Court [has] developed, for its own governance in the cases confessedly within its jurisdiction, a series of rules under which it has avoided passing upon a large part of all the constitutional questions pressed upon it for decision." . . . In part the rules summarized in the Ashwander opinion have derived from the historically defined, limited nature and function of courts and from the recognition that, within the framework of our adversary system, and adjudicatory process is most securely founded when it is exercised under the impact of a lively conflict between antagonistic demands, actively pressed, which make resolution of the controverted issue a practical necessity.

. . .

These considerations press with special urgency in cases challenging legislative action or state judicial action as repugnant to the Constitution. "The best teaching of this Court's experience admonishes us not to entertain constitutional questions in advance of the strictest necessity." . . . The various doctrines of "standing," "ripeness," and "mootness," which this Court has evolved with particular, though not exclusive, reference to such cases are but several manifestations—each having its own "varied application"—of the primary conception that federal judicial power is to be exercised to strike down legislation, whether state or federal, only at the instance of one who is himself immediately harmed, or immediately threatened with harm, by the challenged action.

. . .

. . . Although we have held that a state declaratory-judgment suit may constitute a case or controversy within our appellate jurisdiction, it is to be reviewed here only "so long as the case retains the essentials of an adversary proceeding, involving a real, not a hypothetical, controversy, which is finally determined by the judgment below." . . . It was with respect to a state-originating declaratory judgment proceeding that we said, . . . that "the extent to which the declaratory judgment procedure may be used in the federal courts to control state action lies in the sound discretion of the Court. . . ." Indeed, we have recognized, in such cases, that ". . . the discretionary element characteristic of declaratory jurisdiction, and imported perhaps from equity jurisdiction and practice without the remedial phrase, offers a convenient instrument for making . . . effective . . . the policy against premature constitutional decision.

. . .

Insofar as appellants seek to justify the exercise of our declaratory power by the threat of prosecution, facts which they can no more negative by complaint and demurrer than they could by stipulation preclude our determining their appeals on the merits. . . . It is clear that the mere existence of a state penal statute would constitute insufficient grounds to support a federal court's adjudication of its constitutionality in proceedings brought against the State's prosecuting officials if real threat of enforcement is wanting. . . . If the prosecutor expressly agrees not to prosecute, a suit against him for declaratory and injunctive relief is not such an adversary case as will be reviewed here. . . . Eighty years of Connecticut history demonstrate a similar, albeit tacit agreement. The fact that Connecticut has not chosen to press the enforcement of this statute deprives these controversies of the immediacy which is an indispensable condition of constitutional adjudication. This Court cannot be umpire to debates concerning harmless, empty shadows. To find it necessary to pass on these statutes now, in order to protect appellants from the hazards of prosecution, would be to close our eyes to reality.

Nor does the allegation by the Poes and Doe that they are unable to obtain information concerning contraceptive devices from Dr. Buxton, "for the sole reason that the delivery and use of such information and advice may or will be claimed by the defendant State's Attorney to constitute offenses," disclose a necessity for present constitutional decision. It is true that this Court has several times passed upon criminal statutes challenged by persons who claimed that the effects of the statutes were to deter others from maintaining profitable or advantageous relations with the complainants. . . . But in these cases the deterrent effect complained of was one which was grounded in a realistic fear of prosecution. We cannot agree that if Dr. Buxton's compliance with these statutes is uncoerced by the risk of their enforcement, his patients are entitled to a declaratory judgment concerning the statutes' validity. And, with due regard to Dr. Buxton's standing as a physician and to his personal sensitiveness, we cannot accept, as the basis of constitutional adjudication, other than as chimerical the fear of enforcement of provisions that have during so many years gone uniformly and without exception unenforced.

Justiciability is of course not a legal concept with a fixed content or susceptible of scientific verification. Its utilization is the resultant of many subtle pressures, including the appropriateness of the issues for decision by this Court and the actual hardship to the litigants of denying them the relief sought. Both these factors justify withholding adjudication of the constitutional issue raised under the circumstances and in the manner in which they are now before the Court.

(Dismissed.)
Justice Brennan concurred.
Justices Black, Douglas, Harlan, and Stewart dissented.

Discretionary Review—A Barrier to Constitutional Decision Making

Rescue Army v *Municipal Court of Los Angeles*
331 U.S. 549, 67 S.Ct. 1409, 91 L.Ed. 1666 (1947)

This case involved a municipal ordinance of the City of Los Angeles which set out a comprehensive scheme for the regulation of all solicitations. Of specific concern to the Rescue Army was article 4 which governed charitable solicitations. The Rescue Army brought this action to prohibit continuation of criminal proceeding against one of its officers, Murdock, who had been convicted in Los Angeles Municipal Court on two separate occasions for violations of specified sections of the ordinance. Both of these convictions were reversed by the state courts. So, in essence, the Rescue Army sought a writ of prohibition against the Municipal Court on the grounds that the sections in question were an unconstitutional interference with freedom of religion.

The Supreme Court decision was a statement of discretionary review. It was felt that on the merits of the case on appeal substantial questions were presented concerning the constitutional validity of ordinances of the City of Los Angeles governing solicitation of contributions for charity. The Supreme Court, however, faced difficult problems in determining exactly which sections of the ordinance had been used by the state courts in earlier decisions regarding Officer Murdock. Therefore, the Court decided to follow its previous policy of ''strict necessity in disposing with constitutional issues.'' Justice Rutledge, in delivering the opinion of the Court, said:

> The earliest exemplifications, too well known for repeating the history here, arose in the Court's refusal to render advisory opinions and in applications of the related jurisdictional policy drawn from the case and controversy limitation. . . . The same policy has been reflected continuously not only in decisions but also in rules of court and in statutes made applicable to jurisdictional matters including the necessity for reasonable clarity and definiteness, as well as for timeliness, in raising and presenting constitutional questions. Indeed perhaps the most effective implement for making the policy effective has been the certiorari jurisdiction conferred upon this Court by Congress.
>
> . . .
>
> The policy's ultimate foundations, some if not all of which also sustain the jurisdictional limit, lie in all that goes to make up the unique place and character, in our scheme, of judicial review of governmental action for constitutionality. They are found in the delicacy of that function, particularly in view of possible consequences for others stemming also from constitutional roots; the comparative finality of those consequences; the consideration due to the judgment of other repositories of constitutional power concerning the scope of their authority; the necessity, if government is to function constitutionally, for each to keep within its power, including the courts; the inherent limitations of the judicial process, arising especially from its largely negative character and limited resources of enforcement; withal in the paramount importance of constitutional adjudication in our system.
>
> All these considerations and perhaps others, transcending specific procedures, have united to form and sustain the policy. Its execution has involved a continuous choice between the obvious advantages it produces for the functioning of government in all its coordinate parts and the very real disadvantages, for the assurance of rights, which deferring decision very often entails. On the other hand it is not altogether speculative that a contrary policy, of accelerated decision, might do equal or greater harm for the security of private rights, without attaining any of the benefits of tolerance and harmony for the functioning of the various authorities in our scheme. For premature and

relatively abstract decisions, which such a policy would be most likely to promote, have their part too in rendering rights uncertain and insecure.

Justice Rutledge then continues this discussion with a review of the application of this policy. In closing he notes:

Our decision of course should be without prejudice to any rights which may arise upon final determination of the Municipal Court proceeding, relative to review in this Court of that determination. With that reservation we think the only course consistent, upon this record, at once with preservation of appellants' rights and with adherence to our long-observed policy, is to decline to exercise jurisdiction in this cause.

(Appeal dismissed.)
Justice Black concurred.
Justices Murphy and Douglas dissented.

In a denial of the petition for a writ of certiorari in *Maryland* v *Baltimore Radio,* 338 U.S. 912, 70 S.Ct. 252, 94 L.Ed. 562 (1950), Justice Frankfurter discussed the various reasons for the denial of consideration of the high court. All of the possible reasons for denial were not listed by the author, but rather the magnitude of the possibilities as well as the individuality of any justice's reason for denial were discussed. According to Justice Frankfurter, the reasons for the denial of a hearing may vary with each justice, even though the result of denial is the same. Further, if a dissent is written and included in the denial, it is not necessarily true that the writer was the sole justice in disagreement with the denial. The purposes of expediting the work of the United States Supreme Court and reasons for the denial of most cases are not indicated in the denials.

A citizen of the United States has a constitutionally protected freedom to travel and this freedom can only be regulated narrowly through Congressional power. In *Kent* v *Dulles,* 357 U.S. 116, 78 S.Ct. 1113, 2 L.Ed. 2d 1204 (1958), the United States Supreme Court considered together the appeals of two persons who had been denied passports because of their refusal to make an affidavit concerning associational activities with the Communist Party. The denial was based, in both cases, on a regulation promulgated by the secretary of state under the authority of the president. The Court found that the secretary of state had surpassed his power to restrict travel, since there had been no congressional authorization of the restriction placed on Communists by the United States Congress. Further, only two reasons for the restriction of travel could be validly pursued by the secretary of state: the noncitizen status of the applicant for a passport and the criminal motivation of the applicant. Since only these two restrictions had been authorized by the Congress, the determination of a citizen's memberships and association in order to get a passport was an unwarranted intrusion on the citizen's liberty.

Dombrowski v *Pfister*

380 U.S. 479, 85 S.Ct. 1116, 14 L.Ed. 2d 22 (1965)

Dombrowski was the executive director of the Southern Conference Educational Fund, Inc., which was active in fostering black civil rights in the South. Dombrowski and others sought declaratory relief and an injunction restraining the governor of Louisiana, police, law enforcement officers, and the chairman of the Legislative Joint Committee on Un-American Activities in Louisiana from prosecuting or threatening to prosecute them for alleged violations of the Louisiana Subversive Activities and Communist Control Law and the Communist Propaganda Control Law. The complaint alleged a violation of First and Fourteenth Amendment rights because the breadth of the statute allows sweeping and improper application of the law.

A federal district court dismissed the complaint because of a "failure to state a claim upon which relief can be granted." The judges thought that constitutional rights were in danger but there was no case of irreparable damage threatened.

In delivering the opinion of the court, Justice Brennan states:

It is generally to be assumed that state courts and prosecutors will observe constitutional limitations as expounded by this Court, and that the mere possibility of erroneous initial application of constitutional standards will usually not amount to the irreparable injury necessary to justify a disruption of orderly state proceedings. In *Douglas* v *City of Jeannette,* 319 U.S. (1957)... for example, the Court upheld a district court's refusal to enjoin application of a city ordinance to religious solicitation, even though the ordinance was that very day held unconstitutional as so applied on review of a criminal conviction under it.... Since injunctive relief looks to the future, and it was not alleged that Pennsylvania courts and prosecutors would fail to respect the *Murdock* ruling, the Court found nothing to justify an injunction. And in a variety of other contexts the Court has found no special circumstances to warrant cutting short the normal adjudication of constitutional defenses in the course of a criminal prosecution. In such cases it does not appear that the plaintiffs "have been threatened with any injury other than that incidental to every criminal proceeding brought lawfully and in good faith, or that a federal court of equity by withdrawing the determination of guilt from the state courts could rightly afford petitioners any protection which they could not secure by prompt trial and appeal pursued to this Court."

Of major concern to the Court in this case was the claim of the appellant that irreparable injury from prosecution under this statute would result.

Appellants' allegations and offers of proof outline the chilling effect on free expression of prosecutions initiated and threatened in this case. Early in October 1963 appellant Dombrowski and intervenors Smith and Waltzer were arrested by Louisiana state and local police and charged with violations of the two statutes. Their offices were raided and their files and records seized. Later in October a state judge quashed the arrest warrants as not based on probable cause, and discharged the appellants. Subsequently, the court granted a motion to suppress the seized evidence on the ground that the raid was illegal. Louisiana officials continued, however, to threaten prosecution of the appellants, who thereupon filed this action in November. Shortly after the three-judge court was convened, a grand jury was summoned in the Parish of Orleans to hear evidence looking to indictments of the individual appellants. On appellants' application Judge Wisdom issued a temporary restraining order against prosecutions pending hearing and decision of the case in the District Court. Following a hearing the District Court, over Judge Wisdom's dissent, dissolved the temporary restraining order and, at the same time, handed down an order dismissing the complaint. Thereafter the grand jury returned indictments under the Subversive Activities and Communist Control Law against the individual appellants.

It was the feeling of the Court that "injury other than that incidental to every criminal proceeding brought lawfully and in good faith" would follow prosecution under these statutes. The Supreme Court therefore stated:

We conclude that on the allegations of the complaint, if true, abstention and the denial of injunctive relief may well result in the denial of any effective safeguards against the loss of protected freedoms of expression, and cannot be justified.

(Judgment reversed.)
Justices Black and Stewart did not participate.
Justices Clark and Harlan dissented.

Political Questions

Baker v Carr
369 U.S. 186, 82 S.Ct. 691, 7 L.Ed. 2d 663 (1962)

Tennessee apportioned both of its legislative houses in 1901. A provision of the enacting legislation directed subsequent reapportionment every 10 years based on the number of qualified voters in each county as determined by census. During the 60 years between the 1901 apportionment and this case the population shifted into urban areas in Tennessee. Also during the 6 decades proposals to reapportion the state and redistribute the legislative seats failed to pass the legislature. This case was initiated by Baker and others living in urban areas under the federal civil rights act. They charged that they were being denied equal protection of the laws because their votes did not carry the same value as other state residents. Baker and the others asked that state officials be required to hold the election of state legislators at large or if not, then the legislators should be selected from constituencies determined by the 1950 census. The suit was dismissed by the federal district court which acknowledged that there was an abridgement of civil rights, but the court could not remedy the situation. On appeal, the United States Supreme Court reversed.

After discussion on the issues of jurisdiction and justiciability, Justice Brennan concludes for the Court:

> We come, finally, to the ultimate inquiry whether our precedents as to what constitutes a nonjusticiable "political question" bring the case before us under the umbrella of that doctrine. A natural beginning is to note whether any of the common characteristics which we have been able to identify and label descriptively are present. We find none: The question here is the consistency of state action with the Federal Constitution. We have no question decided, or to be decided, by a political branch of government coequal with this Court. Nor do we risk embarrassment of our government abroad, or grave disturbance at home if we take issue with Tennessee as to the constitutionality of her action here challenged. Nor need the appellants, in order to succeed in this action, ask the Court to enter upon policy determinations for which judicially manageable standards are lacking. Judicial standards under the Equal Protection Clause are well developed and familiar, and it has been open to courts since the enactment of the Fourteenth Amendment to determine, if on the particular facts they must, that a discrimination reflects *no* policy, but simply arbitrary and capricious action.
>
> This case does, in one sense, involve the allocation of political power within a state, and the appellants might conceivably have added a claim under the Guaranty Clause. Of course, as we have seen, any reliance on that clause would be futile. But because any reliance on the Guaranty Clause could not have succeeded it does not follow that appellants may not be heard on the equal protection claim which in fact they tender. True, it must be clear that the Fourteenth Amendment claim is not so enmeshed with those political question elements which render Guaranty Clause claims not justiciable as actually to present a political question itself. But we have found that not to be the case here.
>
>   . . .
>
> When the challenges to state action respecting matters of "the administration of the affairs of the State and the officers through whom they are conducted" have rested on claims of constitutional deprivation which are amena-

ble to judicial correction, this Court has acted upon its view of the merits of the claim.... And only last Term, in *Gomillion* v *Lightfoot,* 364 U.S. 339 [1960], ... we applied the Fifteenth Amendment to strike down a redrafting of municipal boundaries which effected a discriminatory impairment of voting rights, in the face of what a majority of the Court of Appeals thought to be a sweeping commitment to state legislatures of the power to draw and redraw such boundaries.

It was the conclusion of the court that the allegations of the complaint's stating a denial of equal protection presented a justiciable constitutional cause of action upon which appellants are entitled to a trial and a decision.

(Judgement reversed.)
Justice Whittaker did not participate in the consideration of the case.
Justices Douglas, Clark, and Stewart concurred separately.
Justices Frankfurter and Harlan dissented.

In *Colegrove* v *Green,* 328 U.S. 549, 66 S.Ct. 1198, 90 L.Ed. 1432 (1946), voters in Illinois were about to vote in an election of congressmen. Voters in congressional districts that had much larger populations than other congressional districts sued in federal court to enjoin holding the upcoming elections as long as the districts were apportioned as they were. The voters claimed violation of the Constitution and the Reapportionment Act of 1911. The federal district court dismissed the case and on appeal the United States Supreme Court affirmed.

Only seven justices participated in the decision. Justice Frankfurter wrote the opinion of the court, but his opinion was joined only by Justices Reed and Burton. His major contention was that the demands of the petitioners were beyond the Court's competence to grant, added to by the Court's traditional aloofness in determination of similar issues.

Effective working of our government revealed this issue to be of a peculiarly political nature.

Therefore, these three justices wished to keep the Courts out of the "political thicket."

Justice Rutledge who concurred in the opinion felt that the issue was justiciable but that the delicacy of the case forced the Court to "decline to exercise its jurisdiction." On the other hand, Justices Black, Douglas, and Murphy felt that the Court not only had jurisdiction in this matter but "that petitioners had standing to sue, since the facts alleged show that they had been injured as individuals."

In *Coleman* v *Miller,* 307 U.S. 433, 59 S.Ct. 972, 83 L.Ed. 1385 (1939), the United States Supreme Court affirmed the congressional responsibility for the political questions arising from the process of amending the United States Constitution. The Kansas legislature rejected a proposed "Child Labor" amendment to the Constitution in its 1924 term. The amendment was reintroduced to the body in the 1937 term; 40 senators were present and.the vote on the resolution for adoption was evenly divided with 20 senators favoring adoption and 20 senators rejecting adoption. The lieutenant governor broke the tie in favor of the resolution for adoption. The resolution was later adopted by a majority of the members in the state House of Representatives. Twenty-one members of the state legislature brought a mandamus proceeding in the Supreme Court of Kansas requesting the denial of the adoption of the resolution and the restraint of the officers of the legislature in forwarding the authenticated resolution to the governor. The petition claimed that the ratification of the amendment was invalid because of (1) the lieutenant governor's overstepping the bounds of his authority by casting the deciding vote and (2) the "unreasonable" length of time between the legislative rejection and adoption of the amendment. The petitioners claimed that the amendment had "lost its vitality" by the time it was finally ratified by the state legislature. The United States Supreme Court affirmed the lower court's decision to deny the writ of mandamus. According to the Court, the propriety of the lieutenant governor's actions was a state question and properly determined to be correct by the state Supreme Court. The federal question concerning the vitality of the amendment remained and the Court classified this problem as a "political question." The nature of the amendment process granted in the Constitution demands that the United States Congress remain in control of the process during the determination by the states of the acceptability of the proposed amendment to the Constitution. Further, all "political questions" should be considered by the political body in charge of the process. Therefore, the vitality of the amendment and the legality of the ratification of the amendment by the state legislature are political questions to be answered by the United States Congress.

Adam Clayton Powell was elected to the House of Representatives for the 90th Congress. He met the constitutional requirements in Article I, Section 2, Clause 2, but he was nevertheless not permitted to take his seat pursuant to a House Resolution after finding that he wrongfully diverted House funds to himself, avoided valid New York court processes, and made false reports of expenditures to the House. Claiming that his exclusion was unconstitutional, Powell sued to be seated and for back pay. In discussing the issue of whether the Court should stay out of the case because it involved a political question, Chief Justice Warren stated for the majority:

Respondents' alternate contention is that the case presents a political question because judicial resolution of petitioner's claim would produce a "potentially embarrassing confrontation between coordinate branches" of the Federal Government. But, as our interpretation of Art. I,§5, discloses, a determination of Petitioner Powell's right to sit would require no more than an interpretation of the Constitution. Such a determination falls within the traditional role accorded courts to interpret the law, and does not involve a "lack of respect due [a] coordinate branch of Government," nor does it involve an initial determination of a kind clearly for nonjudicial discretion. . . . Our system of government requires that federal courts on occasion interpret the Constitution in a manner at variance with the construction given the document by another branch. The alleged conflict that such an adjudication may cause cannot justify the courts' avoiding their constitutional responsibility. *Powell* v *McCormack,* 395 U.S. 486, 89 S.Ct. 1944, 23 L.Ed. 2d 491 (1969).

QUESTIONS

1. What is the basis for the judicial review authority asserted in *Marbury* v *Madison?*

2. "Jurisdiction" is a term that is used in all of the cases in this chapter. What is "jurisdiction of the federal court?" What are the guidelines? Discuss original and appellate jurisdiction.

3. Discuss the differences between "advisory opinion" and "ripeness of the controversy." Is there an "advisory opinion" problem in *Massachusetts* v *Mellon?*

4. Does the Supreme Court hesitate to issue an opinion on the constitutionality of statutes in *Dombrowski* v *Pfister?* Is there a difference in the Court's rulings on constitutionality in regard to state statutes versus local statutes?

5. What has caused the traditional aloofness of the Court in deciding "political questions"?

3

THE FEDERAL SYSTEM

The materials in this chapter present the basic concepts pertaining to the sharing of powers in a federal system of government. In each section of this chapter answers to questions on the scope or breadth of national power, specified versus implied powers, international relations, and incorporation have been addressed by the United States Supreme Court. The cases are of extreme importance in a study of constitutional law.

The concept of federalism has been deeply involved with the expanding rights afforded to individuals in the state. These rights are discussed in subsequent chapters, but an analysis of federalism as it applies to the Fourteenth Amendment is appropriate here.

Prior to the Civil War individuals were protected against federal actions by the Constitution and the Bill of Rights. There were some significant protections of individual liberty against state action in the prohibitions against *ex post facto* laws, impairment of contractual obligations, and bills of attainder. Beyond these protection of the individual was left up to the state laws and state courts. A change occurred with the adoption of Thirteenth, Fourteenth, and Fifteenth Amendments which contained the potential limitation of state power over the individual. One amendment, the Fourteenth, has been used increasingly to prohibit the states from denying to the individual privileges and immunities of United States citizenship, due process of the law, and equal protection of the law. These protections have gradually made the substantive protections and procedural safeguards of the Bill of Rights applicable to both *state* and *federal* attempts to restrict individual liberty.

The remainder of this introduction to the federal system presents an overview of the concept of incorporation of the Bill of Rights into the Fourteenth Amendment. It should be once again reiterated that many of the United States Supreme Court decisions alluded to will be found in succeeding chapters which discuss the individual rights contained in the appropriate amendments.

The emancipation of slaves and the protection of free blacks from discrimination were the reasons behind the adoption of the Thirteenth, Fourteenth, and Fifteenth Amendments. The Thirteenth Amendment was a clear response to providing a constitutional basis for the elimination of slavery which was recognized in Article 1, Section 2 providing for the apportionment of the House of Representatives membership; Article 1, Section 9 which until 1808 prohibited Congress from regulating "The Migration or Importation of such Persons as any of the States now existing shall think proper to admit;" and Article 4, Section 2 which compelled states to return persons held for service under the laws of one state to be returned if they escaped to another state.

President Lincoln's Emancipation Proclamation applied only to slaves in states in rebellion against the United States. The Thirteenth Amendment made slavery and involuntary servitude illegal, except as a punishment for crime. In the first case construing the Thirteenth Amendment, the United States Supreme Court decided that the amendment prohibited only slavery and other servitudes that were forms of slavery, such as coolie labor systems and peonage. The amendment was therefore not a general protection of personal liberty against state action. *Slaughter-House Cases,* 83 U.S. 36 (1873).

The Thirteenth Amendment was ratified in 1865, but the condition of the black in the South was still in danger because of the so-called "black codes" which:

1. prohibited blacks from owning, leasing, or renting agricultural lands,

2. barred blacks from occupations other than husbandry, and

3. provided for the return of free blacks to their employers.

The 1866 Civil Rights Act declared that free blacks had full citizen's rights, specifically gave them the right to enter the occupation of their choice, and permitted them to own or lease land.

The debate over the Act was acrimonious, with those opposing it arguing that the Thirteenth Amendment did not authorize congressional interference with all state laws discriminating against the blacks. President Andrew Johnson vetoed the law, but this was overridden by the Republican Congress. Because of the debate over the power of Congress to pass such laws, the Fourteenth Amendment was submitted in the same session of Congress which adopted the 1866 Civil Rights Act. However, the amendment contained language that was not solely for the protection of ex-slaves. The clauses—due process, equal protection, and privileges and immunities—were imprecise. Consequently, throughout its history there have been doubts voiced concerning the protection that the Fourteenth

Amendment provides in protecting individuals against state intrusions on personal liberty.

An historically interesting point concerns the ratification of the Fourteenth Amendment. Doubters to its ratification claim that 28 of the 37 states did not freely ratify the amendment because some of the southern states were coerced into ratification. The Supreme Court has, however, consistently refused to inquire into whether any amendment is properly ratified on the ground that it is a political question with Congress having the ultimate authority in exercising the control over the adoption procedures.

The Fifteenth Amendment, ratified in 1870, was designed explicitly to provide constitutional protections for the blacks' right to vote by providing that states may not abridge the rights of citizens to vote "on account of race, color, or previous condition of servitude."

The Incorporation Doctrine and the Fourteenth Amendment

The Fourteenth Amendment has radically changed individual rights in states by incorporation of selected provisions of the Bill of Rights. Early decisions interpreting the Fourteenth Amendment construed it narrowly on the ground that it was meant to protect the rights of former slaves. However, gradually the guarantees in the Bill of Rights against federal intrusion on individual rights have been incorporated into the Fourteenth Amendment to be applicable also in the states.

With the exception of the First Amendment provisions, the Second Amendment through the Eight Amendment could easily be applicable in both the state and federal governments. Why was this not so? In *Barron* v *Baltimore,* 23 U.S. 243 (1833), the United States Supreme Court declared that the whole Bill of Rights was directed not toward the states but solely toward the federal government. Because of this blanket prohibition, the doctrine of selective incorporation was developed.

Due Process of the Law

In the *Slaughter-House Cases,* the United States Supreme Court expressed doubts whether the provisions of the Fourteenth Amendment's prohibition against depriving a person of his life, liberty, or property without due process of law were adequate to protect individual liberty. The position of the Supreme Court took a radical change over succeeding decades.

One of the longest standing judicial philosophies of interpreting the Due Process Clause of the Fourteenth Amendment was that it incorporates only "fundamental" values. These values may or may not be included in the Bill of Rights and as a consequence may or may not be coextensive with particular provisions in the Bill of Rights. Exponents of this view appeal to a higher law, to a set of overreaching principles of correctness which are neither articulated nor are capable of being set out in words, but which the Court has a duty to discover. Under this view, its advocates argued that the states have the responsibility to conduct fair trials and the only time for federal interference is when there is some kind of demonstrable unfairness. The concept of "fundamental" values has prevailed until recent years.

The view today has shifted to the concept that the Due Process Clause of the Fourteenth Amendment incorporates selected provisions of the Bill of Rights. The Court today still rejects the idea that the Bill of Rights is incorporated *in toto* into the Due Process Clause but the most important protections of the Bill of Rights have been made applicable to the states through the process of selective incorporation. The process of selective incorporation of the right to counsel for state indigent defendants is discussed in Chapter 8 and other rights incorporated are covered in the Chapters 9, 10, 11, and 12.

Before leaving the subject of incorporation, a word of caution is in order. Most state constitutions contain the same broad individual liberty protections as those contained in the United States Constitution. Consider for a minute freedom of speech. For example, from the question whether or not the Fourteenth Amendment's Due Process Clause protects freedom of speech, one does not necessarily proceed to the question asking whether or not inhabitants of particular states are to have any freedom in what they say. In other words, to the extent that a particular provision has not been incorporated into the Fourteenth Amendment, people are left to rely on state constitutions for protection. In interpreting their own constitutions, state courts have the final say.

In the final analysis, the real issue involving the incorporation doctrine is seldom whether or not the right exists in the states. Rather, it is whether or not residents of the states must rely solely on state constitutions, interpreted solely by state courts for protection of their individual rights. The real question when incorporation is at issue is whether the power of the United States Supreme Court, and not the state courts, can make final decisions in some cases in which reasonable men may have differing views on what constitutes adequate protection of liberty.

BROAD VERSUS NARROW VIEW OF NATIONAL POWERS

McCulloch v *Maryland*
4 Wheat (17 U.S.) 316, 4 L.Ed. 579 (1819)

An 1818 Maryland statute made it unlawful for any bank operating in Maryland to issue bank notes without state authority, "except upon stamped paper" issued by the state. The fees specified by the act for issuance of the "stamped paper" varied with the value of the note, but in general they amounted to about 2 percent of the face value. The statute also provided that a bank could be relieved of payment of fees on individual notes by paying a lump sum of $15,000 per year. A penalty was provided for violators by providing that officers and the cashier of the violating bank were to be fined $500 for each offense. McCulloch was the cashier of the Bank of the United States, Baltimore branch. He issued notes without payment of the required fees, was arrested, and was convicted. The highest state court in Maryland, Maryland Court of Appeals, affirmed. The United States Supreme Court heard the case on a writ of error. Because of the constitutional significance of the issue, the Court waived its usual rule of permitting only two attorneys to argue the case for each party. Six attorneys argued the case over a nine-day period. The opinion was delivered three days after the close of the argument.

Chief Justice Marshall delivered the opinion of the Court:

In the case now to be determined, the defendant, a sovereign state, denies the obligation of a law enacted by the legislature of the Union, and the plaintiff, on his part, contests the validity of an act which has been passed by the legislature of that state. The Constitution of our country, in its most interesting and vital parts, is to be considered; the conflicting powers of the government of the Union and of its members, as marked in that Constitution, are to be discussed; and an opinion given, which may essentially influence the great operations of the government. No tribunal can approach such a question without a deep sense of its importance, and of the awful responsibility involved in its decision. But it must be decided peacefully, or remain a source of hostile legislation, perhaps of hostility of a still more serious nature; and if it is to be so decided, by this tribunal alone can the decision be made. On the Supreme Court of the United States has the Constitution of our country devolved this important duty.

The first question made in the cause is, has Congress power to incorporate a bank?

It has been truly said that this can scarcely be considered as an open question, entirely unprejudiced by the former proceedings of the nation respecting it. The principle now contested was introduced at a very early period of our history, has been recognized by many successive legislatures, and has been acted upon by the judicial department, in cases of peculiar delicacy, as a law of undoubted obligation.

. . .

. . . The government proceeds directly from the people; is "ordained and established" in the name of the people; and is declared to be ordained, "in order to form a more perfect union, establish justice, ensure domestic tranquility, and secure the blessings of liberty to themselves and to their posterity." The assent of the states, in their sovereign capacity, is implied in calling a convention, and thus submitting that instrument to the people. But the people were at perfect liberty to accept or reject it; and their act was final. It required not the affirmance, and could not be negatived, by the state governments. The Constitution, when thus adopted, was of complete obligation, and bound the state sovereignties.

. . .

Among the enumerated powers, we do not find that of establishing a bank or creating a corporation. But there is no phrase in the instrument which, like the articles of confederation, excludes incidental or implied powers; and which requires that everything granted shall be expressly and minutely described. Even the Tenth Amendment, which was framed for the purpose of quieting the excessive jealousies which had been excited, omits the word "expressly," and declares only that the powers "not delegated to the United States, nor prohibited to the states, are reserved to the states, are reserved to the states or to the people"; thus leaving the question, whether the particular power which may become the subject of contest has been delegated to the one government, or prohibited to the other, to depend on a fair construction of the whole instrument.

. . .

Although, among the enumerated powers of government, we do not find the word "bank" or "incorporation," we find the great powers to lay and collect taxes; to borrow money; to regulate commerce; to declare and conduct a war; and to raise and support armies and navies. The sword and the purse, all the external relations, and no inconsiderable portion of the industry of the nation, are entrusted to its government.

. . .

The government which has a right to do an act, and has imposed on it the duty of performing that act, must, according to the dictates of reason, be allowed to select the means; and those who contend that it may not select any appropriate means, that one particular mode of effecting the object is excepted, take upon themselves the burden of establishing that exception.

. . .

. . . the good sense of the public has pronounced, without hesitation, that the power of punishment appertains to sovereignty, and may be exercised whenever the sovereign has a right to act, as incidental to his constitutional powers. It is a means for carrying into execution all sovereign powers, and may be used although not indispensably necessary. It is a right incidental to the power, and conducive to its beneficial exercise.

If this limited construction of the word "necessary" must be abandoned in order to punish, whence is derived the rule which would reinstate it, when the government would carry its powers into execution by means not vindictive in their nature? If the word "necessary" means "needful," "requisite," "essential," "conducive to," in order to let in the power of punishment for the infraction of law; why is it not equally comprehensive when required to authorize the use of means which facilitate the execution of the powers of government without the infliction of punishments?

It being the opinion of the Court that the act incorporating the bank is constitutional, and that the power of establishing a branch in the state of Maryland might be properly exercised by the bank itself, we proceed to inquire:

2. Whether the state of Maryland may, without violating the Constitution, tax that branch?

That the power of taxation is one of vital importance; that it is retained by the states; that it is not abridged by the grant of a similar power to the government of the Union; that it is to be concurrently exercised by the two governments: are truths which have never been denied. But, such is the paramount character of the Constitution that its capacity to withdraw any subject from the action of even this power, is admitted.

. . .

This great principle is, that the Constitution and the laws made in pursuance thereof are supreme; that they control the constitution and laws of the respective states, and cannot be controlled by them.

. . .

It may be objected to this definition, that the power of taxation is not confined to the people and property of a state. It may be exercised upon every object brought within its jurisdiction.

This is true. But to what source do we trace this right? It is obvious that it is an incident of sovereignty, and is co-extensive with that to which it is an incident. All subjects over which the sovereign power of a state extends, are objects of taxation; but those over which it does not extend, are, upon the soundest principles, exempt from taxation. This proposition may almost be pronounced self-evident.

. . .

If the states may tax one instrument, employed by the government in the execution of its powers, they may tax any and every other instrument. They may tax the mail; they may tax the mint; they may tax patent-rights; they may tax the papers of the custom-house; they may tax judicial process; they may tax all the means employed by the government, to an excess which would defeat all the ends of the government. This was not intended by the American people. This did not design to make their government dependent on the states.

. . .

. . . This is not all. If the controlling power of the states be established; if their supremacy as to taxation be acknowledged; what is to restrain their exercising this control in any shape they may please to give it? Their sovereignty is not confined to taxation. That is not the only mode in which it might be displayed. The question is, in truth, a question of supremacy; and if the right of the states to tax the means employed by the general government be conceded, the declaration that the Constitution, and the laws made in pursuance thereof, shall be the supreme law of the land, is empty and unmeaning declamation.

. . .

It has also been insisted, that, as the power of taxation in the general and state governments is acknowledged to be concurrent, every argument which would sustain the right of the general government to tax banks chartered by the states, will equally sustain the right of the states to tax banks chartered by the general government.

But the two cases are not on the same reason. The people of all the states have created the general government, and have conferred upon it the general power of taxation. The people of all the states, and the states themselves are represented in Congress, and, by these representatives, exercise this power. When they tax the chartered institutions of the states, they tax their constituents; and these taxes must be uniform. But, when a state taxes the operations of the government of the United States, it acts upon institutions created not by their own constitutients, but by the people over whom they claim no control. It acts upon the measures of a government created by others as well as themselves, for the benefit of others in common with themselves. The difference is that which always exists, and always must exist, between the action of the whole on a part, and the action of a part on the whole—between the laws of a government declared to be supreme, and those of a government which, when in opposition to those laws, is not supreme.

But if the full application of this argument could be admitted, it might bring into question the right of Congress to tax the state banks, and could not prove the right of the states to tax the Bank of the United States.

The Court has bestowed on this subject its most deliberate consideration. The result is a conviction that the states have no power, by taxation or otherwise, to retard, impede, burden, or in any manner control the operations of the constitutional laws enacted by Congress to carry into execution the powers vested in the general government. This is, we think, the unavoidable consequence of that supremacy which the Constitution has declared.

We are unanimously of opinion that the law passed by the legislature of Maryland, imposing a tax on the Bank of the United States, is unconstitutional and void.

This opinion does not deprive the states of any resources which they originally possessed. It does not extend to a tax paid by the real property of the bank, in common with the other real property within the state, nor to a tax imposed on the interest which the citizens of Maryland may hold in this institution, in common with other property of the same description throughout the state. But this is a tax on the operations of the bank, and is, consequently, a tax on the operation of an instrument employed by the government of the Union to carry its powers into execution. Such a tax must be unconstitutional.

(Judgment reversed.)

CONCEPT OF SPECIFIED POWERS

Kansas v *Colorado*

206 U.S. 46, 27 S.Ct. 655, 51 L.Ed. 956 (1907)

A suit was filed by Kansas to enjoin Colorado from diverting the waters of the Arkansas River. The United States intervened asserting that the United States has superior authority and supervisory control over the waters and the resulting controversy between the states. The question of the original jurisdiction of the United States Supreme Court over cases and controversies of a jurisdictional nature was crucial to the power of the Supreme Court to intervene in the case. Justice Brewer delivered the opinion of the Court:

Turning now to the controversy as here presented, it is whether Kansas has a right to the continuous flow of the waters of the Arkansas river, as that flow existed before any human interference therewith, or Colorado the right to appropriate the waters of that stream so as to prevent that continuous flow, or that the amount of the flow is subject to the superior authority and supervisory control of the United States.

. . .

Turning to the enumeration of the powers granted to Congress by the eighth section of the first article of the Constitution, it is enough to say that no one of them, by any implication, refers to the reclamation of arid lands. The last paragraph of the section which authorizes Congress to make all laws which shall be necessary and proper for carrying into execution the foregoing powers, and all other powers vested by this Constitution in the government of the United States, or in any department or officer thereof, is not the delegation of a new and independent power, but simply provision for making effective the powers theretofore mentioned.

. . .

We are not here confronted with a question of the extent of the powers of Congress, but one of the limitations imposed by the Constitution on its action, and it seems to us clear that the same rule and spirit of construction must also be recognized. If powers granted are to be taken as broadly granted and as carrying with them authority to pass those acts which may be reasonably necessary to carry them into full execution; in other words, if the Constitution in its grant of powers is to be so construed that Congress shall be able to carry into full effect the powers granted, it is equally imperative that, where prohibition or limitation is placed upon the power of Congress, that prohibition or limitation should be enforced in its spirit and to its entirety. It would be a strange rule of construction that language granting powers is to be liberally construed, and that language of restriction is to be narrowly and technically construed. Especially is this true when, in respect to grants of powers, there is, as heretofore noticed, the help found in the last clause of the eighth section, and no such helping clause in respect to prohibitions and limitations. The true spirit of constitutional interpretation in both directions is to give full, liberal construction to the language, aiming ever to show fidelity to the spirit and purpose.

This very matter of the reclamation of arid lands illustrates this: At the time of the adoption of the Constitution within the known and conceded limits of the United States there were no large tracts of arid land, and nothing which called for any further action than that which might be taken by the legislature of the state in which any particular tract of such land was to be found; and the Constitution, therefore, makes no provision for a national control of the arid regions or their reclamation. But, as our national territory has been enlarged, we have within our borders extensive tracts of arid lands which ought to be reclaimed, and it may well be that no power is adequate for their reclamation other than that of the national government. But, if no such power has been granted, none can be exercised.

It does not follow from this that the national government is entirely power-less in respect to this matter. These arid lands are largely within the territories, and over them, by virtue of the second paragraph of Section 3 of Article IV, hertofore quoted, or by virtue of the power vested in the national government to acquire territory by treaties, Congress had full power of legislation, subject to no restrictions other than those expressly named in the Constitution, and, therefore, it may legislate in respect to all arid lands within their limits. As to those lands within the limits of the states, at least of the Western states, the national government is the most considerable owner and has power to dispose of and make all needful rules and regulations respecting its property. We do not mean that its legislation can override state laws in respect to the general subject of reclamation. While arid lands are to be found mainly, if not only, in the Western and newer states, yet the powers of the national government within the limits of those states are the same (no greater and no less) than those within the limits of the original thirteen; and it would be strange if, in the absence of a definite grant of power, the national government could enter the territory of the states along the Atlantic and legislate in respect to improving, by irrigation or otherwise, the lands within their borders. Nor do we under-stand that hitherto Congress has acted in disregard to this limitation.

. . .

The federal government has certain responsibilities to its citizens which cannot be blocked by the lack of state approval. In *Arizona* v *California,* 283 U.S. 423, 51 S.Ct. 522, 75 L.Ed. 1154 (1931), the United States Supreme Court consid-ered an argument by Arizona that an interstate agreement approved by the United States Congress but not approved by Arizona was an unconstitutional abridgement of that state's right since it involved building a dam which partly lay in Arizona. The Court found that since the purpose of the act was the navigation of an interstate navigable waterway, the Colorado River, the Congress had the authority to approve the agreement as long as its purpose was the navigation of the waterway. Further infringement on the Arizona land and water was not argued, but the Court stated that if an unnecessary infringement on the rights of the state of Arizona could be shown, this was the proper concern for further legal action. Under the facts of this case, however, the interstate compact fell within the Constitution's provisions.

INTERNATIONAL RELATIONS EXCEPTION

United States v Curtis-Wright Export Corporation
299 U.S. 304, 57 S.Ct. 216, 81 L.Ed. 255 (1936)

A joint resolution of Congress stated that "if the President finds that the prohibition of the sale of arms and munitions of war in the United States to those countries now engaged in armed conflict in the Chaco may contribute to the reestablishment of peace between those two countries and if . . . he (the President) may deem it necessary, and he makes proclamation to that effect, it shall be unlawful to sell except, under such limitations as the President prescribes" arms and munitions to the combatants. The resolution provided penalities of fine or imprisonment or both.

Curtis-Wright Corporation was indicted for conspiracy to violate the Joint Congressional Resolution and the Presidental Proclamation issued under the resolution's authority. A federal district court sustained a demurrer to the indictment basically on the ground that the Joint Resolution provided for an unconstitutional delegation of legislative authority to the executive. A direct appeal was taken to the United States Supreme Court.

Justice Sutherland delivered the opinion of the Court:

. . . The whole aim of the resolution is to affect a situation entirely external to the United States, and falling within the category of foreign affairs. The determination which we are called to make, therefore, is whether the Joint Resolution, as applied to that situation, is vulnerable to attack under the rule that forbids a delegation of the lawmaking power. In other words, assuming (but not deciding) that the challenged delegation, if it were confined to internal affairs, would be invalid, may it nevertheless be sustained on the ground that its exclusive aim is to afford a remedy for a hurtful condition within foreign territory?

It will contribute to the elucidation of the question if we first consider the differences between the powers of the federal government in respect of foreign or external affairs and those in respect of domestic or internal affairs.

. . .

The two classes of powers are different, both in respect of their origin and their nature. The broad statement that the federal government can exercise no powers except those specifically enumerated in the Constitution, and such implied powers as are necessary and proper to carry into effect the enumerated powers, is categorically true only in respect of our internal affairs.

. . .

. . . That this doctrine applies only to powers which the states had is self-evident. And since the states severally never possessed international powers, such powers could not have been carved from the mass of state powers but obviously were transmitted to the United States from some other source. During the Colonial period, those powers were possessed exclusively by and were entirely under the control of the Crown. By the Declaration of Independence, "the Representatives of the United States of America" declared the United (not the several) Colonies to be free and independent states, and as such to have "full Power to levy War, conclude Peace, contract Alliances, establish Commerce and to do all other Acts and Things which Independent States may of right do."

. . .

After a discussion of the acquisition of the powers of external sovereignty gained by the colonies collectively as a result of their separation from Great Britain, Justice Sutherland states:

Not only, as we have shown, is the federal power over external affairs in origin and essential character different from that over internal affairs, but participation in the exercise of the power is significantly limited. In this vast external realm, with its important, complicated, delicate and manifold problems, the President alone has the power to speak or listen as a representative of the nation. He *makes* treaties with the advice and consent of the Senate; but he alone negotiates. Into the field of negotiation the Senate cannot intrude; and Congress itself is powerless to invade it.

. . .

In the light of the foregoing observations, it is evident that this court should not be in haste to apply a general rule which will have the effect of condemning legislation like that under review as constituting an unlawful delegation of legislative power. The principles which justify such legislation find overwhelming support in the unbroken legislative practice which has prevailed almost from the inception of the national government to the present day.

. . .

. . . A legislative practice such as we have here, evidenced not by only occasional instances, but marked by the movement of a steady stream for a century and a half of time, goes a long way in the direction of proving the presence of unassailable ground for the constitutionality of the practice, to be found in the origin and history of the power involved, or in its nature, or in both combined.

. . .

The uniform, long-continued and undisputed legislative practice just disclosed rests upon an admissible view of the Constitution which, even if the practice found far less support in principle than we think it does, we should not feel at liberty at this late day to disturb.

We deem it unnecessary to consider, *seriatim,* the several clauses which are said to evidence the unconstitutionality of the Joint Resolution as involving an unlawful delegation of legislative power. It is enough to summarize by saying that, both upon principle and in accordance with precedent, we conclude there is sufficient warrant for the broad discretion vested in the President to determine whether the enforcement of the statute will have a beneficial effect upon the re-establishment of peace in the affected countries; whether he shall make proclamation to bring the resolution into operation; whether and when the resolution shall cease to operate and to make proclamation accordingly; and to prescribe limitations and exceptions to which the enforcement of the resolution shall be subject.

(Reversed.)
(Justice Reynolds dissented.)

FEDERALISM AND THE INCORPORATION DOCTRINE

Palko v *Connecticut*

302 U.S. 319, 58 S.Ct. 149, 82 L.Ed. 288 (1937)

Palko was indicted in Fairfield County, Connecticut, for the crime of first-degree murder. In a jury trial he was found guilty of second degree murder and sentenced to life imprisonment in the state prison. On appeal to the Connecticut Supreme Court of Errors by the state prosecutor in pursuance to Connecticut law, the conviction was reversed because of various errors in the trial which prejudiced the state. Thereafter Palko was retried, convicted of first-degree murder, and sentenced to death. On appeal to the United States Supreme Court, Palko claimed that the effect of the second trial was to place him twice in jeopardy for the same offense and in so doing, the Connecticut law was in violation of the Fourteenth Amendment.

Justice Cardozo delivered the opinion of the Court:

1. The execution of the sentence will not deprive appellant of his life without the process of law assured to him by the Fourteenth Amendment of the Federal Constitution.

The argument for appellant is that whatever is forbidden by the Fifth Amendment is forbidden by the Fourteenth also. . . . To retry a defendant, though under one indictment and only one, subjects him, it is said, to double jeopardy in violation of the Fifth Amendment, if the prosecution is one on behalf of the United States. From this the consequence is said to follow that there is a denial of life or liberty without due process of law, if the prosecution is one on behalf of the people of a state.

. . .

We do not find it profitable to mark the precise limits of the prohibition of double jeopardy in federal prosecutions. The subject was much considered in *Kepner* v *United States,* 195 U.S. 100, 24 S.Ct. 797, 49 L.Ed. 114, 1 Ann.Cas. 655, decided in 1904 by a closely divided court. The view was there expressed for a majority of the court that the prohibition was not confined to jeopardy in a new and independent case. It forbade jeopardy in the same case if the new trial was at the instance of the government and not upon defendant's motion.

. . .

We have said that in appellant's view the Fourteenth Amendment is to be taken as embodying the prohibitions of the Fifth. His thesis is even broader. Whatever would be a violation of the original Bill of Rights (Amendments 1 to 8) if done by the federal government is now equally unlawful by force of the Fourteenth Amendment if done by a state. There is no such general rule.

The Fifth Amendment provides, among other things, that no person shall be held to answer for a capital or otherwise infamous crime unless on presentment or indictment of a grand jury. This court has held that, in prosecutions by a state, presentment or indictment by a grand jury may give way to informations at the instance of a public officer. *Hurtado* v *California,* 110 U.S. 516, . . . the Fifth Amendment provides also that no person shall be compelled in any criminal case to be a witness against himself. This court has said that, in prosecutions by a state, the exemption will fail if the state elects to end it. . . . As to the Fourth Amendment, one should refer to *Weeks* v *United States,* 232 U.S. 383, . . . and as to other provisions of the Sixth, to *West* v *Louisiana,* 194 U.S. 258.

. . .

On the other hand, the Due Process Clause of the Fourteenth Amendment may make it unlawful for a state to abridge by its statutes the freedom of speech which the First Amendment safeguards against encroachment by the Congress . . . or the like freedom of the press . . . or the free exercise of religion . . . or the right of peaceable assembly, without which speech would be unduly trammeled . . . or the right of one accused of crime to the benefit of counsel. . . . In these and other situations immunities that are valid as against the federal government by force of the specific pledges of particular amendments have been found to be implicit in the concept of ordered liberty, and thus, through the Fourteenth Amendment, become valid as against the states. . . . We deal with the statute before us and no other. The state is not attempting to wear the accused out by a multitude of cases with accumulated trials. It asks no more than this, that the case against him shall go on until there shall be a trial free from the corrosion of substantial legal error. . . . This is not cruelty at all, nor even vexation in any immoderate degree. If the trial had been infected with error adverse to the accused, there might have been review at his instance, and as often as necessary to purge the vicious taint. A reciprocal privilege, subject at all times to the discretion of the presiding judge . . . has now been granted to the state. There is here no seismic innovation. The edifice of justice stands, its symmetry, to many, greater than before.

2. The conviction of appellant is not in derogation of any privileges or immunities that belong to him as a citizen of the United States.

There is argument in his behalf that the Privileges and Immunities Clause of the Fourteenth Amendment as well as the Due Process Clause has been flouted by the judgment.

(Judgment affirmed.)
(Justice Butler dissented.)

The United States Supreme Court in *Twining* v *New Jersey,* 211 U.S. 78, 29 S.Ct. 14, 53 L.Ed. 97 (1908), failed to incorporate the privilege against self-incrimination in the Due Process Clause of the Fourteenth Amendment. *Twining* was convicted of a felony after the trial judge instructed the jury that Twining's failure to testify on his behalf could be used to impute evidence of guilty. The United States Supreme Court accepted the appeal in order to determine the validity of the defendant's argument that the exemption against self-incrimination was a fundamental right necessary under due process of the law. The Court rejected this argument, even though the majority opinion stressed the inherent fairness of the exemption. The question put to the Court was much more narrow than that of wisdom and fairness. The Court was asked to determine if the privilege against self-incrimination was so intertwined in due process that its denial constituted the denial of due process. The Court could not find this inherent necessity and affirmed the conviction.

The indigent's right to counsel under the Sixth Amendment was reaffirmed and strengthened by the United States Supreme Court in *Johnson* v *Zerbst,* 304 U.S. 458, 58 S.Ct. 1019, 82 L.Ed. 1461 (1938). Johnson was tried and convicted without the assistance of counsel. Then questioned by the court as to his readiness for trial, Johnson answered affirmatively. On a writ of habeas corpus, the United States Supreme Court considered his case and the ancilliary question of the intelligent waiver of constitutional rights. It found that since all other alternatives to appeal had been looked over due to the lack of legal knowledge by the defendant, then the habeas corpus appeal was proper. It further found the Sixth Amendment's right to counsel was so necessary to an effective defense that any waiver of this right must be intelligent and knowing on the part of the defendant. Without this provision, the ignorant are at the double disadvantage—

legal rights are ignored in addition to reliance on improperly trained legal skills for a defense. For these reasons, the judgment was reversed and the case remanded to the district court for proper action.

Adamson v *California*

332 U.S. 46, 67 S.Ct. 1672, 91 L.Ed. 1093 (1947)

Adamson was convicted of first-degree murder in California and sentenced to death. The defendant did not testify during his trial. As permitted by California law, the failure of a defendant to explain or deny evidence against him may be commented upon by the court and by counsel and be considered by the court and jury. On appeal, the United States Supreme Court considered whether or not the California provision was unconstitutional under the Fourteenth Amendment.

Justice Reed delivered the opinion of the Court:

. . . This forces an accused who is a repeated offender to choose between the risk of having his prior offenses disclosed to the jury or of having it draw harmful inferences from uncontradicted evidence that can only be denied or explained by the defendant.

· · ·

We shall assume, but without any intention thereby of ruling upon the issue, that state permission by law to the court, counsel, and jury to comment upon and consider the failure of defendant "to explain or to deny by his testimony any evidence or facts in the case against him" would infringe defendant's privilege against self-incrimination under the Fifth Amendment if this were a trial in a court of the United States under a similar law. Such an assumption does not determine appellant's rights under the Fourteenth Amendment. It is settled law that the clause of the Fifth Amendment, protecting a person against being compelled to be a witness against himself, is not made effective by the Fourteenth Amendment as a protection against state action on the ground that freedom from testimonial compulsion is a right of national citizenship, or because it is a personal privilege or immunity secured by the federal Constitution as one of the rights of man that are listed in the Bill of Rights.

Appellant secondly contends that if the privilege against self-incrimination is not a right protected by the Privileges and Immunities Clause of the Fourteenth Amendment against state action, this privilege, to its full scope under the Fifth Amendment, inheres in the right to a fair trial. A right to a fair trial is a right admittedly protected by the Due Process Clause of the Fourteenth Amendment. Therefore, appellant argues, the Due Process Clause of the Fourteenth Amendment protects his privilege against self-incrimination. The Due Process Clause of the Fourteenth Amendment, however, does not draw all the rights of the federal Bill of Rights under its protection. That contention was made and rejected in *Palko* v *Connecticut,* 302 U.S. 319, 323. . . . It was rejected with citation of the cases excluding several of the rights, protected by the Bill of Rights, against infringement by the National Government. Nothing has been called to our attention that either the framers of the Fourteenth Amendment or the states that adopted intended its Due Process Clause to draw within its scope the earlier amendments to the Constitution. *Palko* held that such provisions of the Bill of Rights as were "implicit in the concept of ordered liberty," 302 U.S. at page 325, 58 S.Ct. at pages 151, 152, became secure from state interference by the clause. But it held nothing more.

. . .

Generally, comment on the failure of an accused to testify is forbidden in American jurisdictions. This arises from state constitutional or statutory provisions similar in character to the federal provisions. . . . California, however, is one of a few states that permit limited comment upon a defendant's failure to testify. That permission is narrow. The California law is set out in note 3 and authorizes comment by court and counsel upon the "failure of the defendant to explain or to deny by his testimony any evidence or facts in the case against him." This does not involve any presumption, rebuttable or irrebuttable, either of guilt or of the truth of any fact, that is offered in evidence. . . . It allows inferences to be drawn from proven facts. Because of this clause, the court can direct the jury's attention to whatever evidence there may be that a defendant could deny and the prosecution can argue as to inferences that may be drawn from the accused's failure to testify. . . . There is here no lack of power in the trial court to adjudge and no denial of a hearing. California has prescribed a method for advising the jury in the search for truth. However sound may be the legislative conclusion that an accused should not be compelled in any criminal case to be a witness against himself, we see no reason why comment should not be made upon his silence. It seems quite natural that when a defendant has opportunity to deny or explain facts and determines not to do so, the prosecution should bring out the strength of the evidence by commenting upon defendant's failure to explain or deny it. The prosecution evidence may be of facts that may be beyond the knowledge of the accused. If so, his failure to testify would have little if any weight. But the facts may be such as are necessarily in the knowledge of the accused. In that case a failure to explain would point to an inability to explain.

Appellant sets out the circumstances of this case, however, to show coercion and unfairness in permitting comment. The guilty person was not seen at the place and time of the crime. There was evidence, however, that entrance to the place or room where the crime was committed might have been obtained through a small door. It was freshly broken. Evidence showed that six fingerprints on the door were petitioner's. Certain diamond rings were missing from the deceased's possession. There was evidence that appellant, some time after the crime, asked an unidentified person whether the latter would be interested in purchasing a diamond ring. As has been stated, the information charged other crimes to appellant and he admitted them. His argument here is that he could not take the stand to deny the evidence against him because he would be subjected to a cross-examination as to former crimes to impeach his veracity and the evidence so produced might well bring about his conviction. Such cross-examination is allowable in California. . . . Therefore, appellant contends the California statute permitting comment denies him due process.

It is true that if comment were forbidden, an accused in this situation could remain silent and avoid evidence of former crimes and comment upon his failure to testify. We are of the view, however, that a state may control such a situation in accordance with its own ideas of the most efficient administration of criminal justice. The purpose of due process is not to protect an accused against a proper conviction but against an unfair conviction. When evidence is before a jury that threatens conviction, it does not seem unfair to require him to choose between leaving the adverse evidence unexplained and subjecting himself to impeachment through disclosure of former crimes.

. . .

(Judgment affirmed.)

Justice Frankfurter concurring:

For historical reasons a limited immunity from the common duty to testify was written into the federal Bill of Rights, and I am prepared to agree that, as part of that immunity, comment on the failure of an accused to take the witness stand is forbidden in federal prosecutions. It is so, of course, by explicit act of Congress. . . . But to suggest that such a limitation can be drawn out of "due process" in its protection of ultimate decency in a civilized society is to suggest that the Due Process Clause fastened fetters of unreason upon the states. This opinion is concerned solely with a discussion of the Due Process Clause of the Fourteenth Amendment.

. . .

The short answer to the suggestion that the provision of the Fourteenth Amendment, which ordains "nor shall any State deprive any person of life, liberty, or property, without due process of law," was a way of saying that every state must thereafter initiate prosecutions through indictment by a grand jury, must have a trial by a jury of twelve in criminal cases, and must have trial by such a jury in common law suits where the amount in controversy exceeds $20, is that it is a strange way of saying it. . . . The notion that the Fourteenth Amendment was a covert way of imposing upon the states all the rules which it seemed important to eighteenth-century statesmen to write into the Federal Amendments, was rejected by judges who were themselves witnesses of the process by which the Fourteenth Amendment became part of the Constitution.

. . .

Indeed, the suggestion that the Fourteenth Amendment incorporates the first eight amendments as such is not unambiguously urged. Even the boldest innovator would shrink from suggesting to more than half the states that they may no longer initiate prosecutions without indictments by grand jury, of that thereafter all the states of the Union must furnish a jury of 12 for every case involving a claim above $20. There is suggested merely a selective incorporation of the first eight amendments into the Fourteenth Amendment. . . . If all that is meant is that due process contains within itself certain minimal standards which are "of the very essence of a scheme of ordered liberty" . . . putting upon this court the duty of applying these standards from time to time, then we have merely arrived at the insight which our predecessors long ago expressed. . . . This guidance bids us to be duly mindful of the heritage of the past, with its great lessons of how liberties are won and how they are lost. As judges charged with the delicate task of subjecting the government of a continent to the Rule of Law we must be particularly mindful that it is "a *constitution* we are expounding," so that it should not be imprisoned in what are merely legal forms even though they have the sanction of the eighteenth century.

A construction which gives to due process no independent function but turns it into a summary of the specific provisions of the Bill of Rights would, as has been noted, tear up by the roots much of the fabric of law in the several states, and would deprive the states of opportunity for reforms in legal process designed for extending the area of freedom.

. . .

. . . It seems pretty late in the day to suggest that a phrase so laden with historic meaning should be given an improvised content consisting of some but not all of the provisions of the first eight amendments, selected on an undefined basis, with improvisation of content for the provisions so selected.

And so, when, as in a case like the present, a conviction in a state court is here for review under a claim that a right protected by the Due Process Clause of the Fourteenth Amendment has been denied, the issue is not whether an infraction of one of the specific provisions of the first eight amendments is disclosed by the record. The relevant question is whether the criminal proceedings which resulted in conviction deprived the accused of the due process of law to which the United States Constitution entitled him. . . . These standards of justice are not authoritatively formulated anywhere as though they were prescriptions in a pharmacopoeia. But neither does the application of the Due Process Clause imply that judges are wholly at large. The judicial judgment in applying the Due Process Clause must move within the limits of accepted notions of justice and is not to be based upon the idiosyncrasies of a merely personal judgment. The fact that judges among themselves may differ whether in a particular case a trial offends accepted notions of justice is not disproof that general rather than idiosyncratic standards are applied. An important safeguard against such merely individual judgment is an alert deference to the judgment of the state court under review.

Justice Black dissenting:

This decision reasserts a constitutional theory spelled out in *Twining* v *New Jersey,* 211 U.S. 78, 29 S.Ct. 14, 53 L.Ed. 97 (1908), that this Court is endowed by the Constitution with boundless power under "natural law" periodically to expand and contract constitutional standards to conform to the Court's conception of what at a particular time constitutes "civilized decency" and "fundamental principles of liberty and justice." Invoking this *Twining* rule, the Court concludes that although comment upon testimony in a federal court would violate the Fifth Amendment, identical comment in a state court does not violate today's fashion in civilized decency and fundamentals and is therefore not prohibited by the federal Constitution as amended.

. . . I would not reaffirm the *Twining* decision. I think that decision and the "natural law" theory of the Constitution upon which it relies degrade the constitutional safeguards of the Bill of Rights and simultaneously appropriate for this Court a broad power which we are not authorized by the Constitution to exercise. Furthermore, the *Twining* decision rested on previous cases and broad hypotheses which have been undercut by intervening decisions of this Court.

. . .

. . . I am attaching to this dissent an appendix which contains a resume, by no means complete, of the Amendment's history. In my judgment that history conclusively demonstrates that the language of the first section of the Fourteenth Amendment, taken as a whole, was thought by those responsible for its submission to the people, and by those who opposed its submission, sufficiently explicit to guarantee that thereafter no state could deprive its citizens of the privileges and protections of the Bill of Rights.

I cannot consider the Bill of Rights to be an outworn eighteenth-century "strait jacket" as the *Twining* opinion did. Its provisions may be thought outdated abstractions by some. And it is true that they were designed to meet ancient evils. But they are the same kind of human evils that have emerged from century to century wherever excessive power is sought by the few at the expense of the many. In my judgment the people of no nation can lose their liberty so long as a Bill of Rights like ours survives and its basic purposes are conscientiously interpreted, enforced, and respected so as to afford continuous protection against old, as well as new, devices and practices which might thwart those purposes. . . . If the choice must be between the selective process of the *Palko* decision applying some of the Bill of Rights to the states or the *Twining* rule applying none of them, I would choose the *Palko* selective process. But rather than accept either of these choices, I would follow what I believe was the original purpose of the Fourteenth Amendment—to extend to all the people of the nation the complete protection of the Bill of Rights. To hold that this Court can determine what, if any, provisions of the Bill of Rights will be enforced, and if so to what degree, is to frustrate the great design of a written Constitution.

Since *Marbury* v *Madison*, 1 Cranch 137, . . . was decided, the practice has been firmly established for better or worse, that courts can strike down legislative enactments which violate the Constitution. This process, of course, involves interpretation, and since words can have many meanings, interpretation obviously may result in contraction or extension of the original purpose of a constitutional provision thereby affecting policy. But to pass upon the constitutionality of statutes by looking to the particular standards enumerated in the Bill of Rights and other parts of the Constitution is one thing; to invalidate statutes because of application of "natural law" deemed to be above and undefined by the Constitution is another. "In the one instance, courts proceeding within clearly marked constitutional boundaries seek to execute policies written into the Constitution; in the other they roam at will in the limitless area of their own beliefs as to reasonableness and actually select policies, a responsibility which the Constitution entrusts to the legislative representatives of the people.

Rochin v California
342 U.S. 165, 72 S.Ct. 205, 96 L.Ed. 183 (1952)

Acting on information that Rochin was selling narcotics, three deputy sheriffs entered Rochin's home and found him sitting on his bed partly dressed. The deputies saw two capsules on a night stand beside the bed. Rochin grabbed the capsules and swallowed them. The deputies sought unsuccessfully to extract the capsules. Rochin was then taken to a hospital where he was medically forced to vomit. Stomach pumping produced the vomit in which the two capsules were found.

Rochin was later convicted of possessing a morphine preparation, the chief evidence against him being the two capsules. The United States Supreme Court granted certiorari.

Justice Frankfurter delivered the opinion of the Court.

The vague contours of the Due Process Clause do not leave judges at large. We may not draw on our merely personal and private notions and disregard the limits that bind judges in their judicial function. . . . The Due Process Clause places upon this Court the duty of exercising a judgment, within the narrow confines of judicial power in reviewing state convictions, upon interests of society pushing in opposite directions.

Due process of law thus conceived is not to be derided as resort to a revival of "natural law." To believe that this judicial exercise of judgment could be avoided by freezing "due process of law" at some fixed stage of time or thought is to suggest that the most important aspect of constitutional adjudication is a function for inanimate machines and not for judges, for whom the independence safeguarded by Article III of the Constitution was designed and who are presumably guided by established standards of judicial behavior.

. . .

Restraints on our jurisdiction are self-imposed only in the sense that there is from our decisions no immediate appeal short of impeachment or constitutional amendment. But that does not make due process of law a matter of judicial caprice. The faculties of the Due Process Clause may be indefinite and vague, but the mode of their ascertainment is not self-willed.

. . .

Applying these general considerations to the circumstances of the present case, we are compelled to conclude that the proceedings by which this conviction was obtained do more than offend some fastidious squeamishness or private sentimentalism about combatting crime too energetically. This is conduct that shocks the conscience. Illegally breaking into the privacy of the petitioner, the struggle to open his mouth and remove what was there, the forcible extraction of his stomach's contents—this course of proceeding by agents of government to obtain evidence is bound to offend even hardened sensibilities. They are methods too close to the rack and the screw to permit of constitutional differentiation.

. . .

. . . It would be a stultification of the responsibility which the course of constitutional history has cast upon this Court to hold that in order to convict a man the police cannot extract by force what is in his mind but can extract what is in his stomach.

To attempt in this case to distinguish what lawyers call "real evidence" from verbal evidence is to ignore the reasons for excluding coerced confessions. . . . Coerced confessions offend the community's sense of fair play and decency. So here, to sanction the brutal conduct which naturally enough was condemned by the court whose judgment is before us, would be to afford brutality the cloak of law. Nothing would be more calculated to discredit law and thereby to brutalize the temper of a society.

(Judgment reversed.)

Justice Black, concurring:

. . . I think a person is compelled to be a witness against himself not only when he is compelled to testify, but also when as here, incriminating evidence is forcibly taken from him by a contrivance of modern science.

. . .

In view of a majority of the Court, however, the Fifth Amendment imposes no restraint of any kind on the states. They nevertheless hold that California's use of this evidence violated the Due Process Clause of the Fourteenth Amendment. Since they hold as I do in this case, I regret my inability to accept their interpretation without protest. But I believe that faithful adherence to the specific guarantees in the Bill of Rights ensures a more permanent protection of individual liberty than that which can be afforded by the nebulous standards stated by the majority.

If the Due Process Clause does vest this Court with such unlimited power to invalidate laws, I am still in doubt as to why we should consider only the notions of English-speaking peoples to determine what are immutable and fundamental principles of justice. Moreover, one may well ask what avenues of investigation are open to discover "canons" of conduct so universally favored that this Court should write them into the Constitution? All we are told is that the discovery must be made by an "evaluation based on a disinterested inquiry pursued in the spirit of science, on a balanced order of facts.

· · ·

... These cases, and others, show the extent to which the evanescent standards of the majority's philosophy have been used to nullify state legislative programs passed to suppress evil economic practices. What paralyzing role this same philosophy will play in the future economic practices.... Of even graver concern, however, is the use of the philosophy to nullify the Bill of Rights. I long ago concluded that the accordion-like qualities of this philosophy must inevitably imperil all the individual liberty safeguards specifically enumerated in the Bill of Rights. Reflection and recent decisions of this Court sanctioning abridgment of the freedom of speech and press have strengthened this conclusion.

Justice Douglas, concurring:

... The Court rejected the view that compelled testimony should be excluded and held in substance that the accused in a state trial can be forced to testify against himself. I disagree. Of course an accused can be compelled to be present at the trial, to stand, to sit, or turn this way or that, and to try on a cap or a coat.... I think that words taken from his lips, capsules taken from his stomach, blood taken from his veins are all inadmissible provided they are taken from him without his consent. They are inadmissible because of the command of the Fifth Amendment.

That is an unequivocal, definite, and workable rule of evidence for state and federal courts. But we cannot in fairness free the state courts from that command and yet excoriate them for flouting the "decencies of civilized conduct" when they admit the evidence. That is to make the rule turn not on the Constitution but on the idiosyncrasies of the judges who sit here.

In *Roe* v *Wade*, 410 U.S. 113, 93 S.Ct. 705, 35 L.Ed. 2d 147 (1973), it was held that the Due Process Clause of the Fourteenth Amendment was violated by a state criminal abortion statute which only exempted from its criminal provisions abortion necessary to save the life of the mother. The Court recognized that the right of privacy does exist as a constitutional doctrine and is broad enough to encompass a woman's decision whether or not to terminate pregnancy.

Griffin v *California*

380 U.S. 609, 85 S.Ct. 1229, 14 L.Ed. 2d 106 (1965)

(See the introductory factual situation in the opinion which follows for the criminal rule in issue.)

Justice Douglas delivered the opinion of the Court:

If this were a federal trial, reversible error would have been committed, *Wilson* v *United States,* 149 U.S. 60, ... so holds. It is said, however, that the Wilson decision rested not on the Fifth Amendment, but on an Act of Congress, now 18 U.S.C. §3481. That indeed is the fact, as the opinion of the Court in the Wilson case states. ... But that is the beginning, not the end, of our inquiry. The question remains whether, statute or not, the comment rule, approved by California, violates the Fifth Amendment.

We think it does. It is in substance a rule of evidence that allows the state the privilege of tendering to the jury for its consideration the failure of the accused to testify. No formal offer of proof is made as in other situations; but the prosecutor's comment and the court's acquiescence are the equivalent of an offer of evidence and its acceptance.

. . .

If the words "Fifth Amendment" are substituted for "act" and for "statute" the spirit of the Self-Incrimination Clause is reflected. For comment on the refusal to testify is a remnant of the "inquisitorial system of criminal justice," *Murphy* v. *Waterfront Comm.,* 378 U.S. 52, 55, 84 S.Ct. 1594, 1596, 12 L.Ed. 2d 678, which the Fifth Amendment outlaws. It is a penalty imposed by courts for exercising a constitutional privilege. It cuts down on the privilege by making its assertion costly. It is said, however, that the inference of guilt for failure to testify as to facts peculiarly within the accused's knowledge is in any event natural and irresistible, and that comment on the failure does not magnify that inference into a penalty for asserting a constitutional privilege. ... What the jury may infer, given no help from the court, is one thing. What it may infer when the court solemnizes the silence of the accused into evidence against him is quite another. That the inference of guilty is not always so natural or irresistible is brought out in the *Modesto* opinion itself:

> Defendant contends that the reason a defendant refuses to testify is that his prior convictions will be introduced in evidence to impeach him ([Cal.] Code Civ. Proc. §2051) and not that he is unable to deny the accusations. It is true that the defendant might fear that his prior convictions will prejudice the jury, and therefore another possible inference can be drawn from his refusal to take the stand.
>
> . . .

We said in *Malloy* v *Hogan,* supra, 378 U.S. p. 11, ... that "the same standards must determine whether an accused's silence in either a federal or state proceeding is justified." We take that in its literal sense and hold that the Fifth Amendment, in its direct application to the federal government and in its bearing on the states by reason of the Fourteenth Amendment, forbids either comment by the prosecution on the accused's silence or instructions by the court that such silence is evidence of guilt.

(Judgment reversed.)

Justice Harlan concurring:

I agree with the Court that within the federal judicial system the Fifth Amendment bars adverse comment by federal prosecutors and judges on a defendant's failure to take the stand in a criminal trial, a right accorded him by that amendment. And given last Term's decision in *Malloy* v *Hogan,* 378 U.S. 1, 84 . . . that the Fifth Amendment applies to the states in all its refinements, I see no legitimate escape from today's decision and therefore concur in it. I do so, however, with great reluctance, since for me the decision exemplifies the creeping paralysis with which this Court's recent adoption of the "incorporation" doctrine is infecting the operation of the federal system.

Justice Stewart, with whom Justice White joins, dissenting:

Moreover, no one can say where the balance of advantage might lie as a result of the attorneys' discussion of the matter. No doubt the prosecution's argument will seek to encourage the drawing of inferences unfavorable to the defendant. However, the defendant's counsel equally has an opportunity to explain the various other reasons why a defendant may not wish to take the stand, and thus rebut the natural if uneducated assumption that it is because the defendant cannot truthfully deny the accusations made.

I think the California comment rule is not a coercive device which impairs the right against self-incrimination, but rather a means of articulating and bringing into the light of rational discussion a fact inescapably impressed on the jury's consciousness. The California procedure is not only designed to protect the defendant against unwarranted inferences which might be drawn by an uninformed jury; it is also an attempt by the state to recognize and articulate what it believes to be the natural probative force of certain facts. Surely no one would deny that the state has an important interest in throwing the light of rational discussion on that which transpires in the course of a trial, both to protect the defendant from the very real dangers of silence and to shape a legal process designed to ascertain the truth.

The California rule allowing comment by counsel and instruction by the judge on the defendant's failure to take the stand is hardly an idiosyncratic aberration. The Model Code of Evidence, and the Uniform Rules of Evidence both sanction the use of such procedures. The practice has been endorsed by resolution of the American Bar Association and the American Law Institute, and has the support of the weight of scholarly opinion.

QUESTIONS

1. What was the major area of concern in the *McCulloch* v *Maryland* decision? What new precedents were set by this case? How did the necessary and proper clause enter this decision?

2. Article I, Section 8 of the Constitution was interpreted in *Kansas* v *Colorado*. Can any of these powers be interpreted to encompass reclamation of arid land? Why did the Court rule that they could not?

3. How does the Court interpret the relationship between specified powers and foreign affairs? Why?

4. Justice Black and Justice Frankfurter delivered concurring opinions in *Rochin* v *California* and yet they were on opposite sides in most of the other cases covered in the section on federalism and the incorporation doctrine in this chapter. What was the basis for this difference of interpretation? How were these two justices able to concur in Rochin? What is the outgrowth of this dispute?

4

CONSTITUTIONAL NATIONAL POWERS—AN OVERVIEW

To survive as a powerful, viable nation, strong government was a necessity in the opinion of the framers of the Constitution. However, strong government has to be isolated from a government that becomes so powerful that it jeopardizes the civil liberties of its citizens. In wrestling with this dilemma, the founding fathers attempted to reconcile the fear by drawing up the Constitution. The Constitution provided restraints on governmental power while strengthening the powers of the central government over those contained in the preceding Articles of Confederation. The real protection against accumulation of excessive governmental powers was in the division of powers between the states and central government, although there is an extensive list of prohibitions of government power in the Bill of Rights against a variety of conditions.

In the attempts to allocate power between states and federal governments, the Constitution divides power by specifying those powers of the central government (Congress: Article I, Section 8) and then providing in the Tenth Amendment that powers not specifically delegated are ''reserved to the states respectively, or to the people.'' To further protect against an oppressive government, the powers given to the central government were diffused among three separate branches of government.

The grants and distribution of powers in this chapter view governmental activities that are justified by these grants as the limits implied by the grants. The case decisions have shaped the development of the federal system beginning with the case of *McCulloch* v *Maryland,* 170.S. (4 Wheat) 316 (1819), which was concerned primarily with a state tax on a federal bank. How well the United States Supreme

Court has acted as the arbitrator has been the subject of controversy. The cases covered in this chapter discuss much congressional legislation that was declared unconstitutional by the Court even though there was presumably great support for the legislation among the populace who nevertheless presented arguments that the legislation infringed on legitimate states' rights. The role of the Court in deciding the issues involving federal versus state power is apparent on the face of the cases which follow.

The sources and scope of legislative powers are contained in Article 1, Section 8 of the Constitution. But one should not be misled into believing that all of Congress' powers are derived from this article. Additional powers are found elsewhere in the Constitution. For example, Article 1, Section 4 states that Congress has the power to make or change regulations covering "the times, places, and manner of holding elections for senators and representatives." Article III grants Congress the power to establish federal courts and establish the appellate jurisdiction of the United States Supreme Court.

Congress also derives tremendous powers from the concept of sovereignty which basically implies that there are certain powers which are inherent in being sovereign. The Supreme Court has recognized this concept in *American Insurance Company* v *Canter*, 26 U.S. (1 Pet.) 243 (1828)

Perhaps the power of governing a territory belonging to the United States, which has not, by becoming a state, acquired the means of self-government, may result necessarily from the facts, that it is not within the jurisdiction of any particular state, and is within the power and jurisdiction of the United States. The right to govern may be the inevitable consequence of the right to acquire territory. Whichever may be the source, whence the power is derived, the possession of it is unquestioned.

This power is seen in the handling of aliens through legislation enacted by Congress.

Beginning with *Gibbons* v *Ogden,* 22 U.S. (9 Wheat) 1 (1824), coming to grips with the question of the expansion of congressional power to regulate interstate commerce has been a difficult problem area for the Congress and the courts. In his decision Chief Justice Marshall attempted to define commerce in broad, expansive terms as being commercial intercourse, the power to regulate navigation, and control of interstate transportation. In short, the nation's regulatory powers extended across state lines and followed into the state itself in order to protect the free movement of interstate commerce.

A question of the scope of the commerce power which was not answered by Marshall involved the issue whether production as well as distribution of goods was included. Beginning in 1895 the Supreme Court began to chop away at the expansive doctrine of the commerce power. The result was a severe blow to economic reform, especially in the 1920's and 1930's.

Several kinds of attacks were leveled at legislation aimed at economic reform.

The Court distinguished various kinds of production as being peculiar to different levels of government. Thus, the Court came to distinguish manufacturing, mining, and farming in local terms and, therefore, subject to state regulation.

The Tenth Amendment was also used to prevent national regulatory legislation from invading the sacrosanct state powers. As a consequence, any attempt to use the commerce power which might affect production was unconstitutional.

Faced with a completely hostile Supreme Court in the 1930's, President Franklin Roosevelt attempted unsuccessfully to persuade the Congress to adopt his famous "court packing plan." However, the Supreme Court appeared to understand the hostility of the country and, in fact, barely escaped humiliation. Beginning with *NLRB* v *Jones and Laughlin Steel Corporation,* 301 U.S. 1 (1937), the Court began to retreat from its previous position by analyzing that what had previously been indirect effects on commerce now might have direct effect and, therefore, come within the Commerce Clause regulation. *Hammer* v *Dagenhart,* 247 U.S. 251 (1918), was expressly overruled in 1941. And with *Wickard* v *Filburn,* 317 U.S. 111 (1942), a new Supreme Court majority firmly established national control of interstate commerce by indicating that even potential effects of strictly local commerce were within the reach of national economic control.

The Commerce Clause has also had a significant impact in the area of civil rights. In the early 1960's a concerted attack was made on racial segregation by both black and white groups in the United States. The line of assault of the proponents involved attempts to have the United States Supreme Court declare that the Fourteenth Amendment's Equal Protection Clause standing alone prohibited racial discrimination by private owners in facilities offering public accommodations. Although there were numerous cases reaching the Supreme Court in which convictions of violating state trespass laws of persons engaged in sit-ins were reversed because the state enforcement of such laws was discriminatory and in violation of the Equal Protection Clause, the Fourteenth Amendment issue was sidestepped. The Court was highly reluctant to invoke the Amendment where there was no federal legislation prohibiting private racial discrimination.

Congress then passed the Civil Rights Act of 1964 which cited the Commerce Clause as well as the Fourteenth Amendment as constitutional authority allowing it to regulate racial discrimination problems falling under the act. The Congress adopted this route because the Supreme Court's decision in the *Civil Rights Cases,* 109 U.S. 3 (1883), adopted a very narrow interpretation of the Thirteenth and Fourteenth Amendments. If the Court refused to overrule the decision, then the 1964 Act would be valid under the Commerce Clause if private racial discrimination interferes with interstate commerce whether it be in housing, employment, or public accommodations.

The constitutionality of the Public Accommodations Clause was attacked and upheld in *Heart of Atlanta Motel* v *United States,* 379 U.S. 241 (1964). A remote application of the Act was applied to private recreation areas in *Daniel* v *Paul,*

395 U.S. 298 (1969). The impact on public dining facilities is found in *Katzen-bach* v *McClung,* 379 U.S. 294 (1964).

Congressional power to tax is the first of the enumerated powers of Congress in Article 1, Section 8. In Section 9 of the same article an exception to the taxation power is provided which forbids the national government from levying taxes on exports. This same section also qualifies the manner in which other kinds of taxes may be levied and distinguishes between direct and indirect taxes. Direct taxes are to be apportioned among the states based on population determined by a census. Indirect taxes are to be levied geographically and uniformly so that the taxes are collected throughout the country on a uniform basis and rate.

Into which category does the federal income tax fall? In *Hylton* v *United States,* 3 U.S. (3 Dall.) 171 (1796), the Supreme Court reasoned that only land and capitation taxes could be regarded as direct taxes. Following this reasoning, the Court struck down a federal income tax in *Pollack* v *Farmer's Loan and Trust,* 158 U.S. 601 (1895). The Court reasoned that *Hylton* did not limit the kind of direct taxes, but it included income from taxes of land and other property. Because an income tax was a direct tax and because of the unrealistic option of apportioning such a tax, because of the *Pollock* decision, Congress was denied the opportunity to enact a federal income tax until the Sixteenth Amendment was ratified in 1913.

Taxes, however, are not solely utilized to raise revenues. They may be used to regulate. The taxing and spending of revenues may be used to foster or hinder activities. *United States* v *Butler,* 297 U.S. 1 (1936), is not included in the cases, but it is a classic response by the Supreme Court to the regulatory uses of taxation. The position of current judicial philosophy in regard to taxing to regulate is set forth in *United States* v *Kahriger,* 345 U.S. 22 (1953), in which the Court appears to appreciate the regulatory capacity of taxing power. However, taxing to regulate may run into the tangle of the protection of individual rights as the dissenters in *Kahriger* feared. In *Marchetti* v *United States,* 390 U.S. 39 (1968), and *Grosso* v *United States,* 390 U.S. 62 (1968), the fear of a taxation scheme to regulate ran into the privilege against self-incrimination argument and the taxes were declared to be unconstitutional.

Up to now the discussion has been about federal powers in the domestic arena. Another problem area is the impact of international arrangements on the operation of the federal system. The section on treaty making addresses this doctrine, with one case striking down a state law that conflicted with a federal treaty giving foreign heirs title to property in a state. The second decision, *Missouri* v *Holland,* 252 U.S. 416 (1920), strongly suggests that treaties which contradict express constitutional promises are null and void.

The war-making power of Congress and presidential powers are closely tied, even though only Congress is given the power to declare war. The scope of executive power is at best ambiguous. What the executive power means has been a subject of controversy throughout the nation's history. Certainly it is deeply involved when there is a strong president in office who exerts the full meaning of executive power. This is fully exemplified in President Truman's involvement in *Youngstown Sheet and Tube Co.* v *Sawyer,* 343 U.S. 579 (1952).

Throughout the nation's history the president has accumulated great power in the field of foreign affairs. As the United States has grown more powerful, the use of military forces became more and more an arm of the president in carrying out his responsibility for foreign affairs. Experience has demonstrated that as the commander in chief of the Armed forces the president could involve the nation in shooting wars without Congress' carrying out its constitutional function of declaring war. Also, the student will note that in handling foreign relations the president has vast control over the secrecy of information as a matter of executive privilege to protect potential damage to relations with other countries, and has been only recently found, to prevent embarrassing internal political situations.

Congress can regulate interstate transportation under the Commerce Clause. How is the Congress about to protect the legitimate interests of the states in such matters as safety devices for interstate movement inside the state? What is the amount of permissible interference with interstate commerce that may be allowed? *Bibb* v *Navajo Freight Lines, Inc.,* 359 U.S. 520 (1959), is an excellent example of the Supreme Court's striking down an unjustifiable burden on interstate commerce. The Supreme Court has attempted to strike a balance between legitimate state needs and the free flow of commerce. In general, the greater the state burden on interstate commerce, the stronger the state justification must be for imposing the burden.

The Commerce Clause as it regulates interstate commerce is constantly undergoing Supreme Court interpretation. On March 17, 1977, the United States Supreme Court held that a Mississippi tax on the privilege of doing business in Mississippi did not violate the Commerce Clause when it applied to an interstate activity (transportation by motor transport in Mississippi to Mississippi dealers of automobiles manufactured outside of the state) with a substantial connection with the taxing state, and does not discriminate against interstate commerce, and is fairly related to the services provided by the state. (*Complete Auto Transit Inc.* v *Brady.* 45 L.W. 4529 March 27, (1977).

There are only two constitutional clauses that involve the movement of people, and one was overturned by the Thirteenth Amendment (Article IV, Section 3). Article IV, Section 2 mandates that authorities in one state who apprehend a fugitive from legal processes in another state shall return him upon demand to the state from which he fled. As later declared by the Supreme Court this is a moral obligation only, but no force of law attaches to the constitutional provision [*Kentucky* v *Dennison,* 65 U.S. (24 How.) 66 (1861)].

The right of the average person's free travel has come about from utilization of other clauses to impute this right. In *Edwards* v *California,* 314 U.S. 160 (1941), the Supreme Court regarded people as commerce so as to come within the Commerce Clause. Note that over two decades later the court used this clause to eliminate racial discrimination in public accommodations in the 1964 Civil

Rights Act. Travel restrictions were involved in *Shapiro* v *Thompson*, 394 U.S. 618 (1969), which struck down a state law requiring a one-year residency requirement as a prerequisite for seeking welfare payments. Some three years prior to *Shapiro* the Court had held in *United States* v *Guest*, 383 U.S. 745 (1966), that the right to travel was a fundamental right.

What power does the state have in making interstate commerce pay its fair share to protecting the legitimate police power interests that the state possesses? License fees and property taxes are common sources of state revenue. In the early history of the nation a good deal of effort was devoted to determining the kinds of goods that could be taxed by the state as distinguished from those moving in interstate commerce. *Brown* v *Maryland*, 25 U.S. (Wheat.) 419 (1827), established the classic rule that the immunity of goods from state taxation continued on imported goods until the goods had been removed from their "original package" and mixed with the mass of domestic property so as to lose their character as an imported commodity. Although this test has led to problems, it remains as an effective guide in those cases raising questions concerning state taxes on foreign imports.

The question of foreign commerce taxation is closely associated with the entire trade problem, especially when the state makes an effort to stabilize the produce markets in the state. The conflict between the free flow of interstate trade and the state need to prevent the destructive competition within the state are found in the cases of *H. P. Wood and Sons* v *Du Mond*, 336 U.S. 525, (1949), and *Parker* v *Brown*, 317 U.S. 341 (1943).

COMMERCE

The Underpinnings

Gibbons v *Ogden*

22 U.S. (9 Wheat.) 1, 6 L.Ed. 23 (1824)

Gibbons, A New Jersey citizen, operated two steamboats between Elizabethtown, New Jersey, and New York City. Ogden filed a bill in the New York Chancery Court seeking an injunction to restrain Gibbons from operating the boats. Prior to this dispute the New York legislature enacted a statute granting exclusive rights to Robert Fulton and Robert Livingston to operate steam vessels on New York waters. Ogden received exclusive rights from Livingston to navigate between New Jersey and New York City. Gibbons was operating his boats with a license granted under an act of Congress. He argued that the New York laws conflicted with the Constitution and federal laws. Nevertheless, the injunction was granted ordering Gibbons to cease operating his boats in New York waters. The state courts affirmed and on appeal to the United States Supreme Court the decree was reversed.

Chief Justice Marshall delivered the opinion of the Court:

The appellant contends that this decree is erroneous, because the laws which purport to give the exclusive privilege it sustains, are repugnant to the Constitution and laws of the United States. They are said to be repugnant—1st. To that clause in the Constitution which authorizes Congress to regulate commerce.

. . .

This instrument (Constitution) contains an enumeration of powers expressly granted by the people to their government. It has been said that these powers ought to be construed strictly. But why ought they to be so construed? Is there one sentence in the Constitution which gives countenance to this rule? In the last of the enumerated powers, that which grants, expressly, the means of carrying all others into execution, Congress is authorized "to make all laws which shall be necessary and proper" for the purpose. But this limitation on the means which may be used, is not extended to the powers which are conferred; nor is there one sentence in the Constitution which has been pointed out by the gentlemen of the bar, or which we have been able to discern, that prescribes this rule. We do not, therefore, think ourselves justified in adopting it. What do gentlemen mean by a strict construction? If they contend only against that enlarged construction which would extend words beyond their natural and obvious import, we might question the application of the term, but should not controvert the principle. If they contend for that narrow construction which, in support of some theory not to be found in the Constitution, would deny to the government those powers which the words of the grant, as usually understood, import, and which are consistent with the general views and objects of the instrument; for that narrow construction, which would cripple the government and render it unequal to the objects for which it is declared to be instituted, and to which the powers given, as fairly understood, render it competent; then we cannot perceive the propriety of this strict construction, nor adopt it as the rule by which the Constitution is to be expounded. As men, whose intentions require no concealment, generally employ the words which most directly and aptly express the ideas they intend to convey, the enlightened patriots who framed our Constitution, and the people who adopted it, must be understood to have employed words in their natural sense, and to have intended what they have said. If, from the imperfection of human language, there should be serious doubts respecting the extent of any given power, it is a well-settled rule that the objects for which it was given, especially when those objects are expressed in the instrument itself, should have great influence in the construction. We know of no reason for excluding this rule from the present case. The grant does not convey power which might be beneficial to the grantor, if retained by himself, or which can enure solely to the benefit of the grantee, but is an investment of power for the general advantage, in the hands of agents selected for that purpose; which power can never be exercised by the people themselves, but must be placed in the hands of agents or be dormant. We know of no rule for construing the extent of such powers, other than is given by the language of the instrument which confers them, taken in connection with the purposes for which they were conferred.

The words are: "Congress shall have power to regulate commerce with foreign nations, and among the several states, and with the Indian tribes."

The subject to be regulated is commerce; and our Constitution being, as was aptly said at the bar, one of enumeration, and not of definition, to ascertain the extent of the power it becomes necessary to settle the meaning of the word. The counsel for the appellee would limit it to traffic, to buying and selling, or the interchange of commodities, and do not admit that it comprehends navigation. This would restrict a general term, applicable to many objects, to one of its significations. Commerce, undoubtedly, is traffic, but it is something more; it is intercourse. It describes the commercial intercourse between nations, and parts of nations, in all its branches, and is regulated by prescribing rules for carrying on that intercourse. The mind can scarcely conceive a system for regulating commerce between nations, which shall exclude all laws concerning navigation, which shall be silent on the admission of the vessels of the one nation into the ports of the other, and be confined to prescribing rules for the conduct of individuals, in the actual employment of buying and selling, or of barter.

If commerce does not include navigation, the government of the Union has no direct power over that subject, and can make no law prescribing what shall constitute American vessels, or requiring that they shall be navigated by American seamen. Yet this power has been exercised from the commencement of the government, has been exercised with the consent of all, and has been understood by all to be a commercial regulation. All America understands, and has uniformly understood, the word "commerce" to comprehend navigation. It was so understood and must have been so understood, when the Constitution was framed. The power over commerce, including navigation, was one of the primary objects for which the people of America adopted their government, and must have been contemplated in forming it. The convention must have used the word in that sense; because all have understood it in that sense, and the attempt to restrict it comes too late.

. . .

The word used in the Constitution, then, comprehends, and has been always understood to comprehend, navigation within its meaning; and a power to regulate navigation is as expressly granted as if that term had been added to the word "commerce."

. . .

To what commerce does this power extend? The Constitution informs us, to commerce "with foreign nations, and among the several states, and with the Indian tribes."

It has, we believe, been universally admitted that these words comprehend every species of commercial intercourse between the United States and foreign nations. No sort of trade can be carried on between this country and any other, to which this power does not extend. It has been truly said, that commerce, as the word is used in the Constitution, is a unit, every part of which is indicated by the term.

If this be the admitted meaning of the word, in its application to foreign nations, it must carry the same meaning throughout the sentence, and remain a unit, unless there be some plain intelligible cause which alters it.... The subject to which the power is next applied, is to commerce "among the several states." The word "among" means intermingled with. A thing which is among others, is intermingled with them. Commerce among the states cannot stop at the external boundary line of each state, but may be introduced into the interior. It is not intended to say that these words comprehend that commerce which is completely internal, which is carried on between man and man in a state, or between different parts of the same state, and which does not extend to or affect other states. Such a power would be inconvenient, and is certainly unnecessary. Comprehensive as the word "among" is, it may very properly be restricted to that commerce which concerns more states than one. The phrase is not one which would probably have been selected to indicate the completely interior traffic of a state, because it is not an apt phrase for that purpose; and the enumeration of the particular classes of commerce to which the power was to be extended, would not have been made had the intention been to extend the power to every description. The enumeration presupposes something not enumerated, and that something, if we regard the language or the subject of the sentence, must be the exclusively internal commerce of a state. The genius and character of the whole government seem to be, that its action is to be applied to all the external concerns of the nation, and to those internal concerns which affect the states generally; but not to those which are completely within a particular state, which do not affect other states, and with which it is not necessary to interfere, for the purpose of executing some of the general powers of the government. The completely internal commerce of a state, then, may be considered as reserved for the state itself.

But, in regulating commerce with foreign nations, the power of Congress does not stop at the jurisdictional lines of the several states. It would be a very useless power if it could not pass those lines. The commerce of the United States with foreign nations, is that of the whole United States. Every district has a right to participate in it. The deep streams which penetrate our country in every direction, pass through the interior of almost every state in the Union, and furnish the means of exercising this right. If Congress has the power to regulate it, that power must be exercised whenever the subject exists. If it exists within the states, if a foreign voyage may commence or terminate at a port within a state, then the power of Congress may be exercised within a state.

. . .

We are now arrived at the inquiry, What is this power?

It is the power to regulate; that is, to prescribe the rule by which commerce is to be governed. This power, like all others vested in Congress, is complete in itself, may be exercised to its utmost extent, and acknowledges no limitation, other than are prescribed in the Constitution. These are expressed in plain terms, and do not affect the questions which arise in this case, or which have been discussed at the bar. If, as has always been understood, the sovereignty of Congress, though limited to specified objects, is plenary as to those objects, the power over commerce with foreign nations, and among the several states is vested in Congress as absolutely as it would be in a single government, having in its constitution the same restrictions on the exercise of the power as are found in the Constitution of the United States. The wisdom and discretion of Congress, their identity with the people, and the influence which their constituents possess at election, are, in this, as in may other instances, as that, for example, of declaring war, the sole restraints on which they have relied, to secure them from its abuse. They are the restraints on which the people must often rely solely, in all representative governments.

The power of Congress, then, comprehends navigation within the limits of every state in the Union; so far as that navigation may be, in any manner, connected with "commerce with foreign nations, or among the several states, or with the Indian tribes." It may, of consequence, pass the juridictional line of New York, and act upon the very waters to which the prohibition now under consideration applies.

. . .

This principle is, if possible, still more clear, when applied to commerce "among the several states." They either join each other in which case they are separated by a mathematical line, or they are remote from each other, in which case other states lie between them. What is commerce "among" them; and how is it to be conducted? Can a trading expedition between two adjoining states commence and terminate outside of each? And if the trading intercourse be between two states remote from each other, must it not commence in one, terminate in the other, and probably pass through a third? Commerce among the states must, of necessity, be commerce with the states. In the regulation of trade with the Indian tribes, the action of the law, especially when the Constitution was made, was chiefly within a state. The power of Congress, then, whatever it may be, must be exercised within the territorial jurisdiction of the several states. The sense of the nation, on this subject, is unequivocally manifested by the provisions made in the laws for transporting goods, by land, between Baltimore and Providence, between New York and Philadelphia, and between Philadelphia and Baltimore.

. . .

The Court is aware that, in stating the train of reasoning by which we have been conducted to this result, much time has been consumed in the attempt to demonstrate propositions which may have been thought axioms. It is felt that the tediousness inseparable from the endeavor to prove that which is already clear, is imputable to a considerable part of this opinion. But it was unavoidable. The conclusion to which we have come, depends on a chain of principles which it was necessary to preserve unbroken; and, although some of them were thought nearly self-evident, the magnitude of the question, the weight of character belonging to those from whose judgment we dissent, and the argument at the bar, demanded that we should assume nothing.

Powerful and ingenious minds, taking, as postulates, that the powers expressly granted to the government of the Union are to be contracted, by construction, into the narrowest possible compass, and that the original powers of the states are retained, if any possible construction will retain them, may, by a course of well-digested, but refined and metaphysical reasoning, founded on these premises, explain away the Constitution of our country, and leave it a magnificent structure indeed, to look at, but totally unfit for use. They may so entangle and perplex the understanding, as to obscure principles which were before thought quite plain, and induce doubts where, if the mind were to pursue its own course, none would be perceived. In such a case, it is peculiarly necessary to recur to safe and fundamental principles to sustain those principles, and, when sustained, the make them the tests of the arguments to be examined.

(Decree reversed.)
Justice Johnson concurred.

The Congress has the power to control matters that concern intrastate commerce if such matters also effect interstate commerce. In *Houston, East and West Railway* v *United States,* 234 U.S. 342, 34 S.Ct. 833, 58 L.Ed. 1341 (1914), the court supported a decision by the Interstate Commerce Commission which ordered the end to unfair favoritism to intrastate commerce by the appellant railroad. The railroad charged much higher rates of fare between Shreveport, Louisiana, and points within Texas than were charged for similar distances within the state of Texas. The ICC ordered that the higher charges for interstate transportation be equalized to the lower rate in effect for intrastate transportation. The railroad appealed this decision, claiming that the ICC lacked jurisdiction to consider intrastate commerce. The United States Supreme Court disagreed with this argument. "All matters having such a close and substantial relation to interstate commerce" must fall within the purview of the government if effective regulation of interstate commerce is to result.

Limitations on Commerce Power

Bailey v *Drexel Furniture Company*
259 U.S. 20, 42 S.Ct. 449, 66 L.Ed. 817 (1922)

In 1919 the Congress enacted the Child Labor Tax Law which imposed an excise tax of 10 percent yearly on the net profits of every person employing child labor in a wide range of manufacturing and production businesses. The act was identical to that in *Hammer* v *Dagenhart,* 247 U.S. 251, 38 S.Ct. 529, 62 L.Ed. 610 (1918) except the tax applied whether or not the goods were shipped in interstate commerce. Drexel Furniture Company paid the tax under protest. It then secured a court judgment to have the tax refunded. On appeal the United States Supreme Court held the Child Labor Tax Law invalid.

Chief Justice Taft delivered the opinion of the Court:

The law is attacked on the ground that it is a regulation of the employment of child labor in the states—an exclusively state function under the federal Constitution and within the reservations of the Tenth Amendment. It is defended on the ground that it is a mere excise tax levied by the Congress of the United States under its broad power of taxation conferred by Section 8, Article I, of the federal Constitution. We must construe the law and interpret the intent and meaning of Congress from the language of the Act. The words are to be given their ordinary meaning unless the context shows that they are differently used. Does this law impose a tax with only that incidental restraint and regulation which a tax must inevitably involve? Or does it regulate by the use of the so-called tax as a penalty? If a tax, it is clearly an excise. If it were an excise on a commodity or other thing of value, we might not be permitted under previous decisions of this Court to infer solely from its heavy burden that the Act intends a prohibition instead of a tax. But this Act is more. It provides a heavy exaction for a departure from a detailed and specified course of conduct in business. That course of business is that employers shall employ in mines and quarries, children of an age greater than 16 years; in mills and factories, children of an age greater than 14 years, and shall prevent children of less than 16 years in mills and factories from working more than 8 hours a day or 6 days in the week. If an employer departs from this prescribed course of business, he is to pay to the government one-tenth of his entire net income in the business for a full year. The amount is not to be proportioned in any degree to the extent or frequency of the departures, but is to be paid by the employer in full measure whether he employs 500 children for a year, or employs only one for a day. Moreover, if he does not know the child is within the named age limit, he is not to pay; that is to say, it is only where he knowingly departs from the prescribed course that payment is to be exacted. Scienters are associated with penalties, not with taxes. The employer's factory is to be subject to inspection at any time not only by the taxing officers of the Treasury, the Department normally charged with the collection of taxes, but also by the Secretary of Labor and his subordinates, whose normal function is the advancement and protection of the welfare of the workers. In the light of these features of the Act, a Court must be blind not to see that the so-called tax is imposed to stop the employment of children within the age limits prescribed. Its prohibitory and regulatory effect and purpose are palpable. All others can see and understand this. How can we properly shut our minds to it?

It is the high duty and function of this Court in cases regularly brought to its bar to decline to recognize or enforce seeming laws of Congress, dealing with subjects not intrusted to Congress, but left or committed by the supreme law of the land to the control of the states. We cannot avoid the duty, even though it require us to refuse to give effect to legislation designed to promote the highest good. The good sought in unconstitutional legislation is an insidious feature, because it leads citizens and legislators of good purpose to promote it, without thought of the serious breach it will make in the ark of our covenant, or the harm which will come from breaking down recognized standards. In the maintenance of local self-government, on the one hand, and the national power, on the other, our country has been able to endure and prosper for near a century and a half.

Out of a proper respect for the acts of a co-ordinate branch of the government, this Court has gone far to sustain taxing acts as such, even though there has been ground for suspecting, from the weight of the tax, it was intended to destroy its subject. But in the Act before us the presumption of validity cannot prevail, because the proof of the contrary is found on the very face of its provisions. Grant the validity of this law, and all that Congress would need to do, hereafter, in seeking to take over to its control any one of the great number of subjects of public interest, jurisdiction of which the states have never parted with, and which are reserved to them by them by the Tenth Amendment, would be to enact a detailed measure of complete regulation of the subject and enforce it by a so-called tax upon departures from it. To give such magic to the word "tax" would be to break down all constitutional limitation of the powers of Congress and completely wipe out the sovereignty of the states.

The difference between a tax and a penalty is sometimes difficult to define, and yet the consequences of the distinction in the required method of their collection often are important. Where the sovereign enacting the law has power to impose both tax and penalty, the difference between revenue production and mere regulation may be immaterial, but not so when one sovereign can impose a tax only, and the power of regulation rests in another. Taxes are occasionally imposed in the discretion of the Legislature on proper subjects with the primary motive of obtaining revenue from them and with the incidental motive of discouraging them by making their continuance onerous. They do not lose their character as taxes because of the incidental motive. But there comes a time in the extension of the penalizing features of the so-called tax when it loses its character as such and becomes a mere penalty, with the characteristics of regulation and punishment. Such is the case in the law before us. Although Congress does not invalidate the contract of employment or expressly declare that the employment within the mentioned ages is illegal, it does exhibit its intent practically to achieve the latter result by adopting the criteria of wrongdoing and imposing its principal consequence on those who transgress its standard.

The case before us cannot be distinguished from that of *Hammer* v *Dagenhart,* 247 U.S. 251, . . . Congress there enacted a law to prohibit transportation in interstate commerce of goods made at a factory in which there was employment of children within the same ages and for the same number of hours a day and days in a week as are penalized by the Act in this case.

. . .

In the case at the bar, Congress in the name of a tax which on the face of the Act is a penalty seeks to do the same thing, and the effort must be equally futile.

The analogy of the *Dagenhart* Case is clear. The congressional power over interstate commerce is, within its proper scope, just as complete and unlimited as the congressional power to tax, and the legislative motive in its exercise is just as free from judicial suspicion and inquiry. Yet when Congress threatened to stop interstate commerce in ordinary and necessary commodities, unobjectionable as subjects of transportation, and to deny the same to the people of a state in order to coerce them into compliance with Congress' regulation of state concerns, the Court said this was not in fact regulation of interstate commerce, but rather that of state concerns and was invalid. So here the so-called tax is a penalty to coerce people of a state to act as Congress wishes them to act in respect of a matter completely the business of the state government under the federal Constitution. This case requires as did the *Dagenhart* Case the application of the principle announced by Chief Justice Marshall in *McCullouch* v *Maryland,* 4 Wheat. 316, . . . in a much-quoted passage:

> Should Congress, in the execution of its powers, adopt measures which are prohibited by the Constitution; or should Congress, under the pretext of executing its powers, pass laws for the accomplishment of objects not intrusted to the government; it would become the painful duty of this tribunal, should a case requiring such a decision come before it, to say that such an act was not the law of the land.

For the reasons given, we must hold the Child Labor Tax Law invalid.

. . .

(Judgement affirmed.)
Justice Clark dissented.

The United States Supreme Court found the 1914 Narcotic Drug Act to be constitutional in its decision of *United States* v *Doremus,* 249 U.S. 86, 39 S.Ct. 214, 63 L.Ed. 493 (1919). The Act, which imposed an excise tax on dispensers of narcotic drugs and regulated the sale of the drugs, was challenged by Doremus, who was a physician who had paid the excise tax but had failed to use the official forms in the sale of 500 heroin tablets. The convicted physician claimed that the requirement of the use of official forms in the sale of narcotics was outside the taxing and revenue collecting powers of the Congress. The Court did not delve into the purposes of such regulatory requirements, since, on the face of the legislation, the revenue collection was served by the other, peripheral, requirements. Therefore, the 1914 Narcotic Drug Act was held to be in accord with the taxing power of the Congress.

The federal power to regulate commerce does not encompass all matters which effect the interstate commerce, but only those which have direct effects on such commerce. This opinion was reiterated in *Carter* v *Carter Coal Company,* 298 U.S. 238, 56 S.Ct. 855, 80 L.Ed. 1160 (1936). The Congress passed legislation which set minimum wages and maximum working hours of miners whose coal was shipped in interstate commerce. A tax was levied on coal operators who failed to meet these wage and hour restrictions. The United States Supreme Court found the Act to be an unconstitutional abridgement of local governmental power. Since the wages and working hours of miners are only indirectly related to the trading of coal in interstate commerce, they do not fall within the commerce power of the Congress. Rather, such matter are directly related to production—not trade, and as such are within the regulatory powers of local governments.

The Commerce Power—A Vast Expansion for National Needs

National Labor Relations Board v *Jones and Laughlin Steel Corporation*

301 U.S. 1, 57 S.Ct. 615, 81 L.Ed. 893 (1937)

In 1935 Congress passed the National Labor Relations Act to replace the collective bargaining guarantees of the NIRA which had been declared unconstitutional previously. The National Labor Relations Act, also known as the Wagner Act, recognized the right of collective bargaining and empowered the National Labor Relations Board (NLRB) to prevent unfair labor practices in violation of the Act which lead to strikes and therefore a burden on interstate commerce. A labor organization alleged that Jones and Laughlin engaged in discriminatory practices by discharging union members because of union activities. The NLRB found that Jones and Laughlin had committed unfair labor practices and ordered reinstatement and other relief. Jones and Laughlin refused to comply claiming that the Wagner Act in regulating labor relations was not regulating interstate commerce and, therefore, the Act was unconstitutional. The United States Circuit Court refused to enforce the NLRB order. On appeal to the United States Supreme Court, the Circuit Court decision was reversed.

In delivering the opinion of the Court, Chief Justice Hughes states that the operations of the Jones and Laughlin Steel Corporation:

... in Pittsburgh and Aliquippa might be likened to the heart of a self-contained, highly integrated body. They drew in the raw materials from Michigan, Minnesota, West Virginia, Pennsylvania in part through arteries and by means controlled by the respondent; they transform the materials and then pump them out to all parts of the nation through the vast mechanism which the respondent has elaborated.

. . .

Following this line of reasoning the Chief Justice evaluated the scope of the act and the effects of unfair labor practices:

The close and intimate effect which brings the subject within the reach of federal power may be due to activities in relation to productive industry although the industry when separately viewed is local. This has been abundantly illustrated in the application of the federal Anti-Trust Act.

. . .

Experience has abundantly demonstrated that the recognition of the right of employees to self-organization and to have representatives of their own choosing for the purpose of collective bargaining is often an essential condition of industrial peace. Refusal to confer and negotiate has been one of the most prolific causes of strife. This is such an outstanding fact in the history of labor disturbances that it is a proper subject of judicial notice and requires no citation of instances.

. . .

Our conclusion is that the order of the Board was within its competency and that the Act is valid as applied here.

. . .

(Judgement reversed.)
Justices McReynolds, Van Devanter, Sutherland, and Butler dissented.

Trading need not be great in magnitude in order to fall within the laws regulating interstate commerce. In *National Labor Relations Board* v *Fainblatt,* 306 U.S. 601, 59 S.Ct. 668, 83 L.Ed. 1014 (1939), the United States Supreme Court found the Labor Act to be applicable to a small clothing shop in New Jersey which was employed by a New York company for piece work. Even though the shop employed only 60 women, it met the qualifications of interstate commerce. According to the Court, ''there are not a few industries in the United States which, though conducted in relatively small units, contribute in the aggregate a vast volume of interstate commerce.''

In *Steward Machine Company* v *Davis,* 301 U.S. 548, 57 S.Ct. 883, 81 L.Ed. 1279 (1937), the right to the Congress to fill a national need through a tax, which could be averted by appropriate state agencies, if such agencies acted to fill the national need, was affirmed. Title IX of the Social Security Act of 1935 imposed a tax on employers which would be used to set up unemployment compensations on a national scale. However, the employer's tax would be drastically reduced if the state in which his business operated also required an unemployment tax which would be used to administer a state program of assistance. It was contended by the appellant that this provision of the law coerced the states into the development of unemployment programs. The United States Supreme Court made a distinction between coercion and motivation and found that the Social Security Act of 1935 provided the states with the motivation necessary to institute a program catering to the needs of the unemployed. According to the majority opinion, since the federal legislation stimulated state legislation for the fulfillment of the same national and state need, it was within the acceptance realm of federal motivation to state programs.

The United States Supreme Court broke with previous decisions regarding the power of Congress to regulate commerce in *United States* v *Darby,* 312 U.S. 100, 61 S.Ct. 451, 85 L.Ed. 609 (1941). Legislation prohibiting the trading of goods in interstate commerce produced by companies that failed to meet minimum wage/maximum working hour regulations was upheld by the Court. It was decided that the congressional power to regulate interstate commerce extended into all matters relating to such commerce and was not limited to harmful or deleterious products alone. The manner of production was found to be as important a consideration in promoting fair interstate commerce as the actual product resulting from the industry. Since there is no express constitutional restriction on the power of the Congress in regulating commerce, the Court could not find a judicial reason for limiting the realm of legislative control. See also *Wickard* v *Filburn,* 317 U.S. 111, 63 S.Ct. 82, 87 L.Ed. 122 (1942).

Civil Rights and the Commerce Power—1964 Civil Rights Act: Employment Practices

Heart of Atlanta Motel v *United States*

379 U.S. 241, 85 S.Ct. 348, 13 L.Ed. 2d 258 (1964)

The defendant owned and operated an Atlanta motel of 216 guest rooms which were available to transients. It was in downtown Atlanta and was accessible to the various federal interstate highways and numerous state highways. The motel solicited out-of-state business by using various kinds of advertising media. It accepted large numbers of convention guests from outside Georgia. About 75 percent of its registered guests were from outside Georgia. Prior to passage of Title II of the 1964 Civil Rights Act the motel refused to rent rooms to blacks and alleged that it continued to do so. The motel brought suit in an effort to perpetuate this policy by seeking a declaratory judgment that the Act was unconstitutional. A three-judge federal circuit court sustained the validity of the Act. The United States Supreme Court affirmed.

Justice Clark delivered the opinion of the court. In deciding this case the Court considered many important aspects, including the application of Title II to the Heart of Atlanta Motel, the basis for congressional action, and the power of Congress over interstate travel.

Application of Title II to Heart of Atlanta Motel

It is admitted that the operation of the motel brings it within the provisions of §201 (a) of the Act and that appellant refused to provide lodging for transient Negroes because of their race or color and that it intends to continue that policy unless restrained.

The sole question posed is, therefore, the constitutionality of the Civil Rights Act of 1964 as applied to these facts. The legislative history of the Act indicates that Congress based the Act on Section 5 and the Equal Protection

Clause of the Fourteenth Amendment as well as its power to regulate interstate commerce under Article I, Section 8, Clause 3, of the Constitution.

The Basis of Congressional Action

While the Act as adopted carried no congressional findings the record of its passage through each house is replete with evidence of the burdens that discrimination by race or color places upon interstate commerce. . . . This testimony included the fact that our people have become increasingly mobile with millions of people of all races traveling from state to state; that Negroes in particular have been the subject of discrimination in transient accommodations, having to travel great distances to secure the same; that often they have been unable to obtain accommodations and have had to call upon friends to put them up overnight, . . . and that these conditions have become so acute as to require the listing of available lodging for Negroes in a special guidebook which was itself "dramatic testimony to the difficulties" Negroes encounter in travel.

. . .

The Power of Congress Over Interstate Travel

It is said that the operation of the motel here is of a purely local character. But, assuming this to be true, "[i]f it is interstate commerce that feels the pinch, it does not matter how local the operation which applies the squeeze." . . . Thus the power of Congress to promote interstate commerce also includes the power to regulate the local incidents thereof, ... One need only examine the evidence which we have discussed above to see that Congress may—as it has—prohibit racial discrimination by motels serving travelers, however "local" their operations may appear.

Nor does the Act deprive appellant of liberty or property under the Fifth Amendment. The commerce power invoked here by the Congress is a specific and plenary one authorized by the Constitution itself.

There is nothing novel about such legislation. Thirty-two States now have it on their books either by statute or executive order and many cities provide such regulation. . . . It has been repeatedly held by this Court that such laws do not violate the Due Process Clause of the Fourteenth Amendment.

We, therefore, conclude that the action of the Congress in the adoption of the Act as applied here to a motel which concededly serves interstate travelers is within the power granted it by the Commerce Clause of the Constitution, as interpreted by this Court for 140 years. It may be argued that Congress could have pursued other methods to eliminate the obstructions it found in interstate commerce caused by racial discrimination. But this is a matter of policy that rests entirely with the Congress, not with the courts. How obstructions in commerce may be removed—what means are to be employed—is within the sound and exclusive discretion of the Congress. It is subject only to one caveat—that the means chosen by it must be reasonably adapted to the end permitted by the Constitution. We cannot say that its choice here was not so adapted. The Constitution requires no more.

(Judgment affirmed.)

The Civil Rights Act of 1964 prohibited racial discrimination by restaurants that either serve interstate travelers or make use of food which has moved in interstate commerce. The constitutionality of this provision was challenged by a restaurant owner who met the second requirement in *Katzenbach* v *McClung*, 379 U.S. 294, 85 S.Ct. 377, 13 L.Ed. 2d 290 (1964). According to the restaurant owner, the Congress has no power to regulate racial discrimination by food establishments through the Commerce Clause of the Constitution, since no real effect on interstate commerce can be shown. The United States Supreme Court did not find this argument compelling; based on intensive congressional hearings, the Congress had determined that racial discrimination deleteriously effected the interstate commerce of the nation, and the Court allowed this determination to stand as fast. With this settled, the power of the Congress to enforce the disputed provision of the Civil Rights Act of 1964 was affirmed.

In *Daniel* v *Paul*, 395 U.S. 298, 89 S.Ct. 1697, 23 L.Ed. 2d 318 (1969), the United States Supreme Court found that the appellees were operating a recreational area in violation of Title II of the Civil Rights Act of 1964. The area provided sporting activities as well as a snack bar and was regularly visited by persons in interstate commerce. Further, "a major portion" of the food served at the snack bar had traveled in interstate commerce and many of the elements required in the recreational activities had been purchased through interstate commerce. Even though a nominal "membership fee" was charged, there was no communal government or ownership of the facility. Only persons of the Caucasian race were allowed to buy membership and participate in the activities. The Court found that the area was not within the "private club" exception to the Civil Rights Act and was very much an "entertainment facility" which was supported by interstate commerce. For these reasons, the facility was within the jurisdiction of the Civil Rights Act and its provisions against racial discrimination.

POLICE PROBLEM REGULATION

Interstate Commerce—Exclusion of Harmful Activities

United States v *Sullivan*

332 U.S. 689, 68 S.Ct. 331, 92 L.Ed. 297 (1948)

Sullivan was a Columbus, Georgia, druggist who purchased a properly labeled bottle of 1,000 tablets of sulfathiazole from an Atlanta wholesaler. The drugs were shipped to Atlanta from Chicago 6 months earlier. Three months after Sullivan bought the drug he made 2 retail sales of 12 tablets each. He placed the tablets in a small pillbox marked "sulfathiazole." No danger warnings and no directions were included on the label as required by The Federal Food, Drug and Cosmetic Act of 1968, Section 301(k). Sullivan was charged with misbranding because he failed to place the warnings and directions on the boxes. The United States Supreme Court reversed the judgment of the United States Court of Appeals which had reversed Sullivan's conviction by the federal district court.

Justice Black delivered the opinion of the Court:

Third. When we seek the meaning of §301(k) from its language we find that the offense it creates and which is here charged requires the doing of some act with respect to a drug (1) which results in its being misbranded, (2) while the article is held for sale "after shipment in interstate commerce." Respondent has not seriously contended that the "misbranded" portion of §301(k) is ambiguous. Section 502(f), as has been seen, provides that a drug is misbranded unless the label contains adequate directions and adequate warnings. The labeling here did not contain the information which §502(f) requires. There is a suggestion here that, although alteration, mutilation, destruction, or obliteration of the bottle label would have been a "misbranding," transferring the pills to nonbranded boxes would not have been, so long as the labeling on the empty bottle was not disturbed. Such an argument cannot be sustained. For the chief purpose of forbidding the destruction of the label is to keep it intact for the information and protection of the consumer. That purpose would be frustrated when the pills the consumer buys are not labeled as required, whether the label has been torn from the original container or the pills have been transferred from it to a nonlabeled one. We find no ambiguity in the misbranding language of the Act.

Furthermore, it would require great ingenuity to discover ambiguity in the additional requirement of §301(k) that the misbranding occur "while such article is held for sale after shipment in interstate commerce." The words accurately describe respondent's conduct here. He held the drugs for sale after they had been shipped in interstate commerce from Chicago to Atlanta. It is true that respondent bought them over six months after the interstate shipment had been completed by their delivery to another consignee. But the language used by Congress broadly and unqualifiedly prohibits misbranding articles held for sale after shipment in interstate commerce, without regard to how long after the shipment the misbranding occurred, how many intrastate sales had intervened, or who had received the articles at the end of the interstate shipment. Accordingly we find that the conduct of the respondent falls within the literal language of 301(k).

Fourth. Given the meaning that we have found the literal language of §301(k) to have, it is thoroughly consistent with the general aims and purposes of the Act. For the Act as a whole was designed primarily to protect consumers from dangerous products. . . . Its purpose was to safeguard the consumer by applying the Act to articles from the moment of their introduction into interstate commerce all the way to the moment of their delivery to the ultimate consumer.

. . .

Fifth. It is contended that the Act as we have construed it is beyond any authority granted Congress by the Constitution and that it invades the powers reserved to the states. A similar challenge was made against the Pure Food and Drug Act of 1906 . . . and rejected. . . . That Act did not contain §301(l), but it did prohibit misbranding and authorized seizure of misbranded articles after they were shipped from one state to another, so long as they remained "unsold." The authority of Congress to make this requirement was upheld as a proper exercise of its powers under the Commerce Clause. There are two variants between the circumstances of that case and this one. In the McDermott case the labels involved were on the original containers; here the labels are required to be put on other than the original containers—the boxes to which the tablets were transferred. Also, in the *McDermott* case the possessor of the labeled cans held for sale had himself received them by way of an interstate sale and shipment; here, while the petitioner had received the sulfathiazole by way of an intrastate sale and shipment, he bought it from a wholesaler who had received it as the direct consignee of an interstate shipment. These variants are not sufficient we think to detract from the applicability of the *McDermott* holding to the present decision. In both cases alike the question relates to the constitutional power of Congress under the Commerce Clause to regulate the branding of articles that have completed an interstate shipment and are being held for future sales in purely local or intrastate commerce. The reasons given for the McDermott holding therefore are equally applicable and persuasive here. And many cases decided since the McDermott decision lend support to the validity of §301(k).

. . .

(Judgment reversed.)
Justice Rutledge concurred.
Justices Frankfurter, Reed, and Jackson dissented.

Taxation Power

The Internal Revenue Act of 1951 provided that each person engaged in the business of accepting wagers pay an excise tax of 10 percent on all of the monies wagered; pay a special $50 tax each year; and register with the Collector of Internal Revenue his name, place of each business where wagers are accepted for him, residence, and the name and residence of every person who accepts wagers for him. In *United States* v *Kahriger,* 345 U.S. 22, 73 S.Ct. 510, 97 L.Ed. 754 (1953), the Court reversed the federal district court decision to grant Kahriger's motion to dismiss the charges on the ground that the Act was unconstitutional. The Court also did not find a violation of the privileges against self-incrimination in the registration feature of the Act.

The congressional power to tax citizens does not include the power to impose penalties through taxes. In *United States* v *Constantine,* 296 U.S. 287, 56 S.Ct. 223, 80 L.Ed. 233 (1935), the Court considered the legality of a federal excise tax that imposed a tax from 10 to 50 times higher on illegally operated liquor businesses than the tax imposed on legal operations. The fact that the tax was specifically imposed on businesses that operated ''contrary to the laws of a state . . . or municipality'' and that the tax was grossly disproportionate to the normal federal excise tax on liquor dealers led the Court to the assumption that the tax was being used as a penalty on illegal operations. This is not a constitutional use of the power of taxation held by the Congress.

The Court declined to analyze the purposes of a tax on particularly noxious weapons, including short-barreled machine guns, machine guns, and mufflers and silencers. In *Sonzinsky* v *United States,* 300 U.S. 506, 57 S.Ct. 554, 81 L.Ed. 772 (1937), the Court denied an argument that the tax was actually a penalty meant to inhibit the trade of such articles. Since the tax was an operational one that did not accompany ''offensive regulation,'' it fell within the taxing power of the Congress and the analysis of motives of the legislation did not fall within the judicial power.

Marchetti v *United States,* 390 U.S. 39, 88 S.Ct. 697, 19 L.Ed. 2d 889 (1968), questioned the Court's decision in *United States* v *Kahriger, supra* and called for a new consideration on the continuing force of like cases ''in light of our most recent decisions.''

Mr. Justice Harlan stated We find this reasoning no longer persuasive. The question is not whether petitioner holds a ''right'' to violate state law, but whether, having done so, he may be compelled to give evidence against himself. The constitutional privilege was intended to shield the guilty and imprudent as well as the innocent and foresighted; if such an inference of antecedent choice were alone enough to abrogate the privilege's protection, it would be excluded from the situations in which it has historically been guaranteed, and withheld from those who most require it.

. . . We can only conclude, under the wagering tax system as presently written, that petitioner properly asserted the privilege against self-incrimination, and that his assertion should have provided a complete defense to this prosecution. This defense should have reached both the substantive counts for failure to register and to pay the occupational tax, and the count for conspiracy to evade payment of the tax. We emphasize that we do not hold that these wagering tax provisions are as such constitutionally impermissible; we hold only that those who properly assert the constitutional privilege as to these provisions may not be criminally punished for failure to comply with their requirements. If, in different circumstances, a taxpayer is not confronted by substantial hazards of self-incrimination, or if he is otherwise outside the privilege's protection, nothing we decide today would shield him from the various penalties prescribed by the wagering tax statutes.

In *Grosso* v *United States,* 390 U.S. 62, 88 S.Ct. 709 19 L.Ed. 2d 906 (1968), the conviction of the appellant on charges of conspiracy to defraud the government by failing to pay a special occupational tax on gamblers and willfull failure to pay a special excise tax on wagering was reversed. The appellant contended that compliance with the federal statutes imposing such taxes would result in self-incrimination, since the state in which his gambling took place had enacted a comprehensive statute prohibiting gambling. Because the federal tax forms required detailed evidence of gambling, and the forms were frequently given to local prosecutors, the compliance with the federal statutes would result in self-incrimination by the appellant. Further, the Court held that the activities of the appellant had in no way foreclosed his right against self-incrimination. For these reasons, the convictions were reversed.

Treaty-Making Power

Missouri v Holland
252 U.S. 416, 40 S.Ct. 382, 64 L.Ed. 641 (1920)

Pursuant to a 1916 treaty between the United States and Great Britain governing the preservation and protection of certain species of birds, in 1918 Congress passed a Migratory Bird Act which authorized the secretary of agriculture to issue regulations concerning the killing, capturing, and selling birds named in the treaty when they migrated through the United States and Canada. The state of Missouri filed a suit in the federal district court to restrain Holland, a game warden, from enforcing the Act and regulations of the secretary of agriculture claiming that the Act was unconstitutional because it violated the Tenth Amendment and invaded the sovereignty of Missouri. Missouri appealed from an adverse holding by the district court, and the United States Supreme Court affirmed.

Justice Holmes delivered the opinion of the Court:

... It is unnecessary to go into any details, because, as we have said, the question raised is the general one whether the treaty and statute are void as an interference with the rights reserved to the states.

To answer this question it is not enough to refer to the Tenth Amendment, reserving the powers not delegated to the United States, because by Article II, Section 2, the power to make treaties is delegated expressly, and by Article 6 treaties made under the authority of the United States, along with the Constitution and laws of the United States made in pursuance thereof, are declared the supreme law of the land. If the treaty is valid there can be no dispute about the validity of the statute under Article I, Section 8, as a necessary and proper means to execute the powers of the government. The language of the Constitution as to the supremacy of treaties being general, the question before us is narrowed to an inquiry into the ground upon which the present supposed exception is placed.

It is said that a treaty cannot be valid if it infringes upon the Constitution, that there are limits, therefore, to the treaty-making power, and that one such limit is that what an act of Congress could not do unaided, in derogation of the powers reserved to the states, a treaty cannot do.

. . .

Whether the two cases cited were decided rightly or not they cannot be accepted as a test of the treaty power. Acts of Congress are the supreme law of the land only when made in pursuance of the Constitution, while treaties are declared to be so when made under the authority of the United States. It is open to question whether the authority of the United States means more than the formal acts prescribed to make the convention. We do not mean to imply that there are no qualifications to the treaty-making power; but they must be ascertained in a different way. It is obvious that there may be matters of the sharpest exigency for the national well-being that an act of Congress could not deal with but that a treaty followed by such an act could, and it is not lightly to be assumed that, in matters requiring national action, ''a power which must belong to and somewhere reside in every civilized government'' is not to be found. . . . What was said in that case with regard to the powers of the states applies with equal force to the powers of the nation in cases where the states individually are incompetent to act. We are not yet discussing the particular case before us but only are considering the validity of the test proposed. With regard to that we may add that when we are dealing with words that also are a constituent act, like the Constitution of the United States, we must realize that they have called into life a being the development of which could not have been foreseen completely by the most gifted of its begetters. It was enough for them to realize or to hope that they had created an organism; it has taken a century and has cost their successors much sweat and blood to prove that they created a nation. The case before us must be considered in the light of our whole experience and not merely in that of what was said a hundred years ago. The treaty in question does not contravene any prohibitory words to be found in the Constitution. The only question is whether it is forbidden by some invisible radiation from the general terms of the Tenth Amendment. We must consider what this country has become in deciding what that amendment has reserved.

The state as we have intimated founds it claims of exclusive authority upon an assertion of title to migratory birds, an assertion that is embodied in statute. No doubt it is true that as between a state and its inhabitants the state may regulate the killing and sale of such birds, but it does not follow that its authority is exclusive of paramount powers. To put the claim of the state upon title is to lean upon a slender reed. Wild birds are not in the possession of anyone; and possession is the beginning of ownership. The whole foundation of the state's rights is the presence within their jurisdiction of birds that yesterday had not arrived, tomorrow may be in another state and in a week a thousand miles away. If we are to be accurate we cannot put the case of the state upon higher ground than that the treaty deals with creatures that for the moment are within the state borders, that it must be carried out by officers of the United States within the same territory, and that but for the treaty the state would be free to regulate this subject itself.

As most of the laws of the United States are carried out within the states and as many of them deal with matters which in the silence of such laws the state might regulate, such general grounds are not enough to support Missouri's claim. Valid treaties of course "are as binding within the territorial limits of the states as they are elsewhere throughout the dominion of the United States." . . . No doubt the great body of private relations usually falls within the control of the state, but a treaty may override its power.

· · ·

Here a national interest of very nearly the first magnitude is involved. It can be protected only by national action in concert with that of another power. The subject matter is only transitorily within the state and has no permanent habitat therein. But for the treaty and the statute there soon might be no birds for any powers to deal with. We see nothing in the Constitution that compels the government to sit by while a food supply is cut off and the protectors of our forests and our crops are destroyed. It is not sufficient to rely upon the states. The reliance is vain, and were it otherwise, the question is whether the United States is forbidden to act. We are of opinion that the treaty and statute must be upheld.

· · ·

(Judgment affirmed.)
Justices Van Devanter and Pitney dissented.

The treaty-making power of the federal government is absolute in relation to the individual states. This was illustrated in *Hauenstein* v *Lynham*, 100 U.S. 483, 25 L.Ed. 628 (1880). The appellants claimed that the state of Virginia had unconstitutionally denied him ownership of an estate left by his heir, who was a citizen of the United States and Virginia. Acting under a state statute, the estate of the deceased was denied the rightful heirs because they were not citizens of the United States. A treaty made subsequent to the statute made all property of citizens of either Switzerland or the United States transferrable according to the will of the property owner. The United States Supreme Court affirmed the federal government's right to make treaties with foreign nations and further held that "the Constitution, laws, and treaties of the United States are as much a part of the law of every state as its own local laws and Constitution.'' Any statute contrary to a treaty, whether enacted prior or subsequent to the enactment of the treaty, is void.

War Power

Woods v *Miller*

333 U.S. 138, 68 S.Ct. 421, 92 L.Ed. 596 (1948)

Congress passed the Housing and Rent Act of 1947 to alleviate inflationary trends in rents because of the housing shortage that resulted from the lack of construction during World War II. The Act set a maximum rent level in specified areas. The day after the Act became effective Miller violated the Act by increasing tenant rents from 40 percent to 60 percent. Woods then instituted this suit to enjoin the increases as violating the Act. The district court declined to issue the injunction under the theory that a presidental proclamation on December 31, 1946, terminated the hostilities and inaugurated ''peace-in-fact'' although it did not mark termination of the war. Therefore, Congress went beyond the legitimate exercise of its war powers and the Act was invalid. On direct appeal to the United States Supreme Court the judgment was reversed.

Justice Douglas delivered the opinion of the Court:

We conclude, in the first place, that the war power sustains this legislation. The Court said in *Hamilton* v *Kentucky Distilleries and Warehouse* Co., 251 U.S. 146, . . . , that the war power includes the power ''to remedy the evils which have arisen from its rise and progress'' and continues for the duration of that emergency. Whatever may be the consequences when war is officially terminated, the war power does not necessarily end with the cessation of hostilities. We recently held that it is adequate to support the preservation of rights created by wartime legislation. . . . But it has a broader sweep. In *Hamilton* v *Kentucky Distilleries* . . . prohibition laws which were enacted after the Armistice in World War I were sustained as exercises of the war power because they conserved manpower and increased efficiency of production in the critical days during the period of demobilization, and helped to husband the supply of grains and cereals depleted by the war effort.

. . .

The constitutional validity of the present legislation follows *a fortiori* from those cases. The legislative history of the present Act makes abundantly clear that there has not yet been eliminated the deficit in housing which in considerable measure was caused by the heavy demobilization of veterans and by the cessation or reduction in residential construction during the period of hostilities due to the allocation of building materials to military projects. Since the war effort contributed heavily to that deficit, Congress has the power even after the cessation of hostilities to act to control the forces that a short supply of the needed article created. If that were not true, the Necessary and Proper Clause, Article I, Section 8, Clause 18 would be drastically limited in its application to the several war powers. The Court has declined to follow that course in the past. . . . We decline to take it today. The result would be paralyzing. It would render Congress powerless to remedy conditions the creation of which necessarily followed from the mobilization of men and materials for successful prosecution of the war. So to read the Constitution would be to make it self-defeating.

We recognize the force of the argument that the effects of war under modern conditions may be felt in the economy for years and years, and that if the war power can be used in days of peace to treat all the wounds which war inflicts in our society, it may not only swallow up all other powers of Congress but largely obliterate the Ninth and the Tenth Amendments as well. There are no such implications in today's decision. We deal here with the consequences of a housing deficit greatly intensified during the period of hostilities by the war effort. Any power, of course, can be abused. But we cannot assume that Congress is not alert to its constitutional responsibilities. And the question whether the war power has been properly employed in cases such as this is open to judicial inquiry.

. . .

The question of the constitutionality of action taken by Congress does not depend on recitals of the power which it undertakes to exercise. Here it is plain from the legislative history that Congress was invoking its war power to cope with a current condition of which the war was a direct and immediate cause. Its judgment on that score is entitled to the respect granted like legislation enacted pursuant to the police power.

. . .

Under the present Act the housing expediter is authorized to remove the rent controls in any defense-rental area if in his judgment the need no longer exists by reason of new construction or satisfaction of demand in other ways. The powers thus delegated are far less extensive than those sustained. . . . Nor is there here a grant of unbridled administrative discretion. The standards prescribed pass muster under our decision.

. . .

Objection is made that the Act by its exemption of certain classes of housing accommodations violates the Fifth Amendment. A similar argument was rejected under the Fourteenth Amendment when New York made like exemptions under the rent-control statute which was here for review. . . . Certainly Congress is not under greater limitations. It need not control all rents or none. It can select those areas or those classes of property where the need seems the greatest. . . . This alone is adequate answer to the objection, equally applicable to the original Act sustained in *Bowles* v *Willingham, supra*, that the present Act lacks uniformity in application.

The fact that the property regulated suffers a decrease in value is no more fatal to the exercise of the war power . . . than it is where the police power is invoked to the same end.

. . .

(Judgment reversed.)
Justices Frankfurter and Jackson concurred.

Presidential Power

Youngstown Sheet and Tube Co. v Sawyer

343 U.S. 579, 72 S.Ct. 863, 96 L.Ed. 1153 (1952)

In early 1952 President Truman was threatened with a nationwide steel strike which he believed would jeopardize the national defense. To avoid the strike he issued an executive order on April 3, 1952, directing Secretary of Commerce Sawyer to take possession of most of the nation's steel mills and keep them operating, which Secretary Sawyer did. The presidents of the companies seized became operating managers for the United States. President Truman accounted for his actions to Congress the next morning. Congress did nothing. Youngstown and the other seized steel companies sought a declaratory judgment and injunctive relief against Secretary of Commerce Sawyer to regain possession. The federal district court granted the relief; the Court of Appeals stayed the injunction; the Supreme Court affirmed the district court.

In stating the opinion of the Court, Justice Black cites two crucial issues:

. . . *First*. Should final determination of the constitutional validity of the President's order be made in this case which has proceeded no further than the preliminary injunction stage? *Second*. If so, is the seizure order within the constitutional power of the President? . . .''

Speaking to the issue of final determination at this point, Justice Black states:

''Moreover, seizure and governmental operation of these going businesses were bound to result in many present and future damages of such nature as to be difficult, if not incapable, of measurement. Viewing the case this way, and in light of the facts presented, the district court saw no reason for delaying decision of the constitutional validity of the orders.''

. . .

Determination of the issue of constitutional power came from these words:

The President's power, if any, to issue the order must stem either from an act of Congress or from the Constitution itself. There is no statute that expressly authorizes the President to take possession of property as he did here. Nor is there any act of Congress to which our attention has been directed from which such a power can fairly be implied. Indeed, we do not understand the government to rely on statutory authorization for this seizure. There are two statutes which do authorize the President to take both personal and real property under certain conditions. However, the government admits that these conditions were not met and that the President's order was not rooted in either of the statutes. The government refers to the seizure provisions of one of these statutes [§201(b) of the Defense Production Act] as "much too cumbersome, involved, and time-consuming for the crisis which was at hand."

It was therefore decided in this case that:

The President's order does not direct that a congressional policy be executed in a manner prescribed by Congress—it directs that a presidential policy be executed in a manner prescribed by the President. The preamble of the order itself, like that of many statutes, sets out reasons why the President believes certain policies should be adopted, proclaims these policies as rules of conduct to be followed, and again, like a statute, authorizes a government official to promulgate additional rules and regulations consistent with the policy proclaimed and needed to carry that policy into execution. The power of Congress to adopt such public policies as those proclaimed by the order is beyond question. It can authorize the taking of private property for public use. It can make laws regulating the relationships between employers and employees, prescribing rules designed to settle labor disputes, and fixing wages and working conditions in certain fields of our economy. The Constitution did not subject this law-making power of Congress to presidential or military supervision or control.

It is said that other presidents without congressional authority have taken possession of private business enterprises in order to settle labor disputes. But even if this be true, Congress has not thereby lost its exclusive constitutional authority to make laws necessary and proper to carry out the powers vested by the Constitution "in the government of the United States, or in any department or officer thereof."

The founders of this nation entrusted the law-making power to the Congress alone in both good and bad times. It would do no good to recall the historical events, the fears of power, and the hopes for freedom that lay behind their choice. Such a review would but confirm our holding that this seizure order cannot stand.

(District Court judgment affirmed.)
Justices Jackson, Douglas, Clark, Frankfurter and Burton concurred separately. The Chief Justice and Justices Reed and Menton dissented.

United States v Nixon

418 U.S. 683, 94 S.Ct. 3090, 41 L.Ed. 2d 1039 (1974)

Several of President Nixon's staff and political supporters were indicted for various offenses including conspiracy to defraud the government and to obstruct justice. President Nixon was named as an unindicted conspirator. The special prosecutor, Leon Jaworski, filed a motion under the federal rules for a *subpoena duces tecum* for the production before trial of specifically identified tapes and documents. The President filed a motion to quash the motion claiming executive privilege. The district court concluded that there was adequate showing for needing the materials and ordered them to be produced. On a special writ of certiorari, the United States Supreme Court held that President Nixon had to comply with the subpoena.

Chief Justice Burger delivered the opinion of the Court:

Having determined that the requirements of Rule 17(c) were satisfied, we turn to the claim that the subpoena should be quashed because it demands "confidential conversations between a president and his close advisors that it would be inconsistent with the public interest to produce." . . . The first contention is a broad claim that the separation of powers doctrine precludes judicial review of a president's claim of privilege. The second contention is that if he does not prevail on the claim of absolute privilege, the Court should hold as a matter of constitutional law that the privilege prevails over the *subpoena duces tecum.*

In the performance of assigned constitutional duties each branch of the government must initially interpret the Constitution, and the interpretation of its powers by any branch is due great respect from the others. The president's counsel, as we have noted, reads the Constitution as providing an absolute privilege of confidentiality for all presidential communications. Many decisions of this Court, however, have unequivocally reaffirmed the holding of *Marbury* v *Madison,* 1 Cranch, 137 . . . , that "it is emphatically the province and duty of the judicial department to say what the law is." . . . We therefore reaffirm that it is "emphatically the province and the duty" of this Court "to say what the law is" with respect to the claim of privilege presented in this case.

. . .

The second ground asserted by the President's counsel in support of the claim of absolute privilege rests on the doctrine of separation of powers. Here it is argued that the independence of the Executive Branch within its own sphere, . . . insulates a president from a judicial subpoena in an ongoing criminal prosecution, and thereby protects confidential presidental communications.

However, neither the doctrine of separation of powers, nor the need for confidentiality of high-level communications, without more, can sustain an absolute, unqualified presidential privilege of immunity from judicial process under all circumstances. The president's need for complete candor and objectivity from advisors calls for great deference from the courts. However, when the privilege depends solely on the broad, undifferentiated claim of public interest in the confidentiality of such conversations, a confrontation with other values arises. Absent a claim of need to protect military, diplomatic, or sensitive national security secrets, we find it difficult to accept the argument that even the very important interest in confidentiality of presidential communications is significantly diminished by production of such material for *in camera* inspection with all the protection that a district court will be obliged to provide.

· · ·

We conclude that when the ground for asserting privilege as to subpoenaed materials sought for use in a criminal trial is based only on the generalized interest in confidentiality, it cannot prevail over the fundamental demands of due process of law in the fair administration of criminal justice. The generalized assertion of privilege must yield to the demonstrated, specific need for evidence in a pending criminal trial.

(Judgment affirmed.)
Justice Rehnquist did not participate.

QUESTIONS

1. Why is the scope of *Gibbons* and *Ogden* so often compared with that of *McCulloch* v *Maryland?* How are these decisions similar? How are they different?

2. Discuss the Civil Rights Act of 1964 in relation to interstate commerce discussed in the cases in the section on civil rights and the commerce power.

3. Compare the cases of *Missouri* v *Holland* and *Woods* v *Miller*.

4. How much power does the Court have in relation to the power of the president? Is there adequate recourse for either party in this system of checks and balances?

5

THE CIVIL-
MILITARY
CONFLICT

A state of war is associated with the deprivation of individual liberty even though the war power does not remove constitutional liberties. See *Home Building and Loan Association* v *Blaisdell*, 290 U.S. 398 (1934). The cases of *Ex Parte Milligan*, 71 U.S. (4 Wall) 2 (1866), and *Korematsu* v *United States*, 323 U.S. 214 (1944), attest to the infringement of constitutional guarantees during periods of war.

Military control over military personnel has, as a rule, been covered under applicable military regulations in the Uniform Code of Military Justice. However, controversies have arisen concerning the question of whether an individual remains subject to military law where crimes were committed while a member of one of the various services but the individual is currently not in the service. The United States Supreme Court has also been active in the determination of whether a military court-martial has jurisdiction to try a member of the armed forces for the commission of a crime cognizable by the civilian courts but alleged to have been committed off post and while on leave. In *O'Callahan* v *Parker*, 395 U.S. 258 (1969), the Court answered this in the negative.

Closely allied with the war power in a world of national turmoil are the various rights that United States citizenship confers. The question of whether or not a person who deserts the military service during wartime can be deprived of his citizenship has been posed to the Supreme Court. Once again, a negative answer was given. The various ramifications of being a United States citizen are vast and far-reaching. Some of the problems involving this topic are covered in the several cases making up the section on rights of citizenship.

MILITARY LAW

Reid v *Covert*
Kinsella v *Krueger*

354 U.S. 1, 77 S.Ct. 1222, 1 L.Ed. 2d 1148 (1957)

Mrs. Covert, a civilian, killed her husband, a sergeant, at an air force base in England where they were residing. Mrs. Smith, also a civilian, killed her army major husband at a post in Japan where they were living. Both were tried for murder under the Uniform Code of Military Justice (UCMJ) which asserted jurisdiction over them by virtue of Article 2 (11), which subjects to the UCMJ "all persons serving with, employed by, or accompanying the armed forces without the continental limits of the United States." At the time of the offenses, the United States was permitted to exercise exclusive jurisdiction over offenses by American servicemen or their dependents for offenses committed in both Britain and Japan by virtue of executive agreements between the United States and those countries.

The cases were consolidated before the United States Supreme Court.

Justice Black announced the judgment of the Court and delivered an opinion in which the Chief Justice and Justices Douglas and Brennan joined.

These cases raise basic constitutional issues of the utmost concern. They call into question the role of the military under our system of government. They involve the power of Congress to expose civilians to trial by military tribunals, under military regulations and procedures, for offenses against the United States thereby depriving them of trial in civilian courts, under civilian laws and procedures and with all the safeguards of the Bill of Rights. These cases are particularly significant because for the first time since the adoption of the Constitution wives of soldiers have been denied trial by jury in a court of law and forced to trial before courts-martial.

. . .

At the beginning we reject the idea that when the United States acts against citizens abroad it can do so free of the Bill of Rights. The United States is entirely a creature of the Constitution. Its power and authority have no other source. It can only act in accordance with all the limitations imposed by the Constitution. When the government reaches out to punish a citizen who is abroad, the shield which the Bill of Rights and other parts of the Constitution provide to protect his life and liberty should not be stripped away just because he happens to be in another land.

. . .

Among those provisions, Article III, Section 2 and the Fifth and Sixth Amendments are directly relevant to these cases.

. . .

This Court and other federal courts have held or asserted that various constitutional limitations apply to the government when it acts outside the continental United States. While it has been suggested that only those constitutional rights which are "fundamental" protect Americans abroad, we can find no warrant, in logic or otherwise, for picking and choosing among the remarkable collection of "thou shalt nots" which were explicitly fastened on all departments and agencies of the federal government by the Constitution and its amendments. Moreover, in view of our heritage and the history of the adoption of the Constitution and the Bill of Rights, it seems peculiarly anomalous to say that trial before a civilian judge and by an independent jury picked from the common citizenry is not a fundamental right.

. . .

Article I, Section 8, Clause 14 empowers Congress "to make rules for the government and regulations of the land and naval forces." It has been held that this creates an exception to the normal method of trial in civilian courts as provided by the Constitution and permits Congress to authorize military trial of members of the armed services without all the safeguards given an accused by Article III and the Bill of Rights. But if the language of Clause 14 is given its natural meaning, the power granted does not extend to civilians—even though they may be dependents living with servicemen on a military base. The term "land and naval forces" refers to persons who are members of the armed services and not to their civilian wives, children, and other dependents. It seems inconceivable that Mrs. Covert or Mrs. Smith could have been tried by military authorities as members of the "land and naval forces" had they been living on a military post in this country. Yet this constitutional term surely has the same meaning everywhere. The wives of servicemen are no more members of the "land and naval forces" when living at a military post in England or Japan than when living at a base in this country or in Hawaii or Alaska.

The government argues that the Necessary and Proper Clause (18) when taken in conjunction with Clause 14 allows Congress to authorize the trial of Mrs. Smith and Mrs. Covert by military tribunals and under military law. The government claims that the two clauses together constitute a broad grant of power "without limitation" authorizing Congress to subject all persons, civilians and soldiers alike, to military trial if "necessary and proper" to govern and regulate the land and naval forces. It was on a similar theory that Congress once went to the extreme of subjecting persons who made contracts with the military to court-martial jurisdiction with respect to frauds related to such contracts. In the only judicial test a circuit court held that the legislation was patently unconstitutional.

. . .

It is true that the Constitution expressly grants Congress power to make all rules necessary and proper to govern and regulate those persons who are serving in the "land and naval forces." But the Necessary and Proper Clause cannot operate to extend military jurisdiction to any group of persons beyond that class described in Clause 14—"the land and naval forces." Under the grand design of the Constitution civilian courts are the normal repositories of power to try persons charged with crimes against the United States. And to protect persons brought before these courts, Article III and the Fifth, Sixth, and Eighth Amendments establish the right to trial by jury, to indictment by a grand jury, and a number of other specific safeguards. By way of contrast the jurisdiction of military tribunals is a very limited and extraordinary jurisdiction derived from the cryptic language in Article I, Section 8, and, at most, was intended to be only a narrow exception to the normal and preferred method of trial in courts of law. Every extension of military jurisdiction is an encroachment on the jurisdiction of the civil courts, and, more important, acts as a deprivation of the right to jury trial and of other treasured constitutional protections.

. . .

Further light is reflected on the scope of Clause 14 by the Fifth Amendment. . . . Since the exception in this Amendment for "cases arising in the land or naval forces" was undoubtedly designed to correlate with the power granted Congress to provide for the "government and Regulation" of the armed services, it is a persuasive and reliable indication that the authority conferred by Clause 14 does not encompass persons who cannot fairly be said to be "in" the military service.

Even if it were possible, we need not attempt here to precisely define the boundary between "civilians" and members of the "land and naval forces." We recognize that there might be circumstances where a person could be "in" the armed services for purposes of Clause 14 even though he had not formally been inducted into the military or did not wear a uniform. But the wives, children, and other dependents of servicemen cannot be placed in that category, even though they may be accompanying a serviceman abroad at government expense and receiving other benefits from the government.

. . .

In light of this history, it seems clear that the founders had no intention to permit the trial of civilians in military courts, where they would be denied jury trials and other constitutional protections, merely by giving Congress the power to make rules which were "necessary and proper" for the regulation of the "land and naval forces." Such a latitudinarian interpretation of these clauses would be at war with the well-established purpose of the founders to keep the military strictly within its proper sphere, subordinate to civil authority. The Constitution does not say that Congress can regulate "the land and naval forces and all other persons whose regulation might have some relationship to maintenance of the land and naval forces." There is no indication that the founders contemplated setting up a rival system of military courts to compete with civilian courts for jurisdiction over civilians who might have some contact or relationship with the armed forces. Courts-martial were not to have concurrent jurisdiction with courts of law over nonmilitary America.

. . .

Courts-martial are typically *ad hoc* bodies appointed by a military officer from among his subordinates. They have always been subject to varying degrees of "command influence." In essence, these tribunals are simply executive tribunals whose personnel are in the executive chain of command. Frequently, the members of the court-martial must look to the appointing officer for promotions, advantageous assignments, and efficiency ratings—in short, for their future progress in the service. Conceding to military personnel that high degree of honesty and sense of justice which nearly all of them undoubtedly have, the members of a court-martial, in the nature of things, do not and cannot have the independence of jurors drawn from the general public or of civilian judges.

We recognize that a number of improvements have been made in military justice recently by engrafting more and more of the methods of civilian courts on courts-martial. In large part these ameliorations stem from the reaction of civilians, who were inducted during the two world wars, to their experience with military justice. Notwithstanding the recent reforms, military trial does not give an accused the same protection which exists in the civil courts. Looming far above all other deficiencies of the military trial, of course, is the absence of trial by jury before an independent judge after an indictment by a grand jury. Moreover the reforms are merely statutory; Congress—and perhaps the president—can reinstate former practices, subject to any limitations imposed by the Constitution, whenever it desires. As yet it has not been clearly settled to what extent the Bill of Rights and other protective parts of the Constitution apply to military trials.

(Judgment: Mrs. Covert and Mrs. Smith were ordered released from custody.)
Justice Frankfurter concurring in the result:

. . . (T)his Court, applying appropriate methods of constitutional interpretation, has long held, and in a variety of situations, that in the exercise of a power specifically granted to it, Congress may sweep in what may be necessary to make effective the explicitly worded power. . . . This is the significance of the Necessary and Proper Clause, which is not to be considered so much a separate clause in Article I, Section 8, as an integral part of each of the preceding 17 clauses. Only thus may be avoided a strangling literalness in construing a document that is not an enumeration of static rules but the living framework of government designed for an undefined future.

. . .

Everything that may be deemed, as the exercise of an allowable judgment by Congress, to fall fairly within the conception conveyed by the power given to Congress "to make rules for the government and regulation of the land and naval forces" is constitutionally within that legislative grant and not subject to revision by the independent judgment of the Court. To be sure, every event or transaction that bears some relation to "the land and naval forces" does not *ipso facto* come within the tolerant conception of that legislative grant. The issue in these cases involves regard for considerations not dissimilar to those involved in a determination under the Due Process Clause. Obviously, the practical situations before us bear some relation to the military. Yet the question for this Court is not merely whether the relation of these women to the ''land and naval forces'' is sufficiently close to preclude the necessity of finding that Congress has been arbitrary in its selection of a particular method of trial. For, although we must look to Article I, Section 8, Clause 14 as the immediate justifying power, it is not the only clause of the Constitution to be taken into account. The Constitution is an organic scheme of government to be dealt with as an entirety. A particular provision cannot be dissevered from the rest of the Constitution. Our conclusion in these cases therefore must take due account of Article III and the Fifth and Sixth Amendments. We must weigh all the factors involved in these cases in order to decide whether these women dependents are so closely related to what Congress may allowably deem essential for the effective ''government and regulation of the land and naval forces'' that they may be subjected to court-martial jurisdiction in these capital cases, when the consequence is loss of the protections afforded by Article III and the Fifth and Sixth Amendments.

. . .

The prosecution by court-martial for capital crimes committed by civilian dependents of members of the armed forces abroad is hardly to be deemed, under modern conditions, obviously appropriate to the effective exercise of the power to ''make rules for the government and regulation of the land and naval forces'' when it is a question of deciding what power is granted under Article I and therefore what restriction is made on Article III and the Fifth and Sixth Amendments. I do not think that the proximity, physical and social, of these women to the ''land and naval forces'' is, with due regard to all that has been put before us, so clearly demanded by the effective ''government and regulation'' of those forces as reasonably to demonstrate a justification for court-martial jurisdiction over capital offenses.

. . .

I therefore conclude that, in capital cases, the exercise of court-martial jurisdiction over civilian dependents in time of peace cannot be justified by Article I, considered in connection with the specific protections of Article III and the Fifth and Sixth Amendments.

Justice Harlan concurred in the result.
Justice Clark and Burton joined dissenting.
Justice Whittaker took no part in the consideration or decision of these cases.

O'Callahan v *Parker*

395 U.S. 258, 89 S.Ct. 1683, 23 L.Ed. 2d 291 (1969)

O'Callahan, an American soldier, was stationed in Hawaii. While in civilian clothes on an evening pass he broke into the Honolulu hotel room of a young girl and assaulted and attempted to rape her. He was subsequently convicted of various violations of the Uniform Code of Military Justice (UCMJ). Habeas corpus relief was sought in the United States Supreme Court after being denied in the federal district court and court of appeals.

Justice Douglas delivered the opinion of the Court:

The Constitution gives Congress power to "make rules for the government and regulation of the land and naval forces," Article I Section 8, Clause 14, and it recognizes that the exigencies of military discipline require the existence of a special system of military courts in which not all of the specific procedural protections deemed essential in Article III trials need apply. The Fifth Amendment specifically exempts "cases arising in *the land or naval forces,* or in the militia, when in actual service in time of war or public danger" from the requirement of prosecution by indictment and from the right to trial by jury. [Emphasis supplied.] . . . The result has been the establishment and development of a system of military justice with fundamental differences from the practices in the civilian courts.

. . .

A court-martial is tried, not by a jury of the defendant's peers which must decide unanimously, but by a panel of officers empowered to act by a two-thirds vote. The presiding officer at a court-martial is not a judge whose objectivity and independence are protected by tenure and undiminishable salary and nurtured by the judicial tradition, but is a military law officer. Substantially different rules of evidence and procedure apply in military trials. Apart from those differences, the suggestion of the possibility of influence on the actions of the court-martial by the officer who convenes it, selects its members and the counsel on both sides, and who usually has direct command authority over its members is a pervasive one in military law, despite strenuous efforts to eliminate the danger.

A court-martial is not yet an independent instrument of justice but remains to a significant degree a specialized part of the overall mechanism by which military discipline is preserved.

That a system of specialized military courts, proceeding by practices different from those obtaining in the regular courts and in general less favorable to defendants, is necessary to an effective national defense establishment, few would deny. But the justification for such a system rests on the special needs of the military, and history teaches that expansion of military discipline beyond its proper domain carries with it a threat to liberty. This Court, mindful of the genuine need for special military courts, has recognized their propriety in their appropriate sphere.

. . .

These cases decide that courts-martial have no jurisdiction to try those who are not members of the armed forces, no matter how intimate the connection between their offense and the concerns of military discipline. From these cases, the government invites us to draw the conclusion that once it is established that the accused is a member of the armed forces, lack of relationship between the offense and identifiable military interests is irrelevant to the jurisdiction of a court-martial.

. . .

We have concluded that the crime to be under military jurisdiction must be service-connected, lest "cases arising in the land or naval forces, or in the militia, when in actual service in time of war or public danger, "used in the Fifth Amendment, be expanded to deprive every member of the armed services of the benefits on an indictment by a grand jury and a trial by a jury of his peers. The power of Congress to make "rules for the government and regulations of the land and naval forces," Article I, Section 8, Clause 14, need not be sparingly read in order to preserve those two important constitutional guarantees. For it is assumed that an express grant of general power to Congress is to be exercised in harmony with express grant of general power to Congress is to be exercised in harmony with express guarantees of the Bill of Rights. We are advised on oral argument that Article 134 is construed by the military to give it power to try a number of the armed services for income tax evasion. This article has been called "a catchall" that "incorporates almost every federal penal statute into the Uniform Code." . . . The catalogue of cases put within reach of the military is indeed long; and we see no way of saying to servicemen and servicewomen in any case the benefits of indictment and of trial by jury, if we conclude that this petitioner was properly tried by court-martial.

In the present case petitioner was properly absent from his military base when he committed the crimes with which he is charged. There was no connection—not even the remotest one—between his military duties and the crimes in question. The crimes were not committed on a military post or enclave; nor was the person whom he attacked performing any duties relating to the military. However, the situs of the crime is not an armed camp under military control, as are some of our far-flung outposts.

Finally, we deal with peacetime offenses, not with authority stemming from the war power. Civil courts were open. The offenses were committed within our territorial limits, not in the occupied zone of a foreign country. The offenses did not involve any question of the flouting of military authority, the security of a military post, or the integrity of military property.

We have accordingly decided that since petitioner's crimes were not service-connected, he could not be tried by court-martial but rather was entitled to trial by the civilian courts.

(Judgment reversed.)
Justice Harlan was joined by Justices Steward and White who dissented:

In the light of the language and history of Article I, Section 8, Clause 14, of the Constitution, and this Court's hitherto consistent interpretation of this provision, I do not believe that the resolution of the controversy before us calls for any balancing of interests. But if one does engage in a balancing process, one cannot fairly hope to come up with a meaningful answer unless the interests on both sides are fully explored. The Court does not do this. Rather, it chooses to ignore strong and legitimate governmental interests which support the exercise of court-martial jurisdiction even over "nonmilitary" crimes.

The United States has a vital interest in creating and maintaining an armed force of honest, upright, and well-disciplined persons, and in preserving the reputation, morale, and integrity of the military services. Furthermore, because its personnel must, perforce, live and work in close proximity to one another, the military has an obligation to protect each of its members from the misconduct of fellow servicemen. The commission of offenses against the civil order manifests qualities of attitude and character equally destructive of military order and safety. The soldier who acts the part of Mr. Hyde while on leave is, at best, a precarious Dr. Jekyll when back on duty.

. . .

The government, thus, has a proper concern in keeping its own house in order, by deterring members of the armed forces from engaging in criminal misconduct on or off the base, and by rehabilitating offenders to return them to useful military service.

The exercise of military jurisdiction is also responsive to other practical needs of the armed forces. A soldier detained by the civil authorities pending trial, or subsequently imprisoned, is to that extent rendered useless to the service. Even if he is released on bail or recognizance, or ultimately placed on probation, the civil authorities may require him to remain within the jurisdiction, thus making him unavailable for transfer with the rest of his unit or as the service otherwise requires.

. . .

The Court does not explain the scope of the "service-connected" crimes as to which court-martial jurisdiction is appropriate, but it appears that jurisdiction may extend to "nonmilitary" offenses in appropriate circumstances. Thus, the Court intimates that it is relevant to the jurisdictional issue in this case that petitioner was wearing civilian clothes rather than a uniform when he committed the crime. . . . And it also implies that plundering, abusing, and stealing from civilians may sometimes constitute a punishable abuse of military position, *ante,* at 1689, n. 14, and that officers may be court-martialed for purely civilian crimes because "(i)n the eighteenth century . . . the "honor" of an officer was thought to give a specific military connection to a crime otherwise without military significance." . . . But if these are illustrative cases, the Court suggests no general standard for determining when the exercise of court-martial jurisdiction is permissible.

Korematsu v *United States*
323 U.S. 214, 65 S.Ct. 193, 89 L.Ed. 194 (1944)

Korematsu was a Japanese-American. On May 9, 1942, an order of General DeWitt, Western Command, United States Army, directed that all persons of

Japanese ancestry should be excluded from specified areas. Korematsu remained in San Leandro, California, one of the areas mentioned in the order. He was convicted in a federal district court for acts contrary to the civilian exclusion order. At no time was a question of Korematsu's loyalty raised. The conviction was affirmed by the Court of Appeals, and the United States Supreme Court granted certiorari.

Justice Black delivered the opinion of the Court:

It should be noted, to begin with, that all legal restrictions which curtail the civil rights of a single racial group are immediately suspect. That is not to say that all such restrictions are unconstitutional. It is to say that courts must subject them to the most rigid scrutiny. Pressing public necessity may sometimes justify the existence of such restrictions; racial antagonism never can.

One of the series of orders and proclamations, a curfew order, which like the exclusion order here was promulgated pursuant to Executive Order 9066, subjected all persons of Japanese ancestry in prescribed West Coast military areas to remain in their residences from 8 p.m. to 6 a.m. . . . In *Hirabayashi* v *United States,* 320 U.S. 81, . . . , we sustained a conviction obtained for violation of the curfew order.

. . .

The 1942 Act was attacked in the Hirabayashi Case as an unconstitutional delegation of power; it was contended that the curfew order and other orders on which it rested were beyond the war powers of the Congress, the military authorities, and of the president, as commander in chief of the Army; and finally that to apply the curfew order against none but citizens of Japanese ancestry ammounted to a constitutionally prohibited discrimination solely on account of race. . . . We upheld the curfew order as an exercise of the power of the government to take steps necessary to prevent espionage and sabotage in an area threatened by Japanese attack.

In the light of the principles we announced in the Hirabayashi Case, we are unable to conclude that it was beyond the war power of Congress and the Executive to exclude those of Japanese ancestry from the West Coast war area at the time they did. . . . The military authorities, charged with the primary responsibility of defending our shores, concluded that curfew provided inadequate protection and ordered exclusion. They did so, . . . in accordance with congressional authority to the military to say who should, and who should not, remain in the threatened areas.

Here, as in the Hirabayashi Case, . . . "we cannot reject as unfounded the judgment of the military authorities and of Congress that there were disloyal members of that population, whose number and strength could not be precisely and quickly ascertained."

. . .

Like curfew, exclusion of those of Japanese origin was deemed necessary because of the presence of an unascertained number of disloyal members of the group, most of whom we have no doubt were loyal to this country.

. . .

We uphold the exclusion order as of the time it was made and when the petitioner violated it.

. . .

Since the petitioner has not been convicted of failing to report or to remain in an assembly or relocation center, we cannot in this case determine the validity of those separate provisions of the order.

. . .

It is said that we are dealing here with the case of imprisonment of a citizen in a concentration camp solely because of his ancestry, without evidence or inquiry concerning his loyalty and good disposition toward the United States. Our task would be simple, our duty clear, were this a case involving the imprisonment of a loyal citizen in a concentration camp because of racial prejudice. . . . We are dealing specifically with nothing but an exclusion order. Korematsu was not excluded from the military area because of hostility to him or his race. He was excluded because we are at war with the Japanese Empire, because the properly constituted military authorities feared an invasion of our West Coast and felt constrained to take proper security measures, because they decided that the military urgency of the situation demanded that all citizens of Japanese ancestry be segregated from the West Coast temporarily, and finally, because Congress, reposing its confidence in this time of war in our military leaders—as inevitably it must—determined that they should have the power to do just this. There was evidence of disloyalty on the part of some, the military authorities considered that the need for action was great, and time was short. We cannot—by availing ourselves of the calm perspective of hindsight—now say that at that time these actions were unjustified.

(Judgment affirmed. Justice Frankfurther concurred. Justice Roberts dissented.) Justice Murphy dissenting:

This exclusion of "all persons of Japanese ancestry, both alien and non-alien," from the Pacific Coast area on a plea of military necessity in the absence of martial law ought not to be approved. Such exclusion goes over "the very brink of constitutional power" and falls into the ugly abyss of racism.

. . .

It was Justice Murphy's feeling that to exclude the members of one race without reasonable cause was unjustifiable:

. . . And that relation is lacking because the exclusion order necessarily must rely for its reasonableness upon the assumption that *all* persons of Japanese ancestry may have a dangerous tendency to commit sabotage and espionage and to aid our Japanese enemy in other ways. It is difficult to believe that reason, logic, or experience could be marshalled in support of such an assumption.

. . .

Justice Jackson dissenting:

. . . My duties as a justice as I see them do not require me to make a military judgment as to whether General DeWitt's evacuation and detention program was a reasonable military necessity. I do not suggest that the courts should have attempted to interfere with the Army in carrying out its task. But I do not think they may be asked to execute a military expedient that has no place in law under the Constitution. I would reverse the judgment and discharge the prisoner.

MARTIAL LAW

Ex parte Milligan

71 U.S. (4 Wall) 2, 18 L.Ed. 281 (1866)

Milligan, a United States civilian citizen, was arrested by military authorities and tried, convicted, and sentenced to be executed by a military commission in Indiana. The United States Supreme Court heard the case because of a certificate of division between the judges of the district court for Indiana and the Circuit Court of Appeals.

Justice Davis delivered the opinion of the Court:

The controlling question in the case is this: Upon the facts stated in Milligan's petition, and the exhibits filed, had the military commission mentioned in it jurisdiction, legally, to try and sentence him? Milligan, not a resident of one of the rebellious states, or a prisoner of war, but a citizen of Indiana for 20 years past, and never in the military or naval service, is, while at his home, arrested by the military power of the United States, imprisoned and, on certain criminal charges preferred against him, tried, convicted, and sentenced to be hanged by a military commission, organized under the direction of the military commander of the military district of Indiana. Had this tribunal the legal power and authority to try, and punish this man?

No graver question was ever considered by this Court, nor one which more nearly concerns the rights of the whole people; for it is the birthright of every American citizen when charged with crime, to be tried and punished according to law. The power of punishment is alone through the means which the laws have provided for that purpose, and if they are ineffectual, there is an immunity from punishment, no matter how great an offender the individual may be, or how much his crimes may have shocked the sense of justice of the country, or endangered its safety. By the protection of the law human rights are secured; withdrawn that protection, and they are at the mercy of wicked rulers, or the clamor of an excited people. If there was law to justify this military trial, it is not our province to interfere; if there was not, it is our duty to declare the nullity of the whole proceedings.

. . .

But it is said that the jurisdiction is complete under the "laws and usages of war."

It can serve no useful purpose to inquire what those laws and usages are, whence they originated, where found, and on whom they operate; they can never be applied to citizens in states which have upheld the authority of the government, and where the courts are open and their process unobstructed. This Court has judicial knowledge that in Indiana the federal authority was always unopposed, and its courts always open to hear criminal accusations and redress grievances; and no usage of war could sanction a military trial there for any offense whatever of a citizen in civil life, in nowise connected with the military service. Congress could grant no such power; and to the honor of our national legislature be it said, it has never been provoked by the state of the country even to attempt its exercise. One of the plainest constitutional provisions was, therefore, infringed when Milligan was tried by a court not ordained and established by Congress, and not composed of judges appointed during good behavior.

. . .

It is claimed that martial law covers with its broad mantle the proceedings of this military commission. The proposition is this: That in a time of war the commander of an armed force (if in his opinion the exigencies of the country demand it, and of which he is to judge), has the power, within the lines of his military district, to suspend all civil rights and their remedies, and subject citizens as well as soldiers to the rule of his will; and in the exercise of his lawful authority cannot be restrained, except by his superior officer or the president of the United States.

. . .

The statement of this proposition shows its importance; for, if true, republican government is a failure, and there is an end of liberty regulated by law. Martial law, established on such a basis, destroys every guaranty of the Constitution, and effectually renders the "military independent of and superior to the civil power"—the attempt to do which by the King of Great Britain was deemed by our fathers such an offense, that they assigned it to the world as one of the causes which impelled them to declare their independence. Civil liberty and this kind of martial law cannot endure together; the antagonism is irreconcilable and, in the conflict, one or the other must perish.

This nation, as experience has proved, cannot always remain at peace, and has no right to expect that it will always have wise and humane rulers, sincerely attached to the principles of the Constitution. Wicked men, ambitious of law, may fill the place once occupied by Washington and Lincoln; and if this right is conceded, and the calamities of war again befall us, the dangers to human liberty are frightful to contemplate. If our fathers had failed to provide for just such a contingency, they would have been false to the trust reposed in them. They knew—the history of the world told them—the nation they were founding, be its existence short or long, would be involved in war; how often or how long continued, human foresight could not tell; and that unlimited power, wherever lodged at such a time, was especially hazardous to free men. For this, and other equally weighty reasons, they secured the inheritance they had fought to maintain, by incorporating in a written Constitution the safeguards which time had proved were essential to its preservation. Not one of these safeguards can the president or Congress or the Judiciary disturb, except the one concerning the writ of habeas corpus.

It is essential to the safety of every government that, in a great crisis, like the one we have just passed through, there should be a power somewhere of suspending the writ of habeas corpus. In every war, there are men of previously good character, wicked enough to counsel their fellow citizens to resist the measures deemed necessary by a good government to sustain its just authority and overthrow its enemies; and their influence may lead to dangerous combinations. In the emergency of the times, an immediate public investigation according to law may not be possible; and yet, the peril to the country may be too imminent to suffer such persons to go at large. Unquestionably, there is then an exigency which demands that the government, if it should see fit, in the exercise of a proper discretion, to make arrests, should not be required to produce the person arrested in answer to a writ of habeas corpus. The Constitution goes no further. It does not say after a writ of habeas corpus is denied a citizen, that he shall be tried otherwise than by the course of common law. If it had intended this result, it was easy by the use of direct words to have accomplished it.

· · ·

It follows, from what has been said on this subject, that there are occasions when martial rule can be properly applied. If, in foreign invasion or civil war, the courts are actually closed, and it is impossible to administer criminal justice according to law, then, on the theater of actual military operations, where war really prevails, there is a necessity to furnish a substitute for the civil authority, thus overthrown, to preserve the safety of the army and society; and as no power is left but the military, it is allowed to govern by martial rule until the laws can have their free course. As necessity creates the rule, so it limits its duration; for, if this government is continued after the courts are reinstated, it is a gross usurpation of power. Martial rule can never exist where the courts are open, and in the proper and unobstructed exercise of their jurisdiction. It is also confined to the locality of actual war. Because, during the late Rebellion it could have been enforced in Virginia, where the national authority was overturned and the courts driven out, it does not follow that it should obtain in Indiana, where that authority was never disputed, and justice was always administered. And so in the case of a foreign invasion, martial rule may become a necessity, in one state, when, in another, it would be "mere lawless violence." We are not without precedents in English and American history illustrating our views of this question; but it is hardly necessary to make particular reference to them.

· · ·

The two remaining questions in this case must be answered in the affirmative. The suspension of the privilege of the writ of habeas corpus does not suspend the writ itself. The writ issues as a matter of course; and on the return made to it the court decides whether the party applying is denied the right of proceeding any further with it.

If the military trial of Milligan was contrary to law, then he was entitled, on the facts stated in his petition, to be discharged from custody by the terms of the act of Congress of March 3d, 1863. The provisions of this law having been considered in a previous part of this opinion, we will not restate the views there presented. Milligan avers he was a citizen of Indiana, not in the military or naval service, and was detained in close confinement, by order of the president, from the 5th day of October, 1864, until the 2d day of January, 1865, when the circuit court for the district of Indiana, with a grand jury, convened in session at Indianapolis; and afterwards, on the 27th day of the same month, adjourned without finding an indictment or presentment against him. If these averments were true (and their truth is conceded for the purposes of this case), the Court was required to liberate him on taking certain oaths prescribed by the law, and entering into recognizance for his good behavior.

But it is insisted that Milligan was a prisoner of war, and, therefore, excluded from the privileges of the statute. It is not easy to see how he can be treated as a prisoner of war, when he lived in Indiana for the past 20 years, was arrested there, and had not been, during the late troubles, a resident of any of the states in rebellion. If in Indiana he conspired with bad men to assist the enemy, he is punishable for it in the courts of Indiana; but, when tried for the offense, he cannot plead the rights of war; for he was not engaged in legal acts of hostility against the government, and only such persons, when captured, are prisoners of war. If he cannot enjoy the immunities attaching to the character of a prisoner of war, how can he be subject to their pains and penalties?

(Judgment reversed.)

Chief Justice Chase, joined by Justices Wayne, Swayne, and Miller, wrote a concurring opinion.

In *Duncan* v *Kahanamoku*, 327 U.S. 304, 66 S.Ct. 606, 90 L.Ed 688 (1946), the Court overturned the conviction of a civilian for nonmilitary offenses by a military court. These convictions had occurred pursuant to the declaration of martial law by the territorial governor of Hawaii immediately following the attack on Pearl Harbor. The ability to declare martial law in this situation was derived from the Hawaiian Organic Act. This Act authorized that the powers of the government were to be turned over to the commanding general.

Per Justice Black the Court felt that:

. . . The phrase "martial law" as employed in that Act, therefore, while intended to authorize the military to act vigorously for the maintenance of an orderly civil government and for the defense of the island against actual or threatened rebellion or invasion, was not intended to authorize the supplanting of courts by military tribunals. Yet the government seeks to justify the punishment of both White and Duncan on the ground of such supposed congressional authorization. We hold that both petitioners are now entitled to be released from custody.

In *Middendorf* v *Henry,* 425 U.S. 25, 96 S.Ct. 1281, 47 Ed.2d 566 (1976), the District Court ruled that counsel was required in a summary court-martial, by way of the Fifth and Sixth Amendments of the United States Constitution, contrary to a congressional determination that counsel was not necessary in this situation. The Court of Appeals vacated this judgment and remanded the case for consideration in light of its opinion in *Daigle* v *Warner,* 490 F. 2d 358 (1974), which held that the Sixth Amendment was not applicable in this situation, and that the Fifth Amendment was not absolute in every case. They qualified their stand on the Due Process Clause of the Fifth Amendment in line with *Gagnon* v *Scarpelli,* 411 U.S. 788 (1973), where the accused "makes a request based on a timely and colorable claim (1) that he has a defense and (2) that there are mitigating circumstances, and the assistance of counsel is necessary to his defense."

The Supreme Court reversed this decision on the grounds that ". . . presence of counsel will turn a brief, informal hearing . . . into an attenuated proceeding which consumes the resources of the military to a degree which Congress could properly have felt to be beyond what is warranted by the relative insignificance of the offenses being tried."

LAW OF WAR

In re Yamashita

327 U.S. 1, 66 S.Ct. 340, 90 L.Ed. 499 (1946)

Yamashita was the commanding general of the Japanese army in the Philippine Islands. He was also the military general of the Islands. After the war he was charged with violating the law of war by permitting troops under his command to commit atrocities and other high crimes against the people of the United States and its allies. Yamashita was tried, found guilty, and sentenced to death by a military tribunal. In his petition for a writ of habeas corpus, Yamashita claimed *inter alia* that no military commission could try him for violation of the law of war after cessation of hostilities between the United States and Japan.

Chief Justice Stone delivered the opinion of the Court:

In *Ex parte Quirin,* 317 U.S. 1, . . . , we had occasion to consider at length the sources and nature of the authority to create military commissions for the trial of enemy combatants for offenses against the law of war. We there pointed out that Congress, in the exercise of the power conferred upon it by

Article I, Section 8, Clause 10 of the Constitution to "define and punish . . . offenses against the law of nations . . . ," of which the law of war is a part, had by the Articles of War . . . recognized the "military commission" appointed by military command, as it had previously existed in United States Army practice, as an appropriate tribunal for the trial and punishment of offenses against the law of war.

. . .

We further pointed out that Congress, by sanctioning trial of enemy combatants for violations of the law of war by military commission, had not attempted to codify the law of war or to mark its precise boundaries. Instead, by Article 15 it had incorporated, by reference, as within the preexisting jurisdiction of military commissions created by appropriate military command, all offenses which are defined as such by the law of war, and which may constitutionally be included within that jurisdiction. It thus adopted the system of military common law applied by military tribunals so far as it should be recognized and deemed applicable by the courts, and as further defined and supplemented by the Hague Convention, to which the United States and the Axis powers were parties.

We also emphasized in *Ex parte Quirin,* as we do here, that on application for habeas corpus we are not concerned with the guilt or innocence of the the petitioner for the offense charged.

. . .

We cannot say that there is no authority to convene a commission after hostilities have ended to try violations of the law of war committed before their cessation, at least until peace has been officially recognized by treaty or proclamation of the political branch of the government. In fact, in most instances the practical administration of the system of military justice under the law of war would fail if such authority were thought to end with the cessation of hostilities. For only after their cessation could the greater number of offenders and the principal ones be apprehended and subjected to trial.

No writer on international law appears to have regarded the power of military tribunals, otherwise competent to try violations of the law of war, as terminating before the formal state of war has ended. In our own military history there have been numerous instances in which offenders were tried by military commission after the cessation of hostilities and before the proclamation of peace, for offenses against the law of war committed before the cessation of hostilities.

. . .

Petitioner further urges that by virtue of Article 63 of the Geneva Convention of 1929, 47 Stat. 2052, he is entitled to the benefits afforded by the 25th and 38th Articles of War to members of our own forces. Article 63 provides: "Sentence may be pronounced against a prisoner of war only by the same courts and according to the same procedure as in the case of persons belonging to the armed forces of the detaining Power." Since petitioner is a prisoner of war, and as the 25th and 38th Articles of War apply to the trial of any person in our own armed forces, it is said that Article 63 requires them to be applied to the trial of petitioner. But we think examination of Article 63 in its setting in the Convention plainly shows that it refers to sentence "pronounced against a prisoner of war" for an offense committed while a prisoner of war, and not for a violation of the law of war committed while a combatant.

(Writ denied.)

Mr. Justice Murphy, dissenting:

The significance of the issue facing the Court today cannot be overemphasized. An American military commission has been established to try a fallen military commander of a conquered nation for an alleged war crime. The authority for such action grows out of the exercise of the power conferred upon Congress by Article I, Section 8, Clause 10 of the Constitution to "define and punish . . . offenses against the law of nations. . . ." The grave issue raised by this case is whether a military commission so established and so authorized may disregard the procedural rights of an accused person as guaranteed by the Constitution, especially by the due process clause of the Fifth Amendment.

The answer is plain. The Fifth Amendment guarantee of due process of law applies to "any person" who is accused of a crime by the federal government or any of its agencies. No exception is made as to those who are accused of war crimes or as to those who possess the status of an enemy belligerent.

. . .

The existence of these rights, unfortunately, is not always respected. They are often trampled under by those who are motivated by hatred, aggression, or fear. But in this nation individual rights are recognized and protected, at least in regard to governmental action. They cannot by ignored by any branch of the government, even the military, except under the most extreme and urgent circumstances.

The failure of the military commission to obey the dictates of the due process requirements of the Fifth Amendment is apparent in this case. The petitioner was the commander of an army totally destroyed by the superior power of this nation. While under heavy and destructive attack by our forces, his troops committed many brutal atrocities and other high crimes. Hostilities ceased and he voluntarily surrendered. At that point he was entitled, as an individual protected by the Due Process Clause of the Fifth Amendment, to be treated fairly and justly according to the accepted rules of law and procedure. He was also entitled to a fair trial as to any alleged crimes and to be free from charges of legally unrecognized crimes that would serve only to permit his accusers to satisfy their desires for revenge.

A military commission was appointed to try the petitioner for an alleged war crime. The trial was ordered to be held in territory over which the United States has complete sovereignty. No military necessity or other emergency demanded the suspension of the safeguards of due process. Yet petitioner was rushed to trial under an improper charge, given insufficient time to prepare an adequate defense, deprived of the benefits of some of the most elementary rules of evidence and sentenced to be hanged.

Justice Rutledge dissented.
Justice Jackson took no part in the decision.

In *MacKenzie* v *Hare,* 239 U.S. 299, 36 S.Ct. 106, 60 L.Ed. 297 (1915), Mrs. MacKenzie, a United States citizen and resident of the United States, married an Englishman and resided with him in the United States. A federal statute in effect at that time provided that an American woman who married a foreigner shall take the nationality of the husband. When the maritial relationship is terminated, she may resume her American citizenship. MacKenzie sought to register for a California election and was refused on the ground she was not an American citizen. Her denial of a writ of mandamus in the California courts was upheld by the United States Supreme Court.

In *Trop* v *Dulles,* 356 U.S. 86, 78 S.Ct. 590, 2 L.Ed. 2d 630 (1958), Trop, a private in the Army, was convicted by a military court-martial of desertion and dishonorable discharged. The Nationality Act of 1940, Section 401(g) as amended, stated that a citizen shall lose his citizenship by reason of his conviction and dishonorable discharge for wartime desertion. The federal district court and Court of Appeals, Second Circuit, denied Trop's request for a judgment that he had not lost his citizenship. The United States Supreme Court granted certiorari and declared the Nationality Act provision to be unconstitutional.

Kennedy v *Mendoza-Martinez* and *Rusk* v *Cort,* 372 U.S. 144, 83 S.Ct. 554, 9 L.Ed. 2d 644 (1963), concerned the loss of citizenship.

These two cases were consolidated. Provisions of the Immigration and Nationality Act of 1952 and the Nationality Act of 1940 provide that native-born Americans who depart from or remain outside the jurisdiction of the United States in time of war or national emergency in order to avoid military service shall lose their citizenship. The federal district court granted a declaratory judgment in favor of Mendoza-Martinez and Cort in both the District of Columbia and California. The United States Attorney General appealed to the United States Supreme Court.

The Court held that the provisions of this Act violated the Fifth and Sixth Amendments by imposing punishment "without a prior trial and all its incidents, including notice, confrontation, trial by jury, assistance of counsel and compulsory process for obtaining witnesses."

The constitutionality of the Immigration and Nationality Act of 1952 was questioned in *Schneider* v *Rusk,* 377 U.S. 163, 84 S.Ct. 1187, 12 L.Ed. 2d 218 (1964). This Act provided that a naturalized citizen "shall lose his nationality by having two continuous residences for three years in the territory of a foreign state of which he was formerly a national or in which the place of his birth is situated.: It was the decision of the court that:

. . . A native-born citizen is free to reside abroad indefinitely without suffering loss of citizenship. The discrimination aimed at naturalized citizens drastically limits their rights to live and work abroad in a way that other citizens may. It creates indeed a second-class citizenship. Living abroad, whether the citizen be naturalized or native-born, is no badge of lack of allegiance and in no way evidences a voluntary renunciation of nationality and allegiance. It may indeed be compelled by family, business, or other legitimate reasons.

(Judgment reversed.)

QUESTIONS

1. How does the Court describe "military necessity"? What factors must the Court consider in regard to a question of "military necessity"?

2. What is the jurisdiction of the military court? Are military decisions subject to direct appellate court review? Was this a factor in the Court's decision in the cases in the section on martial law in this chapter? Discuss.

3. Define "expatriation." Compare the case of *in re Yamashita* with those cases found in the note. What are the similarities? What are the differences?

6

FIRST AMENDMENT RIGHTS

Congress shall make no law respecting an establishment of religion, or prohibiting the free exercise thereof; or abridging the freedom of speech, or of the press, or the right of the people peaceably to assemble, and to petition the Government for a redress of grievances.

This chapter addresses two constitutional rights that have been the subject of continuous constitutional interpretation throughout the history of our nation—speech and religion. These two areas are sometimes grouped together under the title of "freedom of expression," but for a clearer presentation an analysis of each is set forth in this chapter. The reader will note immediately the large number of constitutional cases that have addressed these two areas. They attest their importance in a democratic scheme of government. Freedom of speech will be covered first.

Both of these rights are, to all appearances, clear, unequivocal bans to (1) governmental efforts to suppress or limit in any way what Americans say, to whom they wish to speak, and when they wish to utter their remarks and (2) governmental efforts to establish a particular religion or to prohibit a person from exercising his religious preference in any way.

To begin, freedom of speech is so taken for granted by Americans that it is difficult to recall that it did not come about easily. Many tend to forget that freedom of speech has not been so free from government interference as the language in the First Amendment suggests.

For all practical purposes, Americans can say what they want, when they want, and where they want. Every day Americans write letters to all kinds of government agencies criticizing their activities. Americans make speeches on almost every topic. They argue vociferously with their government's policies. Newspapers publish what they wish. All of this is done without having to seek advance governmental approval as to the purpose of the expression. As a general rule, Americans have no fear of punishment for failure to secure prior approval of written or spoken communication. There are, however, certain kinds of expression which almost everyone agrees should not be free from some governmental regulation. For example, agreements to commit criminal acts, false advertising, and fraudulent statements that are used to cheat a person out of his property are subject to regulation.

Questions that involve impairment of speech are, as a general rule, examined in the context of a case or controversy. Restrictions on speech must be evaluated by the Court in light of the government's responsibility to meet the public interest as well as the individual's First Amendment guarantee of freedom of speech. It is important to remember that the general scheme of operation in considering a case or controversy involving free speech requires judicial exposure only after the legislative enactment and alleged offense against that enactment. Some people take the view that courts should not interfere with "reasonable" legislative judgments concerning the dangerousness of speech or the manner of its expression. In their view this is most appropriately within the purview of the legislature because it has the most insight and appreciation of what restrictions on speech or expression are in the public interest. According to this argument, the courts are just too far removed to adequately assess social needs.

Another view takes the position that a system of government such as ours places great reliance on courts to solve problems. This is the "judicial review" concept. It permits the courts to review legislative judgments because it is felt that the courts are the best avenue for evaluation of legislative judgments in respect to historical perspective and constitutional demands. A second reason is of a more practical nature: Judicial review is inevitable because the United States Supreme Court has adopted this device as a constitutional doctrine.

A third view often expressed criticizes the idea that courts examine laws after there has been a legislative judgment. This view postulates that this has caused too great a dependence on the courts to vindicate the value of free speech. Legislatures need to understand and appreciate the history, values, and philosophy of the First Amendment in order to prevent the issue of freedom of speech from arising. If the legislature had this appreciation, suppressive laws would not be enacted. This view has frequently been criticized because it does not take sufficient cognizance of political pressures and reality.

In the cases that follow one notes that free speech is absolutely necessary because of the importance of several values deemed significant in our society. First, free expression promotes individual dignity. Second, it encourages the competition of ideas. Third, it provides a safety valve for individuals to make their ideas and grievances known. Fourth, free expression is indispensable as an aid to intelligent choice. There may be other values of importance, but these have been expressed in varying forms in the cases interpreting freedom of expression.

Several aspects of the First Amendment's protection of speech have caused a considerable body of constitutional law to be developed. "Seditious speech" and "advocacy of the overthrow of the government" are discussed in light of the First Amendment's guarantee of freedom of expression. The obscenity issue provides another problem of freedom of expression. It is one illustration of a form of expression whose control involves different considerations from those involved in seditious utterances. Constitutional implications in controlling obscenity are enormous, and consequently, case after case has had to be decided by the United States Supreme Court in this complex, and politically important, problem.

The question on the ways in which speech may be regulated must be addressed once it is established that certain kinds of speech may be controlled constitutionally. One way would be to punish after the act has been accomplished in the manner of criminal law. A much more difficult problem is presented by prior restraint, which is an attempt to prevent the speech from even taking place. Because of the fear of censorship and all its evils, such as those kinds of statutes which require a license before showing a motion picture, strict judicial requirements have been developed to protect against threats to constitutionally protected expression.

As will be seen, controlling speech is not necessarily related to its contents. There are various modes of speech in today's society that may be the subject to regulation, for example: voice amplification trucks, handbill distribution, and the parade. Each of these posess a difficult problem of accommodating the various social interests and freedom of speech. Also, in this context, the troublesome issue arises over the obligation of the police to protect the person whose words arouse an audience against him and thus jeopardize his safety.

In a study of the constitutional interpretation of the First Amendment, one must remember that until the eighteenth century and the invention of the printing press, suppression of speech was the rule rather than the exception. Typically, during the pre-seventeenth-century period a special license was required before a book, pamphlet, leaflet, or play could be published. This technique effectively stifled any political expression because the government merely refused to issue a license for materials it thought to be offensive.

During the seventeenth century English governmental policies were changed to provide subsidies to printers who spoke favorably of the government. The Parliament imposed a tax on periodicals, leaflets, and the like in an effort to silence some publications. This was gradually eliminated. By the middle of the eighteenth century most controls on the press were removed, licensing was totally denounced, and few successful prosecutions under sedition laws occurred.

The issue of prior restraint of speech is considered to be a greater danger to freedom of expression than imposition of criminal penalties. Such informal techniques of prior restraint as officially informing distributors of books that certain publications may be "objectionable" and that a governmental commission may recommend prosecution of persons who sell them to young people have been held to be constitutionally invalid. *Bantam Books, Inc.* v *Sullivan*, 372 U.S. 58 (1963).

Particularly troublesome are attempts to censor motion pictures. Recently the United States Supreme Court held that a statutory scheme of censorship could be consistent with the First Amendment. In *Freedman* v *Maryland*, 380 U.S. 51 (1965), municipalities were given some control in censorship, but important minimum procedural safeguards were imposed to lessen the dangers of a prior licensing system.

> The censor will within a specified brief period either issue a license or go to a court to restrain showing the film. Any restraint imposed in advance of a final judicial determination on the merits must . . . be limited to . . . the shortest fixed period compatible with sound judicial resolutions. . . . [T]he procedure must also assure a prompt final judicial decision.
>
>   . . .

Also, a municipality may not be selective of those persons who may use its parks and streets for discussion of public issues if the facilities are available for public use. The extent to which a municipality is required to make its facilities available for public discussion has not been decided.

Turning to the second aspect of the First Amendment, freedom of religion, one finds numerous issues that have been established in our constitutional law. "Congress shall make no law respecting the establishment of religion, or prohibiting the free exercise thereof . . ." are the opening words of the Bill of Rights and they clearly express a commitment to the freedom of religion. This liberty expresses the convictions of the founding fathers that as a Union of citizens, all of whom had varying religious, cultural, and ethnic backgrounds, there should be no suppression of religion or other infringement of a person's method of worship.

Litigation, public debates, and political squabbles over the issue of religious freedom demonstrate the complexity of issues surrounding religious practices even in the face of the seemingly clear pronouncement in the First Amendment. There is unanimous agreement that Congress is restricted from passing laws that infringe on a person's freedom to believe or not believe as he wishes or that are aimed at establishing a national church. However, the true clauses stating that Congress is prohibited from making a law "respecting an establishment of religion, or prohibiting free exercise thereof" can be interpreted in various ways.

As a basis for the cases that follow a short historical overview will be of some assistance. Of the persons who founded America, most were of the Protestant faith in one form or another. Persecution in England in the form of attempts to modify the Anglican Church of England caused Puritans to migrate to North America. Other Protestant sects soon followed. These various sects, for example, the Society of Friends and the Baptists, demanded that there be freedom of worship for all and a complete separation of church and state which was not the situation in the colonies.

As more religious sects migrated, the typical pattern was for each to establish a colony. Intolerance of another's beliefs was common in the colonies. At the time of the Constitutional Convention numerous states had established churches and many had a religious test administered for a person to hold public office. It thus appears that the founding fathers were concerned with preventing religious tests for holding national office. It also appears that their religious diversity was the basis for demanding that the Constitution guarantee religious liberty as a constitutional amendment. Thus the demands took the form of the Free Exercise and Establishment Clauses in the First Amendment.

The cases in this chapter begin with a discussion of the Establishment Clause. Most nations in the world maintain an established church or give various advantages to members of a particular faith, for example, the Anglican Church in England, the Lutheran Church in Sweden, and the Roman Catholic Church in Italy. Buddhism is for practical purposes a merging of state and church in Burma. The same may be said about Muslim nations. In the United States the First Amendment prohibits the government from supporting or establishing a state church or permitting preferential treatment of one religion over others.

During recent years there has, however, been great controversy in the application of the Establishment Clause in instances in which the government has made efforts to aid religious groups on a nondiscriminatory basis. There has been large-scale debate over this practice in light of the doctrine that there may be no aid and no preference given to any religion. The argument asserts that this governmental activity constitutes a state support of religion. Starting with the "released time" case of less than 30 years ago, there has been vigorous opposition to United States Supreme Court decisions respecting the Establishment Clause. The outcry reached a peak when the Supreme Court ruled that Bible reading and prayer in public schools were unconstitutional. Vigorous debate has followed this decision and there has been a movement to amend the Constitution to allow such religious exercises.

When discussing the First Amendment's Establishment Clause, it is important to bear in mind that it does not mean that laws that are based on religious or moral principles are automatically unconstitutional. For example, laws regulating many family relationships are based on religious ideals, but they are not thereby unconstitutional. As stated previously, the Establishment Clause generally forbids government from aiding one religion preferentially over others and that there can be no aid to all religions even in a nondiscriminate manner.

The basic idea that there can be no preferential treatment is not often subject to controversy, but there are situations that involve the application of this principle and have caused some debate. During the Vietnam conflict many individuals applied for a conscientious objector status on religious grounds to avoid active military service. Such exemption was frequently given even though these individuals received different treatment from those practicing other religions which hold different beliefs and tenets. The materials presented in this section cover the prohibition of preferential and nonpreferential aid, transportation to church-related schools, government support of religious practices, prayer, and Bible reading, released time for religious instruction, and material aid to church-related schools.

The Free Exercise Clause protects religious beliefs, thought, and speech and is a special application of the principle of freedom of speech. This section of the chapter examines a troublesome problem—when religious beliefs violate otherwise valid criminal laws or when, because of his practice of his religious beliefs, an individual is subjected to some type of economic detriment. Because of the sensitive nature of this area of the Constitution, reconciling state interests and individual beliefs has caused numerous controversies.

It is a basic premise of our government that a person cannot be required to hold a particular religious belief and that he cannot be punished for holding an "improper" religious conviction. Because this canon is so ingrained in our governmental scheme, there are no cases dealing with attempts to punish religious beliefs not accompanied by some action. One particularly difficult issue has arisen which involves required participation in flag salutes by Jehovah's Witnesses.

Religious education is subject to state minimum standards, but the state cannot insist that all children be given a secular public education. Religious proselytizing in the form of speech and funds solicitation has involved some unique constitutional problems. In general, the Constitution protects door-to-door religious solicitations and the sale of religious publications.

Some of the most difficult issues involving religious freedom have involved the practice of nonspeech aspects dictated by religious convictions. One of the most easily recognizable examples of this issue is when a person's religious convictions conflict with civil authority and result in criminal punishment. Few would argue that there should be an across-the-board criminal defense to exempt a person from criminal responsibility. Societal needs require some regularization, such as driving on the right-hand side of the road or stopping at traffic lights. Also, religion cannot be used as an excuse for serious crimes, such as murder.

However, there is some substantial merit in the argument that religious convictions may excuse violations of otherwise valid criminal laws. This argument does not claim that religion provides a blanket excuse, but that the unsequential demands of the state should yield to religious conscience. In other words, the courts should weigh religious freedom with individual needs. This balancing process is, however, very difficult. To the present time the United States Supreme Court has not accepted religious convictions as a defense to a valid criminal charge, although as the following cases indicate, the controversy still rages.

When there is a likelihood of difficulties involving religious conviction, Congress has recognized religious beliefs as excuses in laws that would otherwise impose general obligations. For example, the Selective Service laws have always recognized religious conscientious objection to active military service. Such legal exceptions prevent constitutional issues from arising. On occasion, however, there has been a direct clash between religious beliefs and the criminal law. Polygamy and pacifism provide excellent insight into the problem, as seen in *Reynolds* v *United States,* 98 U.S. 145 (1878), and *United States* v *Seegar,* 380 U.S. 163 (1965).

Other issues arise regarding Sunday closing laws (Blue Laws) and the ancillary issue of refusal to perform work on the Sabbath, which is a day other than Sunday for some religions (Seventh-Day Adventists and Jews). So far the United States Supreme Court has not been convinced the laws placing indirect burdens on religion violate the Free Exercise Clause.

On more and more occasions, the question is being asked about the use of drugs in the practice of a person's religion. No case has been decided by the United States Supreme Court on this point. In a California court decision, *People* v *Woody,* 61 Cal. 2d 716 (1964), the California Supreme Court held that a California statute outlawing the possession of a narcotic, peyote, which was indispensable to the practice of a religious belief was unconstitutional as applied to the possession for a valid religious purpose. In short, the application of the law to a religious use of peyote violated the First Amendment's Free Exercise Clause. The California opinion cited *Sherbert* v *Verner,* 374 U.S. 398 (1963), extensively and emphasized that the California statute placed a heavy burden upon a legitimate religious practice. Since the religious use of the peyote was a very slight danger to the state, there was no compelling state interest that overrode the full administration of the Free Expression Clause.

In summary, the United States Supreme Court has adopted the position, after much litigation, that the protection given to the free exercise of religion is almost unlimited, providing there is no compelling secular interest in overriding the protection. It has similarly established that the First Amendment forbids preferential assistance to one religion over another. Despite holdings to the contrary, there are some Supreme Court decisions that do permit aid in one form or another to religions. The standards for determining when there may be permissible aid to religions is still a matter of debate.

SPEECH

Schenck v *United States*

249 U.S. 47, 39 S.Ct. 247, 63 L.Ed. 470 (1919)

Schenck and others were charged with conspiracy of causing and attempting to cause insubordination in the United States armed forces by circulating printed matter to men called for military service. The defendants argued that the First Amendment forbade Congress from making any law abridging the freedom of speech or the press. They were convicted in the lower court and the United States Supreme Court affirmed.

Justice Holmes delivered the opinion of the Court:

The document in question upon its first printed side recited the first section of the Thirteenth Amendment, said that the idea embodied in it was violated by the conscription act and that a conscript is little better than a convict. In impassioned language it intimated that conscription was despotism in its worst form and a monstrous wrong against humanity in the interest of Wall Street's chosen few. It said, "Do not submit to intimidation," but in form at least confined itself to peaceful measures such as a petition for the repeal of the act. The other and later printed side of the sheet was headed "Assert Your Rights." It stated reasons for alleging that any one violated the Constitution when he refused to recognize "your right to assert your opposition to the draft," and went on, "If you do not assert and support your rights, you are helping to deny or disparage rights which it is the solemn duty of all citizens and residents of the United States to retain." It described the arguments on the other side as coming from cunning politicians and a mercenary capitalist press, and even silent consent to the conscription law as helping to support an infamous conspiracy. It denied the power to send our citizens away to foreign shores to shoot up the people of other lands, and added that words could not express the condemnation such cold ruthlessness deserves, etc., etc., winding up, "You must do your share to maintain, support, and uphold the rights of the people of this country." Of course the document would not have been sent unless it had been intended to have some effect, and we do not see what effect it could be expected to have upon persons subject to the draft except to influence them to obstruct the carrying of it out. The defendants do not deny that the jury might find against them on this point.

But it is said, suppose that that was the tendency of this circular, it is protected by the First Amendment to the Constitution. Two of the strongest expressions are said to be quoted respectively from well-known public men. It well may be that the prohibition of laws abridging the freedom of speech is not confined to previous restraints, although to prevent them may have been the main purpose. . . . The most stringent protection of free speech would not protect a man in falsely shouting fire in a theater and causing a panic. It does not even protect a man from an injunction against uttering words that may have all the effect of force. . . . The question in every case is whether the words used are used in such circumstances and are of such a nature as to create a clear and present danger that they will bring about the substantive evils that Congress has a right to prevent. It is a question of proximity and degree. The statute of 1917 in section 4 . . . punishes conspiracies to obstruct as well as actual obstruction. If the act (speaking or circulating a paper), its tendency, and the intent with which it is done are the same, we perceive no ground for saying that success alone warrants making the act a crime. . . . Indeed that case might be said to dispose of the present contention if the precedent covers all media concludendi. But as the right to free speech was not referred to specially, we have thought fit to add a few words.

. . .

(Judgment affirmed.)

Gitlow was a member of the left-wing section of the Socialist Party which adopted a left-wing manifesto calling for a Communist revolution, urging mass political strikes, and condemning moderate Socialism for recognizing the need for a parliamentary state. Gitlow arranged to have the document published and mailed. The defendant was charged under the New York "criminal anarchy" statute which prohibited "advocacy, advising, or teaching the duty; necessity, or propriety of overthrowing or overturning organized government by violence," and the distribution or publication of such matter. Gitlow was convicted even though there was no evidence of any effect stemming from publication and distribution of the manifesto. The United States Supreme Court affirmed the conviction even though it recognized the fundamental personal liberties in the First Amendment which are protected against state intrusion by the Fourteenth. *Gitlow* v *New York* 268 U.S. 652, 45 S.Ct. 625, 69 L.Ed. 1138 (1925).

In *Whitney* v *California,* 274 U.S. 357, 47 S.Ct. 641, 71 L.Ed. 1095 (1927), the Supreme Court upheld the Syndicalism Act in regard to its constitutionality. The case centered around Charlotte Whitney who, along with others, formed the Communist Labor Party. This party espoused revolutionary goals and methods of achieving them. She was found guilty under the California syndicalism law which provided criminal punishment for becoming a member or helping to form an organization that advocated "teaching or abetting and aiding in the commission of a crime, sabotage, . . . or unlawful acts of force or violence or unlawful methods of terrorism as a means of accomplishing a change in industrial ownership or control or effecting any political change."

Delivering the opinion of the Court Justice Sanford states:

It is clear that the Syndicalism Act is not repugnant to the Due Process Clause by reason of vagueness and uncertainty of definition.

Neither is the Syndicalism Act repugnant to the Equal Protection Clause, on the ground that as its penalties are confined to those who advocate a resort to violent and unlawful methods as a means of changing industrial and political conditions, it arbitrarily discriminates between such persons and those who may advocate a resort to these methods as a means of maintaining such conditions.

. . .

The essence of the offense denounced by the Act is the combining with others in an association for the accomplishment of the desired ends through the advocacy and use of criminal and unlawful methods. It partakes of the nature of a criminal conspiracy. . . . That such united and joint action involves even greater danger to the public peace and security than the isolated utterances and acts of individuals is clear. We cannot hold that, as here applied, the Act is an unreasonable or arbitrary exercise of the police power of the state, unwarrantably infringing any right of free speech, assembly, or association, or that those persons are protected from punishment by the Due Process Clause who abuse such rights by joining and furthering an organization thus menacing the peace and welfare of the state.

. . .

In *Nebraska Press Association* v *Stuart,* 427 U.S. 539, 96 S.Ct. 2791, 49 L.Ed. 2d 683 (1976), news media were restrained from publishing or broadcasting accounts of admissions or confessions made by an accused to law enforcement officials or third parties, except members of the press. The trial for multiple murders attracted widespread news coverage. The trial court's order was affirmed by the Nebraska Supreme Court. The United States Supreme Court reversed the state decision stating, "Our analysis ends as it began, with a confrontation between prior restraint imposed to protect one constitutional guarantee and the explicit command of another that the freedom to speak and publish shall not be abridged." After affirming that the guarantee of freedom of expression is not absolute, the Court noted that there is a strong presumption against prior restraint. "We hold that . . . the barriers have not been overcome; to the extent that this order restrained publication of such material, is clearly invalid." There was no finding that measures short of prior restraint on the press would not have protected the accused's rights. The Nebraska Supreme Court's attempt to restrain evidence adduced at a preliminary hearing, that was plainly incorrect according to the United States Supreme Court in *Sheppard* v *Maxwell,* 384 U.S. 333 (1966), which stated that "there is nothing that proscribes the press from reporting events that transpire in the courtroom."

In *Near* v *Minnesota,* 283 U.S. 697, 51 S.Ct. 625, 75 L.Ed. 1357 (1931), the publisher of a small newspaper in Minnesota was tried under a Minnesota statute which provided for abating as a public nuisance any "malicious, scandalous, and defamatory newspaper, magazine, or periodical." An injunction was issued to abate the nuisance, and the constitutionality of this statute was upheld by the state supreme court. On appeal the United States Supreme Court reversed this decision. In delivering the opinion of the Court, Chief Justice Hughes stated:

This statute, for the suppression as a public nuisance of a newspaper or periodical, is unusual, if not unique, and raises questions of grave importance transcending the local interests involved in the particular action. It is no longer open to doubt that the liberty of the press and of speech is within the liberty safeguarded by the Due Process Clause of the Fourteenth Amendment from invasion by state action. It was found impossible to conclude that this essential personal liberty of the citizen was left unprotected by the general guaranty of fundamental rights of persons and property. . . . Charges of reprehensible conduct, and in particular of official malfeasance, unquestionably create a public scandal, but the theory of the constitutional guaranty is that even a more serious public evil would be caused by authority to prevent publication.

. . .

In *United States* v *O'Brien,* 391 U.S. 367, 88 S.Ct. 1673, 20 L.Ed. 2d 672 (1968), the defendant was convicted for burning his Selective Service registration certificate. He committed this act knowing that it violated federal law. The United States Supreme Court rejected O'Brien's argument that the statute was unconstitutional because it violated his freedom of speech which includes all modes of "communication of ideas by conduct." The Court held

> that when "speech" and "nonspeech" elements are combined in the same course of conduct, a sufficiently important governmental interest in regulating the nonspeech element can justify incidental limitations on First Amendment freedoms. . . . (W)e think it clear that a government regulation is sufficiently justified if it is within the constitutional power of government; if the governmental interest is unrelated to the suppression of free expression; and if the incidental restriction on alleged First Amendment freedom is no greater than is essential to the furtherance of that interest. . . . O'Brien can be constitutionally convicted for violating it.

Street burned an American flag in protest to the shooting of civil rights leader James Meredith. He was convicted for violating the New York malicious mischief statute which made it a misdemeanor publically to mutilate, defile, deface or to trample upon, or cast contempt by words or acts on any flag of the United States. The United States Supreme Court found it unnecessary to decide Street's argument that the New York statute was void for vagueness because the statute was applied unconstitutionally "because it permitted him to be punished merely for speaking defiant or contemptuous words about the American flag." Justice Harlan noted that there may be four situations in which Street could have been punished: (1) when the state has an interest in deterring Street from vocally inciting others to perpetuate unlawful acts; (2) to protect Street when his words would so inflame a gathering so as to attack him; (3) to protect others who might be shocked by Street's defiling the American flag; (4) to protect the interest in assuming that Street showed proper respect for the national emblem, regardless of the import of the words or others. None of these justified Street's conviction speaking as he did. *Street* v *New York,* 394 U.S. 576, 89 S.Ct. 1354, 22 L.Ed. 2d 572 (1969).

Justice Fortas in *Tinker* v *Des Moines School District,* 393 U.S. 503, 89 S.Ct. 733, 21 L.Ed. 2d 731 (1969), wrote that suspending students from school for wearing black armbands in protest to the Vietnam conflict directly involves

> primary First Amendment rights akin to "pure speech." . . . , school officials do not possess absolute authority over their students. Students in school as

well as out of school are "persons" under our Constitution. . . . A student's rights, therefore, do not embrace merely the classroom hours. When he is in the cafeteria, or on the playing field, or on the campus during the authorized hours, he may express his opinions even on controversial subjects like the conflict in Vietnam, if he does so without "materially and substantially (interfering) with the requirements of appropriate discipline in the operation of the school" and without colliding with the rights of others.

SPEECH

Subversive Activities: Advocacy and Membership

Brandenburg v *Ohio*

395 U.S. 944, 89 S.Ct. 1827, 23 L.Ed. 1137 (1969)

Brandenburg, a Ku Klux Klan leader, was convicted under the Ohio Criminal Syndicalism Act for advocating terrorism as a means of industrial and political reform. He challenged the constitutionality of the statute on the ground that it violated the First and Fourteenth Amendments of the United States Constitution. The United States Supreme Court in a *per curiam* opinion reversed the conviction and in so doing overruled *Whitney* v *California, supra.*

The Ohio Criminal Syndicalism Statute was enacted in 1919. From 1917 to 1920, identical or quite similar laws were adopted by 20 states and 2 territories. . . . In 1927, this Court sustained the constitutionality of California's Criminal Syndicalism Act, . . . the text of which is quite similar to that of the laws of Ohio. . . . The Court upheld the statute on the ground that, without more, "advocating" violent means to effect political and economic change involves such danger to the security of the state that the state may outlaw it. . . . But *Whitney* has been thoroughly discredited by later decisions. These later decisions have fashioned the principle that the constitutional guarantees of free speech and free press do not permit a state to forbid or proscribe advocacy of the use of force or of law violation except where such advocacy is directed to inciting or producing imminent lawless action and is likely to incite or produce such action. As we said . . . "the mere abstract teaching . . . of the moral propriety or even moral necessity for a resort to force and violence, is not the same as preparing a group for violent action and steeling it to such action." . . . A statute which fails to draw this distinction impermissibly intrudes upon the freedoms guaranteed by the First and Fourteenth Amendments. It sweeps within its condemnation speech which our Constitution has immunized from governmental control.

. . .

Measured by this test, Ohio's Criminal Syndicalism Act cannot be sustained. The Act punished persons who "advocate or teach the duty, necessity, or propriety" of violence "as a means of accomplishing industrial or political reform''; or who publish or circulate or display any book or paper containing such advocacy; or who ''justify'' the commission of violent acts ''with intent to exemplify, spread, or advocate the propriety of the doctrines of criminal syndicalism''; or who ''voluntarily assemble'' with a group formed ''to teach or advocate the doctrine of criminal syndicalism.'' Neither the indictment nor the trial judge's instructions to the jury in any way refined the statute's bald definition of the crime in terms of mere advocacy not distinguished from incitement to imminent lawless action.

Accordingly, we are here confronted with a statute which, by its own words and as applied, purports to punish mere advocacy and to forbid, on pain of criminal punishment, assembly with others merely to advocate the described type of action. Such a statute falls within the condemnation of the First and Fourteenth Amendments. The contrary teaching of *Whitney* v *California, supra,* cannot be supported, and that decision is therefore overruled.

(Judgment reversed.)
Justices Black and Douglas concurred.

The Smith Act, which prohibited the teaching and advocacy of the overthrow of the United States government by force and violence and which prohibited the organization of the Communist Party of the United States of America in order to achieve such an overthrow, was held to be constitutional in *Dennis* v *United States,* 341 U.S. 494, 71 S.Ct. 857, 95 L.Ed. 1137 (1951). The United States Supreme Court affirmed the convictions of petitioners for a violation of the Act with the use of a dual test: the ''clear and present danger test'' was used in conjunction with the ''grave and probable danger test.'' Under these tests, the courts are to evaluate any restriction on the First Amendment's guarantee of free speech in light of the possible consequences of the unrestricted speech. If they find that the government has a legitimate responsibility in preventing consequences of speech which are both grave and probable, then the freedom of speech may be restricted. In this case, the Court found a violent and forceful overthrow of the United States government to be dangerous as well as somewhat probable if the freedom to advocate and teach such goals were not restricted.

The United States Supreme Court's decision in *Noto* v *United States,* 367 U.S. 290, 81 S.Ct. 1517, 6 L.Ed. 2d 836 (1961), reached the conclusion that the petitioner had been unconstitutionally restricted through the membership clause of the Smith Act. The ''advocacy of action'' found to be necessary for conviction under the Smith Act was not present in the *Noto* case. Although the Court found evidence of the advocacy of violent overthrow as an inevitably necessary means of establishing Communism in the United States, it could not find the systematic conduct and utterances necessary for the ''advocacy of action'' required for conviction.

Dr. Spock, a well-known pediatrician and war resister, was convicted of conspiracy to counsel, aid, and abet Selective Service registrants to disobey duties imposed by the Selective Service Act of 1967. In considering *United States* v *Spock,* 416 F. 2d 16 (1st Cir. 1969), the Court found the activities of the petitioner lacking in the elements required for the establishment of the conspiracy. The defendant's criminal intent in such a case must be judged *strictissimi juris* so that his adherence to the legitimate goals of an organization will not be confused with illegal goals to which he does not adhere. Dr. Spock's activities toward war resistance did not meet the evidentiary standards required to convict; he had made no prior or subsequent unambiguous statements showing criminal intent; he had committed no illegal act contemplated by the alleged conspiracy; and he had committed no legal act clearly designed to render a contemplated illegal act effective. His conviction, then, was reversed.

Maintenance of Public Order

Picketing is a constitutionally protected expression, according to the majority opinion in *Thornhill* v *Alabama,* 310 U.S. 88, 60 S.Ct. 736, 84 L.Ed. 1093 (1940). A law prohibiting the picketing of commercial establishments for the purpose of injuring business was found to be an unconstitutional abridgment of the First Amendment freedom of speech "on its face." The United States Supreme Court decided that "proof of an abuse of power in the particular case has never been deemed a requisite for attack on the constitutionality of a statute purporting to license the dissemination of ideas. . . ." The dissemination of facts concerning a labor dispute must be considered within the free discussion protected by the Constitution, and a law that prohibits this cannot stand.

A New Hampshire statute provided that "no person shall address any offensive, derisive, or annoying word to any other person who is lawfully in any street or other public place, nor call him by any offensive or derisive name." In *Chaplinsky* v *New Hampshire,* 315 U.S. 568, 62 S.Ct. 766, 86 L.Ed. 1031 (1942), these words were interpreted to ban words that were likely to cause the average addressee to fight and to ban plain face-to-face words that were likely to cause a breach of peace. The defendant, a Jehovah's Witness, had gotten into a fight on the sidewalk after he called a policeman "a damned Fascist" and "a God damned racketeer." His conviction of violating the statute was affirmed on appeal to the United States Supreme Court.

Justice Murphy delivered the opinion of the Court:

> Allowing the broadest scope to the language and purpose of the Fourteenth Amendment, it is well understood that the right of free speech is not absolute at all times and under all circumstances.
>
> . . .
>
> We are unable to say that the limited scope of the statute as thus construed contravenes the constitutional right of free expression. It is a statute narrowly drawn and limited to define and punish specific conduct lying within the domain of state power, the use in a public place of words likely to cause a breach of the peace.
>
> . . .

This conclusion necessarily disposes of appellant's contention that the statute is so vague and indefinite as to render a conviction thereunder a violation of due process. A statute punishing verbal acts, carefully drawn so as not unduly to impair liberty of expression, is not too vague for a criminal law.

. . .

In *Terminiello* v *Chicago,* 337 U.S. 1, 69 S.Ct. 894, 93 L.Ed. 1131 (1949), the defendant was convicted of violating Chicago's "breach of the peace" ordinance. Terminiello's arrest grew out of a speech in which he vigorously and viciously denounced the Roosevelt Administration as Communists; called leftists "scum"; villified Jews, and berated racial and political groups. Several disturbances broke out, windows were broken, stink bombs thrown, rocks tossed, and attempts made to enter the auditorium. The police controlled the crowd as best it could. On appeal to the United States Supreme Court, Terminiello's conviction was reversed.

Stating the opinion of the Court, Justice Douglas concludes:

But it is said that throughout the appellate proceedings the Illinois courts assumed that the only conduct punishable and punished under the ordinance was conduct constituting "fighting words." . . . Petitioner was not convicted under a statute so narrowly construed. For all anyone knows he was convicted under the parts of the ordinance (as construed) which, for example, make it an offense merely to invite dispute or to bring about a condition of unrest. We cannot avoid that issue by saying that all Illinois did was to measure petitioner's conduct, not the ordinance, against the Constitution. Petitioner raised both points—that his speech was protected by the Constitution; that the inclusion of his speech within the ordinance was a violation of the Constitution. We would, therefore, strain at technicalities to conclude that the constitutionality of the ordinance as construed and applied to petitioner was not before the Illinois courts.

. . .

An individual's right to freedom of expression must always be weighed against the government's responsibility to preserve order. In *Feiner* v *New York,* 340 U.S. 315, 71 S.Ct. 303, 95 L.Ed. 295 (1951), the United States Supreme Court held that the petitioner's speech was not protected when it passed the bounds of persuasion and became incitement to riot. Feiner's speech caused a crisis situation, where traffic was disrupted and some listeners became excited and angry. The police sensed the crisis and asked Feiner to stop speaking. Upon his refusal, he was arrested for disorderly conduct. In affirming the conviction, the Court reaffirmed the power of the police to prevent an immediate threat to public safety in order to preserve peace and order.

Any constitutional statute that restricts the speech of citizens must be narrowly construed to meet a serious responsibility of the state. A Georgia statute, which prohibited the use of opprobrious or abusive words concerning a person and in his presence that may tend to cause a "breach of the peace," was found by the United States Supreme Court to lack the narrow construction necessary to bring such a statute within constitutional bounds. In *Gooding* v *Wilson,* 405 U.S. 518, 92 S.Ct. 518, 31 L.Ed. 2d 408 (1972), the Georgia statute was found unconstitutional. If the state's purpose in such a restriction of speech is the prevention of any "breach of the peace," the wording must be construed to mean only those "fighting" words that would tend to cause an immediate breach of the peace. The Court found that the statute in question had never been so construed and that, rather, previous convictions under the statute had been sustained even though no possibility of an immediate breach of the peace caused by "fighting" words existed. In order to preserve all citizens' guaranteed freedom of speech, any restriction on speech must be "narrowly limited," and speech should generally be allowed a wide range of acceptability.

The United States Supreme Court was faced with the constitutionality of a statute that was interpreted subsequent to its application in the case of *Shuttlesworth* v *Birmingham,* 394 U.S. 147, 89 S.Ct. 935, 22 L.Ed. 2d 162 (1969). Reverend Shuttlesworth attempted to comply with a Birmingham city ordinance requiring the issuance of a permit prior to any public demonstration, but his request for such a permit was summarily refused. The city ordinance requiring the permit was a very broad one that failed to specify narrow limits to guide the licensing authority in the issuing of permits. After being refused a permit having no avenues for the quick expedition of a review, Shuttlesworth and his cohorts proceeded with the scheduled procession, which caused neither traffic obstruction nor other public nuisance. During this procession he was arrested for violation of the city ordinance. On appeal, the Supreme Court of Alabama affirmed the conviction after strictly interpreting the city ordinance in order to bring it within the First Amendment's freedom of expression. Again on appeal, the United States Supreme Court found that even though the Supreme Court of Alabama provided an interpretation of the statute narrow enough to make it constitutional, the Shuttlesworth conviction could not stand under it. As the ordinance had been written and construed at the time of the arrest, it was so general that it unconstitutionally prohibited the free exercise of expression as guaranteed in the First Amendment.

In *Cox* v *Louisiana,* 379 U.S. 536, 85 S.Ct. 453, 13 L.Ed. 2d 471 (1965), the defendant was convicted of violating a Louisiana "disturbing the peace" statute. The United States Supreme Court held that there was "no conduct which the state had a right to prohibit as a breach of the peace."

Cox, a field secretary for CORE, led approximately 1,500 to 2,000 black college students in an orderly fashion to a sidewalk across the street from a courthouse. They were approximately 101 feet from the steps the steps of the courthouse. The group did not obstruct the street. Cox made a speech protesting the arrests of 23 fellow students and appealed to the protesters to sit in at various segregated lunch counters. The sheriff deemed this appeal to be inflamatory and sought to break up the demonstration. The crowd did not disperse and after about 2 to 5 minutes tear gas was used to disperse the crowd. Cox, a white man, was arrested and convicted for breach of the peace. No others were arrested. It was the assertion of the state that "violence was about to erupt," but virtually all testimony proved otherwise. The Court also noted that the statute was "unconstitutionally vague in its overly broad scope." On these two grounds the Supreme Court reversed the decision of the lower court.

Police authorities cannot use their predictive abilities in order to stop the free expression of ideas, according to the United States Supreme Court in *Gregory* v *Chicago,* 394 U.S. 111, 89 S.Ct. 946, 22 L.Ed. 2d 134 (1969). The petitioners in this case carried on an orderly public demonstration for the purpose of espousing school desegregation. Upon arriving at the destination of the march, the demonstrators' language increased in intensity and hostility, thus alerting the accompanying police to possible difficulties. The police ordered an end to the demonstration, and upon the refusal of the demonstrators, the petitioners were arrested for disorderly conduct. According to the United States Supreme Court, the arrests and convictions were unconstitutional, since there was no evidence of disorderly conduct and since the arrests were precipitated by the suspicions of the police concerning probable future occurrences rather than actual illegal conduct.

The "Symbolic Speech" Cases

A city ordinance that prohibited "annoying" conduct by three or more persons meeting on a public sidewalk was struck down in *Coates* v *City of Cincinnati,* 402 U.S. 611, 91 S.Ct. 1686, 29 L.Ed. 2d 214 (1971). The details of the "annoying" conduct that resulted in the convictions of the appellants were not presented to the United States Supreme Court. However, the majority of the Court found the ordinance unconstitutional on its face for two reasons. First, the ordinance required that citizens conduct themselves according to "an unascertainable standard in violation of the due process standard of vagueness." Second, notwithstanding the vagueness of the wording of the ordinance, the state was making the exercise of the constitutionally guaranteed right of free assembly and association a crime. Thus, the First and Fourteenth Amendments were violated by the ordinance. The details of the appellants' behaviors would not, under any circumstances, have been capable of justifying such a blatant violation of the Constitution. Appellants' convictions were reversed.

Decency and Morality—The Obscenity Problem

Roth v *United States*
Alberts v *California*
345 U.S. 476, 77 S.Ct. 1304, 1 L.Ed. 2d 1498 (1957)

Roth was indicted under a federal statute for sending "obscene, lewd, lascivious, or filthy" matter or advertisements through the mails. Among the items advertised were sets of nude photographs and a quarterly publication dealing in literary erotica. Roth was acquitted of the charges involving nude photographs, but he was convicted on the sale and advertisement of the periodical. Albert was convicted of the same general crimes under the California obscenity statute. On appeal, the United States Supreme Court affirmed setting out some basic guidelines for determining what constitutes obscenity.

Justice Brennan delivered the opinion of the Court:

The constitutionality of a criminal obscenity statute is the question in each of these cases. In Roth, the primary constitutional question is whether the federal obscenity statute violates the provision of the First Amendment that "Congress shall make no law . . . abridging the freedom of speech, or of the press. . . ." In Alberts, the primary constitutional question is whether the obscenity provisions of the California Penal Code invade the freedoms of speech and press as they may be incorporated in the liberty protected from state action by the Due Process Clause of the Fourteenth Amendment.

. . .

The dispositive question is whether obscenity is utterance within the area of protected speech and press.

. . .

The guaranties of freedom of expression in effect in 10 of the 14 states which by 1792 had ratified the Constitution, gave no absolute protection for every utterance.

. . .

. . . At the time of the adoption of the First Amendment, obscenity law was not as fully developed as libel law, but there is sufficiently contemporaneous evidence to show that obscenity, too, was outside the protection intended for speech and press.

. . .

All ideas having even the slightest redeeming social importance—unorthodox ideas, controversial ideas, even ideas hateful to the prevailing climate of opinion—have the full protection of the guaranties, unless excludable because they encroach upon the limited area of more important interests. But implicit in the history of the First Amendment is the rejection of obscenity as utterly without redeeming social importance.

. . .

It is strenuously urged that these obscenity statutes offend the constitutional guaranties because they punish incitation to impure sexual *thoughts,* not shown to be related to any overt antisocial conduct which is or may be incited in the persons stimulated to such *thoughts. . . .* It is insisted that the constitutional guaranties are violated because convictions may be had without proof either that obscene material will perceptibly create a clear and present danger of antisocial conduct, or will probably induce its recipients to such conduct. But, in light of our holding that obscenity is not protected speech, the complete answer to this argument is in the holding of this Court in *Beauharnais* v *People of State of Illinois,* 343 U.S. 250,.

. . .

However, sex and obscenity are not synonymous. Obscene material is material which deals with sex in a manner appealing to prurient interest. The portrayal of sex, *e.g.*, in art, literature, and scientific works, is not itself sufficient reason to deny material the constitutional protection of freedom of speech and press. Sex, a great and mysterious motive force in human life, has indisputably been a subject of absorbing interest to mankind through the ages; it is one of the vital problems of human interest and public concern.

. . .

Both trial courts below sufficiently followed the proper standard. Both courts used the proper definition of obscenity.

. . .

In summary, then, we hold that these statutes, applied according to the proper standard for judging obscenity, do not offend constitutional safeguards against convictions based upon protected material, or fail to give men in acting adequate notice of what is prohibited.

Roth's argument that the federal obscenity statute unconstitutionally encroaches upon the powers reserved by the Ninth and Tenth Amendments to the states and to the people to punish speech and press where offensive to decency and morality is hinged upon his contention that obscenity is expression not excepted from the sweep of the provision of the First Amendment that *"Congress* shall make *no law* abridging the freedom of speech, or of the press. . . ." [Emphasis added.] That argument falls in light of our holding that obscenity is not expression protected by the First Amendment. We therefore hold that the federal obscenity statute punishing the use of the mails for obscene material is a proper exercise of the postal power delegated to Congress by Article I, Section 8, Clause 7.

. . .

(Other issues raised were found not to have merit.)
(Judgments affirmed.)
Chief Justice Warren concurred.
Justice Harlan concurred in the result in *Alberts* but dissented in *Roth*.
Justices Black and Douglas dissented.

In *Kingsley International Pictures Corp.* v *Regents,* 360 U.S. 684, 79 S.Ct. 1362, 3 L.Ed. 2d 1512 (1959), the United States Supreme Court found a portion of a New York state statute to be an unconstitutional abridgment of the freedoms guaranteed in the First and Fourteenth Amendments. The statute required that a license issued by the Regents of the State of New York be issued prior to the exhibition of a motion picture. According to the statute, no license would be issued if the film in question portrayed immoral behavior as proper or desirable. The film in question in this case was *Lady Chatterly's Lover,* which, according to the licensing body, pictorially presented adultery as a behavior that could be proper and desirable in certain circumstances. On this basis, a license for commercial exhibition was denied. On appeal, the appellate division reversed the Regents' decision, but the Court of Appeals upholding the Regents, ordered that no license be issued. The United States Supreme Court found that the section of the statute in question hindered the free expression of ideas unnecessarily. One permissible restriction on the free expression of ideas is the prohibition of incitement to illegal behavior, but the mere advocacy of such behaviors falls short of this constitutional restriction. Since *Lady Chatterly's Lover* failed to incite adultery and only presented an idea of the acceptability of adultery under certain circumstances, the denial of a license by the Board of Regents was unconstitutional.

Through the majority opinion in *Jacobellis* v *Ohio*, 378 U.S. 184, 84 S.Ct. 1676, 12 L.Ed. 2d 793 (1964), the United States Supreme Court denied the "community" aspect in the determination of the obscenity of any particular film. The Court decided that since the boundaries of any community are elusive, and further, since those persons who have a commercial interest in films or literature may draw customers from outside these boundaries, then a community orientation to the standards used to determine obscenity would be an ineffective, as well as unconstitutional restriction on freedom of expression. National standards of decency in literature and films were substituted for the community standards through this case.

Young v *American Mini Theatres*, 427 U.S. 50, 96 S.Ct. 2440, 49 L.Ed. 2d 310 (1976), questioned the constitutionality of zoning ordinances adopted by the city of Detroit which differentiates between theaters showing sexually explicit "adult" movies and those which do not. It was the ruling of the Supreme Court that there was no violation of the First Amendment rights and that ". . . the city's interest in the present and future character of its neighborhoods adequately supports its classification of motion pictures . . . the zoning ordinances requiring that adult motion picture theaters not be located within 1,000 feet of two other regulated uses do not violate the Equal Protection Clause of the Fourteenth Amendment."

The government has no right to make the personal possession of obscene materials a crime, according to the majority opinion in *Stanley* v *Georgia*, 394 U.S. 557, 89 S.Ct. 1243, 22 L.Ed. 2d 542 (1969). The petitioner was charged with such possession after obscene films were found in his home during a police search for bookmaking paraphernalia. Basing its decision on the First and Fourteenth Amendments, the Court found that any restriction on the private reading or viewing of citizens in their own residences would be unconstitutional. The Constitution protects the individual's freedoms within his own home, regardless of the need for the administration of valid criminal laws.

Miller v *California*
413 U.S. 15, 93 S.Ct. 2607, 37 L.Ed. 2d 419 (1973)

Miller was convicted of violating the California obscenity laws which were written to include the definition as set forth in the *Roth* test. He conducted a mass mailing of "adult" materials. The brochures advertised four books that primarily consisted of pictures and drawings explicitly depicting men and women in groups of two or more engaging in a variety of sexual activities with the genitals often displayed prominently. The persons who made the initial complaint to the police received five of the brochures unsolicited through the mails. The United States Supreme Court changed the constitutional test for determining obscenity.

Chief Justice Burger delivered the opinion of the Court:

Apart from the initial formulation in the *Roth* case, no majority of the Court has at any given time been able to agree on a standard to determine what constitutes obscene, pornographic material subject to regulation under the states' police power.... We have seen "a variety of views among the members of the Court unmatched in any other course of constitutional adjudication."... This is not remarkable, for in the area of freedom of speech and press the courts must always remain sensitive to any infringement on genuinely serious literary, artistic, political, or scientific expression. This is an area in which there are few external verities.

The case we now review was tried on the theory that the California Penal Code §311 approximately incorporates the three-stage *Memoirs* test. But now the *Memoirs* test has been abandoned as unworkable by its author and no member of the Court today supports the *Memoirs* formulation.

This much has been categorically settled by the Court, that obscene material is unprotected by the First Amendment.... The First and Fourteenth Amendments have never been treated as absolutes.... We acknowledge, however, the inherent dangers of undertaking to regulate any form of expression. State statutes designed to regulate obscene materials must be carefully limited.... As a result, we now confine the permissible scope of such regulation to works which depict or describe sexual conduct. That conduct must be specifically defined by the applicable state law, as written or authoritatively construed. A state offense must also be limited to works which, taken as a whole, appeal to the prurient interest in sex, which portray sexual conduct in a patently offensive way, and which, taken as a whole, do not have serious literary, artistic, political, or scientific value.

The basic guidelines for the trier of fact must be: (a) whether "the average person, applying contemporary community standards" would find that the work, taken as a whole, appeals to the prurient interest;... (b) whether the work depicts or describes, in a patently offensive way, sexual conduct specifically defined by the applicable state law; and (c) whether the work, taken as a whole, lacks serious literary, artistic, political, or scientific value. We do not adopt as a constitutional standard the "*utterly* without redeeming social value" test,... that concept has never commanded the adherence of more than three Justices at one time.... If a state law that regulates obscene material is thus limited, as written or construed, the First Amendment values applicable to the states through the Fourteenth Amendment are adequately protected by the ultimate power of appellate courts to conduct an independent review of constitutional claims when necessary.

We emphasize that it is not our function to propose regulatory schemes for the states. That must await their concrete legislative efforts. It is possible, however, to give a few plain examples of what a state statute could define for regulation under part (b) of the standard announced in this opinion,

(a) Patently offensive representations or descriptions of ultimate sexual acts, normal or perverted, actual or simulated.

(b) Patently offensive representation or descriptions of masturbation, excretory functions, and lewd exhibition of the genitals.

Under the holdings announced today, no one will be subject to prosecution for the sale or exposure of obscene materials unless these materials depict or describe patently offensive "hard-core" sexual conduct specifically defined by the regulating state law, as written or construed. We are satisfied that these specific prerequisites will provide fair notice to a dealer in such materials that his public and commercial activities may bring prosecution. . . . If the inability to define regulated materials with ultimate, god-like precision altogether removes the power of the states or the Congress to regulate, then "hard-core" pornography may be exposed without limit to the juvenile, the passerby, and the consenting adult alike, as, indeed, Mr. Justice Douglas contends. In this belief, however, Mr. Justice Douglas now stands alone.

. . .

It is certainly true that the absence, since *Roth,* of a single majority view of this Court as to proper standards for testing obscenity has placed a strain on both state and federal courts. But today, for the first time since *Roth* was decided in 1957, a majority of this Court has agreed on concrete guidelines to isolate "hard-core" pornography from expression protected by the First Amendment.

. . .

This may not be an easy road, free from difficulty. But no amount of "fatigue" should lead us to adopt a convenient "institutional" rationale—an absolutist, "anything goes" view of the First Amendment—because it will lighten our burdens. "Such an abnegation of judicial supervision in this field would be inconsistent with our duty to uphold the constitutional guarantees." . . . Nor should we remedy "tension between state and federal courts" by arbitrarily depriving the states of a power reserved to them under the Constitution, a power which they have enjoyed and exercised continuously from before the adoption of the First Amendment to this day.

. . .

. . . When triers of fact are asked to decide whether "the average person, applying contemporary community standards" would consider certain materials "prurient," it would be unrealistic to require that the answer be based on some abstract formulation. The adversary system, with lay jurors as the usual ultimate factfinders in criminal prosecutions, has historically permitted triers of fact to draw on the standards of their community, guided always by limiting instructions on the law. To require a state to structure obscenity proceedings around evidence of a *national* ''community standard'' would be an exercise in futility.

We conclude that neither the state's alleged failure to offer evidence of ''national standards,'' nor the trial court's charge that the jury consider state community standards, were constitutional errors. Nothing in the First Amendment requires that a jury must consider hypothetical and unascertainable ''national standards'' when attempting to determine whether certain materials are obscene as a matter of fact.

. . .

It is neither realistic nor constitutionally sound to read the First Amendment as requiring that the people of Maine or Mississippi accept public depiction of conduct found tolerable in Las Vegas, or New York City. . . . People in different states vary in their tastes and attitudes, and this diversity is not to be strangled by the absolutism of imposed uniformity.

. . .

The dissenting Justices sound the alarm of repression. But, in our view, to equate the free and robust exchange of ideas and political debate with commercial exploitation of obscene material demeans the grand conception of the First Amendment and its high purposes in the historic struggle for freedom. It is a ''misuse of the great guarantees of free speech and free press. . . .'' The First Amendment protects works which, taken as a whole, have serious literary, artistic, political, or scientific value, regardless of whether the government or a majority of the people approve of the ideas these works represent. ''The protection given speech and press was fashioned to assure unfettered interchange of *ideas* for the bringing about of political and social changes desired by the people.'' . . . But the public portrayal of hard-core sexual conduct for its own sake, and for the ensuing commercial gain, is a different matter.

There is no evidence, empirical or historical, that the stern nineteenth-century American censorship of public distribution and display of material relating to sex, . . . in any way limited or affected expression of serious literary, artistic, political, or scientific ideas. On the contrary, it is beyond any question that the era following Thomas Jefferson to Theodore Roosevelt was an ''extraordinarily vigorous period,'' not just in economics and politics, but in *belles lettres* and in ''the outlying fields of social and political philosophies.'' We do not see the harsh hand of censorship of ideas—good or bad, sound or unsound—and ''repression'' of political liberty lurking in every state regulation of commercial exploitation of human interest in sex.

Mr. Justice Brennan finds ''it is hard to see how state-ordered regimentation of our minds can ever be forestalled.'' . . . These doleful anticipations assume that courts cannot distinguish commerce in ideas, protected by the First

Amendment, from commercial exploitation of obscene material. Moreover, state regulation of hard-core pornography so as to make it unavailable to nonadults, a regulation which Mr. Justice Brennan finds constitutionally permissible, has all the elements of "censorship" for adults; indeed even more rigid enforcement techniques may be called for with such dichotomy of regulation. . . . One can concede that the "sexual revolution" of recent years may have had useful byproducts in striking layers of prudery from a subject long irrationally kept from needed ventilation. But it does not follow that no regulation of patently offensive "hard-core" materials is needed or permissible; civilized people do not allow unregulated access to heroin because it is a derivative of medicinal morphine.

In sum, we (a) reaffirm the *Roth* holding that obscene material is not protected by the First Amendment; (b) hold that such material can be regulated by the states, subject to the specific safeguards enunciated above, without a showing that the material is "*utterly* without redeeming social value"; and (c) hold that obscenity is to be determined by applying "contemporary community standards," . . . not "national standards."

(Judgment affirmed.)

Justices Douglas, Brennan, Stewart, and Marshall dissented.

Prior Restraint

Near v *Minnesota*

283 U.S. 697, 51 S.Ct. 625, 75 L.Ed. 1357 (1931)

Supra, p. 226

Kingsley Books, Inc. v *Brown*

354 U.S. 436, 77 S.Ct. 1325, 1 L.Ed. 2d 1469 (1957)

A New York law provided that the chief executive officer or legal officer of a municipality could invoke a "limited injunctive remedy" under closely prescribed procedural guidelines against the sale and distribution of written and printed matter found after a trial to be obscene. An order could then be obtained for seizure of the materials if they were not voluntarily surrendered. The statute also provided for an *ex parte* injunction *pendente lite* to be obtained prior to trial; however, the person sought to be enjoined was entitled to a trial within one day after the issues were joined. The party was also entitled to a decision within two days after the conclusion of the trial. The publisher consented to an injunction *pendente lite* in a proceeding under the statute. After trial the books in issue found to be obscene were enjoined from further distribution, and their destruction was ordered. The order was affirmed in the state courts. On appeal to the United States Supreme Court, the publisher argued that the injunction remedy was unconstitutional because it placed a prior restraint on freedom of expression.

Justice Frankfurter delivered the opinion of the Court:

The judicial angle of vision in testing the validity of a statute like 22-a is "the operation and effect of the statute in substance." . . . The phrase "prior restraint" is not a self-wielding sword. Nor can it serve as a talismanic test. The duty of closer analysis and critical judgment in applying the thought behind the phrase has thus been authoritatively put by one who brings weighty learning to his support of constitutionally protected liberties: "What is needed," writes Professor Paul A. Freund, "is a pragmatic assessment of its operation in the particular circumstances. The generalization that prior restraint is particularly obnoxious in civil liberties cases must yield to more particularistic analysis."

. . .

Criminal enforcement and the proceeding under 22-a interfere with a book's solicitation of the public precisely at the same stage. In each situation the law moves after publication; the book need not in either case have yet passed into the hands of the public. The *Alberts* record does not show that the matter there found to be obscene had reached the public at the time that the criminal charge of keeping such matter for sale was lodged, while here as a matter of fact copies of the booklets whose distribution was enjoined had been on sale for several weeks when process was served. In each case the bookseller is put on notice by the complaint that sale of the publication charged with obscenity in the period before trial may subject him to penal consequences. In the one case he may suffer fine and imprisonment for violation of the criminal statute, in the other, for disobedience of the temporary injunction. The bookseller may of course stand his ground and confidently believe that in any judicial proceeding the book could not be condemned as obscene, but both modes of procedure provide an effective deterrent against distribution prior to adjudication of the book's content—the threat of subsequent penalization.

. . .

Nor are the consequences of a judicial condemnation for obscenity under 22-a more restrictive of freedom of expression than the result of conviction for a misdemeanor. In Alberts, the defendant was fined $500, sentenced to 60 days in prison, and put on probation for 2 years on condition that he not violate the obscenity statute. Not only was he completely separated from society for 2 months but he was also seriously restrained from trafficking in all obscene publications for a considerable time. Appellants, on the other hand, were enjoined from displaying for sale or distributing only the particular booklets theretofore published and adjudged to be obscene. Thus, the restraint upon appellants as merchants in obscenity was narrower than that imposed on Alberts.

Section 22-a's provision for the seizure and destruction of the instruments of ascertained wrongdoing expresses resort to a legal remedy sanctioned by the long history of Anglo-American law.

. . .

It only remains to say that the difference between *Near v State of Minnesota* and this case is glaring in fact. The two cases are no less glaringly different when judged by the appropriate criteria of constitutional law. Minnesota empowered its courts to enjoin the dissemination of future issues of a publication because its past issues had been found offensive. In the language of Mr. Chief Justice Hughes, "This is of the essence of censorship." . . . As such, it was found unconstitutional. This was enough to condemn the statute wholly apart from the fact that the proceeding in *Near* involved not obscenity but matters deemed to be derogatory to a public officer. Unlike *Near,* 22-a is concerned solely with obscenity and, as authoritatively construed, it studiously withholds restraint upon matters not already published and not yet found to be offensive.

(Judgment affirmed.)
The Chief Justice and Justices Black, Douglas, and Brennan dissented.

A New York City ordinance required any person who wished to hold a public worship meeting on public grounds to receive a permit from the police commissioner prior to the meeting. The appellant, in *Kunz* v *New York,* 340 U.S. 290, 71 S.Ct. 312, 95 L.Ed. 280 (1951), received such a permit, but it was later revoked because of a violation of another section of the ordinance, which prohibited the ridicule of any religious belief. The appellant applied for the annual permit for the next two years, but he was denied on both occasions. He was later arrested and convicted for holding a public religious meeting without a permit. His appeal stemmed from the conviction. The United States Supreme Court ruled the New York statute to be an unconstitutional restraint on the First Amendment freedom of speech. The denial of the requests for a permit by the police commissioner constituted prior restraint of speech, and since no appropriate guidelines for the administrative action were included in the ordinance, the restraint was unconstitutional.

In *Poulos* v *New Hampshire,* 345 U.S. 395, 73 S.Ct. 760, 97 L.Ed. 1105 (1953), the petitioner's conviction for a violation of a city ordinance requiring all persons using public parks as religious forums to receive a permit prior to the religious meeting was considered. Poulos, a Jehovah's Witness, applied for a permit and was denied. He held the planned religious demonstration in the public park without a permit and was subsequently arrested and convicted. The United States Supreme Court affirmed. The ordinance was found by the Court to be a regulating one instead of a restrictive one. In order to maintain order, the city required permits for the religious use of public parks, but the licensing authorities were given no discretion in restricting the religious groups that could use the parks or the speech of those granted permits. Thus, the Court found the ordinance to be constitutional. The petitioner further claimed that the absence of any redress to the administrative decision, other than state judicial proceedings, violated his constitutional freedom of speech. On the contrary, the United States Supreme

Court found that the state had provided sufficient means to circumvent the arbitrary and wrongful decisions of the administrative body.

An ordinance for the City of Dallas, Texas, established a motion picture board with the authority to classify films as suitable or unsuitable for young persons who had not reached their sixteenth birthday. The ordinance required that a movie classified as being "not suitable for young persons" must be so stated clearly in advertising. Admission to such films was prohibited to those under sixteen without his guardian or spouse. Violation of the ordinance was a misdemeanor. In the case of *Interstate Circuit, Inc.* v *Dallas,* 390 U.S. 676, 88 S.Ct. 1298, 20 L.Ed. 2d 225 (1968), the classification board classified the movie *Viva Maria* as "not suitable for young persons." The classification was upheld by the county court, and the exhibitor was enjoined from its showing except under the imposed restriction. The Texas Court of Appeals affirmed. The Supreme Court reversed this holding on the grounds that the statute was "unconstitutionally vague."

. . . As the Court said in *Joseph Burstyn, Inc.* v *Wilson,* 343 U.S., at 502, 72 S.Ct. at 781, "[i]t does not follow that the Constitution requires absolute freedom to exhibit every motion picture of every kind at all times and all places." What does follow at the least, as the cases above illustrate, is that the restrictions imposed cannot be so vague as to set "the censor . . . adrift upon a boundless sea . . . ," id., at 504, 72 S.Ct. at 782. In short, as Justice Frankfurter said,

Legislation must not be so vague, the language so loose, as to leave to those who have to apply it too wide a discretion . . . and we have indicated more generally that because of its strong and abiding interest in youth, a state may regulate the dissemination to juveniles of, and their access to, material objectionable as to them, but which a state clearly could not regulate as to adults. . . . Here we conclude only that "the absence of narrowly drawn, reasonable, and definite standards for the officials to follow," . . . is fatal.

Civil Rights Demonstrations and Freedom of Speech

Adderley v *Florida*

385 U.S. 39, 87 S.Ct. 242, 17 L.Ed. 2d 149 (1966)

Adderley and other students went from the Florida A & M campus to the county jail in Tallahassee to protest the arrest of students who had previously protested state and local racial segregation policies and jail segregation. The sheriff notified them that if they did not leave the jail grounds, they would be arrested for trespassing. Some departed, but Adderley and 31 other students remained and were arrested. They were convicted of trespassing "committed with a malicious and mischievous intent." The United States Supreme Court granted certiorari and affirmed the convictions.

Justice Black delivered the opinion of the Court:

Petitioners have insisted from the beginning of this case that it is controlled by and must be reversed because of our prior cases of *Edwards* v *South Carolina*, 372 U.S. 229,... , and *Cox* v *State of Louisiana*, 379 U.S. 536,.... We cannot agree.

... In *Edwards*, the demonstrators went to the South Carolina state capitol grounds to protest. In this case they went to the jail. Traditionally, state capitol grounds are open to the public. Jails, built for security purposes, are not.... This Court in *Edwards* took pains to point out at length the indefinite, loose, and broad nature of this charge; indeed, this Court pointed out... that the South Carolina Supreme Court had itself declared that the "breach of the peace" charge is "not susceptible of exact definition." South Carolina's power to prosecute, it was emphasized,... would have been different had the state proceeded under a "precise and narrowly drawn regulatory statute evincing a legislative judgment that certain specific conduct be limited or proscribed," such as, for example, "limiting the periods during which the State House grounds were open to the public...." The South Carolina breach-of-the-peace statute was thus struck down as being so broad and all-embracing as to jeopardize speech, press, assembly, and petition, under the constitutional doctrine... followed in many subsequent cases. And it was on this same ground of vagueness that... the Louisiana breach-of-the-peace law used to prosecute Cox was invalidated.

The Florida trespass statute under which these petitioners were charged cannot be challenged on this ground. It is aimed at conduct of one limited kind, that is, for one person or persons to trespass upon the property of another with a malicious and mischievous intent. There is no lack of notice in this law, nothing to entrap or fool the unwary.

... The use of these terms in the statute, instead of contributing to uncertainty and misunderstanding, actually makes its meaning more understandable and clear.

. . .

Under the foregoing testimony the jury was authorized to find that the state had proven every essential element of the crime, as it was defined by the state court. That interpretation is, of course, binding on us, leaving only the question of whether conviction of the state offense, thus defined, unconstitutionally deprives petitioners of their rights to freedom of speech, press, assembly, or petition. We hold it does not.... There is no evidence at all that on any other occasion had similarly large groups of the public been permitted to gather on this portion of the jail grounds for any purpose. Nothing in the Constitution of the United States prevents Florida from even-handed enforcement of its general trespass statute against those refusing to obey the sheriff's order to remove themselves from what amounted to the curtilage of the jailhouse. The state, no less than a private owner of property, has power to preserve the property under its control for the use to which it is lawfully dedicated. For this reason there is no merit to the petitioners' argument that they had a constitutional right to stay

on the property, over the jail custodian's objections, because this "area chosen
for the peaceful civil rights demonstration was not only 'reasonable' but also
particularly appropriate. . . ." Such an argument has as its major unarticulated
premise the assumption that those who want to propagandize protests or views
have a constitutional right to do so whenever and however and wherever they
please. That concept of constitutional law was vigorously and forthrightly
rejected in two of the cases petitioners rely on. . . . We reject it again. The
United States Constitution does not forbid a state to control the use of its own
property for its own lawful nondiscriminatory purpose.

(Judgment affirmed.)
The Chief Justice and Justices Douglas, Brennan, and Fortas dissented.

In *Greer* v *Spock,* 424 U.S. 828, 96 S.Ct. 1211, 47 L.Ed. 2d 505 (1976). By
Fort Dix regulation 210–26 the Fort Dix Military Reservation of the United
States banned speeches and demonstrations of a partisan political nature. Also,
the distribution or posting of any literature—personal or otherwise—is prohibited
by regulation 210–27. In 1972 Dr. Benjamin Spock and others who were candi-
dates of minor political parties wrote to the commanding officer of Fort Dix
stating their intent to enter the reservation to speak and distribute literature. Their
request was rejected. Subsequently, a suit was filed in the United States District
Court of New Jersey to enjoin the enforcement of the Fort Dix regulation. The
District Court denied relief, but the Court of Appeals overruled that order. Spock
then held a rally at Fort Dix. The District Court issued a permanent injunction
prohibiting military authorities from interfering. The Court of Appeals affirmed
this order.
The Supreme Court overruled and reversed this decision, stating,

In short, it is the primary business of the Armies and Navies to fight or be
ready to fight wars should the occasion arise. And it is consequently the
business of a military installation like Fort Dix to train soldiers, not to provide
a public forum.
    Such a policy is wholly consistent with the American constitutional tradition
of a politically neutral military establishment under civilian control.
                                        . . .
This case, therefore, simply does not raise any question of unconstitutional
application of the regulation to any specific situation. The United States Supreme
Court struck down a state law making a "breach of peace" unlawful in *Edwards*
v *South Carolina,* 372 U.S. 229, 83 S.Ct. 680, 9 L.Ed. 2d 697 (1963). The
statute generally defined a "breach of peace" as any act in violation of any
ordinance meant to maintain community order or any "disturbance of public
tranquility." The appellants were convicted under the statute after a public
demonstration protesting racial discrimination held on the grounds of the South
Carolina State House. There was no threat of violence, no violation of any traffic

or other ordinance, and there was ample police protection. For these reasons, the Court could discern no danger to the public order, but only a peaceful assembly of citizens in protest. According to the United States Supreme Court, the demonstration was a "classic and pristine form" of the peaceful, public expression of grievances protected by the Constitution. The law which prohibited such a demonstration was so general that it was unconstitutional.

In *Brown* v *Louisiana*, 383 U.S. 131, 86 S.Ct. 719, 15 L.Ed. 2d 637 (1966), the United States Supreme Court overturned the convictions of the appellants for a "breach of the peace" under Louisiana law. The petitioners, both of whom were black, entered a public library which had previously been segregated. The men requested services, which were given. After conducting their business, they sat in the room silently. The police arrested them for a "breach of the peace" and for the refusal "to disperse and move on [when so ordered by any officer or authorized person]." The Court found that the convictions were inappropriately based on the state law prohibiting such behavior. The appellants' occupation of the public reading room could not be construed to be a crime under the statute. Further, the freedom of expression guaranteed by the Constitution is not limited to verbal expressions; it also encompasses appropriate actions such as "silent and reproachful presence in a place where the protestant has every right to be" in order to protest the unconstitutional segregation of a public facility. The appellants in this case were making use of their constitutional freedoms, and the inappropriate application of the state "breach-of-peace" statute abridged these freedoms.

Even though a shopping center is not publicly owned, it must not be considered "private" property in the same sense that other facilities that are not open to public use are. In *Amalgamated Food Employees Union* v *Logan Valley Plaza, Inc.*, 391 U.S. 308, 88 S.Ct. 1601, 20 L.Ed. 2d 603 (1968), the United States Supreme Court found that a group of demonstrators who were peacefully picketing a shopping center supermarket because it was non-union were unlawfully convicted of a violation of the state's trespass laws. The appellants were exercising their First Amendment freedoms in "a manner and for a purpose generally consonant with the use to which the property is actually put." Governments may regulate the expression of ideas on public property in order to prevent the disruption of the normal business carried on on the property. Similarly, private property that is generally open to the public may also fall within the state's regulations. However, any state that acts to deny completely the public use of such properties for the expression of First Amendment rights is unconstitutionally abridging these rights. Since the appellants' activities could not be construed to be a disruption to the business of the supermarket in question, the convictions were overturned.

In *Hudgens* v *NLRB*, 424 U.S. 507, 96 S.Ct. 1029, 47 L.Ed. 2d 196 (1976), strikers of a labor union picketed in front of their employer's store which was located in the confines of a privately owned shopping center. The general manager of the shopping center told the strikers that they could not picket within the mall or on the parking lot and if they continued to do so they would be subject to arrest. The picketers left, but they returned 30 minutes later. The general manager once again threatened arrest. The strikers then departed.

The union filed an unfair labor practice charge with the National Labor Relations Board against Hudgens, the owner of the shopping center. The Board issued a cease-and-desist order against Hudgens, thus beginning a series of events which saw the case go to the Court of Appeals, back to the NLRB, back to the Court of Appeals, and finally to the Supreme Court.

Upon reaching the Supreme Court of the United States, a confusing situation existed because of the infinite number of theories upon which this case had been decided. In the opinion of the Court the major question to be answered was whether the respective rights and liabilities of the parties should be decided under the criteria of the National Labor Relations Act alone, under a First Amendment standard, or under a combination of the two. After lengthy discussion by the Court in which the members considered the constitutional guarantee of free speech and the area of a shopping center as the "functional equivalent of a municipality," it was the decision of the Court to vacate the judgment and remand the case to the Court of Appeals with directions to remand to the National Labor Relations Board, "so that the case may be considered under the statutory criteria of the National Labor Relations Act alone."

Defamation

New York Times Company v *Sullivan*
376 U.S. 254, 84 S.Ct. 710, 11 L.Ed. 2d 686 (1964)

During the early civil rights drives in Alabama *The New York Times* published a full-page advertisement which made several charges indirectly implicating Sullivan with activities directed against civil rights demonstrators. Some of the statements were false and inaccurate, although none mentioned Sullivan by name or title of Commissioner of Public Affairs who was responsible for supervision of the Montgomery Police Department. The jury awarded Sullivan $500,000 damages in his libel suit against *The New York Times*. On appeal of the finding to the United States Supreme Court, the Court was required for the first time to determine the extent to which the constitutional protections for speech and press limited a state's power to award damages in a libel action brought by a public official against critics of his official conduct.

Justice Brennan delivered the opinion of the Court:

> ... We reverse the judgment. We hold that the rule of law applied by the Alabama courts is constitutionally deficient for failure to provide the safeguards for freedom of speech and of the press that are required by the First and Fourteenth Amendments in a libel action brought by a public official against critics of his official conduct. We further hold that under the proper

safeguards the evidence presented in this case is constitutionally insufficient to support the judgment for respondent.

We may dispose at the outset of two grounds asserted to insulate the judgment of the Alabama courts from constitutional scrutiny. The first is the proposition relied on by the State Supreme Court—that "The Fourteenth Amendment is directed against state action and not private action." That proposition has no application to this case. Although this is a civil lawsuit between private parties, the Alabama courts have applied a state rule of law which petitioners claim to impose invalid restrictions on their constitutional freedoms of speech and press.

. . .

The second contention is that the constitutional guarantees of freedom of speech and of the press are inapplicable here, at least so far as the *Times* is concerned, because the allegedly libelous statements were published as part of a paid, "commercial" advertisement.

. . .

That the *Times* was paid for publishing the advertisement is as immaterial in this connection as is the fact that newspapers and books are sold. . . . Any other conclusion would discourage newspapers from carrying "editorial advertisements" of this type, and so might shut off an important outlet for the promulgation of information and ideas by persons who do not themselves have access to publishing facilities—who wish to exercise their freedom of speech even though they are not members of the press. . . . The effect would be to shackle the First Amendment in its attempt to secure "the widest possible dissemination of information from diverse and antagonistic sources." . . . To avoid placing such a handicap upon the freedoms of expression, we hold that if the allegedly libelous statements would otherwise be constitutionally protected from the present judgment, they do not forfeit that protection because they were published in the form of a paid advertisement.

Under Alabama law as applied in this case, a publication is "libelous per se" if the words "tend to injure a person . . . in his reputation" or to "bring [him] into public contempt"; the trial court stated that the standard was met if the words are such as to "injure him in his public office, or impute misconduct to him in his office, or want of official integrity, or want of fidelity to a public trust. . . ." The jury must find that the words were published "of and concerning" the plaintiff, but where the plaintiff is a public official his place in the governmental hierarchy is sufficient evidence to support a finding that his reputation has been affected by statements that reflect upon the agency of which he is in charge. Once "libel per se" has been established, the defendant has no defense as to stated facts unless he can persuade the jury that they were true in all their particulars. . . . His privilege of "fair comment" for expressions of opinion depends on the truth of the facts upon which the comment is based. . . . Unless he can discharge the burden of proving truth, general damages are presumed, and may be awarded without proof of pecuniary injury. A showing of actual malice is apparently a prerequisite to recovery of punitive damages, and the defendant may in any event forestall a punitive award by a retraction meeting the statutory requirements. Good motives and belief in truth do not negate an inference of malice, but are relevant only in mitigation of punitive damages if the jury chooses to accord them weight.

· · ·

The question before us is whether this rule of liability, as applied to an action brought by a public official against critics of his official conduct, abridges the freedom of speech and of the press that is guaranteed by the First and Fourteenth Amendments.

In deciding the question now, we are compelled by neither precedent nor policy to give any more weight to the epithet "libel" than we have to other "mere labels" of state law. . . . It must be measured by standards that satisfy the First Amendment.

· · ·

The constitutional guarantees require, we think, a federal rule that prohibits a public official from recovering damages for a defamatory falsehood relating to his official conduct unless he proves that the statement was made with "actual malice"—that is, with knowledge that it was false or with reckless disregard of whether it was false or not.

· · ·

Such a privilege for criticism of official conduct is appropriately analogous to the protection accorded a public official when *he* is sued for libel by a private citizen. . . . Analogous considerations support the privilege for the citizen-critic of government. It is as much his duty to criticize as it is the official's duty to administer.

· · ·

We conclude that such a privilege is required by the First and Fourteenth Amendments.

We hold today that the Constitution delimits a state's power to award damages for libel in actions brought by public officials against critics of their official conduct. . . . Since the trial judge did not instruct the jury to differentiate between general and punitive damages, it may be that the verdict was wholly an award of one or the other. But it is impossible to know, in view of the general verdict returned. Because of this uncertainty, the judgment must be reversed and the case remanded.

· · ·

Since respondent may seek a new trial, we deem that considerations of effective judicial administration require us to review the evidence in the present record to determine whether it could constitutionally support a judgment for respondent. This Court's duty is not limited to the elaboration of constitutional principles; we must also in proper cases review the evidence to make certain that those principles have been constitutionally applied. This is such a case, particularly since the question is one of alleged trespass across "the line

between speech unconditionally guaranteed and speech which may legitimately be regulated.''

. . .

Applying these standards, we consider that the proof presented to show
actual malice lacks the convincing clarity which the constitutional standard
demands, and hence that it would not constitutionally sustain the judgment for
respondent under the proper rule of law. The case of the individual petitioners
requires little discussion. Even assuming that they could constitutionally be
found to have authorized the use of their names on the advertisement, there
was no evidence whatever that they were aware of any erroneous statements or
were in any way reckless in that regard. The judgment against them is thus
without constitutional support.

. . .

As to the *Times,* we similarly conclude that the facts do not support a
finding of actual malice.

. . .

We also think the evidence was constitutionally defective in another respect:
it was incapable of supporting the jury's finding that the allegedly libelous
statements were made ''of and concerning'' respondent.

. . .

(Judgment reversed.)
Justices Black, Douglas, and Goldberg concurred.

In *Time, Inc.* v *Firestone,* 424 U.S. 448, 96 S.Ct. 958, 47 L.Ed. 2d 154, (1976),
Time, Inc. had been ordered to pay a $100,000 libel judgment by the Supreme
Court of Florida for printing an item that purported to describe the result of a
divorce suit between Mr. and Mrs. Firestone. Time, Inc. petitioned the Supreme
Court to review this claim on the grounds that their First and Fourteenth Amend-
ment rights had been violated.

Time, Inc. contended that the article was not published ''with actual malice''
as defined in *New York Times* v *Sullivan,* 376 U.S. 254 (1964). Supporting this
argument Time submitted that the respondent was a ''public figure'' and that
their article was simply ''a report of a judicial proceeding.'' Both of these
arguments were rejected by the Court.

The major issue upon which the Court submitted its opinion was the finding of
fault as established by *Gertz* v *Robert Welch, Inc.* 418 U.S. 323 (1974), which
stated that there must also be evidence of some fault on the part of the defendant
charged with publishing defamatory material. The Court asserted that there might
be sufficient indication that the lower court found the petitioner at fault within the
meaning of Gertz, but that it is mandatory that they make a determination of this
''critical fact'' evident. It was therefore the opinion of the Court that, ''. . . in the
absence of a finding in some element of the state court system that there was
fault, we are not inclined to canvas the record to make such a determination in the
first instance. . . . Accordingly the judgment of the Supreme Court of Florida is

vacated and the case remanded for further proceedings not inconsistent with this opinion.''

A Louisiana statute, which prohibited criticism of a public official if such criticism consisted of true statements made with malice or false statements made with ill will or without the reasonable belief that such statements were true, was struck down by the Court in *Garrison* v *Louisiana,* 379 U.S. 64, 85 S.Ct. 209, 13 L.Ed. 2d 125 (1964). The United States Supreme Court found that the statute was an unconstitutional abridgment of the First Amendment freedom of expression, since it placed the criticism of public officials acting in their governmental capacity easily within the libel statutes. Following the rule cited in the *New York Times* v *Sullivan* decision, the Court held that no one could be charged with libel against a public official unless their statements were false and were made without regard to their falsity or truth.

Two cases decided together, *Curtis Publishing Company* v *Butts* and *Associated Press* v *Walker,* 388 U.S. 130, 87 S.Ct. 1975, 18 L.Ed. 2d 18 L.Ed. 2d 1094 (1967), concerned the application of libel laws in the protection of "public figures" who were not public officials. The first case involved a story, published by the *Saturday Evening Post,* which accused the appellee, a collegiate athletic director, of arranging the outcome of a college football game. The second case involved the publication of a news dispatch which stated that appellee had led a riotous charge against federal law enforcers who were enforcing a federal decree for the desegregation of a state university. The libel conviction against Curtis Publishing Company was affirmed, but the conviction of Associated Press was reversed. The reasons for the decisions cited by the Justices consisted of three different "rules" to be applied in the cases of libel of "public figures." First, the *New York Times* rule was reiterated by two Justices; only false statements made with the knowledge or disregard for their falsity could be the subject of libel against a "public figure." Second, the "absolutist" rule was cited by two Justices; the freedom of the press is absolute and no charges of libel are applicable. The third rule, cited by four Justices, made statements which resulted from unreasonable standards of journalism libelous if such statements were detrimental to "public figures." For these various reasons, the decisions for the affirmation of the conviction of Curtis Publishing Company and the reversal of the conviction of the Associated Press were reached.

In *Pickering* v *Board of Education,* 391 U.S. 563, 88 S.Ct. 1731, 20 L.Ed. 2d 811 (1968), the United States Supreme Court held that the dismissal of a public school teacher for writing a letter critical of the school board was an abridgment of the teacher's guaranteed freedom of expression. The Court applied the *New York Times* rule once again, even though the person accused of libel was a public employee. Since the employment of the teacher was only tangentially related to the public issue in question, his membership in the "general public" category was retained. Without the proof that the statements made were false and were made knowingly or with reckless disregard for the truth, the punishment of dismissal could not stand.

Loyalty Oaths

Watkins v United States

354 U.S. 178, 77 S.Ct. 1173, 1 L.Ed. 2d 1273 (1957)

In 1954 Watkins, a labor organizer and former union organizer, appeared before a subcommittee of the House Committee on Un-American Activities to testify about Communist Party activities by himself and others. He admitted to cooperating with the Communist Party and volunteered to identify individuals who were still active in the Party. He was then asked questions about past activities of persons he thought were no longer Party members. Believing that these questions were not relevant to the purpose of the subcommittee's investigation and that it had no right to merely expose a person's past activities, Watkins refused to answer. He was later found in contempt of the subcommittee by two federal courts. On appeal, the United States Supreme Court reversed the "contempt of Congress conviction."

Chief Justice Warren delivered the opinion of the Court:

A far more difficult task evolved from the claim by witnesses that the committees' interrogations were infringements upon the freedoms of the First Amendment. Clearly, an investigation is subject to the demand that the Congress shall make no law abridging freedom of speech or press or assembly. While it is true that there is no statute to be reviewed, and that an investigation is not a law, nevertheless an investigation is part of law making. It is justified solely as an adjunct to the legislative process. The First Amendment may be invoked against infringement of the protected freedoms by law or by law making.

Abuses of the investigative process may imperceptibly lead to abridgment of protected freedoms. . . . Those who are identified by witnesses and thereby placed in the same glare of publicity are equally subject to public stigma, scorn, and obloquy. . . . That this impact is partly the result of nongovernmental activity by private persons cannot relieve the investigators of their responsibility for initiating the reaction.

. . .

The Committee on Un-American Activities, as a whole or by subcommittee, is authorized to make from time to time investigations of (1) the extent, character, and objects of un-American propaganda activities in the United States, (2) the diffusion within the United States of subversive and un-American propaganda that is instigated from foreign countries or of a domestic origin and attacks the principle of the form of government as guaranteed by our Constitution, and (3) all other questions in relation thereto that would aid Congress in any necessary remedial legislation.

In fulfillment of their obligation under this statute, the courts must accord to the defendants every right which is guaranteed to defendants in all other criminal cases. . . . this raises a special problem in that the statute defines the crime as refusal to answer "any question pertinent to the question under inquiry." Part of the standard of criminality, therefore, is the pertinency of the questions propounded to the witness.

The most serious doubts as to the Subcommittee's "question under inquiry," however, stem from the precise questions that petitioner has been charged with refusing to answer. Under the terms of the statute, after all, it is these which must be proved pertinent. Petitioner is charged with refusing to tell the Subcommittee whether or not he knew that certain named persons had been members of the Communist Party in the past. The Subcommittee's counsel read the list from the testimony of a previous witness who had identified them as Communists. Although this former witness was identified with labor he had not stated that the persons he named were involved in union affairs. Of the 30 names propounded to petitioner, 7 were completely unconnected with organized labor. One operated a beauty parlor. Another was a watchmaker. Several were identified as "just citizens" or "only Communists." When almost a quarter of the persons on the list are not labor people, the inference becomes strong that the subject before the Subcommittee was not defined in terms of Communism in labor.

The final source of evidence as to the "question under inquiry" is the Chairman's response when petitioner objected to the questions on the grounds of lack of pertinency. The Chairman then announced that the Subcommittee was investigating "subversion and subversive propaganda." This is a subject at least as broad and indefinite as the authorizing resolution of the Committee, if not more so.

Having exhausted the several possible indicia of the "question under inquiry," we remain unenlightened as to the subject to which the questions asked petitioner were pertinent. Certainly, if the point is that obscure after trial and appeal, it was not adequately revealed to petitioner when he had to decide at his peril whether or not to answer. Fundamental fairness demands that no witness be compelled to make such a determination with so little guidance. Unless the subject matter has been made to appear with undisputable clarity, it is the duty of the investigative body, upon objection of the witness on grounds of pertinency, to state for the record the subject under inquiry at that time and the manner in which the propounded questions are pertinent thereto. To be meaningful, the explanation must describe what the topic under inquiry is and the connective reasoning whereby the precise questions asked relate to it.

(Judgment reversed.)
Justice Clark dissented.
Justices Burton and Whittaker did not participate in the decision.

The power of the Congress to conduct legislative investigations is not an absolute one, according to the United States Supreme Court decision in *Kilbourn* v *Thompson,* 103 U.S. 168, 26 L.Ed. 377 (1881). Kilbourn, the manager of a "real estate pool," was called before a committee of the House of Representatives that had been formed to investigate the dealings between the "real estate pool" and a bankrupt banking firm. Upon the refusal of Kilbourn to answer certain questions concerning his business, the House ordered his imprisonment. On appeal to the Court, Kilbourn's imprisonment was found to be an unconstitutional use of the legislative power of the Congress. According to the Court, the Congress did not have a sufficient purpose to the investigation and had, therefore, exceeded the constitutional powers of investigation.

The Congress has a limited constitutional authorization for investigation, and when it steps outside the boundaries of its power to investigate, it loses the concomitant authority to punish. In *United States* v *Rumely,* 345 U.S. 41, 73 S.Ct. 543, 97 L.Ed. 770 (1953), the United States Supreme Court considered the conviction of the respondent for contempt of Congress. A committee of the House of Representatives was authorized by the Congress to study "all lobbying activities, intended to influence, encourage, promote, or retard legislation." During this investigation the respondent was called before the House to testify as to the persons who had made bulk purchases of books of a political nature. She refused to do so and was cited for contempt. The Court reversed the conviction on the grounds that the committee requiring the testimony had exceeded the purposes of the authorizing resolution of the Congress. Further, the material requested by the committee concerned "personal and private affairs," and "inquiry" into such matters is precluded by the Constitution. If the practice of investigation into the reading habits of the public were continued, said the Court, the Congress could use its investigative powers to inhibit the First Amendment freedoms.

In *Sweezy* v *New Hampshire,* 354 U.S. 234, 77 S.Ct. 1203, 1 L.Ed. 2d 1311 (1957), a contempt conviction was reversed by the United States Supreme Court. Pursuant to the 1951 Subversive Activities Act of the State of New Hampshire, the legislature authorized the attorney general of that state to investigate "subversive" persons and activities as a one-man committee of the legislature. The attorney general questioned the petitioner, a man who considered himself to be a "classical Marxist" and a "socialist." The petitioner was cooperative in all matters, except the portion of the questioning that concerned certain of his university lectures and his knowledge of the Progressive Party. Upon his refusal to answer questions in these areas, he was cited for contempt. The Supreme Court overruled this contempt citation for two reasons: First, the attorney general could not show that the legislature considered the university lectures and the information concerning the Progressive Party to be within the scope of the investigation. Second, such information could not constitutionally be the subject of an investigative inquiry. The areas probed by the attorney general invaded the area protected by the First Amendment without a coinciding need of the state for "self-protection." Further, the Progressive Party had not been shown to be anything other than a political organization, and as such, could not be subjected to investigation by a political body, such as the state legislature.

While conducting a one-man probe of subversive activities in New Hampshire, the attorney general of that state called the defendant, Uphaus, the Executive Director of World Fellowship, Inc., a New Hampshire corporation that maintained a summer camp in the state. The attorney general also subpoenaed corporate records containing the names of all persons who attended the camp during 1954 and 1955. The defendant refused to comply and the attorney general petitioned the state court to mandate compliance. Uphaus still refused claiming the irrevelancy of the documents and to compel him to produce them would violate his First Amendment rights. He was adjudged to be in civil contempt and ordered to jail until he complied. On appeal, the United States Supreme Court affirmed the lower court's decision in *Uphaus* v *Wyman,* 360 U.S. 72, 79 S.Ct. 1040, 3 L.Ed. 2d 1090 (1959).

In the light of such a record we conclude that the state's interest has not been "pressed, in this instance, to a point where it has come into fatal collision with the overriding" constitutionally protected rights of appellant and those he may represent.

. . .

An investigation into the subversive activities of New Hampshire citizens by the attorney general of that state led to the questioning of the appellant concerning his membership in the Communist Party. The appellant testified that he had been involved in the Communist Party in the past, but was not currently a member and had no knowledge of the party activities since the termination of his association with the party. He refused to testify as to his knowledge of and activities with the Communist Party during the period of his membership. His citation for contempt was overturned by the United States Supreme Court in *De Gregory* v *Attorney General,* 383 U.S. 825, 86 S.Ct. 1148, 16 L.Ed. 2d 292 (1966). The Court found the subject of the questioning to be too remote to justify the intrusion by the attorney general into the political associations of appellant. Since there was no "overriding and compelling state interest" in the information which could possibly result from the investigation, the Court found the contempt citation to be an unconstitutional abridgment of the appellant's First Amendment freedom of association.

RELIGION

Establishment of Religion

Everson v *Board of Education*
330 U.S. 1, 67 S.Ct. 504, 91 L.Ed. 711 (1947)

A New Jersey statute contained a provision that permitted school boards to reimburse parents of both public and parochial school students for transportation costs incurred for traveling to and from school on public transportation. Exempted were those schools operated for profit. Everson, a school district taxpayer, challenged the idea of reimbursement to parochial school students claiming that the state act amounted to establishment of religion. His claims were rejected in the state courts. On appeal, the United States Supreme Court affirmed.

Justice Black delivered the opinion of the Court:

First. The due process argument that the state law taxes some people to help others carry out their private purposes is framed in two phases. The first phase is that a state cannot tax A to reimburse B for the cost of transporting his children to church schools. This is said to violate the Due Process Clause because the children are sent to these church schools to satisfy the personal desires of their parents, rather than the public's interest in the general education of all children. This argument, if valid, would apply equally to prohibit state payment for the transportation of children to any nonpublic school, whether operated by a church, or any other nongovernment individual or group. But, the New Jersey legislature has decided that a public purpose will be served by using tax-raised funds to pay the bus fares of all school children, including those who attend parochial schools. The New Jersey Court of Errors and Appeals has reached the same conclusion. The fact that a state law, passed to satisfy a public need, coincides with the personal desires of the individuals most directly affected is certainly an inadequate reason for us to say that a legislature has erroneously appraised the public need.

Insofar as the second phase of the due process argument may differ from the first, it is by suggesting that taxation for transportation of children to church schools constitutes support of a religion by the state. But if the law is invalid for this reason, it is because it violates the First Amendment's prohibition against the establishment of religion by law. This is the exact question raised by appellant's second contention, to consideration of which we now turn.

Second. The New Jersey statute is challenged as a "law respecting an establishment of religion." The First Amendment, as made applicable to the states by the Fourteenth . . . commands that a state "shall make no law respecting an establishment of religion, or prohibiting the free exercise thereof." These words of the First Amendment reflected in the minds of early Americans a vivid mental picture of conditions and practices which they fervently wished to stamp out in order to preserve liberty for themselves and for their posterity.
· · ·

The meaning and scope of the First Amendment, preventing establishment of religion or prohibiting the free exercise thereof, in the light of its history and the evils it was designed forever to suppress, have been several times elaborated by the decisions of this Court prior to the application of the First Amendment to the states by the Fourteenth.
· · ·

We must consider the New Jersey statute in accordance with the foregoing limitations imposed by the First Amendment. But we must not strike that state statute down if it is within the state's constitutional power even though it approaches the verge of that power. . . . New Jersey cannot consistently with the "Establishment of Religion" Clause of the First Amendment contribute tax-raised funds to the support of an institution which teaches the tenets and faith of any church. On the other hand, other language of the Amendment commands that New Jersey cannot hamper its citizens in the free exercise of their own religion. Consequently, it cannot exclude individual Catholics, Lutherans, Mohammedans, Baptists, Jews, Methodists, nonbelievers, Presbyterians, or the members of any other faith, *because of their faith, or lack of it,* from receiving the benefits of public welfare legislation.

· · ·

Measured by these standards, we cannot say that the First Amendment prohibits New Jersey from spending tax-raised funds to pay the bus fares of parochial school pupils as a part of a general program under which it pays the fares of pupils attending public and other schools.

· · ·

This Court has said that parents may, in the discharge of their duty under state compulsory education laws, send their children to a religious rather than a public school if the school meets the secular educational requirements which the state has power to impose. . . . It appears that these parochial schools meet New Jersey's requirements. The state contributes no money to the schools. It does not support them. Its legislation, as applied, does no more than provide a general program to help parents get their children, regardless of their religion, safely and expeditiously to and from accredited schools.

The First Amendment has erected a wall between church and state. That wall must be kept high and impregnable. We could not approve the slightest breach. New Jersey has not breached it here.

(Judgment affirmed.)
Justices Rutledge, Frankfurter, Jackson, and Burton dissented.

In *McGowan* v *Maryland,* 366 U.S. 420, 81 S.Ct. 1101, 6 L.Ed. 2d 393 (1961), the United States Supreme Court upheld the Maryland Sunday closing law in finding that the purpose and effect of the laws were not religious and did not violate the Establishment Clause. The Court found that such legislation ''does not ban federal or state regulation of conduct whose reason or effect merely happens to coincide or harmonize with the tenets of some or all religions. In many instances, the Congress or state legislatures conclude that the general welfare of society wholly apart from any religious consideration, demands such regulation.'' But the Court also admonished that such laws may be in violation of the Establishment Clause if it can be shown that the state in attempting to use its power to aid religion.

In *Board of Education* v *Allen,* 392 U.S. 236, 88 S.Ct. 1923, 20 L.Ed. 2d 1060 (1968), a New York law required public school authorities to lend textbooks to all students in grades 7 through 12, including students attending private schools. The United States Supreme Court rejected the argument that the law transgressed the Establishment Clause and the Free Exercise of Religion

Clause. In rejecting these arguments, the Court stated that the law was aimed at providing a secular education:

> Against this background of judgment and experience, . . . we cannot agree with appellants either that all teaching in a sectarian school is religious or that the processes of secular and religious training are so intertwined that secular textbooks furnished to students by the public are in fact instrumental in the teaching of religion.

In the case of *McCollum* v *Board of Education,* 333 U.S. 203, 68 S.Ct. 461, 92 L.Ed. 649 (1948), the Illinois compulsory education law permitting religious teachers employed by private religious groups to come weekly into school buildings and for 30 minutes substitute their religious teaching for the secular education provided was questioned. McCollum sought a writ of mandamus to compel the Board of Education to adopt and enforce rules and regulations prohibiting all instruction in and teaching of all religious education in public schools in the district. McCollum argued that the joint public school–religious group program violated the First and Fourteenth Amendments. The state courts denied the writ. On appeal, the United States Supreme Court reversed.

In the majority opinion, delivered by Justice Black, the decision in *Everson* was further qualified:

> . . . The majority in the Everson case, and the minority . . . agreed that the First Amendment's language, properly interpreted, had erected a wall of separation between church and state. They disagreed as to the facts shown by the record and as to the proper application of the First Amendment's language to those facts.

Concluding its opinion, the Court states:

> Here not only are the state's tax-supported public school buildings used for the dissemination of religious doctrines. The state also affords sectarian groups an invaluable aid in that it helps to provide pupils for their religious classes through use of the state's compulsory public school machinery. This is not separation of church and state.

In *Zorach* v *Clauson,* 343 U.S. 306, 72 S.Ct. 679, 96 L.Ed. 954 (1952), the New York City "released time" program that permitted public schools to release students during the school day so that they could leave the building and go to religious centers to receive religious instruction was challenged as being a state support of religion. In upholding the law, the United States Supreme Court stated that there is no requirement that the government be hostile to religion. Rather, it must be neutral when it comes to competition among sects.

It may not coerce anyone to attend church, to observe a religious holiday, or to take religious instruction. But it can close its doors or suspend its operations as to those who want to repair to their religious sanctuary for worship or instruction. No more than that is undertaken here. . . . We follow the *McCollum* case. But we cannot expand it to cover the present released time program. . . . We cannot read into the Bill of Rights such a philosophy of hostility to religion.

Engle v *Vitale*

370 U.S. 421, 82 S.Ct. 1261, 8 L.Ed. 2d 601 (1962)

A local school board in New York directed that a nondenominational prayer drawn up by the New York Board of Regents be read aloud daily by each class. The prayer was: "Almight God, we acknowledge our dependence upon Thee, and we beg Thy blessings upon us, our parents, our teachers, and our country." Engle and others brought an action against the board of education to compel the board to retract its order. The state courts upheld the board's order. On certiorari, the United States Supreme Court reversed.

Justice Black delivered the opinion of the Court:

We think that by using its public school system to encourage recitation of the Regents' prayer, the State of New York has adopted a practice wholly inconsistent with the Establishment Clause. There can, of course, be no doubt that New York's program of daily classroom invocation of God's blessings as prescribed in the Regents' prayer is a religious activity. It is a solemn avowal of divine faith and supplication for the blessings of the Almighty.

. . .

The petitioners contend among other things that the state laws requiring or permitting use of the Regents' prayer must be struck down as a violation of the Establishment Clause because that prayer was composed by governmental officials as a part of a governmental program to further religious beliefs. For this reason, petitioners argue, the state's use of the Regents' prayer in its public school system breaches the constitutional wall of separation between church and state. We agree with that contention since we think that the constitutional prohibition against laws respecting an establishment of religion must at least mean that in this country it is no part of the business of government to compose official prayers for any group of the American people to recite as a part of a religious program carried on by government.

It is a matter of history that this very practice of establishing governmentally composed prayers for religious services was one of the reasons which caused many of our early colonists to leave England and seek religious freedom in America.

. . .

There can be no doubt that New York's state prayer program officially establishes the religious beliefs embodied in the Regents' prayer. The respondents' argument to the contrary, which is largely based upon the contention that the Regents' prayer is "nondenominational" and the fact that the program, as modified and approved by state courts, does not require all pupils to recite the prayer but permits those who wish to do so to remain silent or be excused from the room, ignores the essential nature of the program's constitutional defects. Neither the fact that the prayer may be denominationally neutral nor the fact that its observance on the part of the students is voluntary can serve to free it from the limitations of the Establishment Clause, as it might from the Free Exercise Clause, of the First Amendment, both of which are operative against the states by virtue of the Fourteenth Amendment.

. . .

The Establishment Clause, unlike the Free Exercise Clause, does not depend upon any showing of direct governmental compulsion and is violated by the enactment of laws which establish an official religion whether those laws operate directly to coerce nonobserving individuals or not. . . . But the purposes underlying the Establishment Clause go much further than that. Its first and most immediate purpose rested on the belief that a union of government and religion tends to destroy government and to degrade religion. . . . Another purpose of the Establishment Clause rested upon an awareness of the historical fact that governmentally established religions and religious persecutions go hand in hand. . . . The New York laws officially prescribing the Regents' prayer are inconsistent both with the purposes of the Establishment Clause and with the Establishment Clause itself.

It has been argued that to apply the Constitution in such a way as to prohibit state laws respecting an establishment of religious services in public schools is to indicate a hostility toward religion or toward prayer. Nothing, of course, could be more wrong. The history of man is inseparable from the history of religion. And perhaps it is not too much to say that since the beginning of that history many people have devoutly believed that "more things are wrought by prayer than this world dreams of." It was doubtless largely due to men who believed this that there grew up a sentiment that caused men to leave the cross-currents of officially established state religions and religious persecution in Europe and come to this country filled with the hope that they could find a place in which they could pray when they pleased to the God of their faith in the language they chose. And there were men of this same faith in the power of prayer who led the fight for adoption of our Constitution and also for our Bill of Rights with the very guarantees of religious freedom that forbid the sort of governmental activity which New York has attempted here. These men knew that the First Amendment, which tried to put an end to governmental control of religion and of prayer, was not written to destroy either. They knew rather that it was written to quiet well-justified fears which nearly all of them felt arising out of an awareness that governments of the past had shackled men's tongues to make them speak only the religious thoughts that government wanted them to speak and to pray only to the God that government wanted them to pray to.

It is neither sacrilegious nor antireligious to say that each separate government in this country should stay out of the business of writing or sanctioning official prayers and leave that purely religious function to the people themselves and to those the people choose to look to for religious guidance.

(Judgment reversed.)
Justice Frankfurter did not participate in the consideration and decision.
Justice Douglas concurred.
Justice Steward dissented.

In *School District* v *Shempp,* 374 U.S. 203, 83 S.Ct. 1560, 10 L.Ed. 2d 844 (1963), compulsory reading of ten Bible verses and recitation of the Lord's Prayer each day in a public school were declared to be a violation of the Constitution. ''Applying the Establishment Clause principles to the (case) at bar we find that the states are requiring [these] activities as part of the curricular activities of students who are required by law to attend school.'' The Court also rejected the idea that the concept of governmental neutrality when it comes to religion permits the majority to exert its religious preference on the minority by using state machinery to practice its beliefs.

A Wisconsin law requiring attendance at public or private schools until the age of 16 years old was contested in *Wisconsin* v *Yoder,* 406 U.S. 205, 92 S.Ct. 1526 32 L.Ed. 2d 15 (1972). Yoder and others were members of the Old Order Amish religion. They refused to send their children, ages 14 and 15, to school beyond the eighth grade. For violating the law, Yoder and the other parents were fined $5 each. Their argument in response to the charges was that the compulsory school attendance violated their religious beliefs. The state acknowledged the sincerity of the beliefs, risk of censure in the community, and the prospect of starvation for themselves and their children by continuing to send them to school. The Wisconsin Supreme Court reversed the convictions. On appeal by the state, the United States Supreme Court affirmed the Wisconsin Supreme Court's holding.

Free Exercise of Religion

West Virginia State Board of Education v *Barnette*
319 U.S. 624, 63 S.Ct. 1178, 87 L.Ed. 1628 (1943)

Following a United States Supreme Court decision (*Minersville School District* v *Gobitis, infra.*) upholding the constitutionality of a Pennsylvania town regulation requiring students and teachers to salute the flag, the West Virginia legislature passed an act requiring all state schools to teach specific subjects to foster and perpetuate the ideals, principles, and spirit of Americanism. Pursuant to this enactment, the State Board of Education mandated that all students salute the flag as part of usual school activities. A student who did not comply would be cited for insubordination and expelled. Afterward he would be treated as a delinquent. Parents were liable for prosecution and a fine of $50 and 30 days in jail. Barnette sought to enjoin compulsory flag saluting because it would require his children to violate a religious commandment not to worship any graven image. The complaint was dismissed by the Board of Education. A federal district court granted the injunction and the Board appealed. The United States Supreme Court upheld the federal district court ruling.

Justice Jackson delivered the opinion of the Court:

The freedom asserted by these appellees does not bring them into collision with rights asserted by any other individual. . . . The sole conflict is between authority and rights of the individual. The state asserts power to condition access to public education on making a prescribed sign and profession and at the same time to coerce attendance by punishing both parent and child. The latter stand on a right of self-determination in matters that touch individual opinion and personal attitude.

As the present Chief Justice said in dissent in the *Gobitis* case, the state may "require teaching by instruction and study of all in our history and in the structure and organization of our government, including the guaranties of civil liberty which tend to inspire patriotism and love of country." . . . Here, however, we are dealing with a compulsion of students to declare a belief. . . . The issue here is whether this slow and easily neglected route to aroused loyalties constitutionally may be shortcut by substituting a compulsory salute and slogan.

There is no doubt that, in connection with the pledges, the flag salute is a form of utterance. Symbolism is a primitive but effective way of communicating ideas. The use of an emblem or flag to symbolize some system, idea, institution, or personality, is a shortcut from mind to mind. Causes and nations, political parties, lodges, and ecclesiastical groups seek to knit the loyalty of their followings to a flag or banner, a color or design. The state announces rank, function, and authority through crowns and maces, uniforms and black robes; the church speaks through the cross, the crucifix, the altar and shrine, and clerical raiment. Symbols of state often convey political ideas just as religious symbols come to convey theological ones. Associated with many of these symbols are appropriate gestures of acceptance or respect: a salute, a bowed or bared head, a bended knee. A person gets from a symbol the meaning he puts into it, and what is one man's comfort and inspiration is another's jest and scorn.

Whether the First Amendment to the Constitution will permit officials to order observance of ritual of this nature does not depend upon whether as a voluntary exercise we would think it to be good, bad, or merely innocuous. Any credo of nationalism is likely to include what some disapprove or to omit what others think essential, and to give off different overtones as it takes on different accents or interpretations.

. . .

Nor does the issue as we see it turn on one's possession of particular religious views or the sincerity with which they are held. While religion supplies appellees' motive for enduring the discomforts of making the issue in this case, many citizens who do not share these religious views hold such a compulsory rite to infringe constitutional liberty of the individual. It is not necessary to inquire whether nonconformist beliefs will exempt from the duty to salute unless we first find power to make the salute a legal duty.

. . .

The Fourteenth Amendment, as now applied to the states, protects the citizen against the state itself and all of its creatures—boards of education not excepted. These have, of course, important, delicate, and highly discretionary functions, but none that they may not perform within the limits of the Bill of Rights. That they are educating the young for citizenship is reason for scrupulous protection of constitutional freedoms of the individual, if we are not to strangle the free mind at its source and teach youth to discount important principles of our government as mere platitudes.

. . .

The very purpose of a Bill of Rights was to withdraw certain subjects from the vicissitudes of political controversy, to place them beyond the reach of majorities and officials, and to establish them as legal principles to be applied by the courts. One's right to life, liberty, and property, to free speech, a free press, freedom of worship and assembly, and other fundamental rights may not be submitted to vote; they depend on the outcome of no elections.

National unity as an end which officials may foster by persuasion and example is not in question. The problem is whether under our Constitution compulsion as here employed is a permissible means for its achievement.

Struggles to coerce uniformity of sentiment in support of some end thought essential to their time and country have been waged by many good as well as by evil men. Nationalism is a relatively recent phenomenon but at other times and places the ends have been racial or territorial security, support of a dynasty or regime, and particular plans for saving souls. As first and moderate methods to attain unity have failed, those bent on its accomplishment must resort to an ever-increasing severity. . . . Ultimate futility of such attempts to compel coherence is the lesson of every effort from the Roman drive to stamp out Christianity as a disturber of its pagan unity, the Inquisition, as a means to religious and dynastic unity, the Siberian exiles as a means to Russian unity, down to the fast-failing efforts of our present totalitarian enemies. Those who begin coercive elimination of dissent soon find themselves exterminating dissenters. Compulsory unification of opinion achieves only the unanimity of the graveyard.

It seems trite but necessary to say that the First Amendment to our Constitution was designed to avoid these ends by avoiding these beginnings. There is no mysticism in the American concept of the state or of the nature or origin of its authority. We set up government by consent of the governed, and the Bill of

Rights denies those in power any legal opportunity to coerce that consent. Authority here is to be controlled by public opinion, not public opinion by authority.

The case is made difficult not because the principles of its decision are obscure but because the flag involved is our own. Nevertheless, we apply the limitations of the Constitution with no fear that freedom to be intellectually and spiritually diverse or even contrary will disintegrate the social organization. To believe that patriotism will not flourish if patriotic ceremonies are voluntary and spontaneous instead of a compulsory routine is to make an unflattering estimate of the appeal of our institutions to free minds. We can have intellectual individualism and the rich cultural diversities that we owe to exceptional minds only at the price of occasional eccentricity and abnormal attitudes. When they are so harmless to others or to the state as those we deal with here, the price is not too great. But freedom to differ is not limited to things that do not matter much. That would be a mere shadow of freedom. The test of its substance is the right to differ as to things that touch the heart of the existing order.

If there is any fixed star in our constitutional constellation, it is that no official, high or petty, can prescribe what shall be orthodox in politics, nationalism, religion, or other matters of opinion or force citizens to confess by word or act their faith therein. If there are any circumstances which permit an exception, they do not now occur to us.

. . .

(Judgment affirmed.)
Justices Black, Douglas, and Murphy concurred.
Justices Roberts, Reed, and Frankfurter dissented.

The United States Supreme Court allowed a state statute requiring all public school children to salute the national flag to stand in *Minersville School District* v *Gobitis,* 310 U.S. 586, 60 S.Ct. 1010 84 L.Ed. 1375 (1940). The Gobitis children were members of the Jehovah's Witnesses, a religious sect that forbade the salute to any flag, since the Bible was viewed as the "supreme authority" and allegiance to a national flag conflicted with this belief. Upon refusal to participate in the daily ritual of a flag salute, the Gobitis children were expelled from public school. The United States Supreme Court reversed a Court of Appeals decision to grant relief to the Gobitis family. Although the Court stated that "every possible leeway should be given to the claims of religious faith when a man's conception of religious duty conflicts with the secular interests of his fellow man," it found that the state had a responsibility to promote national cohesiveness. The requirement of the flag salute of public school children did not violate their protected religious freedoms, since "the mere possession of religious convictions which contradict the relevant concerns of a political discharge of political responsibilities." According to the Court, the flag salute could be validly considered by the state to be a "political responsibility."

No state can pass a law that favors persons who believe in the existence of God, according to the majority opinion in *Torcaso* v *Watkins,* 367 U.S. 488, 81 S.Ct. 1680, 6 L.Ed. 2d 982 (1961). On this basis, a Maryland statute which required public officials to express a belief in God was held unconstitutional. Further, the Court stated that no law can favor believers over atheists, or persons of one religion over persons of other religions. The Constitution not only prohibits the establishment of a state religion, but it also prohibits the aid or denial of aid on the basis of religious expression.

The Fourteenth Amendment makes the First Amendment applicable to the states, according to the decision in *Pierce* v *Society of Sisters,* 268 U.S. 510, 45 S.Ct. 571, 69 L.Ed. 1070 (1925). The state cannot abridge the freedom of religion guaranteed its citizens by the First Amendment. A state statute that required all children within the state to attend public schools was, therefore, unconstitutional. Further, the statute interfered with the property rights of private schools because it was "arbitrary, unreasonable, and unlawful interference" in the business of private education. The parents of children have a constitutional right to send their children to religious schools which otherwise meet the reasonable state requirements concerning education. (See *Kunz* v *New York* in Chapter 5.)

Martin v *City of Struthers*

319 U.S. 141, 63 S.Ct. 862, 87 L.Ed. 1313 (1943)

A City of Struthers' ordinance made it illegal for any person to distribute handbills, circulars, or other advertisements, or to ring a doorbell, sound the knocker, or otherwise summon the inmates of a home to have them receive the same. The defendant was a Jehovah's Witness who delivered leaflets advertising a religious meeting. She was convicted of violating the ordinance and fined $100. She appealed her conviction to the United States Supreme Court arguing that the ordinance as construed and applied was beyond the power of the state because it violated the right to freedom of the press and religion as guaranteed by the First and Fourteenth Amendments.

Justice Black delivered the opinion of the Court:

The right of freedom of speech and press has broad scope. The authors of the First Amendment knew that novel and unconventional ideas might disturb the complacent, but they chose to encourage a freedom which they believed essential if vigorous enlightenment was ever to triumph over slothful ignorance. This freedom embraces the right to distribute literature, . . . and necessarily protects the right to receive it. The privilege may not be withdrawn even if it creates the minor nuisance for a community of cleaning litter from its streets. . . . Yet the peace, good order, and comfort of the community may imperatively require regulation of the time, place, and manner of distribution.

. . .

We are faced in the instant case with the necessity of weighing the conflicting interests of the appellant in the civil rights she claims, as well as the right of the individual householder to determine whether he is willing to receive her message, against the interest of the community which by this ordinance offers to protect the interests of all of its citizens, whether particular citizens want that protection or not. The ordinance does not control anything but the distribution of literature, and in that respect it substitutes the judgment of the community for the judgment of the individual householder. It submits the distributor to criminal punishment for annoying the person on whom he calls, even though the recipient of the literature distributed is in fact glad to receive it. In considering legislation which thus limits the dissemination of knowledge, we must "be astute to examine the effect of the challenged legislation" and must "weigh the circumstances and . . . appraise the substantiality of the reasons advanced in support of the regulation."

. . .

Ordinances of the sort now before us may be aimed at the protection of the householders from annoyance, including intrusion upon the hours of rest, and at the prevention of crime. . . . In the instant case, for example, it is clear from the record that the householder to whom the appellant gave the leaflet which led to her arrest was more irritated than pleased with her visitor. The City, which is an industrial community most of whose residents are engaged in the iron and steel industry, has vigorously argued that its inhabitants frequently work on swing shifts, working nights and sleeping days so that casual bell pushers might seriously interfere with the hours of sleep although they call at high noon. In addition, burglars frequently pose as canvassers, either in order that they may have a pretense to discover whether a house is empty and hence ripe for burglary, or for the purpose of spying out the premises in order that they may return later. Crime prevention may thus be the purpose of regulatory ordinances.

Freedom to distribute information to every citizen wherever he desires to receive it is so clearly vital to the prevention of a free society that, putting aside reasonable police and health regulations of time and manner of distribution, it must be fully preserved. The dangers of distribution can so easily be controlled by traditional legal methods, leaving to each householder the full right to decide whether he will receive strangers as visitors, that stringent prohibition can serve no purpose but that forbidden by the Constitution, the naked restriction of the dissemination of ideas.

Traditionally the American law punishes persons who enter onto the property of another after having been warned by the owner to keep off. General trespass after warning statutes exist in at least 20 states, while similar statutes of narrower scope are on the books of a least 12 states more. We know of no state which, as does the Struthers ordinance in effect, makes a person a criminal trespasser if he enters the property of another for an innocent purpose without an explicit command from the owners to stay away. The National Institute of Municipal Law Officers has proposed a form of regulation to its member cities which would make it an offense for any person to ring the bell of a householder who has appropriately indicated that he is unwilling to be disturbed. This or any similar regulation leaves the decision as to whether distributors of literature may lawfully call at a home where it belongs—with the homeowner himself. A city can punish those who call at a home in defiance of the previously expressed will of the occupant and, in addition, can by identification devices control the abuse of the privilege by criminals posing as canvassers. In any case the problem must be worked out by each community for itself with due respect for the constitutional rights of those desiring to distribute literature and those desiring to receive it, as well as those who choose to exclude such distributors from the home.

The Struthers ordinance does not safeguard these constitutional rights. For this reason, and wholly aside from any other possible defects, on which we do not pass but which are suggested in other opinions filed in this case, we conclude that the ordinance is invalid because in conflict with the freedom of speech and press.

(Judgment reversed.)
Justice Murphy concurred.

In *United States* v *Seeger,* 380 U.S. 163, 85 S.Ct. 850, 13 L.Ed. 2d 733 (1965), the status of conscientious objector was denied to defendant Seeger. The Universal Military Training and Service Act, 50 U.S.C.A. App. 456(j), exempts from combat military service those persons who are conscientiously opposed to participation in war in any form by reason of their religious beliefs and training. Seeger was convicted in federal district court for refusal to submit to induction. Although he claimed to be a conscientious objector, he did not subscribe to the belief necessary to be declared a conscientious objector, i.e., his refusal had to be impelled from a ''belief in relation to a Supreme Being,'' as distinguished from a personal moral code based on his political, social, or philosophical views. Although he professed belief in goodness, virtue, and religious faith in a purely ethical creed, his request for exemption was denied because it did not meet the standard set forth in the law. Seeger was convicted of refusing to be inducted. The United States Court of Appeals and the United States Supreme Court upheld the claim of exemption.

In summary, Seeger professed ''religious belief'' and ''religious faith.'' He did not disavow any belief ''in relation to a Supreme Being''; indeed he stated that ''the cosmic order does perhaps, suggest a creative intelligence.'' He decried the tremendous ''spiritual'' price man must pay for his willingness to destroy human life. In light of his beliefs and the unquestioned sincerity with which he held them, we think the Board, had it applied the test we propose today, would have granted him the exemption. We think it clear that the beliefs which prompted his objection occupy the same place in his life as the belief in a traditional deity holds in the lives of his friends, the Quakers. . . . It may be that Seeger did not clearly demonstrate what his beliefs were with regard to the usual understanding of the term "Supreme Being." But as we have said Congress did not intend that to be the test. We therefore affirm the judgment.

In *Braunfeld* v *Brown,* 366 U.S. 599, 81 S.Ct. 1144, 6 L.Ed. 2d 563 (1961), the United States Supreme Court found a Pennsylvannia statute requiring the Sunday closing of all retail business establishments to be valid on its face. Braunfeld, an Orthodox Jew, operated a clothing and furniture business. Since his religious beliefs prevented him from working on Saturday, the Jewish Sabbath, he opened his store for business on Sunday. He sought a permanent injunction against the enforcement of the state statute requiring the closing of his business on Sunday. His arguments before the Court included the claim that the law hindered the practice of his religion, since he was not able to stay open on Saturday and the law disallowed his operation on Sunday. His competitors, then, were allowed six working days in the week and a day of Sabbath, but he could enjoy the economic benefits of only five working days if he complied with his religious precepts and the state law. The Court, however, stated that the state has the power to regulate matters affecting its citizenry, and if the state were required to allow each citizen the same economic opportunities, regardless of religious restrictions on their activity, that the regulation of matters within the state's jurisdiction would be complex and inefficient. Since the regulation before the Court in this case was an indirect effect on the combination of the state law and the religious law, the appellant's right to freedom to expression was not being infringed upon. Only such laws whose indirect effects are utilized by the state in order to impede the observance of religious activities or to discriminate between religious bodies can be found unconstitutional.

PRESS

Gitlow v *New York*

268 U.S. 652, 45 S.Ct., 625, 69 L.Ed. 1138 (1925)

Supra p-127

New York Times Company v *United States*

403 U.S. 670, 91 S.Ct. 2140, 29 L.Ed. 2d 822 (1971)

This case is referred to as the "Pentagon Papers Case." The *Times* had possession of a multi-volume analysis of a major defense study. The volumes were turned over the the *Times* by Daniel Ellsberg, a contributor to the study. In companion actions the United States government sought an injunction restraining publication by the *Times* and *The Washington Post.* The federal district courts refused to restrain publication and the government appealed. The Court of Appeals in New York (Second Circuit) remanded the case for further hearing and the

District of Columbia Court of Appeals affirmed the ruling of one district court. Both the government and *The New York Times* sought review by the United States Supreme Court which affirmed the District of Columbia Circuit and reversed the Second Circuit.

Per Curiam

We granted certiorari in these cases, 403 U.S. 942, 943, 91 S.Ct. 2270, 2271, 29 L.Ed. 2d 853 (1971), in which the United States seeks to enjoin *The New York Times* and *The Washington Post* from publishing the contents of a classified study entitled "History of U.S. Decision-Making Process on Vietnam Policy."

Any system of prior restraints of expression comes to this Court bearing a heavy presumption against its constitutional validity." *Bantam Books, Inc.* v *Sullivan,* 372 U.S. 58, 70, 83 S.Ct. 631, 639, 9 L.Ed. 2d 584 (1963); see also *Near* v *Minnesota ex rel.* Olson, 283 U.S. 697, 51 S.Ct. 625, 75 L.Ed. 1357 (1931). The government "thus carries a heavy burden of showing justification for the imposition of such a restraint." *Organization for a Better Austin* v *Keefe,* 402 U.S. 415, 419, 91 S.Ct. 1575, 1578, 29 L.Ed. 2d 1 (1971). The District Court for the Southern District of New York in *The New York Times* Case, 328 F.Supp. 324, and the District Court for the District of Columbia and the Court of Appeals for the District of Columbia Circuit, 446 F.2d 1327, in *The Washington Post* Case held that the government had not met that burden. We agree.

The judgment of the Court of Appeals for the District of Columbia Circuit is therefore affirmed. The order of the Court of Appeals for the Second Circuit is reversed, 444 F.2d 544, and the case is remanded with directions to enter a judgment affirming the judgment of the District Court for the Southern District of New York. The stays entered June 25, 1971, by the Court are vacated. The judgments shall issue forth.

So ordered.

Judgment of the Court of Appeals for the District of Columbia Circuit affirmed; order of the Court of Appeals for the Second Circuit reversed and case remanded with directions.

Justice Black joined by Justice Douglas concurred separately.

Justice Douglas joined by Justice Black concurred separately.

Justice Brennan concurred separately.

Justice Stewart joined by Justice White concurred separately.

Justice White joined by Justice Stewart concurred separately.

Justice Marshall concurred separately.

Chief Justice Burger dissented separately

Justice Harlan, Chief Justice Burger, and Justice Blackmun dissented separately.

United States v *Caldwell*

408 U.S. 665, 92 S.Ct. 2646, 33 L.Ed. 2d 626 (1972)

In one of several cases, Paul Branzburg, a reporter for the *Louisville Courier–Journal*, wrote an article on the processing of hashish from marijuana. At a grand jury investigation of drug traffic, he was ordered by a judge to answer grand jury questions seeking the identity of the persons he saw manufacturing hashish. Branzburg refused and brought suit to restrain Judge Hayes from imposing a comtempt holding. The Kentucky Court of Appeals denied Branzburg's petition and argument that he had immunity from disclosure of the testimony from the guarantees of the freedom of the press.

Pappas and Caldwell refused to testify before grand juries regarding what they observed and heard while visiting Black Panther headquarters during a civil dispute. No articles were ever published following the events. Caldwell refused to answer questions about interviews with the militants. The United States Supreme Court granted certiorari and held that requiring newsmen to answer questions before federal and state grand juries does not abridge the speech and press guarantees of the First Amendment.

Opinion of the Court by Justice White, announced by the Chief Justice:

The issue in these cases is whether requiring newsmen to appear and testify before state or federal grand juries abridges the freedom of speech and press guaranteed by the First Amendment. We hold that it does not.

. . .

Petitioners Branzburg and Pappas and respondent Caldwell press First Amendment claims that may be simply put: that to gather news it is often necessary to agree either not to identify the source of information published or to publish only part of the facts revealed, or both; that if the reporter is nevertheless forced to reveal these confidences to a grand jury, the source so identified and other confidential sources of other reporters will be measurably deterred from furnishing publishable information, all to the detriment of the free flow of information protected by the First Amendment. . . . The heart of the claim is that the burden on news gathering resulting from compelling reporters to disclose confidential information outweighs any public interest in obtaining the information.

. . .

The sole issue before us is the obligation of reporters to respond to grand jury subpoenas as other citizens do and to answer questions relevant to an investigation into the commission of crime.

. . .

It is clear that the First Amendment does not invalidate every incidental burdening of the press that may result from the enforcement of civil or criminal statutes of general applicability.

. . .

The prevailing view is that the press is not free to publish with impunity everything and anything it desires to publish. Although it may deter or regulate what is said or published, the press may not circulate knowing or reckless falsehoods damaging to private reputation without subjecting itself to liability for damages, including punitive damages, or even criminal prosecution. A newspaper or a journalist may also be punished for contempt of court, in appropriate circumstances.

. . .

It has generally been held that the First Amendment does not guarantee the press a constitutional right of special access to information not available to the public generally.

. . .

. . . Newsmen have no constitutional right of access to the scenes of crime or disaster when the general public is excluded, and they may be prohibited from attending or publishing information about trials if such restrictions are necessary to assure a defendant a fair trial before an impartial tribunal.
. . . In 1958, a news gatherer asserted for the first time that the First Amendment exempted confidential information from public disclosure pursuant to a subpoena issued in a civil suit, . . . but the claim was denied, and this argument has been almost uniformly rejected since then although there are occasional dicta that, in circumstances not presented here, a newsman might be excused. . . . These courts have applied the presumption against the existence of an asserted testimonial privilege . . . and have concluded that the First Amendment interest asserted by the newsman was outweighed by the general obligation of a citizen to appear before a grand jury or at trial, pursuant to a subpoena, and give what information he possesses. The opinions of the state courts in *Branzburg* and *Pappas* are typical of the prevailing view, although a few recent cases, such as *Caldwell,* have recognized and given effect to some form of constitutional newsman's privilege.

. . .

Finally, as we have earlier indicated, news gathering is not without its First Amendment protections, and grand jury investigations if instituted or conducted other than in good faith, would pose wholly different issues for resolution under the First Amendment. Official harassment of the press undertaken not for purposes of law enforcement but to disrupt a reporter's relationship with his news sources would have no justification. Grand juries are subject to judicial control and subpoenas to motions to quash. We do not expect courts will forget that grand juries must operate within the limits of the First Amendment as well as the Fifth.

(Judgment affirmed.)   . . .
Justices Stewart, Brennan, Marshall, and Douglas dissented.

QUESTIONS

1. Compare the cases dealing with advocacy and membership in subversive organizations to the cases in the section dealing with civil rights demonstrations. Is there any common ground showed by these decisions?

2. What is "prior restraint?" Do these decisions affect any of the others?

3. Interpret *Young* v *American Mini Theatres* in terms of the local community. What is the major goal of this decision?

4. How does the *Time, Inc.* v *Firestone* decision affect the press? What are the future implications of this decision?

5. Discuss the evolution of the Court's decisions in the area of religious freedoms. What is the position of the Court in regard to freedom of religion?

7

EQUAL PROTECTION OF THE LAW (FOURTEENTH AMENDMENT)

The year 1870 brought the judicial construction of the Thirteenth, Fourteenth, and Fifteenth Amendments which concerned the racial minorities in this country. These amendments were originally intended to benefit black freedmen, but they reach every race and individual whether Japanese, Arab, or Anglo-Saxon. Specifically, the Fourteenth Amendment provides that no state is permitted to "deny to any person within its jurisdiction the equal protection of the laws." In short, this provision ensures that minorities shall not be permitted to be the object of discrimination.

In the last half of the twentieth century no political issues have had greater significance than the problem of racial discrimination. In 1954 the United States Supreme Court established in the landmark case of *Brown* v *Board of Education,* 347 U.S. 483 (1954), that segregation in public schools is unconstitutional. This decision led to a march toward the ideal of elimination of discrimination because of ethnic or racial backgrounds.

Throughout the history of the Fourteenth Amendment there has not been a great deal of controversy regarding the meaning of its express ban on state discrimination against racial groups. The Fourteenth Amendment does not expressly cover, however, discrimination by private persons or organizations. The ban is directed toward the state's open support of discrimination. This is indi-

175

cated in the specific language of the amendment which protects the individual or offers him some type of redress. Consequently, the major issue involves *what amounts to state action*. The cases and materials in this chapter show the expanding nature of the concept of state action. One can note that the expansion has been particularly rapid since World War II which can be described as a period of social concern and identity consciousness. This national awakening acted as a stimulus for the 1954 decision declaring public school segregation to be unconstitutional. Since this decision, minority group treatment has been at the forefront of the social issues facing this country. Discrimination because of race, creed, or ethnic considerations has been attacked as being morally wrong, dangerous, and wasteful from an economic perspective.

The problem of equal protection under the law involves three separate considerations:

1. The right of Americans to live their own lives and be as arbitrary as they wish in their decisions.

2. The state power to regulate such matters as housing and employment.

3. The Constitutional mandate as it affects the concept of "state action."

The Constitution does not prohibit private acts of discrimination, but the states have enacted laws making private acts of discrimination in housing, employment, and public accommodations illegal under the state police and regulatory powers. In other words, the basic conflict arises over the right of minorities not to be discriminated against because of race, creed, or national origin.

Among other cases in this chapter, issues involving free sectarian schools, the role of education in America, the extent to which the Constitution guarantees equal educational opportunity, and the extent to which the government may go to promote equal education for all students will be explored. The problems of racial discrimination and classification are closely tied together with the issue of segregation in the public schools. The American public school system has been a major agency for ensuring the workability of self-government and the perpetuation of freedom. It has been the unifying force for bringing the American people together into an integrated society. It has provided unprecedented opportunities to all who have had access to it. Unfortunately, whole segments of our society have been denied the benefits of an education because of inadequate educational opportunities.

Until 1954 the "separate but equal" doctrine of *Plessy* v *Ferguson*, 163 U.S. 537 (1896), was the law of the land. This concept died with the *Brown* decision announced by Chief Justice Earl Warren who stated that separate educational facilities are inherently unequal. Therefore, those individuals compelled to seek an education in such a system "are deprived of equal protection of the laws guaranteed by the Fourteenth Amendment."

Transition from segregation to integration has been extremely difficult. The

Brown decision and how to carry it out have been the subject of bitter controversy. In 1955 the second *Brown* v *Board of Education,* 349 U.S. 294 (1955), decreed that public schools had to be desegregated "with all deliberate speed." In some states, usually those that have small black populations, desegregation took place with little difficulty. In other states desegregation met with massive resistance and was often accompanied by violence. In some places in the South desegration is still an issue, but the battleground is shifting to the massive *de facto* segregation that exists in cities in the North.

The 1964 Civil Rights Act and the 1965 Elementary and Secondary Education Act made an attempt to ensure equality in education opportunity and thus encourage school desegregation. Title IV of the Civil Rights Act authorizes the United States commissioner of education to make personnel and information available to aid in desegregation upon the request of a school board. He is also authorized to conduct training courses on specific problems involving desegregation of schools, make grants to schools to assist them in alleviating problems, and provide grants for hiring outside consultants. The commissioner was also directed to report on the status of equality of educational opportunity. One of the most important powers given to the commissioner is the duty to withhold federal funds from school districts unless there is compliance with a final court order or a promise to comply if one is rendered.

The scope of the Equal Protection Clause of the Fourteenth Amendment has become increasingly important in the criminal courts. Its use has been expanded in order to fully protect those individuals who, for reasons of racial, sexual, or religious status, have not previously been provided with the full benefits of advice and counsel so readily available to more affluent defendants. There is often an interplay between various constitutional amendments (for example, the Sixth Amendment's provision for counsel and the Fifth Amendment's privilege against self-incrimination) which comes into being in this often complex and confusing area of criminal due process of the law. The materials presented in this chapter must not be read in isolation. Instead, they must be related to the impact on criminal procedure as the United States Supreme Court has seen fit to interpret the Fourth, Fifth, and Sixth Amendments.

United States v *Guest*
383 U.S. 745, 86 S.Ct. 1170, 16 L.Ed. 2d 239 (1966)

Six defendants, including Guest, were indicted by a United States grand jury for conspiracy to violate the rights of black citizens by depriving them of specific rights secured by the laws and Constitution of the United States. The United States District Court sustained the defendant's motion to dismiss the indictment on the ground that it did not charge an offense against the laws of the United States. On a direct appeal to the United States Supreme Court by the United States, the Court primarily dealt with issues of statutory construction rather than constitutional power.

Justice Stewart delivered the opinion of the Court:

The second numbered paragraph of the indictment alleges that the defendants conspired to injure, oppress, threaten, and intimidate Negro citizens of the United States in the free exercise and enjoyment of:

> The right to the equal utilization, without discrimination upon the basis of race, of public facilities in the vicinity of Athens, Georgia, owned, operated, or managed by or on behalf of the State of Georgia or any subdivision thereof.

Correctly characterizing this paragraph as embracing rights protected by the Equal Protection Clause of the Fourteenth Amendment, the District Court held as a matter of statutory construction that 18 U.S.C. 241 does not encompass any Fourteenth Amendment rights, and further held as a matter of constitutional law that "any broader construction of 241 . . . would render it void for indefiniteness." . . . In so holding, the District Court was in error, as our opinion in *United States* v *Price,* 383 U.S. 787, . . . , decided today, makes abundantly clear.

Moreover, inclusion of Fourteenth Amendment rights within the compass of 18 U.S.C. 241 does not render the statute unconstitutionally vague. Since the gravamen of the offense is conspiracy, the requirement that the offender must act with a specific intent to interfere with the federal rights in question is satisfied. . . . And the rights under the Equal Protection Clause described by this paragraph of the indictment have been so firmly and precisely established by a consistent line of decisions in this Court, that the lack of specification of these rights in the language of §241 itself can raise no serious constitutional question on the ground of vagueness or indefiniteness.

This case, however, requires no determination of the threshold level that state action must attain in order to create rights under the Equal Protection Clause. This is so because, contrary to the argument of the litigants, the indictment in fact contains an express allegation of state involvement sufficient at least to require the denial of a motion to dismiss.

. . .

The fourth numbered paragraph of the indictment alleged that the defendants conspired to injure, oppress, threaten, and intimidate black citizens of the United States in the free exercise and enjoyment of:

> the right to travel freely to and from the State of Georgia and to use highway facilities and other instrumentalities of interstate commerce within the *State of Georgia.*

The District Court was in error in dismissing the indictment as to this paragraph.

. . .

Although there have been recurring differences in emphasis within the Court as to the source of the constitutional right of interstate travel, there is no need here to canvass those differences further. All have agreed that the right exists.

. . .

This does not mean, of course, that every criminal conspiracy affecting an individual's right of free interstate passage is within the sanction of 18 U.S.C. 241.... If the predominant purpose of the conspiracy is to impede or prevent the exercise of the right of interstate travel, or to oppress a person because of his exercise of that right, then, whether or not motivated by racial discrimination, the conspiracy becomes a proper object of the federal law under which the indictment in this case was brought. Accordingly, it was error to grant the motion to dismiss on this branch of the indictment.

(Judgment reversed.)
Justice Clark, joined by Justices Fortas and Black, concurred:

The Court carves out of its opinion the question of the power of Congress, under Section 5 of the Fourteenth Amendment, to enact legislation implementing the Equal Protection Clause or any other provision of the Fourteenth Amendment.

. . .

... I believe, [it is] both appropriate and necessary under the circumstances here to say that there now can be no doubt that the specific language of Section 5 empowers the Congress to enact laws punishing all conspiracies—with or without state action—that interfere with Fourteenth Amendment rights.

Justice Harlan concurred in part and dissented in part:

I join Parts I and II of the Court's opinion, but I cannot subscribe to Part III in its full sweep.

. . .

Preliminarily, nothing in the Constitution expressly secures the right to travel.

. . .

Justice Brennan, joined by Justice Douglas and the Chief Justice, dissented in part and concurred in part.

RACIAL DISCRIMINATION AND CLASSIFICATION

Loving v *Virginia*

388 U.S. 1, 87 S.Ct. 1817, 18 L.Ed. 2d 1010 (1967)

The state of Virginia adopted a statute that prevented marriages between persons of different races. Loving, a white man, married a black woman in the District of Columbia. They later moved to Virginia where they lived as husband and wife. They were indicted under the Virginia antimiscegenation statute that prohibited interracial marriages involving white persons. The question of the constitutionality of the Virginia statutory scheme prohibiting interracial marriages was ultimately appealed to the United States Supreme Court after conviction of the Lovings.

Chief Justice Warren delivered the opinion of the Court:

Virginia is now one of 16 states which prohibit and punish marriages on the basis of racial classifications. Penalties for miscegenation arose as an incident to slavery and have been common in Virginia since the colonial period. The present statutory scheme dates from the adoption of the Racial Integrity Act of 1924, passed during the period of extreme nativism which followed the end of the First World War.

There can be no question but that Virginia's miscegenation statutes rest solely upon distinctions drawn according to race. The statutes proscribe generally accepted conduct if engaged in by members of different races. Over the years, this Court has consistently repudiated "[d]istinctions between citizens solely because of their ancestry" as being "odious to a free people whose institutions are founded upon the doctrine of equality." . . . At the very least, the Equal Protection Clause demands that racial classifications, especially suspect in criminal statutes, be subjected to the "most rigid scrutiny," . . . and, if they are ever to be upheld, they must be shown to be necessary to the accomplishment of some permissible state objective, independent of the racial discrimination which it was the object of the Fourteenth Amendment to eliminate. Indeed, two members of this Court have already stated that they "cannot conceive of a valid legislative purpose . . . which makes the color of a person's skin the test of whether his conduct is a criminal offense."

. . .

There is patently no legitimate overriding purpose independent of invidious racial discrimination which justifies this classification. . . . There can be no doubt that restricting the freedom to marry solely because of racial classifications violates the central meaning of the Equal Protection Clause.

These statutes also deprive the Lovings of liberty without due process of law in violation of the Due Process Clause of the Fourteenth Amendment. The freedom to marry has long been recognized as one of the vital personal rights essential to the orderly pursuit of happiness by free men.

Marriage is one of the "basic civil rights of man," fundamental to our very existence and survival. . . . To deny this fundamental freedom on so unsupportable a basis as the racial classifications embodied in these statutes, classifications so directly subversive of the principle of equality at the heart of the Fourteenth Amendment, is surely to deprive all the state's citizens of liberty without due process of law. The Fourteenth Amendment requires that the freedom of choice to marry not be restricted by invidious racial discriminations. Under our Constitution, the freedom to marry or not marry a person of another race resides with the individual and cannot be infringed by the state.

(Convictions reversed.)
Justice Stewart concurred.

The United States Supreme Court found a city ordinance permitting picketing for one topic and denying it for another an unconstitutional barrier to the Fourteenth Amendment's guarantee to equal protection under the law. In *Police Department of Chicago* v *Mosley,* 408 U.S. 92, 92 S.Ct. 2286, 33 L.Ed. 2d 212 (1972), the Court considered an ordinance that limited picketing within 150 feet of a school. The subject matter of the expression, rather than the medium itself, was regulated by the ordinance contrary to the First and Fourteenth Amendments. Legal protection was extended by the ordinance to the individual in a manner dependent solely on the content of an expressive activity, thus restricting freedom of speech as well as the equality of legal protection. The Court found that the ordinance in question failed to offer the citizens their constitutional right to express ideas not concerned with labor disputes. The state's argument that the regulation of "time, place, and manner" of picketing as being within the government's responsibility to maintain order was found inadequate. These interests must be directly and undisputedly connected to the expressive activity in question, rather than to its content. The judgment was affirmed.

In *Takahashi* v *Fish and Game Commission,* 334 U.S. 410, 68 S.Ct. 1138, 92 L.Ed. 1478 (1948), the limitation of the occupational activity of persons ineligible for federal citizenship was found to be a denial of the alien's right to equal protection of the law.

The United States Supreme Court found California's attempt to limit the fishing occupation to those eligible for federal citizenship unconstitutional for two reasons. First, the states are not given the power to regulate the activities of legal aliens in this country. The control of immigration is constitutionally given to the federal government. The Court found that in trying to use the federal classification of aliens to limit them within the state boundaries, California overstepped its constitutional prerogative. Second, the state could show no compelling "special public interest" in denying aliens the right to fish commercially. California's argument that its citizens are the collective owners of all fish within three miles of the state's shore failed to convince the Court of the necessity for denying access to those fish *only* to legal aliens. The judgment was reversed.

In *Gomillion* v *Lightfoot,* 364 U.S. 339, 81 S.Ct. 125, 5 L.Ed. 2d 110 (1960), an Alabama statute changed the Tuskegee city boundaries from a square to a 28-sided figure that excluded from the city almost all its black voters but no white voters. The mayor, Lightfoot, was sued by Gomillion, a black, challenging the constitutionality of the act. The complaint was dismissed by the federal district court, and the Court of Appeals affirmed. The United States Supreme Court granted certiorari.

It was the ruling of the Court that when a state exercises power wholly within the domain of state interest, it is insulated from federal judicial review. But such insulation is not carried over when state power is used as an instrument for circumventing a federally protected right. This principle has had many applications. It has long been recognized in cases which have prohibited a state from exploiting a power acknowledged to be absolute in an isolated context to justify the imposition of an "unconstitutional condition." What the Court has said in those cases is equally applicable here, viz., that "acts generally lawful may become unlawful when done to accomplish an unlawful end, . . . a constitutional power cannot be used by way of condition to attain an unconstitutional result."

An ordinance regulating business procedures cannot be used as a means of discrimination against a particular group of persons. A San Francisco law that limited laundry operations to buildings made of stone or brick was found unconstitutional in *Yick Wo* v *Hopkins,* 118 U.S. 356, 6 S.Ct. 1064, 30 L.Ed 220 (1886). Occupational permits were denied to persons firmly entrenched in the occupation on the basis of the ordinance. The Court found that the law, even though fair on its face, was adopted and applied solely as a means of discrimination against a particular racial group. Under these circumstances, the enforcement of the law is a denial of equal protection and is, therefore, unconstitutional. The peculiar facts of this situation showed that only persons of Chinese descent were held liable under the provisions of the permit law and that persons operating businesses under similar conditions who were not Chinese were not denied permits. This established the pattern of discrimination for the Court.

ENFORCEMENT OF RACIAL DISCRIMINATION DECISIONS

Plessy v *Ferguson*
163 U.S. 537, 16 S.Ct. 1138, 41 L.Ed. 256 (1896)

In 1890 the Louisiana legislature enacted a statute requiring that all railway passenger coaches have separate but equal sections for white and black passengers. Plessy was arrested because he refused to leave a seat in the white section of a coach. During the trial Plessy petitioned the state supreme court to enjoin Ferguson, the trial judge, from proceeding with the charge against him. The Louisiana Supreme Court refused. Plessy then took the case to the United States Supreme Court on a writ of error.

Justice Brown delivered the opinion of the Court:

The constitutionality of this act is attacked upon the ground that it conflicts both with the Thirteenth Amendment of the Constitution, abolishing slavery, and the Fourteenth Amendment, which prohibits certain restrictive legislation on the part of the states.

1. That it does not conflict with the Thirteenth Amendment, which abolished slavery and involuntary servitude, except as a punishment for crime, is too clear for argument. Slavery implies involuntary servitude, a state of bondage; the ownership of mankind as a chattel, or, at least, the control of the labor and services of one man for the benefit of another, and the absence of a legal right to the disposal of his own person, property, and services.
. . .

A statute which implies merely a legal distinction between the white and colored races—a distinction which is founded in the color of the two races, and which must always exist so long as white men are distinguished from the other race by color—has no tendency to destroy the legal equality of the two races, or reestablish a state of involuntary servitude.

. . .

2. By the Fourteenth Amendment, all persons born or naturalized in the United States, and subject to the jurisdiction thereof, are made citizens of the United States and of the state wherein they reside; and the states are forbidden from making or enforcing any law which shall abridge the privileges or immunities of citizens of the United States, or shall deprive any person of life, liberty, or property without due process of law, or deny to any person within their jurisdiction the equal protection of the laws.

. . .

The object of the amendment was undoubtedly to enforce the absolute equality of the two races before the law, but, in the nature of things, it could not have been intended to abolish distinctions based upon color, or to enforce social, as distinguished from political, equality, or a commingling of the two races upon terms unsatisfactory to either. Laws permitting, and even requiring, their separation, in places where they are liable to be brought into contact, do not necessarily imply the inferiority of either race to the other, and have been generally, if not universally, recognized as within the competency of the state legislatures in the exercise of their police power.

. . .

The distinction between laws interfering with the political equality of the black and those requiring the separation of the two races in schools, theaters, and railway carriages has been frequently drawn by this Court.

. . .

While we think the enforced separation of the races, as applied to the internal commerce of the state, neither abridges the privileges or immunities of the colored man, deprives him of his property without due process of law, nor denies him the equal protection of the laws, within the meaning of the Fourteenth Amendment, we are not prepared to say that the conductor, in assigning passengers to the coaches according to their race, does not act at his peril, or that the provision of the second section of the act that denies to the passengers compensation in damages for a refusal to receive him into the coach in which he properly belongs is a valid exercise of the legislative power. . . . The power to assign to a particular coach obviously implies the power to determine to which race the passenger belongs, as well as the power to determine who, under the laws of the particular state, is to be deemed a white, and who a colored, person. This question, though indicated in the brief of the plaintiff in error, does not properly arise upon the record in this case, since the only issue made is as to the unconstitutionality of the act, so far as it requires the railway to provide separate accommodations, and the conductor to assign passengers according to their race.

. . .

... Legislation is powerless to eradicate racial instincts, or to abolish distinctions based upon physical differences, and the attempt to do so can only result in accentuating the difficulties of the present situation. If the civil and political rights of both races be equal, one cannot be inferior to the other civilly or politically. If one race be inferior to the other socially, the Constitution of the United States cannot put them upon the same plane.

(Judgment affirmed.)
Justice Harlan dissented:

In respect of civil rights, common to all citizens, the Constitution of the United States does not, I think, permit any public authority to know the race of those entitled to be protected in the enjoyment of such rights. Every true man has pride of race, and under appropriate circumstances, when the rights of others, his equals before the law, are not to be affected, it is his privilege to express such pride and to take such action based upon it as to him seems proper. But I deny that any legislative body or judicial tribunal may have regard to the race of citizens when the civil rights of those citizens are involved. Indeed, such legislation as that here in question is inconsistent not only with that equality of rights which pertains to citizenship, national and state, but with the personal liberty enjoyed by every one within the United States.

The present decision, it may well be apprehended, will not only stimulate aggressions, more or less brutal and irritating, upon the admitted rights of colored citizens, but will encourage the belief that it is possible, by means of state enactments, to defeat the beneficent purposes which the people of the United States had in view when they adopted the recent amendments of the Constitution, by one of which the blacks of this country were made citizens of the United States and of the states in which they respectively reside, and whose privileges and immunities, as citizens, the states are forbidden to abridge.

. . .

I am of opinion that the statute of Louisiana is inconsistent with the personal liberty of citizens, white and black, in that state, and hostile to both the spirit and letter of the Constitution of the United States. If laws of like character should be enacted in the several states of the Union, the effect would be in the highest degree mischievous. Slavery, as an institution tolerated by law, would, it is true, have disappeared from our country; but there would remain a power in the states, by sinister legislation, to interfere with the full enjoyment of the blessings of freedom, to regulate civil rights, common to all citizens, upon the basis of race, and to place in a condition of legal inferiority a large body of American citizens, now constituting a part of the political community, called the "People of the United States," for whom, and by whom through representatives, our government is administered. Such a system is inconsistent with the guaranty given by the Constitution to each state of a republican form of government, and may be stricken down by congressional action, or by the courts in the discharge of their solemn duty to maintain the supreme law of the land, anything in the Constitution or laws of any state to the contrary notwithstanding.

Justice Brennan did not participate in the case.

Brown v *Board of Education*

347 U.S. 483, 74 S.Ct. 686, 98 L.Ed. 873 (1954)

Minor blacks of four states (Kansas, South Carolina, Delaware, and Virginia) in this class action sought to obtain admission to public schools on a nonsegregated basis. In each instance they were denied admission to schools attended by white children under laws mandating or permitting segregation. In every state except Delaware relief was denied. Each state, however, still stated that it adhered to the separate but equal doctrine. On appeal to the federal courts the plaintiffs again were denied relief. The United States Supreme Court granted certiorari.

Chief Justice Warren delivered the opinion of the Court:

Reargument was largely devoted to the circumstances surrounding the adoption of the Fourteenth Amendment in 1868. It covered exhaustively consideration of the Amendment in Congress, ratification by the states, then existing practices in racial segregation, and the views of proponents and opponents of the Amendment. This discussion and our own investigation convince us that, although these sources cast some light, it is not enough to resolve the problem with which we are faced. At best, they are inconclusive. The most avid proponents of the post-War Amendments undoubtedly intended them to remove all legal distinctions among "all persons born or naturalized in the United States." Their opponents, just as certainly, were antagonistic to both the letter and the spirit of the Amendments and wished them to have the most limited effect. What others in Congress and the state legislatures had in mind cannot be determined with any degree of certainty.

An additional reason for the inconclusive nature of the Amendment's history, with respect to segregated schools, is the status of public education at that time. In the South, the movement toward free common schools, supported by general taxation, had not yet taken hold. Education of white children was largely in the hands of private groups. Education of Negroes was almost nonexistent, and practically all of the race were illiterate. In fact, any education of blacks was forbidden by law in some states. Today, in contrast, many Negroes have achieved outstanding success in the arts and sciences as well as in the business and professional world. It is true that public school education at the time of the Amendment had advanced further in the North, but the effect of the Amendment on northern states was generally ignored in the congressional debates. Even in the North, the conditions of public education did not approximate those existing today. The curriculum was usually rudimentary; ungraded schools were common in rural areas; the school term was but three months a year in many states; and compulsory school attendance was virtually unknown. As a consequence, it is not surprising that there should be so little in the history of the Fourteenth Amendment relating to its intended effect on public education.

In the first cases in this Court construing the Fourteenth Amendment, decided shortly after its adoption, the Court interpreted it as proscribing all state-imposed discriminations against the Negro race. The doctrine of "separate but equal" did not make its appearance in this Court until 1896 in the case of *Plessy* v *Ferguson, supra,* involving not education but transportation. American courts have since labored with the doctrine for over half a century.

In approaching this problem, we cannot turn the clock back to 1868 when the Amendment was adopted, or even to 1896 when *Plessy* v *Ferguson* was written. We must consider public education in the light of its full development and its present place in American life throughout the nation. Only in this way can it be determined if segregation in public schools deprives these plaintiffs of the equal protection of the laws.

Today, education is perhaps the most important function of state and local governments. Compulsory school attendance laws and the great expenditures for education both demonstrate our recognition of the importance of education to our democratic society. It is required in the performance of our most basic public responsibilities, even service in the armed forces. It is the very foundation of good citizenship. Today it is a principal instrument in awakening the child to cultural values, in preparing him for later professional training, and in helping him to adjust normally to his environment. In these days, it is doubtful that any child may reasonably be expected to succeed in life if he is denied the opportunity of an education. Such an opportunity, where the state has undertaken to provide it, is a right which must be made available to all on equal terms.

We come then to the question presented: Does segregation of children in public schools solely on the basis of race, even though the physical facilities and other "tangible" factors may be equal, deprive the children of the minority group of educational opportunities? We believe that it does.

In *Sweatt* v *Painter, . . . ,* 339 U.S. 629, . . . , in finding that a segregated law school for blacks could not provide them equal educational opportunities, this Court relied in large part on "those qualities which are incapable of objective measurement but which make for greatness in a law school." In *McLaurin* v *Oklahoma State Regents,* 339 U.S. 637, . . . , the Court, in requiring that a black admitted to a white graduate school be treated like all other students, again resorted to intangible considerations: ". . . his ability to study, to engage in discussions and exchange views with other students, and, in general, to learn his profession." Such considerations apply with added force to children in grade and high schools. To separate them from others of similar age and qualifications solely because of their race generates a feeling of inferiority as to their status in the community that may affect their hearts and minds in a way unlikely ever to be undone. The effect of this separation on their educational opportunities was well stated by a finding in the Kansas case by a court which nevertheless felt compelled to rule against the black plaintiffs:

> Segregation of white and colored children in public schools has a detrimental effect upon the colored children. The impact is greater when it has the sanction of the law; for the policy of separating the races is usually interpreted as denoting the inferiority of the black group. A sense of inferiority affects the motivation of a child to learn. Segregation with the sanction of law, therefore, has a tendency to [retard] the educational and mental development of black children and to deprive them of some of the benefits they would receive in a racial[ly] integrated school system.

Whatever may have been the extent of psychological knowledge at the time of *Plessy* v *Ferguson,* this finding is amply supported by modern authority. Any language in *Plessy* v *Ferguson* contrary to this finding is rejected.

We conclude that in the field of public education the doctrine of ''separate but equal'' has no place. Separate educational facilities are inherently unequal. Therefore, we hold that the plaintiffs and others similarly situated for whom the actions have been brought are, by reason of the segregation complained of, deprived of the equal protection of the laws guaranteed by the Fourteenth Amendment. This disposition makes unnecessary any discussion whether such segregation also violates the Due Process Clause of the Fourteenth Amendment.

Because these are class actions, because of the wide applicability of this decision, and because of the great variety of local conditions, the formulation of decrees in these cases presents problems of considerable complexity. On reargument, the consideration of appropriate relief was necessarily subordinated to the primary question—the constitutionality of segregation in public education. We have now announced that such segregation is a denial of the equal protection of the laws. In order that we may have the full assistance of the parties in formulating decrees, the cases will be restored to the docket, and the parties are requested to present further argument on Questions 4 and 5 previously propounded by the Court for the reargument this Term. The Attorney General of the United States is again invited to participate. The attorneys general of the states requiring or permitting segregation in public education will also be permitted to appear as *amici curiae* upon request to do so by September 15, 1954, and submission of briefs by October 1, 1954.

(Judgment reversed.)

Brown v *Board of Education,* 349 U.S. 294, 75 S.Ct. 753, 99 L.Ed. 2d 1083 (1955), considered the manner in which relief was to be accorded in the immediately preceding case. The decree of the Court was that ''the judgments . . . are remanded to the district courts to take such proceedings and enter such orders

and decrees consistent with this opinion as are necessary and proper to admit to
public schools on a racially nondiscriminatory basis with all deliberate speed the
parties to these cases. . . .''

The Court's stipulations required the courts to have ''the defendants make a
prompt and reasonable start toward full compliance with our May 17, 1954,
ruling. Once such a start has been made, the courts may find that additional time
is necessary to carry out the ruling in an effective manner. *The burden rests upon
the defendants to establish that such time is necessary in the public interest and is
consistent with good faith compliance at the earliest practicable date''* [Author's
italics].

Cooper v *Aaron*

358 U.S. 1, 78 S.Ct. 1401, 3 L.Ed. 2d 5 (1958)

As a result of the United States Supreme Court's decisions in the *Brown* v
Board of Education cases a plan was drawn up in 1955 calling for the complete
desegregation of the Little Rock school system by 1963. The first stage called for
admission of nine black students to Central High School on September 3, 1957.
Evidence indicated that the majority of citizens believed that desegregation was
in the best interests of the students. The Arkansas legislature, however, took
several steps to thwart desegregation. Finally, Governor Faubus sent National
Guard troops to prevent blacks from attending the high school. This action
hardened opposition to the desegregation plan. Subsequently the federal district
court enjoined Governor Faubus and the National Guard from interfering with the
Little Rock school plan. Black students then entered the school under police
protection, but they were later withdrawn because it became too difficult for the
police to control the crowds gathered around the school. President Eisenhower
sent federal troops to enforce the court order.

Cooper petitioned the federal district court to postpone implementation of the
plan because of the foregoing situation. The district court granted the petition.
The Court of Appeals reversed. The United States Supreme Court granted certiorari and upheld the Court of Appeals.

In an unusual show of concern all nine justices signed the opinion of the Court:

In affirming the judgment of the Court of Appeals which reversed the
District Court we have accepted without reservation the position of the school
board, the superintendent of schools, and their counsel that they displayed
entire good faith in the conduct of these proceedings and in dealing with the
unfortunate and distressing sequence of events which has been outlined. We
likewise have accepted the findings of the District Court as to the conditions at
Central High School during the 1957–1958 school year, and also the findings
that the educational progress of all the students, white and colored, of that
school has suffered and will continue to suffer if the conditions which prevailed last year are permitted to continue.

The significance of these findings, however, is to be considered in light of the fact, indisputably revealed by the record before us, that the conditions they depict are directly traceable to the actions of legislators and executive officials of the State of Arkansas, taken in their official capacities, which reflect their own determination to resist this Court's decision in the *Brown* Case and which have brought about violent resistance to that decision in Arkansas. In its petition for certiorari filed in this Court, the school board itself describes the situation in this language: "The legislative, executive, and judicial departments of the state government opposed the desegregation of Little Rock schools by enacting laws, calling out troops, making statements villifying federal law and federal courts, and failing to utilize state law enforcement agencies and judicial processes to maintain public peace."

The constitutional rights of respondents are not to be sacrificed or yielded to the violence and disorder which have followed upon the actions of the governor and legislature. As this Court said some 41 years ago in a unanimous opinion in a case involving another aspect of racial segregation: "It is urged that this proposed segregation will promote the public peace by preventing race conflicts. Desirable as this is, and important as is the preservation of the public peace, this aim cannot be accomplished by laws or ordinances which deny rights created or protected by the federal Constitution." . . . Thus law and order are not here to be preserved by depriving the black children of their constitutional rights. The record before us clearly establishes that the growth of the Board's difficulties to a magnitude beyond its unaided power to control is the product of state action. Those difficulties, as counsel for the Board forthrightly conceded on the oral argument in this Court, can also be brought under control by state action.

The controlling legal principles are plain. The command of the Fourteenth Amendment is that no "state" shall deny to any person within its jurisdiction the equal protection of the laws. "A state acts by its legislative, its executive, or its judicial authorities. It can act in no other way."

· · ·

. . . Thus the prohibitions of the Fourteenth Amendment extend to all action of the state denying equal protection of the laws; whatever the agency of the state taking the action, . . . or whatever the guise in which it is taken, ... In short, the constitutional rights of children not to be discriminated against in school admission on grounds of race or color declared by this Court in the *Brown* Case can neither be nullified openly and directly by state legislators or state executive or judicial officers, nor nullified indirectly by them through evasive schemes for segregation whether attempted "ingeniously or ingenuously."

· · ·

What has been said, in the light of the facts developed, is enough to dispose of the case. However, we should answer the premise of the actions of the governor and legislature that they are not bound by our holding in the *Brown* Case. It is necessary only to recall some basic constitutional propositions which are settled doctrine.

Article VI of the Constitution makes the Constitution the ''supreme law of the land.'' In 1803, Chief Justice Marshall, speaking for a unanimous Court, referring to the Constitution as ''the fundamental and paramount law of the nation,'' declared in the notable case of *Marbury* v *Madison*, . . . that ''it is emphatically the province and duty of the judicial department to say what the law is.'' This decision declared the basic principle that the federal judiciary is supreme in the exposition of the law of the Constitution, and that principle has ever since been respected by this Court and the country as a permanent and indispensable feature of our constitutional system. It follows that the interpretation of the Fourteenth Amendment enunciated by this Court in the *Brown* Case is the supreme law of the land, and Article VI of the Constitution makes it of binding effect on the states ''any thing in the Constitution or laws of any state to the contrary notwithstanding.'' Every state legislator and executive and judicial officer is solemnly committed by oath taken pursuant to Article VI, Section 3 ''to support this Constitution.'' Chief Justice Taney, speaking for a unanimous Court in 1859, said that this requirement reflected the framers' ''anxiety to preserve it [the Constitution] in full force, in all its powers, and to guard against resistance to or evasion of its authority, on the part of a state.''

. . .

No state legislator or executive or judicial officer can war against the Constitution without violating his undertaking to support it. . . . A governor who asserts a power to nullify a federal court order is similarly restrained. If he had such power, said Chief Justice Hughes, in 1932, also for a unanimous Court, ''it is manifest that the fiat of a state governor, and not the Constitution of the United States, would be the supreme law of the land; that the restrictions of the federal Constitution upon the exercise of state power would be but impotent phrases.''

. . .

It is, of course, quite true that the responsibility for public education is primarily the concern of the states, but it is equally true that such responsibilities, like all other state activity, must be exercised consistently with federal constitutional requirements as they apply to state action. The Constitution created a government dedicated to equal justice under law. The Fourteenth Amendment embodied and emphasized that ideal. State support of segregated schools through any arrangement, management, funds, or property cannot be squared with the Amendment's command that no state shall deny to any person within its jurisdiction the equal protection of the laws. The right of a student not to be segregated on racial grounds in schools so maintained is indeed so fundamental and pervasive that it is embraced in the concept of due process of law. . . . The basic decision in *Brown* was unanimously reached by this Court only after the case had been briefed and twice argued and the issues had been given the most serious consideration. Since the first *Brown* opinion three new Justices have come to the Court. They are at one with the Justices still on the Court who participated in that basic decision as to its correctness, and that decision is now unanimously reaffirmed. The principles announced in that decision and the obedience of the states to them, according to the command of the Constitution, are indispensable for the protection of the freedoms guaranteed by our fundamental charter for all of us. Our constitutional ideal of equal justice under law is thus made a living truth.

(Judgment affirmed.)

New Kent County, located in rural Virginia, adopted a "freedom of choice" plan for school desegregation in order to remain eligible for HEW financial aid. No white child elected to go to the black school which about 85 percent of the black student population continued to attend. The children were bused over overlapping routes in order to maintain this racial makeup.

In *Green* v *County School Board,* 391 U.S. 430, 88 S.Ct. 1689, 20 L.Ed. 2d 716 (1968), the United States Supreme Court found that the purpose of achieving fully integrated schools "with all deliberate speed" could not be achieved by the freedom of choice plan. Instead of providing all with a freedom to choose their educational institution, *Brown* was to provide for the movement toward "racially nondiscriminatory" school systems. This was to be assisted by the courts through the 1955 *Brown* decision which injected flexibility into the solutions of the multifaceted problems associated with integration. However, the County School Board failed to adopt either policy until ten years after the decisions, thus indicating a commitment to the unconstitutional dual educational system. The "freedom of choice" plan may be used under the correct circumstances. In this case, it was used as an end in itself rather than as a plan to effectuate the orderly transition to a unitary system. The County School Board was required to establish a more effective plan toward that goal.

In *Griffin* v *County School Board,* 377 U.S. 218, 84 S.Ct. 1226, 12 L.Ed. 2d 256 (1964), the United States Supreme Court decided that a governmental body could not constitutionally close its school system and assist in funding a private school system so that school segregation would be continued. When the closing of a school system is solely for the purpose of maintaining racial segregation in education, that closing is unconstitutional. The children of the county affected by such closing are being denied equal protection under the law.

EQUAL PROTECTION IN CRIMINAL CASES

Alexander v *Louisiana*

405 U.S. 625, 92 S.Ct. 1221, 31 L.Ed. 2d 536 (1972)

Alexander, a Black, was convicted of rape and sentenced to life imprisonment. Prior to his trial, Alexander petitioned to quash his indictment on two grounds: (1) Blacks were included on the grand jury list and venire only in token numbers and (2) females were systematically excluded from the grand jury list, venire, and impaneled grand jury. He therefore argued that the indictment against him was invalid because it was returned by a grand jury impaneled from a venire made up contrary to the requirements of the Equal Protection and Due Process clauses of the Fourteenth Amendment. His motions were denied and his conviction was affirmed by the Louisiana courts. The United States Supreme Court granted certiorari.

Justice White delivered the opinion of the Court:

For over 90 years, it has been established that a criminal conviction of a Negro cannot stand under the Equal Protection Clause of the Fourteenth Amendment if it is based on an indictment of a grand jury from which Negroes were excluded by reason of their race, ... Although a defendant has no right to demand that members of his race be included on the grand jury that indicts him, ... he is entitled to require that the state not deliberately and systematically deny to members of his race the right to participate as jurors in the administration of justice.... It is only the application of these settled principles that is at issue here.

This is not a case where it is claimed that there have been no Negroes called for service within the last 30 years, ... only one Negro chosen within the last 40 years, ... or no Negroes selected ''within the memory of witnesses who had lived [in the area] all their lives,'' .... Rather, petitioner argues that, in his case, there has been a consistent process of progressive and disproportionate reduction of the number of Negroes eligible to serve on the grand jury at each stage of the selection process until ultimately an all-white grand jury was selected to indict him.

In Lafayette Parish, 21 percent of the population was Negro and 21 or over, therefore presumptively eligible for grand jury service. Use of questionnaires by the jury commissioners created a pool of possible grand jurors which was 14 percent Negro, a reduction by one-third of possible black grand jurors. The commissioners then twice called this group to create a list of 400 prospective jurors, 7 percent of whom were Negro—a further reduction to 5 percent on petitioner's grand jury venire and to zero on the grand jury that actually indicted him. Against this background, petitioner argues that the substantial disparity between the proportion of blacks chosen for jury duty and the proportion of blacks in the eligible population raises a strong inference that racial discrimination and not chance has produced this result because elementary principles of probability make it extremely unlikely that a random selection process would, at each stage, have so consistently reduced the number of Negroes.

This Court has never announced mathematical standards for the demonstration of ''systematic'' exclusion of blacks but has, rather, emphasized that a factual inquiry is necessary in each case that takes into account all possible explanatory factors. The progressive decimation of potential black grand jurors is indeed striking here, but we do not rest our conclusion that petitioner has demonstrated a prima facie case of invidious racial discrimination on statistical improbability alone, for the selection procedures themselves were not racially neutral. The racial designation on both the questionnaire and the information card provided a clear and easy opportunity for racial discrimination. At two crucial steps in the selection process, when the number of returned questionnaires was reduced to 2,000 and when the final selection of the 400 names was made, these racial identifications were visible on the forms used by the jury commissioners, although there is no evidence that the commissioners consciously selected by race.

. . .

Petitioner also challenges the Louisiana statutory exemption of women who do not volunteer for grand jury service. . . . This claim is novel in this Court, and, when urged by a male, finds no support in our past cases. The strong constitutional and statutory policy against racial discrimination has permitted Negro defendants in criminal cases to challenge the systematic exclusion of blacks from the grand juries that indicted them. Also, those groups arbitrarily excluded from grand or petit jury service are themselves afforded an appropriate remedy. . . . But there is nothing in past adjudications suggesting that petitioner himself has been denied equal protection by the alleged exclusion of women from grand jury service. Although the Due Process Clause guarantees petitioner a fair trial, it does not require the states to observe the Fifth Amendment's provision for presentment or indictment by a grand jury. In *Duncan* v *Louisiana,* 391 U.S. 115, . . . , the Court held that because trial by jury in criminal cases under the Sixth Amendment is "fundamental to the American scheme of justice," . . . such a right was guaranteed to defendants in state courts by the Fourteenth Amendment, but the Court has never held that federal concepts of a "grand jury," binding on the federal courts under the Fifth Amendment, are obligatory for the states.

. . .

Against this background and because petitioner's conviction has been set aside on other grounds, we follow our usual custom of avoiding decision of constitutional issues unnecessary to the decision of the case before us. . . . The state may or may not recharge petitioner, a properly constituted grand jury may or may not return another indictment, and petitioner may or may not be convicted again.

. . .

(Judgment reversed.)
Justices Powell and Rehnquist did not participate in this case.
Justice Douglas concurred.

Swain v *Alabama*

380 U.S. 202, 85 S.Ct. 824, 13 L.Ed. 2d 759 (1965)

Swain, a black was convicted of rape in Talladega County, Alabama, and was sentenced to death. He sought to quash the indictment because both the venire and petit jury were chosen by a method of invidious discrimination. He also claimed that the exercise of peremptory challenges to systematically exclude blacks deprived him of equal protection of the law. The Alabama courts affirmed the conviction and the United States Supreme Court granted certiorari.

Justice White delivered the opinion of the Court:

We consider first petitioner's claims concerning the selection of grand jurors and the petit jury venire.

. . .

Venires drawn from the jury box made up in this manner unquestionably contained a smaller proportion of the Negro community than of the white community. But a defendant in a criminal case is not constitutionally entitled to demand a proportionate number of his race on the jury which tries him nor on the venire or jury rule from which petit jurors are drawn. . . . We cannot say that purposeful discrimination based on race alone is satisfactorily proved by showing that an identifiable group in a community is underrepresented by as much as 10 percent. . . . There is no evidence that the commissioners applied different standards of qualifications to the Negro community than they did to the white community. Nor was there any meaningful attempt to demonstrate that the same proportion of Negroes qualified under the standards being administered by the commissioners. It is not clear from the record that the commissioners even knew how many Negroes were in their respective areas, or on the jury roll or on the venires drawn from the jury box. The overall percentage disparity has been small, and reflects no studied attempt to include or exclude a specified number of Negroes. Undoubtedly the selection of prospective jurors was somewhat haphazard and little effort was made to ensure that all groups in the community were fully represented. But an imperfect system is not equivalent to purposeful discrimination based on race. We do not think that the burden of proof was carried by petitioner in this case.

Petitioner makes a further claim relating to the exercise of peremptory challenges to exclude Negroes from serving on petit juries.

The essential nature of the peremptory challenge is that it is one exercised without a reason stated, without inquiry and without being subject to the court's control. . . . While challenges for cause permit rejection of jurors on a narrowly specified, provable, and legally cognizable basis of partiality, the peremptory permits rejection for a real or imagined partiality that is less easily designated or demonstrable. . . . It is often exercised upon the "sudden impressions and unaccountable prejudices we are apt to conceive upon the bare looks and gestures of another," . . . upon a juror's "habits and associations," . . . or upon the feeling that "the bare questioning [a juror's] indifference may sometimes provoke a resentment." . . . It is no less frequently exercised on grounds normally thought irrelevant to legal proceedings or official action, namely, the race, religion, nationality, occupation, or affiliations of people summoned for jury duty. For the question a prosecutor or defense counsel must decide is not whether a juror of a particular race or nationality is in fact partial, but whether one from a different group is less likely to be. It is well known that these factors are widely explored during the *voir dire,* by both prosecutor and accused. . . . This Court has held that the fairness of trial by jury requires no less. *Aldridge, supra.* Hence veniremen are not always judged solely as individuals for the purpose of exercising peremptory challenges. Rather they are challenged in light of the limited knowledge counsel has of them, which may include their group affiliations, in the context of the case to be tried.

With these considerations in mind, we cannot hold that the striking of Negroes in a particular case is a denial of equal protection of the laws. In the quest for an impartial and qualified jury, Negro and white, Protestant and Catholic, are alike subject to being challenged without cause. To subject the prosecutor's challenge in any particular case to the demands and traditional standards of the Equal Protection Clause would entail a radical change in the nature and operation of the challenge. The challenge, *pro tanto,* would no longer be peremptory, each and every challenge being open to examination, either at the time of the challenge or at a hearing afterwards. The prosecutor's judgment underlying each challenge would be subject to scrutiny for reasonableness and sincerity. And a great many uses of the challenge would be banned.

In the light of the purpose of the peremptory system and the function it serves in a pluralistic society in connection with the institution of jury trial, we cannot hold that the Constitution requires an examination of the prosecutor's reasons for the exercise of his challenges in any given case. The presumption in any particular case would be that the prosecutor is using the state's challenges to obtain a fair and impartial jury to try the case before the court. The presumption is not overcome and the prosecutor therefore subjected to examination by allegations that in the case at hand all Negroes were removed from the jury or that they were removed because they were Negroes. Any other result, we think, would establish a rule wholly at odds with the peremptory challenge system as we know it. Hence the motion to strike the trial jury was properly denied in this case.

Petitioner, however, presses a broader claim in this Court. His argument is that not only were the Negroes removed by the prosecutor in this case but that there never has been a Negro on a petit jury in either a civil or criminal case in Talladega County and that in criminal cases prosecutors have consistently and systematically exercised their strikes to prevent any and all Negroes on petit jury venires from serving on the petit jury itself. This systematic practice, it is claimed, is invidious discrimination for which the peremptory system is insufficient justification.

We agree that this claim raises a different issue and it may well require a different answer. We have decided that it is permissible to insulate from inquiry the removal of Negroes from a particular jury on the assumption that the prosecutor is acting on acceptable considerations related to the case he is trying, the particular defendant involved, and the particular crime charged. But when the prosecutor in a county, in case after case, whatever the circumstances, whatever the crime and whoever the defendant or the victim may be, is responsible for the removal of Negroes who have been selected as qualified jurors by the jury commissioners and who have survived challenges for cause, with the result that no Negroes ever serve on petit juries, the Fourteenth Amendment claim takes on added significance. . . . In these circumstances, giving even the widest leeway to the operation of irrational but trial-related suspicions and antagonisms, it would appear that the purpose of the peremptory challenge is being perverted. If the state has not seen fit to leave a single Negro on any jury in a criminal case, the presumption protecting the prosecutor may well be overcome, Such proof might support a reasonable inference that blacks are excluded from juries for reasons wholly unrelated to the outcome of the particular case on trial and that the peremptory system is being used to deny the Negro the same right and opportunity to participate in the administration of justice enjoyed by the white population. These ends the peremptory challenge is not designed to facilitate or justify.

We need pursue this matter no further, however, for even if a state's systematic striking of Negroes in the selection of petit juries raises a prima facie case under the Fourteenth Amendment, we think it is readily apparent that the record in this case is not sufficient to demonstrate that the rule has been violated by the peremptory system as it operates in Talladega County.

. . .

(Judgment affirmed.)
Justice Harlan concurred. Justice Black concurred in the result.
Justice Goldberg, joined by the Chief Justice and Justice Douglas, dissented.

In *Douglas* v *California,* 372 U.S. 353, 83 S.Ct. 814 9 L.Ed. 2d 811 (1963), the United States Supreme Court found unconstitutional a California appellate procedure that allowed the state appellate court to deny counsel to an indigent on appeal if, in the court's judgment, counsel would be of no value to the defendant or the court. The majority opinion stated that the indigent defendant would receive inferior legal assistance under this ruling since the appellate court must determine the worthiness of his appeal without written briefs or arguments from counsel. This prejudgment of the merits of an indigent's appeal denies him the equal protection under the law based on his financial status. On a first appeal, counsel must be appointed for the indigent defendant.

The United States Supreme Court insisted on the equality of the right to appeal through two similar cases: *Griffin* v *Illinois,* 351 U.S. 12, 76 S.Ct. 585, 100 L.Ed. 891 (1956), which concerned appeal from a felony conviction, and *Mayer* v *City of Chicago,* 404 U.S. 189, 92 S.Ct. 410, 30 L.Ed. 2d 372 (1971), which concerned appeal from a misdemeanor conviction. The primary doctrine supported in both cases is the right of all defendants, regardless of financial status, to an adequate appeal procedure. The kind of appeal a convicted person obtains should not depend only on his ability or inability to pay. The court put forth more specific guidelines to use. First, a verbatim transcript is not necessarily provided free of charge to an indigent. Only when the full and complete record of the trial proceeding is mandatory to an effective appeal is the state required to provide it. Other, more inexpensive alternatives to full transcripts may be substituted when the alternative provides the counsel and appellate court all information having to do with the grounds of appeal. The distinction between felony and misdemeanor appeals was found wanting by the court. "The size of the defendant's pocketbook bears no more relationship to his guilt or innocence in a nonfelony than a felony case." Further, the consequences of a misdemeanor conviction can be very serious to the indigent defendant, and, therefore, a record of "sufficient completeness" should be provided to indigent defendants in both felony and nonfelony cases.

Williams v *Illinois*
399 U.S. 235, 90 S.Ct. 2018, 26 L.Ed. 2d 586 (1970)

Williams was convicted of petty theft, sentenced to one year in jail, and fined $500. He was also taxed $5 in court costs. According to Illinois law, if he could not pay the fine and court costs by the end of the one year, he was to remain in jail and work off the monetary obligations at the rate of $5 per day. In short, Williams could spend an extra 101 days in confinement if he could not pay the $505.

The Illinois courts rejected William's claim that he should be released after the one sentence, that he was indigent, and if he were released he would be able to find a job to pay the fine and the court costs. The Illinois Supreme Court held "there is no denial of equal protection of the law when an indigent is imprisoned to satisfy payment of the fine." The United States Supreme Court granted certiorari.

Chief Justice Burger delivered the opinion of the Court:

In addition to renewing the constitutional argument rejected by the state courts, appellant advanced a host of other claims which, in light of our disposition, we find unnecessary to reach or decide. Appellant challenges the constitutionality of § 1-7(k) of the Illinois Criminal Code and argues primarily that the Equal Protection Clause of the Fourteenth Amendment prohibits imprisonment of an indigent beyond the maximum term authorized by the statute governing the substantive offense when that imprisonment flows directly from his present inability to pay a fine and court costs. In response the state asserts its interest in the collection of revenues produced by payment of fines and contends that a "work off" system, as provided by § 1-7(k), is a rational means of implementing that policy. That interest is substantial and legitimate but for present purposes it is not unlike the state's interest in collecting a fine from an indigent person in circumstances where no imprisonment is included in the judgment. The state argues further that the statute is not constitutionally infirm simply because the legislature could have achieved the same result by some other means. With that general proposition we have no quarrel but that generality does not resolve the issue.

As noted earlier, appellant's incarceration beyond the statutory maximum stems from separate albeit related reasons: nonpayment of a fine and nonpayment of court costs. We find that neither of those grounds can constitutionally support the type of imprisonment imposed here, but we treat the fine and costs together because disposition of the claim on fines governs our disposition on costs.

The need to be open to reassessment of ancient practices other than those explicitly mandated by the Constitution is illustrated by the present case since the greatly increased use of fines as a criminal sanction has made nonpayment a major cause of incarceration in this country. Default imprisonment has traditionally been justified on the ground it is a coercive device to ensure obedience to the judgment of the court. Thus, commitment for failure to pay has not been viewed as a part of the punishment or as an increase in the penalty; rather, it has been viewed as a part of the punishment or as an increase in the penalty; rather, it has been viewed as a means of enabling the court to enforce collection of money that a convicted defendant was obligated by the sentence to pay. The additional imprisonment, it has been said, may always be avoided by payment of the fine.

We conclude that when the aggregate imprisonment exceeds the maximum period fixed by the statute and results directly from an involuntary nonpayment of a fine or court costs we are confronted with an impermissible discrimination that rests on ability to pay, and accordingly, we vacate the judgment below.

A state has wide latitude in fixing the punishment for state crimes. Thus, appellant does not assert that Illinois could not have appropriately fixed the penalty, in the first instance, at one year and 101 days. Nor has the claim been advanced that the sentence imposed was excessive in light of the circumstances of the commission of this particular offense. However, once the state has defined the outer limits of incarceration necessary to satisfy its penological interests and policies, it may not then subject a certain class of convicted defendants to a period of imprisonment beyond the statutory maximum solely by reason of their indigency.

It is clear, of course, that the sentence was not imposed upon appellant because of his indigency but because he had committed a crime. And the Illinois statutory scheme does not distinguish between defendants on the basis of ability to pay fines. But, as we said in *Griffin* v *Illinois*, "a law nondiscriminatory on its face may be grossly discriminatory in its operation."

. . .

The mere fact that an indigent in a particular case may be imprisoned for a longer time than a non-indigent convicted of the same offense does not, of course, give rise to a violation of the Equal Protection Clause. Sentencing judges are vested with wide discretion in the exceedingly difficult task of determining the appropriate punishment in the countless variety of situations that appear. The Constitution permits qualitative differences in meting out punishment and there is no requirement that two persons convicted of the same offense receive identical sentences.

Nothing in today's decision curtails the sentencing prerogative of a judge because, as noted previously, the sovereign's purpose in confining an indigent beyond the statutory maximum is to provide a coercive means of collecting or "working out" a fine. After having taken into consideration the wide range of factors underlying the exercise of his sentencing function, nothing we now hold precludes a judge from imposing on an indigent, as on any defendant, the maximum penalty prescribed by law.

It bears emphasis that our holding does not deal with a judgment of confinement for nonpayment of a fine in the familiar pattern of alternative sentence of "$30 and 30 days." We hold only that a state may not constitutionally imprison beyond the maximum duration fixed by statute a defendant who is financially unable to pay a fine.

. . . We hold . . . that the Equal Protection Clause of the Fourteenth Amendment requires that the statutory ceiling placed on imprisonment for any substantive offense be the same for all defendants irrespective of their economic status.

We are not unaware that today's holding may place a further burden on states in administering criminal justice. Perhaps a fairer and more accurate statement would be that new cases expose old infirmities which apathy or absence of challenge has permitted to stand. But the constitutional imperatives of the Equal Protection Clause must have priority over the comfortable convenience of the *status quo*. "Any supposed administrative inconvenience would be minimal, since . . . [the unpaid portion of the judgment] could be reached through the ordinary processes of garnishment in the event of default."

. . .

Nothing we hold today limits the power of the sentencing judge to impose alternative sanctions permitted by Illinois law; the definition of such alternatives, if any, lies with the Illinois courts. We therefore vacate the judgment appealed from and remand to the Supreme Court of Illinois for further proceedings not inconsistent with this opinion.

(Judgment vacated.)
Justice Harlan wrote a concurring opinion.

QUESTIONS

1. What is equal protection of the Law?
2. What is the current trend in school desegregation? How does it affect your area?

3. Discuss the future of programs for school desegregation in light of constitutional rights.

4. How will the decision discussed in the section on equal protection in criminal cases affect voir dire proceedings?

8

OTHER FUNDAMENTAL RIGHTS

The right to privacy of Americans is newly emerging in the field of constitutional law. In *Griswold* v *Connecticut,* 381 U.S. 479 (1965), the individual's right to live without governmental interference is guaranteed in situations where there is no showing of a legitimate governmental interest. These rights of privacy are not only limited to the kind of situations in the *Griswold* Case. The claimed infringement of personal liberty in *Griswold* did not involve any express infringement of the Bill of Rights. In this situation the controversy is whether there are personal liberties, such as marital privacy, that are so fundamental that they deserve protection, especially in cases in which there is a questionable legislative judgment and not simply an express constitutional provision applicable. In Justice Douglas' opinion there is no express provision in the Bill of Rights, but there is an implicit one that protects individual privacy. He and Justice Goldberg relied on the Ninth Amendment which states: "The enumeration in the Constitution of certain rights shall not be construed to deny or disparage others retained by the people."

It should be pointed out that the United States Supreme Court's function of protecting individual liberty under our constitutional scheme of government is likely to continue. It is also likely to be a continuing controversial issue whether there is an express constitutional provision or not.

The right of privacy has found expression in the protection from unreasonable searches and seizures found in the Fourth Amendment. Government interference with individuals in locating and seizing evidence without either a search warrant or probable cause has been the constant subject of judicial scrutiny. In the area of electronic surveillance and eavesdropping the Supreme Court has addressed itself to the privacy issue by severely limiting the situations in which the government can wiretap or overhear conversations of individuals. Expressed in the Supreme Court decisions in this area of criminal procedure is the fear of government and its agents invading individual privacy without adequate safeguards to ensure that it is not done indiscriminately. These problems are discussed in detail in this chapter.

The right of franchise is crucial in a democratic system of government. Unfortunately, millions of Americans have been denied this right throughout our history. Democracy is identified with the increase in suffrage because the right to vote is the basic ingredient in a governmental form that makes elected officials responsible directly to the people. If citizens are denied the right to vote, they are deprived of the most effective method of ensuring equal opportunities in such fields as education, employment, and housing.

In America it has taken some 300 years to establish the right to universal equal suffrage. Because the right to vote largely has been denied to whole segments of our citizens, Congress has used the Constitution to regulate the times, places, and manner of federal elections (Article I, Section 4). It has also used its powers under the Fourteenth and Fifteenth Amendments to eliminate some state restrictions on the right to vote and to authorize federal officials to act when voting rights are denied in violation of these amendments. However, this use of congressional power to set voting qualifications has raised serious questions in our federal scheme of government.

First of all, the issue arises whether or not the national government can intervene in state elections when the state legislature permits discrimination in its elections—who should determine who should vote, the state or the federal government? Equally involved here are the ancillary issues of who determines the voting qualifications and how far the federal government should go in establishing and enforcing these regulations.

In 1962 the second major issue regarding the right to vote—equality of each vote—was before the Supreme Court. No question is more fundamental in a democratic society than the manner in which the people choose their representatives. A series of decisions beginning with *Baker* v *Carr,* 369 U.S. 186 (1962), held that a person has a right to equal protection in having his votes counted and this right is violated by having unequally apportioned districts. These decisions led to numerous state apportionment suits and massive state legislative reapportioning activity. It should also be mentioned that these cases caused the beginning of a national debate on the role of the Supreme Court in the political process itself. The debate continues today with such issues arising as: How far should the Supreme Court go in setting up apportionment guidelines? What constitutes unfair apportionment? Should only the states determine what constitutes fair apportionment? These questions become increasingly important when it is remembered that the basic power to set voting qualifications is given to the states by the Constitution. Nevertheless, Article I empowers Congress to regulate the "times, places, and manner of holding elections." Also, state powers are restricted by the Thirteenth, Fourteenth, Fifteenth, Seventeenth, and Nineteenth Amendments. With these in mind, we can see that the vital question of the right to vote becomes one involving which governmental body must determine not only who can vote but also how to count the votes equally.

Before analyzing the following landmark decisions of the United States Supreme Court regarding franchisement, let us look at a short historical perspective that will lay the groundwork for their consideration. During the first 50 years of our history property ownership by males was required in all 13 Colonies as a qualification to vote. As a consequence only about 1 out of 30 people had the right to vote. Subsequently, when North Carolina finally relinquished this requirement in 1856, property ownership was abandoned by all the states. As a substitute, taxpaying was required. Some states still retain this voter qualification in order to vote in local bond elections.

Changes in the economic and social structure in the United States have served as a strong emphasis for broadening the franchise. New social classes have been born as the result in industrial expansion with consequent agitation for the opportunity to participate in the concept of self-government through elected representatives. At the turn of the twentieth century women's rights organizations became more and more active in social, educational, and political reform movements. With the adoption of the Nineteenth Amendment in 1920, suffrage was granted to women in all states rather than just the few that had previously extended the franchise to women. Distinctions between social classes have been eliminated in many of the highly structured, almost feudal, states. The elimination of racial discrimination in jobs, housing, and education provided a stimulus for securing equality in voting rights. Politicans were also interested in the bloc of voters that came into the American political scene from foreign immigration.

Federal legislation in regards to voting rights has been particularly active, especially since 1957, when the first legislation enforcing the Fifteenth Amendment since 1871 was enacted. Specifically, the 1957 Civil Rights Act reiterated the declaration that all qualified citizens should be permitted to vote in all elections without regard to race, creed, or color. A significant feature of the 1957 Act was the provision allowing the United States Attorney General to commence suits dealing with voting rights. This meant that private persons no longer had to institute suits to secure their right to vote. This was especially important because it prevented large legal expenses, as well as economic and physical intimidation. A major drawback of the Act was that the Attorney General had no express authority to correct widespread and continuing patterns of voter discrimination. In short, bringing and winning a suit involving an individual who had been denied the right to vote had little effect on the total problem.

The 1960 Civil Rights Act corrected this situation by permitting the Attorney General, once a suit involving denial of voting rights had been established, to ask the court to determine if there was a pattern or practice of discrimination. If this was found by the court, any person in the class discriminated against could apply to the court to issue an order stating that he was qualified to vote. The 1960 Act also required the preservation, production, and presentation of voting records. It also empowered the United States Attorney General who brings a suit to require a state to be a party.

In 1965 the most comprehensive attempt was made to ensure the right to vote to all groups and to correct inadequacies in previous legislation. In particular, the 1965 Voting Rights Act dealt with subtle and wide devices aimed at disenfranchising the black man. It permits limited federal regulation of voter registration in states and subdivisions where:

1. Literacy tests or other similar devices were used on November 1, 1964.

2. Less than 50 percent of voting-age residents were registered to vote or voted in the 1964 presidential election.

Once these determinations are made by the United States Attorney General and the census director, any state or subdivision is forbidden from denying any person the right to vote because of his failure to comply with the literacy test or other discriminatory device.

If the state or subdivision persists in the discriminatory practices, federal examiners are authorized to be assigned to the area to conduct voter registration of qualified persons who previously have been deprived of the right to vote because of race, creed, or color. The major change in the 1965 Act was that there was no longer a need for elaborate proof of actual discrimination to put the law's provisions into movement.

In *South Carolina* v *Katzenbach,* 383 U.S. 301 (1966), the United States Supreme Court upheld the Act's provision for appointment of voting registrars and suspension of literacy tests in all or part of the affected areas of Alabama, Georgia, Louisiana, Mississippi, North Carolina, and South Carolina.

The 1966 Act also had an impact on voter qualifications in the North. It provided that a person who had completed the sixth grade of an accredited school in the United States or Puerto Rico could not be denied the right to vote because of an inability to read, write, understand, or interpret any matter in the English language. The main thrust of this provision was to halt New York's requirement of literacy in English as applied to Puerto Ricans residing in New York. Over substantial objections to the constitutionality of this provision, the Supreme Court in *Katzenbach* v *Morgan,* 384 U.S. 681 (1966), upheld this provision, stating that Congress has the power to ascertain that New York's requirement as applied to Spanish-speaking people was a form of subtle discrimination forbidden by the Fourteenth Amendment's Equal Protection Clause.

PRIVACY

Griswold v *Connecticut*

381 U.S. 479, 85 S.Ct. 1678, 14 L.Ed. 2d 510 (1965)

According to Connecticut statutes it was illegal to use birth-control devices. Also outlawed was furnishing information or giving instructions by anyone on the use of such devices. Griswold, the director of a planned parenthood organization, and the organization's medical director were convicted of providing such services to married persons and fined $100. The convictions were affirmed in the state courts, and an appeal was taken to the United States Supreme Court.

Justice Douglas delivered the opinion of the Court:

> Coming to the merits, we are met with a wide range of questions that implicate the Due Process Clause of the Fourteenth Amendment. . . . We do not sit as a super-legislature to determine the wisdom, need, and propriety of laws that touch economic problems, business affairs, or social conditions. This law, however, operates directly on an intimate relation of husband and wife and their physician's role in one aspect of that relation.
>
> The association of people is not mentioned in the Constitution nor in the Bill of Rights. The right to educate a child in a school of the parents' choice—whether public or private or parochial—is also not mentioned. Nor is the right to study any particular subject or any foreign language. Yet the First Amendment has been construed to include certain of those rights.
>
> · · ·
>
> In *NAACP* v *State of Alabama,* 357 U.S. 449, . . . , we protected the "freedom to associate and privacy in one's associations," noting that freedom of association was a peripheral First Amendment right.
>
> · · ·
>
> The Fourth and Fifth Amendments were described . . . as protection against all governmental invasions "of the sanctity of a man's house and the privacies of life." We recently referred . . . to the Fourth Amendment as creating a "right to privacy, no less important than any other right carefully and particularly reserved to the people."
>
> · · ·
>
> The present case, then, concerns a relationship lying within the zone of privacy created by several fundamental constitutional guarantees. And it concerns a law which, in forbidding the *use* of contraceptives rather than regulating their manufacture or sale, seeks to achieve its goals by means having a maximum destructive impact upon that relationship. Such a law cannot stand in light of the familiar principle, so often applied by this Court, that a "governmental purpose to control or prevent activities constitutionally subject to state regulation may not be achieved by means which sweep unnecessarily broadly and thereby invade the area of protected freedoms." . . . Would we allow the police to search the sacred precincts of marital bedrooms for telltale signs of the use of contraceptives? The very idea is repulsive to the notions of privacy surrounding the marriage relationship.
>
> We deal with a right of privacy older than the Bill of Rights—older than our political parties, older than our school system. Marriage is a coming together for better or for worse, hopefully enduring, and intimate to the degree of being sacred. It is an association that promotes a way of life, not causes; a harmony in living, not political faiths; a bilateral loyalty, not commercial or social

projects. Yet it is an association for as noble a purpose as any involved in our prior decisions.

(Judgment reversed.)

Justice Goldberg, joined by the Chief Justice and Justice Brennan, concurred:

I agree with the Court that Connecticut's birth-control law unconstitutionally intrudes upon the right of marital privacy, and I join in its opinion and judgment. Although I have not accepted the view that "due process" as used in the Fourteenth Amendment includes all of the first eight amendments, . . . I do agree that the concept of liberty protects those personal rights that are fundamental, and is not confined to the specific terms of the Bill of Rights. My conclusion that the concept of liberty is not so restricted and that it embraces the right of marital privacy though that right is not mentioned explicitly in the Constitution is supported both by numerous decisions of this Court, referred to in the Court's opinion, and by the language and history of the Ninth Amendment.

· · ·

In the course of its opinion the Court refers to no less than six amendments to the Constitution: the First, the Third, the Fourth, the Fifth, the Ninth, and the Fourteenth. But the Court does not say which of these amendments, if any, it thinks is infringed by this Connecticut law.

· · ·

The Court also quotes the Ninth Amendment, and my Brother Goldberg's concurring opinion relies heavily upon it. But to say that the Ninth Amendment has anything to do with this case is to turn somersaults with history. The Ninth Amendment, like its companion the Tenth, which this Court held "states but a truism that all is retained which has not been surrendered," . . . was framed by James Madison and adopted by the states simply to make clear that the adoption of the Bill of Rights did not alter the plan that the *federal* government was to be a government of express and limited powers, and that all rights and powers not delegated to it were retained by the people and the individual states. Until today no member of the Court has ever suggested that the Ninth Amendment meant anything else, and the idea that a federal court could ever use the Ninth Amendment to annul a law passed by the elected representatives of the people of the State of Connecticut would have caused James Madison no little wonder.

In *Paul* v *Davis,* 424 U.S. 693, 96 S.Ct. 1155, 47 L.Ed. 2d 405, (1976), the Court narrowed the power of private citizens to sue public officials. Davis had been listed as an "active shoplifter" in a five-page flyer distributed to local merchants by the Louisville, Kentucky, police. Davis had been arrested but had not been brought to trial. The charges against him were dismissed. Shortly after the flyer was distributed, he asserted that the listing would impair his future job opportunities and make him fearful of going into stores. The Court ruled that he would have a good case for a libel suit but that there was no violation of his civil rights.

TRAVEL

Aptheker v *Secretary of State*
378 U.S. 500, 84 S.Ct. 1659, 12 L.Ed. 2d 992 (1964)

Aptheker was a member of the Communist Party. According to the Subversive Activities Control Act of 1950, Section 6, it was unlawful for a registered Communist Party member to apply for, be issued, or attempt to use a United States passport. Aptheker had his passport revoked by State Department officials. He and another citizen similarly situated sought review of the action in the State Department, but the revocation was upheld. He then sought relief in the federal courts, claiming the Section 6 deprived the two of their liberty to travel under the Fifth Amendment. The federal district court sustained the constitutionality of Section 6, and they appealed to the United States Supreme Court.
Justice Goldberg delivered the opinion of the Court:

In 1958 in *Kent* v *Dulles,* 357 U.S. 116, . . . , this Court declared that the right to travel abroad is ''an important aspect of the citizen's ''liberty'' guaranteed in the Due Process Clause of the Fifth Amendment. . . . In *Kent,* however, the Court concluded that Congress had not conferred authority upon the Secretary of State to deny passports because of alleged Communist beliefs and associations. Therefore, although the decision protected the constitutional right to travel, the Court did not examine ''the extent to which it can be curtailed.''

. . .

Although previous cases have not involved the constitutionality of statutory restrictions upon the right to travel abroad, there are well-established principles by which to test whether the restrictions here imposed are consistent with the liberty guaranteed in the Fifth Amendment. It is a familiar and basic principle, recently reaffirmed in *NAACP* v *Alabama,* 377 U.S. 288, . . . , that ''a governmental purpose to control or prevent activities constitutionally subject to state regulation may not be achieved by means which sweep unnecessarily broadly and thereby invade the area of protected freedoms.''

. . .

This principle requires that we consider the congressional purpose underlying Section 6 of the Control Act. The government emphasizes that the legislation in question flows, as the statute itself declares, from the congressional desire to protect our national security. That Congress under the Constitution has power to safeguard our nation's security is obvious and unarguable. . . . At the same time the Constitution requires that the powers of government ''must be so exercised as not, in attaining a permissible end, unduly to infringe a constitutionally protected freedom. *Cantwell* v *Connecticut, supra, ."*

. . .

Section 6 provides that any member of a Communist organization which has registered or has been ordered to register commits a crime if he attempts to use or obtain a United States passport. . . . Thus the terms of Section 6 apply whether or not the member actually knows or believes that he is associated with what is deemed to be a "Communist-action" or a "Communist-front" organization. . . . The provision therefore sweeps within its prohibition both knowing and unknowing members.

. . .

In addition to the absence of criteria linking the bare fact of membership to the individual's knowledge, activity, or commitment, Section 6 also excludes other considerations which might more closely relate the denial of passports to the stated purpose of the legislation. The prohibition of Section 6 applies regardless of the purposes for which an individual wishes to travel. Under the statute it is a crime for a notified member of a registered organization to apply for a passport to travel abroad to visit a sick relative, to receive medical treatment, or for any other wholly innocent purpose. In determining whether there has been an abridgment of the Fifth Amendment's guarantee of liberty, this Court must recognize the danger of punishing a member of a Communist organization "for his adherence to lawful and constitutionally protected purposes, because of other and unprotected purposes which he does not necessarily share." . . . In addition it must be noted that Section 6 applies to a member regardless of the security-sensitivity of the areas in which he wishes to travel.

. . . `

In determining the constitutionality of Section 6, it is also important to consider that Congress has within its power "less drastic" means of achieving the congressional objective.

In our view, the foregoing considerations compel the conclusion that Section 6 of the Control Act is unconstitutional on its face. The section, judged by its plain import and by the substantive evil which Congress sought to control, sweeps too widely and too indiscriminately across the liberty guaranteed in the Fifth Amendment. The prohibition against travel is supported only by a tenuous relationship between the bare fact of organizational membership and the activity Congress sought to proscribe. The broad and enveloping prohibition indiscriminately excludes plainly relevant considerations such as the individual's knowledge, activity, commitment, and purposes in and places for travel. The section therefore is patently not a regulation "narrowly drawn to prevent the supposed evil," . . . yet here, as elsewhere, precision must be the touchstone of legislation so affecting basic freedoms.

(Judgment reversed.)   . . .
Justices Douglas and Black wrote concurring opinions.

Justice Clark, joined by Justice Harlan, dissented.
Justice White joined Justice Harlan in part in dissent.

According to the United States Supreme Court's opinion in *Zemel* v *Rusk,* 381 U.S. 1, 85 S.Ct. 1271, 14 L.Ed. 2d 179 (1965), an American citizen does not have the absolute right to travel wherever he wishes. Within two months after the Cuban missile crisis, Zemel requested permission from Secretary of State Rusk to travel to Cuba. This was in compliance with a ruling by the State Department. Rusk denied the request and Zemel appealed, claiming that the 1926 Passport Act, which authorized the Secretary to issue passports under presidentially promulgated rules, was an unconstitutional delegation of authority. The Court supported the right of the president to restrict travel in certain areas through the State Department, but the Court remained loyal to the requirement of due process before the travel restrictions could be enacted.

Shapiro v *Thompson*
394 U.S. 618, 89 S.Ct. 1322, 22 L.Ed. 2 600 (1969)

Thompson, a 19-year-old unwed mother of one child and pregnant with another, moved to Connecticut from Massachusetts in June 1966. She filed for public assistance in August, 1966, under the Aid to Families and Dependent Children program. She was denied aid because she failed to meet the state's one-year residency requirement to become eligible for public assistance. She filed suit against Shapiro, the welfare commissioner in Connecticut, seeking to strike down the residency requirement. The federal district court struck down the requirement because of its chilling effect on travel. Shapiro appealed to the United States Supreme Court where several similar cases were consolidated.

Justice Brennan delivered the opinion of the Court:

Primarily, appellants justify the waiting-period requirement as a protective device to preserve the fiscal integrity of state public assistance programs. It is asserted that people who require welfare assistance during their first year of residence in a state are likely to become continuing burdens on state welfare programs. Therefore, the argument runs, if such people can be deterred from entering the jurisdiction by denying them welfare benefits during the first year, state programs to assist long-time residents will not be impaired by a substantial influx of indigent newcomers.

There is weighty evidence that exclusion from the jurisdiction of the poor who need or may need relief was the specific objective of these provisions.
. . .

We do not doubt that the one-year waiting period device is suited to discourage the influx of poor families in need of assistance. . . . But the purpose of inhibiting migration by needy persons into the state is constitutionally impermissible.

Thus, the purpose of deterring the in-migration of indigents cannot serve as justification for the classification created by the one-year waiting period, since that purpose is constitutionally impermissible. If a law has "no other purpose . . . than to chill the assertion of constitutional rights by penalizing those who choose to exercise them, then it [is] patently unconstitutional."

. . .

We recognize that a state has a valid interest in preserving the fiscal integrity of its programs. It may legitimately attempt to limit its expenditures, whether for public assistance, public education, or any other program. But a state may not accomplish such a purpose by invidious distinctions between classes of its citizens. It could not, for example, reduce expenditures for education by barring indigent children from its schools. Similarly, in the cases before us, appellants must do more than show that denying welfare benefits to new residents saves money. The saving of welfare costs cannot justify an otherwise invidious classification.

In sum, neither deterrence of indigents from migrating to the state nor limitation of welfare benefits to those regarded as contributing to the state is a constitutionally permissible state objective.

Appellants next advance as justification certain administrative and related governmental objectives allegedly served by the waiting-period requirement. They argue that the requirement (1) facilitates the planning of the welfare budget; (2) provides an objective test of residency; (3) minimizes the opportunity for recipients fraudulently to receive payments from more than one jurisdiction; and (4) encourages early entry of new residents into the labor force.

The argument tht the waiting-period requirement facilitates budget predictability is wholly unfounded. . . . In these circumstances, there is simply no basis for the claim that the one-year waiting requirement serves the purpose of making the welfare budget more predictable.

. . .

The argument that the waiting period serves as an administratively efficient rule of thumb for determining residency similarly will not withstand scrutiny.

. . .

Similarly, there is no need for a state to use the one-year waiting period as a safeguard against fraudulent receipt of benefits; for less drastic means are available, and are employed, to minimize that hazard.

. . .

We conclude therefore that appellants in these cases do not use and have no need to use the one-year requirement for the governmental purposes suggested. . . . Since the classification here touches on the fundamental right of interstate movement, its constitutionality must be judged by the stricter standard of whether it promotes a *compelling* state interest. Under this standard, the waiting-period requirement clearly violates the Equal Protection Clause.

. . . In terms of federal power, the discrimination created by the one-year requirement violates the Due Process Clause of the First Amendment. "[W]hile the Fifth Amendment contains no equal protection clause, it does forbid discrimination that is 'so unjustifiable as to be violative of due process.' '' . . . For the reasons we have stated in invalidating the Pennsylvania and Connecticut provisions, the District of Columbia provision is also invalid—the Due Process Clause of the Fifth Amendment prohibits Congress from denying public assistance to poor persons otherwise eligible solely on the ground that they have not been residents of the District of Columbia for one year at the time their applications are filed.

(Judgments affirmed.)
Justice Stewart concurred.

Wesberry v *Sanders*

376 U.S. 1, 84 S.Ct. 526, 11 L.Ed. 2d 481 (1964)

The Georgia congressional districting statute that permitted some districts to have over twice the population as others was challenged by Westberry and others as being unconstitutional. The district court dismissed the complaint and the plaintiffs appealed to the United States Supreme Court.
Justice Black delivered the opinion of the Court:

This brings us to the merits. We agree with the District Court that the 1931 Georgia apportionment grossly discriminates against voters in the Fifth Congressional District. A single congressman represents from two to three times as many Fifth-District voters as are represented by each of the congressmen from the other Georgia congressional districts. The apportionment statute thus contracts the value of some votes and expands that of others. If the federal Constitution intends that when qualified voters elect members of Congress each vote be given as much weight as any other vote, then this statute cannot stand.

We hold that, construed in its historical context, the command of Article I, Section 2, that representatives be chosen ''by the people of the several states'' means that as nearly as is practicable one man's vote in a congressional election is to be worth as much as another's. This rule is followed automatically, of course, when representatives are chosen as a group on a statewide basis, as was a widespread practice in the first 50 years of our nation's history. It would be extraordinary to suggest that in such statewide elections the votes of inhabitants of some parts of a state, for example, Georgia's thinly populated Ninth District, could be weighted at two or three times the value of the votes of people living in more populous parts of the state, for example, the Fifth District around Atlanta.

. . .

It is in the light of . . . history that we must construe Article I, Section 2, of the Constitution, which, carrying out the ideas of Madison and those of like views, provides that representatives shall be chosen ''by the people of the several states'' and shall be ''apportioned among the several states . . . according to their respective numbers.'' It is not surprising that our Court has held that this Article gives persons qualified to vote a constitutional right to vote and to have their votes counted. . . . Not only can this right to vote not be denied outright, it cannot, consistently with Article I, be destroyed by alteration of ballots, . . . or diluted by stuffing of the ballot box, ... No right is more precious in a free country than that of having a voice in the election of those who make the laws under which, as good citizens, we must live. Other rights, even the most basic, are illusory if the right to vote is undermined. Our Constitution leaves no room for classification of people in a way that unnecessarily abridges this right. In urging the people to adopt the Constitution, Madison said in No. 57 of *The Federalist*:

> Who are to be the electors of the Federal Representatives? Not the rich more than the poor; not the learned more than the ignorant; not the haughty heirs of distinguished names, more than the humble sons of obscure and unpropitious fortune. The electors are to be the great body of the people of the United States. . . ."

Readers surely could have fairly taken this to mean, "one person, one vote."

· · ·

While it may not be possible to draw congressional districts with mathematical precision, that is no excuse for ignoring our Constitution's plain objective of making equal representation for equal numbers of people the fundamental goal for the House of Representatives. That is the high standard of justice and common sense which the Founders set for us.

(Judgment reversed.) · · ·
Justice Clark concurred in part and dissented in part.
Justices Harlan and Stewart dissented separately.

Reynolds v *Sims*

377 U.S. 533, 84 S.Ct. 1362, 12 L.Ed. 2d 506 (1964)

The apportionment scheme of the Alabama legislature was challenged by Alabama voters. The Alabama constitution required the legislature to reapportion the House of Represenatives and Senate decennially on a population basis provided that each county shall be entitled to at least one representative, and no county will be given more than one senator. No reapportionment had taken place since 1901. As a result there was malapportionment. The Alabama Supreme Court did not intervene although it recognized legislative noncompliance. The federal district court held that the Alabama apportionment was violative of equal protection of the law under the Fourteenth Amendment.

It was found that under the Alabama scheme, based on 1960 census figures, only about 25 percent of the state's population resided in districts that represented a majority in the Senate. Only 25.7 percent lived in counties that could elect a majority of the House of Representatives. There was a population variance ratio of about 41 to 1 for the Senate and about 16 to 1 for the House.

Chief Justice Warren delivered the opinion of the Court:

. . . Nevertheless, *Wesberry* clearly established that the fundamental principle of representative government in this country is one of equal representation for equal numbers of people, without regard to race, sex, economic status, or place of residence within a state. Our problem, then, is to ascertain, in the insant cases, whether there are any constitutionally cognizable principles which would justify departures from the basic standard of equality among voters in the apportionment of seats in state legislatures.

Legislators represent people, not trees or acres. Legislators are elected by voters, not farms or cities or economic interests. As long as ours is a representative form of government, and our legislatures are those instruments of government elected directly by and directly representative of the people, the right to elect legislators in a free and unimpaired fashion is a bedrock of our political system. It could hardly be gainsaid that a constitutional claim had been asserted by an allegation that certain otherwise qualified voters had been entirely prohibited from voting for members of their state legislature. . . . It would appear extraordinary to suggest that a state could be constitutionally permitted to enact a law providing that certain of the state's voters could vote two, five, or ten times for their legislative representatives, while voters living elsewhere could vote only once. And it is inconceivable that a state law to the effect that, in counting votes for legislators, the votes of citizens in one part of the state would be multiplied by two, five, or ten, while the votes of persons in another area would be counted only at face value, could be constitutionally sustainable. Of course, the effect of state legislative districting schemes which give the same number of representatives to unequal numbers of constitutients is identical. Overweighting and overvaluation of the votes of those living here have the certain effect of dilution and undervaluation of the votes of those living there.

. . .

Logically, in a society ostensibly grounded on representative government, it would seem reasonable that a majority of the people of a state could elect a majority of that state's legislators. To conclude differently, and to sanction minority control of state legislative bodies, would appear to deny majority rights in a way that far surpasses any possible denial of minority rights that might otherwise be thought to result.

. . .

We hold that, as a basic constitutional standard, the Equal Protection Clause requires that the seats in both houses of a bicameral state legislature must be apportioned on a population basis.

. . .

Since neither of the houses of the Alabama Legislature, under any of the three plans considered by the District Court, was apportioned on a population basis, we would be justified in proceeding no further. However, one of the proposed plans, that contained in the so-called 67-Senator Amendment, at least superficially resembles the scheme of legislative representation followed in the federal Congress.

. . .

Political subdivisions of states—counties, cities, or whatever—never were and never have been considered as sovereign entities. Rather, they have been traditionally regarded as subordinate governmental instrumentalities created by the state to assist in the carrying out of state governmental functions. The relationship of the states to the federal government could hardly be less analogous.

By holding that as a federal constitutional requisite both houses of a state legislature must be apportioned on a population basis, we mean that the Equal Protection Clause requires that a state make an honest and good faith effort to construct districts, in both houses of its legislature, as nearly of equal population as is practicable.

. . . Somewhat more flexibility may therefore be constitutionally permissible with respect to state legislative apportionment than in congressional districting. Lower courts can and assuredly will work out more concrete and specific standards for evaluating state legislative apportionment schemes in the context of actual litigation. For the present, we deem it expedient not to attempt to spell out any precise constitutional tests. What is marginally permissible in one state may be unsatisfactory in another, depending on the particular circumstances of the case. Developing a body of doctrine on a case-by-case basis appears to us to provide the most satisfactory means of arriving at detailed constitutional requirements in the area of state legislative apportionment.

. . .

A state may legitimately desire to maintain the integrity of various political subdivisions, insofar as possible, and provide for compact districts of contiguous territory in designing a legislative apportionment scheme. Valid considerations may underlie such aims. Indiscriminate districting, without any regard for political subdivision or natural or historical boundary lines, may be little more than an open invitation to partisan gerrymandering. Single-member districts may be the rule in one state, while another state might desire to achieve some flexibility by creating multimember or floterial districts. Whatever the means of accomplishment, the overriding objective must be substantial equality of population among the various districts, so that the vote of any citizen is approximately equal in weight to that of any other citizen in the state.

A consideration that appears to be of more substance in justifying some deviations from population-based representation in state legislatures is that of ensuring some voice to political subdivisions, as political subdivisions. Several factors make more than insubstantial claims that a state can rationally consider according political subdivisions some independent representation in at least one body of the state legislature, as long as the basic standard of equality of population among districts is maintained.

. . .

We do not consider here the difficult question of the proper remedial devices which federal courts should utilize in state legislative apportionment cases. Remedial techniques in this new and developing area of the law will probably often differ with the circumstances of the challenged apportionment and a variety of local conditions. It is enough to say now that, once a state's legislative apportionment scheme has been found to be unconstitutional, it would be the unusual case in which a court would be justified in not taking appropriate action to ensure that no further elections are conducted under the invalid plan.

. . .

(Judgment affirmed and remanded.)
Justices Clark and Stewart concurred.
Justice Harlan dissented.

A state is not obligated to abide by any one method of selecting governmental officials, according to the majority opinion in *Fortson* v *Morris,* 385 U.S. 231, 87 S.Ct. 446, 17 L.Ed. 2d 330 (1966). The Georgia constitution allows the state legislature to elect the governor of the state if no candidate receives the majority of votes cast in the election. When this situation arose in 1966, a federal district court enjoined the legislature from electing the governor on the basis of the Equal Protection Clause of the Fourteenth Amendment. The United States Supreme Court reversed this judgment since it found that all citizens were afforded equal protection through the election procedures.

Hadley v *Junior College District,* 397 U.S. 50, 90 S.Ct. 791, 25 L.Ed. 2d 45 (1970), held that equality in voting power is an essential constitutional right in any popular election. A junior college district, made up of numerous school districts, was barred from allowing the election of representatives to a board in such a manner that more populous districts were always at a disadvantage to smaller districts. Although the court did not require "mathematical exactitude" in the election of the small number of representatives, it did affirm the spirit of the "one man, one vote" rule. When certain districts are consistently denied the proper percentage of representatives, this rule is violated and the method of election is unconstitutional.

QUESTIONS

1. In what other situations could the privacy right as stated in *Griswold* be invoked?

2. According to what constitutional right or rights can the decision of the Supreme Court in *Aptheker* v *Secretary of State* be compared to *Shapiro* v *Thompson?*

3. How has the right of franchise, seen through the Supreme Courts decisions, protected the public from gerrymandering?

9

FOURTH AMENDMENT— SEARCH AND SEIZURE

No changes in constitutional interpretation have been as widespread and traumatic as in the field of search and seizure under the Fourth and Fourteenth Amendments. Within the short time span from 1960 to the present the criminal law and procedure upheaval has radically altered police practices, prosecutorial processes, court procedures, and correctional handling of persons.

Of the various amendments to the United States Constitution, only four directly circumscribe the governmental exercise of power in the criminal field. Of these four—the Fourth, Fifth, Sixth and Eighth Amendments—the Fourth in its regulation of searches and seizures has invoked far-reaching changes in the processing of persons through the complex of criminal justice agencies.

The Fourth Amendment's prohibition against unreasonable searches and seizures interposes a wall between the individual and the power of law enforcement functionaries to search and seize whenever, whomever, and wherever they may wish. Additionally, the Fourth Amendment protects the privacy of the individual through the prohibition against unreasonable search and seizure. The Fourth Amendment guarantees individual privacy of persons whose homes and offices can be violated by the police only when a proper search warrant has been issued by a judicial official. The Amendment also permits police intrusion when certain unusual circumstances occur, for example, the search of a person who has been lawfully arrested or when a moving vehicle has been stopped under peculiar circumstances.

As mentioned previously, enforcement of the protection against unreasonable searches and seizures has met with strong objections, primarily on the grounds that enforcement of the restrictions would unduly restrict the efficient operations of law enforcement. This opposition reached its crescendo in 1961 when the United States Supreme Court in *Mapp* v *Ohio*, 367 U.S. 643 (1961), decided that evidence which had been obtained as a result of an illegal search and seizure was inadmissible in criminal trials in the states by virtue of the Fourteenth Amendment. The *Mapp* decision made the exclusion of the evidence in state trials the same as had been in the federal criminal trials since 1914.

A short discussion of the English common law will help to put the concerns of the founding fathers in context. The English common law was extremely strict in regard to the rules to be followed before a warrant could be issued. The warrant had to describe in great detail the places to be searched and the persons or things to be seized. A point that caused great consternation among the American colonists involved a Parliament law that allowed a relaxation of the warrant requirements in the colonies. The exceptions to the English practice summarized below greatly influenced the subsequent development of American rights in the field of search and seizure.

Writ of Assistance. To enforce the Trade Acts, the English Parliament authorized by statute, general search warrants, called *writs of assistance*, which permitted English customs officials to randomly conduct searches for contraband. A particularly offensive aspect of the *writ* was the authority given to the English officials to search any house or ship, to open boxes and trunks, and break down doors in order to seize goods at will.

In 1760 the law that authorized the *writs of assistance* was reviewed. James Otis in a famous argument opposing issuance of the writs stated that the "writ is the worst instrument of arbitrary power, the most destructive of English liberty, and the fundamental principles of laws, that ever was found in an English lawbook."

The English Townshend Revenue Act of 1767 specifically permitted the issuance of writs of assistance. Subsequently the First Continental Congress cited the Townshend Act as one of the acts violating the rights of the colonists. The states gradually adopted constitutional provisions embodying the concept enunciated by Otis of guaranteeing the right of the individual to be free from the threat of unreasonable searches and seizures. In short, before a search warrant could be issued, there had to be a sufficient foundation for issuing it, and some specificity in describing the persons and places to be searched and the particular things to be seized. By the close of the Revolutionary War most of the states had such a provision in their constitutions. When the Bill of Rights was adopted in 1791, such a provision was considered to be indispensable as a protection against governmental tyranny.

The material in this chapter will analyze the Fourth Amendment's prohibition against unreasonable searches and seizures by looking at the scope of the Amendment, what constitutes lawful searches, the procedural rules for issuance of a search warrant, and exceptions to the search warrant requirement which include the search incident to a lawful arrest. The materials will also address some peculiar problems associated with the ban on unreasonable searches and seizures such as searches of vehicles (which are a controversial problem from the constitutional standpoint), administrative searches, electronic eavesdropping, and the use of informants as an aid to detecting criminal conduct.

SCOPE

Weeks v *United States*

232 U.S. 383, 34 S.Ct. 341, 58 L.Ed. 652 (1914)

Weeks was convicted of illegal use of the mails for transporting lottery coupons. He was sentenced and fined. He was arrested without a warrant. At the time of the arrest other officers went to his house, let themselves in by a key found in a place indicated by a neighbor, and searched the defendant's room where certain incriminating papers were found. These were turned over to a United States marshal. Later on the same day the marshal returned to the house, knocked, and was granted entry by what was probably a boarder. The marshal searched Weeks' room and seized and carried away some papers found in a chiffonier drawer. Neither the officers nor the marshal had a search warrant. The defendant sought to suppress the evidence.

Justice Day delivered the opinion of the Court:

The defendant assigns error, among other things, in the court's refusal to grant his petition for the return of his property, and in permitting the papers to be used at the trial.

. . .

The defendant contends that such appropriation of his private correspondence was in violation of rights secured to him by the Fourth and Fifth Amendments to the Constitution of the United States. We shall deal with the Fourth Amendment, which provides: The effect of the Fourth Amendment is to put the courts of the United States and federal officials, in the exercise of their power and authority, under limitations and restraints as to the exercise of such power and authority, and to forever secure the people, their persons, houses, papers, and effects, against all unreasonable searches and seizures under the guise of law. This protection reaches all alike, whether accused of crime or not, and the duty of giving to it force and effect is obligatory upon all intrusted under our federal system with the enforcement of the laws. The tendency of those who execute the criminal laws of the country to obtain conviction by means of unlawful seizures and enforced confessions, the latter often obtained after subjecting accused persons to unwarranted practices destructive of rights secured by the federal Constitution, should find no sanction in the judgments of the courts, which are charged at all times with the support of the Constitution, and to which people of all conditions have a right to appeal for the maintenance of such fundamental rights.

. . .

The case in the aspect in which we are dealing with it involves the right of the court in a criminal prosecution to retain for the purposes of evidence the letters and correspondence of the accused, seized in his house, in his absence and without his authority, by a United States marshal holding no warrant for his arrest and none for the search of his premises. The accused, without awaiting his trial, made timely application to the court for an order for the return of these letters, as well or other property. This application was denied, the letters retained and put in evidence, after a further application at the beginning of the trial, both applications asserting the rights of the accused under the Fourth and Fifth Amendments to the Constitution. If letters and private documents can thus be seized and held and used in evidence against a citizen accused of an offense, the protection of the Fourth Amendment, declaring his right to be secure against such searches and seizures, is of no value, and, so far as those thus placed are concerned, might as well be stricken from the Constitution. The efforts of the courts and their officials to bring the guilty to punishment, praiseworthy as they are, are not to be aided by the sacrifice of those great principles established by years of endeavor and suffering which have resulted in their embodiment in the fundamental law of the land. The United States marshal could only have invaded the house of the accused when armed with a warrant issued as required by the Constitution, upon sworn information, and describing with reasonable particularity the thing for which the search was to be made. Instead, he acted without sanction of law, doubtless prompted by the desire to bring further proof to the aid of the government, and under color of his office undertook to make a seizure of private papers in direct violation of the constitutional prohibition against such action. Under such circumstances, without sworn information and particular description, not even an order of court would have justified such procedure; much less was it within the authority of the United States marshal to thus invade the house and privacy of the accused. . . . To sanction such proceedings would be to affirm by judicial decision a manifest neglect, if not an open defiance, of the prohibitions of the Constitution, intended for the protection of the people against such unauthorized action.

. . .

We therefore reach the conclusion that the letters in question were taken from the house of the accused by an official of the United States, acting under color of his office, in direct violation of the constitutional rights of the defendant; that having made a reasonable application for their return, which was heard and passed upon by the court, there was involved in the order refusing the application a denial of the constitutional rights of the accused, and that the court should have restored these letters to the accused. In holding them and permitting their use upon the trial, we think prejudicial error was committed.

As to the papers and property seized by the policemen, it does not appear that they acted under any claim of federal authority such as would make the amendment applicable to such unauthorized seizures. The record shows that what they did by way of arrest and search and seizure was done before the finding of the indictment in the federal court; under what supposed right or authority does not appear. What remedies the defendant may have against them we need not inquire, as the Fourth Amendment is not directed to individual misconduct of such officials. Its limitations reach the federal government and its agencies.

. . .

(Judgment reversed.)

Wolf v *Colorado*

338 U.S. 25, 69 S.Ct. 1359, 93 L.Ed. 1782 (1949)

The issue in this case was: Does a conviction by a state court for a state offense deny the due process of the law required by the Fourteenth Amendment, solely because evidence that was admitted at the trial was obtained under circumstances that would have rendered it inadmissible in a prosecution for a violation of federal law in a United States Court because of an infraction of the Fourteenth Amendment as applied in *Weeks* v *United States?* (See preceding case.)

Justice Frankfurter delivered the opinion of the Court:

The security of one's privacy against arbitrary intrusion by the police—which is at the core of the Fourth Amendment—is basic to a free society. It is therefore implicit in "the concept of ordered liberty" and as such enforceable against the states through the Due Process Clause.

. . .

... [W]e have no hesitation in saying that were a state affirmatively to sanction such police incursion into privacy it would run counter to the guaranty of the Fourteenth Amendment. But the ways of enforcing such a basic right raise questions of a different order. How such arbitrary conduct should be checked, what remedies against it should be afforded, the means by which the right should be made effective, are all questions that are not to be so dogmatically answered as to preclude the varying solutions which spring from an allowable range of judgment on issues not susceptible of quantitative solution.

In *Weeks* v *United States,* this Court held that in a federal prosecution the Fourth Amendment barred the use of evidence secured through an illegal search and seizure.... The decision was a matter of judicial implication. Since then it has been frequently applied and we stoutly adhere to it. But the immediate question is whether the basic right to protection against arbitrary intrustion by the police demands the exclusion of logically relevant evidence obtained by an unreasonable search and seizure because, in a federal prosecution for a federal crime, it would be excluded.... When we find that in fact most of the English-speaking world does not regard as vital to such protection the exclusion of evidence thus obtained, we must hesitate to treat this remedy as an essential ingredient of the right. The contrariety of views of the states is particularly impressive in view of the careful reconsideration which they have given the problem in the light of the Weeks decision.

. . .

As of today 30 states reject the Weeks doctrine, 17 states are in agreement with it.

. . .

The jurisdictions which have rejected the *Weeks* doctrine have not left the right to privacy without other means of protection. Indeed, the exclusion of evidence is a remedy which directly serves only to protect those upon whose person or premises something incriminating has been found. We cannot, therefore, regard it as a departure from basic standards to remand such persons, together with those who emerge scatheless from a search, to the remedies of private action and such protection as the internal discipline of the police, under the eyes of alert public opinion, may afford. . . . There are, moreover, reasons for excluding evidence unreasonably obtained by the federal police which are less compelling in the case of police under state or local authority.

. . .

We hold, therefore, that in a prosecution in a state court for a state crime the Fourteenth Amendment does not forbid the admission of evidence obtained by an unreasonable search and seizure. And though we have interpreted the Fourth Amendment to forbid the admission of such evidence, a different question would be presented if Congress under its legislative powers were to pass a statute purporting to negate the Weeks doctrine. We would then be faced with the problem of the respect to be accorded the legislative judgment on an issue as to which, in default of that judgment, we have been forced to depend upon our own. Problems of a converse character, also not before us, would be presented should Congress under Section 5 of the Fourteenth Amendment undertake to enforce the rights there guaranteed by attempting to make the *Weeks* doctrine binding upon the states.

(Judgment affirmed.)
Justice Black concurred.
Justices Rutledge, Murphy, and Douglas dissented.

In *Ker* v *California,* 374 U.S. 23, 83 S.Ct. 1623, 10 L.Ed. 2d 726 (1963), the United States Supreme Court in a five to four decision ruled that evidence obtained as a result of an unannounced entry by the state police could be used in a state court where admissibility is governed by constitutional law, even though such evidence might not be allowed in a federal trial because its use would violate a federal statute. Justice Clark for the majority noted that although the standards of reasonableness are the same under the Fourth and Fourteenth

Amendments, the federal system compels distinguishing between evidence held to be inadmissible under the Supreme Court's supervision and that held to be inadmissible because of the prohibition of the United States Constitution. Clark went on to state that a lawful arrest by state officers for state offenses is determined by state law as long as there is no constitutional violation. In a separate finding the Court also found that the California law permitting breaking in by law enforcement officers without proper notice is permissible when exigent circumstances require.

United States v *Watson*

423 U.S. 411, 96 S.Ct. 820, 46 L.Ed 2d 598, (1976)

A postal inspector received from a reliable informant a stolen credit card which Watson had given to the informant. The card was to be used for the mutual benefit of the informant and Watson, who agreed to furnish additional cards. The inspector suggested that a later meeting be arranged between Watson and the informant at a restaurant. At the meeting and upon a prearranged signal from the informant that Watson had additional cards, postal officers made a warrantless arrest of Watson, removed him from the restaurant, and gave him the Miranda warnings. No cards were revealed during the search of Watson's person. A consent search of his automobile nearby revealed two additional cards in the name of other persons.

On appeal to the Court of Appeals, Ninth Circuit, the defendant's motion to suppress was granted after denial of suppression of the evidence by the District Court. Writing for the majority in upholding the admissibility of evidence, Mr. Justice White held that "contrary to the Court of Appeals view, Watson's arrest was not invalid because executed without a warrant," but was valid on probable cause since it was made by postal officers acting in strict compliance with governing statutes and regulations. Therefore, there was no Fourth Amendment violation.

The majority next concluded that because Watson's arrest was valid, his consent to search the vehicle was not the product of an illegal arrest. This was also contrary to the Court of Appeals' holding that the voluntariness of the consent was presumed on the coercion of a illegal arrest. Nor were there any other circumstances which were relied upon by the Court of Appeals that were adequate to invalidate Watson's consent. As White noted:

> We are satisfied in addition that the remaining factors relied upon by the Court of Appeals to invalidate Watson's consent are inadequate to demonstrate that, in the totality of the circumstances, Watson's consent was not his own "essentially free and unconstrained choice" because his "will ha[d] been overborne and his capacity for self-determination critically impaired." . . . There was no overt act or threat of force against Watson proved or claimed. There were no promises made to him and no indication of more subtle forms of coercion that might flaw his judgment. He had been arrested and was in custody, but his consent was given while on a public street, not in the confines

of the police station. Moreover, the fact of custody alone has never been enough in itself to demonstrate a coerced confession or consent to search. Similarly, . . . the absence of proof that Watson knew he could withhold his consent, though it may be a factor in the overall judgment, is not to be given controlling significance. There is no indication in this record that Watson was a newcomer to the law, mentally deficient, or unable in the face of a custodial arrest to exercise a free choice. He was given Miranda warnings and was further cautioned that the results of the search of his car could be used against him. He persisted in his consent.

In these circumstances, to hold that illegal coercion is made out from the fact of arrest and the failure to inform the arrestee that he could withhold consent would not be consistent with Schneckloth and would distort the voluntariness standard that we reaffirmed in that case.

Justice Stevens did not participate in consideration of the case.
Justices Powell and Stewart concurred.
Justices Marshall and Brennan dissented.

Chimel v California
395 U.S. 752, 89 S.Ct. 2034, 23 L.Ed. 2d 685 (1969)

Three police officers having a warrant to arrest Chimel went to his home one afternoon. Upon being admitted by his wife, they waited until he returned home from work. They then served the warrant and proceeded to conduct a search of the entire house for over an hour. They recovered several items—mostly coins, which could be used as evidence in the case against Chimel. At the later trial the evidence was admitted as evidence over Chimel's objection. Upon appeal of the conviction and affirmance by the California appellate courts, the United States Supreme Court reversed.

Justice Stewart delivered the opinion of the Court:

In 1950, . . . came *United States* v *Rabinowitz,* 339 U.S. 56, . . . , the decision upon which California primarily relies in the case now before us. In *Rabinowitz,* federal authorities had been informed that the defendant was dealing in stamps bearing forged overprints. On the basis of that information they secured a warrant for his arrest, which they executed at his one-room business office. At the time of the arrest, the officers "searched the desk, safe, and file cabinets in the office for about an hour and a half," . . . and seized 573 stamps with forged overprints. The stamps were admitted into evidence at the defendant's trial, and this Court affirmed his conviction, rejecting the contention that the warrantless search had been unlawful. The Court held that the search in its entirety fell within the principle giving law enforcement authorities "(t)he right 'to search the place where the arrest is made in order to find and seize things connected with the crime . . .'" *Harris* was regarded as "ample authority" for that conclusion. . . . The opinion rejected the rule . . .

that "in seizing goods and articles, law enforcement agents must secure and use search warrants wherever reasonably practicable." The test, said the Court, "is not whether it is reasonable to procure a search warrant, but whether the search was reasonable."

. . .

Rabinowitz has come to stand for the proposition, *inter alia,* that a warrant-less search "incident to a lawful arrest" may generally extend to the area that is considered to be in the "possession" or under the "control" of the person arrested. And it was on the basis of that proposition that the California courts upheld the search of the petitioner's entire house in this case. That doctrine, however, at least in the broad sense in which it was applied by the California courts in this case, can withstand neither historical nor rational analysis.

Even limited to its own facts, the *Rabinowitz* decision was, as we have seen, hardly founded on an unimpeachable line of authority. As Mr. Justice Frankfurter commented in dissent in that case, the "hint" contained in *Weeks* was, without persuasive justification, "loosely turned into dictum and finally elevated to a decision." . . . And the approach taken in cases such as *Go-Bart, Lefkowitz, and Trupiano* was essentially disregarded by the *Rabinowitz* Court.

Nor is the rationale by which the state seeks here to sustain the search of the petitioner's house supported by a reasoned view of the background and purpose of the Fourth Amendment. Mr. Justice Frankfurter wisely pointed out in his *Rabinowitz* dissent that the Amendment's proscription of "unreasonable searches and seizures" must be read in light of "the history that gave rise to the words"—a history of "abuses so deeply felt by the Colonies as to be one of the potent causes of the Revolution. . . ." The Amendment was in large part a reaction to the general warrants and warrantless searches that had so alien-ated the colonists and had helped speed the movement for independence. In the scheme of the Amendment, therefore, the requirement that "no warrants shall issue, but upon probable cause," plays a crucial part. . . . Even in the *Agnello* case the Court relied upon the rule that "(b)elief, however well founded, that an article sought is concealed in a dwelling house, furnishes no justification for a search of that place without a warrant. And such searches are held unlawful notwithstanding facts unquestionably showing probable cause." . . . Clearly, the general requirement that a search warrant be obtained is not lightly to be dispensed with, and "the burden is on those seeking [an] exemption [from the requirement] to show the need for it."

. . .

A similar analysis underlies the "search incident to arrest" principle, and marks its proper extent. When an arrest is made, it is reasonable for the arresting officer to search the person arrested in order to remove any weapons that the latter might seek to use in order to resist arrest or effect his escape. Otherwise, the officer's safety might well be endangered, and the arrest itself frustrated. In addition, it is entirely reasonable for the arresting officer to search for and seize any evidence on the arrestee's person in order to prevent its concealment or destruction. And the area into which an arrestee might reach in order to grab a weapon or evidentiary items must, of course, be governed by a like rule. A gun on a table or in a drawer in front of one who is arrested can be as dangerous to the arresting officer as one concealed in the clothing of the person arrested. There is ample justification, therefore, for a search of the arrestee's person and the area "within his immediate control"—construing that phrase to mean the area from within which he might gain possession of a weapon or destructible evidence.

There is no comparable justification, however, for routinely searching any room other than that in which an arrest occurs—or, for that matter, for searching through all the desk drawers or other closed or concealed areas in that room itself. Such searches, in the absence of well-recognized exceptions, may be made only under the authority of a search warrant. The "adherence to judicial processes" mandated by the Fourth Amendment requires no less.

. . .

It is argued in the present case that it is "reasonable" to search a man's house when he is arrested in it. But that argument is founded on little more than a subjective view regarding the acceptability of certain sorts of police conduct, and not on considerations relevant to Fourth Amendment interests. Under such an unconfined analysis, Fourth Amendment protection in this area would approach the evaporation point. It is not easy to explain why, for instance, it is less subjectively "reasonable" to search a man's house when he is arrested on his front lawn—or just down the street—than it is when he happens to be in the house at the time of arrest.

. . .

It would be possible, of course, to draw a line between *Rabinowitz* and *Harris* on the one hand, and this case on the other. For *Rabinowitz* involved a single room, and *Harris* a four-room apartment, while in the case before us an entire house was searched. But such a distinction would be highly artificial. The rationale that allowed the searches and seizures in *Rabinowitz* and *Harris* would allow the searches and seizures in this case. No consideration relevant to the Fourth Amendment suggests any point of rational limitation, once the search is allowed to go beyond the area from which the person arrested might obtain weapons or evidentiary items. The only reasoned distinction is one between a search of the person arrested and the area within his reach on the one hand, and more extensive searches on the other.

The petitioner correctly points out that one result of decisions such as *Rabinowitz* and *Harris* is to give law enforcement officials the opportunity to engage in searches not justified by probable cause, by the simple expedient of arranging to arrest suspects at home rather than elsewhere. We do not suggest that the petitioner is necessarily correct in his assertion that such a strategy was utilized here, but the fact remains that had he been arrested earlier in the day, at his place of employment rather than at home, no search of his house could have been made without a search warrant. In any event, even apart from the possibility of such police tactics, the general point so forcefully made by Judge Learned Hand . . . remains:

> After arresting a man in his house, to rummage at will among his papers in search of whatever will convict him, appears to us to be indistinguishable from what might be done under a general warrant; indeed, the warrant would give more protection, for presumably it must be issued by a magistrate. True, by hypothesis the power would not exist, if the supposed offender were not found on the premises; but it is small consolation to know that one's papers are safe only so long as one is not at home." ...

Rabinowitz and *Harris* have been the subject of critical commentary for many years, and have been relied upon less and less in our own decisions. It is time, for the reasons we have stated, to hold that on their own facts, and insofar as the principles they stand for are inconsistent with those that we have endorsed today, they are no longer to be followed.

Application of sound Fourth Amendment principles to the facts of this case produces a clear result. The search here went far beyond the petitioner's person and the area from within which he might have obtained either a weapon or something that could have been used as evidence against him. There was no constitutional justification, in the absence of a search warrant, for extending the search beyond that area. The scope of the search was, therefore, "unreasonable" under the Fourth and Fourteenth Amendments and the petitioner's conviction cannot stand.

(Judgment reversed.)
Justice Harlan concurred.
Justices White and Black dissented.

In *United States* v *Harris*, 403 U.S. 573, 91 S.Ct. 2075, 29 L.Ed. 2d 723 (1971), an informant furnished information to a federal tax collector. A warrant was issued and Harris was arrested and subsequently charged with possession of untaxed liquor. He moved to suppress the evidence claiming that the affidavit in support of the search warrant did not establish adequate facts to believe the informant. In a five-man majority, the United States Supreme Court found the affidavit to be sufficient even though it was largely based on hearsay evidence from an informant who was described as a prudent person who had recent personal knowledge of the whiskey sales by Harris. Chief Justice Burger noted for the majority that "while a bare statement by an affiant that he believed the informant to be truthful would not, before, in itself, provide a factual basis for crediting the report of an unnamed informant, we conclude that the affidavit in the present case contains an ample factual basis for believing the informant, which when coupled with his own knowledge of the respondent's background, afforded a basis upon which a magistrate could reasonably issue a warrant. The accusation ... was plainly a declaration against interest since it could readily warrant a prosecution and could sustain a conviction against the informant himself."

In *Vale* v *Louisiana*, 399 U.S. 30, 90 S.Ct. 1969, 26 L.Ed. 2d 409 (1970), police officers upon reasonably believing that a narcotics sale had just taken place arrested Vale on the front steps of his residence. He was advised that they were going to search the house. An officer conducted a cursory search to ascertain if anyone else was present. A quantity of narcotics was found in a rear bedroom. In striking down the seizure Justice Stewart for the majority stated that there was "no precedent of this Court (to) sustain the constitutional validity of the search before us." The search must be contemporaneous with the arrest and confined to the immediate vicinity. If the search was to be upheld, the arrest must at least occur inside the house, not somewhere outside. A belief that an article is to be found inside of a dwelling does not furnish justification for the search no matter how well founded the belief.

Stone v *Powell*
428 U.S. 465, 96 S.Ct. 3037, 49 L.Ed. 2d 1067, (1976)

Several defendants were convicted of criminal offenses in California state courts. Their convictions were affirmed on appeals within California. In each case, the prosecutor relied upon evidence obtained by searches and seizures alleged by the defendants to have been illegal. Subsequently each defendant sought federal relief by filing a writ of habeas corpus under 28 U.S.C. 2254. The question presented to the United States Supreme Court was whether a federal court should consider, in ruling on a petition for habeas corpus relief, a claim that the evidence obtained by an unconstitutional search or seizure was introduced at his trial, when the defendant was previously afforded an opportunity for full and fair litigation of the issue in the state courts.

Justice Powell delivered the opinion for the Court:

In sum, we conclude, that where the state has provided an opportunity for full and fair litigation of a Fourth Amendment claim, a state prisoner may not be granted federal habeas corpus relief on the ground that the evidence obtained in an unconstitutional search or seizure was introduced at his trial. In this context the contribution of the exclusionary rule, if any, to the effectuation of the Fourth Amendment is minimal and the substantial societal costs of application of the rule persist with special force.

In discussing the exclusionary rule, it was stated that, "Application of the rule thus deflects the truth finding process and often frees the guilty.

. . .

Evidence obtained by police officers in violation of the Fourth Amendment is excluded at trial in the hope that the frequency of future violations will decrease. Despite the absence of supportive empirical evidence, we have assumed that the immediate effect of exclusion will be to discourage law enforcement officials from violating the Fourth Amendment." While stating that the Court still adheres to the rule, it went on to emphasize that there "is no reason to believe, however, that the overall educative effect of the exclusionary rule would be appreciably diminished if search and seizure claims could not be raised in federal habeas corpus review of state convictions. . . ." The view that the deterrence of the Fourth Amendment violations would be furthered rests on the dubious assumption that law enforcement authorities would fear that federal habeas corpus review might reveal flaws in a search or seizure that went undetected at trial and on appeal.

Justices Brennan, Marshall, and White dissented.

In *United States* v *Edwards,* 415 U.S. 800, 94 S.Ct. 1234, 39 L.Ed. 2d 771 (1974), the United States Supreme Court held that the Fourth Amendment would not be extended to exclude from evidence the clothing taken from a defendant while he was in custody at the city jail following his arrest.

In *Cupp* v *Murphy,* 412 U.S. 29, 93 S.Ct. 2000, 36 L.Ed. 2d 900 (1973), Murphy was questioned concerning the murder of his estranged wife. He went voluntarily to the police station for this questioning and his attorney was present. The police noted a dark mark on his finger and asked if they could take sample scrapings from his fingernails. He refused, but the police took the samples over his protest and without a warrant. The incriminating evidence was admitted at his trial and he was convicted. On appeal the Supreme Court ruled that the seizure of samplings did not violate the Fourth Amendment; therefore, the search was permissible even though there was no formal arrest.

In *Stoner* v *California,* 376 U.S. 483, 84 S.Ct. 889, 11 L.Ed. 2d 856 (1964), the United States Supreme Court held that the search of a defendant's hotel room without his consent and with neither a search warrant nor arrest warrant is a violation of his constitutional rights, even though the permission of the hotel clerk was received.

In *Bumper* v *North Carolina,* 391 U.S. 543, 88 S.Ct. 1788, 20 L.Ed. 2d 797 (1968), the defendant, a black, was charged with rape. Before his arrest, law enforcement officers came to his grandmother's house where he was staying. The officers told the grandmother, "I have a search warrant to search your house." She allowed the officers to enter the house and they found a rifle that was introduced at Bumper's trial after his motion to suppress was denied. The Supreme Court ruled that a search cannot be justified as lawful on the sole basis of consent when "consent" has been given only after the official conducting the search has asserted that he possesses a warrant.

Vehicle Searches

Preston v *United States*

376 U.S. 364, 84 S.Ct. 881, 11 L.Ed. 2d 777 (1964)

Preston was arrested for vagrancy and his automobile was searched after it had been taken from the scene of the arrest. During the search of the automobile two loaded revolvers were found in the glove compartment. Unable to open the trunk lid, officers entered the trunk space by removing the rear seat. Additional incriminative items were seized from the trunk space. The seized articles were entered into evidence over Preston's objection and the defendant was convicted. On certiorari the United States Supreme Court reversed.

Justice Black delivered the opinion of the Court:

The Amendment provides:

> The right of the people to be secure in their persons, houses, papers, and effects, against unreasonable searches and seizures, shall not be violated, and no warrants shall issue but upon probable cause, supported by oath or affirmation, and particularly describing the place to be searched, and the persons or things to be seized.

The question whether evidence obtained by state officers and used against a defendant in a federal trial was obtained by unreasonable search and seizure is to be judged as if the search and seizure had been made by federal officers. . . . Our cases make it clear that searches of motorcars must meet the test of reasonableness under the Fourth Amendment before evidence obtained as a result of such searches is admissible. . . . Common sense dictates, of course, that questions involving searches of motorcars or other things readily moved cannot be treated as identical to questions arising out of searches of fixed structures like houses. For this reason, what may be an unreasonable search of a house may be reasonable in the case of a motorcar. . . . But even in the case of motorcars, the test still is, was the search unreasonable. Therefore we must inquire whether the facts of this case are such as to fall within any of the exceptions to the constitutional rule that a search warrant must be had before a search may be made.

It is argued that the search and seizure were justified as incidental to a lawful arrest. Unquestionably, when a person is lawfully arrested, the police have the right, without a search warrant, to make a contemporaneous search of the person of the accused for weapons or for the fruits of or implements used to commit the crime. . . . This right to search and seize without a search warrant extends to things under the accused's immediate control, . . . and, to an extent depending on the circumstances of the case, to the place where he is arrested. . . . The rule allowing contemporaneous searches is justified, for example, by the need to seize weapons and other things which might be used to assault an officer or effect an escape, as well as by the need to prevent the destruction of evidence of the crime—things which might easily happen where the weapon or evidence is on the accused's person or under his immediate control. But these justifications are absent where a search is remote in time or place from the arrest. Once an accused is under arrest and in custody, then a search made at another place, without a warrant, is simply not incident to the arrest. . . . Here, we may assume, as the government urges, that, either because the arrests were valid or because the police had probable cause to think the car stolen, the police had the right to search the car when they first came on the scene. But this does not decide the question of the reasonableness of a search at a later time and at another place. . . . The search of the car was not undertaken until petitioner and his companions had been arrested and taken in custody to the police station and the car had been towed to the garage. At this point there was no danger that any of the men arrested could have used any weapons in the car or could have destroyed any evidence of a crime— assuming that there are articles which can be the "fruits" or "implements" of the crime of vagrancy. . . . Nor, since the men were under arrest at the police station and the car was in police custody at a garage, was there any danger that the car would be moved out of the locality or jurisdiction. . . . We think that the search was too remote in time or place to have been as incidental to the arrest and conclude, therefore, that the search of the car without a warrant failed to meet the test of reasonableness under the Fourth Amendment, rendering the evidence obtained as a result of the search inadmissible.

(Judgment reversed.)

Is a warrantless search of a vehicle based upon probable cause that it contained contraband in violation of the Fourth Amendment? *Carroll* v *United States,* 267 U.S. 132, 45 S.Ct. 280, 69 L.Ed. 543 (1925), was the first major United States Supreme Court decision involving a search of a moving vehicle. The Court held in a seven to two opinion that a search and seizure are valid without a warrant if based upon a reasonable belief that the automobile or other vehicle contains contraband. In analyzing the realities of the automobile as a place to be searched, the Court further noted that, "[F]reedom from unreasonable searches and seizures . . . has been construed, practically since the beginning of government, as recognizing a necessary difference between a search of a store, dwelling house, or other structure in respect of which a proper official warrant readily may be obtained and a search of a ship, motorboat, wagon, or automobile for contraband goods, where it is not practical to secure a warrant, because the vehicle can quickly be moved out of the locality or jurisdiction in which the warrant must be sought."

Chambers v *Maroney*
399 U.S. 42, 90 S.Ct. 1975, 26 L.Ed. 2d 419 (1970)

Two armed men robbed a service station attendant at gunpoint. The money was carried away in a right-hand glove. Within an hour after witnesses gave a description of the getaway car, police stopped a vehicle matching the description. Chambers was one of the four male occupants who was wearing clothing matching the description given by the witnesses. The occupants were placed under arrest, but no search of the automobile was conducted at the scene. The car was taken to the police station where an immediate search was conducted without success. Later a second search revealed evidence of items taken from the attendant. The defendant was convicted of robbery and on appeal the United States Supreme Court affirmed.

Justice White delivered the opinion of the Court:

> We pass quickly the claim that the search of the automobile was the fruit of an unlawful arrest. Both the courts below thought the arresting officers had probable cause to make the arrest. We agree.
>
> · · ·
>
> Even so, the search that produced the incriminating evidence was made at the police station some time after the arrest and cannot be justified as a search incident to an arrest: "Once an accused is under arrest and in custody, then a search made at another place, without a warrant, is simply not incident to the arrest."
>
> · · ·
>
> In terms of the circumstances justifying a warrantless search, the Court has long distinguished between an automobile and a home or office. After surveying the law from the time of the adoption of the Fourth Amendment onward, the Court held that automobiles and other conveyances may be searched without a warrant in circumstances that would not justify the search without a warrant of a house or an office, provided that there is probable cause to believe that the car contains articles that the officers are entitled to seize.
>
> · · ·
>
> In enforcing the Fourth Amendment's prohibition against unreasonable searches and seizures, the Court has insisted upon probable cause as a minimum requirement for a reasonable search permitted by the Constitution. As a general rule, it has also required the judgment of a magistrate on the probable-cause issue and the issuance of a warrant before a search is made. Only in exigent circumstances will the judgment of the police as to probable cause serve as a sufficient authorization for a search. *Carroll* holds a search warrant unnecessary where there is probable cause to search an automobile stopped on the highway; the car is movable, the occupants are alerted, and the car's contents may never be found again if a warrant must be obtained. Hence an immediate search is constitutionally permissible.
>
> Arguably, because of the preference for a magistrate's judgment, only the immobilization of the car should be permitted until a search warrant is obtained; arguably, only the "lesser" intrusion is permissible until the magistrate authorizes the "greater." But which is the "greater" and which the "lesser" intrusion is itself a debatable question and the answer may depend on a variety of circumstances. For constitutional purposes, we see no difference between on the one hand seizing and holding a car before presenting the probable cause issue to a magistrate and on the other hand carrying out an immediate search without a warrant. Given probable cause to search, either course is reasonable under the Fourth Amendment.
>
> On the facts before us, the blue station wagon could have been searched on

the spot when it was stopped since there was probable cause to search and it was fleeting target for a search. The probable-cause factor still obtained at the station house and so did the mobility of the car unless the Fourth Amendment permits a warrantless seizure of the car and the denial of its use to anyone until a warrant is secured. In that event there is little to choose in terms of practical consequences between an immediate search without a warrant and the car's immobilization until a warrant is obtained. The same consequences may not follow where there is unforeseeable cause to search a house. . . . But as *Carroll* held for the purposes of the Fourth Amendment there is a constitutional difference between houses and cars.

(Judgment affirmed.)
Justices Stewart and Harlan concurred.

In *South Dakota* v *Opperman,* 428 U.S. 364, 96 S.Ct. 3092, 49 L.Ed. 2d 1000, (1976), Opperman's car had been impounded for several parking violations. Following standardized procedures, the Vermillion, South Dakota, police inventoried the vehicle and in doing so found marijuana in the glove compartment. The defendant was later arrested for possession of marijuana. He sought to suppress the evidence at the trial. His motion was denied by the South Dakota Supreme Court which reversed the conviction on the ground that the evidence was obtained in violation of the Fourth Amendment's prohibition against unreasonable searches and seizures. The United States Supreme Court reversed the South Dakota Supreme Court indicating that the police procedures did not violate the Fourth Amendment because the case did not involve an unreasonable search and seizure. Mr. Chief Justice Burger emphasized that the expectation of privacy regarding automobiles is diminished by the public nature of auto travel. Such expectation is considerably less than relating to one's home or office. In concluding, Burger stated:

> The Vermillion police were indisputably engaged in a caretaking search of a lawfully impounded automobile. . . . The inventory was conducted only after the car had been impounded for multiple parking violations. The owner, having left his car illegally parked for an extended period, and thus subject to impoundment, was not present to make other arrangements for the safekeeping of his belongings. The inventory itself was prompted by the presence in plain view of a number of valuables inside the car. . . . [T]here is no suggestion whatever that this standard procedure, essentially like that followed throughout the country, was a pretext concealing an investigation's police motive.

In *Texas* v *White,* 423 U.S. 67, 96 S.Ct. 304, 46 L.Ed. 2d 209, (1975), the Supreme Court held that where there was probable cause at the scene the probable-cause factor was still present at the station house after questioning the arrested defendant. Therefore, inventory search of an automobile, even though not consented to and without a warrant, was valid.

Stop and Frisk

Terry v *Ohio*

392 U.S. 1, 88 S.Ct. 1868, 20 L.Ed. 2d 889 (1968)

McFadden, a Cleveland, Ohio, police detective, observed three men who appeared to be "casing" a store. He testified that he had never seen them before and was unable to articulate what precisely drew his attention to them. McFadden had about 39 years on the force of which 35 were as a detective. He spent about 30 years in the area in question looking for shoplifters and pickpockets. He further explained that he had developed routine habits of observing people, and according to him, the three men did not look right. McFadden observed the men for about 10 to 12 minutes in the process of "casing" the job for a stickup. Considering it his duty, he then decided to investigate further. He approached the men and fearing for his life because "they may have a gun," spun the two remaining men around and "patted" them down over the outside clothing. He felt what he thought was a gun and reaching inside an outer garment he, seized the gun. The defendant, Terry, was convicted of carrying a concealed weapon. He appealed the conviction to the United States Supreme Court which affirmed.

Chief Justice Warren delivered the opinion of the Court:

... We granted certiorari to determine whether the admission of the revolver in evidence violated petitioner's rights under the Fourth Amendment, made applicable to the states by the Fourteenth.

. . .

... The question is whether in all the circumstances of this on-the-street encounter, his right to personal security was violated by an unreasonable search and seizure.

. . .

We would be less than candid if we did not acknowledge that this question thrusts to the fore difficult and troublesome issues regarding a sensitive area of police activity—issues which have never before been squarely presented to this Court. Reflective of the tensions involved are the practical and constitutional arguments pressed with great vigor on both sides of the public debate over the power of the police to "stop and frisk"—as it is sometimes euphemistically termed—suspicious persons.

Our first task is to establish at what point in this encounter the Fourth Amendment becomes relevant. That is, we must decide whether and when Officer McFadden "seized" Terry and whether and when he conducted a "search." There is some suggestion in the use of such terms as "stop" and "frisk" that such police conduct is outside the purview of the Fourth Amendment because neither action rises to the level of a "search" or "seizure" within the meaning of the Constitution. We emphatically reject this notion. . . . It must be recognized that whenever a police officer accosts an individual and restrains his freedom to walk away, he has "seized" that person. And it is nothing less than sheer torture of the English language to suggest that a careful exploration of the outer surfaces of a person's clothing all over his or her body in an attempt to find weapons is not a "search." Moreover, it is simply fantastic to urge that such a procedure performed in public by a policeman while the citizen stands helpless, perhaps facing a wall with his hands raised, is a "petty indignity." It is a serious intrusion upon the sanctity of the person, which may inflict great indignity and arouse strong resentment, and it is not to be undertaken lightly.

The danger in the logic which proceeds upon distinctions between a "stop" and an "arrest," or "seizure" of the person and between a "frisk" and a "search" is twofold. It seeks to isolate from constitutional scrutiny the initial stages of the contact between the policeman and the citizen. And by suggesting a rigid all-or-nothing model of justification and regulation under the Amendment, it obscures the utility of limitations upon the scope, as well as the initiation, of police action as a means of constitutional regulation. This Court has held in the past that a search which is reasonable at its inception may violate the Fourth Amendment by virtue of its intolerable intensity and scope.

· · ·

In view of these facts, we cannot blind ourselves to the need for law enforcement officers to protect themselves and other prospective victims of violence in situations where they may lack probable cause for an arrest.

· · ·

We must still consider, however, the nature and quality of the intrusion on individual rights which must be accepted if police officers are to be conceded the right to search for weapons in situations where probable cause to arrest for crime is lacking. Even a limited search of the outer clothing for weapons constitutes a severe, though brief, intrusion upon cherished personal security, and it must surely be an annoying, frightening, and perhaps humiliating experience.

· · ·

We conclude that the revolver seized from Terry was properly admitted in evidence against him. At the time he seized petitioner and searched him for weapons, Officer McFadden had reasonable grounds to believe that petitioner was armed and dangerous, and it was necessary for the protection of himself and others to take swift measures to discover the true facts and neutralize the threat of harm if it materialized. The policeman carefully restricted his search to what was appropriate to the discovery of the particular items which he sought. Each case of this sort will, of course, have to be decided on its own facts. We merely hold today that where a police officer observes unusual conduct which leads him reasonably to conclude in light of his experience that criminal activity may be afoot and that the persons with whom he is dealing may be armed and presently dangerous, where in the course of investigating this behavior he identifies himself as a policeman and makes reasonable inquiries, and where nothing in the initial stages of the encounter serves to dispel his reasonable fear for his own or others' safety, he is entitled for the protection of himself and others in the area to conduct a carefully limited search of the outer clothing of such persons in an attempt to discover weapons which might be used to assault him.

Such a search is a reasonable search under the Fourth Amendment, and any weapons seized may properly be introduced in evidence against the person from whom they were taken.

(Judgment affirmed.)
Justices Harlan and White concurred.
Justice Douglas dissented.

Williams was convicted of possessing a handgun and heroin found after an officer received information from an informant that Williams was dealing in heroin and had a gun in his waist. The officer reached inside the car and seized the gun from Williams' waistband which was where the informant said the gun was. Upholding the search and seizure, Justice Rehnquist stated that "applying [Terry's] principles to the present case we believe Sergeant Connolly acted justifiably in responding to the informant's tip." The information carried an indicia of reliability to justify the forcible stop of Williams. The informer was not anonymous but personally known to Connolly and the information was readily verifiable at the scene. *Adams* v *Williams,* 407 U.S. 143, 92 S.Ct. 1921, 32 L.Ed. 2d 612 (1972).

United States v *Robinson,* 414 U.S. 218, 94 S.Ct. 467, 38 L.Ed. 2d 427 (1973), raised the issue of how extensive a search may be after a lawful arrest. The defendant was arrested for the motor vehicle violation of operating a vehicle with an expired operator's license. He was given a full-custody search which revealed what later turned out to be heroin. The United States Supreme Court sustained the complete field search once the arrest of the person was made. Justice Rehnquist concluded:

The authority to search the person incident to a lawful custody arrest, while based upon the need to disarm and discover evidence does not depend on what a court may later decide was the probability in a particular arrest situation that weapons or evidence would in fact be found upon the person of the suspect. A custodial arrest of a suspect based on probable cause is a reasonable intrusion under the Fourth Amendment; that intrusion being lawful, a search incident to the arrest requires no additional justification. . . . [W]e hold that in the case of a lawful custodial arrest a full search of the person is not only an exception to the warrant requirement of the Fourth Amendment, but is also "reasonable" search under that Amendment.

Administrative Searches

Camara v Municipal Court of San Francisco
387 U.S. 523, 87 S.Ct. 1727, 18 L.Ed. 2d 930 (1967)

The San Francisco Housing Code authorized city departmental employees, if necessary for the performance of their duties and upon presentation of their credentials, to enter any building, structure, or premises in the city if necessary to carry out their duties. Camara refused several times to permit an inspection without a warrant of part of an apartment building he was leasing. He was convicted of violating the ordinance. On appeal in the state courts his request for a writ of prohibition to stop the action against him was refused. He finally appealed to the United States Supreme Court and secured a reversal.

Justice White delivered the opinion of the Court:

In *Frank* v *State of Maryland,* 359 U.S. 360 . . . this Court upheld, by a five-to-four vote, a state court conviction of a homeowner who refused to permit a municipal health inspector to enter and inspect his premises without a search warrant. In *Ohio ex rel. Eaton* v *Price,* 364 U.S. 263 . . . a similar conviction was affirmed by an equally divided Court. Since those closely divided decisions, more intensive efforts at all levels of government to contain and eliminate urban blight have led to increasing use of such inspection techniques, while numerous decisions of this Court have more fully defined the Fourth Amendment's effect on state and municipal action. . . . In view of the growing nationwide importance of the problem, we noted probable jurisdiction in this case . . . to re-examine whether administrative inspection programs, as presently authorized and conducted, violate Fourth Amendment rights as those rights are enforced against the states through the Fourteenth Amendment.

. . .

In summary, we hold that administrative searches of the kind at issue here are significant intrusions upon the interests protected by the Fourth Amendment, that such searches when authorized and conducted without a warrant procedure lack the traditional safeguards which the Fourth Amendment guarantees to the individual, and that the reasons put forth in *Frank* v *State of Maryland* and in other cases for upholding these warrantless searches are insufficient to justify so substantial a weakening of the Fourth Amendment's protections. Because of the nature of the municipal programs under consideration, however, these conclusions must be the beginning, not the end, of our inquiry. The *Frank* majority gave recognition to the unique character of these inspection programs by refusing to require search warrants; to reject that disposition does not justify ignoring the question whether some other accommodation between public need and individual rights is essential.

Since our holding emphasizes the controlling standard of reasonableness, nothing we say today is intended to foreclose prompt inspections, even without a warrant, that the law has traditionally upheld in emergency situations. . . . On the other hand, in the case of most routine area inspections, there is no compelling urgency to inspect at a particular time or on a particular day. Moreover, most citizens allow inspections of their property without a warrant. Thus, as a practical matter and in light of the Fourth Amendment's requirement that a warrant specify the property to be searched, it seems likely that warrants should normally be sought only after entry is refused unless there has been a citizen complaint or there is other satisfactory reason for securing immediate entry.

. . .

In this case, appellant has been charged with a crime for his refusal to permit housing inspectors to enter his leasehold without a warrant. There was no emergency demanding immediate access; in fact, the inspectors made three trips to the building in an attempt to obtain appellant's consent to search. Yet no warrant was obtained and thus appellant was unable to verify either the need for or the appropriate limits of the inspection. . . . Assuming the facts to be as the parties have alleged, we therefore conclude that appellant had a constitutional right to insist that the inspectors obtain a warrant to search and that appellant may not constitutionally be convicted for refusing to consent to the inspection. It appears from the opinion of the District Court of Appeal that under these circumstances a writ of prohibition will issue to the criminal court under California law.

(Conviction reversed.)
Justices Clark, Harlan, and Stewart dissented.

In *Frank* v *Maryland,* 359 U.S. 360, 79 S.Ct. 804, 3 L.Ed. 2d 877 (1959), the United States Supreme Court upheld a conviction of a person who refused to permit a warrantless inspection of a private premise for the purposes of locating and abating a suspected public nuisance. This opinion was generally interpreted as carrying out an additional exception to the rule that warrantless searches are unreasonable under the Fourth Amendment. According to the majority in *Frank,* the inspections in issue only touch the periphery "of the important interests safeguarded by the Fourth Amendment's protection against official intrusions, but it is hedged about with safeguards designed to make the least possible demand on the individual occupant and to cause only the slight restriction of his claims of privacy."

In *Colonnade Catering Corporation* v *United States,* 397 U.S. 72, 90 S.Ct. 744, 25 L.Ed. 2d 60 (1970), a federal statute authorized a fine for a person to refuse to admit Treasury Officers to inspect for specified taxable articles or for refusing to permit examination of such articles. Several officers upon refusal broke into a storeroom and removed articles. In holding that the guarantees of the Fourth Amendment are breached if an inspector enters to inspect for various violations of regulatory law without the official authority evidenced by a warrant, the United States Supreme Court concluded: "Under the existing statutes, Congress selected a standard that does not include forcible entries without a warrant. It resolved the issue, not by authorizing forcible, warrantless entries, but by making it an offense for a licensee to refuse admission to the inspector."

Investigative Searches

Davis v Mississippi
394 U.S. 721, 89 S.Ct. 1394, 22 L.Ed. 2d 676 (1969)

Davis and 24 other black youths were taken to police headquarters for questioning about a rape by a black youth. They were fingerprinted and released without a charge. About 40 or 50 other black young people were also questioned in school, on the street, or at police headquarters. A set of fingerprints found at the crime scene matched those of Davis. The evidence was introduced at the trial of Davis for the rape and he was convicted. Davis argued that the fingerprint evidence should have been excluded as being secured in violation of the Fourth Amendment. On appeal the United States Supreme Court reversed the conviction.

Justice Brennan delivered the opinion of the Court:

We turn then to the question whether the detention of petitioner during which the fingerprints used at trial were taken constituted an unreasonable seizure of his person in violation of the Fourth Amendment. The opinion of the Mississippi Supreme Court proceeded on the mistaken premise that petitioner's prints introduced at trial were taken during his brief detention on December 3. In fact, as both parties before us agree, the fingerprint evidence used at trial was obtained on December 14, while petitioner was still in detention following his December 12 arrest. The legality of his arrest was not determined by the Mississippi Supreme Court. However, on oral argument here, the state conceded that the arrest on December 12 and the ensuing detention through December 14 were based on neither a warrant nor probable cause and were therefore constitutionally invalid. The state argues, nevertheless, that this invalidity should not prevent us from affirming petitioner's conviction. The December 3 prints were validly obtained, it is argued, and "it should make no difference in the practical or legal sense which [fingerprint] card was sent to the F.B.I. for comparison." It may be that it does make a difference in light of the objectives of the exclusionary rule, . . . but we need not decide the question since we have concluded that the prints of December 3 were not validly obtained.

. . .

Detentions for the sole purpose of obtaining fingerprints are no less subject to the constraints of the Fourth Amendment. It is arguable, however, that, because of the unique nature of the fingerprinting process, such detentions might, under narrowly defined circumstances, be found to comply with the Fourth Amendment even though there is no probable cause in the traditional sense. See *Camara* v *Municipal Court,* 387 U.S. 523, 87 S.Ct. 1727, 18 L.Ed. 2d 930 (1967). Detention for fingerprinting may constitute a much less serious intrusion upon personal security than other types of police searches and detentions. Fingerprinting involves none of the probing into an individual's private life and thoughts that marks an interrogation or search. Nor can fingerprint detention be employed repeatedly to harass any individual, since the police need only one set of each person's prints. Furthermore, fingerprinting is an inherently more reliable and effective crime-solving tool than eyewitness identifications or confessions and is not subject to such abuses as the improper line-up and the "third degree." Finally, because there is no danger of destruction of fingerprints, the limited detention need not come unexpectedly or at an inconvenient time. For this same reason, the general requirement that the authorization of a judicial officer be obtained in advance of detention would seem not to admit of any exception in the fingerprinting context.

We have no occasion in this case, however, to determine whether the requirements of the Fourth Amendment could be met by narrowly circumscribed procedures for obtaining, during the course of a criminal investigation, the fingerprints of individuals for whom there is no probable cause to arrest. For it is clear that no attempt was made here to employ procedures which might comply with the requirements of the Fourth Amendment: the detention at police headquarters of petitioner and the other young Negroes was not authorized by a judicial officer; petitioner was unnecessarily required to undergo two fingerprinting sessions; and petitioner was not merely fingerprinted during the December 3 detention but also subjected to interrogation.
. . .

(Judgment reversed.)
Justices Harlan concurred.
Justices Black and Stewart dissented.
Justice Fortas did not participate in the decision.

In *United States* v *Dionisio,* 410 U.S. 1, 93 S.Ct. 764, 35 L.Ed. 2d 67 (1973), about twenty defendants were ordered by an Illinois grand jury to record their voices. Dianisio refused and was held in contempt claiming that the disclosure would violate Fourth and Fifth Amendment rights. On appeal to the United States Supreme Court the issue of whether or not a grand jury must establish the reasonableness of the request for investigative evidence before the evidence needs to be supplied came into focus. The majority concluded that compulsion to testify before a grand jury differs from the seizure effected by an arrest or investigative stop. "A grand jury subpoena to testify is not the kind of governmental intrusion on privacy which the Fourth Amendment affords protection once the Fifth Amendment is satisfied." Neither the summons nor the directive to give a voice exemplar infringes on any right protected by the Fourth Amendment and therefore there is no requirement to satisfy even the minimal requirement of reasonableness.

Remedial Actions

Mapp v Ohio

367 U.S. 643, 81 S.Ct. 1684, 6 L.Ed. 2d 1081 (1961)

Several Cleveland, Ohio, police officers went to the Mapp residence looking for a fugitive who was believed to be in Mrs. Mapp's home. They were refused entrance after a request. They had no warrant. After a second request the officers forced their way in. Mrs. Mapp was physically assaulted and handcuffed when she reached for a piece of paper the officers said was a search warrant. Upon a search of the whole home, some obscene materials were found. She was later convicted for possessing these materials. On appeal to the United States Supreme Court Mrs. Mapp claimed that the evidence used against her was seized illegally. Her conviction was reversed.

Justice Clark delivered the opinion of the Court:

The state says that even if the search were made without authority, or otherwise unreasonably, it is not prevented from using the unconstitutionally seized evidence at trial, citing . . . in which this Court did indeed hold "that in a prosecution in a state court for a state crime the Fourteenth Amendment does not forbid the admission of evidence obtained by an unreasonable search and seizure." On this appeal, . . . it is urged once again that we review that holding.

Seventy-five years ago, in *Boyd* v *United States,* . . . considering the Fourth and Fifth Amendments as running "almost into each other" on the facts before it, this Court held that the doctrines of those Amendments

apply to all invasions on the part of the government and its employees of the sanctity of a man's home and the privacies of life. . . .

Less than 30 years after *Boyd,* this Court in *Weeks* v *United States,* 232 U.S. 383, . . . , stated that use of the seized evidence involved "a denial of the constitutional rights of the accused." This Court has ever since required of federal law officers a strict adherence to that command which this Court has held to be a clear, specific, and constitutionally required—even if judicially implied—deterrent safeguard without insistence upon which the Fourth Amendment would have been reduced to "a form of words."

· · ·

In 1949, 35 years after *Weeks* was announced, this Court, in *Wolf* v *People of State of Colorado,* again for the first time, discussed the effect of the Fourth

Amendment upon the states through the operation of the Due Process Clause of the Fourteenth Amendment. It said:

> [W]e have no hesitation in saying that were a state affirmatively to sanction such police incursion into privacy it would run counter to the guaranty of the Fourteenth Amendment. . . .

Nevertheless, after declaring that the "security of one's privacy against arbitrary intrusion by the police" is "implicit in 'the concept of ordered liberty' and as such enforceable against the states through the Due Process Clause," . . . and announcing that it "stoutly adhere[d] to the Weeks decision, the Court decided that the *Weeks* exclusionary rule would not then be imposed upon the states as "an essential ingredient of the right." . . . The Court's reasons for not considering essential to the right to privacy, as a curb imposed upon the states by the Due Process Clause, that which decades before had been posited as part and parcel of the Fourth Amendment's limitation upon federal encroachment of individual privacy, were bottomed on factual considerations.

While they are not basically relevant to a decision that the exclusionary rule is an essential ingredient of the Fourth Amendment as the right it embodies is vouchsafed against the states by the Due Process Clause, we will consider the current validity of the factual grounds upon which *Wolf* was based.

The Court in *Wolf* first stated that "[t]he contrariety of views of the states" on the adoption of the exclusionary rule of *Weeks* was "particularly impressive"; . . . and in, this connection that it could not "brush aside the experience of states which deem the incidence of such conduct by the police too slight to call for a deterrent remedy . . . by overriding the [states'] relevant rules of evidence." . . . While in 1949, prior to the Wolf Case, almost two-thirds of the states were opposed to the use of the exclusionary rule, now, despite the Wolf Case, more than half of those since passing upon it, by their own legislative or judicial decision, have wholly or partly adopted or adhered to the *Weeks* rule. . . . Significantly, among those now following the rule is California, which, according to its highest court, was "compelled to reach that conclusion because other remedies have completely failed to secure compliance with the constitutional provisions. . . ." In connection with this California case, we note that the second basis elaborated in *Wolf* in support of its failure to enforce the exclusionary doctrine against the states was that "other means of protection" have been afforded "the right to privacy." . . . The experience of California that such other remedies have been worthless and futile is buttressed by the experience of other states. The obvious futility of relegating the Fourth Amendment to the protection of other remedies has, moreover, been recognized by this Court since *Wolf*.

. . .

However, the force of that reasoning has been largely vitiated by later decisions of this Court. These include the recent discarding of the "silver platter'' doctrine which allowed federal judicial use of evidence seized in violation of the Constitution by state agents; . . . the relaxation of the formerly strict requirements as to standing to challenge the use of evidence thus seized, so that now the procedure of exclusion, "ultimately referable to constitutional safeguards,'' is available to anyone even "legitimately on [the] premises'' unlawfully searched . . . and finally, the formulation of a method to prevent state use of evidence unconstitutionally seized by federal agents.

. . .

It, therefore, plainly appears that the factual considerations supporting the failure of the Wolf Court to include the *Weeks* exclusionary rule when it recognized the enforceability of the right to privacy against the states in 1949, while not basically relevant to the constitutional consideration, could not, in any analysis, now be deemed controlling. . . . Today we once again examine *Wolf's* constitutional documentation of the right to privacy free from unreasonable state intrusion, and, after its dozen years on our books, are led by it to close the only courtroom door remaining open to evidence secured by official lawlessness in flagrant abuse of that basic right, reserved to all persons as a specific guarantee against that very same unlawful conduct. We hold that all evidence obtained by searches and seizures in violation of the Constitution is, by that same authority, inadmissible in a state court.

In non-exclusionary states, federal officers, being human, were by it invited to and did, as our cases indicate, step across the street to the state's attorney with their unconstitutionally seized evidence. Prosecution on the basis of that evidence was then had in a state court in utter disregard of the enforceable Fourth Amendment. If the fruits of an unconstitutional search had been inadmissible in both state and federal courts, this inducement to evasion would have been sooner eliminated.

Federal–state cooperation in the solution of crime under constitutional standards will be promoted, if only by recognition of their now mutual obligation to respect the same fundamental criteria in their approaches. "However much in a particular case insistence upon such rules may appear as a technicality that inures to the benefit of a guilty person, the history of the criminal law proves that tolerance of shortcut methods in law enforcement impairs its enduring effectiveness.''

. . .

There are those who say, as did Justice (then Judge) Cardozo, that under our constitutional exclusionary doctrine "[t]he criminal is to go free because the constable has blundered.'' . . . In some cases this will undoubtedly be the result. But, as was said in *Elkins,* "there is another consideration—the imperative of judicial integrity.'' . . . The criminal goes free, if he must, but it is the law that sets him free. Nothing can destroy a government more quickly than its failure to observe its own laws, or worse, its disregard of the charter of its own existence.

. . .

The ignoble shortcut to conviction left open to the state tends to destroy the entire system of constitutional restraints on which the liberties of the people rest. Having once recognized that the right to privacy embodied in the Fourth Amendment is enforceable against the states, and that the right to be secure against rude invasions of privacy by state officers is, therefore, constitutional in origin, we can no longer permit that right to remain an empty promise. Because it is enforceable in the same manner and to like effect as other basic rights secured by the Due Process Clause, we can no longer permit it to be revocable at the whim of any police officer who, in the name of law enforcement itself, chooses to suspend its enjoyment. Our decision, founded on reason and truth, gives to the individual no more than that which the Constitution guarantees him, to the police officer no less than that to which honest law enforcement is entitled, and, to the courts, that judicial integrity so necessary in the true administration of justice.

(Judgment reversed.)
Justice Black concurred.

A memorandum was written by Justice Stewart.
Justices Harlan, Whittaker, and Frankfurter dissented.

In *Wong Sun* v *United States,* 371 U.S. 471, 83 S.Ct. 407, 9 L.Ed. 2d 441 (1963), several federal narcotics officers forced open the door of Toy's laundry and followed him into his living quarters. His wife and child were asleep at the time. As Toy reached a night stand and started to reach into the night stand drawer, one officer drew his pistol, pulled Toy's hand away, and handcuffed him. Toy then told the federal agents that Yee was selling narcotics. The agents immediately went to Yee who gave the agents some heroin. Yee indicated that Wong Sun and Toy brought the heroin to him. Subsequently Wong Sun and Toy were charged for narcotics violations and released. Some days later Wong Sun was interrogated after being advised of his Fifth Amendment rights. Wong Sun made an unsigned confession. After conviction, Wong Sun appealed to the United States Supreme Court which reversed his conviction.

It was the Court's opinion that upon the small amount of information provided the officer, no warrant could have been issued. Therefore, the arrests were made without ''probable cause or reasonable grounds'' in direct violation of the Fourth Amendment.

Michigan police officers forcibly took Collins from Illinois to Michigan to be tried. He was convicted. He then appealed to the United States Supreme Court, claiming that conviction under such circumstances deprived him of the right to due process under the Fourteenth Amendment. The Supreme Court in upholding the conviction stated that due process is satisfied when a defendant is given a fair trial in accordance with constitutional due process and when he is present is fairly appraised of the charges against him. Justice Black concluded that, ''There is

nothing in the Constitution that requires a court to permit a guilty person rightfully convicted to escape justice because he was brought to trial against his will."
Frisbie v *Collins,* 342 U.S. 519, 72 S.Ct. 509, 96 L.Ed. 541 (1952).

In *United States* v *Calandra,* 414 U.S. 338, 94 S.Ct. 613, 38 L.Ed. 2d 561 (1974), the name of the defendant as possibly being involved in criminal activities was discovered as a result of an illegal search and seizure involving another case. A grand jury was subsequently empaneled to investigate loan-sharking and Calandra was subpoenaed because his name was found on the card. He refused to answer questions and was held in contempt. In rejecting his argument that he could refuse to answer questions at the grand jury hearing because of an illegal search and seizure, the Court concluded: "In sum, we believe that allowing a grand jury witness to invoke the exclusionary rule would unduly interfere with the effective and expeditious discharge of the grand jury's duties."

ELECTRONIC EAVESDROPPING

Olmstead v United States
277 U.S. 438, 48 S.Ct. 564, 72 L.Ed. 944 (1928)

Olmstead and several others were convicted of violating the National Prohibition Act. In order to find evidence against them, federal agents tapped telephone lines at points between the defendants' offices and their homes. They were convicted despite their objections that this evidence was illegally seized and therefore inadmissible under the Fourth and Fifth Amendments. On appeal the United States Supreme Court affirmed.

Chief Justice Taft delivered the opinion of the Court:

There is no room in the present case for applying the Fifth Amendment, unless the Fourth Amendment was first violated. There was no evidence of compulsion to induce the defendants to talk over their many telephones. They were continually and voluntarily transacting business without knowledge of the interception. Our consideration must be confined to the Fourth Amendment.

. . .

The well-known historical purpose of the Fourth Amendment, directed against general warrants and writs of assistance, was to prevent the use of governmental force to search a man's house, his person, his papers, and his effects, and to prevent their seizure against his will.

The United States takes no such care of telegraph or telephone messages as of mailed sealed letters. The Amendment does not forbid what was done here. There was no searching. There was no seizure. The evidence was secured by the use of the sense of hearing and that only. There was no entry to the houses or offices of the defendants.

The language of the Amendment cannot be extended and expanded to include telephone wires, reaching to the whole world from the defendant's house or office. The intervening wires are not part of his house or office, any more than are the highways along which they are stretched.

Congress may, of course, protect the secrecy of telephone messages by making them, when intercepted, inadmissible in evidence in federal criminal trials, by direct legislation, and thus depart from the common law of evidence. But the courts may not adopt such a policy by attributing an enlarged and unusual meaning to the Fourth Amendment.

. . .

We think, therefore, that the wire tapping here disclosed did not amount to a search or seizure within the meaning of the Fourth Amendment.

What has been said disposes of the only question that comes within the terms of our order granting certiorari in these cases. But some of our number, departing from that order, have concluded that there is merit in the twofold objection, overruled in both courts below, that evidence obtained through interception of telephone messages by government agents was inadmissible, because the mode of obtaining it was unethical and a misdemeanor under the law of Washington.

. . .

The common-law rule is that the admissibility of evidence is not affected by the illegality of the means by which it was obtained.

. . .

Nor can we, without the sanction of congressional enactment, subscribe to the suggestion that the courts have a discretion to exclude evidence, the admission of which is not unconstitutional, because unethically secured. This would be at variance with the common-law doctrine generally supported by authority. There is no case that sustains, nor any recognized textbook that gives color to, such a view. Our general experience shows that much evidence has always been receivable, although not obtained by conformity to the highest ethics. The history of criminal trials shows numerous cases of prosecutions of oathbound conspiracies for murder, robbery, and other crimes, where officers of the law have disguised themselves and joined the organizations, taken the oaths, and given themselves every appearance of active members engaged in the promotion of crime for the purpose of securing evidence. Evidence secured by such means has always been received.

(Judgment affirmed.)
Justice Brandeis dissented.

In *On Lee* v *United States,* 343 U.S. 747, 72 S.Ct. 697, 96 L.Ed. 1270 (1952), an undercover agent was wired for sound, and a small microphone attached to the agent transmitted all sounds to another agent who had a receiving set. On Lee made several incriminating statements to the undercover agent. The statements were introduced in On Lee's trial by permitting the receiving agent to testify to what he heard over the receiver. On Lee's conviction was upheld with Justice Jackson concluding, "We find no violation of the Fourth Amendment here." The Court also emphasized that the undercover agent merely agreed to have the conversation recorded which did not amount to an unreasonable search and seizure.

In *Lopez* v *United States,* 373 U.S. 427, 83 S.Ct. 1381, 10 L.Ed. 2d 462 (1963), a federal tax agent recorded a conversation with Lopez which amounted to a bribe. The recording of the conversation was admitted into evidence in the trial and Lopez was convicted. The United States Supreme Court held that the recorded conversation was admissible at the trial at which the agent also testified. As Justice Harlan stated for the majority: "Instead the device was used only to obtain the most reliable evidence possible of a conversation in which the government's own agent was a participant and which the agent was fully entitled to disclose. And the device was not planted by means of an unlawful physical invasion of the (defendant's) premises under circumstances that would violate the Fourth Amendment."

In *Berger* v *New York,* 388 U.S. 41, 87 S.Ct. 1873, 18 L.Ed. 2d 1040 (1967), New York judges were permitted by state statute to authorize wiretaps and buggings if specific procedural steps were followed—oath and affirmation that there is reasonable cause to believe that evidence of a crime may be obtained. The officers applying for the warrants also had to describe with some particularity the discussions to be overheard and the purpose of the wiretap; Berger, convicted on such wiretap evidence, contended that the statute was unconstitutional because it did require a particular description of the things to be seized and failed to require probable cause. The United States Supreme Court reversed the conviction holding that the statute violates the Fourth and Fourteenth Amendments because of its blanket grant of authority to eavesdrop and wiretap without adequate judicial supervision or protective procedures. It stated that the language of the New York statute was too broad in its sweep and resulted in a trespassing intrusion into constitutionally protected areas and therefore violated the Fourth and Fourteenth Amendments.

Katz v *United States*
389 U.S. 347, 88 S.Ct. 507, 19 L.Ed. 2d 576 (1967)

F.B.I. agents recorded the defendant's end of telephone conversations while he placed calls from a telephone booth. The conversations were overheard by placing an electronic listening and recording device on the outside of the booth. The recordings were admitted as evidence in the trial of Katz for violation of a federal statute. The United States Supreme Court, on appeal by Katz, reversed the conviction.

Justice Stewart delivered the opinion of the Court:

The petitioner has phrased those questions as follows:

A. Whether a public telephone booth is a constitutionally protected area so that evidence obtained by attaching an electronic listening-recording device to the top of such a booth is obtained in violation of the right to privacy of the user of the booth.

B. Whether physical penetration of a constitutionally protected area is necessary before a search and seizure can be said to be violative of the Fourth Amendment to the United States Constitution.

We decline to adopt this formulation of the issues. In the first place the correct solution of Fourth Amendment problems is not necessarily promoted by incantation of the phrase "constitutionally protected area." Secondly, the Fourth Amendment cannot be translated into a general constitutional "right to privacy." That Amendment protects individual privacy against certain kinds of governmental intrusion, but its protections go further, and often have nothing to do with privacy at all. Other provisions of the Constitution protect personal privacy from other forms of governmental invasion. But the protection of a person's *general* right to privacy—his right to be let alone by other people—is, like the protection of his property and of his very life, left largely to the law of the individual states.

Because of the misleading way the issues have been formulated, the parties have attached great significance to the characterization of the telephone booth from which the petitioner has strenuously argued that the booth was a "constitutionally protected area." The government has maintained with equal vigor that it was not. But this effort to decide whether or not a given "area," viewed in the abstract, is "constitutionally protected" deflects attention from the problem presented by this case. For the Fourth Amendment protects people, not places. What a person knowingly exposes to the public, even in his own home or office, is not a subject of Fourth Amendment protection. . . . But what he seeks to preserve as private, even in an area accessible to the public, may be constitutionally protected.

. . .

The government stresses the fact that the telephone booth from which the petitioner made his calls was constructed partly of glass, so that he was visible after he entered it as he would have been if he had remained outside. But what he sought to exclude when he entered the booth was not the intruding eye—it was the uninvited ear. He did not shed his right to do so simply because he made his calls from a place where he might be seen. No less than an individual in a business office, in a friend's apartment, or in a taxicab, a person in a telephone booth may rely upon the protection of the Fourth Amendment. One who occupies it, shuts the door behind him, and pays the toll that permits him to place a call is surely entitled to assume that the words he utters into the mouthpiece will not be broadcast to the world. To read the Constitution more narrowly is to ignore the vital role that the public telephone has come to play in private communication.

. . .

We conclude that the underpinnings of *Olmstead* and *Goldman* have been so eroded by our subsequent decisions that the "trespass" doctrine there enunciated can no longer be regarded as controlling. The government's activities in electronically listening to and recording the petitioner's words violated the privacy upon which he justifiably relied while using the telephone booth and thus constituted a "search and seizure" within the meaning of the Fourth Amendment. The fact that the electronic device employed to achieve that end did not happen to penetrate the wall of the booth can have no constitutional significance.

The question remaining for decision, then, is whether the search and seizure conducted in this case complied with constitutional standards. In that regard, the government's position is that its agents acted in an entirely defensible manner: They did not begin their electronic surveillance until investigation of the petitioner's activities had established a strong probability that he was using the telephone in question to transmit gambling information to persons in other states, in violation of federal law. Moreover, the surveillance was limited, both in scope and in duration, to the specific purpose of establishing the contents of the petitioner's unlawful telephonic communications. The agents confined their surveillance to the brief periods during which he used the telephone booth, and they took great care to overhear only the conversations of the petitioner himself.

The government urges that, because its agents relied upon the decisions in *Olmstead* and *Goldman,* and because they did no more here than they might properly have done with prior judicial sanction, we should retroactively validate their conduct. That we cannot do. It is apparent that the agents in this case acted with restraint. Yet the inescapable fact is that this restraint was imposed by the agents themselves, not by a judicial officer. They were not required, before commencing the search, to present their estimate of probable cause for detached scrutiny by a neutral magistrate. They were not compelled, during the conduct of the search itself, to observe precise limits established in advance by a specific court order. Nor were they directed, after the search had been completed, to notify the authorizing magistrate in detail of all that had been seized. In the absence of such safeguards, this Court has never sustained a search upon the sole ground that officers reasonably expected to find evidence of a particular crime and voluntarily confined their activities to the least intrusive means consistent with that end. Searches conducted without warrants have been held unlawful "notwithstanding facts unquestionably showing probable cause," . . . for the Constitution requires "that the deliberate, impartial judgment of a judicial officer . . . be interposed between the citizen and the police. . . ." "Over and again this Court has emphasized that the mandate of the [Fourth] Amendment requires adherence to judicial processes," . . . and that searches conducted outside the judicial process, without prior approval by judge or magistrate, are *per se* unreasonable under the Fourth Amendment— subject only to a few specifically established and well-delineated exceptions.

. . .

(Judgment reversed.)
Justice Marshall did not participate in the decision. Justice Harlan concurred.
Justice Black dissented.

In 1968 a major loophole was closed in the wiretapping controversy when the
United States Supreme Court held in *Lee* v *Florida,* 394 U.S. 378, 88 S.Ct.
2069, 20 L.Ed. 2d 1166 (1968), that Section 605 of the Federal Communications
Act forbids anyone, unless authorized by the sender, to intercept a telephone
message and no person shall divulge or publish its contents or substance to any
person. Evidence seized by state agents in violation of this prohibition could not
be used in state proceedings.

F.B.I. records of an electronic surveillance that were used in the conviction of
Alderman were discovered after the conviction. The United States Supreme
Court ruled that persons are entitled to object to illegally secured evidence and to
inspect the records of the recorded conversation, without first submitting the
materials to be screened *in camera* by the trial judge. As Justice White emphasized, "Unavoidably, this is a matter of judgment, but in our view the task is
too complex, and the margin of error too great, to rely wholly on the *in camera*
judgment of the trial court to identify those records which might have contributed
to the government's case. *Alderman* v *United States,* 394 U.S. 165, 89 S.Ct.
961, 22 L.Ed. 2d 176 (1969).

In *Gelbard* v *United States,* 408 U.S. 41, 92 S.Ct. 2357, 33 L.Ed. 2d 179
(1972), Gelbard was called before a federal grand jury to answer questions based
on information secured as a result of a judge-approved wiretap. The United
States Supreme Court held that a grand jury may invoke the statutory prohibition
found in Title III of the Crime Control Act of 1968 against the use of evidence in
grand jury evidence which is derived from the interception of oral or wire
communications. In ruling this way, the Court concluded that the statutory prohibition may be used as a defense to a contempt charge brought on by a refusal to
obey court orders to testify.

INFORMANTS

Roviaro v *United States*
353 U.S. 53, 77 S.Ct. 623, 1 L.Ed. 2d 639 (1957)

Roviaro was charged with illegally selling heroin and illegally transporting
heroin. The sales were allegedly to a "John Doe." Prior to the trial, the defendant requested the name, address, and occupation of "John Doe." The trial court
denied the request after objection by the government. At the trial itself the
request by the defendant was once again denied. The defendant was convicted on
both counts. On appeal the government did not defend the nondisclosure of John
Doe's identity in regard to the first charge, but it sought to sustain confidentiality

on the conviction of the second. The United States Supreme Court reversed the conviction.

Justice Burton delivered the opinion of the Court:

What is usually referred to as the informer's privilege is in reality the government's privilege to withhold from disclosure the identity of persons who furnish information of violations of law to officers charged with enforcement of that law. . . . The purpose of the privilege is the furtherance and protection of the public interest in effective law enforcement. The privilege recognizes the obligation of citizens to communicate their knowledge of the commission of crimes to law-enforcement officials and, by preserving their anonymity, encourages them to perform that obligation.

The scope of the privilege is limited by its underlying purpose. Thus, where the disclosure of the contents of a communication will not tend to reveal the identity of an informer, the contents are not privileged. Likewise, once the identity of the informer has been disclosed to those who would have cause to resent the communication, the privilege is no longer applicable.

A further limitation on the applicability of the privilege arises from the fundamental requirements of fairness. Where the disclosure of an informer's identity, or of the contents of his communication, is relevant and helpful to the defense of an accused, or is essential to a fair determination of a cause, the privilege must give way. In these situations the trial court may require disclosure and, if the government withholds the information, dismiss the action. Most of the federal cases involving this limitation on the scope of the informer's privilege have arisen where the legality of a search without a warrant is in issue and the communications of an informer are claimed to establish probable cause. In these cases the government has been required to disclose the identity of the informant unless there was sufficient evidence apart from his confidential communication.

Three recent cases in the courts of appeals have involved the identical problem raised here—the government's right to withhold the identity of an informer who helped to set up the commission of the crime and who was present at its occurrence. . . . In each case it was stated that the identity of such an informer must be disclosed whenever the informer's testimony may be relevant and helpful to the accused's defense.

We believe that no fixed rule with respect to disclosure is justifiable. The problem is one that calls for balancing the public interest in protecting the flow of information against the individual's right to prepare his defense. Whether a proper balance renders nondisclosure erroneous must depend on the particular circumstances of each case, taking into consideration the crime charged, the possible defenses, the possible significance of the informer's testimony, and other relevant factors.

. . .

The circumstances of this case demonstrate that John Doe's possible testimony was highly relevant and might have been helpful to the defense. So far as petitioner knew, he and John Doe were alone and unobserved during the crucial occurrence for which he was indicted. Unless petitioner waived his constitutional right not to take the stand in his own defense, John Doe was his one material witness. Petitioner's opportunity to cross-examine Police Officer Bryson and Federal Narcotics Agent Durham was hardly a substitute for an opportunity to examine the man who had been nearest to him and took part in the transaction. Doe had helped to set up the criminal occurrence and had played a prominent part in it. His testimony might have disclosed an entrapment. He might have thrown doubt upon petitioner's identity or on the identity of the package. He was the only witness who might have testified to petitioner's possible lack of knowledge of the contents of the package that he ''transported'' from the tree to John Doe's car. The desirability of calling John Doe as a witness, or at least interviewing him in preparation for trial, was a matter for the accused rather than the government to decide.

. . .

This is a case where the government's informer was the sole participant, other than the accused, in the transaction charged. The informer was the only witness in a position to amplify or contradict the testimony of government witnesses. Moreover, a government witness testified that Doe denied knowing petitioner or ever having seen him before. We conclude that, under these circumstances, the trial court committed prejudicial error in permitting the government to withhold the identity of its undercover employee in the face of repeated demands by the accused for his disclosure.

(Judgment reversed.)
Justices Black and Whittaker did not participate in considering the case.
Justice Clark dissented.

In *Lewis* v *United States,* 385 U.S. 206, 87 S.Ct. 424, 17 L.Ed. 2d 312 (1966), an undercover agent made purchases of marijuana on two different occasions from Lewis. Subsequently Lewis was arrested and charged with two counts of narcotics law violations. He was convicted on both. The United States Supreme Court ruled that the Fourth Amendment was not violated when a federal narcotics agent who misrepresented his identity and stated his willingness to purchase narcotics was invited into the defendant's home where a narcotics transaction was consummated. The narcotics were thereafter introduced in evidence against the defendant in a criminal trial.

In support of his application for a search warrant, F.B.I. agent Moore stated in an affidavit that he received information from another F.B.I. agent and a confidential informant, who had been reliable in the past, that a large number of stolen furs were concealed in a particular Chicago residence. Moore further supported the affidavit by statements of other reliable confidential informants in Chicago to the effect that Rugendorf had stolen the furs in question. The affidavit also alleged that the informant's description of the stolen furs matched the description of the furs stolen from the only reported fur burglary in the last six months. Pursuant to the warrant, a search was made of the residence and the furs were found. At his trial Rugendorf moved to suppress the evidence by challenging the legal sufficiency of the affidavit. On appeal from his conviction, the United States Supreme Court affirmed. Thus, *Rugendorf* v *United States*, 376 U.S. 528, 84 S.Ct. 825, 11 L.Ed. 2d 887 (1964), affirmed that ''as hearsay alone does not render an affidavit insufficient, the commissioner need not have required the informants . . . to be produced . . . so long as there was a substantial basis for crediting the hearsay.''

In *Hoffa* vs *United States*, 335 U.S. 293, 87 S.Ct., 408, 17 L.Ed. 2d 374 (1966), Partin was a paid federal government informant to whom Jimmy Hoffa confided. Hoffa did not know Partin's undercover status. During Hoffa's trial for attempting to bribe jurors a substantial part of the government's evidence against him was Partin's testimony. The Unites States Supreme Court affirmed Hoffa's conviction stating:

Where the argument falls is in its misapprehension of the fundamental nature and scope of Fourth Amendment protection. What the Fourth Amendment protects is the security a man relies upon when he places himself or his property within a constitutionally protected area, be it his home or his office, his hotel room or his automobile.
. . .

Neither this Court nor any member of it has ever expressed the view that the Fourth Amendment protects a wrongdoer's misplaced belief that a person to whom he voluntarily confides his wrongdoing will not reveal it.

In *United States* v *White*, 401 U.S. 745, 97 S.Ct. 1122, 28 L.Ed. 2d 453 (1971), an informer carrying a concealed radio transmitter engaged the defendant in conversations in the latter's home, in a restaurant, and in the informer's car. Agents overheard the conversations by the use of radio equipment. At the trial the informer was not produced, but the testimony of the overhearing agents was admitted, and the defendant was convicted. No warrants and no court orders were ever obtained. Citing *Hoffa* v *United States*, the United States Supreme Court held that the agents could testify by holding that there was no reasonable expectation of privacy. The Court also noted that the informant who worked in conjunction with the police, voluntarily as one of the parties to the conversation, relayed the conversation by means of the radio transmitter to the agents. In regard to the defendant's right to privacy claim, it was stated: ''If the law gives no protection to the wrongdoer whose trusted accomplice is or becomes a police agent, neither should it protect him when the same agent has recorded or trasmitted the conversations which are later offered in evidence to prove the state's case.''

In *McCray* v *Illinois*, 386 U.S. 300, 87 S.Ct. 1056, 18 L.Ed. 2d 62, (1967), there was a warrantless search following an arrest without a warrant. The arrest by the police was based on information furnished by a reliable informant. The officers during the trial refused to reveal the identity of the informant, although they did provide information in regard to the reliability of the informant and the underlying circumstances upon which the informant's conclusion was based. The United States Supreme Court held that the facts of the case did not require that the identity of the informant be revealed, although in some instances it may be mandatory. The Court noted:

> Where the issue is not guilt or innocence, but, as here, the question of probable cause for an arrest or search, the Illinois Supreme Court has held that the police officers need not invariably be required to disclose an informant's identity if the trial judge is convinced by evidence submitted in open court and subject to cross-examination that the officers did rely in good faith upon credible information supplied by a reliable informant. This Illinois evidentiary rule is consistent with the law of many other states.

. . .

QUESTIONS

1. What is the scope of search and seizure as defined by the latest Supreme Court decisions? What areas have these decisions encompassed?

2. Compare the case of *U.S.* v *Watson* to the other cases involving vehicle search. What are the prerequisites for a vehicle search as defined by the Court?

3. Discuss the decisions in the Section on stop and frisk. What is the probable cause requirement? Is it necessary according to the Court?

4. What is the basis of the *Mapp* decision? Why is this considered a landmark case?

5. According to the Court decisions regarding informants, what position will be taken in future cases? Will the trend be pro or con?

10

FIFTH AMENDMENT PRIVILEGE AGAINST SELF- INCRIMINATION

The privilege against self-incrimination—no person "shall be compelled in any criminal case to be a witness against himself"—has been one of the most misunderstood and controversial provisions in the Constitution. It is one of the most significant of the personal liberties guaranteed by the Constitution to Americans. The privilege ensures that no one can be compelled to give an answer to a question if the answer may implicate him in an offense or convict him of a crime. The privilege guarantees that no defendant must take the stand and be subject to cross-examination.

In general, those who support the concept of the Fifth Amendment privilege consider it one of the most important provisions in the Bill of Rights. They view the idea of compelling a person to contribute to his own conviction as degrading and repugnant to human decency and dignity. Those who have negative beliefs about the privilege claim that when an individual "pleads the Fifth Amendment," he is making an admission of guilt.

These two views have led to a great debate in the post-World War II era. One needs only to remember the televised congressional investigations into communist activities and organized crime in which the privilege was invoked on a wide scale—with sometimes humorous results. However, the impact of the Fifth

Amendment privilege is probably felt strongest in the day-to-day operations of the state and federal criminal justice system.

Once again, the experiences in seventeenth-century England were a basis for including the Fifth Amendment privilege in the Constitution to protect individuals from being forced to incriminate themselves. In the seventeenth century it was the practice in England to question accused persons and other suspects. At the trial it was the customary procedure for the prosecutor and the judge to interrogate the defendant. In the infamous Star Chamber Court individuals merely suspected of some offense were interrogated without ever having a formal accusation made. The question most often was directed to having the defendant admit to some crime. Very frequently persuasion in the forms of torture or threats was used if the suspect did not respond with the desired answers.

The privilege against self-incrimination had an early beginning in the American Colonies. Laws on this subject date from 1641 in Massachusetts and 1650 in Connecticut. However, because of abuses of the privileges in the colonies, the Bill of Rights of Virginia, which subsequently became a model for the Fifth Amendment, provided that no one can be "compelled to give evidence against himself."

Currently only two states, Iowa and New Jersey, do not have a guarantee against self-incrimination in their state constitutions. Both of these states have the privilege guaranteed by statute. Because these are state laws, interpretation of the privilege is by state courts and consequently such interpretations may be different from those of federal courts. The question, therefore, comes up whether the Fifth Amendment privilege is binding on the states through the doctrine of incorporation. The *Malloy* v *Hogan,* 378 U.S. 1 (1964), decision of the United States Supreme Court extracted in the following cases held that the Fourteenth Amendment's Due Process Clause does incorporate the Fifth Amendment privilege.

Suppose that a person does claim the Fifth Amendment privilege. Is he harmed by its invocation? The question then becomes: Why should an innocent person not take the stand? Can the trier-of-fact draw any inferences from a failure to take the stand? Although there may be many reasons why a person does not take the stand to testify, such as previous conviction of a felony or he may be of low intelligence and therefore easily confused when cross-examined, there is a tendency on the part of jurors to infer guilt when a defendant refuses to testify.

The danger of refusing to testify is compounded when the prosecutor or judge calls the jury's attention to the fact that the defendant refused to take the witness stand and then tells the jury to infer that because the defendant knew the facts of the case and chose to say nothing, he must be guilty. In *Griffin* v *California,* 380 U.S. 609 (1965), the Supreme Court declared that this kind of conduct violated the Fifth Amendment privilege.

It should be pointed out here that a witness who is not a defendant has the same self-incrimination privilege as a defendant, but in the case of a witness the refusal to take the stand or answer would be damaging or favorable to the person for or against whom the witness is testifying.

The privilege against self-incrimination is subject to the limitation of the waiver doctrine. It may be lost if the person freely chooses to take the stand and testify in his own behalf. When he does this, he is not permitted to refuse to answer relevant questions on the grounds his answers may tend to incriminate him. Also, once a witness responds to questions with incriminating answers, he is no longer able to claim the privilege to further questions on the same subject. The defendant, in short, has a clear choice: refuse to take the stand or take it and waive the privilege.

A witness is in a somewhat more difficult position. He can be compelled to be a witness but not give answers which may incriminate him. He can be compelled to answer all relevant questions which do not incriminate him. The problem arises where the witness is unsure if an answer will incriminate him. He does not wish to take the chance that he will incriminate himself and therefore waive his privilege, as seen above. For this reason, witnesses often claim the privilege as soon as possible even though the questions are seemingly inconsequential and not incriminating.

Analyzing the Fifth Amendment one notes that the privilege indicates that a person cannot be compelled to incriminate himself ''in any criminal case.'' He is protected in the criminal case because he can refrain from taking the stand. The protection has been considerably broadened in scope over the decades by the United States Supreme Court decisions. The clause applies to witnesses not only in criminal cases but also in civil cases and in other appearances before bodies authorized to compel sworn testimony. These hearings are generally before various administrative agencies, the grand jury, or a legislative committee. A valuable protection for the witness is that the privilege may be claimed when the answer may *tend* to incriminate him. If the answer would furnish a link in the chain of evidence against him, the witness need not answer. Additionally, if the question is for the purpose of searching out other evidence outside the purposes of the hearing which may and can be used against him, he may refuse to answer.

Violation of the Fifth Amendment privilege is commonly used as a basis for exclusions of admissions and confessions made by a person who is interrogated by police without having been first warned of his right to not answer any questions in addition to being denied his right to counsel. Chapter 2 discusses this problem in greater detail.

Once a person becomes a witness, can he refuse to answer questions whenever he chooses by claiming the Fifth Amendment privilege? The answer is no because there must be some basis for the claim of the privilege. The privilege does not protect the witness merely because he will be embarrassed. Similarly, testimony that may implicate a relative or close friend is not privileged. The privilege is personal and applies only to natural persons. It therefore cannot be used on behalf of a corporation or an organization. The privilege also applies to testimonial compulsion and not to real evidence secured from the person such as blood, urine or body fluid specimens, fingerprints, handwriting exemplars, and voice speaking for identification.

The privilege is also limited by the doctrine of immunity in which a person may be compelled to answer incriminating questions if he is granted immunity from prosecution by the government for any crime in which he may be implicated by his answers. A number of federal and state statutes provide that if a witness is granted immunity from subsequent prosecution with respect to any matter about which he testifies, he can be forced to provide answers to incriminating questions. The theory behind the immunity doctrine is that the witness is protected to the same extent by the grant of immunity as by the Fifth Amendment. If he has nothing to lose, then the witness can be compelled to testify.

Double Jeopardy

The Fifth Amendment forbids successive prosecutions for the same offense in the federal courts of the United States. It has only been within the last decade that the federal double jeopardy protection has been made applicable to the states by the Due Process Clause of the Fourteenth Amendment. *Benton* v *Maryland,* 395 U.S. 784, 89 S.Ct. 2056, 23 L.Ed. 2d 707 (1969).

In a criminal trial, jeopardy attaches when a defendant is formally charged with an offense and the trial has commenced before a competent court. A trial commences in jury trial when the jury is impaneled and sworn and in a court trial when the first witness is sworn. Several situations arise in which the defense of double jeopardy bars retrial:

1. conviction or acquittal of the defendant.

2. if a mistrial is declared by the judge without legal cause and the jury is discharged without the defendant's consent.

3. dismissal by the judge after the trial has commenced without legal cause.

4. discharge of a joint defendant, in many states, to be a witness for the state.

Certain situations that may arise after the criminal process has commenced and that terminate the proceeding do not amount to jeopardy. A mistaken view held by some is that any dismissal of a criminal proceeding results in jeopardy for the defendant. One must start with the basic premise that jeopardy does not attach until the trial commences before a court of competent jurisdiction. Therefore, if a judge fails to hold a suspect to answer for the crime charged in an accusatory pleading at the *preliminary hearing,* the person can be rearrested and put to trial for the same offense. Similarly, if a judge dismisses an accusation (information or indictment) for specified reasons set forth in the law of most states, the defendant can be reindicted or new information filed charging him with the same offense without subjecting him to jeopardy.

The trial itself, under certain circumstances, may be terminated without subjecting the defendant to jeopardy for a retrial. For example, if a defendant is granted a motion for a mistrial at his request, he may then be tried again for the same offense. Similarily, if a jury is discharged for some legal necessity, such as a failure to agree on a verdict, a defendant may be retried. A dismissal of a charge because of a variance between the pleading and the proof does not amount to jeopardy. Also, a defendant may be retried if the jury is discharged because of the illness or absence of a juror.

If a defendant makes a motion for a new trial after conviction and the motion is granted, or if the defendant appeals his conviction and it is reversed, he may be tried again for the same offense of which he was initially tried without doing damage to the prohibition against double jeopardy.

The constitutional cases in this section dealing with double jeopardy look into some ramifications of the double jeopardy protections of the Fifth Amendment, such as increased punishments given or an allowable retrial of a case. The important aspect of the Fifth Amendment privilege, however, is that since 1969 it has been incorporated into the Due Process Clause of the Fourteenth Amendment. State procedures must now at least measure up to the federal standards of this important constitutional protection.

SELF-INCRIMINATION

Brown v Mississippi
287 U.S. 278, 56 S.Ct. 461, 80 L.Ed. 682 (1936)

Brown and several other defendants were suspected of the slaying of Stewart. They were arraigned, assigned counsel, and pleaded not guilty. It was found at the trial that the only evidence sufficient to submit the case to the jury were confessions. The confessions while in police custody were claimed to have been extracted by brutal torture and were false. The torture used by the police officers as found by the United States Supreme Court involved hanging, whipping, and beating one of the defendants until he confessed.

Other defendants were stripped, laid over chairs, and beaten with straps with buckles on them until they confessed.

After the torture, the sheriffs of two counties along with several other persons, came to the jail to hear the "free and voluntary" confessions of the defendants. One sheriff admitted that he heard and knew about the beatings. Nevertheless, the two sheriffs and other witnesses who heard the confessions and observed the miserable condition of the defendants testified to the free and voluntary nature of the confessions.

At the state trial there was adequate evidence presented to question the voluntary nature of the confessions. Nevertheless, the defendants were convicted. The Mississippi Supreme Court affirmed. In certiorari to the United States Supreme Court the Court reversed the judgment.

Chief Justice Hughes delivered the opinion of the Court:

The state stresses . . . that "exemption from compulsory self-incrimination in the courts of the states is not secured by any part of the federal Constitution," and the statement in *Snyder* v *Massachusetts*, 291 U.S. 97, . . . , that "the privilege against self-incrimination may be withdrawn and the accused put upon the stand as a witness for the state." But the question of the right of the state to withdraw the privilege against self-incrimination is not here involved. The compulsion to which the quoted statements refer is that of the processes of justice by which the accused may be called as a witness and required to testify. Compulsion by torture to extort a confession is a different matter.

The state is free to regulate the procedure of its courts in accordance with its own conceptions of policy, unless in so doing it "offends some principle of justice so rooted in the traditions and conscience of our people as to be ranked as fundamental." . . . The state may abolish trial by jury. It may dispense with indictment by a grand jury and substitute complaint or information. . . . But the freedom of the state in establishing its policy is the freedom of constitutional government and is limited by the requirement of due process of law. Because a state may dispense with a jury trial, it does not follow that it may substitute trial by ordeal. The rack and torture chamber may not be substituted for the witness stand. The state may not permit an accused to be hurried to conviction under mob domination—where the whole proceeding is but a mask—without supplying corrective process. . . . The state may not deny to the accused the aid of counsel. . . . Nor may a state, through the action of its officers, contrive a conviction through the pretense of a trial which in truth is "but used as a means of depriving a defendant of liberty through a deliberate deception of court and jury by the presentation of testimony known to be perjured." . . . And the trial equally is a mere pretense where the state authorities have contrived a conviction resting solely upon confessions obtained by violence. The Due Process Clause requires "that state action, whether through one agency or another, shall be consistent with the fundamental principles of liberty and justice which lie at the base of all our civil and political institutions." . . . It would be difficult to conceive of methods more revolting to the sense of justice than those taken to procure the confessions of these petitioners, and the use of the confessions thus obtained as the basis for conviction and sentence was a clear denial of due process.

It is in this view that the further contention of the state must be considered. That contention rests upon the failure of counsel for the accused, who had objected to the admissibility of the confessions, to move for their exclusion after they had been introduced and the fact of coercion had been proved. It is a contention which proceeds upon a misconception of the nature of petitioners' complaint. That complaint is not of the commission of mere error, but of a wrong so fundamental that it made the whole proceeding a mere pretense of a trial and rendered the conviction and sentence wholly void.

. . .

In the instant case, the trial court was fully advised by the undisputed evidence of the way in which the confessions had been procured. The trial court knew that there was no other evidence upon which conviction and sentence could be based. Yet it proceeded to permit conviction and to pronounce sentence. The conviction and sentence were void for want of the essential elements of due process, and the proceeding thus vitiated could be challenged in any appropriate manner. . . . It was challenged before the Supreme Court of the state by the express invocation of the Fourteenth Amendment. That court entertained the challenge, considered the federal question thus presented, but declined to enforce petitioners' constitutional right. The court thus denied a federal right fully established and specially set up and claimed, and the judgment must be reversed.

(Judgment reversed.)

Massiah v United States
377 U.S. 201, 84 S.Ct. 1199, 12 L.Ed. 2d 246 (1964)

Massiah was indicted by a federal grand jury for possession of narcotics. He pleaded not guilty and was released on bail. Colson, a codefendant, decided to cooperate with the government agents in their continuing investigation of Massiah's narcotics activities. Colson agreed to have a radio transmitter installed in his automobile so that Murphy, a federal agent, could overhear Colson's conversations from some distance. Massiah made several incriminating statements to Colson which were listened to by Murphy. At Massiah's trial these conversations were allowed before the jury over Massiah's objections. He was convicted. The United States Supreme Court granted certiorari.

Justice Stewart delivered the opinion of the Court:

The petitioner argues that it was an error of constitutional dimensions to permit the agent Murphy at the trial to testify to the petitioner's incriminating statements which Murphy had overheard under the circumstances disclosed by this record. This argument is based upon two distinct and independent grounds. First, we are told that Murphy's use of the radio equipment violated the petitioner's rights under the Fourth Amendment, and consequently, that all evidence which Murphy thereby obtained was . . . inadmissible against the petitioner at the trial. Secondly, it is said that the petitioner's Fifth and Sixth Amendment rights were violated by the use in evidence against him of incriminating statements which government agents had deliberately elicited from him after he had been indicted and in the absence of his retained counsel.

Because of the way we dispose of the case, we do not reach the Fourth Amendment issue.

In *Spano* v *New York,* 360 U.S. 315,... , this Court reversed a state criminal conviction because a confession had been wrongly admitted into evidence against the defendant at his trial. In that case the defendant had already been indicted for first-degree murder at the time he confessed. The Court held that the defendant's conviction could not stand under the Fourteenth Amendment. While the Court's opinion relied upon the totality of the circumstances under which the confession had been obtained, four concurring Justices pointed out that the Constitution required reversal of the conviction upon the sole and specific ground that the confession had been deliberately elicited by the police after the defendant had been indicted, and therefore at a time when he was clearly entitled to a lawyer's help. It was pointed out that under our system of justice the most elemental concepts of due process of law contemplate that an indictment be followed by a trial, "in an orderly courtroom, presided over by a judge, open to the public, and protected by all the procedural safeguards of the law." ... It was said that a Constitution which guarantees a defendant the aid of counsel at such a trial could surely vouchsafe no less to an indicted defendant under interrogation by the police in a completely extrajudicial proceeding. Anything less, it was said, might deny a defendant "effective representation by counsel at the only stage when legal aid and advice would help him." ... Ever since this Court's decision in the Spano Case, the New York courts have unequivocally followed this constitutional rule. "Any secret interrogation of the defendant, from and after the finding of the indictment, without the protection afforded by the presence of counsel, contravenes the basic dictates of fairness in the conduct of criminal causes and the fundamental rights of persons charged with crime."

. . .

This view no more than reflects a constitutional principle established as long ago as *Powell* v *Alabama,* 287 U.S. 45,... , where the Court noted that "... during perhaps the most critical period of the proceedings ... that is to say, from the time of their arraignment until the beginning of their trial, when consultation, thorough-going investigation, and preparation [are] vitally important, the defendants ... [are] as much entitled to such aid [of counsel] during that period as at the trial itself." ... And since the Spano decision the same basic constitutional principle has been broadly reaffirmed by this Court.

Here we deal not with a state court conviction, but with a federal case, where the specific guarantee of the Sixth Amendment directly applies.

. . .

We hold that the petitioner was denied the basic protections of that guarantee when there was used against him at his trial evidence of his own incriminating words, which federal agents had deliberately elicited from him after he had been indicted and in the absence of his counsel. It is true that in the Spano Case the defendant was interrogated in a police station, while here the damaging testimony was elicited from the defendant without his knowledge while he was free on bail. But, as Judge Hays pointed out in his dissent in the Court of Appeals, "If such a rule is to have any efficacy it must apply to indirect and surreptitious interrogations as well as those conducted in the jailhouse. In this case, Massiah was more seriously imposed upon . . . because he did not even know that he was under interrogation by a government agent."

. . .

The Solicitor General, in his brief and oral argument, has strenuously contended that the federal law enforcement agents had the right, if not indeed the duty, to continue their investigation of the petitioner and his alleged criminal associates even though the petitioner had been indicted. He points out that the government was continuing its investigation in order to uncover not only the source of narcotics found on the *S.S. Santa Maria,* but also their intended buyer. He says that the quantity of narcotics involved was such as to suggest that the petitioner was part of a large and well-organized ring, and indeed that the continuing investigation confirmed this suspicion, since it resulted in criminal charges against many defendants. Under these circumstances the Solicitor General concludes that the government agents were completely "justified in making use of Colson's cooperation by having Colson continue his normal associations and by surveilling them."

We may accept and, at least for present purposes, completely approve all that this argument implies, Fourth Amendment problems to one side. We do not question that in this case, as in many cases, it was entirely proper to continue an investigation of the suspected criminal activities of the defendant and his alleged confederates, even though the defendant had already been indicted. All that we hold is that the defendant's own incriminating statements, obtained by federal agents under the circumstances here disclosed, could not constitutionally be used by the prosecution as evidence against *him* at his trial.

(Judgment reversed.)
Justice White, joined by Justices Clark and Harlan, dissented.

Malloy v Hogan

378 U.S. 1, 84 S.Ct. 1489, 12 L.Ed. 2d 653 (1964)

Malloy was sent to jail for contempt for refusal to answer questions before a court-appointed referee to look into gambling in Connecticut. He refused to answer a number of questions on the grounds that he might incriminate himself. The questions could have led to gathering evidence from other persons about whom he was asked, which in turn might prove incriminating to him. His refusal resulted in the contempt citation. The state courts upheld the citation. The United States Supreme Court granted certiorari.

Justice Brennan delivered the opinion of the Court:

We hold today that the Fifth Amendment's exception from compulsory self-incrimination is also protected by the Fourteenth Amendment against abridgment by the states. Decisions of the Court since *Twining* and *Adamson* have departed from the contrary view expressed in those cases.

. . .

The respondent sheriff concedes in its brief that under our decisions, particularly those involving coerced confessions, "the accusatorial system has become a fundamental part of the fabric of our society and, hence, is enforceable against the states." The state urges, however, that the availability of the federal privilege to a witness in a state inquiry is to be determined according to a less stringent standard than is applicable in a federal proceeding. We disagree. We have held that the guarantees of the First Amendment, . . . the prohibition of unreasonable searches and seizures of the Fourth Amendment, . . . and the right to counsel guaranteed by the Sixth Amendment, . . . are all to be enforced against the states under the Fourteenth Amendment according to the same standards that protect those personal rights against federal encroachment. In the coerced confession cases, involving the policies of the privilege itself, there has been no suggestion that a confession might be considered if used in a federal but not a state tribunal. The Court thus has rejected the notion that the Fourteenth Amendment applies to the states only in a "watered-down, subjective version of the individual guarantees of the Bill of Rights." . . . What is accorded is a privilege of refusing to incriminate one's self, and the feared prosecution may be by either federal or state authorities." It would be incongruous to have different standards determine the validity of a claim of privilege based on the same feared prosecution, depending on whether the claim was asserted in a state or federal court. Therefore, the same standards must determine whether an accused's silence in either a federal or state proceeding is justified.

We turn to the petitioner's claim that the State of Connecticut denied him the protection of his federal privilege. It must be considered irrelevant that the petitioner was a witness in a statutory inquiry and not a defendant in a criminal prosecution, for it has long been settled that the privilege protects witnesses in similar federal inquiries. . . . We recently elaborated the content in Hoffman:

> The privilege afforded not only extends to answers that would in themselves support a conviction . . . but likewise embraces those which would furnish a link in the chain of evidence needed to prosecute. . . . [I]f the witness, upon interposing his claim, were required to prove the hazard . . . he would be compelled to surrender the very protection which the privilege is designed to guarantee. To sustain the privilege, it need only be evident from the implication of the question, in the setting in which it is asked, that a responsive answer to the question or an explanation of

why it cannot be answered might be dangerous because injurious disclosure could result. . . .

We also said that, in applying that test, the judge must be

perfectly clear, from a careful consideration of all the circumstances in the case, that the witness is mistaken, and that the answer[s] *cannot possibly* have such tendency to incriminate. . . .

The State of Connecticut argues that the Connecticut courts properly applied the federal standards to the facts of this case. We disagree.

(Judgment reversed.)
(Justice Douglas joined in the opinion of the Court but adhered to his concurrence in *Gideon* v *Wainwright,* 372 U.S. 335.)
Justices Harlan, White, Clark, and Stewart dissented.

Escobedo v *Illinois*
378 U.S. 478, 84 S.Ct. 1758, 12 L.Ed. 2d 977 (1964)

Escobedo was arrested for murder without a warrant. He made no statements to the police and was later released pursuant to a writ of habeas corpus. Further evidence was developed and Escobedo was rearrested. He refused to confess and was interrogated for hours, all the time asking to see his attorney. On one occasion his requests were denied even though he and his attorney waved to each other. Ultimately, Escobedo made some incriminating statements and gave a written statement. During this entire process Escobedo was not advised of his right to have an attorney. All of the police questioning took place before Escobedo was indicted. His conviction was affirmed in the state courts. On certiorari to the United States Supreme Court the conviction was reversed.
Justice Goldberg delivered the opinion of the Court:

The critical question in this case is whether, under the circumstances, the refusal by the police to honor petitioner's request to consult with his lawyer during the course of an interrogation constitutes a denial of ''the assistance of counsel'' in violation of the Sixth Amendment to the Constitution as ''made obligatory upon the states by the Fourteenth Amendment,'' . . . and thereby renders inadmissible in a state criminal trial any incriminating statement elicited by the police during the interrogation.

· · ·

In *Massiah* v *United States,* 377 U.S. 201, . . . , this Court observed that ''a Constitution which guarantees a defendant the aid of counsel at . . . trial could surely vouchsafe no less to an indicted defendant under interrogation by the police in a completely extrajudicial proceeding. Anything less . . . might deny a defendant 'effective representation by counsel at the only stage when legal aid and advice would help him.' "

The interrogation here was conducted before petitioner was formally indicted. But in the context of this case, that fact should make no difference. When petitioner requested, and was denied, an opportunity to consult with his lawyer, the investigation had ceased to be a general investigation of "an unsolved crime." . . . Petitioner had become the accused, and the purpose of the interrogation was to "get him" to confess his guilt despite his constitutional right not to do so. At the time of his arrest and throughout the course of the interrogation, the police told petitioner that they had convincing evidence that he had fired the fatal shots. Without informing him of his absolute right to remain silent in the face of this accusation, the police urged him to make a statement. . . . Petitioner, a layman, was undoubtedly unaware that under Illinois law an admission of "mere" complicity in the murder plot was legally as damaging as an admission of firing of the fatal shots. . . . The "guiding hand of counsel" was essential to advise petitioner of his rights in this delicate situation. . . . This was the "stage when legal aid and advice" were most critical to petitioner.

· · ·

. . . This Court also has recognized that "history amply shows that confessions have often been extorted to save law enforcement officials the trouble and effort of obtaining valid and independent evidence."

· · ·

We have also learned the companion lesson of history that no system of criminal justice can, or should, survive if it comes to depend for its continued effectiveness on the citizens' abdication through unawareness of their constitutional rights. If the exercise of constitutional rights will thwart the effectiveness of a system of law enforcement, then there is something very wrong with that system.

We hold, therefore, that where, as here, the investigation is no longer a general inquiry into an unsolved crime but has begun to focus on a particular suspect, the suspect has been taken into police custody, the police carry out a process of interrogations that lends itself to eliciting incriminating statements, the suspect has requested and been denied an opportunity to consult with his lawyer, and the police have not effectively warned him of his absolute constitutional right to remain silent, the accused has been denied "the assistance of counsel" in violation of the Sixth Amendment to the Constitution as "made obligatory upon the states by the Fourteenth Amendment," . . . and that no statement elicited by the police during the interrogation may be used against him at a criminal trial.

· · ·

Nothing we have said today affects the powers of the police to investigate "an unsolved crime," . . . by gathering information from witnesses and by other "proper investigative efforts." . . . We hold only that when the process shifts from investigatory to accusatory—when its focus is on the accused and its purpose is to elicit a confession—our adversary system begins to operate, and, under the circumstances here, the accused must be permitted to consult with his lawyer.

(Judgment reversed.)
Justices White, Clark, Stewart, and Harlan dissented.

Miranda v Arizona

384 U.S. 436, 86 S.Ct. 1602, 16 L.Ed. 2d 694 (1966)

Miranda was found guilty by an Arizona court of kidnappng and attacking a young woman. On the morning of March 13, he was arrested and taken to the police station. At the time of his arrest, Miranda had a ninth-grade education, had an emotional illness, was poor, and was 23 years old. At the station house he was picked out of a police lineup. Interrogation of him by the police began at about 11:30 a.m. Initially, he denied his guilt but after two hours of questioning, he confessed orally in great detail. This confession was reduced to a brief statement in Miranda's handwriting, in which he described the crime and admitted to its commission. At the top of the statement was a paragraph stating that the confession was made voluntarily without any promises of immunity and with full knowledge of his legal rights.

At the trial the confession was admitted into evidence over Miranda's objection. On appeal the United States Supreme Court reversed the lower court decision.

Chief Justice Warren delivered the opinion of the Court:

Our holding . . . briefly stated it is this: the prosecution may not use statements, whether exculpatory or inculpatory, stemming from custodial interrogation of the defendant unless it demonstrates the use of procedural safeguards effective to secure the privilege against self-incrimination. By custodial interrogation, we mean questioning initiated by law enforcement officers after a person has been taken into custody or otherwise deprived of his freedom of action in any significant way. As for the procedural safeguards to be employed, unless other fully effective means are devised to inform accused persons of their right of silence and to assure a continuous opportunity to exercise it, the following measures are required. Prior to any questioning, the person must be warned that he has a right to remain silent, that any statement he does make may be used as evidence against him, and that he has a right to the presence of an attorney, either retained or appointed. The defendant may waive effectuation of these rights, provided the waiver is made voluntarily, knowingly, and intelligently. If, however, he indicates in any manner and at any stage of the process that he wishes to consult with an attorney before speaking there can be no questioning. Likewise, if the individual is alone and indicates in any manner that he does not wish to be interrogated, the police may not question him. The mere fact that he may have answered some questions or volunteered some statements on his own does not deprive him of the right to refrain from answering any further inquiries until he has consulted with an attorney and thereafter consents to be questioned.

The constitutional issue we decide in each of these cases is the admissibility of statements obtained from a defendant questioned while in custody or otherwise deprived of his freedom of action in any significant way. In each, the defendant was questioned by police officers, detectives, or a prosecuting attorney in a room in which he was cut off from the outside world. In none of these cases was the defendant given a full and effective warning of his rights at the outset of the interrogation process. In all the cases, the questioning elicited oral admissions, and in three of them, signed statements as well which were admitted at their trials. They all thus share salient features—incommunicado interrogation of individuals in a police-dominated atmosphere, resulting in self-incriminating statements without full warnings of constitutional rights.

. . .

Even without employing brutality, the "third degree," or the specific stratagems . . . , the very fact of custodial interrogation exacts a heavy toll on individual liberty and trades on the weakness of individuals.

. . .

In these cases, we might not find the defendants' statements to have been involuntary in traditional terms. Our concern for adequate safeguards to protect precious Fifth Amendment rights is, of course, not lessened in the slightest.

. . .

The question in these cases is whether the privilege is fully applicable during a period of custodial interrogation.

In this Court, the privilege has consistently been accorded a liberal construction. . . . We are satisfied that all the principles embodied in the privilege apply to informal compulsion exerted by law enforcement officers during in-custody questioning.

. . .

Because of the adoption of Congress of Rule 5(a) of the Federal Rules of Criminal Procedure, and the Court's effectuation of that Rule in *McNabb* v *United States*, 318 U.S. 332, . . . , and *Mallory* v *United States*, 354 U.S. 449, . . . , we have had little occasion in the past quarter century to reach the constitutional issues in dealing with federal interrogations. . . . In *McNabb*, . . . , and in *Mallory*, . . . , we recognize both the dangers of interrogation and the appropriateness of prophylaxis stemming from the very fact of interrogation itself.

The Fifth Amendment privilege is so fundamental to our system of constitutional rule and the expedient of giving an adequate warning as to the availability of the privilege so simple, we will not pause to inquire in individual cases whether the defendant was aware of his rights without a warning being given. Assessments of the knowledge the defendant possessed, based on information as to his age, education, intelligence, or prior contact with authorities, can never be more than speculation; a warning is a clearcut fact. More important, whatever the background of the person interrogated, a warning at the time of the interrogation is indispensable to overcome its pressures and to ensure that the individual knows he is free to exercise the privilege at that point in time.

The warning of the right to remain silent must be accompanied by the explanation that anything said can and will be used against the individual in court. This warning is needed in order to make him aware not only of the privilege, but also of the consequences of foregoing it. It is only through an awareness of these consequences that there can be any assurance of real understanding and intelligent exercise of the privilege. Moreover, this warning may serve to make the individual more accurately aware that he is faced with a phase of the adversary system—that he is not in the presence of persons acting solely in his interest.

An individual need not make a pre-interrogation request for a lawyer. While such request affirmatively secures his right to have one, his failure to ask for a lawyer does not constitute a waiver. No effective waiver of the right to counsel during interrogation can be recognized unless specifically made after the warnings we here delineate have been given. The accused who does not know his rights and therefore does not make a request may be the person who most needs counsel.

. . .

Accordingly we hold that an individual held for interrogation must be clearly informed that he has the right to consult with a lawyer and to have the lawyer with him during interrogation under the system for protecting the privilege we delineate today.

. . .

If an individual indicates that he wishes the assistance of counsel before any interrogation occurs, the authorities cannot rationally ignore or deny his request on the basis that the individual does not have or cannot afford a retained attorney.

. . .

In order fully to apprise a person interrogated of the extent of his rights under this system then, it is necessary to warn him not only that he has the right to consult with an attorney, but also that if he is indigent a lawyer will be appointed to represent him.

. . .

Once warnings have been given, the subsequent procedure is clear. If the individual indicates in any manner, at any time prior to or during questioning, that he wishes to remain silent, the interrogation must cease. At this point he has shown that he intends to exercise his Fifth Amendment privilege; any statement taken after the person invokes his privilege cannot be other than the product of compulsion, subtle or otherwise. Without the right to cut off questioning, the setting of in-custody interrogation operates on the individual to overcome free choice in producing a statement after the privilege has been once invoked.

. . .

If the interrogation continues without the presence of an attorney and a statement is taken, a heavy burden rests on the government to demonstrate that the defendant knowingly and intelligently waived his privilege against self-incrimination and his right to retained or appointed counsel.

. . .

The right of the individual to consult with an attorney during this period is expressly recognized.

. . .

Because of the nature of the problem and because of its recurrent significance in numerous cases, we have to this point discussed the relationship of the Fifth Amendment privilege to police interrogation without specific concentration on the facts of the cases before us. We turn now to these facts to consider the application to these cases of the constitutional principles discussed above. In each instance, we have concluded that statements were obtained from the defendant under circumstances that did not meet constitutional standards for protection of the privilege.

. . .

Therefore, in accordance with the foregoing, the judgments of the Supreme Court of Arizona in No. 759, of the New York Court of Appeals in No. 760, and of the Court of Appeals for the Ninth Circuit in No. 761 are reversed. The judgment of the Supreme Court of California in No. 584 is affirmed.

. . .

(Judgment of the Arizona Court reversed.)
Justice Clark, Harlan, Stewart, and White dissented.

Beckwith v *United States*
425 U.S. 341, 96 S.Ct. 1612, 48 L.Ed. 2d 1, (1976)

During the course of a noncustodial interview with agents of the Internal Revenue Service, Beckwith, a taxpayer, made some statements that were subsequently used against him in a criminal tax fraud prosecution. No *Miranda* warnings were given. Evidence indicated that Beckwith's tax liability was under scrutiny by the I.R.S. and the tax investigation had begun to focus upon him. The evidence also indicated that he was in no way taken into custody nor deprived of his freedom of action in any way. Beckwith was convicted of violating federal tax laws and he appealed claiming that the principles in *Miranda* should be extended to cover "interrogation in noncustodial circumstances after a police investigation has focused on the suspect."

In rejecting this claim, Chief Justice Burger stated:

Although the "focuses" of an investigation may indeed have been on Beckwith at the time of the interview in the sense that it was his tax liability which was under scrutiny, he hardly found himself in the custodial situation described by the *Miranda* Court as the basis for its holding. *Miranda* specifically defined "focus," for its purposes, as "questioning initiated by law enforcement officers after a person has been taken into custody or otherwise deprived of his freedom of action in any significant way." . . . It may well be true, as petitioner contends that the "starting point" for the criminal prosecution was the information obtained from petitioner and the records exhibited by him. But this amounts to no more than saying that a tax return signed by the taxpayer can be the "starting point" for a prosecution.

As to the possibility that noncustodial interrogation may indeed be coercive, the majority stated:

We recognize, of course, that noncustodial interrogation might possibly in some situations, by virtue of some special circumstances, be characterized as one where "the behavior . . . law enforcement officials was such as to overbear petitioner's will to resist and bring about confessions not freely self-determined. . . ." When such a claim is raised, it is the duty of an appellate court, including this Court, "to examine the entire record and make an independent determination of the ultimate issue of voluntariness." Proof that some kind of warnings were given would be relevant evidence only on the issue of whether the questioning was in fact coercive.

Justice Stevens did not take part in the decision. Justice Brennan dissented.

Doyle v Ohio
426 U.S. 610, 96 S.Ct. 2240, 49 L.Ed. 2d 91 (1976)

Doyle and another were arrested and subsequently convicted of selling marijuana. After their arrest they were given the *Miranda* warnings. During their trial the defendants took the stand and presented testimony exculpating them from the crime. The testimony had not been previously known to nor given to the police or prosecutor. Over their counsel's objections, they were cross-examined as to why they had not given the exculpatory statements to the arresting officers. The defendants appealed their convictions claiming that the use of their silence at the time of arrest and after they had been Mirandized for impeachment violated the Due Process Clause of the Fourteenth Amendment.

Justice Powell writing for the majority concluded that despite the importance of cross-examination, the *Miranda* decision compels rejection of the state's position. Powell emphased that

The warnings mandated by that case, as a prophylactic means of safeguarding Fifth Amendment rights, . . . require that a person taken into custody be advised immediately that he has the right to remain silent, that anything he says may be used against him, and that he has a right to retained or appointed counsel before submitting to interrogation. Silence in the wake of these warnings may be nothing more than the arrestee's exercise of these *Miranda* rights. Thus, every post-arrest silence is insolubly ambiguous because of what the state is required to advise the person arrested, . . . Moreover, while it is true that the *Miranda* warnings contain no express assurance that silence will carry no penalty, such assurance is implicit to any person who receives the warnings. In such circumstances, it would be fundamentally unfair and a deprivation of due process to allow the arrested person's silence to be used to impeach an explanation subsequently offered at trial.

Basing their opinion upon this analysis, the majority held that the use for impeachment purposes of an accused's silence, at the time of arrest and after receiving *Miranda* warnings, violated the Due Process Clause of the Fourteenth Amendment. Because the state had not claimed that the circumstances in the case would have constituted harmless error, the convictions were revised and remanded for further proceedings consistent with the opinion.

Justices Stevens, Blackmun, and Rhenquist dissented.

In *Brown* v *Illinois,* 422 U.S. 590, 95 S.Ct. 2254, 45 L.Ed. 2d 416 (1975), Brown was arrested without a warrant and without probable cause, taken to the police station, and given his Miranda warnings. While at the police station he made two inculpatory statements concerning a murder. At his trial the motion to suppress these statements on the grounds that they were illegally obtained was denied. The United States Supreme Court held that the fact that the Miranda warnings were given prior to the defendant's statements did not make these statements admissible and that these statements were in fact inadmissible since the first statement was separated from the illegal arrest by less than two hours and the second statement was the result and fruit of the first statement. Thus, the fruit of the poisonous tree doctrine, stemming from the illegal arrest before the Miranda warnings, was declared by the Court.

In *United States* v *Hale,* 422 U.S. 71, 95 S.Ct. 2133, 45 L.Ed. 2d 99 (1975), the Supreme Court held that the trial court committed prejudicial error by allowing cross-examination of the defendant to note the fact that the defendant had been silent during police interrogation. It was the feeling of the Court that the defendant had the right to remain silent because he had no reason to think that any explanation he might make to the police would hasten his release. The Court's decision was made without reaching the constitutional question.

In *Orozco* v *Texas,* 394 U.S. 324, 89 S.Ct. 1095, 22 L.Ed. 2d 311 (1969), the United States Supreme Court held that the questioning of a defendant while at his home in bed was custodial in nature and thereby the fourfold Miranda warnings were mandatory.

In *Michigan* v *Tucker,* 417 U.S. 433, 94 S.Ct. 2357, 41 L.Ed. 2d 182 (1974), the defendant was not given the full *Miranda* warnings. Upon questioning, Tucker provided some information that was later used against him in his trial. The United States Supreme Court, upholding the conviction of Tucker, centered on the scope of the Fifth Amendment and how its protections have been expanded. Since Tucker did not show a resemblance to the kinds of practices protected by the Fifth Amendment, there was no need to exclude the evidence. The deterrent against willful police excesses by exclusion of evidence had no bearing in this case because the police acted in complete good faith. As Justice Rehnquist noted, "Just as the law does not require that a defendant receive a perfect trial, only a fair one, it cannot realistically require that policemen investigating serious crimes make no errors whatsoever. The pressures of law enforcement... would make such an expectation unrealistic. Before we penalize police error, therefore, we must consider whether the sanction serves a valid and useful purpose."

Jackson v *Denno*
378 U.S. 368, 84 S.Ct. 1774, 16 L.Ed. 2d 908 (1966)

After robbing a hotel desk clerk and killing an officer, Jackson was wounded in a gunfight. At the hospital he gave damaging oral and written confessions which were subsequently introduced during his trial. According to New York procedure, when there is a question of the voluntariness of a confession, the issue is submitted to the jury along with other issues. If the confession is found to be voluntary, the jury then affords it weight according to its truth and reliability. If the confession is found to be involuntary, the jury is instructed to disregard it totally. In New York the judge only excluded a confession when it was without a doubt involuntary. Under this procedure, Jackson was found guilty of murder by a jury. The United States Supreme Court granted certiorari and reversed.

Justice White delivered the opinion of the Court:

It is now axiomatic that a defendant in a criminal case is deprived of due process of law if his conviction is founded, in whole or in part, upon an involuntary confession, without regard for the truth or falsity of the confession, ...and even though there is ample evidence aside from the confession to support the conviction. ... Equally clear is the defendant's constitutional right at some stage in the proceedings to object to the use of the confession and to have a fair hearing and a reliable determination on the issue of voluntariness, a determination uninfluenced by the truth or falsity of the confession. ... In our view, the New York procedure employed in this case did not afford a reliable determination of the voluntariness of the confession offered in evidence at the trial, did not adequately protect Jackson's right to be free of a conviction based upon a coerced confession and therefore cannot withstand constitutional attack under the Due Process Clause of the Fourteenth Amendment. We therefore reverse the judgment below denying the writ of habeas corpus.

Under the New York rule, the trial judge must make a preliminary determination regarding a confession offered by the prosecution and exclude it if in no circumstances could the confession be deemed voluntary. But if the evidence presents a fair question as to its voluntariness, as where certain facts bearing on the issue are in dispute or where reasonable men could differ over the inferences to be drawn from undisputed facts, the judge "must receive the confession and leave to the jury under proper instructions, the ultimate determination of its voluntary character and also its truthfulness." . . . If an issue of coercion is presented, the judge may not resolve conflicting evidence or arrive at his independent appraisal of the voluntariness of the confession, one way or the other. These matters he must leave to the jury.

This procedure has a significant impact upon the defendant's Fourteenth Amendment rights. In jurisdictions following the orthodox rule, under which the judge himself solely and finally determines the voluntariness of the confession, or those following the Massachusetts procedure, under which the jury passes on voluntariness only after the judge has fully and independently resolved the issue against the accused, the judge's conclusions are clearly evident from the record since he either admits the confession into evidence if it is voluntary or rejects it if involuntary. Moreover, his findings upon disputed issues of fact are expressly stated or may be ascertainable from the record. In contrast, the New York jury returns only a general verdict upon the ultimate question of guilt or innocence. It is impossible to discover whether the jury found the confession voluntary and relied upon it, or involuntary and supposedly ignored it. Nor is there any indication of how the jury resolved disputes in the evidence concerning the critical facts underlying the coercion issue. Indeed, there is nothing to show that these matters were resolved at all, one way or the other.

. . .

A defendant objecting to the admission of a confession is entitled to a fair hearing in which both the underlying factual issues and the voluntariness of his confession are actually and reliably determined.

. . .

As we have already said, Jackson is entitled to a reliable resolution of these evidentiary conflicts. If this case were here upon direct review of Jackson's conviction, we could not proceed with review on the assumption that these disputes had been resolved in favor of the state for as we have held we are not only unable to tell how the jury resolved these matters but, even if the jury did resolve them against Jackson, its findings were infected with impermissible considerations and accordingly cannot be controlling here. . . . At the very least, *Townsend* v. *Sain,* 372 U.S. 293, . . . , would require a full evidentiary hearing to determine the factual context in which Jackson's confession was given.

However, we think that the further proceedings to which Jackson is entitled should occur initially in the state courts rather than in the federal habeas corpus court.

. . .

It is New York, therefore, not the federal habeas corpus court, which should first provide Jackson with that which he has not yet had and to which he is constitutionally entitled—an adequate evidentiary hearing productive of reliable results concerning the voluntariness of his confession. It does not follow, however, that Jackson is automatically entitled to a complete new trial including a retrial of the issue of guilt or innocence. Jackson's position before the District Court, and here, is that the issue of his confession should not have been decided by the convicting jury but should have been determined in a proceeding separate and apart from the body trying guilt or innocence. So far we agree and hold that he is now entitled to such a hearing in the state court. But if at the conclusion of such an evidentiary hearing in the state court on the coercion issue, it is determined that Jackson's confession was voluntarily given, admissible in evidence, and properly to be considered by the jury, we see no constitutional necessity at that point for proceeding with a new trial, for Jackson has already been tried by a jury with the confession placed before it and has been found guilty.

. . .

Obviously, the state is free to give Jackson a new trial if it so chooses, but for us to impose this requirement before the outcome of the new hearing on voluntariness is known would not comport with the interests of sound judicial administration and the proper relationship between federal and state courts. We cannot assume that New York will not now afford Jackson a hearing that is consistent with the requirements of due process. Indeed New York thought it was affording Jackson such a hearing, and not without support in the decisions of this Court, when it submitted the issue of voluntariness to the same jury that adjudicated guilty. It is both practical and desirable that in cases to be tried hereafter a proper determination of voluntariness be made prior to the admission of the confession to the jury which is adjudicating guilt or innocence. But as to Jackson, who has already been convicted and now seeks collateral relief, we cannot say that the Constitution requires a new trial if in a soundly conducted collateral proceeding, the confession which was admitted at the trial is fairly determined to be voluntary. Accordingly, the judgment denying petitioner's writ of habeas corpus is reversed and the case is remanded to the District Court to allow the state a reasonable time to afford Jackson a hearing or a new trial, failing which Jackson is entitled to his release.

(Judgment reversed.)
Justices Clark, Harlan, and Stewart dissented.
Justice Black dissented in part.

Harris v *New York*

401 U.S. 222, 91 S.Ct. 643, 28 L.Ed. 2d 1 (1971)

Harris was indicted in New York for selling heroin. Several police officers provided details of the sale and collateral matters at the trial. Harris also testified in his own behalf. He made several admissions regarding the alleged sale. On cross-examination Harris was asked if he had made specific statements to the police immediately prior to his arrest—such statements partially contradicted his direct testimony. The statements were given without compliance with the Miranda warnings. The trial judge instructed the jury that the out-of-court statements could be considered only in passing on Harris' credibility as a witness and not evidence of guilt. The jury found Harris guilty and the state appellate courts affirmed. The United States Supreme Court granted certiorari and affirmed.

Chief Justice Burger delivered the opinion of the Court:

Some comments in the *Miranda* opinion can indeed be read as indicating a bar to use of an uncounseled statement for any purpose, but discussion of that issue was not at all necessary to the Court's holding and cannot be regarded as controlling. *Miranda* barred the prosecution from making its case with statements of an accused made while in custody prior to having or effectively waiving counsel. It does not follow from *Miranda* that evidence inadmissible against an accused in the prosecution's case in chief is barred for all purposes, provided of course that the trustworthiness of the evidence satisfies legal standards.

In *Walder* v *United States,* 347 U.S. 62, . . . , the Court permitted physical evidence, inadmissible in the case in chief, to be used for impeachment purposes.

It is one thing to say that the government cannot make an affirmative use of evidence unlawfully obtained. It is quite another to say that the defendant can turn the illegal method by which evidence in the government's possession was obtained to his own advantage, and provide himself with a shield against contradiction of his untruths. Such an extension of the *Weeks* doctrine . . . would be a pervasion of the Fourth Amendment.

[T]here is hardly justification for letting the defendant affirmatively resort to perjurious testimony in reliance on the government's disability to challenge his credibility.

. . .

It is true that Walder was impeached as to collateral matters included in his direct examination, whereas petitioner here was impeached as to testimony bearing more directly on the crimes charged. We are not persuaded that there is a difference in principle that warrants a result different from that reached by the Court in *Walder*. Petitioner's testimony in his own behalf concerning the events of January 7 contrasted sharply with what he told the police shortly after his arrest. The impeachment process here undoubtedly provided valuable aid to the jury in assessing petitioner's credibility, and the benefits of this process should not be lost, in our view, because of the speculative possibility that impermissible police conduct will be encouraged thereby. Assuming that the exclusionary rule has a deterrent effect on proscribed police conduct, sufficient deterrence flows when the evidence in question is made unavailable to the prosecution in its case in chief.

Every criminal defendant is privileged to testify in his own defense, or to refuse to do so. But that privilege cannot be construed to include the right to commit perjury. . . . Having voluntarily taken the stand, petitioner was under an obligation to speak truthfully and accurately, and the prosecution here did no more than utilize the traditional truth-testing devices of the adversary process. Had inconsistent statements been made by the accused to some kind person, it would hardly be contended that the conflict could not be laid before the jury by way of cross-examination and impeachment.

The shield provided by *Miranda* cannot be perverted into a license to use perjury by way of a defense, free from the risk of confrontation with prior inconsistent utterances. We hold, therefore, that petitioner's credibility was appropriately impeached by use of his earlier conflicting statements.

(Judgment affirmed)
Justices Brennan, Douglas, Black, and Marshall dissented.

Andresen v *Maryland*
427 U.S. 463, 96 S.Ct. 2737, 49 L.Ed. 2d 627, (1976)

Agents from the Maryland State's attorney's fraud unit found information that Andresen defrauded some purchasers of real estate. The investigators obtained warrants to search the defendant's offices. The warrants specifically authorized the search and seizure of documents pertaining to the sale of Lot 13T, the realty in question, "together with other fruits, instrumentalities, and evidence of crime at this [time] unknown." In the ensuing search, a number of incriminating documents, including some containing statements made by Andresen, were seized. The defendant was charged, *inter alia*, with false pretenses based on certain misrepresentations made to the purchaser about Lot 13T. In response to motions made by the defendant at the trial, some of the documents were suppressed but others were ruled to be admissible because their admission did not violate the Fourth and Fifth Amendments. Some of the documents admitted referred to lots in the same subdivision other than Lot 13T. The reasoning of the trial judge was that the search and seizure did not force Andresen to be a witness against himself because he had not been required to produce the documents nor was he compelled to authenticate them.

The United States Supreme Court granted certiorari limited to the Fourth and Fifth Amendment issues.

Justice Blackmun who delivered the opinion of the Court concluded that the searches and seizures were not made in violation of the Fourth Amendment. Specifically, it was noted that seizure of the documents not pertaining to Lot 13T did not violate the principle that when police seize "mere evidence," the evidence must be examined in terms of cause to believe that the evidence would aid in a particular apprehension or conviction (see *Warden* v *Hayden,* 387 U.S. 294). As Blackmun stated, "in this case we conclude that the trained special investigators reasonably could have believed that the evidence specifically dealing with another lot in the [same subdivision] could be used to show [defendant's] intent with respect to the Lot 13T transaction." The investigators reasonably could have believed that the evidence dealing with fraudulent conduct respecting the other lots could be used to show Andresen's intent to defraud with respect to Lot 13T and even though the evidence was used to secure additional charges against the defendant, its suppression was not required.

In regard to the defendant's claim that the seizure of the records violated his Fifth Amendment rights, the Court stated: "He bases his argument naturally on dicta in a number of cases which imply, or state, that the search for and seizure of a person's private papers violate the privilege against self-incrimination."

The Court did not agree that broad statements in the cases compel suppression of the defendant's business records.

"Similarly, in this case, [Andresen] was not asked to say or do anything. The records seized contained statements that [Andresen] had voluntarily committed to writing. The search for and seizure of these records were conducted by law enforcement personnel. Finally, when these records were introduced at trial, they were authenticated by a handwriting expert not by [Andresen]. Any compulsion of [Andresen] to speak other than the inherent psychological pressure to respond at trial to unfavorable evidence was not present.

This case thus falls within the principle stated by Mr. Justice Holmes: A party is privileged from producing the evidence but not from its production. . . . Thus, although the Fifth Amendment may protect an individual from complying with a subpoena for the production of his personal records in his possession because the very act of production may constitute a compulsory authentication of incriminating information, . . . a seizure of the same materials by law enforcement officers differs in a crucial respect—the individual against whom the search is directed is not required to aid in the discovery, production, or authentication of incriminating evidence.

Justices Brennan and Marshall dissented.

In *United States* v *Wilson,* 420 U.S. 332, 95 S.Ct. 1013, 43 L.Ed. 2d 232, (1975), the Supreme Court held that "the Double Jeopardy Clause of the Fifth Amendment does not bar the government's appeal from the District Court's postverdict dismissal of the indictment."

Physical Evidence

Schmerber v *California*

384 U.S. 757, 86 S.Ct. 1826, 16 L.Ed. 2d 908 (1966)

Schmerber was convicted of driving an automobile while under the influence of liquor. He was initially arrested while in a hospital receiving treatment for injuries received in an accident involving an automobile he apparently had been driving. At the direction of a police officer, a physician withdrew blood from Schmerber's body. The sample revealed that the alcohol content in the blood indicated that he was intoxicated. This evidence was introduced over Schmerber's objection that its admission deprived him of due process of law under the Fourteenth Amendment, his privilege against self-incrimination, his right to counsel, and his right not to be subjected to unreasonable searches and seizures in violation of the Fourth Amendment. On appeal to the United States Supreme Court, Schmerber's conviction was affirmed.

Justice Brennan delivered the opinion of the Court:

I
The Due Process Clause Claim

Breithaupt was also a case in which police officers caused blood to be withdrawn from the driver of an automobile involved in an accident, and in which there was ample justification for the officer's conclusion that the driver was under the influence of alcohol. There, as here, the extraction was made by a physician in a simple, medically acceptable manner in a hospital environment.

There, however, the driver was unconscious at the time the blood was withdrawn and hence had no opportunity to object to the procedure. We affirmed the conviction there resulting from the use of the test in evidence, holding that under such circumstances the withdrawal did not offend "that 'sense of justice' of which we spoke in *Rochin* v [People of] *California,* 342 U.S. 165, ..." *Breithaupt* thus requires the rejection of petitioner's due process argument, and nothing in the circumstances of this case or in supervening events persuades us that this aspect of *Breithaupt* should be overruled.

II
The Privilege Against Self-Incrimination Claim

Breithaupt summarily rejected an argument that the withdrawal of blood and the admission of the analysis report involved in that state case violated the

Fifth Amendment privilege of any person not to "be compelled in any criminal case to be a witness against himself, ..." But that case, holding that the protections of the Fourteenth Amendment do not embrace this Fifth Amendment privilege, has been succeeded by *Malloy* v *Hogan,* 378 U.S. 1, ... We there held that "(t)he Fourteenth Amendment secures against state invasion the same privilege that the Fifth Amendment guarantees against federal infringement—the right of a person to remain silent unless he chooses to speak in the unfettered exercise of his own will, and to suffer no penalty . . . for such silence." We therefore must now decide whether the withdrawal of the blood and admission in evidence of the analysis involved in this case violated petitioner's privilege. We hold that the privilege protects an accused only from being compelled to testify against himself, or otherwise provide the state with evidence of a testimonial or communicative nature, and that the withdrawal of blood and use of the analysis in question in this case did not involve compulsion to these ends.

. . .

. . . To compel a person to submit to testing in which an effort will be made to determine his guilt or innocence on the basis of physiological responses, whether willed or not, is to evoke the spirit and history of the Fifth Amendment. Such situations call to mind the principle that the protection of the privilege "is as broad as the mischief against which it seeks to guard."

. . .

In the present case, however, no such problem of application is presented. Not even a shadow of testimonial compulsion upon or enforced communication by the accused was involved either in the extraction or in the chemical analysis. Petitioner's testimonial capacities were in no way implicated; indeed, his participation, except as a donor, was irrelevant to the results of the test, which depend on chemical analysis and on that alone. Since the blood test evidence, although an incriminating product of compulsion, was neither petitioner's testimony nor evidence relating to some communicative act or writing by the petitioner, it was not admissible on privilege grounds.

III
The Right to Counsel Claim

This conclusion also answers petitioner's claim that, in compelling him to submit to the test in face of the fact that his objection was made on the advice of counsel, he was denied his Sixth Amendment right to the assistance of counsel. Since petitioner was not entitled to assert the privilege, he has no greater right because counsel erroneously advised him that he could assert it. His claim is strictly limited to the failure of the police to respect his wish, reinforced by counsel's advice, to be left inviolate. No issue of counsel's ability to assist petitioner in respect of any rights he did possess is presented. The limited claim thus made must be rejected.

IV
The Search and Seizure Claim

In *Breithaupt,* as here, it was also contended that the chemical analysis should be excluded from evidence as the product of an unlawful search and seizure in violation of the Fourth and Fourteenth Amendments. The Court did not decide whether the extraction of blood in that case was unlawful, but rejected the claim on the basis of *Wolf* v *People of State of Colorado,* 388 U.S. 25, ... That case had held that the Constitution did not require, in state prosecutions for state crimes, the exclusion of evidence obtained in violation of the Fourth Amendment's provisions. We have since overruled *Wolf* in that respect holding . . . that the exclusionary rule adopted for federal prosecutions in *Weeks* v *United States,* . . . must also be applied in criminal prosecutions in state courts. The question is squarely presented therefore, whether the chemical analysis introduced in evidence in this case should have been excluded as the product of an unconstitutional search and seizure.

Because we are dealing with intrusions into the human body rather than with state interferences with property relationships or private papers—"houses, papers, and effects"—we write on a clean slate. Limitations on the kinds of property which may be seized under warrant, as distinct from the procedures for search and the permissible scope of search, are not instructive in this context. We begin with the assumption that once the privilege against self-incrimination has been found not to bar compelled intrusions into the body for blood to be analyzed for alcohol content, the Fourth Amendment's proper function is to constrain, not against all intrusions as such, but against intrusions which are not justified in the circumstances, or which are made in an improper manner.

. . .

In this case, as will often be true when charges of driving under the influence of alcohol are pressed, these questions arise in the context of an arrest made by an officer without a warrant. Here, there was plainly probable cause for the officer to arrest petitioner and charge him with driving an automobile while under the influence of intoxicating liquor.

. . .

Although the facts which established probable cause to arrest in this case also suggested the required relevance and likely success of a test of petitioner's blood for alcohol, the question remains whether the arresting officer was permitted to draw these inferences himself, or was required instead to procure a warrant before proceeding with the test.

. . .

. . . Particularly in a case such as this, where time had to be taken to bring the accused to a hospital and to investigate the scene of the accident, there was no time to seek out a magistrate and secure a warrant. Given these special facts, we conclude that the attempt to secure evidence of blood-alcohol content in this case was an appropriate incident to petitioner's arrest.

Finally, the record shows that the test was performed in a reasonable manner. Petitioner's blood was taken by a physician in a hospital environment according to accepted medical practices. We are thus not presented with the serious questions which would arise if a search involving use of a medical technique, even of the most rudimentary sort, were made by other than medical personnel or in other than a medical environment—for example, if it were administered by police in the privacy of the station house. To tolerate searches under these conditions might be to invite an unjustified element of personal risk of infection and pain.

We thus conclude that the present record shows no violation of petitioner's right under the Fourth and Fourteenth Amendments to be free of unreasonable searches and seizures. It bears repeating, however, that we reach this judgment only on the facts of the present record. The integrity of an individual's person is a cherished value of our society. That we today hold that the Constitution does not forbid the states minor intrusions into an individual's body under stringently limited conditions in no way indicates that it permits more substantial intrusions, or intrusions under other conditions.

(Judgment affirmed.)
Chief Justice Warren, Justices Black, Douglas, and Fortas dissented.

Public Employees

Garrity v *New Jersey*
385 U.S. 493, 87 S.Ct. 616, 17 L.Ed. 2d 562 (1967)

Upon order of the New Jersey Supreme Court, Garrity and others were questioned because of alleged irregularities in handling cases in municiple courts. New Jersey's attorney general was invested with broad powers of investigation of alleged fixing of traffic tickets. Before being questioned, each person was warned that (1) anything he said could be used against him in any state criminal proceeding, (2) he could refuse to answer any question tending to incriminate him, (3) if he refused to answer, he would be subject to removal from office.

Garrity *et al.* answered the questions without a grant of immunity. In subsequent prosecution for conspiracy to violate state traffic laws, the answers given by Garrity were introduced. He and the others were convicted over their objections that the statements were coerced because if they refused to answer they could lose their jobs with the police department. The New Jersey Supreme Court affirmed the judgment. Certiorari was granted by the United States Supreme Court.

Justice Douglas delivered the opinion of the Court:

We postponed the question of jurisdiction to a hearing on the merits. . . .
The statute whose validity was sought to be "drawn in question," 28 U.S.C.
1257(2), was the forfeiture statute. But the New Jersey Supreme Court refused
to reach that question . . . deeming the voluntariness of the statements as the
only issue presented. . . . The statute is therefore too tangentially involved to
satisfy 28 U.S.C. 1257(2), for the only bearing it had was whether, valid or
not, the fear of being discharged under it for refusal to answer on the one hand
and the fear of self-incrimination on the other was "a choice between the rock
and the whirlpool" which made the statements products of coercion in violation of the Fourteenth Amendment. We therefore dismiss the appeal, treat the
papers as a petition for certiorari (28 U.S.C. 2103), grant the petition, and
proceed to the merits.

We agree with the New Jersey Supreme Court that the forfeiture-of-office
statute is relevant here only for the bearing it has on the voluntary character of
the statements used to convict petitioners in their criminal prosecutions.

The choice imposed on petitioners was one between self-incrimination or
job forfeiture. Coercion that vitiates a confession under *Chambers* v *State of
Florida,* 309 U.S. 227, . . . , and related cases can be "mental as well as
physical": "the blood of the accused is not the only hallmark of an unconstitutional inquisition," . . . may be as telling as coarse and vulgar ones. The
question is whether the accused was deprived of his "free choice to admit, to
deny, or to refuse to answer."

· · ·

It is said that there was a "waiver." That, however, is a federal question for
us to decide.

· · ·

Where the choice is "between the rock and the whirlpool," duress is inherent in deciding to "waive" one or the other.

· · ·

Mr. Justice Holmes in *McAuliffe* v *New Bedford,* 155 Mass. 216, . . . ,
stated a dictum on which New Jersey heavily relies:

> The petitioner may have a constitutional right to talk politics, but he has no constitu-
> tional right to be a policeman. There are few employments for hire in which the
> servant does not agree to suspend his constitutional right of free speech as well as of
> idleness by the implied terms of his contract. The servant cannot complain, as he
> takes the employment on the terms which are offered him. On the same principle the
> city may impose any reasonable condition upon holding offices within its con-
> trol. . . .

The question in this case, however, is not cognizable in those terms. Our
question is whether a state, contrary to the requirement of the Fourteenth
Amendment, can use the threat of discharge to secure incriminatory evidence
against an employee.

We held in *Slochower* v *Board of Education,* 350 U.S. 551, . . . , that a
public school teacher could not be discharged merely because he had invoked

the Fifth Amendment privilege against self-incrimination when questioned by a congressional committee: "The privilege against self-incrimination would be reduced to a hollow mockery if its exercise could be taken as equivalent either to a confession of guilt or a conclusive presumption of perjury. . . . The privilege serves to protect the innocent who otherwise might be ensnared by ambiguous circumstances."

. . .

We conclude that policemen, like teachers and lawyers, are not relegated to a watered-down version of constitutional rights.

There are rights of constitutional stature whose exercise a state may not condition by the exaction of a price. Engaging in interstate commerce is one.

. . .

We now hold the protection of the individual under the Fourteenth Amendment against coerced statements prohibits use in subsequent criminal proceedings of statements obtained under threat of removal from office, and that it extends to all, whether they are policemen or other members of our body politic.

(Judgment reversed.)
Justices Harlan, Clark, Stewart, and White dissented.

The state does not have the power to discharge an officer for refusing to waive his constitutional right against self-incrimination. In *Gardner* v *Broderick,* 392 U.S. 273, 88 S.Ct. 1913, 20 L.Ed. 2d 1082 (1968), the United States Supreme Court found that Gardner had been illegally dismissed from the police force upon his refusal to waive his privilege before a grand jury investigating police corruption. The Court reiterated the importance of the right against self-incrimination even in the case of state officers, just as it had in *Garrity* v *New Jersey,* 385 U.S. 493. Garrity involved the use of compelled testimony against a police officer in a trial court and the Court found the two cases similar since, in both cases, the officers' position of authority was used in attempts to compel testimony at the expense of the individuals' constitutional rights. The Court further stated that Gardner could not have been protected against dismissal had the waiver of immunity not been made a condition of his further employment and prosecution of acts found through specific, narrowly related questions. The provision allowing the dismissal of police officers under such circumstances was found unconstitutional and the previous judgment was reversed.

Special Categories of Persons

Spevack v *Klein*
385 U.S. 511, 87 S.Ct. 625, 17 L.Ed. 2d 574 (1967)

Spevack, a lawyer, refused to honor a *subpoena duces tecum* served on him by refusing to produce demanded financial records and to testify at a judicial inquiry. His sole claim was that production of the records and his testimony would tend to incriminate him. The New York court ordered Spevack disbarred holding that the privilege was not available to him. The United States Supreme Court after granting certiorari, reversed.

Justice Douglas delivered the opinion of the Court:

And so the question emerges whether the principle of *Malloy* v *Hogan* is inapplicable because petitioner is a member of the Bar. We conclude that *Cohen* v *Hurley* should be overruled, that the Self-Incrimination Clause of the Fifth Amendment has been absorbed in the Fourteenth, that it extends its protection to lawyers as well as to other individuals, and that it should not be watered down by imposing the dishonor of disbarment and the deprivation of a livelihood as a price for asserting it. These views, expounded in the dissents in *Cohen* v *Hurley,* need not be elaborated again.

... "Penalty" is not restricted to fine or imprisonment. It means ... the imposition of any sanction which makes assertion of the Fifth Amendment privilege "costly." ... We held in that case that the Fifth Amendment, operating through the Fourteenth, "forbids either comment by the prosecution on the accused's silence or instructions by the court that such silence is evidence of guilt." ... What we said in *Malloy* and *Griffin* is in the tradition of the broad protection given the privilege at least since *Boyd* v *United States,* 116 U.S. 616, ... , where compulsory production of books and papers of the owner of goods sought to be forfeited was held to be compelling him to be a witness against himself.

The threat of disbarment and the loss of professional standing, professional reputation, and of livelihood are powerful forms of compulsion to make a lawyer relinquish the privilege. That threat is indeed as powerful an instrument of compulsion as "the use of legal process to force from the lips of the accused individual the evidence necessary to convict him...." As we recently stated in *Miranda* v *State of Arizona,* 384 U.S. 436, ... , "In this Court, the privilege has consistently been accorded a liberal construction." It is in that tradition that we overrule *Cohen* v *Hurley.* We find no room in the privilege against self-incrimination for classifications of people so as to deny it to some and extend it to others. Lawyers are not excepted from the words "No person ... shall be compelled in any criminal case to be a witness against himself"; and we can imply no exception. Like the school teacher ... and the policemen ... lawyers also enjoy first-class citizenship.

The Court of Appeals alternately affirmed the judgment disbarring petitioner on the grounds that under ... the required records doctrine he was under a duty to produce the withheld records.

· · ·

The documents sought in the subpoena were petitioner's daybook, cash receipts book, cash disbursements book, checkbook stubs, petty cash book and vouchers, general ledger and journal, canceled checks and bank statements, passbooks and other evidences of accounts, record of loans made, payroll records, and state and federal tax returns and worksheets relative thereto.

The *Shapiro* case dealt with a federal price control regulation requiring merchants to keep sales records. The Court called them records with "public aspects," as distinguished from private papers . . . ; and concluded by a divided vote that their compelled production did not violate the Fifth Amendment. We are asked to overrule *Shapiro*. But we find it unnecessary to reach it.

Rule 5, requiring the keeping of records, was broad and general. . . . The detailed financial aspects of contingentfee litigation demanded might possibly by a broad, generous construction of the Rule be brought within its intendment. Our problem, however, is different. Neither the referee of the inquiry, nor counsel for the inquiry, nor the Appellate Division of the New York Supreme Court questioned the applicability of the privilege against self-incrimination *to the records*. . . . The Court of Appeals was the first to suggest that the privilege against self-incrimination was not applicable *to the records*. Petitioner, however, had been disbarred on the theory that the privilege was applicable *to the records,* but that the invocation of the privilege could lead to disbarment. His disbarment cannot be affirmed on the ground that the privilege was not applicable in the first place. . . . For that procedure would deny him all opportunity at the trial to show that the Rule, fairly construed and understood, should not be given a broad sweep and to make a record that the documents demanded by the subpoena had no "public aspects" within the required records rule but were private papers.

(Judgment reversed.)
Justice Fortas wrote a concurring opinion.
Justices Harlan, Clark, Stewart, and White dissented.

In several cases involving investigation of taxpayers with the possibility of civil or criminal liability, the taxpayers transferred documents which their accountants prepared to their respective attorneys in connection with the investigation. The I.R.S. then served summonses on the attorneys directing them to produce the documents. The attorneys refused. In regard to the Fifth Amendment argument that the documents would be privileged if in the possession of the taxpayer, therefore they should also be privileged in the hands of their attorneys. The United States Supreme Court held that compelled production of the documents from the attorneys does not implicate whatever Fifth Amendment privilege that the taxpayer has for producing the documents. The Court indicated that nothing was being compelled from any taxpayer to incriminate himself. The fact that the attorneys are agents does not change the result. The Court also indicated that a different situation is presented if the transfer of possession of the documents was insignificant so as to leave personnel possession of the documents with the taxpayer. In response to an invasion of privacy claim, the Court stated that even if there were a reasonable expectation of privacy regarding the documents, the Fifth Amendment does not protect private information obtained without compelling self-incriminatory testimony. Since the documents in question involved no incriminating testimony, the documents in the hands of attorneys were not immune from protection. *Fisher* v *United States,* 425 U.S. 391, 96 S.Ct. 1569, 48 L.Ed. 2d 39, (1976).

The validity of 18 U.S.C. 6002–6003, the use and derivative use immunity statute, was affirmed by the United States Supreme Court in *Kastigar* v *United States,* 406 U.S. 441, 92 S.Ct. 1653, 32 L.Ed. 2d 212 (1972). Kastigar was granted immunity under the statute in order to testify before a federal grand jury. He refused the immunity on the basis of two arguments: first, that all immunity statutes are unconstitutional abridgments of the privilege against self-incrimination and, second, that any statute authorizing less then transactional immunity (immunity from prosecution of any acts related to the testimony) failed to cover the privilege against self-incrimination. The Court found both arguments wanting. The necessity of immunity statutes was cited, along with the historical and philosophical basis for their constitutionality. Having rejected the first argument, the Court continued in a discussion of the scope of the use and derivative immunity statute when compared with the scope of the Fifth Amendment's privilege against self-incrimination. Upon consideration of the matter, the Court found them to be equal, since neither the privilege nor the statute offers freedom from prosecution. Rather, the transactional immunity statute extends the individual's security from prosecution farther than the original privilege against self-incrimination. The judgment was affirmed.

Zicarelli v New Jersey State Commission of Investigation
406 U.S. 472, 92 S.Ct. 1670, 32 L.Ed. 2d 234 (1972)

This case raises the question concerning cases in which testimony can be compelled from unwilling witnesses who invoke the privilege against self-incrimination under the Fifth Amendment. Zicarelli was subpoenaed to answer questions involving an investigation into organized crime. He refused to answer many of the questions and was granted immunity under a New Jersey statute. Notwithstanding the grant, he still refused. In a contempt hearing, Zicarelli challenged the order to testify because it was insufficient in several respects to compel testimony over a claim of the privilege. Rejecting the claim, he was incarcerated and the state appellate courts affirmed. On appeal the United States Supreme Court affirmed.

Justice Powell delivered the opinion of the Court:

A majority of the members of the Commission have authority to confer immunity on a witness who invokes the privilege against self-incrimination. After the witness testifies under the grant of immunity, the statute provides that:

he shall be immune from having such responsive answer given by him or such responsive evidence produced by him, or evidence derived therefrom used to expose him to criminal prosecution or penalty or to a forfeiture of his estate, except that such person may nevertheless be prosecuted for any perjury committed in such answer or in producing such evidence, or for contempt for failing to give an answer or produce evidence in accordance with the order of the commission. . . .

This is a comprehensive prohibition on the use and derivative use of testimony compelled under a grant of immunity.

. . .

Appellant contends that the immunity provided by the New Jersey statute is unconstitutionally vague because it immunizes a witness only against the use and derivative use of "responsive" answers and evidence, without providing statutory guidelines for determining what is a "responsive" answer. . . . The term "responsive" in ordinary English usage has a well-recognized meaning. It is not, as appellant argues, "so vague that men of common intelligence must necessarily guess at its meaning and differ as to its application."

. . .

Appellant further asserts that he cannot be compelled to testify before the Commission because his testimony would expose him to danger of foreign prosecution. He argues that he has a real and substantial fear of foreign prosecution, and that he cannot be compelled to incriminate himself under foreign law. . . . This Court noted probable jurisdiction to consider appellant's claim that a grant of immunity cannot supplant the Fifth Amendment privilege with respect to an individual who has a real and substantial fear of foreign prosecution. We have concluded, however, that it is unnecessary to reach the constitutional question in this case.

It is well established that the privilege protects against real dangers, not remote and speculative possibilities. At the hearing before the Superior Court of Mercer County, appellant introduced numerous newspaper and magazine articles bearing upon his self-incrimination claim. He called a number of these articles to the court's attention in an effort to demonstrate the basis of a fear of foreign prosecution. These articles labeled appellant the "foremost internationalist" in organized crime, and detailed his alleged participation in unlawful ventures growing out of alleged interests and activities in Canada and the Dominican Republic.

While these articles would lend support to a claim of fear of foreign prosecution in the abstract, they do not support such a claim in the context of the questions asked by the Commission. Of the 100 questions he refused to answer, appellant cites only one specific question as posing a substantial risk of incrimination under foreign law. That question is: "In what geographical area do you have Cosa Nostra responsibilities?"

We think it plain from the context in which the question was asked that it sought an answer concerning geographical areas in New Jersey. . . . Of course, neither the fact that the Commission was not seeking information concerning appellant's activities outside the United States, nor the fact that the question was not designed to elicit such information, is dispositive of appellant's claim that an answer to the question would incriminate him under foreign law. When considering whether a claim of the privilege should be sustained, the Court focuses inquiry on what a truthful answer might disclose, rather than on what information is expected by the questioner. But the context in which a question is asked imparts additional meaning to the question, and clarifies what information is sought. A question to which a claim of the privilege is interposed must be considered "in the setting in which it is asked."

. . .

Considering this question in light of the circumstances in which it was asked, we agree with the conclusion of the Supreme Court of New Jersey that appellant was never in real danger of being compelled to disclose information that might incriminate him under foreign law.

. . .

Appellant is of course free to purge himself of contempt by answering the Commission's questions. Should the Commission inquire into matters that might incriminate him under foreign law and pose a substantial risk of foreign prosecution, and should such inquiry be sustained over a relevancy objection, then a constitutional question will be squarely presented. We do not believe that the record in this case presents such a question.

(Judgment affirmed.)
Justices Brennan and Rehnquist did not participate in the decision.
Justice Douglas and Black dissented.

DOUBLE JEOPARDY

Palko v *Connecticut*
302 U.S. 319, 58 S.Ct. 149, 82 L.Ed. 288 (1937)

Palko was indicted for first degree murder and the jury convicted him of second degree murder and sentenced him to life imprisonment. Under Connecticut procedure, the state was permitted to appeal for errors of law alleged to have been committed by the trial court. The state supreme court reversed the judgment and ordered a new trial. Palko was again brought to trial and was convicted of first degree murder and sentenced to death, his argument of double jeopardy being overruled. On appeal to the United States Supreme Court, the conviction was affirmed.

Justice Cardozo delivered the opinion of the Court:

1. The execution of the sentence will not deprive appellant of his life without the process of law assured to him by the Fourteenth Amendment of the federal Constitution.

The argument for appellant is that whatever is forbidden by the Fifth Amendment is forbidden by the Fourteenth also. The Fifth Amendment, which is not directed to the states, but solely to the federal government, creates immunity from double jeopardy. No person shall be "subject for the same offense to be twice put in jeopardy of life or limb." The Fourteenth Amendment ordains, "nor shall any state deprive any person of life, liberty, or property, without due process of law." To retry a defendant, though under one indictment and only one, subjects him, it is said, to double jeopardy in violation of the Fifth Amendment, if the prosecution is one on behalf of the United States. From this the consequence is said to follow that there is a denial of life or liberty without due process of law, if the prosecution is one on behalf of the people of a state. Thirty-five years ago a like argument was made to this Court . . . and was passed without consideration of its merits as unnecessary to a decision. The question is now here.

We do not find it profitable to mark the precise limits of the prohibition of double jeopardy in federal prosecutions. . . . The view was there expressed for a majority of the Court that the prohibition was not confined to jeopardy in a new and independent case. It forbade jeopardy in the same case if the new trial was at the instance of the government and not upon defendant's motion. . . . All this may be assumed for the purpose of the case at hand, though the dissenting opinions . . . show how much was to be said in favor of a different ruling. Right-minded men, as we learn from those opinions, could reasonably, even if mistakenly, believe that a second trial was lawful in prosecutions subject to the Fifth Amendment, if it was all in the same case. Even more plainly, right-minded men could reasonably believe that in espousing that conclusion they were not favoring a practice repugnant to the conscience of mankind. Is double jeopardy in such circumstances, if double jeopardy it must be called, a denial of due process forbidden to the states? The tyranny of labels . . . must not lead us to leap to a conclusion that a word which in one set of facts may stand for oppression or enormity is of like effect in every other.

We have said that in appellant's view the Fourteenth Amendment is to be taken as embodying the prohibitions of the Fifth. His thesis is even broader. Whatever would be a violation of the original Bill of Rights (Amendments 1 to 8) if done by the federal government is now equally unlawful by force of the Fourteenth Amendment if done by a state. There is no such general rule.

. . .

We reach a different plane of social and moral values when we pass to the privileges and immunities that have been taken over from the earlier articles of the federal Bill of Rights and brought within the Fourteenth Amendment by a process of absorption. These in their origin were effective against the federal government alone. If the Fourteenth Amendment has absorbed them, the process of absorption has had its source in the belief that neither liberty nor justice would exist if they were sacrificed. . . . This is true, for illustration, of freedom of thought and speech. Of that freedom one may say that it is the matrix, the indispensable condition, of nearly every other form of freedom. With rare aberrations a pervasive recognition of that truth can be traced in our history, political and legal. So it has come about that the domain of liberty, withdrawn by the Fourteenth Amendment from encroachment by the states, has been enlarged by latter-day judgments to include liberty of the mind as well as liberty of action. The extension became, indeed, a logical imperative when once it was recognized, as long ago it was, that liberty is something more than exemption from physical restraint, and that even in the field of substantive rights and duties the legislative judgment, if oppressive and arbitrary, may be overridden by the courts.

. . .

Our survey of the cases serves, we think, to justify the statement that the dividing line between them, if not unfaltering throughout its course, has been true for the most part to a unifying principle. On which side of the line the case made out by the appellant has appropriate location must be the next inquiry and the final one. Is that kind of double jeopardy to which the statute has subjected him a hardship so acute and shocking that our polity will not endure it? Does it violate those "fundamental principles of liberty and justice which lie at the base of all our civil and political institutions"? . . . The answer surely must be "no." What the answer would have to be if the state were permitted after a trial free from error to try the accused over again or to bring another case against him, we have no occasion to consider. We deal with the statute before us and no other. The state is not attempting to wear the accused out by a multitude of cases with accumulated trials. It asks no more than this, that the case against him shall go on until there shall be a trial free from the corrosion of substantial legal error. . . . This is not cruelty at all, nor even vexation in any immoderate degree. If the trial had been infected with error adverse to the accused, there might have been review at his instance, and as often as necessary to purge the vicious taint. A reciprocal privilege, subject at all times to the discretion of the presiding judge, . . . has now been granted to the state. There is here no seismic innovation. The edifice of justice stands, its symmetry, to many, greater than before.

2. The conviction of appellant is not in derogation of any privileges or immunities that belong to him as a citizen of the United States.

. . .

(Judgment affirmed.)
Justice Butler dissented.

Benton v Maryland
395 U.S. 784, 89 S.Ct. 2056, 23 L.Ed. 2d 707 (1969)

Benton was tried in a Maryland state court and was found guilty of burglary in a jury trial but was acquitted of a larceny count. Because the grand and petit juries were invalidly chosen, he was given the option of demanding reindictment and retrial. He elected to have his conviction set aside. A new indictment and retrial followed. He was once again charged with the same crimes, larceny and burglary. He successfully moved to have the larceny count dismissed because to try him again would violate his constitutional protection against double jeopardy. The Maryland courts upheld the subsequent convictions on both counts. On appeal, the United States Supreme Court reversed.

Justice Marshall delivered the opinion of the Court:

> In 1937, this Court decided the landmark case of *Palko* v *Connecticut,* 302 U.S. 319,.
>
> . . .
>
> Recently, however, this Court has "increasingly looked to the specific guarantees of the [Bill of Rights] to determine whether a state criminal trial was conducted with due process of law." . . . In an increasing number of cases, the Court "has rejected the notion that the Fourteenth Amendment applies to the states only a 'watered-down, subjective version of the individual guarantees of the Bill of Rights. . . .'" Only last Term we found that the right to trial by jury in criminal cases was "fundamental to the American scheme of justice," . . . and held that the Sixth Amendment right to a jury trial was applicable to the states through the Fourteenth Amendment. For the same reasons, we today find that the double jeopardy prohibition of the Fifth Amendment represents a fundamental ideal in our constitutional heritage, and that it should apply to the states through the Fourteenth Amendment. Insofar as it is inconsistent with this holding, *Palko* v *Connecticut* is overruled.
>
> . . . Our recent cases have thoroughly rejected the *Palko* notion that basic constitutional rights can be denied by the states as long as the totality of the circumstances does not disclose a denial of "fundamental fairness." Once it is decided that a particular Bill of Rights guarantee is "fundamental to the American scheme of justice," . . . the same constitutional standards apply against both the state and federal governments. *Palko's* roots had thus been cut away years ago. We today only recognize the inevitable.
>
> The fundamental nature of the guarantee against double jeopardy can hardly be doubted. Its origins can be traced to Greek and Roman times, and it became established in the common law of England long before this nation's independence. . . . As with many other elements of the common law, it was carried into the jurisprudence of this country through the medium of Blackstone, who codified the doctrine in his Commentaries. "[T]he plea of *autrefois acquit,* or a former acquittal," he wrote, "is grounded on this universal maxim of the common law of England, that no man is to be brought into jeopardy of his life more than once for the same offense." Today, every state incorporates some form of the prohibition in its constitution or common law. As this Court put it in *Green* v *United States,* 355 U.S. 184, . . . , "[t]he underlying idea, one that is deeply ingrained in at least the Anglo–American system of jurisprudence, is that the state with all its resources and power should not be allowed to make repeated attempts to convict an individual for an alleged offense, thereby subjecting him to embarrassment, expense, and ordeal and compelling him to

live in a continuing state of anxiety and insecurity, as well as enhancing the possibility that even though innocent he may be found guilty." This underlying notion has from the very beginning been part of our constitutional tradition. Like the right to trial by jury, it is clearly "fundamental to the American scheme of justice." The validity of petitioner's larceny conviction must be judged, not by the watered-down standard enunciated in *Palko,* but under this Court's interpretations of the Fifth Amendment double jeopardy provisions.

· · ·

Maryland argues that *Green* does not apply to this case because petitioner's original indictment was absolutely void. One cannot be placed in "jeopardy" by a void indictment, the state argues. This argument sounds a bit strange, however, since petitioner could quietly have served out his sentence under this "void" indictment had he not appealed his burglary conviction. Only by accepting the option of a new trial could the indictment be set aside; at worst the indictment would seem only voidable at the defendant's option, not absolutely void. . . . Petitioner was acquitted of larceny. He has, under *Green,* a valid double jeopardy plea which he cannot be forced to waive. Yet Maryland wants the earlier acquittal set aside, over petitioner's objections, because of a defect in the indictment. This it cannot do. Petitioner's larceny conviction cannot stand.

(Judgment reversed.)
Justices White, Harlan, and Stewart dissented.

The right to appeal should be completely "free and unfettered," according to the majority opinion in *North Carolina* v *Alford,* 400 U.S. 25, 91 S.Ct. 160, 27 L.Ed. 2d 162 (1970). For this reason, the Court found that it is unconstitutional to ignore the years of imprisonment spent prior to a successful appeal and subsequent reconviction. Any person who is not acquitted upon reconviction must be granted that time already served on the first conviction toward the sentence imposed upon the second conviction, since multiple punishments are prohibited by the Constitution. The Court also considered the problem of sentencing after reconviction. It found that there is no constitutional prohibition against a more severe sentence than that imposed on the first conviction. This is because the successful appeal "wipes the slate clean" for a new trial and the defendant's rights, as well as the hazards of conviction, are restored. In order to ensure that the court trying the defendant the second time does not punish the defendant for his successful appeal, the Court laid down certain guidelines. First, the judge may sentence the reconvicted defendant in light of all of the information available on his social, physical, and psychological well-being. If, however, the sentence is greater than that originally imposed, the judge must state, in the court record, the reasons for such a sentence, based on information not available to the sentencing judge at the original trial. When the sentencing is completed, then, the time already served on the first conviction, is subtracted from the final sentence. These guidelines were offered by the Court in order to ensure due process and equal protection to those defendants who successfully appeal their convictions. In *North Carolina* v *Alford* the judgment was affirmed.

Ashe v *Swenson*
397 U.S. 436, 90 S.Ct. 1189, 25 L.Ed. 2d 469 (1970)

Three or four armed men broke into a room and robbed six men who were playing poker. Later, four men were arrested and charged with seven different crimes—six counts of robbery of each poker player and theft of an automobile from one player taken for the getaway. Ashe, one of the accused, was tried for robbing Knight, one of the players. The evidence of a robbery occurring was strong, but identification evidence of Ashe was weak, and there was a great deal of contradiction regarding the number of robbers. Ashe was acquitted because of insufficient evidence. Six weeks later Ashe was brought to trial for robbing Roberts, another player. Ashe filed a motion to dismiss based on his previous acquittal. This was overruled and Ashe was subsequently convicted after the prosecutor bolstered his identification evidence. The conviction was upheld in the state courts. On appeal the United States Supreme Court reversed.

Justice Stewart delivered the opinion of the Court:

Viewing the questions presented solely in terms of Fourteenth Amendment due process—whether the course that New Jersey had pursued had "led to fundamental unfairness" . . . this Court declined to reverse the judgment of conviction, because "in the circumstances shown by this record, we cannot say that petitioner's later prosecution and conviction violated due process." . . . The Court found it necessary to decide whether "collateral estoppel"—the principle that bars relitigation between the same parties of issues actually determined at a previous trial—is a due process requirement in a state criminal trial, since it accepted New Jersey's determination that the petitioner's previous acquittal did not in any event give rise to such an estoppel. . . . And in the view the Court took of the issues presented, it did not, of course, even approach consideration of whether collateral estoppel is an ingredient of the Fifth Amendment guarantee against double jeopardy.

The doctrine of *Benton* v *Maryland,* 395 U.S. 784, . . . , puts the issues in the present case in a perspective quite different from that in which the issues were perceived in *Hoag* v *New Jersey,* . . . . The question is no longer whether collateral estoppel is a requirement of due process, but whether it is a part of the Fifth Amendment's guarantee against double jeopardy. And if collateral estoppel is embodied in that guarantee, then its applicability in a particular case is no longer a matter to be left for state court determination within the broad bounds of "fundamental fairness," but a matter of constitutional fact we must decide through an examination of the entire records.

· · ·

The federal decisions have made clear that the rule of collateral estoppel in criminal cases is not to be applied with the hypertechnical and archaic approach of a nineteenth-century pleading book, but with realism and rationality. Where a previous judgment of acquittal was based upon a general verdict, as is usually the case, this approach requires a court to "examine the record of a prior proceeding, taking into account the pleadings, evidence, charge, and other relevant matter, and conclude whether a rational jury could have grounded its verdict upon an issue other than that which the defendant seeks to foreclose from consideration." ... Any test more technically restrictive would, of course, simply amount to a rejection of the rule of collateral estoppel in criminal proceedings, at least in every case where the first judgment was based upon a general verdict of acquittal.

Straightforward application of the federal rule to the present case can lead to but one conclusion. ... The single rationally conceivable issue in dispute before the jury was whether the petitioner had been one of the robbers. And the jury by its verdict found that he had not. The federal rule of law, therefore, would make a second prosecution for the robbery of Roberts wholly impermissible.

The ultimate question to be determined, then, in the light of *Benton* v *Maryland*, ... is whether this established rule of federal law is embodied in the Fifth Amendment guarantee against double jeopardy. We do not hesitate to hold that it is. For whatever else that constitutional guarantee may embrace, *North Carolina* v *Pearce*, ... , it surely protects a man who has been acquitted from having to "run the gantlet" a second time.

. . .

After the first jury had acquitted the petitioner of robbing Knight, Missouri could certainly not have brought him to trial again upon that charge. ... The situation is constitutionally no different here, even though the second trial related to another victim of the same robbery.

In this case the state in its brief has frankly conceded that following the petitioner's acquittal, it treated the first trial as no more than a dry run for the second prosecution: "No doubt the prosecutor felt the state had a provable case on the first charge and, when he lost, he did what every good attorney would do—he refined his presentation in light of the turn of events at the first trial." But this is precisely what the constitutional guarantee forbids.

(Judgment reversed.)
Justices Black, Harlan, Brennan, Douglas, and Marshall concurred in three separate opinions.
Chief Justice Burger dissented.

In *United States* v *Jorn,* 400 U.S. 70, 91 S.Ct. 547, 25 L.Ed. 2d 682 (1971), the appellee had been tried for willfully assisting in preparation of fraudulent tax returns. The judge in the federal district court discharged the jury and aborted the trial so that the witnesses could consult with attorneys. The case was set for retrial, but Jorn demanded dismissal on the grounds that he would be facing double jeopardy. The case was dismissed and the government appealed directly to the Supreme Court which affirmed the district court decision.

Breed, the petitioner, had been tried as an adult in the California State Court after a finding by the juvenile court that he was guilty of violating a criminal statute. The juvenile authority then referred the case to the adult court on the grounds that Breed was unfit for treatment in a juvenile facility. It was the Supreme Court's decision in *Breed* v *Jones,* 421 U.S. 519 95 S.Ct. 1779 44 L.Ed. 2d 346 (1975), that Breed had been placed in double jeopardy by the trial in both the juvenile and superior courts.

QUESTIONS

1. How has the *Miranda* decision affected arrest procedures? What is the current interpretation of *Miranda?*

2. In what areas does *Orozco* v *Texas* extend *Miranda?*

3. Compare *Miranda* to *Harris* v *United States*. How does each holding attempt to deter offensive police conduct?

4. How does *Schmerber* v *California* distinguish between physical and testimonial evidence?

5. Compare *Garrity* v *New Jersey* and *Gardner* v *Broderick*. What was the major difference between these two decisions?

6. What conditions during a trial do not cause jeopardy to be attached? When can it be attached? What cases in the section on double jeopardy specifically allude to this question?

11

SIXTH AMENDMENT

Counsel

During the early twelfth century a defendant was permitted to have counsel only if he could afford one and only for very minor offenses. Since then the law has changed radically, if not slowly, so that now a defendant must be furnished counsel in all cases in which he may be sentenced to a loss of freedom. In the twelfth century defendants had no legal right to appear with counsel. The theory behind this was that the judge would ensure that the defendant received a fair trial and also that the Crown would not bring a charge against a person unless the evidence was so clear that there was no defense available to the defendant.

This denial of counsel changed in 1696 with the English Treason Act which allowed counsel to argue points of law with the permission of the judge. It was not until 1836, however, that the right to counsel for all criminal prosecutions was permitted in England.

Almost all the American colonies had some statutory provision establishing the right to counsel. After the Revolution this right was included in the constitutions of most states, but the right meant only the right to retain counsel at one's own expense.

Even before the adoption of the United States Constitution there were two federal statutes dealing with the right to counsel. The Judiciary Act of 1789 stated that counsel was permitted in United States courts. Another statute passed in 1790 provided that in cases of treason or capital offenses a defendant may employ his own counsel or have one assigned by the court. In 1791, when the

Sixth Amendment was adopted, an accused was guaranteed the right to have the assistance of counsel in all criminal prosecutions. Once again this meant that if the defendant could retain an attorney, he was guaranteed the right to have him represent him.

It was not until 1932 in *Powell* v *Alabama,* 287 U.S. 45 (1932), that an indigent defendant in a capital case had the right to have an attorney appointed for him—the first constitutional interpretation requiring the states to furnish counsel. In 1938 the United States Supreme Court mandated that counsel be furnished to indigent defendants in all federal criminal cases subject to the *caveat* that a defendant may waive the right intelligently, competently, and voluntarily. Even in this situation the judge had the serious responsibility of ensuring that the defendant knew exactly what he was doing. *Johnson* v *Zerbst,* 304 U.S. 458 (1938).

Although *Powell* mandated that the states furnish counsel to indigents in capital cases, and *Johnson* required counsel in all federal cases, *Betts* v *Brady,* 316 U.S. 455 (1942), held that there was not a constitutional right of an indigent defendant to have the state appoint counsel for him. The *Betts* opinion declared that the appointment of counsel was not a fundamental right necessary for a fair trial. In short, the United States Supreme Court looked to see whether the defendant received a fair trial. If he received one, then the need to have representation by an attorney made no difference. Therefore, the argument that the Fourteenth Amendment incorporated the Sixth Amendment's Right to Counsel Clause was rejected.

It was not until 1963 that incorporation of the Right to Counsel Clause was accepted. In *Gideon* v *Wainwright,* 372 U.S. 335, (1963), the Supreme Court decided that indigent defendants had to be offered the assignment of counsel when accused of serious crimes, and that this right was applicable to the states by virtue of the Due Process Clause of the Fourteenth Amendment. Because *Gideon* involved a felony, some states only appointed counsel in felony cases, but other states provided counsel in both felony and misdemeanor cases. This situation was finally rectified in 1972 when the Supreme Court declared that an indigent defendant must be afforded the right to counsel in any case in which he faces a loss of liberty.

The scope of the right to counsel has been expanded to include proceedings before and after trial. In *Miranda* v *Arizona,* 384 U.S. 436 (1966), once a defendant is in custody of the police and a process of interrogation begins to elicit incriminating information, a defendant must be afforded the right to counsel. If he is indigent, he must be notified that the state will appoint counsel for him if he so requests. (See Chapter 10.) The United States Supreme Court has also held that when the state gives a defendant the right to appeal a conviction, it has the obligation of providing legal counsel to an indigent defendant to ensure that he is adequately represented and his case properly argued before the appellate court. If this is not done, then he is denied his rights under the Due Process Clause of the Fourteenth Amendment.

Appointment of Counsel. How is counsel appointed for an indigent defendant? Such appointment is expensive in terms of money and manpower. Three systems of assigning counsel are currently utilized: public defender, voluntary defender, and assigned counsel.

The public defender system is operated from governmental funds and is a governmental agency. The public defender, either upon the request of the court or the indigent defendant, must defend any person who is not financially able to employ an attorney. This system is the primary means of providing counsel to indigents in some of the larger states and urban areas. It has been estimated that in all states the public defender handles about 35 percent of indigent felony trials, with the remainder handled by assigned counsel, despite the fact that 2,750 of the 3,100 counties in this country use some form of the assigned counsel system.[1]

Voluntary defender groups have been used in some areas where private non-governmental organizations have been established for the purpose of representing indigent defendants. In effect, this system is a privately created law office that assigns lawyers to cases or from which the court itself may assign lawyers. This system may also utilize paid trained investigators to assist the legal staff. A major defect of the voluntary defender system is that the uncertainty and inadequacy of income are practical limitations upon its effectiveness.

The third approach used is the assigned counsel system. It is the most widely utilized system. The attorney is appointed by the court on a random or rotating basis from members of the local bar association. A high percentage of the court-appointed attorneys are younger attorneys who frequently have the time and desire to gain some trial experience. As a general rule, compensation is low and inadequate. When the defendant appears at arraignment without counsel, he is asked if he has an attorney. If he cannot afford one, one is appointed. The system of assigned counsel was originally developed with the idea that the bar had the obligation to provide legal services to the needy defendant. This situation has changed radically. The number of cases today requiring counsel has risen rapidly, at a rate disproportionate to the number of available attorneys. A major criticism of the system involves this very condition. It is unfair to require an attorney to be called upon time upon time without adequate compensation.

As a general rule, the assigned counsel's duties end after conviction. If an appeal is taken, a new court-appointed attorney is assigned and he must start from the beginning to familiarize himself with the case. This difficulty may be alleviated by extending the original appointment to cover the first appeal. Once again, however, inadequacy of funds is a nagging problem.

The right to counsel has also been expanded to presence at police lineup identification. Later on in this chapter there are several cases on counsel which

---

[1]The President's Commission on Law Enforcement and Administration of Justice, *Task Force Report: The Courts* (Washington, D.C.: Government Printing Office, 1967), p. 59.

present the current declarations of the United States Supreme Court plus the rationale for expansion of the right to counsel.

Confrontation

The right to confront and cross-examine is essential to the development of the criminal processes. Although the right was developed in the eighteenth century, it was not considered to be a constitutional right guaranteed by the Due Process Clause of the Fourteenth Amendment as a limitation on the states until 1965. The right to confront and cross-examine witnesses guarantees that the defendant will have the opportunity to test the credibility of the testimony of witnesses and other evidence against him. This is particularly important so that the trier-of-fact (jury or judge) can determine the truth not only by what is said, but how it is said.

The right of confrontation is especially important in the jury trial. In the eighteenth century when the jury came from the neighborhood of the defendant, the jury knew about the case and the defendant personally. As the jury system developed, with greater emphasis on determining the facts in the case based on the presentation of evidence, greater reliance was placed on the testimony of witnesses. During this time the defendant was still denied the right to call witnesses in his behalf. If the prosecutor proved his part of the case, it was almost a foregone conclusion that the defendant would be convicted because there was a presumption that if the defendant had the opportunity to rebut the evidence he would merely be perjuring himself. The Treason Act of 1696 in England established the right of confrontation for the defendant in treason trials. The right was subsequently extended to all English defendants.

In the United States the confrontation clause was found in early state constitutions adopted during the Revolutionary War. In 1789 the Sixth Amendment's Confrontation Clause was adopted with little controversy. It was therefore applicable in federal criminal cases. Even though the right to confrontation has been traditionally recognized in state law, it was not until *Pointer* v *Texas,* 380 U.S. 400 (1965), that it was declared by the United States Supreme Court to be a requirement of the Due Process Clause of the Fourteenth Amendment.

Once it is recognized that the right to confrontation exists in criminal cases, should this right be available in other kinds of proceedings? Legislative hearings are frequently conducted into such activities as organized crime, communist activities, and interstate sales of securities during which witnesses are subpoenaed to testify. Frequently these individuals have sought the opportunity to cross-examine their accusers. The efforts have been unsuccessful. In 1960 the United States Supreme Court declared that persons compelled to testify before the United States Civil Rights Commission regarding their alleged denial of black voting rights were not entitled to confront witnesses against them. *Hannah* v *Larche,* 363 U.S. 420 (1960).

Also contained in the Sixth Amendment is the clause that the accused shall have the right to have "compulsory process for obtaining witnesses in his favor.'' This clause has caused little controversy. The rights of confrontation and compulsory process are complementary. They assure that all evidence will be produced, that it is subject to challenge and cross-examination, and that the decisions in the case will be made only on the basis of evidence produced in open court.

Speedy Trial

The principle of a speedy trial dates from the Magna Charta in 1215 and guarantees that an accused cannot be held in jail without trial for an excessively long period of time. This protects the defense by preventing a lapse of time during which witnesses might become unavailable or evidence might be lost which might prove the guilt or innocence of the accused. The speedy trial, by requiring that there by no undue delay, protects the accused against prolonged incarceration. By being brought to trial quickly, a defendant is similarly relieved of some of the suspicion that may be against him by being locked up for an extended period.

The right to a speedy trial begins at the time the formal charge is made. What happens when there is an excessive delay before bringing the accused to trial? One way of forestalling some of the detrimental consequences of delay is to release the accused on bail. Bail is posting of a bond of a set amount to guarantee the presence of the defendant at the trial. When the question of bail arises, the Eighth Amendment (Chapter 12) must be considered because of the guarantee that excessive bail may not be imposed. A main issue arises concerning the meaning of ''excessive.'' Theoretically, the main purpose of bail is to ensure presence at trial. Recent studies have cast some doubts on the efficacy of the bail system, particularly since it affects the poor defendant.[2] It appears to lessen the chances of acquittal of those who cannot raise bail; there is also less chance of lenient treatment for those who are convicted who could not raise bail; poor defendants are kept in jail even though they may never be convicted of any offense, and bail has the tendency to deny release rather than encourage release of indigents.

There are some legitimate reasons for delay before trial. Most common, for example, is the situation where the defense counsel requests more time to prepare a defense.

Jury Trial

A jury is made up of fact-finders. Trial by jury is an important method of ensuring that the processes of criminal justice remain adequately protected in a

[2]Among the various materials see Karl Menninger, *The Crime of Punishment* (New York: Viking, 1968); Alexander B. Smith and Harriet Pollack, *Crime and Justice in a Mass Society* (San Francisco: Rinehart Press, 1973); Frank B. Prassel, *Introduction to American Criminal Justice* (New York: Harper & Row, 1975); *The Challenge of Crime in a Free Society* (Washington, D.C.: Government Printing Office, 1967).

democratic society. The trial by jury is contained in the main body of the Constitution (Article III, Section 2, Clause 3): "The trial of all Crimes except in Cases of Impeachment shall be by Jury." The Sixth Amendment also guarantees that "In all criminal prosecutions, the accused shall enjoy the right of a speedy and public trial, by an impartial jury. . . ." Both of these provisions apply to the federal government. The cases that will be presented on speedy trial discuss the incorporation of the right to a jury trial into the Due Process Clause of the Fourteenth Amendment. The cases also address several other major constitutional issues, such as the number of jurors required and the need for a unanimous verdict in criminal cases.

The fact-finding function of the jury takes place after each side has presented his evidence and has made final arguments to the jury. Next, the judge instructs the jury regarding the applicable law covering the issues presented and makes any other appropriate comments. The members of the jury then retire to the jury room for secret deliberations. They remain there until either a verdict is reached or it is found that they cannot reach a verdict. In a federal criminal trial all 12 jurors must vote for conviction or acquittal. If they cannot, the judge may declare a "hung jury," dismiss the jury and order a new trial before another jury. This procedure is much the same in state criminal trials.

An important function of the jury outside the fact-finding one is that the jury system intimately involves the citizen in the administration of the criminal justice system. The system also helps to remove popular mistrust of the judicial system. A jury trial similarly provides necessary flexibility in legal rules. The law is normally well defined and the judge is expected to enforce it in the same way for all persons. The jury, acting with flexibility in weighing evidence before it, applies the general law by making adjustments to fit the pecularities of the case. The jury also reflects the community attitudes and in this way it operates as a check on the law. Juries have the reputation for refusing to apply the law and temper their decision with individual concern for particularly worthy defendants. Sometimes called *jury nullification,* it is still a democratic way of assuring that the current feeling of a community is injected into the outcome of a trial.

Impartial Jury. Originally juries were called together to decide disputed questions of fact because they knew the accused and the crime. The function of the jury subsequently became one of judging. With the adoption of the Sixth Amendment in 1791, the Constitution reflected the direct application of the English common law as practiced in the eighteenth century in England: A juror should be known neither to the accused nor the plaintiff; he should judge the issue on the evidence presented; and he should avoid any trace of partiality in his judging. Since these requirements are difficult to fulfill, the law does not demand that all jurors be able to fulfill them.

The laws do require, however, that the juror render an unbiased verdict. To allow this the prospective jurors are examined by the opposing parties prior to the beginning of the trial to determine if the jurors are qualified. In some states and the federal courts the judge examines the jurors based on questions submitted to him from the opposing counsel.

Jurors may be challenged and removed for "cause." Removal for "cause" is usually based on grounds contained in statutes, for example, a close relationship with the accused or a witness, family relationship within specified degrees of consanguinity, or actual or possible bias toward one of the parties. In addition to challenge for cause, each side is allocated a specified number of peremptory challenges, challenges and removals of jurors for which no reason need be given. The juror is arbitrarily removed under this kind of challenge.

The peremptory challenge by its very nature can be used to exclude racial groups from juries. In *Swain* v *Alabama,* 380 U.S. 202 (1965), an Alabama prosecutor used the peremptory challenge to remove all blacks from the jury panel which was to try a black defendant. The practice is still used extensively in many southern states. In a challenge to this practice the United States Supreme Court declared that the peremptory striking of blacks from a particular jury did not violate the Due Process Clause of the Fourteenth Amendment. The reason given was that the peremptory challenge was normally exercised on extralegal grounds that did not need to be explained. The Supreme Court did issue a warning, however, when it stated that when the prosecution in case after case is responsible for removal of blacks who have survived all challenges for cause and who are qualified jurors, "with the result that no blacks ever serve on petit juries, the Fourteenth Amendment claim takes on added significance."

Fair and Public Trial

Before the colonists settled America the right to a public trial was well settled in the English common law because of the great distrust for secret trials. This right was transported to America and has become a fixed part of the individual guarantees of criminal due process.

The right to a public trial does not mean that a judge cannot limit the number of spectators at a trial. It means that no court may limit attendance to only court officials. Such factors as the size of the courtroom and notoriety of the trial may cause the judge to set limits on the classes of spectators allowed. He cannot arbitrarily exclude the public. Today the major issue involving the public trial is how public should the trial be. As mentioned, the judge should show considerable discretion in excluding some people from the courtroom. In addition, he should show discretion in his concern for the interests of public safety by excluding unruly persons and in his concern for minors by excluding them when he believes that they should not be present because of the nature of the testimony. Courts differ on these points, but not one court has declared that an accused may be tried when everyone except court officials have been excluded.

What are some of the benefits of a public trial? First, a public trial serves as a notice to witnesses who are not known to the defendant and it may help the defendant in his defense. Second, it permits the spectators to learn about the operations of their government and be more confident in the judicial system. Third, it imposes a restraint on the power of the judiciary by keeping its operations open to scrutiny. Fourth, it permits citizens to view the judicial branch of governmental operations by showing the kinds of cases brought by the prosecution and the manner in which they are presented for public scrutiny.

Pretrial Publicity. Today publicity given by the news media to criminal trials is often widespread and of a sensational nature. Many scholars and leading legal figures feel that two constitutional values—freedom of the press and the right of the accused to have a fair trial—conflict with each other.

Those who argue against placing curbs on the press reports of criminal trials claim that the accused has a right to a public trial *and* the public has a right to know what is happening. There should be no legal restrictions on mass-media coverage of trials because the very nature of the democratic process mandates that there be public awareness of all events.

Those who favor placing curbs on the press reports of criminal trials contend that anything which comes to the potential juror's attention outside the courtroom conceivably could prejudice him against the accused. They also argue that reporting of criminal cases by an overzealous press can and often does create a situation in which the accused cannot receive a fair trial. Many of this belief favor the system used in England in which newspaper accounts of trials are restricted to accurate and fair reporting of trial proceedings. If the accounts are not fair, the newspapers are subject to contempt proceedings. English courts take this responsibility seriously and have held offending newspapers in contempt.

In 1966 the move to adopt court rules limiting public release of information about criminal trials was given impetus by *Sheppard* v *Maxwell,* 384 U.S. 333 (1966). The United States Supreme Court reversed the criminal conviction of the defendant because the pretrial publicity created a "Roman holiday" atmosphere for news reporters.

Television and radio have created a new challenge to assuring that an accused receives a fair trial. In 1963 a defendant was convicted of kidnapping and murder during a bank robbery. He was interviewed over television the morning after his arrest and gave a complete confession during the television broadcast. In reversing the conviction, the United States Supreme Court said that it made no difference if jurors were interviewed to determine whether or not they were influenced by the telecast. The Court further noted that the television spectacle was really the accused's trial, and any subsequent proceedings in a community so pervasively exposed to the impression would be a hollow formality. *Rideau* v *Louisiana,* 373 U.S. 723 (1963).

The case of *Estes* v *Texas,* 381 U.S. 532 (1965), which will be discussed later in this chapter, points to the difficulties that may arise from television coverage in courtrooms. The opinion itself reversed Estes' conviction, but the basis for the decision is somewhat uncertain because of the lack of a clear-cut majority.

COUNSEL

Powell v *Alabama*

287 U.S. 45, 53 S.Ct. 55, 77 L.Ed. 158 (1932)

Powell and two other defendants pleaded not guilty to charges of raping two white girls. After they were apprehended they were taken to Scottsboro, Alabama, where they were met by a large hostile crowd. The sheriff requested the militia to protect the prisoners although the defendants did not appear to be in serious danger from the crowd. After they were indicted the trial judge "appointed" members of this bar (Alabama) to represent them. Prior to this time the judge appointed "all members of the bar" for the purpose of arraigning the defendants. The record of the trial indicated that the appearance of counsel was more charade than an active and vigorous defense of the defendants. After being convicted and sentenced to death, the defendants appealed on the ground that they were denied the right to counsel in a substantial sense. On appeal the United States Supreme Court reversed.

Justice Sutherland delivered the opinion of the Court:

The record shows that on the day when the offense is said to have been committed, these defendants, together with a number of other negroes, were upon a freight train on its way through Alabama. On the same train were seven white boys and the two white girls. A fight took place between the negroes and the white boys, in the course of which the white boys, with the exception of one named Gilley, were thrown off the train. A message was sent ahead, reporting the fight and asking that every black be gotten off the train. The participants in the fight, and the two girls, were in an open gondola car. The two girls testified that each of them was assaulted by six different blacks in turn, and they identified the seven defendants as having been among the number. None of the white boys was called to testify, with the exception of Gilley, who was called in rebuttal.

[W]e confine ourselves, as already suggested, to the inquiry whether the defendants were in substance denied the right of counsel, and if so, whether such denial infringes the Due Process Clause of the Fourteenth Amendment.

First. The record shows that immediately upon the return of the indictment defendants were arraigned and pleaded not guilty. Apparently they were not asked whether they had, or were able to employ, counsel, or wished to have counsel appointed; or whether they had friends or relatives who might assist in that regard if communicated with. That it would not have been an idle ceremony to have given the defendants reasonable opportunity to communicate with their families and endeavor to obtain counsel is demonstrated by the fact that very soon after conviction, able counsel appeared in their behalf.

. . .

It is hardly necessary to say that the right to counsel being conceded, a defendant should be afforded a fair opportunity to secure counsel of his own choice.

. . .

It thus will be seen that until the very morning of the trial no lawyer had been named or definitely designated to represent the defendants. Prior to that time, the trial judge had "appointed all the members of the bar" for the limited "purpose of arraigning the defendants." . . . Such a designation, even if made for all purposes, would, in our opinion, have fallen far short of meeting, in any proper sense, a requirement for the appointment of counsel.

. . . This action of the trial judge in respect of appointment of counsel was little more than an expansive gesture, imposing no substantial or definite obligation upon any one.

. . .

. . . The prompt disposition of criminal cases is to be commended and encouraged. But in reaching that result a defendant, charged with a serious crime, must not be stripped of his right to have sufficient time to advise with counsel and prepare his defense. To do that is not to proceed promptly in the calm spirit of regulated justice but to go forward with the haste of the mob.

. . .

Second. The Constitution of Alabama . . . provides that in all criminal prosecutions the accused shall enjoy the right to have the assistance of counsel; and a state statute requires the court in a capital case, where the defendant is unable to employ counsel, to appoint counsel for him. The state Supreme Court held that these provisions had not been infringed, and with that holding we are powerless to interfere. The question, however, which it is our duty, and within our power, to decide, is whether the denial of the assistance of counsel contravenes the Due Process Clause of the Fourteenth Amendment to the federal Constitution.

. . .

In the light of the facts outlined in the forepart of this opinion—the ignorance and illiteracy of the defendants, their youth, the circumstances of public hostility, the imprisonment and close surveillance of the defendants by the military forces, the fact that their friends and families were all in other states and communication with them necessarily difficult, and above all that they stood in deadly peril of their lives—we think the failure of the trial court to give them reasonable time and opportunity to secure counsel was a clear denial of due process.

But passing that, and assuming their inability, even if opportunity had been given, to employ counsel, as the trial court evidently did assume, we are of opinion that, under the circumstances just stated, the necessity of counsel was so vital and imperative that the failure of the trial court to make an effective appointment of counsel was likewise a denial of due process within the meaning of the Fourteenth Amendment. Whether this would be so in other criminal prosecutions, or under other circumstances, we need not determine. All that it is necessary now to decide, as we do decide, is that in a capital case, where the defendant is unable to employ counsel, and is incapable adequately of making his own defense because of ignorance, feeblemindedness, illiteracy, or the like, it is the duty of the court, whether requested or not, to assign counsel for him as a necessary requisite of due process of law; and that duty is not discharged by an assignment at such a time or under such circumstances as to preclude the giving of effective aid in the preparation and trial of the case. To hold otherwise would be to ignore the fundamental postulate, already adverted to, ''that there are certain immutable principles of justice which inhere in the very idea of free government which no member of the Union may disregard.'' . . . In a case such as this, whatever may be the rule in other cases, the right to have counsel appointed, when necessary, is a logical corollary from the constitutional right to be heard by counsel.

. . .

(Judgment reversed.)
Justices Butler and McReynolds dissented.

Gideon v Wainwright

372 U.S. 335, 83 S.Ct. 792, 9 L.Ed. 2d 799 (1963)

Gideon was charged in Florida with the felony of breaking and entering a pool hall with intent to commit a crime. The offense is frequently classified as burglary in most states. The defendant appeared as indigent and requested appointment of counsel. Per Florida law the judge denied the request because the case was not a capital offense. Gideon conducted his own defense. He was convicted by a jury and sentenced to five years in prison. The conviction was affirmed by the Florida courts. The United States Supreme Court granted certiorari.

Justice Black delivered the opinion of the Court:

. . . Since 1942, when *Betts* v *Brady,* 316 U.S. 455 . . . , was decided by a divided Court, the problem of a defendant's federal constitutional right to counsel in a state court has been a continuing source of controversy and litigation in both state and federal courts. To give this problem another review here, we granted certiorari. . . . Since Gideon was proceeding *in forma pauperis,* we appointed counsel to represent him and requested both sides to discuss in their briefs and oral arguments the following: ''Should this Court's holding in *Betts* v *Brady,* . . . , be reconsidered? . . . Treating due process as ''a concept less rigid and more fluid than those envisaged in other specific and particular provisions of the Bill of Rights,'' the Court held that refusal to appoint counsel under the particular facts and circumstances in the Betts case was not so ''offensive to the common and fundamental ideas of fairness'' as to amount to a denial of due process. Since the facts and circumstances of the two cases are so nearly indistinguishable, we think the *Betts* v *Brady* holding if left standing would require us to reject Gideon's claim that the Constitution guarantees him the assistance of counsel. Upon full reconsideration we conclude that *Betts* v *Brady* should be overruled.

. . .

We think the Court in Betts had ample precedent for acknowledging that those guarantees of the Bill of Rights which are fundamental safeguards of liberty immune from federal abridgment are equally protected against state invasion of the Due Process Clause of the Fourteenth Amendment. This same principle was recognized, explained, and applied in *Powell* v *Alabama*, 287 U.S. 45.

. . .

We accept *Betts* v *Brady's* assumption, based as it was on our prior cases, that a provision of the Bill of Rights which is "fundamental and essential to a fair trial" is made obligatory upon the states by the Fourteenth Amendment. We think the Court in Betts was wrong, however, in concluding that the Sixth Amendment's guarantee of counsel is not one of these fundamental rights. Ten years before *Betts* v *Brady,* this Court, after full consideration of all the historical data examined in Betts, had unequivocally declared that "the right to the aid of counsel is of this fundamental character, ..." While the Court at the close of its Powell opinion did by its language, as this Court frequently does, limit its holding to the particular facts and circumstances of that case, its conclusions about the fundamental nature of the right to counsel are unmistakable.

. . .

In light of these and many other prior decisions of this Court, it is not surprising that the Betts Court, when faced with the contention that "one charged with crime, who is unable to obtain counsel, must be furnished counsel by the state," conceded that "[e]xpressions in the opinions of this court lend color to the argument. . . ." . . . The fact is that in deciding as it did—that "appointment of counsel is not a fundamental right, essential to a fair trial"— the Court in *Betts* v *Brady* made an abrupt break with its own well-considered precedents. In returning to these old precedents, sounder we believe than the new, we but restore constitutional principles established to achieve a fair system of justice. Not only these precedents but also reason and reflection require us to recognize that in our adversary system of criminal justice, any person haled into court, who is too poor to hire a lawyer, cannot be assured a fair trial unless counsel is provided for him. This seems to us to be an obvious truth. Governments, both state and federal, quite properly spend vast sums of money to establish machinery to try defendants accused of crime. Lawyers to prosecute are everywhere deemed essential to protect the public's interest in an orderly society. Similarly, there are few defendants charged with crime, few indeed, who fail to hire the best lawyers they can get to prepare and present their defenses. That government hires lawyers to prosecute and defendants who have the money hire lawyers to defend are the strongest indications of the widespread belief that lawyers in criminal courts are necessities, not luxuries. The right of one charged with crime to counsel may not be deemed fundamental and essential to fair trials in some countries, but it is in ours. From the very beginning, our state and national constitutions and laws have laid great emphasis on procedural and substantive safeguards designed to assure fair trials before impartial tribunals in which every defendant stands equal before the law. This noble ideal cannot be realized if the poor man charged with crime has to face his accusers without a lawyer to assist him. . . . The Court in *Betts* v *Brady* departed from the sound wisdom upon which the Court's holding in *Powell* v *Alabama* rested. Florida, supported by two other states, has asked that *Betts* v *Brady* be left intact. Twenty-two states, as friends of the Court, argue that *Betts* was "an anachronism when handed down" and that it should now be overruled. We agree.

(Judgment reversed.)
Justices Douglas, Clark, and Harlan each concurred separately.

In *Betts* v *Brady,* 316 U.S. 455, 62 S.Ct. 1252, 86 L.Ed. 1595 (1942), the defendant advised the judge at his arraignment on robbery charges that because of lack of funds he was unable to employ counsel. The judge refused to appoint counsel, stating that the practice of the court was to appoint attorneys for indigents only in rape and murder prosecutions. On writ of certiorari to the United States Supreme Court the defendant alleged that his right to counsel as guaranteed by the Fourteenth Amendment was denied. The Court ruled that due process of law does not require a state to furnish counsel to an indigent defendant in every criminal case.

Ross v *Moffitt,* 417 U.S. 600, 94 S.Ct. 2437, 41 L.Ed. 2d 341 (1974), answered the following question: Should an indigent defendant be furnished counsel for discretionary state appeals and applications for review to the United States Supreme Court? *Douglas* v *California,* 372 U.S. 353 (1963) required appointment of counsel for indigents on their first appeal as a matter of right. The Court refused to extend the *Douglas* holding to discretionary appellate review. Justice Rehnquist for the majority observed that its "reading of the Fourteenth Amendment leaves these choices to the state, and respondent was denied no rights secured by the federal Constitution when North Carolina refused to provide counsel to aid him in obtaining discretionary appellate review." The Court further noted: "We do not believe that the Due Process Clause requires North Carolina to provide respondent with counsel on his discretionary appeal to the State Supreme Court. At the trial stage of a criminal proceeding, the right of an indigent defendant to counsel at the trial is fundamental. . . . But there are significant differences between the trial and appellate stages of a criminal proceeding."

In *Coleman* v *Alabama,* 399 U.S. 1, 90 S.Ct. 1999, 26 L.Ed. 2d 387 (1970), the defendants were convicted of assault with intent to commit murder. The circuit court judge denied appointment of counsel at the preliminary hearing on the grounds that nothing occurring at a preliminary hearing in Alabama can substantially prejudice the rights of the accused at his trial. The Supreme Court of the United States ruled that the preliminary hearing was a "critical stage" in a criminal prosecution and therefore the appointment of counsel for an indigent defendant is required.

Hamilton v *Alabama*
368 U.S. 52, 82 S.Ct. 157, 7 L.Ed. 2d 114 (1961)

The defendant was charged with a capital offense in Alabama and was sentenced to death. At his arraignment on the grand jury indictment for the offense he was not represented by an attorney. Under Alabama procedure the defendant was permitted to show that if he was disadvantaged by the lack of counsel at arraignment, he would be given a new trial. The Alabama Supreme Court recognized that the defendant had a right to counsel under Alabama law, but that there was no showing that he suffered any disadvantage. The United States Supreme Court reversed, holding that the arraignment is a critical stage of a criminal proceeding and that denial of counsel is a violation of due process.

Justice Douglas delivered the opinion of the Court:

Arraignment under Alabama law is a critical stage in a criminal proceeding. It is then that the defense of insanity must be pleaded . . . or the opportunity is lost. . . . Thereafter that plea may not be made except in the discretion of the trial judge, and his refusal to accept it is "not revisable" on appeal. . . . Pleas in abatement must also be made at the time of arraignment. . . . It is then that motions to quash based on systematic exclusion of one race from grand juries . . . or on the ground that the grand jury was otherwise improperly drawn . . . must be made.

Whatever may be the function and importance of arraignment in other jurisdictions, we have said enough to show that in Alabama it is a critical stage in a criminal proceeding. What happens there may affect the whole trial. Available defenses may be as irretrievably lost, if not then and there asserted, as they are when an accused represented by counsel waives a right for strategic purposes. . . . In *Powell* v *State of Alabama,* 287 U.S. 45, . . . , the Court said that an accused in a capital case "requires the guiding hand of counsel at every step in the proceedings against him. Without it, though he be not guilty, he faces the danger of conviction because he does not know how to establish his innocence." The guiding hand of counsel is needed at the trial "lest the unwary concede that which only bewilderment or ignorance could justify or pay a penalty which is greater than the law of the state exacts for the offense which they in fact and in law committed." . . . But the same pitfalls or like ones face an accused in Alabama who is arraigned without having counsel at his side. When one pleads to a capital charge without benefit of counsel, we do not stop to determine whether prejudice resulted. . . . In this case, as in those, the degree of prejudice can never be known. Only the presence of counsel could have enabled this accused to know all the defenses available to him and to plead intelligently.

(Judgment reversed.)

Mempa v Rhay
389 U.S. 128, 88 S.Ct. 254, 19 L.Ed. 2d 336 (1967)

Mempa was on probation. The Spokane County, Washington, prosecuting attorney sought to have Mempa's probation revoked because of alleged involvement in a burglary. A probation revocation hearing was held with the defendant and with his stepfather in attendance. Mempa was not represented by an attorney and he was not asked if he wished to have one appointed. There was no inquiry concerning the whereabouts of the attorney who previously represented him. After a short inquiry the judge revoked the probation and sentenced him to ten years in prison. The revocation was upheld by the Washington courts. On appeal the United States Supreme Court reversed.

Justice Marshall delivered the opinion of the Court:

In 1948 this Court held in *Townsend* v *Burke,* 334 U.S. 736, . . . , that the absence of counsel during sentencing after a plea of guilty coupled with "assumptions concerning his criminal record which were materially untrue" deprived the defendant in that case of due process. Mr. Justice Jackson there stated in conclusion, "In this case, counsel might not have changed the sentence, but he could have taken steps to see that the conviction and sentence were not predicated on misinformation or misreading of court records, a requirement of fair play which absence of counsel withheld from this prisoner," . . . . Then in *Moore* v *State of Michigan,* 355 U.S. 155, . . . , where a denial of due process was found when the defendant did not intelligently and understandingly waive counsel before entering a plea of guilty, this Court emphasized the prejudice stemming from the absence of counsel at the hearing on the degree of the crime following entry of the guilty plea and stated, "The right to counsel is not a right confined to representation during the trial on the merits."

. . .

. . . In *Gideon* v *Wainwright,* 372 U.S. 335, . . . , this Court held that the Sixth Amendment as applied through the Due Process Clause of the Fourteenth Amendment was applicable to the states and, accordingly, that there was an absolute right to appointment of counsel in felony cases.

There was no occasion in *Gideon* to enumerate the various stages in a criminal proceeding at which counsel was required, but *Townsend, Moore,* and *Hamilton,* when the *Betts* requirement of special circumstances is stripped away by *Gideon,* clearly stand for the proposition that appointment of counsel for an indigent is required at every stage of a criminal proceeding where substantial rights of a criminal accused may be affected. In particular,

Townsend v *Burke,* . . . , illustrates the critical nature of sentencing in a criminal case and might well be considered to support by itself a holding that the right to counsel applies at sentencing. Many lower courts have concluded that the Sixth Amendment right to counsel extends to sentencing in federal cases.

The state, however, argues that the petitioners were sentenced at the time they were originally placed on probation and that the imposition of sentence following probation revocation is, in effect, a mere formality constituting part of the probation revocation proceeding. It is true that sentencing in Washington offers fewer opportunities for the exercise of judicial discretion than in many other jurisdictions. The applicable statute requires the trial judge in all cases to sentence the convicted person to the maximum term provided by law for the offense of which he was convicted. . . . The actual determination of the length of time to be served is to be made by the Board of Prison Terms and Paroles within six months after the convicted person is admitted to prison.

· · ·

On the other hand, the sentencing judge is required by statute, together with the prosecutor, to furnish the Board with a recommendation as to the length of time that the person would serve, in addition to supplying it with various information about the circumstances of the crime and the character of the individual. . . . We were informed during oral argument that the Board places considerable weight on these recommendations, although it is in no way bound by them. Obviously, to the extent such recommendations are influential in determining the resulting sentence, the necessity for the aid of counsel in marshaling the facts, introducing evidence of mitigating circumstances and in general aiding and assisting the defendant to present his case as to sentence is apparent.

Even more important in a case such as this is the fact that certain legal rights may be lost if not exercised at this stage. . . . Therefore in a case where an accused agreed to plead guilty, although he had a valid defense, because he was offered probation, absence of counsel at the imposition of the deferred sentence might well result in loss of the right to appeal. While ordinarily appeals from a plea of guilty are less frequent than those following a trial on the merits, the incidence of improperly obtained guilty pleas is not so slight as to be capable of being characterized as *de minimis*.

· · ·

In sum, we do not question the authority of the State of Washington to provide for a deferred sentencing procedure coupled with its probation provisions. Indeed, it appears to be an enlightened step forward. All we decide here is that a lawyer must be afforded at this proceeding whether it be labeled a revocation of probation or a deferred sentencing. We assume that counsel appointed for the purpose of the trial or guilty plea would not be unduly burdened by being requested to follow through at the deferred sentencing stage of the proceeding.

(Judgment reversed.)

Argersinger v *Hamlin*
407 U.S. 25, 92 S.Ct. 2006, 32 L.Ed. 2d 530 (1972)

A Florida rule required that counsel be appointed for nonpetty offenses punishable by more than six month's imprisonment and that in the absence of a knowing waiver no person could be imprisoned for any offense unless he was represented by counsel. The defendant, Argersinger, was charged with and convicted of carrying a concealed weapon, a Florida misdemeanor carrying a potential punishment of a $1000 fine and six month's imprisonment, or both. He was sentenced to 90 day's imprisonment. Argersinger's appeal was on the ground that he was indigent and was not provided an attorney at his trial. The conviction was affirmed by the Florida courts. On appeal to the United States Supreme Court his conviction was reversed.

Justice Douglas delivered the opinion of the Court:

While there is historical support for limiting the "deep commitment" to trial by jury to "serious criminal cases," there is no such support for a similar limitation on the right to assistance of counsel.

. . .

The Sixth Amendment . . . extended the right to counsel beyond its common-law dimensions. But there is nothing in the language of the Amendment, its history, or in the decisions of this Court, to indicate that it was intended to embody a retraction of the right in petty offenses wherein the common law previously did require that counsel be provided.

. . .

The requirement of counsel may well be necessary for a fair trial even in a petty-offense prosecution. We are by no means convinced that legal and constitutional questions involved in a case that actually leads to imprisonment even for a brief period are any less complex than when a person can be sent off for six months or more.

. . .

The trial of vagrancy cases is illustrative. While only brief sentences of imprisonment may be imposed, the cases often bristle with thorny constitutional questions.

. . .

Beyond the problem of trials and appeals is that of the guilty plea, a problem which looms large in misdemeanor as well as in felony cases. Counsel is needed so that the accused may know precisely what he is doing, so that he is fully aware of the prospect of going to jail or prison, and so that he is treated fairly by the prosecution.

In addition the volume of misdemeanor cases, far greater in number than felony prosecutions, may create an obsession for speedy dispositions, regardless of the fairness of the result.

. . .

We must conclude, therefore, that the problems associated with misdemeanor and petty offenses often require the presence of counsel to ensure the accused a fair trial. Mr. Justice Powell suggests that these problems are raised even in situations where there is no prospect of imprisonment. . . . We need not consider the requirements of the Sixth Amendment as regards the right to counsel where loss of liberty is not involved, however, for here petitioner was in fact sentenced to jail. And, as we said in *Baldwin* v *New York,* 399 U.S., 66 . . . , "the prospect of imprisonment for however short a time will seldom be viewed by the accused as a trivial or 'petty' matter and may well result in quite serious repercussions affecting his career and his reputation."

. . .

Under the rule we announce today, every judge will know when the trial of a misdemeanor starts that no imprisonment may be imposed, even though local law permits it, unless the accused is represented by counsel. He will have a measure of the seriousness and gravity of the offense and therefore know when to name a lawyer to represent the accused before the trial starts.

The run of misdemeanors will not be affected by today's ruling. But in those that end up in the actual deprivation of a person's liberty, the accused will receive the benefit of "the guiding hand of counsel" so necessary when one's liberty is in jeopardy.

(Judgment reversed.)
The Chief Justice wrote a concurring opinion.
Justice Brennan, joined by Justices Douglas and Stewart, filed a concurring opinion.
Justice Powell, joined by Justice Rehnquist, filed a concurring opinion.

In *Faretta* v *California,* 422 U.S. 806, 95 S.Ct. 2525, 45 L.Ed. 2d, 562 (1975), the defendant was charged with grand theft. Well before the trial, Faretta requested that he be allowed to represent himself. The state court judge ruled that the accused had no constitutional right to conduct his own defense and appointed a public defender. The United States Supreme Court vacated this judgment and remanded the case. The Court held that a defendant in a state criminal trial has a constitutional right to proceed without the assistance of counsel if his decision to do so is made voluntarily and intelligently and that under the circumstances Farretta was deprived of his constitutional right to act as his own defense counsel.

In *Herring* v *New York,* 422 U.S. 853, 95 S.Ct. 2550, 45 L.Ed. 2d 593 (1975), the defense counsel, in the defendant's nonjury criminal trial, was denied the opportunity to make a summation of evidence before the judgment was delivered. This was done in accordance with a New York statute which conferred upon the court in such a trial discretion in regard to the delivery of summations by the parties. The United States Supreme Court held that the Sixth Amendment's guarantee of assistance of counsel, made applicable to the states by the

Fourteenth Amendment, was violated by this New York statute insofar as it allowed the trial judge alone the complete power to deny counsel the opportunity to make a closing summation. The Court, therefore, vacated this judgment and remanded the case.

LINEUPS

United States v Wade

388 U.S. 218, 87 S.Ct. 1926, 18 L.Ed. 2d 1149 (1967)

Wade was first indicted for conspiracy to rob a bank. A subsequent indictment charged him with robbery of the bank. He was arrested and counsel was appointed. Two weeks after the appointment, a lineup was held in which Wade was one of the participants. Wade's attorney was not present, and he had not been notified. At the lineup Wade was identified as the bank robber. At the trial Wade sought to strike the in-court identification of Wade because the out-of-court lineup was without his counsel's being present. Therefore, Wade claimed that his Fifth Amendment privilege against self-incrimination and the Sixth Amendment's provision for assistance of counsel were violated. His conviction was affirmed by the Texas appellate courts. The United States Supreme Court on appeal reversed.

Justice Brennan delivered the opinion of the Court:

We have no doubt that compelling the accused merely to exhibit his person for observation by a prosecuting witness prior to trial involves no compulsion of the accused to give evidence having testimonial significance. It is compulsion of the accused to exhibit his physical characteristics, not compulsion to disclose any knowledge he might have. It is no different from compelling Schmerber to provide a blood sample or Holt to wear the blouse, and, as in those instances, is not within the cover of the privilege. Similarly, compelling Wade to speak within hearing distance of the witnesses, even to utter words purportedly uttered by the robber, was not compulsion to utter statements of a "testimonial" nature; he was required to use his voice as an identifying physical characteristic, not to speak his guilt.

· · ·

The government characterizes the lineup as a mere preparatory step in the gathering of the prosecution's evidence, not different—for Sixth Amendment purposes—from various other preparatory steps, such as systematized or scientific analyzing of the accused's fingerprints, blood sample, clothing, hair, and the like. We think there are differences which preclude such stages being characterized as critical stages at which the accused has the right to the presence of his counsel. Knowledge of the techniques of science and technology is sufficiently available, and the variables in techniques few enough, that the accused has the opportunity for a meaningful confrontation of the government's case at trial though the ordinary processes of cross-examination of the government's expert witnesses and the presentation of the evidence of his own experts. The denial of a right to have his counsel present at such analyses does not therefore violate the Sixth Amendment; they are not critical stages since there is minimal risk that his counsel's absence at such stages might derogate from his right to a fair trial.

But the confrontation compelled by the state between the accused and the victim or witnesses to a crime to elicit identification evidence is peculiarly riddled with innumerable dangers and variable factors which might seriously, even crucially, derogate from a fair trial. The vagaries of eyewitness identification are well-known; the annals of criminal law are rife with instances of mistaken identification.

. . .

Moreover, "[i]t is a matter of common experience that, once a witness has picked out the accused at the lineup, he is not likely to go back on his word later on, so that in practice the issue of identity may (in the absence of other relevant evidence) for all practical purposes be determined there and then, before the trial."

. . .

Since it appears that there is grave potential for prejudice, intentional or not, in the pretrial lineup, which may not be capable of reconstruction at trial, and since presence of counsel itself can often avert prejudice and assure a meaningful confrontation at trial, there can be little doubt that for Wade the postindictment lineup was a critical stage of the prosecution at which he was "as much entitled to such aid [of counsel] . . . as at the trial itself." . . . Thus both Wade and his counsel should have been notified of the impending lineup, and counsel's presence should have been a requisite to conduct of the lineup, absent an "intelligent waiver." . . . No substantial countervailing policy considerations have been advanced against the requirement of the presence of counsel. Concern is expressed that the requirement will forestall prompt identifications and result in obstruction of the confrontations. As for the first, we note that in the two cases in which the right to counsel is today held to apply, counsel had already been appointed and no argument is made in either case that notice to counsel would have prejudicially delayed the confrontations.

. . .

(Judgment reversed and remanded.)
The Chief Justice and Justice Douglas concurred in part and dissented in part. Justice Black agreed with the Chief Justice and Justice Douglas but would have disposed of the case differently.

Kirby v Illinois
406 U.S. 682, 92 S.Ct. 1877, 32 L.Ed. 2d 411 (1972)

A robbery was reported to the Chicago Police Department. The report included the property taken. The next day Kirby was stopped by two police officers for investigation. Some papers bearing the victim's name were found on Kirby.

Kirby was arrested and taken to police headquarters where the victim, Shard, was brought by the police and positively identified Kirby as the robber. No lawyer was present and Kirby did not ask for one. Some six weeks later Kirby was indicted for the crime. At the trial he moved to suppress the out-of-court identification by Shard. After denial of the motion, Kirby was convicted. The Illinois appellate courts upheld the conviction. The United States Supreme Court granted certiorari and also affirmed.

Justice Stewart announced the judgment of the Court and was joined by the Chief Justice and Justices Blackmun and Rehnquist.

In a line of constitutional cases in this Court stemming back to the Court's landmark opinion in *Powell* v *Alabama,* 287 U.S. 45, . . . , it has been firmly established that a person's Sixth and Fourteenth Amendment right to counsel attaches only at or after the time that adversary judicial proceedings have been initiated against him.

· · ·

This is not to say that a defendant in a criminal case has a constitutional right to counsel only at the trial itself. The *Powell* Case makes clear that the right attaches at the time of arraignment, and the Court has recently held that it exists also at the time of a preliminary hearing. *Coleman* v *Alabama, supra.* But the point is that, while members of the Court have differed as to existence of the right to counsel in the contexts of some of the above cases, *all* of those cases have involved points of time at or after the initiation of adversary judicial criminal proceedings—whether by way of formal charge, preliminary hearing, indictment, information, or arraignment.

The only seeming deviation from this long line of constitutional decisions was *Escobedo* v *Illinois,* 378 U.S. 478, ... But *Escobedo* is not apposite here for two distinct reasons. First, the Court in retrospect perceived that the "prime purpose" of Escobedo was not to vindicate the constitutional right to counsel as such, but, like *Miranda,* "to guarantee full effectuation of the privilege against self-incrimination. . . ." Secondly, and perhaps even more important for purely practical purposes, the Court has limited the holding of *Escobedo* to its own facts, . . . and those facts are not remotely akin to the facts of the case before us.

The initiation of judicial criminal proceedings is far from a mere formalism. It is the starting point of our whole system of adversary criminal justice. For it is only then that the government has committed itself to prosecute, and only then that the adverse positions of government and defendant have solidified. It is then that a defendant finds himself faced with the prosecutorial forces of organized society, and immersed in the intricacies of substantive and procedural criminal law. It is this point, therefore, that marks the commencement of the "criminal prosecutions" to which alone the explicit guarantees of the Sixth Amendment are applicable.

In this case we are asked to import into a routine police investigation an absolute constitutional guarantee historically and rationally applicable only after the onset of formal prosecutorial proceedings. We decline to do so. Less than a year after *Wade* and *Gilbert* were decided, the Court explained the rule of those decisions as follows: "The rationale of those cases was that an accused is entitled to counsel at any 'critical stage of the *prosecution,*' and that a postindictment lineup is such a 'critical stage.'" [Emphasis supplied.] We decline to depart from that rationale today by imposing a *per se* exclusionary rule upon testimony concerning an identification that took place long before the commencement of any prosecution whatever.

What has been said is not to suggest that there may not be occasions during the course of a criminal investigation when the police do abuse identification procedures. Such abuses are not beyond the reach of the Constitution. As the Court pointed out in *Wade* itself, it is always necessary to "scrutinize *any* pretrial confrontation. . . ." The Due Process Clause of the Fifth and Fourteenth Amendments forbids a lineup that is unnecessarily suggestive and conducive to irreparable mistaken identification. . . . When a person has not been formally charged with a criminal offense, *Stovall* strikes the appropriate constitutional balance between the right of a suspect to be protected from prejudicial procedures and the interest of society in the prompt and purposeful investigation of an unsolved crime.

(Judgment affirmed.)
The Chief Justice filed a concurring opinion.
Justice Powell concurred in the result.
Justices Brennan, Douglas, Marshall, and White dissented.

Is the suggestiveness of a pretrial lineup automatically the basis for reversal of a conviction? Justice Powell, in *Neil* v *Biggers,* 409 U.S. 188, 93 S.Ct. 375, 34 L.Ed. 2d 401 (1972), noted that even though there has been no violation of due process of under "the totality of circumstances" the lineup procedure used by the police was somewhat suggestive. The points to be looked at are whether the witness had the opportunity to view the suspect at the time of the crime, the degree of the witness's attention accuracy of the prior description, the degree of the certainty of identifications, and the length of time between the crime and the identification.

In *Foster* v *California,* 394 U.S. 440, 89 S.Ct. 1127, 22 L.Ed. 2d 402 (1969), there was the question of whether or not the conduct of a police lineup resulted in a violation of Foster's constitutional rights. After arrest Foster was placed in a lineup before the only witness to the crime. Foster was tall—about six feet. The other two men in the lineup were about five feet five or five feet six inches. The witness could not positively identify Foster. The witness asked to speak with Foster. Foster was brought into a room with no one present except the witness and prosecuting officials. The witness still could not make a positive identification. Ten days later another lineup was held which consisted of five men. Foster was the only man from the first lineup and the witness now made a positive identification. On appeal the Supreme Court ruled that the lineup procedures used were so unfair that they violated due process.

Simmons v *United States*, 390 U.S. 377, 88 S.Ct. 967, 19 L.Ed. 2d 1247 (1968), held that photographs may be used for pretrial identification without violating Sixth Amendment rights.

CONFRONTATION

Pointer v *Texas*

380 U.S. 400, 85 S.Ct. 1065, 13 L.Ed. 2d 923 (1965)

At a preliminary hearing Pointer was accused on a charge of robbery. Pointer was not represented by counsel. He also did not cross-examine the victim who offered testimony against him. The victim then moved from the state. At Pointer's trial the prosecutor established the victim's absence and that he did not intend to return. The prosecutor then offered the transcript of the victim's testimony at the preliminary examination as evidence against Pointer who objected because of the lack of opportunity to confront his accuser. His conviction was upheld by the Texas courts, which rejected the argument that the use of the transcript to convict him denied him his rights under the Sixth and Fourteenth Amendments. The United States Supreme Court granted certiorari.

Justice Black delivered the opinion of the Court:

We hold today that the Sixth Amendment's right of an accused to confront the witnesses against him is likewise a fundamental right and is made obligatory on the states by the Fourteenth Amendment.

It cannot seriously be doubted at this late date that the right of cross-examination is included in the right of an accused in a criminal case to confront the witnesses against him. And probably no one, certainly no one experienced in the trial of lawsuits, would deny the value of cross-examination in exposing falsehood and bringing out the truth in the trial of a criminal case. See, e.g., 5 Wigmore, Evidence 1367 (3d ed. 1940). The fact that this right appears in the Sixth Amendment of our Bill of Rights reflects the belief of the framers of those liberties and safeguards that confrontation was a fundamental right essential to a fair trial in a criminal prosecution. Moreover, the decisions of this Court and other courts throughout the years have constantly emphasized the necessity for cross-examination as a protection for defendants in criminal cases.

. . .

Under this Court's prior decisions, the Sixth Amendment's guarantee of confrontation and cross-examination was unquestionably denied petitioner in this case. As has been pointed out, a major reason underlying the constitutional confrontation rule is to give a defendant charged with crime an opportunity to cross-examine the witnesses against him. . . . This Court has recognized the admissibility against an accused of dying declarations, . . . and of testimony of a deceased witness who has testified at a former trial. . . . Nothing we hold here is to the contrary. The case before us would be quite a different one had Phillips' statement been taken at a full-fledged hearing at which petitioner had been represented by counsel who had been given a complete and adequate opportunity to cross-examine. . . . There are other analogous situations which might not fall within the scope of the constitutional rule requiring confrontation of witnesses. The case before us, however, does not present any situation like those mentioned above or others analogous to them. Because the transcript of Phillips' statement offered against petitioner at his trial had not been taken at a time and under circumstances affording petitioner through counsel an adequate opportunity to cross-examine Phillips, its introduction in a federal court in a criminal case against Pointer would have amounted to denial of the privilege of confrontation guaranteed by the Sixth Amendment. Since we hold that the right of an accused to be confronted with the witnesses against him must be determined by the same standards whether the right is denied in a federal or state proceeding, it follows that use of the transcript to convict petitioner denied him a constitutional right.

. . .

(Judgment reversed.)
Concurring opinions were written by Justices Harlan, Stewart, and Goldberg.

In *Barber* v *Page*, 390 U.S. 719, 88 S.Ct. 1318, 20 L.Ed. 2d 255 (1968), the question was whether the defendant was denied his right of confrontation by the use of a transcript from a preliminary hearing even though the defendant was represented by counsel and could have examined the witness had he so chosen. The witness at the time of the trial was incarcerated in a federal prison in Texas.

Justice Marshall, noting that the State of Oklahoma had made absolutely no effort to secure the witness, reversed the state conviction and stated:

In this case the state authorities made no effort to avail themselves of either of the above alternative means of seeking to secure Woods' presence at petitioner's trial. The Court of Appeals majority appears to have reasoned that because the state would have had to request an exercise of discretion on the part of federal authorities, it was under no obligation to make any such request. Yet as Judge Aldrich, sitting at designation, pointed out in dissent below, "The possibility of a refusal is not the equivalent of asking and receiving a rebuff." . . . In short, a witness is not "unavailable" for purposes of the foregoing exception to the confrontation requirement unless the prosecutorial authorities have made a good-faith effort to obtain his presence at trial. The state made no such effort here, and, so far as this record reveals, the sole reason why Woods was not present to testify in person was because the state did not attempt to seek his presence. The right of confrontation may not be dispensed with so lightly.

Harrington v California
395 U.S. 250, 89 S.Ct. 1726, 23 L.Ed. 2d 284 (1969)

Harrington and three others were convicted of felony-murder. One of the codefendant's confessions was admitted into evidence against Harrington. This same codefendant took the stand and testified placing Harrington at the crime scene. Harrington also testified to the fact and cross-examined the testifying codefendant. Several eyewitnesses also placed Harrington at the scene of the crime. The court then allowed the confessions of the other two codefendants to be admitted into evidence placing Harrington at the crime scene. Harrington claimed that the admission of the confessions of the nontestifying defendants violated his constitutional right of confrontation. The California conviction was upheld in the state courts. The United States Supreme Court on appeal affirmed. Justice Douglas delivered the opinion of the Court:

In *Bruton* v *United States,* 391 U.S. 123 . . . , a confession of a codefendant who did not take the stand was used against Bruton in a federal prosecution. We held that Bruton had been denied his rights under the Confrontation Clause of the Sixth Amendment. Since the Confrontation Clause is applicable as well in state trials by reason of the Due Process Clause of the Fourteenth Amendment . . . the rule of *Bruton* applies here.

. . .

. . . But apart from them the case against Harrington was so overwhelming that we conclude that this violation of *Bruton* was harmless beyond a reasonable doubt, unless we adopt the minority view in *Chapman* that a departure from constitutional procedures should result in an automatic reversal, regardless of the weight of the evidence.

It is argued that we must reverse if we can imagine a single juror whose mind might have been made up because of Cooper's and Bosby's confessions and who otherwise would have remained in doubt and unconvinced. We of course do not know the jurors who sat. Our judgment must be based on our own reading of the record and on what seems to us to have been the probable impact of the two confessions on the minds of an average jury. We admonished in *Chapman* . . . against giving too much emphasis to "overwhelming evidence" of guilt, stating that constitutional errors affecting the substantial rights of the aggrieved party could not be considered to be harmless. By that test we cannot impute reversible weight to the two confessions.

We do not depart from *Chapman;* nor do we dilute it by inference. We reaffirm it. We do not suggest that, if evidence bearing on all the ingredients of the crime is tendered, the use of cumulative evidence, though tainted, is harmless error. Our decision is based on the evidence in this record. The case against Harrington was not woven from circumstantial evidence. It is so over-whelming that unless we say that no violation of *Bruton* can constitute harm-less error.

. . .

(Judgment affirmed.)
Chief Justice Warren and Justices Brennan and Marshall dissented.

SPEEDY TRIAL

Klopfer v *North Carolina*

386 U.S. 213, 87 S.Ct. 988, 18 L.Ed. 2d 1 (1967)

Klopfer was indicted on February 24, 1964, for criminal trespass, a mis-demeanor, which occurred on January 3, 1964. He was brought to trial during March, 1964, but a mistrial was declared because the jury could not reach a verdict. The judge ordered the case continued. At the April 1965 court session, the prosecutor filed a motion to have a *nolle prosequi* "with leave" entered. Klopfer interposed an objection. The state's motion had the effect of indefinitely postponing the prosecution of the case. The judge denied Klopfer's objection. Subsequently the prosecutor decided not to file the *nolle prosequi* and filed a motion to continue the case. Klopfer's case was not listed on the August 1965 court calendar. Klopfer then filed a motion to have the case concluded by letting him know when he would be tried. On August 9, 1965, the judge held an open hearing and the prosecutor filed a *nolle prosequi*. No reason was given for the prosecutor's action and in spite of Klopfer's objection, the order was granted. On appeal to the United States Supreme Court Klopfer claimed that the entry of the *nolle prosequi* deprived him of his right to a speedy trial required by the Four-teenth Amendment. The United States Supreme Court reversed.

Chief Justice Warren delivered the opinion of the Court:

The question involved in this case is whether a state may indefinitely postpone prosecution on an indictment without stated justification over the objection of an accused who has been discharged from custody. It is presented in the context of an application of an unusual North Carolina criminal procedural device known as the "*nolle prosequi* with leave."

. . .

In response to the motion, the trial judge considered the status of petitioner's case in open court on Monday, August 9, 1965, at which time the solicitor moved the court that the state be permitted to take a *nolle prosequi* with leave. Even though no justification for the proposed entry was offered by the state, and, in spite of petitioner's objection to the order, the court granted the state's motion.

On appeal to the Supreme Court of North Carolina, petitioner contended that the entry of the *nolle prosequi* with leave order deprived him of his right to a speedy trial as required by the Fourteenth Amendment to the United States Constitution. Although the Supreme Court acknowledged that entry of the *nolle prosequi* with leave did not permanently discharge the indictment, it nevertheless affirmed.

. . .

The North Carolina Supreme Court's conclusion—that the right to a speedy trial does not afford affirmative protection against an unjustified postponement of trial for an accused discharged from custody—has been explicitly rejected by every other state court which has considered the question. That conclusion has also been implicitly rejected by the numerous courts which have held that a *nolle prossed* indictment may not be reinstated at a subsequent term.

We, too, believe that the position taken by the court below was erroneous. The petitioner is not relieved of the limitations placed upon his liberty by this prosecution merely because its suspension permits him to go "whithersoever he will." The pendency of the indictment may subject him to public scorn and deprive him of employment, and almost certainly will force curtailment of his speech, associations and participation in unpopular causes. By indefinitely prolonging this oppression, as well as the the "anxiety and concern accompanying public accusation," the criminal procedure condoned in this case by the Supreme Court of North Carolina clearly denies the petitioner the right to a speedy trial which we hold is guaranteed to him by the Sixth Amendment of the Constitution of the United States.

. . .

We hold here that the right to a speedy trial is as fundamental as any of the rights secured by the Sixth Amendment. That right has its roots at the very foundation of our English law heritage.

. . .

Coke's Institutes were read in the American colonies by virtually every student of the law. Indeed, Thomas Jefferson wrote that at the time he studied law (1762–1767), "Coke Lyttleton was the universal elementary book of law students." And to John Rutledge of South Carolina, the Institutes seemed "to be almost the foundation of our law." To Coke, in turn, Magna Charta was one of the fundamental bases of English liberty. Thus, it is not surprising that when George Mason drafted the first of the colonial bills of rights, he set forth a principle of Magna Charta, using phraseology similar to that of Coke's explication: "[I]n all capital or criminal prosecutions," the Virginia Declaration of Rights of 1776 provided, "a man hath a right . . . to a speedy trial. . . ." That this right was considered fundamental at this early period in our history is evidenced by its guarantee in the constitutions of several of the states of the new nation as well as by its prominent position in the Sixth Amendment. Today, each of the 50 states guarantees the right to a speedy trial to its citizens.

The history of the right to a speedy trial and its reception in this country clearly establish that it is one of the most basic rights preserved by our Constitution.

(Judgment reversed.)
Justices Stewart concurred.
Justice Harlan concurred in the result.

In *Smith* v *Hooey,* 393 U.S. 374, 89 S.Ct. 575, 21 L.Ed. 2d 607 (1969), a federal prisoner sought a writ of mandamus to compel being tried for a charge in a Texas court. The Texas authorities expressed the opinion that they have no power to compel the presence of the defendant in Texas for trial. The United States Supreme Court held that the right to a speedy trial cannot be so lightly regarded and held that the state must make a good faith effort and a diligent effort to bring the defendant to trial.

Barker v *Wingo*
407 U.S. 514, 92 S.Ct. 2182, 33 L.Ed. 2d 101 (1972)

Barker and Manning were arrested on July 20, 1958, for killing two people. The state needed the testimony of Manning in order to convict Barker and tried them separately. Manning was finally convicted in December 1962 after numerous continuances. Barker's trial was set for March 19, 1963, the first court session after Manning's conviction. On the day of the scheduled trial, continuance was granted to the state until June because a witness was ill. The witness was still ill on the June date and a continuance was granted until the September term over the defendant's objection. The trial finally began on October 19, 1963. Barker was convicted and sentenced to life imprisonment. On appeal to the United States Supreme Court Barker claimed that he was denied the right to a speedy trial. The conviction was affirmed.

Justice Powell delivered the opinion of the Court:

The nature of the speedy trial right does make it impossible to pinpoint a precise time in the process when the right must be asserted or waived, but that fact does not argue for placing the burden of protecting the right solely on defendants. A defendant has no duty to bring himself to trial; the state has that duty as well as the duty of ensuring that the trial is consistent with due process. Moreover, for the reasons earlier expressed, society has a particular interest in bringing swift prosecutions, and society's representatives are the ones who should protect that interest.

. . .

We reject, therefore, the rule that a defendant who fails to demand a speedy trial forever waives his right.

. . .

In ruling that a defendant has some responsibility to assert a speedy trial claim, we do not depart from our holdings in other cases concerning the waiver of fundamental rights, in which we have placed the entire responsibility on the prosecution to show that the claimed waiver was knowingly and voluntarily made.

. . .

We, therefore, reject both of the inflexible approaches—the fixed time period because it goes further than the Constitution requires; the demand-waiver rule because it is insensitive to a right which we have deemed fundamental. The approach we accept is a balancing test, in which the conduct of both the prosecution and the defendant are weighed.

A balancing test necessarily compels courts to approach speedy trials cases on an *ad hoc* basis. We can do little more than identify some of the factors which courts should assess in determining whether a particular defendant has been deprived of his right. Though some might express them in different ways, we identify four such factors: Length of delay, the reason for the delay, the defendant's assertion of his right, and prejudice to the defendant.

The length of the delay is to some extent a triggering mechanism. Until there is some delay which is presumptively prejudicial, there is no necessity for inquiry into the other factors that go into the balance. . . . To take but one example, the delay that can be tolerated for an ordinary street crime is considerably less than for a serious, complex conspiracy charge.

Closely related to length of delay is the reason the government assigns to justify the delay. Here, too, different weights should be assigned to different reasons. A deliberate attempt to delay the trial in order to hamper the defense should be weighted heavily against the government. A more neutral reason such as negligence or overcrowded courts should be weighted less heavily but nevertheless should be considered since the ultimate responsibility for such circumstances must rest with the government rather than with the defendant. Finally, a valid reason, such as a missing witness, should serve to justify appropriate delay.

We have already discussed the third factor, the defendant's responsibility to assert his right. . . . We emphasize that failure to assert the right will make it difficult for a defendant to prove that he was denied a speedy trial.

A fourth factor is prejudice to the defendant. Prejudice, of course, should be assessed in the light of the interests of defendants which the speedy trial right was designed to protect. This Court has identified three such interests: (i) to prevent oppressive pretrial incarceration; (ii) to minimize anxiety and concern of the accused; and (iii) to limit the possibility that the defense will be impaired. Of these, the most serious is the last, because the inability of a defendant adequately to prepare his case skews the fairness of the entire system. If witnesses die or disappear during a delay, the prejudice is obvious. There is also prejudice if defense witnesses are unable to recall accurately events of the distant past. Loss of memory, however, is not always reflected in the record because what has been forgotten can rarely be shown.

We have discussed previously the societal disadvantages of lengthy pretrial incarceration, but obviously the disadvantages for the accused who cannot obtain his release are even more serious. The time spent in jail awaiting trial has a detrimental impact on the individual. It often means loss of a job; it disrupts family life; and it enforces idleness. Most jails offer little or no recreational or rehabilitative programs. The time spent in jail is simple dead time. Moreover, if a defendant is locked up, he is hindered in his ability to gather evidence, contact witnesses, or otherwise prepare his defense. Imposing those consequences on anyone who has not yet been convicted is serious. It is especially unfortunate to impose them on those persons who are ultimately found to be innocent. Finally, even if an accused is not incarcerated prior to trial, he is still disadvantaged by restraints on his liberty and by living under a cloud of anxiety, suspicion, and often hostility.

. . .

We regard none of the four factors identified above as either a necessary or sufficient condition to the finding of a deprivation of the right of speedy trial. Rather, they are related factors and must be considered together with such other circumstances as may be relevant. In sum, these factors have no talismanic qualities; courts must still engage in a difficult and sensitive balancing process. But, because we are dealing with a fundamental right of the accused, this process must be carried out with full recognition that the accused's interest in a speedy trial is specifically affirmed in the Constitution.

(Judgment affirmed.)
Justices White and Brennan concurred.

In *United States* v *Marion,* 404 U.S. 307, 92 S.Ct. 455, 80 L.Ed. 2d 468 (1971), the United States Supreme Court held that unless prejudice is shown, a defendant is not denied the constitutional right to a speedy trial in a situation in which the indictment for the offense is found three years after the occurrence of the alleged criminal acts.

JURY TRIAL

Duncan v *Louisiana*

391 U.S. 145, 88 S.Ct. 1444, 20 L.Ed. 2d 491 (1968)

Duncan was convicted of a simple battery, a misdemeanor punishable by up to 2 years in prison and a $300 fine. Duncan sought a jury trial but was denied one because Louisiana permitted one only when imprisonment at hard labor or death might be imposed. Duncan was fined $150 and received a 60-day sentence. The state courts denied his appeal rejecting the argument that he was denied his constitutional right to have a jury trial. On review the United States Supreme Court reversed.

Justice White delivered the opinion of the Court:

. . . Because we believe that trial by jury in criminal cases is fundamental to the American scheme of justice, we hold that the Fourteenth Amendment guarantees a right of jury trial in all criminal cases which—were they to be tried in a federal court—would come within the Sixth Amendment's guarantee. Since we consider the appeal before us to be such a case, we hold that the Constitution was violated when appellant's demand for jury trial was refused.

The history of trial by jury in criminal cases has been frequently told. It is sufficient for present purposes to say that by the time our Constitution was written, jury trial in criminal cases had been in existence in England for several centuries and carried impressive credentials traced by many to Magna Charta. Its preservation and proper operation as a protection against arbitrary rule were among the major objectives of the revolutionary settlement which was expressed in the Declaration and Bill of Rights of 1789.

· · ·

Jury trial continues to receive strong support. The laws of every state guarantee a right to jury trial in serious criminal cases; no state has dispensed with it; nor are there significant movements underway to do so.

· · ·

We are aware of prior cases in this Court in which the prevailing opinion contains statements contrary to our holding today that the right to jury trial in serious criminal cases is a fundamental right and hence must be recognized by the states as part of their obligation to extend due process of law to all persons within their jurisdiction. . . . None of these cases, however, dealt with a state which had purported to dispense entirely with a jury trial in serious criminal cases.

· · ·

The guarantees of jury trial in the federal and state constitutions reflect a profound judgment about the way in which law should be enforced and justice administered. A right to jury trial is granted to criminal defendants in order to prevent oppression by the government. Those who wrote our constitutions knew from history and experience that it was necessary to protect against unfounded criminal charges brought to eliminate enemies and against judges too responsive to the voice of higher authority. The framers of the constitutions strove to create an independent judiciary but insisted upon further protection against arbitrary action. Providing an accused with the right to be tried by a jury of his peers gave him an inestimable safeguard against the corrupt or overzealous prosecutor and against the compliant, biased, or eccentric judge. If the defendant preferred the common-sense judgment of a jury to the more tutored but perhaps less sympathetic reaction of the single judge, he was to have it. Beyond this, the jury trial provisions in the federal and state constitutions reflect a fundamental decision about the exercise of official power—a reluctance to entrust plenary powers over the life and liberty of the citizen to one judge or to a group of judges. Fear of unchecked power, so typical of our state and federal governments in other respects, found expression in the criminal law in this insistence upon community participation in the determination of guilt or innocence. The deep commitment of the nation to the right of jury trial in serious criminal cases as a defense against arbitrary law enforcement qualifies for protection under the Due Process Clause of the Fourteenth Amendment, and must therefore be respected by the states.

The State of Louisiana urges that holding that the Fourteenth Amendment assures a right to jury trial will cast doubt on the integrity of every trial conducted without a jury. Plainly, this is not the import of our holding. Our conclusion is that in the American states, as in the federal judicial system, a general grant of jury trial for serious offenses is a fundamental right, essential for preventing miscarriages of justice and for assuring that fair trials are provided for all defendants. We would not assert, however, that every criminal trial—or any particular trial—held before a judge alone is unfair or that a defendant may never be as fairly treated by a judge as he would be by a jury. Thus we hold no constitutional doubts about the practices, common in both federal and state courts, of accepting waivers of jury trial and prosecuting petty crimes without extending a right to jury trial. However, the fact is that in most places more trials for serious crimes are to juries than to a court alone; a great many defendants prefer the judgment of a jury to that of a court. Even where defendants are satisfied with bench trials, the right to a jury trial very likely serves its intended purpose of making judicial or prosecutorial unfairness less likely.

Louisiana's final contention is that even if it must grant jury trials in serious criminal cases, the conviction before us is valid and constitutional because here the petitioner was tried for simple battery and was sentenced to only 60 days in the parish prison. We are not persuaded. It is doubtless true that there is a category of petty crimes or offenses which is not subject to the Sixth Amendment jury trial provision and should not be subject to the Fourteenth Amendment jury trial requirement here applied to the states. Crimes carrying possible penalties up to 6 months do not require a jury trial if they otherwise qualify as petty offenses. . . . But the penalty authorized for a particular crime is of major relevance in determining whether it is serious or not and may in itself, if severe enough, subject the trial to the mandates of the Sixth Amendment. . . . The penalty authorized by the law of the locality may be taken "as a gauge of its social and ethical judgments" . . . of the crime in question. In *Clawans* the defendant was jailed for 60 days, but it was the 90-day authorized punishment on which the Court focused in determining that the offense was not one for which the Constitution assured trial by jury. In the case before us the Legislature of Louisiana has made simple battery a criminal offense punishable by imprisonment for up to 2 years and a fine. The question, then, is whether a crime carrying such a penalty is an offense which Louisiana may insist on trying without a jury.

. . .

In determining whether the length of the authorized prison term or the seriousness of other punishment is enough in itself to require a jury trial, we are counseled by *District of Columbia* v *Clawans, supra,* to refer to objective criteria, chiefly the existing laws and practices in the nation. In the federal system, petty offenses are defined as those punishable by no more than 6 months in prison and a $500 fine. In 49 of the 50 states crimes subject to trial without a jury, which occasionally include simple battery, are punishable by no more than 1 year in jail. Moreover, in the late eighteenth century in America crimes triable without a jury were for the most part punishable by no more than a 6-month prison term, although there appear to have been exceptions to this rule. We need not, however, settle in this case the exact location of the line between petty offenses and serious crimes. It is sufficient for our purposes to hold that a crime punishable by 2 years in prison is, based on past and contemporary standards in this country, a serious crime and not a petty offense. Consequently, appellant was entitled to a jury trial and it was error to deny it.

. . .

(Judgment reversed.)
Justices Black, Douglas, and Fortas concurred.
Justices Harlan and Stewart dissented.

In *Johnson* v *Louisiana,* 406 U.S. 356, 92 S.Ct. 1620, 32 L.Ed. 2d 152 (1972), Louisiana law provided that a defendant could be convicted by a vote of 9 of the authorized 12-man jury in specified cases. Johnson was convicted and on appeal argued that he was denied due process and equal protection of the law. The issue was whether or not a state law permitting less than unanimous verdicts in certain types of criminal cases was invalid under the Due Process Clause and the Equal Protection Clause of the Constitution. The United States Supreme Court noted that unanimity was never a requisite of due process and rejected the defendant's argument. Justice White wrote for the majority that three votes to acquit a defendant and nine to convict raises no question of constitutional substance about either the integrity or accuracy of the majority verdict of guilt. "The argument that the prosecution could not be said to have proved the case beyond a reasonable doubt when one or more of a jury's members at the conclusion of the deliberation possesses such a doubt" was not persuasive to the Court. The Court also found nothing invidiously discriminatory about the Louisiana procedure of providing different majorities for conviction of crimes of varying severity.

In *Apodaca* v *Oregon,* 406 U.S. 404, 92 S.Ct. 1628, 32 L.Ed. 2d 184 (1972), the defendants were convicted of various felonies by less than unanimous verdicts (11 to 1 and 10 to 2), the minimum vote permitted by Oregon law. On appeal the defendants claimed that conviction of a crime by less than a unanimous verdict violated the Sixth Amendment. In rejecting the argument, four of the five-man majority believed that the unanimous verdict was not of constitutional significance. Justice Powell, the fifth man for the majority, noted that in order to have a fair trial, state trials need not be identical in every respect with federal trials which require unanimous verdicts. In regard to the resonable doubt argument, the Court noted, "We are quite sure, however, that the Sixth Amendment has never been held to require proof beyond a reasonable doubt in criminal cases."

In *Ham* v *United States,* 409 U.S. 524, 93 S.Ct. 848, 35 L.Ed. 2d 46 (1973), the defendant requested that potential jurors be asked on *voir dire* whether they harbored any kind of racial bias. His request was denied. He was also denied a request to have the jurors questioned about possible bias against a beard worn by the defendant. The United States Supreme Court reversed his conviction, Justice Rehnquist stating that "the Fourteenth Amendment required the judge in this case to interrogate the jurors upon the subject of racial prejudice. Justice Douglas thought it was prejudicial not to permit inquiry into prejudice against beards. He noted, "Nothing is more indicative of the importance currently being attached to hair growth by the general populace than the barrage of cases reaching the courts evidencing the attempt by one segment of society officially to control the plumage of another."

In *Ristaino* v *Ross,* 424 U.S. 589, 96 S.Ct. 1017, 47 L.Ed. 2d 258 (1976), the respondent, a black, was convicted in a state court of violent crimes against a white security guard. The state court trial judge did not rule favorably on the respondent's motion to have a question dealing specifically with racial prejudice asked during *voir dire*. Upon reaching the Supreme Court of the United States, the issue was presented in regard to the *Ham* v *South Carolina* decision. The Court ruled that the respondent was not constitutionally entitled to require the asking of such a question specifically directed at racial prejudice.

Williams v *Florida*
99 U.S. 78, 90 S.Ct. 1893, 26 L.Ed. 2d 446 (1970)

Florida law permitted 6-man juries in all criminal cases except capital cases. The defendant filed a motion for a 12-man jury to try the robbery case against him. The motion was denied, he was convicted, and he was sentenced to life imprisonment. The state courts affirmed the conviction. On appeal to the United States Supreme Court, the defendant argued that he was denied his constitutional right to a jury trial under the Sixth Amendment. He specifically claimed that a 12-man jury is a constitutional requirement. The state conviction was affirmed.

Justice White delivered the opinion of the Court:

We had occasion in *Duncan* v *Louisiana* to review briefly the oft-told history of the development of trial by jury in criminal cases. That history revealed a long tradition attaching great importance to the concept of relying on a body of one's peers to determine guilt or innocence as a safeguard against arbitrary law enforcement. That same history, however, affords little insight into the considerations that gradually led the size of that body to be generally fixed at 12. Some have suggested that the number 12 was fixed upon simply because that was the number of the presentment jury from the hundred from which the petit jury developed. Other, less circular but more fanciful reasons for the number 12 have been given, "but they were all brought forward after the number was fixed," and rest on little more than mystical or superstitious insights in the significance of "12." Lord Coke's explanation that the "*number of 12*" is much respected *in holy writ*, as 12 *apostles*, 12 *stones*, 12 *tribes*, etc.," is typical. In short, while sometime in the fourteenth century the size of the jury at common law came to be fixed generally at 12, that particular feature of the jury system appears to have been an historical accident, unrelated to the great purposes which gave rise to the jury in the first place. The question before us is whether this accidental feature of the jury has been immutably codified into our Constitution.

. . .

We do not pretend to be able to divine precisely what the word "jury" imported to the framers, the First Congress, or the states in 1789. It may well be that the usual expectation was that the jury would consist of 12, and that hence, the most likely conclusion to be drawn is simply that little thought was actually given to the specific question we face today. But there is absolutely no indication in "the intent of the framers" of an explicit decision to equate the constitutional and common-law characteristics of the jury. Nothing in this history suggests, then, that we do violence to the letter of the Constitution by turning to other than purely historical considerations to determine which features of the jury system, as it existed at common law, were preserved in the Constitution. The relevant inquiry, as we see it, must be the function that the particular feature performs and its relation to the purposes of the jury trial. Measured by this standard, the 12-man requirement cannot be regarded as an indispensable component of the Sixth Amendment.

The purpose of the jury trial, as we noted in *Duncan,* is to prevent oppression by the government. "Providing an accused with the right to be tried by a jury of his peers gave him an inestimable safeguard against the corrupt or overzealous prosecutor and against the compliant, biased, or eccentric judge." . . . Given this purpose, the essential feature of a jury obviously lies in the interposition between the accused and his accuser of the common-sense judgment of a group of laymen, and in the community participation and shared responsibility that results from that group's determination of guilt or innocence. The performance of this role is not a function of the particular number of the body that makes up the jury. To be sure, the number should probably be large enough to promote group deliberation, free from outside attempts at intimidation, and to provide a fair possibility for obtaining a representative cross section of the community. But we find little reason to think that these goals are in any meaningful sense less likely to be achieved when the jury numbers 6, than when it numbers 12—particularly if the requirement of unanimity is retained. And, certainly the reliability of the jury as a factfinder hardly seems likely to be a function of its size.

It might be suggested that the 12-man jury gives a defendant a greater advantage since he has more "chances" of finding a juror who will insist on acquittal and thus prevent conviction. But the advantage might just as easily belong to the state, which also needs only 1 juror out of 12 insisting on guilt to prevent acquittal. What few experiments have occurred—usually in the civil area—indicate that there is no discernible difference between the results reached by the two different-sized juries. In short, neither currently available evidence nor theory suggests that the 12-man jury is necessarily more advantageous to the defendant than a jury composed of fewer members.

Similarly, while in theory the number of viewpoints represented on a randomly selected jury ought to increase as the size of the jury increases, in practice the difference between the 12-man and the 6-man jury in terms of the cross section of the community represented seems likely to be negligible. Even the 12-man jury cannot ensure representation of every distinct voice in the community, particularly given the use of the peremptory challenge. As long as arbitrary exclusions of a particular class from the jury rolls are forbidden . . . concern that the cross section will be significantly diminished if the jury is decreased in size from 12 to 6 seems an unrealistic one.

. . .

(Judgment affirmed.)

Chief Justice Burger, Justice Harlan, and Justice Stewart concurred and filed opinion; Justice Black concurred in part and dissented in part and filed opinion in which Justice Douglas concurred; Justice Marshall dissented in part and filed opinion.

Justice Blackmun took no part in consideration of the case.

FAIR AND PUBLIC TRIAL

Illinois v *Allen*

397 U.S. 337, 90 S.Ct. 1057, 25 L.Ed. 2d 353 (1970)

Allen was charged with robbery. He refused appointment of counsel and wished to argue his own defense. During examination of prospective jurors and on several occasions thereafter Allen became abusive and began to argue with the trial judge. He threatened that there would be no trial if he did not get his own way. After numerous outbreaks, the trial judge ordered Allen removed from the courtroom so that the trial could continue. In his absence Allen was convicted and sentenced to 30 years in prison. He ultimately appealed his conviction to the

United States Supreme Court claiming that his constitutional right to remain in the courtroom throughout his trial had been denied. The conviction was upheld. Justice Black delivered the opinion of the Court:

The Court of Appeals felt that the defendant's Sixth Amendment right to be present at his own trial was so "absolute" that, no matter how unruly or disruptive the defendant's conduct might be, he could never be held to have lost that right so long as he continued to insist upon it, as Allen clearly did. Therefore the Court of Appeals concluded that a trial judge could never expel a defendant from his own trial and that the judge's ultimate remedy when faced with an obstreperous defendant like Allen who determines to make his trial impossible is to bind and gag him. We cannot agree that the Sixth Amendment, the cases upon which the Court of Appeals relied, or any other cases of this Court so handicap a trial judge in conducting a criminal trial.

. . .

It is essential to the proper administration of criminal justice that dignity, order, and decorum be the hallmarks of all court proceedings in our country. . . . We think there are at least three constitutionally permissible ways for a trial judge to handle an obstreperous defendant like Allen: (1) bind and gag him, thereby keeping him present; (2) cite him for contempt; (3) take him out of the courtroom until he promises to conduct himself properly.

Trying a defendant for a crime while he sits bound and gagged before the judge and jury would to an extent comply with that part of the Sixth Amendment's purposes that accords the defendant an opportunity to confront the witnesses at the trial. But even to contemplate such a technique, much less see it, arouses a feeling that no person should be tried while shackled and gagged except as a last resort.

In a footnote the Court of Appeals suggested the possible availability of contempt of court as a remedy to make Allen behave in his robbery trial, and it is true that citing or threatening to cite a contumacious defendant for criminal contempt might in itself be sufficient to make a defendant stop interrupting a trial. If so, the problem would be solved easily, and the defendant could remain in the courtroom. Of course, if the defendant is determined to prevent *any* trial, then a court in attempting to try the defendant for contempt is still confronted with the identical dilemma that the Illinois court faced in this case. And criminal contempt has obvious limitations as a sanction when the defendant is charged with a crime so serious that a very severe sentence such as death or life imprisonment is likely to be imposed. In such a case the defendant might not be affected by a mere contempt sentence when he ultimately faces a far more serious sanction. Nevertheless, the contempt remedy should be borne in mind by a judge in the circumstances of this case.

Another aspect of the contempt remedy is the judge's power, when exercised consistently with state and federal law, to imprison an unruly defendant such as Allen for civil contempt and discontinue the trial until such time as the defendant promises to behave himself. This procedure is consistent with the defendant's right to be unavailable after a lapse of time. A court must guard against allowing a defendant to profit from his own wrong in this way.

The trial court in this case decided under the circumstances to remove the defendant from the courtroom and to continue his trial in his absence until and unless he promised to conduct himself in a manner befitting an American courtroom. As we said earlier, we find nothing unconstitutional about this procedure. Allen's behavior was clearly of such an extreme and aggravated nature as to justify either his removal from the courtroom or his total physical restraint. Prior to his removal he was repeatedly warned by the trial judge that he would be removed from the courtroom if he persisted in his unruly conduct, and, as Judge Hastings observed in his dissenting opinion, the record demonstrates that Allen would not have been at all dissuaded by the trial judge's use of his criminal contempt powers. Allen was constantly informed that he could return to the trial when he would agree to conduct himself in an orderly manner. Under these circumstances we hold that Allen lost his right guaranteed by the Sixth and Fourteenth Amendments to be present throughout his trial.

It is not pleasant to hold that the respondent Allen was properly banished from the court for a part of his own trial. But our courts, palladiums of liberty as they are, cannot be treated disrespectfully in impunity. Nor can the accused be permitted by his disruptive conduct indefinitely to avoid being tried on the charges brought against him. It would degrade our country and our judicial system to permit our courts to be bullied, insulted, and humiliated and their orderly progress thwarted and obstructed by defendants brought before them charged with crimes. As guardians of the public welfare, our state and federal judicial systems strive to administer equal justice to the rich and the poor, the good and the bad, the native and foreign born of every race, nationality, and religion. Being manned by humans, the courts are to remain what the founders intended, the citadels of justice, their proceedings cannot and must not be infected with the sort of scurrilous, abusive language and conduct paraded before the Illinois trial judge in this case. The record shows that the Illinois judge at all times conducted himself with that dignity, decorum, and patience that befit a judge. Even in holding that the trial judge had erred, the Court of Appeals praised his "commendable patience under severe provocation."

We do not hold that removing this defendant from his own trial was the only way the Illinois judge could have constitutionally solved the problem he had. We do hold, however, that there is nothing whatever in this record to show that the judge did not act completely within his discretion. Deplorable as it is to remove a man from his own trial, even for a short time, we hold that the judge did not commit legal error in doing what he did.

(Conviction affirmed.)
Justices Brennan and Douglas concurred.

In *Estes* v *Texas*, 381 U.S. 532, 85 S.Ct. 1628, 14 L.Ed. 2d 543 (1965), the issue was whether or not the televised trial of a nationally known swindler deprived him of his constitutional right to a fair trial. There was considerable courtroom disruption with 12 TV cameramen in the courtroom for the pretrial hearings. At the trial the cameramen were assigned to space in the rear of the room. In reversing Estes' conviction, the Court noted that the mere probability of unfairness is adequate for reversal. According to Justice Clark, TV cannot be said to contribute materially to ascertaining the truth. It often interjects irrevelancies into the trial which might cause unfairness. The Court stated, "A defendant on trial . . . is entitled to his day in court, not in a stadium or a city or a nationwide arena." The Court did not totally reject future courtroom TV. It concluded, "But we are not dealing here with future developments in the field of electronics. Our judgment cannot be rested on the hypothesis of tomorrow but must take the facts as they are presented today."

The murder trial of Dr. Sam Sheppard was one of the most widely publicized of this century. It was also the most flagrant example of the news media's influence on a criminal trial. A sensational campaign of unfavorable publicity from newspapers, TV, and radio preceded and carried through the trial. A considerable amount of abuse was directed at Dr. Sheppard. In reversing the conviction of Dr. Sheppard the United States Supreme Court alluded to the "Roman carnival" atmosphere generated by the media. However, Justice Clark for the majority noted that there was nothing that proscribes the press from reporting what occurs in the courtroom but when there is a reasonable chance that a defendant will not receive a fair trial because of prejudicial news reporting, the judge must continue the trial or transfer it to another area where the public will be less likely to be affected. Because Sheppard was not adequately protected from prejudicial publicity, he was denied a fair trial. *Sheppard* v *Maxwell*, 384 U.S. 333, 86 S.Ct. 1507, 16 L.Ed. 2d 600 (1966).

In *Witherspoon* v *Illinois*, 391 U.S. 510, 88 S.Ct. 1770, 20 L.Ed. 2d 776 (1968), the defendant was convicted of murder. The prosecutor was permitted in trials for murder to challenge for cause any juror who shall, upon being examined, state that he or she has conscientious scruples against the death penalty but who is not asked whether he or she could never vote to impose the death penalty or that he or she would refuse to ever consider its imposition in the case to be judged.

Moore v Illinois
408 U.S. 786, 92 S.Ct. 2562, 33 L.Ed. 2d 706 (1972)

Defendant Moore was convicted of murder. Prior to the trial the defense attorney sought to discover all written statements taken from witnesses by the police. The prosecution agreed. At a postconviction hearing, Moore claimed that he was denied a fair trial because six items of evidence were withheld from him. Five of the items were statements which the state failed to produce under the original request. One was a crime scene diagram. The state courts ruled that the state had not suppressed evidence favorable to Moore. The state showed that the entire case file was given to Moore and no additional request was made by Moore. Moore claimed that a specific request was unnecessary for disclosure of exculpating evidence and that he should not be expected to request that which he did not know was in existence. On appeal the United States Supreme Court held that the suppression of the evidence did not amount to a denial of discovery by the defendant and therefore did not constitute a denial of due process.

Justice Blackmun delivered the opinion of the Court:

In *Brady* v *Maryland*, 373 U.S. 83, . . . , the petitioner and a companion were found guilty by a jury of first-degree murder and were sentenced to death. In his summation to the jury Brady's counsel conceded that Brady was guilty, but argued that the jury should return its verdict "without capital punishment." Prior to the trial, counsel had requested that the prosecution allow him to examine the codefendant's extrajudicial statements. Some of these were produced, but another, in which the codefendant admitted the actual homicide, was withheld and did not come to Brady's notice until after his conviction. In a postconviction proceeding, the Maryland Court of Appeals held that this denied Brady due process of law, and remanded the case for retrial on the issue of punishment. This Court affirmed.

The heart of the holding in *Brady* is the prosecution's suppression of evidence, in the face of a defense production request, where the evidence is favorable to the accused and is material either to guilt or to punishment. Important, then, are (a) suppression by the prosecution after a request by the defense, (b) the evidence's favorable character for the defense, and (c) the materiality of the evidence. These are the standards by which the prosecution's conduct in Moore's case is to be measured.

Moore's counsel asked several prosecution witnesses if they had given statements to the police. Each witness (Hill, Powell, Fair) who had given a statement admitted doing so and the statement was immediately tendered. The same inquiry was not made of witness Sanders. He was the only state witness who was not asked the question. At the postconviction hearing the inquiry was made. Sanders admitted making a statement to the police and the statement was tendered.

The record discloses, as the Illinois court states, . . . that the prosecutor at the trial submitted his entire file to the defense. The prosecutor, however, has no recollection that Sanders' statement was in the file. The statement, therefore, either was in that file and not noted by the defense or it was not in the possession of the prosecution at the trial.

We know of no constitutional requirement that the prosecution make a complete and detailed accounting to the defense of all police investigatory work on a case. Here, the elusive "Slick" was an early lead the police abandoned when eyewitnesses to the killing and witnesses to Moore's presence at the Ponderosa were found. Unquestionably, as the state now concedes, Sanders was in error when he indicated to the police that he met Moore at Wanda and Del's about six months prior to April 30, 1962. Moore's incarceration at Leavenworth until March shows that conclusion to have been an instance of mistaken identity. But the mistake was as to the identification of Moore as "Slick," not as to the presence of Moore at the Ponderosa Tap on April 27. "Sanders' testimony to the effect that it was Moore he spoke with at the Ponderosa Tap in itself is not significantly, if at all, impeached. Indeed, it is buttressed by the testimony of bartender Joyce and operator Fair, both of whom elaborated the incident by their description of the man and by Moore's request for a ride to Harvey, Illinois, Fair's providing that ride, and Fair's hearing, on that trip, the reference to one of the men as 'Barbee,' and a second reference to trouble with a bartender in Lansing."

The other four of the first five items—that Jones told police he could identify "Slick" and subsequently testified that Moore was not "Slick"; that the police had a picture of Watts and assigned the lieutenant, unsuccessfully, to find a picture of Moore and told the police that Moore was not "Slick"; and that on the day of the trial Sanders remarked that the man he knew as "Slick" looked heavier than Moore—are in exactly the same category. They all relate to "Slick," not Moore, and quite naturally go off on Sanders' initial misidentification of "Slick" with Moore.

None of the five items serves to impeach in any way the positive identification by Hill and by Powell of Moore as Zitek's killer, or the testimony of Fair and Joyce that Moore was at the Ponderosa Tap on April 27, or the testimony of Fair that the moustached Barbee was accompanying Moore at that time, and that one of the two men made the additional and undisputed admission on the ride to Harvey. We conclude, in the light of all the evidence, that Sanders' misidentification of Moore as "Slick" was not material to the issue of guilt.

(Judgment reversed because the death penalty could not be imposed under the Illinois statutes.)
Justices Marshall delivered an opinion concurring in part and dissenting in part. Justices Stewart, Douglas, and Powell joined in the dissenting part of Justice Marshall's opinion.

United States v Agurs

427 U.S. 97, 96 S.Ct. 2392, 49 L.Ed. 2d 342 (1976)

Agurs was convicted of the first-degree murder of Sewell with a knife. It was disclosed at the trial that before the killing Sewell was carrying two knives, one of which was used to slay him, that Sewell was repeatedly stabbed, and that Agurs' defense was one of self-defense. She claimed that the prosecutor had discovered that Sewell had previously been convicted of assault and of carrying a deadly weapon (apparently a knife). Such information would have tended to support Agurs' claim that she acted in self-defense and that the failure to disclose this information deprived her of a fair trial. The district court denied a motion for a new trial on the ground that the evidence was not material because it shed no new light on Sewell's character and the apparent inconsistency between the self-defense claim and the unscathed condition of Agurs. The Court of Appeals reversed, holding that the evidence was material and should have been disclosed because the jury might have returned a different verdict had the evidence been received.

Mr. Justice Stevens, writing for the majority reversed the Court of Appeals, stated: ''We now consider whether the prosecutor has any constitutional duty to volunteer exculpatory matter to the defense, and if so, what standard of materiality gives rise to that duty.'' Stevens noted that the standards under the Due Process Clause of the Fifth Amendment are equally applicable under the comparable clause in the Fourteenth Amendment.

In addressing the issues of disclosure, the majority concluded:

The problem arises in two principal contexts. First, in advance of trial, and perhaps during the course of a trial as well, the prosecutor must decide what, if anything, he should voluntarily submit to defense counsel. Second, after trial a judge may be required to decide whether a nondisclosure deprived the defendant of his right to due process. Logically the same standard must apply at both times. For unless the omission deprived the defendant of a fair trial, there was no constitutional violation requiring that the verdict be set aside; and absent a constitutional violation, there was no breach of the prosecutor's constitutional duty to disclose.

Nevertheless, there is a significant practical difference between the pretrial decision of the prosecutor and the post-trial decision of the judge. Because we are dealing with an inevitably imprecise standard, and because the significance of an item of evidence can seldom be predicted accurately until the entire record is complete, the prudent prosecutor will resolve doubtful questions in favor of disclosure. But to reiterate a critical point, the prosecutor will not have violated his constitutional duty of disclosure unless his omission is of sufficient significance to result in the denial of the defendant's right to a fair trial.

The Court of Appeals appears to have assumed that the prosecutor has a constitutional obligation to disclose any information that might affect the jury's verdict. That statement of a constitutional standard of materiality approaches the ''sporting theory of justice'' which the Court expressly rejected in *Brady*.

Stevens went on and held that ''whether or not procedural rules authorized such broad discovery might be desirable, the Constitution surely does not demand that much.'' The mere fact that an item of undisclosed information could possibly have helped the defense or might have affected the outcome does not establish materiality in the constitutional sense. In regard to materiality as an issue the majority held.

> On the other hand, since we have rejected the suggestion that the prosecutor has a constitutional duty routinely to deliver his entire file to defense counsel, we cannot consistently treat every nondisclosure as though it were error. It necessarily follows that the judge should not order a new trial every time he is unable to characterize a nondisclosure as harmless under the customary harmless error standard. Under that standard when error is present in the record, the reviewing judge must set aside the verdict and judgment unless his "conviction is sure that the error did not influence the jury, or had but very slight affect." . . . Unless every nondisclosure is regarded as automatic error, the constitutional standard of materiality must impose a higher burden on the defendant.
>
> The proper standard of materiality must reflect our overriding concern with the justice of the finding of guilt. Such a finding is permissible only if supported by evidence establishing guilt beyond a reasonable doubt. It necessarily follows that if the omitted evidence creates a reasonable doubt that did not otherwise exist, constitutional error has been committed. This means that the omission must be evaluated in the context of the entire record. If there is no reasonable doubt about guilt whether or not the additional evidence is considered, there is no justification for a new trial. On the other hand, if the verdict is already of questionable validity, additional evidence of relatively minor importance might be sufficient to create a reasonable doubt.

Justices Marshall and Brennan dissented.

Estelle, in custody and charged with a criminal offense, asked for his civilian clothes to wear at the trial. The request on the morning of the trial was not acted upon. Council during the preliminary examination of jurors expressly referred to Estelle's prison attire. No issue was raised during the trial concerning the jail clothing worn by Estelle. The Texas courts upheld his conviction, but the Federal Court of Appeals reversed. The evidence indicated that it was common practice in the county where the trial took place for defendants to be tried in jail clothes. The evidence also indicated that if an objection was made, a defendant could wear civilian clothes. The practice of the judge who tried the case was to permit civilian attire if an accused so desired.

The United States Supreme Court, Chief Justice Burger delivering the opinion, held that the right to a fair trial is a fundamental liberty secured by the Fourteenth Amendment. "Accordingly, although the state cannot, consistent with the Fourteenth Amendment, compel an accused to stand trial before a jury while dressed in identifiable prison clothes, the failure to make an objection to the court as to being tried in such clothes for whatever reason is sufficient to negate the presence of compulsion necessary to establish a constitutional violation." *Estelle* v *Williams,* 425 U.S. 501, 96 S.Ct. 1961, 48 L.Ed. 2d 126 (1976).

QUESTIONS

1. What circumstances require the appointment of counsel? What practical problems would issue from the requirement that counsel be appointed in all felony criminal cases?

2. How have the rulings concerning right to counsel affected police lineups?

3. Compare *Kirby* v *Illinois* to *Simmons* v *United States*. What are the constitutional problems presented? Discuss the distinction between these constitutional problems.

4. What are the evident differences between *Barber* v *Page* and *Pointer* v *Texas?*

5. By what means has the doctrine that the speedy trial provision of the Sixth Amendment takes affect after the arrest or after formal charges are filed been pronounced?

6. What is the Court's position on jury trials? How did the *Furman* v *Georgia* decision affect this position?

12

EIGHTH AMENDMENT

Bail

A short discussion of the bail system was presented in Chapter 11. The opinions in this section present some innovations in the bail system attempted by the states to overcome the evils of the system. The United States Supreme Court has given its approval to such techniques as can be noted.

Cruel and Unusual Punishment

The origin of the American constitutional prohibition against cruel and unusual punishments can be found in the English Bill of Rights which was promulgated from the abhorrence of torture and extremely cruel sentences meted out by the English Court of the Star Chamber. Even in spite of the English Bill of Rights, punishments of a cruel and inhuman nature persisted into the eighteenth century.

In the colonies in the eighteenth century punishments were severe. After the Revolutionary War state constitutions included clauses indicating that cruel and unusual punishments should not be inflicted. Subsequently, this idea was incorporated into the Eighth Amendment.

Weems v *United States,* 217 U.S. 349 (1910), was the first case in which the United States Supreme Court was asked to determine whether punishment was cruel or unusual and also to establish the significant constitutional doctrine that the Eighth Amendment was to be considered in light of the values of current society. The Court stated that the Eighth Amendment "is not fastened to the absolute but may acquire meaning as public opinion becomes enlightened by humane justice.''

The scope of the kinds of punishment that are considered to be cruel and inhumane has been the subject of controversy and has not been resolved. For example, whipping and flogging have been sustained on the ground that they traditionally have been used.

The death penalty has been the subject of continuing constitutional debate. This section contains the leading cases on the death penalty, *Louisiana en rel Francis* v *Resweber,* 329 U.S. 459 (1947), and *Furman* v *Georgia,* 408 U.S. 238 (1972), and the recent case *Gregg* v *Georgia,* 96 S.Ct. 2909 (1976). Prior to *Furman* the death penalty had been held to be neither cruel nor unusual although it was established that it must be accomplished as swiftly and painlessly as possible. *In re Kemmler,* 136 U.S. 436 (1890), declared that punishments are cruel when they involve torture or a lingering death, ''but the punishment of death is not cruel within the meaning of that word as used in the Constitution. It implies there is something inhuman and barbarous, something more than the mere extinguishment of human life.''

Only a few years before *Furman* the death penalty was attacked as a cruel and unusual punishment in *Rudolph* v *Alabama,* 375 U.S. 889 (1963). In affixing death to a conviction of rape the defendant argued that it was cruel and unusual because it was so disproportionate to the crime. The Supreme Court refused to review the case although three justices were of the opinion that the issue should be heard and decided. The *Furman* opinion did not reach the basic issue of the constitutionality of the death penalty. Rather, the majority addressed themselves to the manner in which the penalty of death was decided and came to the conclusion that the procedure was defective. In *Gregg* it was ruled that if these defective procedures were eliminated, the death penalty should be considered constitutional.

The problem of defining exactly what is a crime is a present-day concern. The *Robinson* v *California,* 370 U.S. 660 (1962), and *Powell* v *Texas,* 392 U.S. 514 (1968), decisions discuss this problem as it pertains to cruel and unusual punishment.

BAIL

Stack v *Boyle*
342 U.S. 1, 72 S.Ct. 1, 96 L.Ed. 3 (1951)

Stack and several others were charged with conspiring to violate the Smith Act. The United States District Court for the Southern District of California set bail at $50,000 for each individual. The defendants sought to have the bail reduced and submitted various financial statements. The government's evidence in rebuttal showed that four persons previously convicted under the Smith Act in the Southern District of New York had forfeited bail. There was no evidence produced relating these persons with Stack and the other defendants in this case. Subsequently the amount of bail was affirmed by the Ninth Circuit Court of Appeals. The United States Supreme Court granted certiorari, vacated the judgment of the Court of Appeals, and remanded the case to the District Court with instructions.

Chief Justice Vinson delivered the opinion of the Court:

First. From the passage of the Judiciary Act of 1789, 1 Stat. 73, 91, to the present Federal Rules of Criminal Procedure, Rule 46(a) (1), 18 U.S.C.A., federal law has unequivocally provided that a person arrested for a noncapital offense *shall* be admitted to bail. This traditional right to freedom before conviction permits the unhampered preparation of a defense, and serves to prevent the infliction of punishment prior to conviction. . . . Unless this right to bail before trial is preserved, the presumption of innocence, secured only after centuries of struggle, would lose its meaning.

The right to release before trial is conditioned upon the accused's giving adequate assurance that he will stand trial and submit to sentence if found guilty.

. . .

Since the function of bail is limited, the fixing of bail for any individual defendant must be based upon standards relevant to the purpose of assuring the presence of that defendant. The traditional standards as expressed in the Federal Rules of Criminal Procedure are to be applied in each case to each defendant. In this case petitioners are charged with offenses under the Smith Act and, if found guilty, their convictions are subject to review with the scrupulous care demanded by our Constitution. . . . Upon final judgment of conviction, petitioners face imprisonment of not more than five years and a fine of not more than $10,000. It is not denied that bail for each petitioner has been fixed in a sum much higher than that usually imposed for offenses with like penalties and yet there has been no factual showing to justify such action in this case. The government asks the courts to depart from the norm by assuming, without the introduction of evidence that each petitioner is a pawn in a conspiracy and will, in obedience to a superior, flee the jurisdiction. To infer from the fact of indictment alone a need for bail in an unusually high amount is an arbitrary act. Such conduct would inject into our own system of government the very principles of totalitarianism which Congress was seeking to guard against in passing the statute under which petitioners have been indicted.

If bail in an amount greater than that usually fixed for serious charges of crimes is required in the case of any of the petitioners, that is a matter to which evidence should be directed in a hearing so that the constitutional rights of each petitioner may be preserved. In the absence of such a showing, we are of the opinion that the fixing of bail before trial in these cases cannot be squared with the statutory and constitutional standards for admission to bail.

Second. The proper procedure for challenging bail as unlawfully fixed is by motion for reduction of bail and appeal to the Court of Appeals from an order denying such motion. Petitioners' motion to reduce bail did not merely invoke the discretion of the District Court setting bail within a zone of reasonableness, but challenged the bail as violating statutory and constitutional standards. As there is no discretion to refuse to reduce excessive bail, the order denying the motion to reduce bail is appealable as a "final decision." . . . In this case, however, petitioners did not take an appeal from the order of the District Court denying their motion for reduction of bail. Instead, they presented their claims under the Eighth Amendment in applications for writs of habeas corpus. While habeas corpus is an appropriate remedy for one held in custody in violation of the Constitution, . . . the District Court should withhold relief in this collateral habeas corpus action where an adequate remedy available in the criminal proceeding has not been exhausted.

. . .

The Court concludes that bail has not been fixed by proper methods in this case and that petitioners' remedy is by motion to reduce bail, with right of appeal to the Court of Appeals. Accordingly, the judgment of the Court of Appeals is vacated and the case is remanded to the District Court with directions to vacate its order denying petitioners' applications for writs of habeas corpus and to dismiss the applications without prejudice. Petitioners may move for reduction of bail in the criminal proceeding so that a hearing may be held for the purpose of fixing reasonable bail for each petitioner.

. . .

Justice Minton did not participate in consideration of this case.
Justice Jackson with whom Justice Frankfurter joined wrote a concurring opinion.

Schilb v *Kuebel*
404 U.S. 357, 92 S.Ct. 479, 30 L.Ed. 2d 502 (1971)

The law in Illinois provides for three ways in which an accused can secure his pretrial release: (1) personal recognizance; (2) execution of a bail bond with a 10 percent deposit of the bail, all but 10 percent of which (1 percent of the total bail) is returned upon successful performance of the bond conditions; (3) execution of a full bail bond secured by a full cash or equivalent deposit. Schilb deposited 10 percent of the required bail after being charged with two traffic offenses. He was convicted of one and acquitted of the other. After he paid his fine, all but 1 percent of the bail was refunded. He then challenged the Illinois bail scheme on due process and equal protection grounds by claiming: (1) that the 1 percent retention is imposed on only one class of those granted pretrial release and (2) that its imposition on an accused found innocent constitutes a court cost against the not guilty.

Justice Blackmun delivered the opinion of the Court:

Prior to 1964 the professional bail bondsman system with all its abuses was in full and odorous bloom in Illinois. Under that system the bail bondsman customarily collected the maximum fee (10 percent of the amount of the bond) permitted by statute, . . . and retained that entire amount even though the accused fully satisfied the conditions of the bond. . . . Payment of this substantial "premium" was required of the good risk as well as of the bad. The results were that a heavy and irretrievable burden fell upon the accused, to the excellent profit of the bondsman, and that professional bondsmen, and not the courts, exercised significant control over the actual workings of the bail system.

One of the stated purposes of the new bail provisions in the 1963 Code was to rectify this offensive situation. The purpose appears to have been accomplished. It is said that the bail bondsman abruptly disappeared in Illinois "due primarily to the success of the 10 percent bail deposit provision."

. . .

Bail, of course, is basic to our system of law, . . . and the Eighth Amendment's proscription of excessive bail has been assumed to have application to the states through the Fourteenth Amendment. . . . But we are not at all concerned here with any fundamental right to bail or with any Eighth Amendment–Fourteenth Amendment question of bail excessiveness. Our concern, instead, is with the 1 percent cost-retention provision. This smacks of administrative detail and of procedure and is hardly to be classified as a "fundamental" right or as based upon any suspect criterion. The applicable measure, therefore, must be the traditional one: Is the distinction drawn by the statutes invidious and without rational basis?

. . .

With this background, we turn to the appellants' primary argument. It is threefold: (1) that the 1 percent retention charge under §110–7(f) is imposed on only one segment of the class gaining pretrial release; (2) that it is imposed on the poor and nonaffluent and not on the rich and affluent; and (3) that its imposition with respect to an accused found innocent amounts to a court cost assessed against the not-guilty person.

We are compelled to note preliminarily that the attack on the Illinois bail statutes, in a very distinct sense, is paradoxical. The benefits of the new system, as compared with the old, are conceded.

. . .

A. It is true that no charge is made to the accused who is released on his personal recognizance.

There is also, however, no retention charge to the accused who deposits the full amount of cash bail or securities or real estate.

This perhaps is a more tenuous distinction, but we cannot conclude that it is constitutionally vulnerable. One who deposits securities or encumbers his real estate precludes the use of that property for other purposes. And one who deposits the full amount of his bail in cash is dispossessed of a productive asset throughout the period of the deposit; presumably, at least, its interim possession by the state accrues to the benefit of the state.

B. The poor man–affluent man argument centers, of course, in *Griffin* v *Illinois,* 351 U.S. 12, . . . , and in the many later cases that "reaffirm allegiance to the basic command that justice be applied equally to all persons."

· · ·

In no way do we withdraw today from the *Griffin* principle. That remains steadfast. But it is by no means certain, as the appellants suggest, that the 10 percent deposit provision under §110-7 is a provision for the benefit of the poor and the less affluent and that the full-deposit provision of §110-8 is one for the rich and the more affluent.

· · ·

Neither is it assured, as the appellants also suggest, that the affluent will take advantage of the full-deposit provision of §110-8, with no retention charge, and that the less affluent are relegated to the 10 percent deposit provision of §110-7 and the 1 percent retention charge.

· · ·

C. The court-cost argument is that the person found innocent but already "put to the expense, disgrace, and anguish of a trial" is "then assessed a cost for exercising his right to release pending trial."

· · ·

Finally, the appellants would point out that Article 110 has its federal counterpart in §3(a) of the Bail Reform Act of 1966, Pub. L. 89-465, 89th Cong., 2d Sess., 80 Stat. 214, and in particular in that portion now codified as 18 U.S.C. §3146 (a)(c). They note that (the original bill) contained a 1 percent retention provision.

· · ·

. . . The federal act, unlike the Illinois one, was not directed against the professional bail bondsman, we are not inclined to read constitutional implications into the absence of the retention provision in the Bail Reform Act of 1966.

Neither are we inclined to read constitutional implications into either the presence or absence of a retention provision in corresponding statutes of states other than Illinois.

· · ·

We refrain from nullifying this Illinois statute that, with its companion sections, has brought reform and needed relief to the state's bail system. The judgment of the Supreme Court of Illinois is affirmed.

Justice Marshall wrote a concurring opinion.
Justice Douglas wrote a dissenting opinion.
Justice Stewart, with whom Justice Brennan joined, wrote a dissenting opinion.

CRUEL AND UNUSUAL PUNISHMENTS

Louisiana ex rel Francis v *Resweber*

329 U.S. 459, 67 S.Ct. 374, 91 L.Ed. 422 (1947)

Resweber was convicted of murder and sentenced to be electrocuted. At the execution he was placed in the electric chair. The switch was thrown but because of a mechanical failure death did not result. He was taken back to prison. Subsequently a new date for electrocution was set. The United States Supreme Court granted certiorari to answer the issues whether the protection of the Due Process Clause of the Fourteenth Amendment would be violated by the second execution pronounced because of the Double Jeopardy Clause of the Fifth Amendment and the cruel and unusual punishment provision of the Eighth Amendment.

Justice Reed, joined by Justices Black and Jackson and the Chief Justice, announced the opinion of the Court:

Applications to the Supreme Court of the state were filed for writs of certiorari, mandamus, prohibition, and habeas corpus directed to the appropriate officials in the state. Execution of the sentence was stayed. By the applications petitioner claimed the protection of the Due Process Clause of the Fourteenth Amendment on the ground that an execution under the circumstances detailed would deny due process to him because of the double jeopardy provision of the Fifth Amendment and the cruel and unusual punishment provision of the Eighth Amendment. These federal constitutional protections, petitioner claimed, would be denied because he had once gone through the difficult preparation for execution and had once received through his body a current of electricity intended to cause death. The Supreme Court of Louisiana denied the applications on the ground of a lack of any basis for judicial relief. That is, the state court concluded there was no violation of state or national law alleged in the various applications. It spoke of the fact that no "current of sufficient intensity to cause death" passed through petitioner's body. It referred specifically to the fact that the applications of petitioner invoked the provisions of the Louisiana Constitution against cruel and inhuman punishments and putting one in jeopardy of life or liberty twice for the same offense. We granted certiorari on a petition, setting forth the aforementioned contentions of rights under the federal Constitution in the unusual circumstances of this case. . . . For matters of state law, the opinion and order of the Supreme Court of Louisiana are binding on this Court. . . . So far as we are aware, this case is without precedent in any court.

To determine whether or not the execution of the petitioner may fairly take place after the experience through which he passed, we shall examine the circumstances under the assumption, but without so deciding, that violation of the principles of the Fifth and Eighth Amendments, as to double jeopardy and cruel and unusual punishment, would be violative of the Due Process Clause of the Fourteenth Amendment. As nothing has been brought to our attention to suggest the contrary, we must and do assume that the state officials carried out their duties under the death warrant in a careful and humane manner. Accidents happen for which no man is to blame. We turn to the question as to whether the proposed enforcement of the criminal law of the state is offensive to any constitutional requirements to which reference has been made.

. . .

We find nothing in what took place here which amounts to cruel and unusual punishment in the constitutional sense. The case before us does not call for an examination into any punishments except that of death. . . . The traditional humanity of modern Anglo–American law forbids the infliction of unnecessary pain in the execution of the death sentence. Prohibition against the wanton infliction of pain has come into our law from the Bill of Rights of 1688. The identical words appear in our Eighth Amendment. The Fourteenth would prohibit by its Due Process Clause execution by a state in a cruel manner.

Petitioner's suggestion is that because he once underwent the psychological strain of preparation for electrocution, now to require him to undergo this preparation again subjects him to a lingering or cruel and unusual punishment. Even the fact that petitioner has already been subjected to a current of electricity does not make his subsequent execution any more cruel in the constitutional sense than any other execution. The cruelty against which the Constitution protects a convicted man is cruelty inherent in the method of punishment, not the necessary suffering involved in any method employed to extinguish life humanely. The fact that an unforseeable accident prevented the prompt consummation of the sentence cannot, it seems to us, add an element of cruelty to a subsequent execution. There is no purpose to inflict unnecessary pain nor any unnecessary pain involved in the proposed execution. The situation of the unfortunate victim of this accident is just as though he had suffered the identical amount of mental anguish and physical pain in any other occurrence, such as, for example, a fire in the cell block. We cannot agree that the hardship imposed upon the petitioner rises to that level of hardship denounced as denial of due process because of cruelty.

(Judgment affirmed.)
Justice Frankfurter wrote a concurring opinion.
Justices Burton, with whom Justices Douglas, Murphy, and Rutledge concurred, wrote a dissenting opinion.

Robinson v *California*

370 U.S. 660, 82 S.Ct. 1417, 8 L.Ed. 2d 758 (1962)

Robinson was convicted in Los Angeles for violation of a statute making it a criminal offense to be addicted to the use of narcotics. On appeal to the United States Supreme Court the state court conviction was reversed.

Justice Stewart delivered the opinion of the Court:

The trial judge instructed the jury that the statute made it a misdemeanor for a person "either to use narcotics, or to be addicted to the use of narcotics."

. . .

The judge further instructed the jury that the appellant could be convicted under a general verdict if the jury agreed *either* that he was of the "status" *or* had committed the "act" denounced by the statute.

. . .

Under these instructions the jury returned a verdict finding the appellant "guilty of the offense charged." An appeal was taken to the Appellate Department of the Los Angeles County Superior Court. . . . Although expressing some doubt as to the constitutionality of "the crime of being a narcotic addict," the reviewing court in an unreported opinion affirmed the judgment of conviction, citing two of its own previous unreported decisions which had upheld the constitutionality of the statute.

. . .

The broad power of a state to regulate the narcotic drugs traffic within its borders is not here in issue. More than 40 years ago, . . . this Court explicitly recognized the validity of that power.

. . .

Such regulation, it can be assumed, could take a variety of valid forms. A state might impose criminal sanctions, for example, against the unauthorized manufacture, prescription, sale, purchase, or possession of narcotics within its borders. In the interest of discouraging the violation of such laws, or in the interest of the general health or welfare of its inhabitants, a state might establish a program of compulsory treatment for those addicted to narcotics. Such a program of treatment might require periods of involuntary confinement.

. . .

It would be possible to construe the statute under which the appellant was convicted as one which is operative only upon proof of the actual use of narcotics within the state's jurisdiction. But the California courts have not so construed this law. Although there was evidence in the present case that the appellant had used narcotics in Los Angeles, the jury were instructed that they could convict him even if they disbelieved that evidence. The appellant could be convicted, they were told, if they found simply that the appellant's "status" or "chronic condition" was that of being "addicted to the use of narcotics." And it is impossible to know from the jury's verdict that the defendant was not convicted upon precisely such a finding.

The instructions of the trial court, implicitly approved on appeal, amounted to "a ruling on a question of state law that is as binding on us as though the precise words had been written" into the statute.

. . .

This statute, therefore, is not one which punishes a person for the use of narcotics, for their purchase, sale or possession, or for antisocial or disorderly behavior resulting from their administration. . . . Rather, we deal with a statute which makes the "status" of narcotic addiction a criminal offense, for which the offender may be prosecuted "at any time before he reforms." California has said that a person can be continuously guilty of this offense, whether or not he has ever used or possessed any narcotics within the state, and whether or not he has been guilty of any antisocial behavior there.

It is unlikely that any state at this moment in history would attempt to make it a criminal offense for a person to be mentally ill, or a leper, or to be afflicted with a venereal disease. A state might determine that the general health and welfare require that the victims of these and other human afflictions be dealt with by compulsory treatment, involving quarantine, confinement, or sequestration. But, in the light of contemporary human knowledge, a law which made a criminal offense of such a disease would doubtless be universally thought to be an infliction of cruel and unusual punishment in violation of the Eighth and Fourteenth Amendments.

. . .

We cannot but consider the statute before us as of the same category. In this Court counsel for the state recognized that narcotic addiction is an illness. Indeed, it is apparently an illness which may be contracted innocently and involuntarily. We hold that a state law which imprisons a person thus afflicted as a criminal, even though he has never touched any narcotic drug within the state or been guilty of any irregular behavior there, inflicts a cruel and unusual punishment in violation of the Fourteenth Amendment.

. . .

We are not unmindful that the vicious evils of the narcotics traffic have occasioned the grave concern of government. There are, as we have said, countless fronts on which those evils may be legitimately attacked. We deal in this case only with an individual provision of a particularized local law as it has so far been interpreted by the California courts.

(Judgment reversed.)
Justice Frankfurter did not participate in the consideration of the case.
Justice Douglas wrote a concurring opinion.
Justices Clark and White each wrote a dissenting opinion.

Powell v *Texas*

392 U.S. 514, 88 S.Ct. 2145, 20 L.Ed. 2d 1254 (1963)

In a nonjury trial Powell was convicted of public drunkenness. In an appeal to the United States Supreme Court, the conviction of Powell was upheld even though he argued that he was compelled by his own sickness to some degree to drink. The United States Supreme Court held that the state statute did not amount to cruel and unusual punishment. The opinion was 5 to 4.

Justice Marshall delivered the opinion of the Court in which the Chief Justice and Justices Black and Harlan joined:

In late December 1966, appellant was arrested and charged with being found in a state of intoxication in a public place, in violation of Vernon's Ann. Texas Penal Code, Art. 477 (1952).

. . .

The trial judge in the county court, sitting without a jury, made certain findings of fact, . . . but ruled as a matter of law that chronic alcoholism was not a defense to the charge. He found appellant guilty, and fined him $50. There being no further right to appeal within the Texas judicial system, appellant appealed to this Court; we noted probable jurisdiction.

. . .

Traditional common-law concepts of personal accountability and essential considerations of federalism lead us to disagree with appellant. We are unable to conclude, on the state of this record or on the current state of medical knowledge, that chronic alcoholics in general, and Leroy Powell in particular, suffer from such an irresistible compulsion to drink and to get drunk in public that they are utterly unable to control their performance of either or both of these acts and thus cannot be deterred at all from public intoxication. And in any event this Court has never articulated a general constitutional doctrine of *mens rea*.

We cannot cast aside the centuries-long evolution of the collection of interlocking and overlapping concepts which the common law has utilized to assess the moral accountability of an individual for his antisocial deeds. The doctrines of *actus reus, mens rea,* insanity, mistake, justification, and duress have historically provided the tools for a constantly shifting adjustment of the tension between the evolving aims of the criminal law and changing religious, moral, philosophical, and medical views of the nature of man. This process of adjustment has always been thought to be the province of the states.

Nothing could be less fruitful than for this Court to be impelled into defining some sort of insanity test in constitutional terms. Yet, that task would seem to follow inexorably from an extension of *Robinson* to this case. If a person in the "condition" of being a chronic alcoholic cannot be criminally punished as a constitutional matter for being drunk in public, it would seem to follow that a person who contends that, in terms of one test, "his unlawful act was the product of mental disease or mental defect,"... would state an issue of constitutional dimension with regard to his criminal responsibility had he been tried under some different and perhaps lesser standard, e.g., the right-wrong test of *M'Naghten's Case*. The experimentation of one jurisdiction in that field alone indicates the magnitude of the problem. . . . But formulating a constitutional rule would reduce, if not eliminate, that fruitful experimentation and freeze the developing productive dialogue between law and psychiatry into a rigid constitutional mold. It is simply not yet the time to write the constitutional formulas cast in terms whose meaning, let alone relevance, is not yet clear either to doctors or to lawyers.

Gregg v *Georgia*

428 U.S. 153, 96 S.Ct. 2909, 50 L.Ed. 2d 30 (1976)

Georgia follows the bifurcated trial process under which there is one trial on the guilt or innocence of the accused and a second trial is set to determine the penalty to death or some lesser sentence. Gregg was convicted of murdering two men during an armed robbery. At the penalty stage, the judge instructed the jury that it could recommend either a death sentence or a life prison sentence on each count; that the jury was free to consider mitigating or aggravating circumstances, if any, as presented by the parties; and that the jury would not be authorized to consider imposing the death sentence unless it first found beyond a reasonable doubt (1) that the murder was committed while the offender was engaged in the commission of other capital felonies, viz., the armed robberies of the victims; (2) that he committed the murder for the purpose of receiving the victims' money and automobile; or (3) that the murder was "outrageously and wantonly vile, horrible, and inhuman" in that it "involved the depravity of the mind of the defendant." The jury found the first and second of these aggravating circumstances and returned a sentence of death.

Gregg challenged the imposition of the death sentence, after some modification of the trial court's record, on the ground that its death sentence under the Georgia statute constituted cruel and unusual punishment under the Eighth and Fourteenth Amendments.

The Georgia statute, amended following *Furman* v *Georgia,* 408 U.S. 238 (1972), retained the death penalty for murder and five other crimes. Guilt or innocence is determined at the first stage of the bifurcated trial. If the trial is by a jury, the trial judge must charge lesser included offenses if the evidence so indicates. If the defendant enters a guilty plea or is found guilty by a judge, before death may be the sentence the judge or jury hears additional mitigating, extenuating, and aggravating evidence if made known by the defendant before trial. Of the ten specified aggravating circumstances listed in the statute, at least one must be proved beyond a reasonable doubt, designated in writing, and made known to the defendant before trial.

In jury cases the trial judge is bound by the recommended sentence. On automatic review of death sentences, the Georgia Supreme Court must consider whether the sentence was influenced by passion, prejudice, or any other arbitrary factor; whether the sentence is excessive or disproportionate to that imposed in similar cases; and whether the evidence supports the finding of the statutory aggravating circumstances. Should the court affirm the death penalty, it is required to include in its decision reference to other similar cases it has considered.

In a 7 to 2 decision (Justices Brennan and Marshall dissented) the United States Supreme Court declared that capital punishment is not unconstitutional *per se*.

Three Justices, Stewart, Powell and Stevens, concluded that the imposition of death as a punishment for murder does not necessarily violate the Eighth and Fourteenth Amendments. While recognizing that punishments that are barbarous and unnecessarily cruel are unconstitutional, the opinion stressed that the Eighth Amendment has been interpreted in a flexible and dynamic manner. The Amendment forbids the use of punishments that are excessive either because they unnecessarily and wantonly involve infliction of pain or are grossly disproportionate to the severity of the offense.

The responsibility of the legislature in assessing a punishment was addressed by the Court when it stated that there is a presumed validity when a punishment is chosen by a democratically elected legislature. "We may not require the legislative to select the least severe penalty so long as the penalty selected is not cruelly inhuman or disproportionate to the crime involved and the heavy burden rests on those who would attack the judgment of the representative of the people."

The opinion of the three justices went on to emphasize that for "nearly two centuries the Court, repeatedly and often expressly has recognized that capital punishment is not involved *per se*." The Court also emphasized that retribution and deterrence are permissible considerations for a legislature to weigh in determining whether capital punishment is warranted. Consequently, the three justices stated that the judgment of the Georgia legislative was correct when it weighed the severity of the crime of murder and decided that the penalty for murder may be death.

The concerns expressed in *Furman* v *Georgia* that the death penalty may not be imposed arbitrarily and capriciously are satisfied by the Georgia statute. The procedures on their face satisfy the *Furman* fears.

The opportunities to provide the defendant with mercy do not render the Georgia statute unconstitutional.

The existence of these discretionary stages is not determinative of the issues before us. At each of these stages an actor in the criminal justice system makes a decision which may remove a defendant from consideration as a candidate for the death penalty. *Furman*, in contrast, dealt with the decision to impose the death sentence on a specific individual who had been convicted of a capital offense. Nothing in any of our cases suggests that the decision to afford an individual defendant mercy violates the Constitution. *Furman* held only that, in order to minimize the risk that the death penalty would be imposed on a capriciously selected group of offenders, the decision to impose it has to be guided by standards so that the sentencing authority would focus on the particularized circumstances of the crime and the defendant.

Justice Stewart, Powell, and Stevens concluded by stating:

> The basic concern of Furman centered on those defendants who were being condemned to death capriciously and arbitrarily. Under the procedures before the Court in that case, sentencing authorities were not directed to give attention to the nature or circumstances of the crime committed or to the character or record of the defendant. Left unguided, juries imposed the death sentence in a way that could only be called freakish. The new Georgia sentencing procedures, by contrast, focus the jury's attention on the particularized nature of the crime and the particularized characteristics of the individual defendant. While the jury is permitted to consider any aggravating or mitigating circumstances, it must find and identify at least one statutory aggravating factor before it may impose a penalty of death. In this way the jury's discretion is channeled. No longer can a jury wantonly and freakishly impose the death sentence; it is always circumscribed by the legislative guidelines. In addition, the review function of the Supreme Court of Georgia affords additional assurance that the concerns that prompted our decision in *Furman* are not present to any significant degree in the Georgia procedure applied here.

Justice White, Chief Justice Burger, and Justice Rehnquist concluded that the Georgia scheme of a bifurcated trial process met the constitutional standards set out in *Furman*. If the statute is carefully followed, indiscriminate and wanton death sentences will not be permitted.

In regard to Gregg's argument that prosecutors have little guidance in determining whether the death penalty is to be sought, i.e., negotiating for a plea to a lesser offense or in declining to charge a capital offense, the three justices voted that the argument is unsupported by any facts.

> Absent facts to the contrary it cannot be assumed that prosecutors will be motivated in their charging decision by factors other than the strength of their case and the likelihood that a jury would impose the death penalty if it convicts. Unless prosecutors are incompetent in their judgments the standards by which they decide whether to charge a capital felony will be the same as those by which the jury will decide the questions of guilt and sentence. Thus defendants will escape the death penalty through prosecutorial charging decisions only because the offense is not sufficiently serious; or because the proof is

insufficiently strong. This does not cause the system to be standardless any more than the jury's decision to impose life imprisonment on a defendant whose crime is deemed insufficiently serious or its decision to acquit someone who is probably guilty but whose guilt is not established beyond a reasonable doubt. Thus the prosecutor's charging decisions are unlikely to have removed from the sample of cases considered by the Georgia Supreme Court any which are truly "similar." If the cases really were "similar" in relevant respects it is unlikely that prosecutors would fail to prosecute them as capital cases; and I am unwilling to assume the contrary.

Petitioner's argument that there is an unconstitutional amount of discretion in the system which separates those suspects who receive the death penalty from those who receive life imprisonment, a lesser penalty, or are acquitted or never charged seems to be in final analysis an indictment of our entire system of justice. Petitioner has argued in effect that no matter how effective the death penalty may be as a punishment, government, created and run as it must be by humans, is inevitably incompetent to administer it. This cannot be accepted as a proposition of constitutional law. Imposition of the death penalty is surely an awesome responsibility for any system of justice and those who participate in it. Mistakes will be made and discriminations will occur which will be difficult to explain. However, one of society's most basic ways in which it achieves the task is through criminal laws against murder. I decline to interfere with the manner in which Georgia has chosen to enforce such laws on what is simply an assertion of lack of faith in the ability of the system of justice to operate in a fundamentally fair manner.

Justice Blackmun concurred in the judgment.

Justice Brennan dissented on the ground that death is a cruel and unusual punishment prohibited by the Eighth Amendment.

Justice Marshall dissented on the ground that the death penalty is unnecessary to promote the goal of deterrence or to further any legitimate notion of retribution. It is therefore excessive and violates the Eighth and Fourteenth Amendments.

Furman v *Georgia,* 408 U.S. 238, 92 S.Ct. 2726, 33 L.Ed. 2d 346 (1972), was a combination of three cases brought to the Supreme Court on a grant of certiorari. The circumstances in each of the three cases were very similar. In Furman's case he was convicted of murder and rape and sentenced to death. In the state trial the jury determined whether the penalty should be death or some lesser punishment. The Georgia courts affirmed the conviction and sentence. The United States Supreme Court reversed and remanded the case for further hearings on the penalty. The 5 to 4 opinion of the Court is extremely complex, with no unifying reason supporting the decision.

Each Justice wrote his own opinion. The conclusions added up to the opinion that the Cruel and Unusual Punishments Clause of the Eighth Amendment makes the death penalty when imposed by the sole discretion of the jury not inherently intolerable but applied "so wantonly and freakishly" that it serves no valid purpose and is therefore cruel and unusual. Through this decision a moratorium on the death penalty was established until the 1976 *Gregg* decision.

QUESTIONS

1. What innovations in the bail system are becoming increasingly evident? Will it be necessary for the Court to direct states to alter their existing systems?

2. What was the impact of the *Gregg* decision? How did it follow the logic proposed in *Furman?*

3. Discuss the social trends that brought about the questioning of the death penalty. Has the Court followed these trends or has it been the creator of them?

13

JUVENILE
PROCEDURES

This chapter is limited to a presentation of what constitutional due process requirements are and will be applied to the various and sundry juvenile court systems currently in operation in the United States.

The system of juvenile justice and juvenile courts has not changed appreciably since 1967, but the case of *In re Gault,* 387 U.S. 1 (1967), did focus attention on juvenile procedures, which varied widely from state to state and from county to county within the same state. Although the basic philosophy of handling juveniles was given lip service, it was never applied equally and it was never applied uniformly. Beginning with *Kent* v *United States,* 383 U.S. 541 (1966), the United States Supreme Court began to express an interest in how juveniles were treated. With *In re Gault,* the Supreme Court began a process of selective incorporation of specific civil rights in the Fourth, Fifth, Sixth, and Eighth Amendments to be applied to the juvenile justice system through the Fourteenth Amendment.

The Fourteenth Amendment's due process of law has been discussed in Chapter 3. As will be noted in the cases in this chapter, the procedural rights afforded to the juvenile parallel those given to the adult criminal defendant: confrontation, counsel, notice, and proof beyond a reasonable doubt. However, the list of adult guarantees not afforded to the juvenile is more conspicuous. At the constitutional level, the United States Supreme Court has not addressed such procedural guarantees as the right to a speedy trial, pretrial publicity for juveniles, bail, and the possibility of cruel and unusual punishments by incarcerating juveniles in hopelessly inadequate detention facilities where there is little hope of treatment and rehabilitation. When it was faced squarely with the necessity of affording various procedural rights, the Supreme Court has denied only the right of trial by jury.

The entire concept of juvenile hearings has radically changed. How it will be altered further depends to a great extent on the juvenile courts' receptivity to change. If the juvenile continues to be treated as a second-class citizen, the rights not yet addressed by the United States Supreme Court may very well become fixtures in the juvenile courts.

Historical Development of Juvenile Institutions

In 1825 the New York House of Refuge was established through the support of private funds as a separate juvenile institution. Until that date the standard practice was to put juvenile and adult offenders in the same prison and treat them in much the same way. Today the same situation exists in many areas in America. The House of Refuge retained, by intent, many of the features of a prison, an emphasis on manufacturing with a stronger emphasis on religion. Similar centers were established in Boston in 1826 and in Philadelphia in 1828.

In 1847 the first state reform school, Lyman School for Boys, was established at Westboro, Massachusetts. Similar schools for boys and girls shortly were set up in other states. In 1853 the Children's Aid Society of New York City inaugurated a foster home program by taking children from almshouses in a process of individual replacement. By 1865 eight states had followed Massachusetts and opened reformatories for juveniles: New York, Pennsylvania, Maine, Connecticut, Michigan, Ohio, New Hampshire, and New Jersey. Other private institutions began to appear. One of the earliest (1863) was the New York Catholic Protectory.

Juvenile Court Development

Although provisions for delinquent youth were recorded as early as 2270 B.C. in the Code of Hammurabi, most of the laws that bind the juvenile courts in the United States have their roots in the English common law. Under that system a child under 7 years of age could not be found guilty of a crime. Once the child reached his seventh birthday, however, he could be treated as an adult if evidence was presented showing that he was sufficiently intelligent to understand the nature and consequences of his misconduct and could distinguish between right and wrong. This situation changed through the years, but as late as 1828 a boy of 13 was hanged for an offense committed when he was 12 years old in New Jersey.

In 1877 Massachusetts called for visiting agents who were to work for child betterment, not punishment, and separate juvenile court procedure. New York and Rhode Island soon followed this general plan, but it was not until 1891 that Judge Harvey Hurd authorized and submitted a bill for the establishment of a juvenile court to the Illinois legislature. In 1899 the first session of Chicago's

Juvenile Court took place to deal with delinquent, neglected, dependent, and destitute children. In 1901 the juvenile court in Denver was set up on the basis of:

1. Separate hearings for children's cases.

2. Informal or chancery procedure, including the use of petitions and summonses.

3. Regular probation service both for investigation and supervisory care.

4. Detention separate from adults.

5. Special court records and probation records, both legal and social.

6. Provision for mental and physical examinations.

Without the presence of points 1, 3, and 5, it was felt that a court could not consider itself to be a juvenile court.

The fame of these two courts spread quickly. Soon all of the states with one exception, Wyoming, had incorporated the juvenile court idea into their judicial systems, but few states provided for the establishment of separate courts. Denver led the way in this field in 1907.

As the juvenile court system spread throughout the country the need for professional help became more and more apparent. Most of the more enlightened courts turned to the "helping professions," i.e., social workers, psychologists, psychiatrists, and medical experts. These people were placed on the payroll to meet the needs of the children (usually between the ages of 5 and 16 to 18—21 in one state) with whom the court dealt.

Today, most United States cities of any size have juvenile courts. Some are good; some are bad. In general, it can be said that the degree of the court's proficiency is in direct relation to the attitude of the community it serves. One of the nation's strongest courts has been that of Cincinnati, Ohio. It was one of the first to incorporate the idea of a "referee" and it was a strong proponent of the federal Juvenile Delinquency Act of 1938. By this time the juvenile court in America had come a long way.

As will be seen from the following cases, the basic approach in handling juveniles may be changing radically because of new constitutional requirements. Juvenile proceedings are becoming more of an adversary proceeding than in the past. Local prosecutors frequently are present in juvenile adjudicatory hearings to argue the case on behalf of the state. Depending on further decisions of the United States Supreme Court in the area of constitutional safeguards for juveniles, juvenile courts may indeed become very similar to, or possibly merged into, adult criminal courts.

Kent v *United States*

383 U.S. 541, 86 S.Ct. 1045, 16 L.Ed. 2d 84 (1966)

The District of Columbia Juvenile Court Act gives exclusive jurisdiction to the juvenile court for law violations. An exception in the law provides that the juvenile court judge can waive jurisdiction and transfer the case to the adult court after there has been a full investigation of the facts. This exception applies when the juvenile is 16 years of age or older and is charged with an offense that would be a felony if committed by an adult. Kent was 16 when he was arrested for rape and robbery after entering a female's apartment. He was taken to the receiving home for children. Kent's attorney asked to have the juvenile court retain jurisdiction after the judge began to consider waiving the juvenile court's jurisdiction and allowing Kent to be remitted to the Federal District Court to be tried as an adult.

Justice Fortas delivered the opinion of the Court:

The Juvenile Court judge did not rule on these motions. He held no hearing. He did not confer with petitioner or petitioner's parents or petitioner's counsel. He entered an order reciting that after "full investigation, I do hereby waive" jurisdiction of petitioner and directing that he be "held for trial for [the alleged] offenses under the regular procedure of the U.S. District Court for the District of Columbia." He made no findings. He did not recite any reason for the waiver. He made no reference to the motions filed by petitioner's counsel. We must assume that he denied, *sub silentio,* the motions for a hearing, the recommendation for hospitalization for psychiatric observation, the request for access to the Social Service file, and the offer to prove that petitioner was a fit subject for rehabilitation under the Juvenile Court's jurisdiction.

. . .

It is clear beyond dispute that the waiver of jurisdiction is a "critically important" action determining vitally important statutory rights of the juvenile. The Court of Appeals for the District of Columbia Circuit has so held. . . . The statutory scheme makes this plain. The Juvenile Court is vested with "original and exclusive jurisdiction" of the child. This jurisdiction confers special rights and immunities. He is, as specified by the statute, shielded from publicity. He may be confined, but with rare exceptions he may not be jailed along with adults. He may be detained, but only until he is 21 years of age. The Court is admonished by the statute to give preference to retraining the child in the custody of his parents "unless his welfare and the safety and protection of the public cannot be adequately safeguarded without . . . removal." The child is protected against consequences of adult conviction such as the loss of civil rights, the use of adjudication against him in subsequent proceedings, and disqualification for public employment.

. . .

The net, therefore, is that petitioner—then a boy of 16—was by statute entitled to certain procedures and benefits as a consequence of his statutory right to the "exclusive" jurisdiction of the Juvenile Court. In these circumstances, considering particularly that decision as to waiver of jurisdiction and transfer of the matter to the District Court was potentially as important to petitioner as the difference between five years' confinement and a death sentence, we conclude, that, as a condition to a valid waiver order, petitioner was entitled to a hearing, including access by his counsel to the social records and probation or similar reports which presumably are considered by the court, and to a statement of reasons for the Juvenile Court's decision. We believe that this result is required by the statute read in the context of constitutional principles relating to due process and the assistance of counsel.

. . .

Ordinarily we would reverse the Court of Appeals and direct the District Court to remand the case to the Juvenile Court for a new determination of waiver. If on remand the decision were against waiver, the indictment in the District Court would be dismissed. See *Black* v *United States, supra*. However, petitioner has now passed the age of 21 and the Juvenile Court can no longer exercise jurisdiction over him. In view of the unavailability of a redetermination of the waiver question by the Juvenile Court, it is urged by petitioner that the conviction should be vacated and the indictment dismissed. In the circumstances of this case, and in light of the remedy which the Court of Appeals fashioned in *Black, supra,* we do not consider it appropriate to grant this drastic relief. Accordingly, we vacate the order of the Court of Appeals and the judgment of the District Court and remand the case to the District Court for a hearing *de novo* on waiver, consistent with this opinion. If that court finds that waiver was inappropriate, petitioner's conviction must be vacated. If, however, it finds that the waiver order was proper when originally made, the District Court may proceed, after consideration of such motions as counsel may make and such further proceedings, if any, as may be warranted, to enter an appropriate judgment.

. . .

(Reversed.)

In re Gault

387 U.S. 1, 87 S.Ct. 1428, 18 L.Ed. 2d 527 (1967)

A woman complained to the Gila County, Arizona, sheriff that Gault, age 15, and another boy made a lewd telephone call to her. Gerald Gault was taken to the Children's Detention Home without his parent's being notified. No steps were taken to tell them that he had been arrested. His mother learned of her son's plight from another son. Both went to the Home and were told by a deputy probation officer why her son was there and that a hearing would be held the next day, June 8, at 3 o'clock. No specific charge was told to the mother.

Deputy Probation Officer Flagg filed a petition, with the juvenile court on June 9. It was not served on the Gaults. The petition made no reference to facts surrounding the incident. At the June 9 hearing, Gerald's father was not present. Mrs. Cook, the complainant, was not present. Neither transcript nor recording was made and a memorandum of the proceeding was not made. In the judge's questioning of Gerald about the phone call in question, a conflict in the testimony about whether Gerald ever made the alleged lewd remarks became evident.

At a subsequent hearing on June 15 the procedure was about the same. Mrs.

Cook was again absent. When Mrs. Gault requested that Mrs. Cook be present, the judge said that she didn't have to be present at that hearing. The judge never did speak with Mrs. Cook although Flagg did on June 9 over the telephone.

The judge committed Gerald to the State Industrial School as a delinquent until he was 21 years of age "unless sooner discharged by due process of law." If he were 18, the maximum punishment for the crime would have been a fine of up to $50 or imprisonment for two months.

In their arguments at a habeas corpus hearing, counsel for Gerald argued that he was denied the following basic rights:

1. Notice of charges.

2. Right to counsel.

3. Right to confrontation and cross-examination.

4. Privilege against self-incrimination.

5. Right to a transcript of the proceedings.

6. Right to appellate review.

The United States Supreme Court did not answer the issue of appellate review.

If Gerald had been over 18, he would not have been subject to juvenile court proceedings. For the particular offense immediately involved, the maximum punishment would have been a fine of $5 to $50, or imprisonment in jail for not more than 2 months. Instead, he was committed to custody for a maximum of 6 years. If he had been over 18 and had committed an offense to which such a sentence might apply, he would have been entitled to substantial rights under the Constitution of the United States as well as under Arizona's laws and constitution. The United States Constitution would guarantee him rights and protections with respect to arrest, search, seizure, and pretrial interrogation. It would assure him of specific notice of the charges and adequate time to decide his course of action and to prepare his defense. He would be entitled to clear advice that he could be represented by counsel, and, at least if a felony were involved, the state would be required to provide counsel if his parents were unable to afford it. If the court acted on the basis of his confession, careful procedures would be required to assure its voluntariness. If the case went to trial, confrontation and opportunity for cross-examination would be guaranteed. So wide a gulf between the state's treatment of the adult and of the child requires a bridge sturdier than mere verbiage, and reasons more persuasive than cliché can provide.

. . .

We now turn to the specific issues which are presented to us in the present case.

Notice of Charges

Appellants allege that the Arizona Juvenile Code is unconstitutional or alternatively that the proceedings before the Juvenile Court were constitutionally defective because of failure to provide adequate notice of the hearings.
. . .

We cannot agree with the court's conclusion that adequate notice was given in this case. Notice, to comply with due process requirements, must be given sufficiently in advance of scheduled court proceedings so that reasonable opportunity to prepare will be afforded, and it must "set forth the alleged misconduct with particularity." It is obvious, as we have discussed above, that no purpose of shielding the child from the public stigma of knowledge of his having been taken into custody and scheduled for hearing is served by the procedure approved by the court below. The "initial hearing" in the present case was a hearing on the merits. Notice at that time is not timely; and even if there were a conceivable purpose served by the deferral proposed by the court below, it would have to yield to the requirements that the child and his parents or guardian be notified, in writing, of the specific charge or factual allegations to be considered at the hearing, and that such written notice be given at the earliest practicable time, and in any event sufficiently in advance of the hearing to permit preparation. Due process of law requires notice of the sort we have described—that is, notice which would be deemed constitutionally adequate in a civil or criminal proceeding. It does not allow a hearing to be held in which a youth's freedom and his parents' right to his custody are at stake without giving them timely notice, in advance of the hearing, of the specific issues that they must meet. Nor, in the circumstances of this case, can it reasonably be said that the requirement of notice was waived.

Right to Counsel

Appellants charge that the Juvenile Court proceedings were fatally defective because the court did not advise Gerald or his parents of their right to counsel, and proceeded with the hearing, the adjudication of delinquency, and the order of commitment in the absence of counsel for the child and his parents or an express waiver of the right thereto. The Supreme Court of Arizona pointed out that "[t]here is disagreement [among the various jurisdictions] as to whether the court must advise the infant that he has a right to counsel." It noted its own decision in *Arizona State Department of Public Welfare* v *Barlow,* 80 Ariz. 249, . . . , to the effect "that *the parents* of an infant in a juvenile proceeding cannot be denied representation by counsel of their choosing." [Emphasis added.] It referred to a provision of the Juvenile Code which it characterized as requiring "that the probation officer shall look after the interests of neglected, delinquent, and dependent children," including representing their interests in court. The court argued that "the parent and the probation officer may be relied upon to protect the infant's interests." Accordingly it rejected the proposition that "due process requires that an infant have a right to counsel." It said that juvenile courts have the discretion, but not the duty, to allow such representation; it referred specifically to the situation in which the juvenile court discerns conflict between the child and his parents as an instance in which this discretion might be exercised. We do not agree. Probation officers, in the Arizona scheme, are also arresting officers. They initiate proceedings and file petitions which they verify, as here, alleging the delinquency of the child; and they testify, as here, against the child. And here the probation officer was also superintendent of the detention home. The probation officer cannot act as counsel for the child. His role in the adjudicatory hearing, by statute and in fact, is an arresting officer and witness against the child. There is no material difference in this respect between adult and juvenile proceedings of the sort here involved. In adult proceedings, this contention has been foreclosed by decisions of this Court. A proceeding where the issue is whether the child will be found to be "delinquent" and subjected to the loss of his liberty for years is comparable in seriousness to a felony prosecution. The juvenile needs the assistance of counsel to cope with problems of law, to make skilled inquiry into the facts, to insist upon regularity of the proceedings, and to ascertain whether he has a defense and to prepare and submit it. The child "requires the guiding hand of counsel at every step in the proceedings against him." Just as in *Kent* v *United States, supra,* 383 U.S., at 561–562, 86 S.Ct., at 1057–1058, we indicated our agreement with the United States Court of Appeals for the District of Columbia Circuit that the assistance of counsel is essential for purposes of waiver proceedings, so we hold now that it is equally essential for the determination of delinquency, carrying with it the awesome prospect of incarceration in a state institution until the juvenile reaches the age of 21.

. . .

We conclude that the Due Process Clause of the Fourteenth Amendment requires that in respect of proceedings to determine delinquency which may result in commitment to an institution in which the juvenile's freedom is curtailed, the child and his parents must be notified of the child's right to be represented by counsel retained by them, or if they are unable to afford counsel, that counsel will be appointed to represent the child.

At the habeas corpus proceeding, Mrs. Gault testified that she knew she could have appeared with counsel at the juvenile hearing. This knowledge is not a waiver of the right to counsel which she and her juvenile son had, as we have defined it. They had a right expressly to be advised that they might retain counsel and to be confronted with the need for specific consideration of whether they did or did not choose to waive the right. If they were unable to afford to employ counsel, they were entitled in view of the seriousness of the charge and the potential commitment, to appointed counsel, unless they chose waiver. Mrs. Gault's knowledge that she could employ counsel was not an "intentional-relinquishment or abandonment" of a fully known right.

Confrontation, Self-Incrimination, Cross-Examination

Appellants urge that the writ of habeas corpus should have been granted because of the denial of the rights of confrontation and cross-examination in the Juvenile Court hearings, and because the privilege against self-incrimination was not observed.

. . .

Our first question, then, is whether Gerald's admission was improperly obtained and relied on as the basis of decision, in conflict with the federal Constitution.

. . .

We conclude that the constitutional privilege against self-incrimination is applicable in the case of juveniles as it is with respect to adults. We appreciate that special problems may arise with respect to waiver of the privilege by or on behalf of children, and that there may well be some differences in technique—but not in principle—depending upon the age of the child and the presence and competence of parents. The participation of counsel will, of course, assist the police, Juvenile Courts, and appellate tribunals in administering the privilege. If counsel was not present for some permissible reason when an admission was obtained, the greatest care must be taken to assure that the admission was voluntary, in the sense not only that it was not coerced or suggested, but also that it was not the product of ignorance of rights or of adolescent fantasy, fright, or despair.

The "confession" of Gerald Gault was first obtained by Officer Flagg, out of the presence of Gerald's parents, without counsel, and without advising him of his right to silence, as far as appears. The judgment of the Juvenile Court was stated by the judge to be based on Gerald's admissions in court. Neither "admission" was reduced to writing, and, to say the least, the process by which the "admissions" were obtained and received must be characterized as lacking the certainty and order which are required of proceedings of such formidable consequences. Apart from the "admission," there was nothing upon which a judgment or finding might be based. There was no sworn testimony. Mrs. Cook, the complainant, was not present. The Arizona Supreme Court held that "sworn testimony must be required of all witnesses including police officers, probation officers, and others who are part of or officially related to the juvenile court structure." We hold that this is not enough. No reason is suggested or appears for a different rule in respect of sworn testimony in juvenile courts than in adult tribunals. Absent a valid confession adequate to support the determination of the Juvenile Court, confrontation and sworn testimony by witnesses available for cross-examination were essential for a finding of "delinquency" and an order committing Gerald to a state institution for a maximum of six years.

(Judgment reversed.)
Justice Stewart dissented.

In re Winship

397 U.S. 358, 90 S.Ct. 1068, 25 L.Ed. 2d 368 (1970)

New York defines a juvenile delinquent as a person over 7 and less than 16 years of age who does any act that if done by an adult would constitute a crime. A judge in the New York Family Court in an adjudication hearing found that a 12-year-old boy had entered and stolen $112 from a locker. This would constitute larceny if committed by an adult. The judge noted that there might not be proof to establish guilt beyond a reasonable doubt, but he rejected the contention that the Fourteenth Amendment required such a quantum of proof. The judge relied on New York law which provided any determination at the end of an adjudicatory hearing that a juvenile did the act or acts must be based on a preponderance of evidence. The United States Supreme Court noted jurisdiction.

Justice Brennan delivered the opinion of the Court:

The requirement that guilt of a criminal charge be established by proof beyond a reasonable doubt dates at least from our early years as a nation. The "demand for a higher degree of persuasion in criminal cases was recurrently expressed from ancient times, [though] its crystallization into the formula 'beyond a reasonable doubt' seems to have occurred as late as 1798. It is now accepted in common law jurisdictions as the measure of persuasion by which the prosecution must convince the trier of all the essential elements of guilt." ... Although virtually unanimous adherence to the reasonable doubt standard in common law jurisdictions may not conclusively establish it as a requirement of due process, such adherence does "reflect a profound judgment about the way in which law should be enforced and justice administered."

. . .

Expressions in many opinions of this Court indicate that it has long been assumed that proof of a criminal charge beyond a reasonable doubt is constitutionally required.

. . .

Moreover, use of the reasonable doubt standard is indispensable to command the respect and confidence of the community in applications of the criminal law. It is critical that the moral force of the criminal law not be diluted by a standard of proof that leaves people in doubt whether innocent men are being condemned. It is also important in our free society that every individual going about his ordinary affairs have confidence that his government cannot adjudge him guilty of a criminal offense without convincing a proper factfinder of his guilt with utmost certainty.

Lest there remain any doubt about the constitutional stature of the reasonable doubt standard, we explicitly hold that the Due Process Clause protects the accused against conviction except upon proof beyond a reasonable doubt of every fact necessary to constitute the crime with which he is charged.

We turn to the question whether juveniles, like adults, are constitutionally entitled to proof beyond a reasonable doubt when they are charged with violation of a criminal law. The same considerations that demand extreme caution in factfinding to protect the innocent adult apply as well to the innocent child. We do not find convincing the contrary arguments of the New York Court of Appeals. *Gault* rendered untenable much of the reasoning relied upon by that court to sustain the constitutionality of §744(b).

. . .

We conclude, as we concluded regarding the essential due process of safeguards applied in *Gault,* that the observance of the standard of proof beyond a reasonable doubt "will not compel the states to abandon or displace any of the substantive benefits of the juvenile process."

Finally, we reject the Court of Appeals' suggestion that there is, in any event, only a "tenuous difference" between the reasonable doubt and preponderance standards. The suggestion is singularly unpersuasive. In this very case, the trial judge's ability to distinguish between the two standards enabled him to make a finding of guilt that he conceded he might not have made under the standard of proof beyond a reasonable doubt. Indeed, the trial judge's action evidences the accuracy of the observation of commentators that "the preponderance test is susceptible to the misinterpretation that it calls on the trier of fact merely to perform an abstract weighing of the evidence in order to determine which side has produced the greater quantum, without regard to its effect in convincing his mind of the truth of the proposition asserted."

. . .

In sum, the constitutional safeguard of proof beyond a reasonable doubt is as much required during the adjudicatory stage of a delinquency proceeding as are those constitutional safeguards applied in *Gault*—notice of charges, right to counsel, the rights of confrontation and examination, and the privilege against self-incrimination. We therefore hold, in agreement with Chief Judge Fuld in dissent in the Court of Appeals, "that, where a 12-year-old child is charged with an act of stealing which renders him liable to confinement for as long as 6 years, then, as a matter of due process . . . the case against him must be proved beyond a reasonable doubt."

. . .

(Judgment reversed.)
(Justice Harlan concurred. Justices Burger, Stewart, and Black dissented.

McKeiver v *Pennsylvania*
403 U.S. 528, 91 S.Ct. 1976, 29 L.Ed. 2d 647 (1971)

(Case 322). McKeiver, age 16, was charged with robbery, larceny, and receiving stolen goods as acts of delinquency, such acts being felonies under Pennsylvania law for adults. Another boy, Terry, age 15, was charged with delinquent acts in the form of assault and battery on a police officer and conspiracy, such acts being misdemeanors under Pennsylvania law. They were tried in separate proceedings and both were found to be delinquent. Counsel for each requested and was denied a jury trial. The Pennsylvania Supreme Court permitted consolidation of both cases on appeal to determine whether there is a constitutional right to a jury trial in juvenile court. The state court answered in the negative and the United States Supreme Court noted jurisdiction.

(Case 128) A number of North Carolina children ranging from 11 to 15 years old were declared delinquent and placed on 2 years' probation. They were denied a request to have a jury trial and the public was excluded from the juvenile courtroom. The North Carolina Supreme Court affirmed and the United States Supreme Court granted certiorari. Cases 322 and 128 were heard together.

Justice Blackmun announced the judgments of the Court and an opinion in which the Chief Justice and Justices Stewart and White joined.

These cases present the narrow but precise issue whether the Due Process Clause of the Fourteenth Amendment assures the right to trial by jury in the adjudicative phase of a state juvenile court delinquency proceeding.

. . .

We must recognize as the Court has recognized before, that the fond and idealistic hopes of the juvenile court proponents and early reformers of three generations ago have not been realized. The devastating commentary upon the system's failures as a whole, contained in the President's Commission on Law Enforcement and Administration of Justice, Task Force Report: Juvenile Delinquency and Youth Crime 7–9 (1967), reveals the depth of disappointment in what has been accomplished. Too often the juvenile court judge falls far short of that stalwart, protective, and communicating figure the system envisaged. The community's unwillingness to provide people and facilities and to be concerned, the insufficiency of time devoted, the scarcity of professional help, the inadequacy of dispositional alternatives, and our general lack of knowledge all contribute to dissatisfaction with the experiment.

The Task Force Report, however, also said, *id.,* at 7, ''To say that juvenile courts have failed to achieve their goals is to say no more than what is true of criminal courts in the United States. But failure is most striking when hopes are highest.''

Despite all these disappointments, all these features, and all these shortcomings, we conclude that trial by jury in the juvenile court's adjudicative stage is not a constitutional requirement. We so conclude for a number of reasons:

1. The Court has refrained, in the cases heretofore decided, from taking the easy way with a flat holding that all rights constitutionally assured for the adult accused are to be imposed upon the state juvenile proceeding. . . .

2. There is a possibility, . . . that the jury trial, . . . will remake the juvenile proceeding into a fully adversary process.

. . .

4. The Court has specifically recognized by dictum that a jury is not a necessary part even of every criminal process that is fair and equitable. . . .

5. The imposition of the jury trial on the juvenile court system would not strengthen greatly, . . . the factfinding function

. . .

8. There is, of course, nothing to prevent a juvenile court judge, in a particular case where he feels the need, or when the need is demonstrated, from using an advisory jury.

9. The fact that a practice is followed by a large number of states is not conclusive in a decision as to whether that practice accords with due process.

. . .

10. Since *Gault* and since *Duncan* the great majority of states, . . . that have faced the issues have concluded that the considerations that led to the result in those two cases do not compel trial by jury in the juvenile court.

. . .

12. If the jury trial were to be injected into the juvenile court system as a matter of right, it would bring with it into that system the traditional delay, the formality, and the clamor of the adversary system and, possibly, the public trial.

. . .

13. Finally, the arguments advanced by the juveniles here are, of course, the identical arguments that underlie the demand for the jury trial for criminal proceedings. The arguments necessarily equate the juvenile proceeding—or at least the adjudicative phase of it—with the criminal trial. Whether they should be so equated is our issue. Concern about the inapplicability of exclusionary and other rules of evidence, about the juvenile court judge's possible awareness of the juvenile's prior record and of the contents of the social file, about repeated appearances of the same familiar witnesses in the persons of juvenile and probation officers and social workers—all to the effect that this will create the likelihood of prejudgment—chooses to ignore it seems to us, every aspect of fairness, of concern, of sympathy, and of paternal attention that the juvenile court system contemplates.

If the formalities of the criminal adjudicative process are to be superimposed upon the juvenile court system, there is little need for its separate existence.

Perhaps that ultimate disillusionment will come one day, but for the moment we are disinclined to give impetus to it.

(Judgment affirmed.)

Justice Harlan concurred because it is his belief that jury trials are not required in state criminal cases by either the Sixth Amendment or due process.

Justice Brennan concurred in the judgment of Case 322 but dissented in Case 128 because a juvenile is entitled to either a jury trial *or* a public trial, but not both.

Justices Douglas, Black, and Marshall dissented because they believed that the parties should be permitted a jury trial in both cases.

QUESTIONS

1. What due process rights are now afforded the juvenile? Will there be any addition to these rights in the future?

2. What is the doctrine of *parens patriae?* How did it develop?

14

PLEA BARGAINING

Plea bargaining, or negotiating a plea, is a process through which the prosecutor and defense attorney negotiate an agreeable handling of some aspect of a criminal trial such as acceptance of a guilty plea to a minor offense instead of a trial or a more serious charge or a plea to a lesser charge with a promise by the prosecutor to recommend to the judge that a light punishment be imposed. No matter how the negotiations occur, the pawn in the process is the defendant.

*Convictions by a plea of guilty in contrast to conviction by trial occurs very frequently in the criminal justice system. For example, in California in 1969, of the 28 percent of the felony arrests that resulted in conviction, approximately 21 percent were on pleas of guilty and 7 percent were by trial.[1] Persons accused of criminal conduct many times negotiate a guilty plea with the prosecutor for reasons beneficial to both parties. The most common form of plea bargaining—pleading guilty to a reduced charge—eliminates the need for an expensive, time-consuming trial and avoids complex issues such as admissibility of evidence. Moreover, a guilty plea assures conviction, whereas a trial by jury may raise some doubts in the minds of the triers-of-fact.[2]

---

*This chapter, to page 377, is from George T. Felkenes, "A Sociological Study of the Prosecutor's Office" (unpublished doctoral dissertation, University of California, Berkeley, 1971), pp. 74–88.

[1]California: Department of Justice, Bureau of Criminal Statistics, *Crime and Delinquency in California* (Sacramento: State Printer, 1969), pp. 17–22.

[2]Donald J. Newman, *Conviction: The Determination of Guilt or Innocence Without Trial* (Boston: Little Brown and Company, 1966), pp. 95–97.

	Drug Arrests			Nondrug Arrests		
	1967	*1968*	*1969*	*1967*	*1968*	*1969*
Yearly total	29,039	41,957	62,849	97,947	107,538	117,728
Total cases disposed of in Superior Court	10,250	13,636	23,819	32,126	34,563	38,143
Total cases convicted in Superior Court	7,492	10,237	18,666	27,229	30,218	31,904
Total cases convicted by plea	4,384	6,419	13,639	27,177	21,615	23,899
Total cases convicted by trial	3,108	3,818	5,027	7,052	8,603	8,005

A defendant's incentives to participate in plea bargaining are generally (1) reduction in the charge, (2) promise of a lenient sentence, (3) dismissal of other charges, or (4) avoidance of any stigmatic label attached to conviction of certain crimes (e.g., sexual psychopath).[3]

Extensive materials have been compiled on the subject of plea bargaining, the most comprehensive report probably being that of Donald Newman for the American Bar Association. His published results in book form (*Conviction: The Determination of Guilt or Innocence Without Trial*) comprehensively examine the plea negotiation process in Kansas, Michigan, and Wisconsin. It was his field study that prompted a series of questions concerning the negotiated guilty plea in this study.

From a practical viewpoint, the advantages of plea bargaining for the prosecutor are undeniable. This fact was recognized by 80 percent of the district attorneys who acknowledged that plea bargaining is justified.[4]

According to most of the district attorneys, plea bargaining is the most expeditious way of gaining convictions in a judicial process overburdened with cases and limited in resources. Only 2 of the 44 attorneys who justified plea bargaining did so because it could provide the defendant with a "break," thus taking into consideration any mitigating facts that the prosecution saw surrounding the crime, for example, whether or not the defendant was a "hard-core" or a marginal offender. (See Table 1.)

The four prosecutors who opposed the negotiated guilty plea expressed in rather strong language that they would have no part of it. They admitted that their

[3]*Ibid.*, p. 97.

[4]Some of the district attorneys distinguished between plea bargaining for felonies and for misdemeanors, stating that the former occurs many times on the arraignment date and the latter on the date of trial. It is assumed that the majority of the attorneys who did not make this distinction were speaking of felonies and misdemeanors collectively.

TABLE 1   Plea Bargaining Justified?

	Number	Percent
Yes	44	80.0
No	4	7.3
No response	7	12.7
Total	55	100.0

TABLE 2   Prevalence of Plea Bargaining

	Number	Percent
Very prevalent, almost every case	34	61.8
Very common	10	18.2
Very rare	1	1.8
No response	10	18.2
Total	55	100.0

consciences predominate over the pragmatic arguments, that they would not use it to clear court calendars, and that they only accept a plea when the defendant says he is actually guilty of that charge to which he is pleading. One district attorney put it this way:

> If someone has committed a crime, he should receive the proper punishment for that crime. I don't think that a defendant should receive a lighter sentence or plead guilty to a lesser crime merely because the courts are congested.

Another opponent denounced it on different grounds:

> It places the administration of justice in the same category as a couple of used-car salesmen buying and selling from one another. It is demeaning.

The prevalence of plea bargaining was verified by nearly two-thirds of the district attorneys who revealed that it occurred very frequently, or, as some said, "in almost every case." An additional 18.2 percent stated that its use was very common (Table 2). Only one prosecutor said that plea bargaining was very rare, and in the light of the contrary responses received especially from other district attorneys in his office it is doubtful that his perception was accurate.[5]

[5]Plea negotiation takes numerous forms and hopefully is used by both the prosecution and the defense to their advantage. The negotiation may be for the purpose of reducing the number of charges brought against the defendant or for lessening the severity of a particular charge. Promises regarding the kinds of sentences are also common, especially when it must be remembered that in all probability the defense attorney has a fairly strong opinion about the guilt of his client but is seeking the best "deal" in the form of sentencing. See Newman, pp. 78–90.

TABLE 3   Officials Involved in Plea Bargaining

	Number	Percent
District attorney, defense attorney, and judge to some extent	26	47.3
District attorney, defense attorney, judge, and police	10	18.2
District attorney and defense attorney	4	7.3
Defendant and others	2	3.6
Everyone	3	5.4
All other	2	3.6
No response	8	14.5
Total	55	99.9

Every respondent acknowledged that the normal participants in the plea bargaining process are the district attorney and the defense attorney. However, there was less agreement on the other parties involved. Almost two-thirds (65.5 percent) included the judge, in that he usually intervenes only to approve or disapprove the agreement reached by the attorneys. Also included by 18.2 percent of the district attorneys were the police, who, while not actually physically present during many bargaining sessions, were occasionally contacted—not so much for their opinion on whether the crime should be reduced, but simply for background facts that would help the attorney make the actual plea decision (Table 3).

The types of crimes most often subject to plea bargaining generally consist of crimes that are most easily reduced or should be reduced under certain circumstances. Most easily reduced are crime against property and minor violent offenses such as simple assault. These crimes, together with crimes that reflect the correctional needs of the defendant, specifically first-offender crimes, were mentioned by 32.7 percent of the district attorneys. Slightly fewer, 27.3 percent, thought that narcotic, marijuana, and drug offenses were reduced most often.[6] Far from identifying specific crimes, one out of five prosecutors believed that all crimes are equally subjected to plea bargaining. (See Table 4.)

When asked the converse question of the least subjected crimes, the district attorneys overwhelmingly (63.6 percent) selected crimes of violence, serious crimes, and capital offenses. Additionally, two individuals indicated that they were hesitant to engage in plea negotiation when the crimes involved a high

---

[6]In regard to narcotics offenses, it appears that the legislatures in particular are upset over the prevalence of charge or sentence reduction by their attempts to set mandatory sentences and specific crime classifications to such a common narcotics offense as possession of marijuana. Newman, pp. 99, 177–178; California: *Health and Safety Code* (1970), Sec. 11715.6. See also the case of *People* v *Temorio,* 89 Cal. Rptr. 249 (1970), in which the California Supreme Court declared Section 11718 of the *Health and Safety Code* unconstitutional. This section stated that in any proceeding under the narcotics division of the *Code,* no allegation of fact, which, if admitted to be true or found to be true, may be dismissed or stricken from the pleading except on the motion of the district attorney. This constituted an invasion of judicial power according to the California Supreme Court.

TABLE 4 *Crimes Most Often Subjected to Plea Bargaining*

	Number	Percent
First-offender crimes, minor felonies, nonviolent crimes, alternative felony–misdemeanors	18	32.7
Narcotics offenses, marijuana, dangerous drugs	15	27.3
All crimes, none more than any other	11	20.0
Homicide	5	9.1
All other	3	5.4
No responses	3	5.4
Total	55	99.9

TABLE 5 *Crimes Least Often Subjected to Plea Bargaining*

	Number	Percent
Crimes of violence, serious crimes, capital crimes	35	63.6
None in particular	4	7.4
Trivial crimes	2	3.6
Crimes with a high degree of publicity	2	3.6
All other	5	9.1
No response	7	12.7
Total	55	100.0

degree of publicity. This may reflect a common attitude, but one which most attorneys are reluctant to admit. (See Table 5.)

If plea bargaining is to take place, it is beneficial to both parties in terms of costs and effort for the bargaining to occur at the earliest practical time in the proceedings. Practicality for the prosecution would entail sufficient time to assume that a good case can be developed and practicality for the defense would entail enough time to study the case to assume that the bargaining is the best arrangement for the client. For this reason, it is apparent that plea bargaining occurs most often before the trial begins. The district attorneys' responses were not specific enough to establish at what particular stage of the proceedings plea bargaining usually occurs. Almost half (49.1 percent) stated that it occurs prior to trial or at the earliest stage of proceedings. In contrast, nearly one-third placed it on the day of the trial or just before the trial,[7] with one attorney stating that the most common time for plea bargaining was when the "counselors were approaching the counsel table prior to jury selection." (See Table 6.)

---

[7]It would appear that the practice of plea bargaining taking place on the day of the trial or just before it begins is largely a jurisdictional policy within specific counties. During an interview with the training officer in each county the comment was made that Los Angeles, Orange, and Ventura counties negotiate up to the time of trial, whereas most of the other county district attorney offices negotiate up to the time the formal charges are made or prior to the time specifically set for trial.

TABLE 6   Stages of the Court Proceeding Where Plea Bargaining Most Often Occurs

	Number	Percent
Prior to trial, earliest stage of proceedings	27	49.1
Day of trial	18	32.7
Any time	1	1.8
No response	9	16.4
Total	55	100.0

More specific responses were received when a question was asked about the stages in which plea bargaining least occurs. Ten of the attorneys gave the expected response that plea bargaining occurred least often after the start of the trial, a major reason for plea bargaining being to prevent an expensive and lengthy trial when both the prosecutor and defense attorneys feel that a trial might not be in the best interests of the defendant. Other specific responses reflect the different procedures followed in the three counties studied. Because of the fact that one county attempted to screen its cases before the preliminary hearing and thus allow only the most substantial and solid ones to advance to the arraignment stage, these district attorneys mentioned that plea bargaining occurred least before arraignment (by inference it occurs most before the preliminary hearing). The other counties do just the reverse: They screen their cases after the preliminary hearing. Thus these attorneys (30.9 percent) said it least occurs before the preliminary hearing. (See Table 7.)

Plea bargaining takes place in various settings. In many cases it occurs in the courtroom in formal conversations between the prosecutors and the defense attorneys. Other times it occurs elsewhere (See Table 9). When the attorneys were asked how often plea bargaining occurs outside the courtroom, their answers were far from unanimous. (See Table 8.) Slightly less than one-quarter

TABLE 7   Stages of the Court Proceedings in Which Plea Bargaining Least Often Occurs

	Number	Percent
Before preliminary hearing	17	30.9
After trial begins	10	18.2
Any time	4	7.3
At time of filing	3	5.4
Before arraignment	3	5.4
All other	4	7.3
No response	14	25.5
Total	55	100.0

TABLE 8   *Plea Bargaining Conducted Outside the Courtroom*

	Number	Percent
Always	3	5.4
Frequently (50 percent or more of the cases)	9	16.4
Occasionally (20 percent of the cases)	7	12.7
Rarely (fewer than 20 percent of the cases)	13	23.6
Other	3	5.4
No response	20	36.4
Total	55	99.9

(23.6 percent) thought that it almost always takes place in the courtroom, mentioning that it usually transpires either before the trial convenes, during the lull periods, or during recesses. On the other hand, slightly less than one-quarter (21.8 percent) said that extracourtroom bargaining happens always or frequently. Part of this disparity may be because of the failure to define the phrase "outside the courtroom," for there was some confusion over its meaning. Another possibility is that some district attorney offices and/or individual district attorneys may by willful choice or habit prefer to conduct the bargaining at different locations. Furthermore, since it is usually the defense attorney who initiates the question of bargaining, he may be the one who determines where the session takes place.

When plea bargaining is conducted outside the courtroom setting, the most frequently mentioned alternative was the district attorney's office (Table 9). The next most frequent places, each representing 9.1 percent, were the hallway outside the courtroom, telephonic communications between the attorney's offices, and the judge's chambers. (Table 9).

The final question asked concerning plea bargaining was: "What factors determine the success or failure of a bargaining session?" Unfortunately, over half of the district attorneys gave rather vague responses to this question such as the "strengths and weaknesses of the case" and "how much each attorney wishes to

TABLE 9   *Usual Setting for Extracourtroom Plea Bargaining*

	Number	Percent
District attorney's office	16	29.1
Hallway outside courtroom	5	9.1
Telephone (public, office, and private)	5	9.1
Judge's chambers	5	9.1
Any private place (restaurants, bar meetings, social gatherings, etc.)	4	7.3
No response, unknown	20	36.4
Total	55	100.1*

*Because of rounding of figures, total does not equal 100.0.

TABLE 10 *Factors Determining the Success or Failure of a Plea Bargaining Session*

	Number	Percent
Strength and weaknesses of the case; how much each attorney wishes to give up; the preponderance of evidence against the defendant	30	54.5
Nature of offense	8	14.5
Previous record of defendant	6	10.9
All other	6	10.9
No response	5	9.1
Total	55	99.9

give up." According to 14.5 percent of the respondents, the nature of the offense controlled the success or failure of the sessions while another 10.9 percent thought that the determining factor was the previous record of the defendant. Interestingly, two prosecutors gave as partial responses the perceived attitudes of the judge and the attorney's own supervisor (Table 10).

Brady v *United States*
397 U.S. 742, 90 S.Ct. 1463, 25 L.Ed. 2d 747 (1970)

Brady was charged with kidnapping in violation of federal law. The victim was injured when released. Therefore, under the federal statute Brady faced death if recommended by the jury. First, Brady pleaded not guilty when represented by counsel. The trial judge would not permit the case to be tried without a jury and Brady apparently made no serious attempt to reduce the possibility of the death penalty by waiving a jury trial. Brady next tried to change his plea to guilty upon learning that his codefendant planned to plead guilty and testify against him. The trial judge accepted Brady's guilty plea after carefully finding that it was voluntary. Brady was then sentenced to imprisonment for 50 years. He next sought relief claiming that his guilty plea was involuntary because the federal statute in effect coerced him to plead guilty because of the fear of the death penalty, because his attorney exerted impermissible pressure on him, and because his guilty plea was reduced by representations with respect to reduction of sentence and clemency. Relief was denied in the state and federal courts. The United States Supreme Court granted certiorari.

Justice White delivered the opinion of the Court:

Plainly, it seems to us, (*U.S.* v) *Jackson* ruled neither that all pleas of guilty encouraged by the fear of a possible death sentence are involuntary pleas nor that such encouraged pleas are invalid whether involuntary or not. *Jackson* prohibited the imposition of the death penalty under §1201(a), but that decision neither fashioned a new standard for judging the validity of guilty pleas nor mandates a new application of the test theretofore fashioned by courts and since reiterated that guilty pleas are valid if both "voluntary" and "intelligent."

. . .

That a guilty plea is a grave and solemn act to be accepted only with care and discernment has long been recognized. Central to the plea and the foundation for entering judgment against the defendant is the defendant's admission in open court that he committed the acts charged in the indictment. He thus stands as a witness against himself and he is shielded by the Fifth Amendment from being compelled to do so—hence the minimum requirement that his plea be the voluntary expression of his own choice. But the plea is more than an admission of past conduct; it is the defendant's consent that judgment of conviction may be entered without a trial—a waiver of his right to trial before a jury or a judge. Waivers of constitutional rights not only must be voluntary but must be knowing, intelligent acts done with sufficient awareness of the relevant circumstances and likely consequences. On neither score was Brady's plea of guilty invalid.

The trial judge in 1959 found the plea voluntary before accepting it; the District Court in 1968, after an evidentiary hearing, found that the plea was voluntarily made; the Court of Appeals specifically approved the finding of voluntariness. We see no reason on this record to disturb the judgment of those courts. Petitioner, advised by competent counsel, tendered his plea after his codefendant, who had already given a confession, determined to plead guilty and became available to testify against petitioner. It was this development that the District Court found to have triggered Brady's guilty plea.

The state to some degree encourages pleas of guilty at every important step in the criminal process. For some people, their breach of a state's law is alone sufficient reason for surrendering themselves and accepting punishment. For others, apprehension and charge, both threatening acts by the government, jar them into admitting their guilt. In still other cases, the postindictment accumulation of evidence may convince the defendant and his counsel that a trial is not worth the agony and expense to the defendant and his family. All these pleas of guilty are valid in spite of the state's responsibility for some of the factors motivating the pleas; the pleas are no more improperly compelled than is the decision by a defendant at the close of the state's evidence at trial that he must take the stand or face certain conviction.

The issue we deal with is inherent in the criminal law and its administration because guilty pleas are not constitutionally forbidden, because the criminal law characteristically extends to judge or jury a range of choice in setting the sentence in individual cases, and because both the state and the defendant often find it advantageous to preclude the possibility of the maximum penalty authorized by law.

. . .

The record before us also supports the conclusion that Brady's plea was intelligently made. He was advised by competent counsel, he was made aware of the nature of the charge against him, and there was nothing to indicate that he was incompetent or otherwise not in control of his mental faculties; once his confederate had pleaded guilty and became available to testify, he chose to plead guilty, perhaps to ensure that he would face no more than life imprisonment or a term of years. Brady was aware of precisely what he was doing when he admitted that he had kidnapped the victim and had not released her unharmed.

Often the decision to plead guilty is heavily influenced by the defendant's appraisal of the prosecution's case against him and by the apparent likelihood of securing leniency should a guilty plea be offered and accepted.

. . .

Although Brady's plea of guilty may well have been motivated in part by a desire to avoid a possible death penalty, we are convinced that his plea was voluntarily and intelligently made and we have no reason to doubt that his solemn admission of guilt was truthful.

(Judgment affirmed.)
Justice Black concurred.

North Carolina v *Alford*
400 U.S. 25, 91 S.Ct. 160, 27 L.Ed. 2d 162 (1970)

Alford was indicted for first degree murder. All witnesses but one who could substantiate his claim of innocence claimed he was guilty. Alford's attorney left the choice up to Alford, but because there was no substantial evidence of innocence, he recommended a guilty plea. The prosecutor accepted the guilty plea to a reduced charge of murder in the second degree. The trial court heard damaging evidence before accepting the guilty plea. Alford pleaded guilty because of the threat of the death penalty and was sentenced to 30 years' imprisonment. After Alford was convicted, the Court of Appeals, on appeal from a denial of a writ of habeas corpus, found Alford's plea involuntary and reversed the conviction. The United States Supreme Court vacated the Court of Appeals' judgment.

We held in *Brady* v *United States,* 397 U.S. 742, . . . , that a plea of guilty which would not have been entered except for the defendant's desire to avoid a possible death penalty and to limit the maximum penalty to life imprisonment or a term of years was not for that reason compelled within the meaning of the Fifth Amendment. *Jackson* established no new test for determining the validity of guilty pleas. The standard was and remains whether the plea represents a voluntary and intelligent choice among the alternative courses of action open to the defendants. . . . That he would not have pleaded except for the opportunity to limit the possible penalty does not necessarily demonstrate that the plea of guilty was not the product of a free and rational choice, especially where the defendant was represented by competent counsel whose advice was that the plea would be to the defendant's advantage. The standard fashioned and applied by the Court of Appeals was therefore erroneous and we would, without more, vacate and remand the case for further proceedings with respect to any other claims of Alford which are properly before that court, if it were not for other circumstances appearing in the record which might seem to warrant an affirmance of the Court of Appeals.

State and lower federal courts are divided upon whether a guilty plea can be accepted when it is accompanied by protestations of innocence and hence contains only a waiver of trial but no admission of guilt. Some courts, giving expression to the principle that "[o]ur law only authorizes a conviction where guilt is shown," . . . require that trial judges reject such pleas. . . . But others have concluded that they should not "force any defense on a defendant in a criminal case," particularly where advancement of the defense might "end in disaster." . . . They have argued that, since "guilt, or the degree of guilt, is at times uncertain and elusive," "[a]n accused, though believing in or entertaining doubts respecting his innocence, might reasonably conclude a jury would be convinced of his guilt and that he would fare better in the sentence by pleading guilty."

. . .

These cases would be directly in point if Alford had simply insisted on his plea but refused to admit the crime. The fact that his plea was denominated a plea of guilty rather than a plea of *nolo contendere* is of no constitutional significance with respect to the issue now before us, for the Constitution is concerned with the practical consequences, not the formal categorizations, of state law.

. . .

Relying on *United States* v *Jackson, supra,* Alford now argues in effect that the state should not have allowed him this choice but should have insisted on proving him guilty of murder in the first degree. The states in their wisdom may take this course by statute or otherwise and may prohibit the practice of accepting pleas to lesser included offenses under any circumstances. But this is not the mandate of the Fourteenth Amendment and the Bill of Rights. The prohibitions against involuntary or unintelligent pleas should not be relaxed, but neither should an exercise in arid logic render those constitutional guarantees counterproductive and put in jeopardy the very human values they were meant to preserve.

(Judgment reversed.)
Justice Black concurred.
Justice Brennan, with whom Justices Douglas and Marshall joined, dissented.

I adhere to the view that, in any given case the influence of such an unconstitution threat "must necessarily be given weight in determining the voluntariness of a plea." . . . And, without reaching the question whether due process permits the entry of judgment upon a plea of guilty accompanied by a contemporaneous denial of acts constituting the crime, I believe that at the very least such a denial of guilt is also a relevant factor in determining whether the plea was voluntarily and intelligently made. With these factors in mind, it is sufficient in my view to state that the facts set out in the majority opinion demonstrate that Alford was ''so gripped by fear of the death penalty'' that his decision to plead guilty was not voluntary but was ''the product of duress as much so as choice reflecting physical constraint.'' Accordingly, I would affirm the judgment of the Court of Appeals.

Santobello v *New York*
404 U.S. 257, 92 S.Ct. 495, 30 L.Ed. 2d 427 (1971)

Santobello was indicted on two felony counts of gambling. He first entered a not guilty plea on both counts. After negotiating, the state prosecutor agreed to permit Santobello to plead guilty to a lesser included offense which carried a maximum prison sentence of one year. The prosecutor agreed to make no recommendation on the sentence. At Santobello's sentencing hearing several months later a new prosecutor recommended that the maximum one-year sentence be imposed. Santobello then moved unsuccessfully to withdraw his guilty plea. The judge stated that he was bound by any agreement and imposed the maximum one-year sentence. The United States Supreme Court granted certiorari.

Justice Burger delivered the opinion of the Court:

The record represents another example of an unfortunate lapse in orderly prosecutorial procedures, in part, no doubt, because of the enormous increase in the workload of the often understaffed prosecutor's offices. The heavy workload may well explain these episodes, but it does not excuse them. The disposition of criminal charges by agreement between the prosecutor and the accused, sometimes loosely called ''plea bargaining,'' is an essential component of the administration of justice. Properly administered, it is to be encouraged. If every criminal charge were subjected to a full-scale trial, the states and the federal government would need to multiply by many times the number of judges and court facilities.

Disposition of charges after plea discussions is not only an essential part of the process but a highly desirable part for many reasons. It leads to prompt and largely final disposition of most criminal cases; it avoids much of the corrosive impact of enforced idleness during pretrial confinement for those who are denied release pending trial; it protects the public from those accused persons who are prone to continue criminal conduct even while on pretrial release; and, by shortening the time between charge and disposition, it enhances whatever may be the rehabilitative prospects of the guilty when they are ultimately imprisoned.

. . .

However, all of these considerations presuppose fairness in securing agreement between an accused and a prosecutor. It is now clear, for example, that the accused pleading guilty must be counseled, absent a waiver. . . . Fed. Rule Crim. Proc. 11, governing pleas in federal courts, now makes clear that the sentencing judge must develop, *on the record,* the factual basis for the plea, as, for example, by having the accused describe the conduct that gave rise to the charge. The plea must, of course, be voluntary and knowing and if it was induced by promises, the essence of those promises must in some way be made known. There is, of course, no absolute right to have a guilty plea accepted. . . . A court may reject a plea in exercise of sound judicial discretion.

This phase of the process of criminal justice, and the adjudicative element inherent in accepting a plea of guilty, must be attended by safeguards to ensure the defendant what is reasonably due in the circumstances. Those circumstances will vary, but a constant factor is that when a plea rests in any significant degree on a promise or agreement of the prosecutor, so that it can be said to be part of the inducement or consideration, such promise must be fulfilled.

On this record, petitioner "bargained" and negotiated for a particular plea in order to secure dismissal of more serious charges, but also on condition that no sentence recommendation would be made by the prosecutor. It is now conceded that the promise to abstain from a recommendation was made, and at this stage the prosecution is not in a good position to argue that its inadvertent breach of agreement is immaterial. The staff lawyers in a prosecutor's office have the burden of "letting the left hand know what the right hand is doing" or has done. That the breach of agreement was inadvertent does not lessen its impact.

We need not reach the question whether the sentencing judge would or would not have been influenced had he known all the details of the negotiations for the plea. He stated that the prosecutor's recommendation did not influence him and we have no reason to doubt that. Nevertheless, we conclude that the interests of justice and appropriate recognition of the duties of the prosecution in relation to promises made in the negotiation of pleas of guilty will be best served by remanding the case to the state courts for further consideration. The ultimate relief to which petitioner is entitled we leave to the discretion of the state court, which is in a better position to decide whether the circumstances of this case require only that there be specific performance of the agreement on the plea, in which case petitioner should be resentenced by a different judge, or whether, in the view of the state court, the circumstances require granting the relief sought by petitioner, i.e., the opportunity to withdraw his plea of guilty. We emphasize that this is in no sense to question the fairness of the sentencing judge; the fault here rests on the prosecutor, not on the sentencing judge.

(Judgment reversed and remanded.)
Justice Douglas concurred.

QUESTIONS

1. How is plea bargaining helpful to care flow? Is plea bargaining a good practice?

2. What effect have the cases discussed in this chapter had on plea bargaining?

3. In the future will there be an increase or a decrease in the number of cases plea bargained?

15

CORRECTIONS

Corrections and the Criminal Justice System*

Pressures for change in the American correctional system are building so fast that even the most complacent are finding them impossible to ignore. The pressures come not only from prisoners but also from the press, the courts, the rest of the criminal justice system, and even practicing correctional personnel.

During the past decade conditions in several prison systems have been found by the courts to constitute cruel and unusual punishment in violation of the Constitution. In its 1971–1972 term the United States Supreme Court decided eight cases directly affecting offenders, and in each of the cases the offender's contention prevailed.

The riots and other disturbances that continue to occur in the nation's prisons and jails confirm the feeling of thoughtful citizens that such institutions contribute little to the national effort to reduce crime. Some maintain that time spent in prisons is in fact counterproductive.

It is clear that a dramatic realignment of correctional methods is called for. It is essential to abate the use of institutions. Meanwhile, much can be done to eliminate the worst effects of the institution—its crippling idleness, anonymous

*This material and that of the following sections are freely extracted from *Corrections, National Advisory Commission on Criminal Justice Standards and Goals* (Washington, D.C.: Government Printing Office, 1973), pp. 1–14. Footnotes have been omitted.

brutality, and destructive impact. Insofar as the institution has to be relied on, it must be small enough, so located, and so operated that it can relate to the problems offenders pose for themselves and the community.

These changes must not be made out of sympathy for the criminal or disregard of the threat of crime to society. They must be made precisely because that threat is too serious to be countered by ineffective methods.

Many arguments for correctional programs that deal with offenders in the community—probation, parole, and others—meet the test of common sense on their own merits. Such arguments are greatly strengthened by the failing record of prisons, reformatories, and the like. The mega-institution, holding more than a thousand adult inmates, has been built in larger number and variety in this country than anywhere else in the world. Large institutions for young offenders have also proliferated here. In such surroundings inmates become faceless people living out routine and meaningless lives. And when institutions are racially skewed and filled with a disproportionate number of ill-educated and vocationally inept persons, they magnify tensions already existing in our society.

The failure of major institutions to reduce crime is incontestable. Recidivism rates are notoriously high. Institutions do succeed in punishing, but they do not deter. They protect the community but that protection is only temporary. They relieve the community of responsibility by removing the offender, but they make successful reintegration into the community unlikely. They change the committed offender, but the change is more likely to be negative than positive.

It is no surprise that institutions have not been successful in reducing crime. The mystery is that they have not contributed even more to the increase of crime. Correctional history has clearly demonstrated that tinkering with the system by changing specific program areas without attention to the larger problems can achieve only incidental and haphazard improvement.

Today's practitioners are forced to use the means of an older time. And dissatisfaction with correctional programs is related to the permanence of yesterday's institutions. We are saddled with the physical remains of last century's prisons and with an ideological legacy that has implicitly accepted the objectives of isolation, control, and punishment, as evidenced by correctional operations, policies, and programs.

Corrections must seek ways to become more attuned to its role of reducing criminal behavior. Changing corrections' role from one of merely housing society's rejects to one of sharing responsibility for their reintegration requires a major commitment on the part of correctional personnel and the rest of the criminal justice system.

Behind these clear imperatives lies the achievable principle of a much greater selectivity and sophistication in the use of crime control and correctional methods. These great powers should be reserved for controlling persons who seriously threaten others. They should not be applied to the nuisances, the troublesome, and the rejected who now clutter our prisons and reformatories and fill our jails and youth detention facilities.

The criminal justice system should become the agency of last resort for social problems. The institution should be the last resort for correctional problems.

Of primary importance as the pressures for change gain force are definition of corrections' goals and objectives, articulation of standards to measure achievement, and establishment of bench marks to judge progress. That is the purpose of this report on corrections.

Corrections in the Criminal Justice System

A substantial obstacle to development of effective corrections is its relationship to the police and the courts—the other subsystems in criminal justice. Corrections inherits any inefficiency, inequity, and improper discrimination that may have occurred in any earlier step of the criminal justice process. Its clients come to it from the other subsystems; it is the consistent heir to their defects.

The contemporary view is to consider society's institutionalized response to crime as the criminal justice system and its activities as the criminal justice process. This model envisions interdependent and interrelated agencies and programs that will provide a coordinated and consistent response to crime. The model, however, remains a model—it does not exist in fact. Although cooperation between the various components has improved noticeably in some localities, it cannot be said that a criminal justice "system" really exists.

Even under the model, each element of the system would have a specialized function to perform. The modern systems concept recognizes, however, that none of the elements can perform its tasks without directly affecting the efforts of the others. Thus, while each component must continue to concentrate on improving the performance of its specialized function, it also must be aware of its interrelationships with the other components. Similarly, when functions overlap, each component must be willing to appreciate and utilize the expertise of the others.

The interrelationships of the various elements must be understood in the context of the purposes for which the system is designed. It is generally agreed that the major goal of criminal law administration is to reduce crime by using procedures consistent with the protection of individual liberty. There is less agreement on the specific means of achieving that goal and the relative priority when one set of means conflicts with another.

For example, the criminal justice system must act in relation to two sets of individuals—those who commit crimes and those who do not. Sanctions thought to deter potential lawbreakers may be destructive to offenders actually convicted. Long sentences of confinement in maximum security penitentiaries once were thought to deter other individuals from committing criminal offenses. It is now recognized that long periods of imprisonment not only breed hostility and resentment, but they also make it more difficult for the offender to avoid further law violations. Long sentences also fuel the tension within prisons and make constructive programs there more difficult. Thus, whatever weight may be given to the deterrent effect of a long prison sentence, the benefits are outweighed by the suffering and alienation of committed offenders beyond any hope of rehabilitation or reintegration.

Offenders, perhaps long before the reformers, viewed the criminal justice apparatus as a system. The "they-versus-us" attitude is symptomatic of their feeling that police, courts, and corrections all represent society. Thus, it is critically important that all elements of the system follow procedures that ensure that offenders are, and believe themselves to be, treated fairly, if corrections is to release individuals who will not return to crime.

Corrections and the Police. The police and corrections are the two elements of the criminal justice system that are farthest apart, both in the sequence of their opinions and, very often, in their attitudes toward crime and criminal offenders. Yet police and corrections serve critical functions in society's response to crime. And cooperation between police and correctional personnel is essential if the criminal justice system is to operate effectively.

Because of their law enforcement and order maintenance roles, police often take the view that shutting up an offender is an excellent, if temporary, answer to a "police problem." The police view the community at large as their responsibility, and removal of known offenders from it shifts the problem to someone else's shoulders.

Police are more intimately involved than correctional staff are with a specific criminal offense. Police officers often spend more time with the victim than with the offender. They are subjected to and influenced by the emotional reactions of the community. It is thus understandable that police may reflect, and be more receptive to, concepts of retribution and incapacitation rather than rehabilitation and reintegration as objectives of corrections.

Correctional personnel more often take a longer view. They seldom are confronted with the victim and the emotions surrounding him. While the police can hope for, and often achieve, a short-range objective—the arrest of a criminal— the correctional staff can only hope for success in the long run. Corrections seeks to assure that an offender will not commit crimes in the future.

Corrections with its long-range perspective is required, if not always willing, to take short-run risks. The release of an offender into the community always contains some risks, whether it is at the end of his sentence or at some time before. These risks, although worth taking from the long-range perspective, are sometimes unacceptable to the police in the short run.

For the most part, the released offenders whom police encounter are those who have turned out to be bad risks. As a result, the police acquire an imprecise and inaccurate view of the risks that correctional officials take. Because correctional failures—the parole or probation violator, the individual who fails to return from a furlough—add a burden to the already overtaxed police resources, misunderstanding increases between police and corrections.

If many of the standards proposed in this report are adopted, the police will perhaps take an even dimmer view of correctional adequacy. If local jails and other misdemeanant institutions are brought within the correctional system and removed from police jurisdiction, corrections will bear the responsibility for a substantially larger number of problems that would otherwise fall to the police. Similarly, as additional techniques are implemented that divert more apparently salvageable offenders out of the criminal justice system at an early stage, those offenders who remain within the system will be the most dangerous and the poorest risks. Obviously, a higher percentage of these offenders are likely to fail in their readjustment to society.

The impact of police practices on corrections, although not so dramatic and tangible as the effects of correctional risk taking on the police, nonetheless is important and often critical to the correctional system's ability to perform its functions properly. For most offenders the policeman is the first point of contact with the law. He is the initiator of the relationship between the offender and the criminal justice system. He is also the ambassador and representative of the society that system serves. To the extent that the offender's attitude toward society and its institutions will affect his willingness to respect society's laws, the police in their initial and continued contact with an offender may have substantial influence on the offender's future behavior.

It is widely recognized that the police make a number of policy decisions. Obviously, they do not arrest everyone found violating the criminal law. Police exercise broad discretion in the decision to arrest, and the exercise of that discretion determines to a large extent the clientele of the correctional system. In fact, police arrest decisions may have a greater impact on the nature of the correctional clientele than do the legislative decisions delineating what kinds of conduct are criminal.

Police decisions to concentrate on particular types of offenses will directly affect correctional programming. A large number of arrests for offenses that do not involve a significant danger to the community may result in misallocation and improper distribution of scarce correctional resources. The correctional system may be ill-prepared to cope with a larger than normal influx of certain types of offenders.

The existence of broad, all-encompassing criminal statutes, including dangerous, nondangerous, and merely annoying offenders, assures broad police arrest discretion. Real or imagined discrimination against racial minorities, youth, or other groups breeds hostility and resentment against the police, which inevitably is reflected when these individuals enter the correctional system.

Carefully developed, written criteria for the use of police discretion in making arrests of criminal offenders would relieve the current uncertainties and misunderstandings between police and correctional personnel. If the goals and purposes of the police in making these decisions are publicized, correctional staff should be able to work more effectively with police departments in arriving at meaningful standards and policies.

Similarly, community-based correctional programs cannot hope to be success-ful without police understanding and cooperation. Offenders in these programs are likely to come in contact with the police. The nature of the contact and the police response may directly affect an offender's adjustment.

Police understandably keep close surveillance on released felons, since they are a more easily identifiable risk than the average citizen. When police make a practice of checking ex-offenders first whenever a crime is committed, the ex-offenders may begin to feel that the presumption of innocence has been altered to a presumption of guilt.

When a felon returning to a community is required to register with the police and his name and address are published in police journals, his difficulties in readjusting to community life are compounded. Mass roundups of ex-offenders or continued street surveillance have limited or questionable advantages for the police and significant disadvantages for correctional programs.

When evidence suggests that an ex-offender is involved in criminal activity, the police obviously must take action. However, the police should recognize that the nature of their contact with ex-offenders, as with citizens in general, is critically important in developing respect for law and legal institutions. To con-duct contacts with the least possible notoriety and embarrassment is good police practice and a help to corrections as well.

It should also be noted that the police can make affirmative contributions to the success of community-based programs. The police officer knows his community; he knows where resources useful for the offender are available; he knows the pitfalls that may tempt the offender. The police officer is himself a valuable community resource that should be available for correctional programs. This, of course, requires the police to take a view of their function as one of preventing future crime as well as enforcing the law and maintaining public order.

Bringing about a better working relationship between the police and correc-tions will not be an easy task. Progress can be made only if both recognize that they are performing mutually supportive, not conflicting, functions. Corrections has been lax in explaining the purposes of its programs to the police. Today, corrections is beginning to realize that much of its isolation in the criminal justice system has been self-imposed. Closer working relationships are developed through mutual understanding, and both police and corrections should im-mediately increase their efforts in this regard. Recruit and in-service training programs for each group should contain discussions of the other's programs. Police should designate certain officers to maintain liaison between correctional agencies and law enforcement in order to help to assure better police–corrections coordination. The problems and recommendations discussed in this section are addressed by the National Advisory Commission on Criminal Justice Standards and Goals in its report on the police. Standards set out in that report's chapter on criminal justice relations, if fully implemented, would materially enhance the working relationships between police and corrections.

Corrections and the Courts.   The court has a dual role in the criminal justice system: It is both a participant in the criminal justice process and the supervisor of its practices. As participant, the court and its officers determine guilt or innocence and impose sanctions. In many jurisdictions the court also serves as a correctional agency by administering the probation system.

In addition to being a participant, the court plays another important role. When practices of the criminal justice system conflict with other values in society, the courts must determine which takes precedence over the other.

In recent years the courts have increasingly found that values reflected in the Constitution take precedence over efficient administration of correctional programs. Some difficulties currently encountered in the relationship between corrections and the courts result primarily from the dual role that courts must play.

The relationship between courts and corrections is clearly understood by both parties when the court is viewed as a participant in the administration of the criminal law. Correctional officers and sentencing judges recognize each other's viewpoints, although they may not always agree. Those practices of the courts that affect corrections adversely are recognized by the courts themselves as areas needing reform.

Both recognize that sentencing decisions by the courts affect the discretion of correctional administrators in applying correctional programs. Sentencing courts generally have accepted the concept of the indeterminate sentence, which grants correctional administrators broad discretion in individualizing programs for particular offenders.

There is growing recognition that disparity in sentencing limits corrections' ability to develop sound attitudes in offenders. The man who is serving a 10-year sentence for the same act for which a fellow prisoner is serving a 3-year sentence is not likely to be receptive to correctional programs. He is, in fact, unlikely to respect any of society's institutions. Some courts have attempted to solve the problem of disparity in sentencing through the use of sentencing councils and other devices. Appellate review of sentencing would further diminish the possiblity of disparity.

The appropriateness of the sentence imposed by the court will determine in large measure the effectiveness of the correctional program. This report recognizes that prison confinement is an inappropriate sanction for the vast majority of criminal offenders. Use of probation and other community-based programs will continue to grow. The essential ingredient in the integration of courts and corrections into a compatible system of criminal justice is the free flow of information on sentencing and its effect on individual offenders.

The traditional attitude of the sentencing judge was that his responsibility ended with the imposition of sentence. Many criminal court judges, often with great personal uneasiness, sentenced offenders to confinement without fully recognizing what would occur after sentence was imposed. In recent years, primarily because of the growing number of lawsuits by prisoners, courts have become increasingly aware of the conditions of prison confinement. Continuing judicial supervision of correctional practices to assure that the program applied is consistent with the court's sentence should result in increased interaction between courts and corrections.

Correctional personnel must recognize that they are to some extent officers of the court. They are carrying out a court order and, like other court officers, are subject to the court's continuing supervision. Corrections has little to lose by this development and may gain a powerful new force for correctional reform.

Legal Rights, the Courts, and Corrections. The United States has a strong and abiding attachment to the rule of law, with a rich inheritance of a government of law rather than men. This high regard for the rule of law has been applied extensively in the criminal justice system up to the point of conviction. But beyond conviction, until recently, largely unsupervised and arbitrary discretion held sway. This was true of sentencing, for which criteria were absent and from which appeals were both rare and difficult. It was true of the discretion exercised by the institutional administrator concerning prison conditions and disciplinary sanctions. It applied to the exercise by the parole board of discretion to release and revoke.

Within the last decade, however, the movement to bring the law, judges, and lawyers into relationships with the correctional system has grown apace. The Commission welcomes this development, and many of the standards and goals prescribed in this report rely heavily on increasing substantive and procedural due process in the authoritative exercise of correctional discretion. Since this is a contentious issue, introductory comments may be appropriate.

The American Law Institute took legal initiative in the criminal justice field in drafting the Model Penal Code, which has stimulated widespread recodifications of substantive criminal law at the federal and state levels. An important subsequent step was the extension of legal aid to the indigent accused, a development achieved by a series of Supreme Court decisions, by the Criminal Justice Act of 1964, and by similar state legislation. This move brought more lawyers of skill and sensitivity into contact with the criminal justice system. Then the remarkable project on Minimum Standards for Criminal Justice, pursued over many years to completion by the American Bar Association, began to have a similar widespread influence.

But for the correctional system, historically and repeatedly wracked by riot and rebellion, the most dramatic impact has been made by the courts' abandonment of their hands-off doctrine in relation to the exercise of discretion by correctional administrators and parole boards.

It was inevitable that the correctional immunity from constitutional requirements should end. The Constitution does not exempt prisoners from its protections. As courts began to examine many social institutions from schools to welfare agencies, prisons and other correctional programs naturally were considered. Once the courts agreed to review correctional decisions, it was predictable that an increasing number of offenders would ask the court for relief. The courts' willingness to become involved in prison administration resulted from intolerable conditions within the prisons.

Over the past decade in particular a new and politically important professional group, the lawyers, has, in effect, been added to corrections, and it is not likely to go away. The Supreme Court of the United States has manifested its powerful concern that correctional processes avoid the infliction of needless suffering and achieve standards of decency and efficiency of which the community need not be ashamed and by which it will be better protected. Stimulated by the initiative of Chief Justice Burger, the American Bar Association has embarked on an ambitious series of programs to involve lawyers in correctional processes, both in institutions and in the community.

Federal and state legislatures have increasingly concerned themselves with correctional codes and other correctional legislation. The National Council on Crime and Delinquency in 1972 drafted its Model Act for the Protection of Rights of Prisoners. But more important than all these, lawyers and prisoners are bringing—and courts are hearing and determining—constitutional and civil rights actions alleging unequal protection of the law, imposition of cruel and unusual punishment, and abuse of administrative discretion.

A series of cases has begun to hold correctional administrators accountable for their decision making, especially when these decisions affect First Amendment rights (religion, speech, communication), the means of enforcing other rights (access to counsel or legal advice, access to legal materials), cruel and unusual punishments, denial of civil rights, and equal protection of the law. The emerging view, steadily gaining support since it was enunciated in 1944 in *Coffin* v *Reichard,* 143 F. 2d 443 (6th Cir. 1944), is that the convicted offender retains all rights that citizens in general have, except those that must be limited or forfeited in order to make it possible to administer a correctional institution or agency— and no generous sweep will be given to pleas of administrative inconvenience. The pace and range of such litigation recently have increased sharply. The hands-off doctrine that used to insulate the correctional administrator from juridical accountability is fast disappearing.

Correctional administrators have been slow to accept this role of the courts and many of the specific decisions. It is understandably difficult to give up years of unquestioned authority. Yet the courts, in intervening, required correctional administrators to reevaluate past policies and practices that had proved unsuccessful. Without the courts' intervention and the resulting public awareness of prison conditions, it is unlikely that the current public concern for the treatment of criminal offenders would have developed. Thus, the courts' intervention has provided corrections with public attention and concern. In the long run, these cases bring new and influential allies to correctional reform.

Increasingly, these new allies of corrections are fitting themselves better for this collaboration. Law schools are beginning to provide training in correctional law. The American Bar Association provides energetic leadership. The Law Enforcement Assistance Administration supports these initiatives. The Federal Judicial Center develops creative judicial training programs, and judicial administration finally is acknowledged as an important organizational problem. Federal and state judges in increasing number attend sentencing institutes. Bridges are being built between the lawyers and corrections.

What it comes to is this: Convicted offenders remain within the constitutional and legislative protection of the legal system. The illogic of attempting to train lawbreakers to obey the law in a system unresponsive to law should have been recognized long ago. Forcing an offender to live in a situation in which all decisions are made for him is no training for life in a free society. Thus, the two sets of alternatives before the judiciary in most cases involving correctional practices are the choice between constitutional principle and correctional expediency and the choice between an institution that runs smoothly and one that really helps the offender. In exercising their proper function as supervisors of the criminal justice system, the courts have upset practices that have stifled any real correctional progress.

The courts will and should continue to monitor correctional decisions and practices. The Constitution requires it. The nature of the judicial process dictates that this supervision will be done case by case. A period of uneven and abrupt change and uncertainty will inevitably result. Some court rulings will indeed make administration of correctional programs more difficult. To hold hearings before making decisions that seriously affect an offender is a time-consuming task. Allowing free correspondence and access to the press by offenders creates the risk of unjustified criticism and negative publicity. Eliminating inmate guards (trusties) requires the expenditure of additional funds for staff. Correctional administrators could ease the transition by adopting on their own initiative new comprehensive procedures and practices that reflect constitutional requirements and progressive correctional policy.

The Need for Cooperation in the System. It is unrealistic to believe that the tensions and misunderstandings among the components of the criminal justice system will quickly disappear. There are—and will continue to be—unavoidable conflicts of view. The police officer who must subdue an offender by force will never see him in the same light as the correctional officer who must win him with reason. The courts, which must retain their independence in order to oversee the practices of both police and corrections, are unlikely to be seen by either as a totally sympathetic partner.

On the other hand, the governmental institutions designed to control and prevent crime are closely and irrevocably interrelated, whether they function cooperatively or at cross-purposes. The success of each component in its specific function depends on the actions of the other two. Most areas of disagreement are the result of inadequate understanding both of the need for cooperation and of the existing relationships. The extent to which this misunderstanding can be minimized will determine in large measure the future course of our efforts against crime.

The Commission recognizes that correctional progress will be made only in the context of a criminal justice system operating as an integrated and coordinated response to crime. Thus, corrections must cooperate fully with the other components in developing a system that uses its resources more effectively. If there are persons who have committed legally proscribed acts but who can be better served outside the criminal justice system at lower cost and at little or no increased risk, then police, courts, corrections, legislators, and the public must work together to establish effective diversion programs for such persons. If persons are being detained unnecessarily or for too long awaiting trial, the elements of the system must work together to remedy that situation. If sentencing practices are counterproductive to their intended purposes, a comprehensive restructuring of sentencing procedures and alternatives must be undertaken.

This perspective is in large measure responsible for the broad scope of this report on corrections. The time is ripe for corrections to provide the benefits of its knowledge and experience to the other components of the system. Such issues as diversion, pretrial release and detention, jails, juvenile intake, and sentencing traditionally have not been considered within the scope of correctional concern. But corrections can no longer afford to remain silent on issues that so vitally affect it. Thus, this report on corrections addresses these and other issues that have previously been considered problems of other components of the criminal justice system. It could be said that they are addressed from a correctional perspective, but in a broader sense they are presented from a criminal justice system point of view.

Obstacles to Correctional Reform

Fragmentation of Corrections. One of the leading obstacles to reforming the criminal justice system is the range and variety of governmental authorities—federal, state, and local—that are responsible for it. This Balkanization complicates police planning, impedes development of expeditious court processes, and divides responsibility for convicted offenders among a multiplicity of overlapping but barely intercommunicating agencies. The organizational structure of the criminal justice system was well-suited to the frontier society in which it was implanted. It has survived in a complex, mobile, urban society for which it is grossly unsuited. Accordingly, this report seriously addresses large-scale organizational and administrative restructuring of corrections.

One set of solutions is to accept the current Balkanization of corrections, recognizing its strong political support in systems of local patronage, and to prescribe defined standards, buttressed by statewide inspection systems to attain those standards. Local jails provide a good example. At the very least, if they are to be retained for the unconvicted, they must be subject to state-controlled inspection processes, to ensure the attainment of minimum standards of decency and efficiency. A further control and support that might be added is state subsidy to facilitate attainment of defined standards and goals by the local jails, the carrot of subsidy being added to the stick of threatened condemnation and closure. However, these measures are but compromises.

The contrasting mode of organizational restructuring of corrections is an integrated state correctional system. There is much support for movement in that direction. For example, it is recommended in this report that supervision of offenders under probation should be separated from the courts' administrative control and integrated with the state correctional system.

If prisons, probation, parole, and other community programs for adult and juvenile offenders are brought under one departmental structure, there is no doubt of that department's improved bargaining position in competition for resources in cabinet and legislature. Other flexibilities are opened up; career lines for promising staff are expanded, to say nothing of interdepartmental in-service training possibilities. Above all, such a structure matches the developing realities of correctional processes.

An increasing interdependence between institutional and community-based programs arises as their processes increasingly overlap; as furlough and work-release programs are expanded; as institutional release procedures grow more sophisticated and graduated; and as more intensive supervisory arrangements are added to probation and parole supervision. Institutional placement, probation, and parole or after care grow closer together and structurally intertwine. This is true for both adult and juvenile offenders.

Development of further alternatives to the traditional institution, and diversion of offenders from it, will increase this pressure toward an integrated statewide correctional system, regionalized to match the demography and distribution of offenders in the state. Administrative regionalization of such structurally integrated statewide correctional systems may be necessary in the more populous or larger states to link each regional system with the needs, opportunities, and social milieu of the particular offender group. Regionalization greatly facilitates maintaining closer ties between the offender and his family (as by visits, furloughs, and work release) than is possible otherwise.

In sum, the task of achieving an effective functional balance between state and local correctional authorities is complex and uncertain, yet it offers opportunity. It will require political statesmanship that transcends partisan, parochial, and patronage interests. But whatever the interagency relationships may be, the enunciation of precisely defined standards and goals for those agencies will aid in attainment of effective and humane correctional processes.

Overuse of Corrections. The correctional administrator (and for the present purposes, the sentencing judge too) is the servant of a criminal justice system very remarkable in its lack of restraint. Historically, the criminal law has been used not only in an effort to protect citizens but also to coerce men to private virtue. Criminal law overreaches itself in a host of "victimless" crimes; that is, crimes without an effective complainant other than the authorities. This application of the law is a major obstacle to development of a rational and effective correctional system.

When criminal law invades the sphere of private morality and social welfare, it often proves ineffective and criminogenic. What is worse, the law then diverts corrections from its clear, socially protective function. The result is unwise legislation that extends the law's reach beyond its competence. Manifestations are seen in relation to gambling, the use of drugs, public drunkenness, vagrancy, disorderly conduct, and the noncriminal aspects of troublesome juvenile behavior. This overreach of criminal law has made hypocrites of us all and has confused the mission of corrections. It has overloaded the entire criminal justice system with inappropriate cases and saddled corrections with tasks it is unsuited to perform.

The unmaking of law is more difficult than the making; to express moral outrage at objectionable conduct and to urge legislative proscription is politically popular. On the other hand, to urge the repeal of sanctions against any objectionable conduct is politically risky since it can be equated in the popular mind with approval of that conduct. But corrections, like the rest of the criminal justice system, must reduce its load to what it has some chance of carrying. Too often we are fighting the wrong war, on the wrong front, at the wrong time, so that our ability to protect the community and serve the needs of the convicted offender is attenuated. It is for this reason that a major emphasis in this report is placed on developing diversions from and alternatives to the correctional system.

It is particularly urgent to evict from corrections many of the alcoholics and drug addicts who now clutter that system. They should be brought under the aegis of more appropriate and less punitive mechanisms of social control. The same is true of truants and other juveniles who are in need of care and protection and have not committed criminal offenses. They should be removed from the delinquency jurisdiction of the courts as well as corrections.

At the same time, the rapid expansion of those diverse community-based supervisory programs called probation and parole is needed. Most states still lack probation and parole programs that are more than gestures toward effective supervision and assistance for convicted offenders. Standards and goals for correctional reform depend largely on the swift, substantial improvement of probation and parole practices.

Overemphasis on Custody. The pervasive overemphasis on custody that remains in corrections creates more problems than it solves. Our institutions are so large that their operational needs take precedence over the needs of the people they hold. The very scale of these institutions dehumanizes, denies privacy, encourages violence, and defies decent control. A moratorium should be placed on the construction of any large correctional institution. We already have too many prisons. If there is any need at all for more institutions, it is for small, community-related facilities in or near the communities they serve.

There is also urgent need for reducing the population of jails and juvenile detention facilities. By using group homes, foster care arrangements, day residence facilities, and similar community-based resources, it should be possible to eliminate entirely the need for institutions to hold young persons prior to court disposition of this cases. Similarly, by other methods discussed in this report, it will be practicable to greatly reduce the use of jails for the adult accused. By placing limitations on detention time and by freely allowing community resources, agencies, and individuals to percolate the walls of the jail, it will be possible to minimize the social isolation of those who must be jailed.

Nevertheless, it must be recognized that at our current level of knowledge (certainly of adult offenders) we lack the ability to empty prisons and jails entirely. There are confirmed and dangerous offenders who require protracted confinement because we lack alternative and more effective methods of controlling or modifying their behavior. At least for the period of incarceration, they are capable of no injury to the community.

Even so, far too many offenders are classified as dangerous. We have not developed a means of dealing with them except in the closed institution. Too often we have perceived them as the stereotype of "prisoner" and have applied to all offenders the institutional conditions essential only for relatively few. Hence, this report stresses the need for development of a broader range of alternatives to the institution, and for the input of greater resources of manpower, money, and materials to that end.

Community-based programs are not merely a substitute for the institution. Often they will divert offenders from entering the institution. But they also have important functions as part of the correctional process. They facilitate a continuum of services from the institution through graduated release procedures— such as furloughs and work release—to community-based programs.

Large institutions for adult and juvenile offenders have become places of endemic violence. Overcrowding and the admixture of diverse ethnic groups, thrown together in idleness and boredom, is the basic condition. Race relations tend to be hostile and ferocious in the racially skewed prisons and jails.

Increasing political activism complicates inmate–staff relations. Knives and other weapons proliferate and are used. Diversion of the less violent and more stable from institutions will leave in the prisons and jails a larger proportion of hardened, dangerous, and explosive prisoners. The correctional administrator thus confronts a stark reality. While making needed changes to benefit the great majority of inmates, he must cope with a volatile concentration of the most difficult offenders, whose hostility is directed against the staff.

For these reasons and others, continuing attention must be paid to conditions within the remaining institutions. Although the institution must be used only as a last resort, its programs must not be neglected. Such attention is essential if the institution is to serve as the beginning place for reintegration and not as the end of the line for the offender.

The principle of community-based corrections also extends to prisons and jails. We must make those institutions smaller, for only then can they cease to hold the anonymous. We must make them more open and responsive to community influences, for only thus can we make it possible for prisoners and staff alike to see what the community expects of them.

Lack of Financial Support. The reforms envisioned in this report will not be achieved without substantially increased government funds being allocated to the criminal justice system and without a larger portion of the total being allocated to corrections. There is little sense in the police arresting more offenders if the courts lack the resources to bring them to trial and if corrections lacks the resources to deal with them efficiently and fairly. Happily, the federal government, followed by many states, already is providing important leadership here.

Budgetary recognition is being given to the significance of crime and the fear it produces in the social fabric. For example, statutory provisions now require that at least 20 percent of the federal funds disbursed by the Law Enforcement Assistance Administration to the states to aid crime control be allocated to corrections. It is clearly a proper role for the federal government to assist states by funds and direct service to increase the momentum of the movement toward community-based corrections and to remedy existing organizational inefficiencies.

Two other obstacles to reform merit mention in this litany of adversity and the means of overcoming it. Like the other impediments to change, these obstacles are not intractable, but like the rest, they must be recognized as genuine problems to be reckoned with if they are not to frustrate progress. They are, first, the community's ambivalence, and second, the lack of knowledge on which planning for the criminal justice system can be firmly based.

Ambivalence of the Community. If asked, a clear majority of the community would probably support halfway houses for those offenders who are not a serious criminal threat but still require some residential control. But repeated experience has shown that a proposal to establish such a facility in the neighborhood is likely to rouse profound opposition. The criminal offender, adult or juvenile, is accorded a low level of community tolerance when he no longer is an abstract idea but a real person. Planning must be done, and goals and standards drafted, in recognition of this fact.

Responsible community relations must be built into all correctional plans. The antidote to intolerance of convicted offenders is the active involvement of wide segments of the community in support of correctional processes. With imagination and a willingness to take some risks, members of minority groups, ex-offenders, and other highly motivated citizens can play an effective supporting role in correctional programs.

Part of this process of opening up the institution to outside influences is the creation of a wider base for staff selection. Obviously, recruitment of members of minority groups is vitally important and must be energetically pursued. Of parallel importance, women must be employed in community-based programs and at every level of the institution (for men and women, for adults and youths) from top administration to line guard. Corrections must become a full equal opportunity employer.

Correctional administrators have tended to isolate corrections from the general public—by high walls and locked doors. In light of the community's ambivalence toward corrections, lack of effort at collaboration with community groups and individual citizens is particularly unfortunate. In almost every community there are individuals and social groups with exceptional concern for problems of social welfare whose energies must be called upon. A lobby for corrections lies at hand, to be mobilized not merely by public information and persuasion, but also by encouraging the active participation of the public in correctional work.

There are yet other advantages in such a determined community involvement in corrections. Obstacles to the employment of ex-offenders will be lowered. Probation and parole caseloads could be reduced if paraprofessionals and volunteers, including ex-offenders, assist. And the "nine-to-five on weekdays" syndrome of some probation and parole services can be cured, so that supervision and support can be available when most needed.

Lack of Knowledge Base for Planning. In this catalog of problems in corrections to be solved, the need for a knowledge base must be seriously considered. Research is the indispensable tool by which future needs are measured and met.

Lack of adequate data about crime and delinquency, about the consequences of sentencing practices, and about the outcome of correctional programs is major obstacle to planning for better community protection. It is a sad commentary on our social priorities that every conceivable statistic concerning sports is collected and available to all who are interested. One can readily find out how many lefthanders hit triples in the 1927 World Series. Yet if we wish to know how many one-to-life sentences were handed out to the 1927 crop of burglars—or the 1972 crop for that matter—the facts are nowhere to be found.

Baseline data and outcome data are not self-generating; no computer is self-activating. Research is of central significance to every correctional agency. It is not, as it so often is regarded, merely a public relations gimmick to be manipulated for political and budgetary purposes. It is an indispensable tool for intelligent decision making and deployment of resources.

It is time we stopped giving mere lip service to research and to the critical evaluation of correctional practices. To fail to propound and to achieve ambitious research and data-gathering goals is to condemn corrections to the perpetual continuance of its present ineptitude.

Ex Parte Hull
312 U.S. 546, 61 S.Ct. 640, 85 L.Ed. 1034 (1941)

Hull was twice convicted of state sex offenses and sentenced to the Michigan state prison. He then sought to file a petition for habeas corpus. He took the papers to a prison official for notorization, but the official refused to accept them for notorization and mailing. Hull was subsequently frustrated in several other attempts to send the petition to the United States Supreme Court. He then managed to have his father file the petition and the Supreme Court issued a rule to show cause why the petition for habeas corpus should not issue. In response, the warden of the prison cited the following prison regulation in justification for his actions:

All legal documents, briefs, petitions, motions, habeas corpus proceedings, and appeals will first have to be submitted to the institutional welfare office and if favorably acted upon be then referred to Perry A. Maynard, legal investigator to the Parole Board, Lansing, Michigan. Documents submitted to Perry Maynard, if in his opinion are properly drawn, will be directed to the court designated or will be directed back to the inmate.

Hull challenged the validity of the regulation.
Justice Murphy delivered the opinion of the Court:

The first question concerns the effect of the regulation quoted in the warden's return.

The regulation is invalid. The considerations that prompted its formulation are not without merit, but the state and its officers may not abridge or impair petitioner's right to apply to a federal court for a writ of habeas corpus. Whether a petition for writ of habeas corpus addressed to a federal court is properly drawn and what allegations it must contain are questions for that court alone to determine.

. . .

However, the invalidity of the prison regulation does not compel petitioner's release. For that reason it is necessary to examine the petition annexed to the response. Although it is here as an exhibit to the response, it may be considered as a motion for leave to file a petition for writ of habeas corpus inasmuch as the warden has not had an opportunity to answer it. The next question, therefore, is whether this petition is premature.

The petition is not premature. . . . Despite the fact that petitioner is now in prison under the sentence for the first offense, he was at liberty on parole at the time he was arrested and charged with the second offense. True, parole regulations obligated him to stay within Jackson County but that is not the imprisonment present in the McNally case. Moreover, petitioner's parole was revoked and he was ordered to serve out his first sentence only because of the second conviction. See Michigan Statutes Annotated, *supra*. There is no reason to suppose that he can compel the parole board to review the record of the second conviction, or to make a declaratory ruling that if that conviction is void his parole will be reinstated. Thus the last question is whether the petition, treated as a motion for leave to file a petition for writ of habeas corpus, is sufficient to necessitate an order requiring the warden to answer.

At bottom, petitioner's case is this: that in the second trial there was a variance between pleading and proof with respect to the date when the offense was committed, and that petitioner thus was denied the fair notice of the charge guaranteed by the Due Process Clause. From exhibits and rather vague statements in the petition, the following appears: that in his opening statement and throughout the trial the prosecutor insisted that the offense occurred on the date charged in the information; that petitioner's defense was that he was elsewhere at the time in question; that some of the testimony tended to fix the date of the offense about a week earlier than that charged in the indictment; that at the close of all the evidence, petitioner's counsel moved for a directed verdict on the ground that there was no evidence to prove that the offense was committed on the date charged in the information; that the trial judge denied this motion and charged the jury that the precise date was immaterial, it being sufficient to show that the offense occurred during the month previous; that the trial judge entered judgment on the jury's verdict of guilty and denied petitioner's motion for a new trial on the same ground urged in the motion for directed verdict; and that the Michigan Supreme Court subsequently denied certiorari.

We conclude that the showing made by the petition and exhibits is insufficient to compel an order requiring the warden to answer. Petitioner was represented by counsel throughout the second trial. Yet there is no claim in the petition that he objected to evidence tending to establish a different date for commission of the offense, or that he claimed surprise, or that he moved for a continuance to enable him to secure other witnesses. He does not allege that at the time of the trial he had an alibi for any other date, nor does he make clear the actual extent of any variance. Furthermore, ascertainment of these facts is impossible since petitioner has not furnished the transcript taken at the second trial. Accordingly, it would be improper to inquire whether petitioner was denied procedural due process in the second trial.

The motion for leave to file a petition for writ of habeas corpus is therefore denied.

Johnson v *Avery*

393 U.S. 483, 89 S.Ct. 747, 21 L.Ed. 2d 718 (1969)

The defendant was serving a life sentence in the Tennessee State Penitentiary and was transferred to maximum security in the prison for violating a prison regulation forbidding advising or assisting another inmate in preparing writs or other legal matters. After six months in maximum security, the defendant filed a motion in the federal district court for law books and a typewriter and to seek relief from his confinement in maximum security. The district court ordered him released from maximum security and restored his status as a regular prisoner. The prison regulation was held to be void. On appeal by Tennessee, the federal Court of Appeals reversed, concluding that the regulation did not interfere with the federal right of habeas corpus. The Court also reasoned that limiting the practice of law to lawyers and the need for prison discipline justified the need for the regulations. The United States Supreme Court granted certiorari.

Justice Fortas delivered the opinion of the Court:

This Court has constantly emphasized the fundamental importance of the writ of habeas corpus in our constitutional scheme, and the Congress has demonstrated its solicitude for the vigor of the Great Writ. The Court has steadfastly insisted that "there is no higher duty than to maintain it unimpaired."

. . .

Since the basic purpose of the writ is to enable those unlawfully incarcerated to obtain their freedom, it is fundamental that access of prisoners to the courts for the purpose of presenting their complaints may not be denied or obstructed. . . . And it has insisted that, for the indigent as well as for the affluent prisoner, postconviction proceedings must be more than a formality.

. . .

Tennessee urges, however, that the contested regulation in this case is justified as a part of the state's disciplinary administration of the prisons. There is no doubt that discipline and administration of state detention facilities are state functions. They are subject to federal authority only where paramount federal constitutional or statutory rights supervene. It is clear, however, that in instances where state regulations applicable to inmates of prison facilities conflict with such rights, the regulations may be invalidated.

There can be no doubt that Tennessee could not constitutionally adopt and enforce a rule forbidding illiterate or poorly educated prisoners to file habeas corpus petitions. Here Tennessee has adopted a rule which, in the absence of any other source of assistance for such prisoners, effectively does just that. The District Court concluded that "[f]or all practical purposes, if such prisoners cannot have the assistance of a 'jail-house lawyer,' their possibly valid constitutional claims will never be heard in any court." . . . The record supports this conclusion.

Tennessee does not provide an available alternative to the assistance provided by other inmates. . . . In its brief the state contends that "[t]here is absolutely no reason to believe that prison officials would fail to notify the court should an inmate advise them of a complete inability, . . . , to prepare a habeas application on his own behalf," but there is no contention that they have in fact ever done so.

This is obviously far short of the showing required to demonstrate that, in depriving prisoners of the assistance of fellow inmates, Tennessee has not, in substance, deprived those unable themselves, with reasonable adequacy, to prepare their petitions, of access to the constitutionally and statutorily protected availability of the writ of habeas corpus. . . . We express no judgment concerning these plans, but their existence indicates that techniques are available to provide alternatives if the state elects to prohibit mutual assistance among inmates.

Even in the absence of such alternatives, the state may impose reasonable restrictions and restraints upon the acknowledged propensity of prisoners to abuse both the giving and the seeking of assistance in the preparation of applications for relief. . . . But unless and until the state provides some reasonable alternative to assist inmates in the preparation of petitions for postconviction relief, it may not validly enforce a regulation such as that here in issue, barring inmates from furnishing such assistance to other prisoners.

The judgment of the Court of Appeals is reversed and the case is remanded for further proceedings consistent with this opinion.

(Judgment reversed.)
Justice Douglas concurred.
Justices White and Black joined in dissenting.

Lee v *Washington*

390 U.S. 333, 88 S.Ct. 944, 19 L.Ed. 2d 1212 (1968)

Alabama law required segregation of races in prisons and jails. In an action for declaratory and injunctive relief, the United States District Court entered a decree declaring the statutes unconstitutional. On appeal to the United States Supreme Court, the judgment was affirmed.

Per Curiam.

This appeal challenges a degree of a three-judge District Court declaring that certain Alabama statutes violate the Fourteenth Amendment to the extent that they require segregation of the races in prisons and jails, and establishing a schedule for desegregation of these institutions. The state's contentions that Rule 23 of the Federal Rules of Civil Procedure, which relates to class actions, was violated in this case and that the challenged statutes are not unconstitutional are without merit. The remaining contention of the state is that the specific orders directing desegregation of prisons and jails make no allowance for the necessities of prison security and discipline, but we do not so read the "Order, Judgment, and Decree" of the District Court, which when read as a whole we find unexceptionable."

(Judgment was affirmed.)
Justices Black, Harlan, and Stewart concurred:

In joining the opinion of the Court, we wish to make explicit something that is left to be gathered only by implication from the Court's opinion. This is that prison authorities have the right, acting in good faith and in particularized circumstances, to take into account racial tensions in maintaining security, discipline, and good order in prisons and jails. We are unwilling to assume that state or local prison authorities might mistakenly regard such an explicit pronouncement as evincing any dilution of this Court's firm commitment to the Fourteenth Amendment's prohibition of racial discrimination.

Baxstrom v *Herold*

383 U.S. 107, 86 S.Ct. 760, 15 L.Ed. 2d 620 (1966)

Baxstrom was convicted of second degree assault and sentenced to two and one-half years in a New York prison. He was subsequently certified as insane and transferred from prison to a state institution used for confining and caring for male prisoners who were declared mentally ill while serving a criminal sentence. When Baxstrom's penal sentence was about to expire, the director of the mental institution filed a petition requesting that Baxstrom be civilly committed pursuant to New York Correction Law, Section 384, *McKinney's Consolidated Laws,* c.43. A short hearing was conducted in the surrogate's chambers and Baxstrom was found to be mentally ill. He was retained at the mental facility.

Several times Baxstrom sought a writ of habeas corpus in a New York court to be declared sane, but even if he was not he asserted that he should be transferred to a civil mental hospital. State appellate courts denied him the requested relief.

The United States Supreme Court granted certiorari.

We hold that petitioner was denied equal protection of the laws by the statutory procedure under which a person may be civilly committed at the expiration of his penal sentence without the jury review available to all other persons civilly committed in New York. Petitioner was further denied equal protection of the laws by his civil commitment to an institution maintained by the Department of Correction beyond the expiration of his prison term without a judicial determination that he is dangerously mentally ill such as that afforded to all so committed except those, like Baxstrom, nearing the expiration of a penal sentence.

Section 384 of the New York Correction Law prescribes the procedure for civil commitment under the expiration of the prison term of a mentally ill person confined in Dannemora. Similar procedures are prescribed for civil commitment of all other allegedly mentally ill persons. . . . All persons civilly committed, however, other than those committed at the expiration of a penal term, are expressly granted the right to *de novo* review by jury trial of the question of their sanity under Section 74 of the Mental Hygiene Law. Under this procedure any person dissatisfied with an order certifying him as mentally ill may demand full review by a jury of the prior determination as to his competency. If the jury returns a verdict that the person is sane, he must be immediately discharged. It follows that the state, having made this substantial review proceeding generally available on this issue, may not, consistent with the Equal Protection Clause of the Fourteenth Amendment, arbitrarily withhold it from some.

The director argues that it is reasonable to classify persons in Baxstrom's class together with those found to be dangerously insane since such persons are not only insane but have proven criminal tendencies as shown by their past criminal records. He points to decisions of the New York Court of Appeals supporting this view.

. . .

We find this contention untenable. Where the state has provided for a judicial proceeding to determine the dangerous propensities of all others civilly committed to an institution of the Department of Correction, it may not deny this right to a person in Baxstrom's position solely on the ground that he was nearing the expiration of a prison term. It may or may not be that Baxstrom is presently mentally ill and such a danger to others that the strict security of a Department of Correction hospital is warranted. All others receive a judicial hearing on this issue. Equal protection demands that Baxstrom receive the same.

The capriciousness of the classification employed by the state is thrown sharply into focus by the fact that the full benefit of a judicial hearing to determine dangerous tendencies is withheld only in the case of civil commitment of one awaiting expiration of penal sentence. A person with a past criminal record is presently entitled to a hearing on the question whether he is dangerously mentally ill so long as he is not in prison at the time civil commitment proceedings are instituted. Given this distinction, all semblance of rationality of the classification, purportedly based upon criminal propensities, disappears.

In order to accord to petitioner the equal protection of the laws, he was and is entitled to a review of the determination as to his sanity in conformity with proceedings granted all others civilly committed under Section 74 of the New York Mental Hygiene Law. He is also entitled to a hearing under the procedure granted all others by Section 85 of the New York Mental Hygiene Law to determine whether he is dangerously mentally ill that he must remain in a hospital maintained by the Department of Correction. The judgment of the Appellate Division of the Supreme Court, in the Third Judicial Department of New York, is reversed and the case is remanded to that court for further proceedings not inconsistent with this opinion.

It is so ordered.

(Reversed and remanded.)
Justice Black concurred in the result.

Morrissey v *Brewer*
408 U.S. 471, 92 S.Ct. 2593, 33 L.Ed. 2d 484 (1972)

Morrissey was convicted of false drawing and uttering checks and was sentenced to not more than seven years imprisonment. He was later paroled. Seven months later he was arrested as a parole violator at the direction of his parole officer. After a review of the parole officer's report, Morrissey's parole was revoked and he was returned to prison. He asserted in his argument in the United States Supreme Court that he received no hearing prior to revocation of his parole. The court granted certiorari to determine whether the Due Process Clause of the Fourteenth Amendment requires that a state afford an individual some opportunity to be heard prior to revoking his parole.

Chief Justice Burger delivered the opinion of the Court:

We begin with the proposition that the revocation of parole is not part of a criminal prosecution and thus the full panoply of rights due a defendant in such a proceeding does not apply to parole revocations. . . . Parole arises after the end of criminal prosecution, including imposition of sentence. Supervision is not directly by the court but by an administrative agency, which is sometimes an arm of the court and sometimes of the executive. Revocation deprives an individual, not of the absolute liberty to which every citizen is entitled, but only of the conditional liberty properly dependent on observance of special parole restrictions.

. . .

Turning to the question [of] what process is due, we find that the state's interests are several. The state has found the parolee guilty of a crime against the people. That finding justifies imposing extensive restrictions on the individual's liberty. Release of the parolee before the end of his prison sentence is made with the recognition that with many prisoners there is a risk that they will not be able to live in society without committing additional antisocial acts. Given the previous conviction and the proper imposition of conditions, the state has an overwhelming interest in being able to return the individual to imprisonment without the burden of a new adversary criminal trial if in fact he has failed to abide by the conditions of his parole.

Yet, the state has no interest in revoking parole without some informal procedural guarantees. . . . A simple factual hearing will not interfere with the exercise of discretion. Serious studies have suggested that fair treatment on parole revocation will not result in fewer grants of parole.

. . . What is needed is an informal hearing structured to assure that the finding of a parole violation will be based on verified facts and that the exercise of discretion will be informed by an accurate knowledge of the parolee's behavior.

We now turn to the nature of the process that is due, bearing in mind that the interest of both state and parolee will be furthered by an effective but informal hearing. In analyzing what is due, we see two important stages in the typical process of parole revocation.

In our view, due process requires that after the arrest, the determination that reasonable gound exists for revocation of parole should be made by someone not directly involved in the case.

. . .

We cannot write a code of procedure; that is the responsibility of each state. . . . Our task is limited to deciding the minimum requirements of due process. They include (a) written notice of the claimed violations of parole; (b) disclosure to the parolee of evidence against him; (c) opportunity to be heard in person and to present witnesses and documentary evidence; (d) the right to confront and cross-examine adverse witnesses (unless the hearing officer specifically finds good cause for not allowing confrontation); (e) a "neutral and detached" hearing body such as a traditional parole board, members of which need not be judicial officers or lawyers; and (f) a written statement by the factfinders as to the evidence relied on and reasons for revoking parole.

. . .

We do not reach or decide the question whether the parolee is entitled to the assistance of retained counsel or to appointed counsel if he is indigent.

We have no thought to create an inflexible structure for parole revocation procedures. The few basic requirements set out above, which are applicable to future revocations of parole, should not impose a great burden on any state's parole system.

. . .

In the peculiar posture of this case, given the absence of an adequate record, we conclude the ends of justice will be best served by remanding the case to the Court of Appeals for its return of the two consolidated cases to the District Court with directions to make findings on the procedures actually followed by the Parole Board in these two revocations. If it is determined that petitioners admitted parole violations to the Parole Board, as respondents contend, and if those violations are found to be reasonable grounds for revoking parole under state standards, that would end the matter. If the procedures followed by the Parole Board are found to meet the standards laid down in this opinion that, too, would dispose of the due process claims for these cases.

(Judgment reversed.)
Justice Marshall joined Justice Brennan in concurring opinion.
Justice Douglas dissented in part and filed an opinion.

In *Wolff* v *McDonnell*, 418 U.S. 539 (1974), the Court discussed the application of procedural rules of due process. Justice White observed, "[I]t is immediately apparent that one cannot automatically apply procedural rules designed for free citizens in an open society, or for parolees or probationers under only limited restraints, to the very different situation presented by a disciplinary proceeding in a state prison.'' The major concern of this case was the use of uncorroborated hearsay in a disciplinary hearing in a state prison. It was held by the Court that in a limited class of cases uncorroborated hearsay could be constitutionally permissible since no other procedural alternative might be available.

Gagnon v *Scarpelli*

411 U.S. 778, 93 S.Ct. 1756, 36 L.Ed. 2d 656 (1953)

Scarpelli was convicted of armed robbery and sentenced to 15 years' imprisonment. The sentence was suspended and he was placed on probation. He was subsequently apprehended in the commission of another crime and his probation was revoked without a hearing. He was then incarcerated and began serving the 15-year sentence. The state courts held that the probation revocation without a hearing denied Scarpelli of due process. The United States Supreme Court granted certiorari.

Justice Powell delivered the opinion of the Court:

Two prior decisions set the bounds of our present inquiry. In *Mempa* v *Rhay,* 389 U.S. 128 (1967), the Court held that a probationer is entitled to be represented by appointed counsel at a combined revocation and sentence hearing.

· · ·

Of greater relevance is our decision last Term in *Morrissey* v *Brewer,* 408 U.S. 471 (1972). There we held that the revocation of parole is not a part of a criminal prosecution.

Even though the revocation of parole is not a part of the criminal prosecution, we held that the loss of liberty entailed is a serious deprivation requiring that the parolee be accorded due process.

· · ·

Petitioner does not contend that there is any difference relevant to the guarantee of due process between the revocation of parole and the revocation of probation, nor do we perceive one.... Accordingly, we hold that a probationer, like a parolee, is entitled to a preliminary and a final revocation hearing, under the conditions specified in *Morrissey* v *Brewer, supra*.

The second, and more difficult, question posed by this case is whether an indigent probationer or parolee has a due process right to be represented by appointed counsel at these hearings.

· · ·

... Despite the informal nature of the proceedings and the absence of technical rules of procedure or evidence, the unskilled or uneducated probationer or parolee may well have difficulty in presenting his version of a disputed set of facts where the presentation requires the examining or cross-examining of witnesses or the offering or dissecting of complex documentary evidence.

By the same token, we think that the Court of Appeals erred in accepting respondent's contention that the state is under a constitutional duty to provide counsel for indigents in all probation or parole revocation cases. While such a rule has the appeal of simplicity, it would impose direct costs and serious collateral disadvantages without regard to the need or the likelihood in a particular case for a constructive contribution by counsel.

We thus find no justification for a new inflexible constitutional rule with respect to the requirement of counsel. We think, rather, that the decision as to the need for counsel must be made on a case-by-case basis in the exercise of a sound discretion by the state authority charged with responsibility for administering the probation and parole system. Although the presence and participation of counsel will probably be both undesirable and constitutionally unnecessary in most revocation hearings, there will remain certain cases in which fundamental fairness—the touchstone of due process—will require that the state provide at its expense counsel for indigent probationers or parolees.

. . .

We return to the facts of the present case. Because respondent was not afforded either a preliminary hearing or a final hearing, the revocation of his probation did not meet the standards of due process prescribed in *Morrissey,* which we have here held applicable to probation revocations. Accordingly, respondent was entitled to a writ of habeas corpus. On remand, the District Court should allow the state an opportunity to conduct such a hearing. As to whether the state must provide counsel, respondent's admission to having committed another serious crime creates the very sort of situation in which counsel need not ordinarily be provided. But because of respondent's subsequent assertions regarding that admission, see *supra,* at 780, we conclude that the failure of the Department to provide respondent with the assistance of counsel should be reexamined in light of this opinion. The general guidelines outlined above should be applied in the first instance by those charged with conducting the revocation hearing.

(Judgment affirmed in part and reversed in part.)
Justice Douglas dissented in part.

In *Haines* v *Kerner,* 404 U.S. 519, 92 S.Ct. 594, 30 L.Ed. 2d 652 (1972), Haines sought damages for claimed injuries and deprivation of rights while placed in solitary confinement as a disciplinary measure after he had struck another inmate with a shovel following an argument. He claimed that physical suffering and aggravation of a preexisting foot injury and a circulatory ailment were caused by being required to sleep on a cell floor with only blankets available. The United States District Court dismissed the complaint and the Court of

Appeals, Seventh Circuit, affirmed. The United States Supreme Court granted certiorari and reversed the lower court.

Jackson v *Indiana*

406 U.S. 715, 92 S.Ct. 1845, 32 L.Ed. 2d 435 (1972)

Jackson was found to be mentally incompetent to stand trial on a robbery charge and, under Indiana law, was directed to be committed until he was sane. The commitment procedures provide that a trial judge who has reason to believe that a defendant is incompetent to stand trial must schedule a competency hearing at which the defendant may introduce evidence and at which court-appointed examining physicians are appointed. If the defendant lacks the comprehension to understand his ability to defend himself and to understand the proceedings, he is committed to a psychiatric institution until he becomes sane.

Other state statutory provisions apply to the civil commitment of the feeble-minded and of persons who have psychiatric disorders. These persons can be released by the appropriate institution superintendent or when they are cured. Jackson was found to lack comprehension sufficient to make a defense and was committed until such time as the health department could certify his sanity. He appealed claiming that the commitment amounted to a life imprisonment without his having been convicted of a crime and that therefore he was deprived of equal protection of the laws because in the absence of criminal charges against him, he would have come under the Indiana civil commitment procedures and would have been entitled to substantially greater rights. Jackson also claimed he was deprived of due process and subjected to cruel and unusual punishment.

The United States Supreme Court reversed the Indiana commitment.

Justice Blackmun delivered the opinion of the Court:

For the reasons set forth below, we conclude that, on the record before us, Indiana cannot constitutionally commit the petitioner for an indefinite period simply on account of his incompetency to stand trial on the charges filed against him. Accordingly, we reverse.

. . .

Equal Protection

Because the evidence established little likelihood of improvement in petitioner's condition, he argues that commitment under §9-1706a in his case amounted to a commitment for life. This deprived him of equal protection, he contends, because, absent the criminal charges pending against him, the state would have had to proceed under other statutes generally applicable to all other citizens: either the commitment procedures for feebleminded persons, or those for mentally ill persons.

. . .

In *Baxstrom* v *Herold*, 383 U.S. 107, . . . , the Court held that a state prisoner civilly committed at the end of his prison sentence on the finding of a surrogate was denied equal protection when he was deprived of a jury trial that the state made generally available to all other persons civilly committed. . . . The Court also held that Baxstrom was denied equal protection by commitment to an institution maintained by the state corrections department for "dangerously mentally ill" persons, without a judicial determination of his "dangerous propensities" afforded all others so committed.

If criminal conviction and imposition of sentence are insufficient to justify less procedural and substantive protection against indefinite commitment than that generally available to all others, the mere filing of criminal charges surely cannot suffice.

. . .

Were the state's factual premise that Jackson's commitment is only temporary a valid one, this might well be a different case. But the record does not support that premise.

. . .

We therefore must turn to the question whether, because of the pendency of the criminal charges that triggered the state's invocation of §9-1706a, Jackson was deprived of substantial rights to which he would have been entitled under either of the other two state commitment statutes. *Baxstrom* held that the state cannot withhold from a few the procedural protections or the substantive requirements for commitment that are available to all others.

. . .

. . . Consequently, we hold that by subjecting Jackson to a more lenient commitment standard and to a more stringent standard of release than those generally applicable to all others not charged with offenses, and by thus condemning him in effect to permanent institutionalization without the showing required for commitment or the opportunity for release afforded by §22-1209 or §22-1907, Indiana deprived petitioner of equal protection of the laws under the Fourteenth Amendment.

Due Process

For reasons closely related to those discussed in Part II above, we also hold that Indiana's indefinite commitment of a criminal defendant solely on account of his incompetency to stand trial does not square with the Fourteenth Amendment's guarantee of due process.

. . .

We hold, consequently, that a person charged by a state with a criminal offense who is committed solely on account of his incapacity to proceed to trial cannot be held more than the reasonable period of time necessary to determine whether there is a substantial probability that he will attain that capacity in the foreseeable future. If it is determined that this is not the case, then the state must either institute the customary civil commitment proceeding that would be required to commit indefinitely any other citizen, or release the defendant. Furthermore, even if it is determined that the defendant probably soon will be able to stand trial, his continued commitment must be justified by progress toward that goal. In light of differing state facilities and procedures and a lack of evidence in this record, we do not think it appropriate for us to attempt to prescribe arbitrary time limits. We note, however, that petitioner Jackson has now been confined for three and one-half years on a record that sufficiently establishes the lack of a substantial probability that he will ever be able to participate fully in a trial.

(Judgment reversed.)
Justices Powell and Rehnquist did not participate.

Gilmore v *Lynch*

319 F. Supp. 105 (U.S.D.C., N.D. Cal., 1970)

Gilmore and other individuals filed an action in the federal district court to contest the validity of a prison regulation limiting the law books available in prison libraries. They also challenged a restriction against the possession of legal documents by an inmate.

Per Curiam

The arguments put forward by each side are simply summarized. Plaintiffs allege that the above rules and regulations, taken individually, are arbitrary and unreasonable, and that taken collectively they deny indigent prisoners, and their jailhouse lawyers, the legal expertise which is necessary if access to the courts by these persons is to be in any way meaningful.

. . .

The rights invoked by plaintiffs herein have been given considerable emphasis by past and present case law. Reasonable access to the courts is a constitutional imperative which has been held to prevail against a variety of state interests. Similarly, the right under the Equal Protection Clause of the indigent and uneducated prisoner to the tools necessary to receive adequate hearing in the courts has received special reenforcement by the federal courts in recent decades.

. . .

Plaintiffs argue, then, that at stake here are two principles of recognized importance, i.e. their rights to reasonable access to the courts, and to equal protection of the laws. But the simple invocation of these phrases will not carry the day for plaintiffs, for they must further show that these rights are not only affected by the regulations under attack, but are infringed to such a degree as to render the justifications offered by the state inadequate and unreasonable as a matter of law. Here, the state alleges that the infringement is minimal, and that its interests are great, and this claim must now be weighed by the Court.

... While recent reforms have immeasurably aided the more affluent of California's prisoners in securing access to legal advice and the courts, the lot of the indigent inmate has been somewhat neglected. This neglect of one class, when contrasted with the attention paid to the rights of others, raises serious equal protection questions. Further, for the reasons above stated, plaintiffs' very clearly defined right to reasonable access to the courts is seriously infringed by the highly restricted nature of the book list set forth in Prison Regulation 300.041, even if that list is theoretically supplemented by the State Law Library.

The countervailing considerations offered by the state do not provide sufficient justification for the regulation.

. . .

The relief to be fashioned by the Court in the instant case presents some problem. On the one hand, a court of equity is traditionally given great discretion in such matters; on the other, judges have always feared to rush in where correctional officials are presumed more fit to tread. Balancing both these considerations, the Court will enjoin the enforcement of Prison Regulation 330.041, but it will not itself undertake the task of devising another system whereby indigent prisoners are given adequate means of obtaining the legal expertise necessary to obtain judicial consideration of alleged grievances cognizable by the courts. The Department of Corrections will, therefore, decide whether to expand the present list of basic codes and references in the manner suggested by this opinion, or whether to adopt some new method of satisfying the legal needs of its charges.

The Court is also asked to enjoin the enforcement restrictions by the State Law Library on prisoner use of its collections. This we will decline to do.

. . .

There remains for this Court's consideration only Director's Rule 2602, which provides that "one inmate may assist another inmate in the preparation of legal documents, but . . . all briefs, petitions, and other legal papers must be and remain in the possession of the inmate to whom they pertain." Plaintiffs allege that this rule prevents meaningful mutual assistance, in that it requires in effect that all writing take place in mess halls, where such is impossible, or in libraries, where access is limited and talking is banned. The Court notes, however, that the rule can be easily interpreted to bar only storage of completed legal papers in the cells of persons to whom they do not pertain. Thus, the "jailhouse lawyer" could compose such documents in his own cell, but once they are completed he must deliver them to the possession of the "client," without any threats to retain them until payment is forthcoming. Assuming such an interpretation of Director's Rule 2602, the Court finds it constitutionally valid.

Accordingly it is hereby ordered that defendants be and are enjoined from enforcing Prison Regulation 330.041. Defendants are further ordered, on or before September 1, to file with this Court new or amended regulations which accord with the principles expressed herein. If plaintiffs desire oral argument on the adequacy of such new or amended regulations, they will properly move for a hearing thereon. Otherwise, the Court will entertain written briefs concerning the proposed regulations, and will make such further decision as it deems appropriate. In the interim, no law books, codes, or references now in prison libraries will be destroyed or removed because they are not on the basic reference list promulgated by Prison Regulation 300.041.

It is so ordered.

Younger v *Gilmore*

404 U.S. 15, 92 S.Ct. 250, 30 L.Ed. 2d 142 (1971)

Per Curiam

On this appeal we postponed the question of jurisdiction pending the hearing of the case on the merits.

. . .

Having heard the case on its merits, we find that this Court does have jurisdiction . . . and affirm the judgment of the District Court for the Northern District of California.

. . .

QUESTIONS

1. For what reason have the courts found correctional institutions in violation of the Constitution? What standards have been defined by these courts?

2. What steps have been taken by the Supreme Court to ensure "due process" in relation to prisoners held in correctional institutions?

3. What importance does the Supreme Court place on in-house attorneys? Discuss.

Appendix A

THE CONSTITUTION OF THE UNITED STATES OF AMERICA

WE THE PEOPLE of the United States, in Order to form a more perfect Union, establish Justice, insure domestic Tranquility, provide for the common defence, promote the general Welfare, and secure the Blessings of Liberty to ourselves and our Posterity, do ordain and establish this Constitution for the United States of America.

ARTICLE I.

SECTION 1.   All legislative Powers herein granted shall be vested in a Congress of the United States, which shall consist of a Senate and House of Representatives.

SECTION 2.   The House of Representatives shall be composed of Members chosen every second Year by the People of the several States, and the Electors in each State shall have the Qualifications requisite for Electors of the most numerous Branch of the State Legislature.

No Person shall be a Representative who shall not have attained to the Age of twenty-five Years, and been seven Years a Citizen of the United States, and who shall not, when elected, be an Inhabitant of that State in which he shall be chosen.

[Representatives and direct Taxes shall be apportioned among the several States which may be included within this Union, according to their respective Numbers, which shall be determined by adding to the whole Number of free Persons, including those bound to

Service for a Term of Years, and excluding Indians not taxed, three fifths of all other Persons.]* The actual Enumeration shall be made within three Years after the first Meeting of the Congress of the United States, and within every subsequent Term of ten Years, in such Manner as they shall by Law direct. The Number of Representatives shall not exceed one for every thirty Thousand,** but each State shall have at Least one Representative; and until such enumeration shall be made, the State of New Hampshire shall be entitled to chuse three, Massachusetts eight, Rhode-Island and Providence Plantations one, Connecticut five, New-York six, New Jersey four, Pennsylvania eight, Delaware one, Maryland six, Virginia ten, North Carolina five, South Carolina five, and Georgia three.

When vacancies happen in the Representation from any State, the Executive Authority thereof shall issue Writs of Election to fill such Vacancies.

The House of Representatives shall chuse their Speaker and other Officers; and shall have the sole Power of Impeachment.

SECTION 3.   The Senate of the United States shall be composed of two Senators from each State, [chosen by the Legislature thereof,]*** for six Years; and each Senator shall have one Vote.

Immediately after they shall be assembled in Consequence of the first Election, they shall be divided as equally as may be into three Classes. The Seats of the Senators of the first Class shall be vacated at the Expiration of the second Year, of the second Class at the Expiration of the fourth Year, and of the third Class at the Expiration of the sixth Year, so that one-third may be chosen every second Year; [and if Vacancies happen by Resignation, or otherwise, during the Recess of the Legislature of any State, the Executive thereof may make temporary Appointments until the next Meeting of the Legislature, which shall then fill such Vacancies.]*

No Person shall be a Senator who shall not have attained to the Age of thirty Years, and been nine Years a Citizen of the United States, and who shall not, when elected, be an Inhabitant of that State for which he shall be chosen.

The Vice President of the United States shall be President of the Senate, but shall have no Vote, unless they be equally divided.

The Senate shall chuse their other Officers, and also a President pro tempore, in the absence of the Vice President, or when he shall exercise the Office of President of the United States.

The Senate shall have the sole Power to try all Impeachments. When sitting for that Purpose, they shall be on Oath or Affirmation. When the President of the United States is tried, the Chief Justice shall preside: And no Person shall be convicted without the Concurrence of two thirds of the Members present.

Judgment in Cases of Impeachment shall not extend further than to removal from Office, and disqualification to hold and enjoy any Office of honor, Trust or Profit under the United States: but the Party convicted shall nevertheless be liable and subject to Indictment, Trial, Judgment and Punishment, according to Law.

SECTION 4.   The Times, Places and Manner of holding Elections for Senators and Representatives, shall be prescribed in each State by the Legislature thereof; but the Congress may at any time by Law make or alter such Regulations, except as to the Place of Chusing Senators.

  The Congress shall assemble at least once in every Year, and such Meeting shall [be on the first Monday in December,]** unless they shall by Law appoint a different Day.

---

*Changed by section 2 of the fourteenth amendment.
**Ratio in 1965 was one to over 410,000.
***Changed by section 1 of the seventeenth amendment.
*Changed by clause 2 of the seventeenth amendment.
**Changed by section 2 of the twentieth amendment.

SECTION 5.   Each House shall be the Judge of the Elections, Returns and Qualifications of its own Members, and a Majority of each shall constitute a Quorum to do Business; but a smaller number may adjourn from day to day, and may be authorized to compel the Attendance of absent Members, in such Manner, and under such Penalties as each House may provide.

Each House may determine the Rules of its Proceedings, punish its Members for disorderly Behavior, and, with the Concurrence of two thirds, expel a Member.

Each House shall keep a Journal of its Proceedings, and from time to time publish the same, excepting such Parts as may in their Judgment require Secrecy; and the Yeas and Nays of the Members of either House on any question shall, at the Desire of one fifth of those Present, be entered on the Journal.

Neither House, during the Session of Congress, shall, without the Consent of the other, adjourn for more than three days, nor to any other Place than that in which the two Houses shall be sitting.

SECTION 6.   The Senators and Representatives shall receive a Compensation for their Services, to be ascertained by Law, and paid out of the Treasury of the United States. They shall in all Cases, except Treason, Felony and Breach of the Peace, be privileged from Arrest during their Attendance at the Session of their respective Houses, and in going to and returning from the same; and for any Speech or Debate in either House, they shall not be questioned in any other Place.

No Senator or Representative shall, during the Time for which he was elected, be appointed to any civil Office under the Authority of the United States, which shall have been created, or the Emoluments whereof shall have been encreased during such time; and no Person holding any Office under the United States, shall be a Member of either House during his Continuance in Office.

SECTION 7.   All Bills for raising Revenue shall originate in the House of Representatives; but the Senate may propose or concur with Amendments as on other Bills.

Every Bill which shall have passed the House of Representatives and the Senate, shall, before it become a Law, be presented to the President of the United States; If he approve he shall sign it, but if not he shall return it, with his Objections to that House in which it shall have originated, who shall enter the Objections at large on their Journal, and proceed to reconsider it. If after such Reconsideration two thirds of that House shall agree to pass the Bill, it shall be sent, together with the Objections, to the other House, by which it shall likewise be reconsidered, and if approved by two thirds of that House, it shall become a Law. But in all such Cases the Votes of both Houses shall be determined by Yeas and Nays, and the Names of the Persons voting for and against the Bill shall be entered on the Journal of each House respectively. If any Bill shall not be returned by the President within ten Days (Sundays excepted) after it shall have been presented to him, the Same shall be a Law, in like Manner as if he had signed it, unless the Congress by their Adjournment prevent its Return, in which Case it shall not be a Law.

Every Order, Resolution, or Vote to which the Concurrence of the Senate and House of Representatives may be necessary (except on a question of Adjournment) shall be presented to the President of the United States; and before the Same shall take Effect, shall be approved by him, or being disapproved by him, shall be repassed by two thirds of the Senate and House of Representatives, according to the Rules and Limitations prescribed in the Case of a Bill.

SECTION 8.   The Congress shall have Power To lay and collect Taxes, Duties, Imposts and Excises, to pay the Debts and provide for the common Defence and general Welfare of the United States; but all Duties, Imposts and Excises shall be uniform throughout the United States;

To borrow money on the credit of the United States;

To regulate Commerce with foreign Nations, and among the several States, and with the Indian Tribes;

To establish an uniform Rule of Naturalization, and uniform Laws on the subject of Bankruptcies throughout the United States;

To coin Money, regulate the Value thereof, and of foreign Coin, and fix the Standard of Weights and Measures;

To provide for the Punishment of counterfeiting the Securities and current Coin of the United States;

To establish Post Offices and post Roads;

To promote the Progress of Science and useful Arts, by securing for limited Times to Authors and Inventors the exclusive Right to their respective Writings and Discoveries;

To constitute Tribunals inferior to the supreme Court;

To define and punish Piracies and Felonies committed on the high Seas, and Offenses against the Law of Nations;

To declare War, grant Letters of Marque and Reprisal, and make Rules concerning Captures on Land and Water;

To raise and support Armies, but no Appropriation of Money to that Use shall be for a longer Term than two Years;

To provide and maintain a Navy;

To make Rules for the Government and Regulation of the land and naval Forces;

To provide for calling forth the Militia to execute the Laws of the Union, suppress Insurrections and repel Invasions;

To provide for organizing, arming, and disciplining the Militia, and for governing such Part of them as may be employed in the Service of the United States, reserving to the States respectively, the Appointment of the Officers, and the Authority of training the Militia according to the discipline prescribed by Congress;

To exercise exclusive Legislation in all Cases whatsoever, over such District (not exceeding ten Miles square) as may, by Cession of particular States, and the acceptance of Congress, become the Seat of the Government of the United States, and to exercise like Authority over all Places purchased by the Consent of the Legislature of the State in which the Same shall be, for the Erection of Forts, Magazines, Arsenals, dock-Yards, and other needful Buildings;—And

To make all Laws which shall be necessary and proper for carrying into Execution the foregoing Powers, and all other Powers vested by this Constitution in the Government of the United States, or in any Department or Officer thereof.

SECTION 9. The Migration or Importation of such Persons as any of the States now existing shall think proper to admit, shall not be prohibited by the Congress prior to the Year one thousand eight hundred and eight, but a tax or duty may be imposed on such Importation, not exceeding ten dollars for each Person.

The privilege of the Writ of Habeas Corpus shall not be suspended, unless when in Cases of Rebellion or Invasion the public Safety may require it.

No Bill of Attainder or ex post facto Law shall be passed.

No capitation, or other direct, Tax shall be laid, unless in Proportion to the Census or Enumeration herein before directed to be taken.

No Tax or Duty shall be laid on Articles exported from any State.

No Preference shall be given by any Regulation of Commerce or Revenue to the Ports of one State over those of another: nor shall Vessels bound to, or from, one State, be obliged to enter, clear, or pay Duties in another.

No Money shall be drawn from the Treasury, but in Consequence of Appropriations made by Law; and a regular Statement and Account of the Receipts and Expenditures of all public Money shall be published from time to time.

No Title of Nobility shall be granted by the United States: And no Person holding any Office of Profit or Trust under them, shall, without the Consent of the Congress, accept of any present, Emolument, Office, or Title, of any kind whatever, from any King, Prince, or foreign State.

SECTION 10.   No State shall enter into any Treaty, Alliance, or Confederation; grant Letters of Marque and Reprisal; coin Money; emit Bills of Credit; make any Thing but gold and silver Coin a Tender in Payment of Debts; pass any Bill of Attainder, ex post facto Law, or Law impairing the Obligation of Contracts, or grant any Title of Nobility.

No State shall, without the Consent of the Congress, lay any Imposts or Duties on Imports or Exports, except what may be absolutely necessary for executing its inspection Laws: and the net Produce of all Duties and Imposts, laid by any State on Imports or Exports, shall be for the Use of the Treasury of the United States; and all such Laws shall be subject to the Revision and Controul of the Congress.

No State shall, without the Consent of Congress, lay any duty of Tonnage, keep Troops, or Ships of War in time of Peace, enter into any Agreement or Compact with another State, or with a foreign Power, or engage in War, unless actually invaded, or in such imminent Danger as will not admit of delay.

ARTICLE II.

SECTION 1.   The executive Power shall be vested in a President of the United States of America. He shall hold his Office during the Term of four Years, and, together with the Vice-President, chosen for the same Term, be elected, as follows.

Each State shall appoint, in such Manner as the Legislature thereof may direct, a Number of Electors, equal to the whole Number of Senators and Representatives to which the State may be entitled in the Congress: but no Senator or Representative, or Person holding an Office of Trust or Profit under the United States, shall be appointed an Elector.

[The Electors shall meet in their respective States, and vote by Ballot for two persons, of whom one at least shall not be an Inhabitant of the same State with themselves. And they shall make a List of all the Persons voted for, and of the Number of Votes for each; which List they shall sign and certify, and transmit sealed to the Seat of the Government of the United States, directed to the President of the Senate. The President of the Senate shall, in the Presence of the Senate and House of Representatives, open all the Certificates, and the Votes shall then be counted. The Person having the greatest Number of Votes shall be the President, if such Number be a Majority of the whole Number of Electors appointed; and if there be more than one who have such Majority, and have an equal Number of Votes, then the House of Representatives shall immediately chuse by Ballot one of them for President; and if no Person have a Majority, then from the five highest on the List the said House shall in like Manner chuse the President. But in chusing the President, the Votes shall be taken by States, the Representation from each State having one Vote; a quorum for this Purpose shall consist of a Member or Members from two thirds of the States, and a Majority of all the States shall be necessary to a Choice. In every Case, after the Choice of the President, the Person having the greatest Number of Votes of the Electors shall be the Vice President. But if there should remain two or more who have equal Votes, the Senate shall chuse from them by Ballot the Vice-President.]*

The Congress may determine the Time of chusing the Electors, and the Day on which they shall give their Votes; which Day shall be the same throughout the United States.

No person except a natural born Citizen, or a Citizen of the United States, at the time of the Adoption of this Constitution, shall be eligible to the Office of President; neither shall any Person be eligible to that Office who shall not have attained to the Age of thirty-five Years, and been fourteen Years a Resident within the United States.

**[In Case of the Removal of the President from Office, or of his Death, Resignation, or Inability to discharge the Powers and Duties of the said Office, the same shall devolve

---

*Superseded by the twelfth amendment.

**This clause has been affected by the twenty-fifth amendment.

on the Vice President, and the Congress may by Law, provide for the Case of Removal, Death, Resignation or Inability, both of the President and Vice President, declaring what Officer shall then act as President, and such Officer shall act accordingly, until the Disability be removed, or a President shall be elected.]

The President shall, at stated Times, receive for his Services, a Compensation, which shall neither be encreased nor diminished during the Period for which he shall have been elected, and he shall not receive within that Period any other Emolument from the United States, or any of them.

Before he enter on the Execution of his Office, he shall take the following Oath or Affirmation:—"I do solemnly swear (or affirm) that I will faithfully execute the Office of President of the United States, and will to the best of my Ability, preserve, protect and defend the Constitution of the United States."

SECTION 2.   The President shall be Commander in Chief of the Army and Navy of the United States, and of the Militia of the several States, when called into the actual Service of the United States; he may require the Opinion in writing, of the principal Officer in each of the executive Departments, upon any subject relating to the Duties of their respective Offices, and he shall have Power to Grant Reprieves and Pardons for Offenses against the United States, except in Cases of Impeachment.

He shall have Power, by and with the Advice and Consent of the Senate, to make Treaties, provided two-thirds of the Senators present concur; and he shall nominate, and by and with the Advice and Consent of the Senate, shall appoint Ambassadors, other public Ministers and Consuls, Judges of the supreme Court, and all other Officers of the United States, whose Appointments are not herein otherwise provided for, and which shall be established by Law: but the Congress may by Law vest the Appointment of such inferior Officers, as they think proper, in the President alone, in the Courts of Law, or in the Heads of Departments.

The President shall have Power to fill up all Vacancies that may happen during the Recess of the Senate, by granting Commissions which shall expire at the End of their next Session.

SECTION 3.   He shall from time to time give to the Congress Information of the State of the Union, and recommend to their Consideration such Measures as he shall judge necessary and expedient; he may, on extraordinary Occasions, convene both Houses, or either of them, and in Case of Disagreement between them, with Respect to the Time of Adjournment, he may adjourn them to such Time as he shall think proper; he shall receive Ambassadors and other public Ministers; he shall take Care that the Laws be faithfully executed, and shall Commission all the Officers of the United States.

SECTION 4.   The President, Vice President and all civil Officers of the United States, shall be removed from Office on Impeachment for, and Conviction of, Treason, Bribery, or other high Crimes and Misdemeanors.

ARTICLE III.

SECTION 1.   The judicial Power of the United States, shall be vested in one supreme Court, and in such inferior Courts as the Congress may from time to time ordain and establish. The Judges, both of the supreme and inferior Courts, shall hold their Offices during good Behaviour, and shall, at stated Times, receive for their Services, a Compensation, which shall not be diminished during their Continuance in Office.

SECTION 2.   The judicial Power shall extend to all Cases, in Law and Equity, arising under this Constitution, the Laws of the United States, and Treaties made, or which shall be made, under their Authority;—to all Cases affecting Ambassadors, other public Ministers and Consuls;—to all Cases of admiralty and maritime Jurisdiction;—to Controversies to which the United States shall be a Party;—to Controversies between two or more States;—between a State and Citizens of another State;—between Citizens of different States;—between Citizens of the same State claiming Lands under Grants of different States, and between a State, or the Citizens thereof, and foreign States, Citizens or Subjects.

In all Cases affecting Ambassadors, other public Ministers and Consuls, and those in which a State shall be Party, the supreme Court shall have original Jurisdiction. In all the other Cases before mentioned, the supreme Court shall have appellate Jurisdiction, both as to Law and Fact, with such Exceptions, and under such Regulations as the Congress shall make.

The trial of all Crimes, except in Cases of Impeachment, shall be by Jury; and such Trial shall be held in the State where the said Crimes shall have been committed; but when not committed within any State, the Trial shall be at such Place or Places as the Congress may by Law have directed.

SECTION 3. Treason against the United States, shall consist only in levying War against them, or in adhering to their Enemies, giving them Aid and Comfort. No Person shall be convicted of Treason unless on the Testimony of two Witnesses to the same overt Act, or on Confession in open Court.

The Congress shall have Power to declare the Punishment of Treason, but no Attainder of Treason shall work Corruption of Blood, or Forfeiture except during the Life of the Person attainted.

ARTICLE IV.

SECTION 1. Full Faith and Credit shall be given in each State to the public Acts, Records, and judicial Proceedings of every other State. And the Congress may by general Laws prescribe the Manner in which such Acts, Records and Proceedings shall be proved, and the Effect thereof.

SECTION 2. The Citizens of each State shall be entitled to all Privileges and Immunities of Citizens in the several States.

A Person charged in any State with Treason, Felony, or other Crime, who shall flee from Justice, and be found in another State, shall on demand of the executive Authority of the State from which he fled, be delivered up, to be removed to the State having Jurisdiction of the Crime.

[No Person held to Service or Labour in one State, under the Laws thereof, escaping into another, shall, in Consequence of any Law or Regulation therein, be discharged from such Service or Labour, but shall be delivered up on Claim of the Party to whom such Service or Labour may be due.]*

SECTION 3. New States may be admitted by the Congress into this Union; but no new State shall be formed or erected within the Jurisdiction of any other State; nor any State be formed by the Junction of two or more States, or parts of States, without the Consent of the Legislatures of the States concerned as well as of the Congress.

The Congress shall have Power to dispose of and make all needful Rules and Regulations respecting the Territory or other Property belonging to the United States; and nothing in this Constitution shall be so construed as to Prejudice any Claims of the United States, or of any particular State.

SECTION 4. The United States shall guarantee to every State in this Union a Repub-

*Superseded by the thirteenth amendment.

lican Form of Government, and shall protect each of them against Invasion; and on Application of the Legislature, or of the Executive (when the Legislature cannot be convened) against domestic Violence.

ARTICLE V.

The Congress, whenever two-thirds of both Houses shall deem it necessary, shall propose Amendments to this Constitution, or, on the Application of the Legislatures of two-thirds of the several States, shall call a Convention for proposing Amendments, which, in either Case, shall be valid to all Intents and Purposes, as part of this Constitution, when ratified by the Legislatures of three-fourths of the several States, or by Conventions in three-fourths thereof, as the one or the other Mode of Ratification may be proposed by the Congress: Provided that no Amendment which may be made prior to the Year One thousand eight hundred and eight shall in any Manner affect the first and fourth Clauses in the Ninth Section of the first Article; and that no State, without its Consent, shall be deprived of its equal Suffrage in the Senate.

ARTICLE VI.

All Debts contracted and Engagements entered into, before the Adoption of this Constitution, shall be as valid against the United States under this Constitution, as under the Confederation.

This Constitution, and the Laws of the United States which shall be made in Pursuance thereof; and all Treaties made, or which shall be made, under the Authority of the United States, shall be the supreme Law of the Land; and the Judges in every State shall be bound thereby, any Thing in the Constitution or Laws of any State to the Contrary notwithstanding.

The Senators and Representatives before mentioned, and the Members of the several State Legislatures, and all executive and judicial Officers, both of the United States and of the several States, shall be bound by Oath or Affirmation, to support this Constitution; but no religious Test shall ever be required as a Qualification to any Office or public Trust under the United States.

ARTICLE VII.

The Ratification of the Conventions of nine States shall be sufficient for the Establishment of this Constitution between the States so ratifying the Same.

DONE in Convention by the Unanimous Consent of the States present the Seventeenth Day of September in the Year of our Lord one thousand seven hundred and Eighty seven and of the Independence of the United States of America the Twelfth.
In Witness whereof We have hereunto subscribed our Names.

ARTICLES IN ADDITION TO, AND AMENDMENT OF, THE CONSTITUTION OF THE UNITED STATES OF AMERICA, PROPOSED BY CONGRESS, AND RATIFIED BY THE LEGISLATURES OF THE SEVERAL STATES, PURSUANT TO THE FIFTH ARTICLE OF THE ORIGINAL CONSTITUTION.*

*Amendment XXI was not ratified by state legislatures, but by state conventions summoned by Congress.

(The first 10 Amendments were ratified December 15, 1791, and form what is known as the "Bill of Rights")

AMENDMENT I

Congress shall make no law respecting an establishment of religion, or prohibiting the free exercise thereof; or abridging the freedom of speech, or the press; or the right of the people peaceably to assemble, and to petition the Government for a redress of grievances.

AMENDMENT II

A well regulated Militia, being necessary to the security of a free State, the right of the people to keep and bear Arms, shall not be infringed.

AMENDMENT III

No Soldier shall, in time of peace be quartered in any house, without the consent of the Owner, nor in time of war, but in a manner to be prescribed by law.

AMENDMENT IV

The right of the people to be secure in their persons, houses, papers, and effects, against unreasonable searches and seizures, shall not be violated, and no Warrants shall issue, but upon probable cause, supported by Oath or affirmation, and particularly describing the place to be searched, and the persons or things to be seized.

AMENDMENT V

No person shall be held to answer for a capital, or otherwise infamous crime, unless on a presentment or indictment of a Grand Jury, except in cases arising in the land or naval forces, or in the Militia, when in actual service in time of War or public danger; nor shall any person be subject for the same offence to be twice put in jeopardy of life or limb; nor shall be compelled in any criminal case to be a witness against himself, nor be deprived of life, liberty, or property, without due process of law; nor shall private property be taken for public use, without just compensation.

AMENDMENT VI

In all criminal prosecutions, the accused shall enjoy the right to a speedy and public trial, by an impartial jury of the State and district wherein the crime shall have been committed, which district shall have been previously ascertained by law, and to be informed of the nature and cause of the accusation; to be confronted with the witnesses against him; to have compulsory process for obtaining witnesses in his favor, and to have the Assistance of Counsel for his defence.

AMENDMENT VII

In suits at common law, where the value in controversy shall exceed twenty dollars, the right of trial by jury shall be preserved, and no fact tried by a jury, shall be otherwise reexamined in any Court of the United States, than according to the rules of the common law.

AMENDMENT VIII

Excessive bail shall not be required, nor excessive fines imposed, nor cruel and unusual punishments inflicted.

AMENDMENT IX

The enumeration in the Constitution, of certain rights, shall not be construed to deny or disparage others retained by the people.

AMENDMENT X

The powers not delegated to the United States by the Constitution, nor prohibited by it to the States, are reserved to the States respectively, or to the people.

AMENDMENT XI
(Ratified February 7, 1795)

The Judicial power of the United States shall not be construed to extend to any suit in law or equity, commenced or prosecuted against one of the United States by Citizens of another State, or by Citizens or Subjects of any Foreign State.

AMENDMENT XII
(Ratified July 27, 1804)

The Electors shall meet in their respective states and vote by ballot for President and Vice-President, one of whom, at least, shall not be an inhabitant of the same state with themselves; they shall name in their ballots the person voted for as President, and in distinct ballots the person voted for as Vice-President, and they shall make distinct lists of all persons voted for as President, and of all persons voted for as Vice-President, and of the number of votes for each, which lists they shall sign and certify, and transmit sealed to the seat of the government of the United States, directed to the President of the Senate;— the President of the Senate shall, in presence of the Senate and House of Representatives, open all the certificates and the votes shall then be counted;—The person having the greatest number of votes for President, shall be the President, if such number be a majority of the whole number of Electors appointed; and if no person have such majority, then from the persons having the highest numbers not exceeding three on the list of those voted for as President, the House of Representatives shall choose immediately, by ballot, the President. But in choosing the President, the votes shall be taken by states, the representation from each state having one vote; a quorum for this purpose shall consist of a member or members from two-thirds of the states, and a majority of all the states shall be necessary to a choice. [And if the House of Representatives shall not choose a President whenever the right of choice shall devolve upon them, before the fourth day of March next following, then the Vice-President shall act as President, as in the case of the death or other constitutional disability of the President.—]* The person having the greatest number of votes as Vice-President, shall be the Vice-President, if such number be a majority of the whole number of Electors appointed, and if no person have a majority, then from the two highest numbers on the list, the Senate shall choose the Vice-President; a quorum for the purpose shall consist of two-thirds of the whole number of Senators, and a majority of the whole number shall be necessary to a choice. But no person constitutionally ineligible to the office of President shall be eligible to that of Vice-President of the United States.

AMENDMENT XIII
(*Ratified December 6, 1865*)

SECTION 1.　Neither slavery nor involuntary servitude, except as a punishment for crime whereof the party shall have been duly convicted, shall exist within the United States, or any place subject to their jurisdiction.

SECTION 2.　Congress shall have power to enforce this article by appropriate legislation.

AMENDMENT XIV
(*Ratified July 9, 1868*)

SECTION 1.　All persons born or naturalized in the United States, and subject to the jurisdiction thereof, are citizens of the United States and of the State wherein they reside. No State shall make or enforce any law which shall abridge the privileges or immunities of citizens of the United States; nor shall any State deprive any person of life, liberty, or property, without due process of law; nor deny to any person within its jurisdiction the equal protection of the laws.

SECTION 2.　Representatives shall be apportioned among the several States according to their respective numbers, counting the whole number of persons in each State, excluding Indians not taxed. But when the right to vote at any election for the choice of electors for President and Vice-President of the United States, Representatives in Congress, the Executive and Judicial officers of a State, or the members of the Legislature thereof, is denied to any of the male inhabitants of such State, being twenty-one years of age,* and citizens of the United States, or in any way abridged, except for participation in rebellion, or other crime, the basis of representation therein shall be reduced in the proportion which the number of such male citizens shall bear to the whole number of male citizens twenty-one years of age in such State.

SECTION 3.　No person shall be a Senator or Representative in Congress, or elector of President and Vice-President, or hold any office, civil or military, under the United States, or under any State, who, having previously taken an oath, as a member of Congress, or as an officer of the United States, or as a member of any State legislature, or as an executive or judicial officer of any State, to support the Constitution of the United

*Superseded by section 3 of the twentieth amendment.
*Changed by section 1 of twenty-sixth amendment.

States, shall have engaged in insurrection or rebellion against the same, or given aid or comfort to the enemies thereof. But Congress may by a vote of two-thirds of each House, remove such disability.

SECTION 4.   The validity of the public debt of the United States, authorized by law, including debts incurred for payment of pensions and bounties for services in suppressing insurrection or rebellion, shall not be questioned. But neither the United States nor any State shall assume or pay any debt or obligation incurred in aid of insurrection or rebellion against the United States, or any claim for the loss or emancipation of any slave; but all such debts, obligations and claims shall be held illegal and void.

SECTION 5.   The Congress shall have power to enforce, by appropriate legislation, the provisions of this article.

AMENDMENT XV
(Ratified February 3, 1870)

SECTION 1.   The right of citizens of the United States to vote shall not be denied or abridged by the United States or by any State on account of race, color, or previous condition of servitude—

SECTION 2.   The Congress shall have power to enforce this article by appropriate legislation.

AMENDMENT XVI
(Ratified February 3, 1913)

The Congress shall have power to lay and collect taxes on incomes, from whatever source derived, without apportionment among the several States, and without regard to any census or enumeration.

AMENDMENT XVII
(Ratified April 8, 1913)

The Senate of the United States shall be composed of two Senators from each State, elected by the people thereof, for six years; and each Senator shall have one vote. The electors in each State shall have the qualifications requisite for electors of the most numerous branch of the State legislatures.

When vacancies happen in the representation of any State in the Senate, the executive authority of such State shall issue writs of election to fill such vacancies: *Provided,* That the legislature of any State may empower the executive thereof to make temporary appointments until the people fill the vancancies by election as the legislature may direct.

This amendment shall not be so construed as to affect the election or term of any Senator chosen before it becomes valid as part of the Constitution.

AMENDMENT XVIII
(Ratified January 16, 1919)

[SECTION 1.   After one year from the ratification of this article the manufacture, sale, or transportation of intoxicating liquors within, the importation thereof into, or the exportation thereof from the United States and all territory subject to the jurisdiction thereof for beverage purposes is hereby prohibited.

[SECTION 2.   The Congress and the several States shall have concurrent power to enforce this article by appropriate legislation.

[SECTION 3.   This article shall be inoperative unless it shall have been ratified as an amendment to the Constitution by the legislatures of the several States as provided in the Constitution, within seven years from the date of the submission hereof to the States by the Congress.]*

AMENDMENT XIX
(Ratified August 18, 1920)

The right of citizens of the United States to vote shall not be denied or abridged by the United States or by any State on account of sex.

Congress shall have power to enforce this article by appropriate legislation.

AMENDMENT XX
(Ratified January 23, 1933)

SECTION 1.   The terms of the President and Vice President shall end at noon on the 20th day of January, and the terms of Senators and Representatives at noon on the 3d day of January, of the years in which such terms would have ended if this article had not been ratified; and the terms of their successors shall then begin.

SECTION 2.   The Congress shall assemble at least once in every year, and such meeting shall begin at noon on the 3d day of January, unless they shall by law appoint a different day.

SECTION 3.   If, at the time fixed for the beginning of the term of the President, the President elect shall have died, the Vice President elect shall become President. If a President shall not have been chosen before the time fixed for the beginning of his term, or if the President elect shall have failed to qualify, then the Vice President elect shall act as President until a President shall have qualified; and the Congress may by law provide for the case wherein neither a President elect nor a Vice President elect shall have qualified, declaring who shall then act as President, or the manner in which one who is to act shall be selected, and such person shall act accordingly until a President or Vice President shall have qualified.

SECTION 4.   The Congress may by law provide for the case of the death of any of the persons from whom the House of Representatives may choose a President whenver the right of choice shall have devolved upon them, and for the case of the death of any of the persons from whom the Senate may choose a Vice President whenever the right of choice shall have devolved upon them.

SECTION 5.   Sections 1 and 2 shall take effect on the 15th day of October following the ratification of this article.

SECTION 6.   This article shall be inoperative unless it shall have been ratified as an amendment to the Constitution by the legislatures of three-fourths of the several States within seven years from the date of its submission.

*Repealed by section 1 of the twenty-first amendment.

AMENDMENT XXI
(Ratified December 5, 1933)

SECTION 1.   The eighteenth article of amendment to the Constitution of the United States is hereby repealed.

SECTION 2.   The transportation or importation into any State, Territory, or possession of the United States for delivery or use therein of intoxicating liquors, in violation of the laws thereof, is hereby prohibited.

SECTION 3.   This article shall be inoperative unless it shall have been ratified as an amendment to the Constitution by conventions in the several States, as provided in the Constitution, within seven years from the date of the submission hereof to the States by the Congress.

AMENDMENT XXII
(Ratified February 27, 1951)

SECTION 1.   No person shall be elected to the office of the President more than twice, and no person who has held the office of President, or acted as President, for more than two years of a term to which some other person was elected President shall be elected to the office of the President more than once. But this Article shall not apply to any person holding the office of President when this Article was proposed by the Congress, and shall not prevent any person who may be holding the office of President, or acting as President, during the term within which this Article becomes operative from holding the office of President or acting as President during the remainder of such term.

SECTION 2.   This article shall be inoperative unless it shall have been ratified as an amendment to the Constitution by the legislatures of three-fourths of the several States within seven years from the date of its submission to the States by the Congress.

AMENDMENT XXIII
(Ratified March 29, 1961)

SECTION 1.   The District constituting the seat of Government of the United States shall appoint in such manner as the Congress may direct:

A number of electors of President and Vice President equal to the whole number of Senators and Representatives in Congress to which the District would be entitled if it were a State, but in no event more than the least populous State; they shall be in addition to those appointed by the States, but they shall be considered, for the purposes of the election of President and Vice President, to be electors appointed by a State; and they shall meet in the District and perform such duties as provided by the twelfth article of amendment.

SECTION 2.   The Congress shall have power to enforce this article by appropriate legislation.

AMENDMENT XXIV
(Ratified January 23, 1964)

SECTION 1.   The right of citizens of the United States to vote in any primary or other election for President or Vice President, for electors for President or Vice President, or for

Senator or Representative in Congress, shall not be denied or abridged by the United States or any State by reason of failure to pay any poll tax or other tax.

SECTION 2.   The Congress shall have power to enforce this article by appropriate legislation.

AMENDMENT XXV
(Ratified February 10, 1967)

SECTION 1.   In case of the removal of the President from office or of his death or resignation, the Vice President shall become President.

SECTION 2.   Whenever there is a vacancy in the office of the Vice President, the President shall nominate a Vice President who shall take office upon confirmation by a majority vote of both Houses of Congress.

SECTION 3.   Whenever the President transmits to the President pro tempore of the Senate and the Speaker of the House of Representatives his written declaration that he is unable to discharge the powers and duties of his office, and until he transmits to them a written declaration to the contrary, such powers and duties shall be discharged by the Vice President as Acting President.

SECTION 4.   Whenever the Vice President and a majority of the principal officers of the executive departments or of such other body as Congress may by law provide, transmit to the President pro tempore of the Senate and the Speaker of the House of Representatives their written declaration that the President is unable to discharge the powers and duties of his office, the Vice President shall immediately assume the powers and duties of the office as Acting President.

Thereafter, when the President transmits to the President pro tempore of the Senate and the Speaker of the House of Representatives his written declaration that no inability exists, he shall resume the powers and duties of his office unless the Vice President and a majority of either the principal officers of the executive department or of such other body as Congress may by law provide, transmit within four days to the President pro tempore of the Senate and the Speaker of the House of Representatives their written declaration that the President is unable to discharge the powers and duties of his office. Thereupon Congress shall decide the issue, assembling within forty-eight hours for that purpose if not in session. If the Congress, within twenty-one days after receipt of the latter written declaration, or, if Congress is not in session, within twenty-one days after Congress is required to assemble, determines by two-thirds vote of both Houses that the President is unable to discharge the powers and duties of his office, the Vice President shall continue to discharge the same as Acting President; otherwise, the President shall resume the powers and duties of his office.

AMENDMENT XXVI
(Ratified July 1, 1971)

SECTION 1.   The right of citizens of the United States, who are eighteen years of age or older, to vote shall not be denied or abridged by the United States or by any State on account of age.

SECTION 2.   The Congress shall have power to enforce this article by appropriate legislation.

Appendix B
TABLE
OF
CITED CASES

INDEX

C

F

G

O

P

T

U

V

W